EARLY MEGIDDO
ON THE EAST SLOPE
(THE "MEGIDDO STAGES")

General view of the East Slope taken in 1927, looking north near stake of Square V17, showing Squares T17 and U17. Note the two large dumps in the background

EARLY MEGIDDO ON THE EAST SLOPE (THE "MEGIDDO STAGES")

A Report on the Early Occupation of the East Slope of Megiddo

Results of the Oriental Institute's Excavations, 1925–1933

by

ELIOT BRAUN

with contributions by

DAVID ILAN

OFER MARDER

YAEL BRAUN

and

SARIEL SHALEV

ORIENTAL INSTITUTE PUBLICATIONS • VOLUME 139

THE ORIENTAL INSTITUTE OF THE UNIVERSITY OF CHICAGO

Library of Congress Control Number: 2013949330
ISBN-10: 1-885923-98-8
ISBN-13: 978-1-885923-98-1
ISSN: 0069-3367

The Oriental Institute, Chicago

Published 2013. Printed in the United States of America.

Oriental Institute Publications, Volume 139

Series Editors

Leslie Schramer

and

Thomas G. Urban

Series Editors' Acknowledgments

The assistance of Brian Keenan is acknowledged in the production of this volume.

Spine Illustration

Bow-rim pithos (see pl. 58)

Printed through Four Colour Imports by
Lifetouch, Loves Park, Illinois, USA

The research and compilation for the manuscript for this final publication were made possible through a generous grant from the
Shelby White-Leon Levy Program for Archaeological Publications.

The paper used in this publication meets the minimum requirements of American National Standard for Information Services — Permanence of Paper for Printed Library Materials, ANSI Z39.48-1984.

∞

For Gideon, Ya'ara, Yael, Michal, Boaz, and Tamar

TABLE OF CONTENTS

List of Abbreviations x

List of Figures xi

List of Plates xii

List of Tables xv

Preface xvii

Acknowledgments xix

Bibliography xxi

Chapter 1. Introduction to the East Slope 1

- The Physical Setting of the East Slope 1
- Parameters of the East Slope 1
- Excavation of the East Slope 1
- The East Slope Today 5
- The East Slope in Archaeological Research 5
  - Earliest Research 5
  - Primary Impact of the 1934 Report 5
  - Terminological Confusion 6
- Curated Assemblages and Documentation 7
  - The Oriental Institute Archive and Artifact Assemblage 7
  - The Israel Antiquities Authority Archive and Artifact Assemblage 7
  - A Limited Database 8
  - The System of Loci 9
  - Photographic Documentation 10
  - Plans and Sections of the East Slope 11
  - Note on the Provenience of Artifacts 21
  - The "Megiddo Stages" 21
- In Appreciation of the Excavators and Staff 23

Chapter 2. Early Deposits on the East Slope 25

- Domestic and Non-mortuary Activity 25
- Stratigraphy of the East Slope: An Overview 25
- Architecture 26
- Part 1: "Late" Architectural Features on the East Slope above the Excavators' "Stages" 27
  - "Post-Stage IV" 27
  - The Very Latest Features on the East Slope 27
  - Additional Late Architectural Features 28
  - The Latest Buildings and Structures 30
  - Structures Likely to Be Contemporary with One or More of the Several Phases of B/+IV/1 34
  - An Area of Activity 38
- Part 2: The Earliest Constructions on the East Slope: Stages IV and V and Below 38
  - The Architecture of Stage IV. 39
  - Intermediate Levels Between Stages +IV and V. 49
  - The Architecture of Stage V. 50

The Earliest Occupation and Utilization of the East Slope: Quarrying and Activity in Caves 56
Deposits Below B/V/1: Interpreting Results of Deep Probes 60
Additional Caves 61
The Stratigraphy of the Earliest Utilization and Occupation of the East Slope: A Summary Statement ... 64
Below Stages V and IV to Bedrock 65

Chapter 3. Artifacts from the East Slope 69
Part 1. Pottery 69
The Assemblage 69
Earlier Publication of the Artifacts 70
Note on Drawing Conventions, Photographs, and Pottery Descriptions 70
Pottery from Before the Early Bronze Age 71
Early Bronze Age I Pottery 72
Early Bronze Age I–II Pottery 93
Early Bronze Age III Pottery 97
Part 2: Bone, Groundstone, Metallurgical Artifacts, and a Pottery Figurine 99
Textile-related Artifacts: Bone Tools, Stone Loom Weights, and Cloth Impression in Pottery 99
Metal and Metal-related Objects 100
Groundstone Artifacts 100

Chapter 4. Sealings, Potters' Marks, and Potmarks from the East Slope 103
Introduction 103
Seal Impressions 103
Catalog of Sealings from the East Slope and Two from the High Mound 104
Potters' Marks 113
Potmarks 117
Potmarks with Zoomorphic Representations 117
Potmarks with Anthropomorphic Representations 117
Potmarks with Representations of Boats 118
Potmarks with Fragmentary, Obscure Representations 120
Discussion 121

Chapter 5. The Chipped Stone Collection from the Oriental Institute's Excavation of the East Slope and the High Mound. *Ofer Marder* 125
Introduction 125
Evaluation of Collection and Contexts 125
Description of the Collection 126
Stratum XX 126
The Early Pottery Neolithic Component 126
The East Slope 127
Additional Chrono-Cultural Components 129
Discussion 130
Acknowledgments 130

Chapter 6. The Early Bronze Age Tombs of Megiddo: A Reappraisal. *David Ilan* 133
Introduction 133
Synthetic Description of the Tombs 133
Formation Processes of the Tombs 138
Interpretations 139

Summary ... 140
Acknowledgments ... 140

Chapter 7. Human Activity on the East Slope: A Summary ... 141
Part 1: The East Slope as a Zone of Intermittent Activity in Ancient Times ... 141
Early Human Utilization of the East Slope ... 141
Early Bronze Age I ... 142
Early Bronze Age II ... 143
Early Bronze Age III ... 143
East Slope in Post Early Bronze Age III (Later) Periods ... 144
Part 2: Early Architecture and Artifacts of the East Slope in Context ... 144
Very Earliest Buildings ... 144
Stage V Buildings (B/V/1 and B/V/2) ... 145
Stage IV Buildings (B/IV/1 and B/IV/2) ... 145
Buildings of the East Slope and the Early Bronze Age I Architectural Traditions of the Southern Levant 145
Early Bronze Age I Artifacts in Context ... 146
Architecture and Artifact Assemblages of Early Bronze Age III ... 147
Part 3: Megiddo in Late Phases of Early Bronze Age I: A Hypothesis ... 147
Monumental Megiddo ... 147
The Sociopolitical Context of Megiddo ... 148
The Arslantepe VI-A Paradigm of Social Organization ... 149
Part 4: Abandoning Earlier Stratigraphic Paradigms ... 150
Part 5: A New Paradigm for the Archaeological Record of the East Slope ... 151
Part 6: The Archaeological Record of the East Slope: An Epitaph ... 152
Part 7: Epilogue ... 152

Appendices
A. Locations of Loci According to the 5 × 5 m Grid ... 153
B. Locations of Walls According to the 5 × 5 m Grid and in Illustrations ... 155
C. Megiddo East Slope Locus Register Based on Notebooks and Locus/Object Cards and Photographs in the Oriental Institute ... 157
Introduction ... 157
The Excavators' Annotations in the Locus Register ... 158

Index of Acquisition and Field Numbers ... 169
Plates

ABBREVIATIONS

GENERAL ABBREVIATIONS

asl	above sea level
ca.	*circa*, approximately
cat.	catalog
cf.	*confer*, compare
cm	centimeter(s)
e.g.	*exempli gratia*, for example
esp.	especially
et al.	*et alii*, and others
etc.	*et cetera*, and so forth
f(f).	and following
fig(s).	figure(s)
ibid.	*ibidem*, in the same place
i.e.	*id est*, that is
mm	millimeter(s)
m	meter(s)
n(n).	note(s)
no(s).	number(s)
N.B.	*nota bene*, take careful note
p(p).	page(s)
pers. comm.	personal communication
pl(s).	plate(s)
sq.	square
reg.	registration

BIBLIOGRAPHIC ABBREVIATIONS

Megiddo Tombs	Guy and Engberg 1938
Megiddo I	Lamon and Shipton 1939
Megiddo II	Loud 1948
Megiddo III	Finkelstein, Ussishkin, and Halpern, eds. 2000
Megiddo IV	Finkelstein, Ussishkin, and Halpern, eds. 2006

LIST OF FIGURES

Frontispiece. Work on the East Slope with two large spoil heaps in the background

1. Map of the principal sites discussed and cited in the text . . . 2
2. Map of Early Bronze Age I sites in the Megiddo region . . . 3
3. Topographical map of Megiddo . . . 4
4. Detail from the excavators' inked Primary Master Plan of the East Slope . . . 13
5. Plan of the East Slope . . . 14
6. Detail of Plan of the East Slope . . . 15
7. Megiddo Special Sheet No. 1 with select structures of late periods on the East Slope . . . 17
8. Section C–D . . . 18
9. Schematic section of the early "Stages" . . . 22
10. Detail of the excavators' Primary Master Plan of the East Slope . . . 28
11. Detail derived from the excavators' Primary Master Plan of the East Slope . . . 29
12. Plan of B/+IV/1a derived from an aerial photograph . . . 31
13. Plan of the earliest phases of B/+IV/1 derived from an aerial photograph . . . 33
14. Plans of the upper and lower phases of B/+IV/2 derived from an aerial photograph . . . 34
15. Plan of B/+IV/3 derived from the Primary Master Plan of the East Slope . . . 37
16. Lamon's original, unpublished plan and section of "Stages IV and V" . . . 40
17. Lamon's plan, enhanced with details and a 5 × 5 meter grid . . . 41
18. Detail of figure 17 indicating stratigraphic phasing . . . 42
19. Lamon's Section A–B through B/IV/1 . . . 44
20. Plans of the earliest and latest phases of B/IV/1 . . . 46
21. Plan of B/V/1 and W20 . . . 52
22. Plan of B/V/1 with W41 and W42 . . . 57
23. Enlarged detail of a segment of Section C–D with indications of a deep probe below B/V/1 . . . 59
24. Plan and section of Locus 1101 . . . 63
25. Gray Burnished Ware: Idealized examples of Early Types 1 and 5 . . . 75
26. Profiles of guttered and everted rims . . . 83
27. Early Bronze Age I bow-rim pithoi-typology . . . 87
28. Generic holemouth rim profiles . . . 91
29. Sherds bearing potters' marks . . . 115
30. Selection of holemouth vessels bearing potmarks from Early Bronze Age contexts at sites in the northern region of the southern Levant . . . 119
31. Potmarks with zoomorphic motifs . . . 121
32. Potmarks with anthropomorphic motifs . . . 122
33. Potmarks with boats and uncertain motifs . . . 123
34. Plan and sections of Tomb 910 . . . 135

LIST OF PLATES

1. Aerial view of the high mound of Megiddo of unknown date
2. View of the mound taken from the southeast, probably in winter
3. View of the spoil heaps and exposed bedrock on the East Slope in winter of 2008, taken from the east
4. Two pages from the 1932 Locus Register
5. Page from the Megiddo Artifact Ledgers of the Palestine Archaeological Museum
6. Photographer, presumably Olaf E. Lind, at work on the summit of the tell
7. Balloon with attached camera used for taking the aerial photographs of the East Slope
8. Pages 47 and 48 of the level books, indicating elevations taken on the East Slope
9. Detail from balloon photograph of the East Slope, first series
10. Detail from balloon photograph of the East Slope, second series
11. Detail from balloon photograph of the East Slope, third series
12. Detail from balloon photograph of the East Slope, fourth series
13. Workers excavating on the East Slope
14. Megiddo Expedition staff
15. Remains of a kiln, Locus 1087
16. Detail of balloon photograph from the first series showing most of the excavators' Square U16 and partial Square U17
17. Detail of balloon photograph from the second series showing the upper terrace
18. Detail of an aerial photograph of B/+IV/c–d
19. Detail of a photograph from the third balloon series showing all the upper terrace with B/IV/1 and B/IV/2 and part of the lower terrace with the southern half of B/V/1
20. Newly annotated copy of a detail of an aerial photograph from the final balloon series
21. Detail of aerial photograph from the final balloon series annotated with locus numbers
22. Detail of aerial photograph from the final balloon series annotated with wall numbers
23. Annotated photograph of B/IV/1 from south
24. Annotated photograph of B/IV/1 from west
25. Annotated photograph of B/IV/1 from north
26. Detail of plate 25 showing a complete holemouth vessel in situ in B/IV/1a
27. Photograph of the northwestern quadrant of the upper terrace, from the southeast
28. Photograph of the southwestern quadrant of the upper terrace, from the northeast
29. Photograph of the southwestern quadrant of the upper terrace, from the south
30. Detail of photograph of B/V/1
31. Photograph of the southern end of B/V/1 with later deposits
32. Photograph of the southern half of B/V/1, from the southwest
33. Photograph showing details of B/V/1 during excavation
34. Annotated photograph showing all of B/V/1 and associated floor of B/V/2
35. Annotated photograph showing details of B/V/2, not on Lamon's plan of Stage V
36. Photograph of B/IV/1, from the north
37. Photograph of bedrock surface of Locus 1199 with quarried features
38. Photograph of the bedrock below B/IV/2 at the southwestern end of the upper terrace
39. Photograph of Tomb 903 Lower
40. Annotated photograph of Locus 1101

41. Photograph of Locus 1142 and Locus 1152
42. Two details of aerial photos, showing exposed bedrock and structures in Square V17
43. Pre-Early Bronze Age I pottery
44. Pottery of a very early (Yiftah'el II) phase of Early Bronze Age I
45. Examples of Gray Burnished Ware
46. Early Bronze Age I Gray Burnished Ware bowls Types 1c and 3
47. Gray Burnished Ware Type 4 and non-Gray Burnished Ware parallels
48. Gray Burnished Type 4 bowl and morphological parallels in non-Gray Burnished Ware fabrics
49. Two Type 3 carinated bowls found in Tomb 1106
50. Examples of Early Bronze Age ceramic painted styles from the East Slope
51. Early Bronze Age I open vessels
52. Early Bronze Age I bowls
53. Early Bronze Age I spouted basins and vats
54. Early Bronze Age I strap handles and juglets
55. Early Bronze Age I gourd jars (*amphoriskoi*)
56. Early Bronze Age I small and medium-size spouted vessels ("teapots")
57. Early Bronze Age I jars and stand
58. Early Bronze Age I bow-rim pithos
59. Early Bronze Age I bow-rim pithoi
60. Early Bronze Age I large jars and pithoi
61. Early Bronze Age I holemouth vessels
62. Assorted Early Bronze Age I ledge handles
63. Assorted Early Bronze Age I ledge handles
64. Egyptian-style, locally produced pottery
65. Early Bronze Age II pottery
66. Early Bronze Age II pottery
67. Select Early Bronze Age III pottery
68. Select Early Bronze Age III pottery
69. Early Bronze Age III fragments of small jars, jug, and pithoi
70. Early Bronze Age III platter-plates
71. Early Bronze Age III large bowls and basins
72. Early Bronze Age I–III holemouth vessels
73. Early Bronze Age III holemouth vessels
74. Varia: bone tools, terra-cotta mold, figurine
75. Objects in basalt
76. Detail of a bow-rim pithos with seal impression
77. Cylinder seal impressions
78. Cylinder seal impressions
79. Seal impressions
80. Cylinder seal impressions
81. Details of bow-rim pithoi with cylinder seal impressions
82. Holemouth sherds with potters' marks
83. Sherds and handle with potters' marks
84. Bowls with incised interiors, from Megiddo and Gezer
85. Potmarks with zoomorphic and anthropomorphic motifs
86. Byblos point and Early Pottery Neolithic sickle blades
87. Byblos point, sickle blades, and bladelet core

88. Canaanean blades and borer
89. Canaanean sickle blades
90. Canaanean blades
91. Atypical fan scraper, retouched flake, and polished graver
92. Atypical fan scraper and fan scraper
93. Head of Yarmukian ceramic figurine. OIM A22559
94. Aerial photograph of East Slope showing location of the Early Bronze Age tombs
95. Entry court and antechamber of Tomb 910 and sharply carved lintels of Tomb 910
96. Chamber A in Tomb 910 and close up of human remains in Chamber A, Tomb 910
97. Isometric rendering of monumental J-4 temple on the high mound
98. Annotated photograph of a portion of partly excavated monumental temple at Megiddo

LIST OF TABLES

1. Gray Burnished Ware types from Megiddo and select parallels 78
2. Handles with incised decoration: Select parallels.......... 82
3. Guttered and everted rim vessels: Select Early Bronze Age parallels.......... 83
4. Spouted basins: Select Early Bronze Age parallels 84
5. Bow rim pithoi: Select parallels.......... 89
6. Storage jars with necks and thickened rims: Select Early Bronze Age I parallels.......... 90
7. Storage jar with neck and thickened rim: Select Early Bronze Age II parallels.......... 90
8. Holemouth jars with ridged rims: Select Early Bronze Age parallels.......... 91
9. Holemouth jar 34.2548 from Locus 1200: Select Early Bronze Age I parallels.......... 92
10. Holemouth jar 34.2548 from Locus 1200: Select Early Bronze Age II parallels 92
11. Inventory of South Levantine Metallic Ware from the East Slope 95
12. Waste frequencies 131
13. Tool frequencies 132
14. Early Bronze Age tombs on the East Slope of Megiddo 136
15. Early Bronze Age pottery from the Early Bronze Age tombs of Megiddo 137
16. Complete vessels from Megiddo Tomb 910 138
17. Human utilization of the East Slope of Megiddo.......... 152

A.1. Locations of loci in Squares T16, U16, T17, and U17.......... 153

B.1. Walls of post-Stage IV structures on the East Slope: Locations and labeled illustrations.......... 155
B.2. Walls of the earliest structures on the East Slope: Locations and labeled illustrations.......... 156

C.1. Excavators' annotated locus list 159
C.2. Loci in figures not noted in excavators' locus list.......... 168

PREFACE

This report completes prior publications by Clarence S. Fisher (1929), P. L. O. Guy (1931), Robert M. Engberg and Geoffrey M. Shipton (1934a), and P. L. O. Guy and Robert M. Engberg (1938) on the earliest utilization and occupation of the slope at the southeast base of the high mound of Megiddo (Tell el-Mutesellim). That area, labeled by the excavators the "East Slope," and identified by them in their notations as "ES," was excavated by the Oriental Institute between the years 1925, when work commenced, and 1933, when the last of it was apparently cleared down to bedrock. While the primary focus of this report is on Square U16 (an area of 25 × 25 m), where most of the early remains (i.e., of the Early Bronze Age and earlier) excluding tombs were encountered, this work also deals with the later remains within that same, limited precinct.

It is somewhat difficult today to comprehend just how greatly the cursory and partial report of that excavation (Engberg and Shipton 1934a) impacted on scholars' perceptions of the late prehistory of the southern Levant. Even today, some eight decades after the last season of work on the East Slope, and in an era when considerably more is understood of the periods represented there, the results of those excavations are still widely cited and, perhaps too often, misunderstood.

As a student of the late prehistory of the southern Levant, with particular interest in the Early Bronze Age, time after time I was drawn to the information on that period that could be gleaned from published results of the Oriental Institute's expedition to Megiddo, particularly in regard to the less-than-monumental remains unearthed on the East Slope, with its houses and what was purportedly a pottery sequence reflecting the chrono-cultural progression of the Chalcolithic and Early Bronze Ages. After having excavated the site of ʿEn Shadud, nearby within the Jezreel Valley, I found myself attempting to understand the significance of that small site in comparison with similar discoveries on the East Slope (Braun 1985). Although I relied heavily on the East Slope report in an attempt to place the material culture of ʿEn Shadud within a chronological and regional context, I remained frustrated by limits in available details and, indeed, by a serious lack of some very basic information on early settlements at Megiddo, a site of fundamental importance to understanding the late prehistory of the entire region. It is that frustration, as well as a sense of the relative importance of the East Slope remains, of themselves and in their influence on archaeological scholarship, that has led me to undertake the present project.

The present report is intended, with benefit of nearly nine decades of hindsight, to complete the work of the pioneering scholars of the Oriental Institute who braved the malarial swamps of the Jezreel Valley early in the twentieth century to unearth the secrets of Megiddo. This volume has a dual purpose. It is meant to present the reader with as complete and accurate a description as possible of the physical finds associated with the earliest human activity encountered on the East Slope of Megiddo, while additionally offering interpretations of them in light of modern scholarship. In the first part it fulfills P. L. O. Guy's (1931, p. 10) promise to fully publish the finds from the East Slope, and in the latter it allows me to integrate that information into the ongoing narrative of the late prehistory of the southern Levant.

This work is arranged in chapters that introduce the reader to the site and the East Slope precinct, describe the principal remains in the field (excluding the tombs, which have been published more fully in Guy and Engberg's 1938 *Megiddo Tombs*), the artifacts recovered from them, and associations between them. *Chapter 1* introduces the excavation and describes the site, research on it, and available sources. *Chapter 2* is devoted to describing and illustrating the stratigraphy and architecture of the East Slope. Artifacts are described, illustrated, and their significance interpreted in *Chapter 3*. *Chapter 4* is devoted to glyptics, potters' marks, and potmarks associated with the Early Bronze Age. In *Chapter 5* Ofer Marder describes the chipped-stone finds from the early periods from the entire site and places them within their chrono-cultural contexts. Corollary research conducted by David Ilan, who came to some similar conclusions concerning Tomb 901, is elaborated in *Chapter 6*. In *Chapter 7* I summarize my interpretations of the excavation results within the context of south Levantine prehistory.

****

Readers may wonder why there are no citations in this work of Tel Aviv University's *Megiddo V* (Finkelstein, Usshishkin and Cline 2013) report, which appeared in print ca. July 2013. That is because the writing of this volume was essentially finished early in 2012, when final additions and corrections to the text were made; well before the appearance of *Megiddo V*. Due to technical difficulties beyond our control the actual publishing was delayed for a somewhat lengthy period. Thus, the present work does not reflect the new information available from that report. Suffice it to note that a preliminary perusal of some portions of Tel Aviv University's report available to me do not substantially change any of my views in the present volume.

Eliot Braun
Har Adar, August 31, 2013

Finkelstein, Israel; David Ussishkin; and E. H. Cline
2013 *Megiddo V. The 2004-2008 Seasons.* Three Volumes. Tel Aviv Monograph Series 31. Winona Lake: Eisenbrauns.

ACKNOWLEDGMENTS

With the publication of this work I wish to acknowledge the important contribution that the Shelby White-Leon Levy Program for Archaeological Publications has made to ancient Near Eastern scholarship and archaeological research in particular. Its grant has allowed me to make available information that has long lain dormant and which was virtually inaccessible to the greater public. Without that support, my long-standing dream of probing the secrets of the Megiddo East Slope excavation would never have come to pass, and for that I am exceedingly grateful.

In Jerusalem I enjoyed the full support of the Israel Antiquities Authority (IAA), which provided me with easy access to its archives and its Megiddo collection of antiquities. I am grateful to its director, Yehoshua (Shuka) Dorfman and Hava Katz, IAA Chief Curator of the State Collection of Antiquities for their help and encouragement in this project. I am particularly indebted to Alegre Savariego, IAA Curator of the Rockefeller Museum Collection, for her unstinting help in finding material and making it readily available for study. Fawzi Ibrahim, Israel Museum Curator of the display in the Rockefeller Museum, kindly gave me access to that material. Arieh Halperin-Rochman and Silvia Krapiwko of the IAA's archives were especially helpful in giving me access to their files and in answering the numerous queries with which I peppered them.

Silvia Krapiwko's considerable skills were invaluable help in rendering most of the objects from Jerusalem and then digitizing them, several others rendered by Carmen Hirsh in Jerusalem, and the large selection of objects drawn by Angela Altenhofen in Chicago. Their fine artistic skills are greatly appreciated. The fruits of Silvia's work are easily seen throughout this volume in the drawings in *Chapter 3*, her finishing touches on many of the photographs, plans, and virtually all other illustrations presented throughout this work. Silvia also photographed several objects found in the illustrations of *Chapter 3*.

Warm thanks go to Edwin C. M. van den Brink (Israel Antiquities Authority) for his critical and helpful readings of early drafts of the manuscript and for sharing information on his excavation in Nahal Zippori near Mizpeh Zevulun. I am very thankful to my daughter, Yael Braun, who checked references and helped proofread one version of the manuscript and who added the information on the tectonics of the Megiddo region (*Chapter 2*). Bella Gershovich (Israel Museum) kindly photographed one of the cylinder seal impressions and made it available for publication here.

In Chicago I was giving unstinting support and I am deeply indebted to Gil Stein, director of the Oriental Institute, for his encouragement in this project. My experience in the Research Archives with its helpful and efficient staff was entirely positive. My first contact was with Raymond Tindel, research associate, registrar, and senior curator (now emeritus) of the Museum, who offered encouragement and put me at ease in the archives. Afterwards I received unstinting help and encouragement from John A. Larson, Oriental Institute Museum archivist, and Helen Mcdonald, Oriental Institute Museum registrar, who went out of their way to make my limited time in Chicago as profitable as possible and who, through the miracle of e-mails, gracefully answered many a query. Additional help came from Geoff Emberling, then Oriental Institute Museum chief curator, who allowed me access to display material, and to David Schloen, assistant professor of Syro-Palestinian archaeology, for his support of the project.

Technical assistance was provided by John Sanders, senior research associate and head of the computer library, and Joshua Trampier, then associate director, CAMEL (Oriental Institue), who helped in scanning oversize documents. Leticia Barda (IAA) kindly helped with the positioning of Early Bronze Age I sites on the maps in *Chapter 7*.

I am also very grateful to fellow scholars who shared information with me. Matthew Adams (Bucknell University) provided preliminary information on his sounding on the lower precincts of Megiddo and made available to me titles of works in press. Amihai Mazar (Hebrew University) and Yael Rotem (Hebrew University) offered information on the potmarks from Beth Shan and their soon-to-be-published site report. Nimrod Getzov (IAA) and Sam Wolff kindly shared information on their excavations at Mishmar Ha-emeq and Tel Megadim, respectively. To Marcella Frangipane (La Sapienza Universitá di Roma) and her team of colleagues I am indebted for an invitation to attend the conference Fifty Years of Excavations and Research at Arslantepe-Malatya (Turkey), held at the La Sapienza campus, December 5–7, 2011, which offered so much important information and so many scholarly insights on a site that appears to have been more than a little analogous to Megiddo in the late fourth millennium B.C.

Thanks are due to E. C. M. van den Brink (Israel Antiquities Authority) for bringing an impression of a cylinder seal from Tell Qashish to my attention and for allowing it to be mentioned in this work. Thanks are also due to the Israel Museum for providing a photograph of the seal impression on sherd 38.982.

I also owe a great debt to an anonymous reader, who took the time and trouble to patiently go over a complicated manuscript, and who has helped to correct some errors and forced me to deal with editorial issues. I am also extremely grateful to Thomas Urban and Leslie Schramer and the Oriental Institute Publications Office for their friendly and professional help in bringing the manuscript to press.

Eliot Braun

BIBLIOGRAPHY

Adams, Matthew J.

2009 "The Early Bronze Cultic Complex at Megiddo, 2004–2008 Seasons." *Albright News* 14: 10.

2013 *Area J*, Part 1: *Introduction* (pp. 21–27), and Part 3: *The Main Sector of Area J* (pp. 47–118), in *Megiddo V: The 2004-2008 Seasons,* edited by I. Finkelstein, D. Ussishkin, E. Cline, M. Adams, E. Arie, N. Franklin, and M. Martin. Monograph Series 31. Tel Aviv: Institute of Archaeology.

Akkermans, Peter M. M. G., and Glenn M. Schwartz

2003 *The Archaeology of Syria: From Complex Hunter-gatherers to Early Urban Societies (ca. 16,000-300 B.C.).* Cambridge World Archaeology. Cambridge: Cambridge University Press.

Albright, William F.

1926 "The Jordan Valley in the Bronze Age." In *Annual of the American Schools of Oriental Research* 6, pp. 13–74.

1935 "Presidential Address: Palestine in the Earliest Historical Period." *Journal of the Palestine Oriental Society* 15: 193–234.

Amiran, Ruth K.

1968 *Early Arad: The Chalcolithic Settlement and Early Bronze City.* Jerusalem: The Israel Exploration Society.

1969 *Ancient Pottery of the Holy Land: From Its Beginnings in the Neolithic Period to the End of the Iron Age.* Jerusalem: Massada Press.

1970 "The Bronze Age: The Beginnings of Urbanization in Canaan." In *Near Eastern Archaeology in the Twentieth Century: Essays in Honor of Nelson Glueck*, edited by James A. Sanders, pp. 83–100. Garden City: Doubleday.

1974 "An Egyptian Jar Fragment with the Name of Narmer from Arad." *Israel Exploration Journal* 24/1: 4–12.

1985 "Canaanite Merchants in Tombs of the Early Bronze Age I at Azor." *ʿAtiqot* (English Series) 17: 190–92.

1992 "An Egyptian Artist from Megiddo and a Local, Canaanean Artist at Tell el Farʿah North — Both of the EB I Period." In *Eighteenth Archaeological Conference in Israel, 12-13 February 1992* (Abstracts), p. 31. Jerusalem: Israel Exploration Society. [In Hebrew]

Anati, Emmanuel; Moshe Avnimelech; Nicu Haas; and Ezra Meyerhof

1973 *Hazorea I.* Centro camuno di studi preistorici, Archivi 5. Capo de Ponti: Edizioni del Centro Camuno di Studi Preistorici.

Bankirer, Rina Y.

2003 "The Flint Assemblage." In *Salvage Excavations at Early Bronze Age Site of Qiryat Ata*, edited by Amir Golani, pp. 171–82. Israel Antiquities Authority Reports 18. Jerusalem: Israel Antiquities Authority.

2006 "The Flint Assemblage." In *The Tel Bet Yeraḥ Excavation, 1994-1995*, edited by Nimrød Getzov pp. 159–68. Israel Antiquities Authority Reports 28. Jerusalem: Israel Antiquities Authority.

Bar-Adon, Pesah

1980 *The Cave of the Treasure: The Finds from the Caves in Nahal Mishmar.* Judean Desert Studies. Jerusalem: The Israel Exploration Society.

Baruch, Uri

1987 "The Early Bronze Age, Chalcolithic and Neolithic Periods." In *Tell Qiri: A Village in the Jezreel Valley; Report of the Archaeological Excavations, 1975-1977*, edited by Amnon Ben-Tor, Y. Portugali, Miriam Avissar, Uri Baruch, and Melvin Hunt, pp. 274–99. Qedem: Monographs of the Institute of Archaeology, the Hebrew University of Jerusalem 24. Jerusalem: The Hebrew University.

Bate, Dorothea M. A.

1938 "Animal Remains." In *Megiddo Tombs,* by P. L. O. Guy and Robert M. Engberg, pp. 209–13. Oriental Institute Publications 33. Chicago: The University of Chicago Press.

Beck, Pirhiya

1967 Problems in the Glyptic Art of Palestine. Ph.D. dissertation, Columbia University.

1975 "The Cylinder Seal Impressions from Megiddo, Stage V, and Related Problems." *Opuscula Atheniensia* 11: 1–16.

2002 "Issues in the Art of Early Bronze Age Palestine." In *Imagery and Representation: Studies in the Art and Iconography of Ancient Palestine; Collected Articles*, edited by Pirhiya Beck, pp. 19–57. Journal of the Institute of Archaeology of Tel Aviv University, Occasional Paper 3. Tel Aviv: Institute of Archaeology, Tel Aviv University.

Ben-Dor, Immanuel

1936 "Pottery of the Middle and Late Neolithic Periods." In *Jericho: City and Necropolis; Report for the Sixth and Concluding Season, 1936*, edited by John Garstang, Immanuel Ben-Dor, and G. M. FitzGerald, pp. 77–91. London: Institute of Archaeology.

Ben-Tor, Amnon

1978 *Cylinder Seals of Third-millennium Palestine*. Bulletin of the American Schools of Oriental Research, Supplement Series 22. Cambridge: American Schools of Oriental Research.

2003 "The Early Bronze Age Cylinder-seal Impressions and a Stamp Seal." In *Tel Qashish: A Village in the Jezreel Valley; Final Report of the Archaeological Excavations, 1978–1987*, edited by Amnon Ben-Tor, Ruhama Bonfil, and Sharon Zuckerman, pp. 165–73. Qedem Reports 5. Jerusalem: The Hebrew University and the Israel Exploration Society.

Ben-Tor, Amnon, and Ruhama Bonfil

2003a "The Stratigraphy of the Early Bronze Age." In *Tel Qashish: A Village in the Jezreel Valley; Final Report of the Archaeological Excavations, 1978–1987*, edited by A. Ben-Tor, R. Bonfil, and S. Zuxkerman, pp. 10–30. Qedem Reports 5. Jerusalem: The Hebrew University and the Israel Exploration Society.

2003b "The Stratigraphy of the Early Bronze Age II–III." In *Tel Qashish: A Village in the Jezreel Valley; Final Report of the Archaeological Excavations, 1978–1987*, edited by Amnon Ben-Tor, Ruhama Bonfil, and Sharon Zuckerman, pp. 130–60. Qedem Reports 5. Jerusalem: The Hebrew University and the Israel Exploration Society.

Ben-Tor, Amnon; Ruhama Bonfil; and Sharon Zuckerman

2003 *Tel Qashish: A Village in the Jezreel Valley; Final Report of the Archaeological Excavations, 1978–1987*. Qedem Reports 5. Jerusalem: The Hebrew University and the Israel Exploration Society.

Bertemes Frenz

1986 "Das Frühe Neolithikum von Kamid el-Loz." In *Bericht über die Ergebnisse der Ausgrabungen in Kamid el-Loz in den Jahren 1977 bis 1981*, edited by Rolf Hachmann, pp. 33–76. Saarbrücker Beiträge zur Altertumskunde 36. Bonn: Rudolf Habelt.

Blockman, N., and I. Groman-Yeroslavski

2006 "The Early Bronze Age Flint Assemblage." In *Megiddo IV: The 1998–2000 Seasons*, edited by Israel Finkelstein, David Ussishkin, and Baruch Halpern, pp. 315–42. Monograph Series 24. Tel Aviv: Tel Aviv University.

Bourke, Stephen; Jamie Lovell; Peta Seaton; Rachael Sparks; Lachlan Mairs; and John Meadows

2007 "A Fourth Season of Renewed Excavation by the University of Sydney at Tulaylāt al-Ghassūl (1999)." *Annual of the Department of Antiquities of Jordan* 51: 35–80.

Bourke, Stephen; Ugo Zoppi; John Meadows; Quan Hua; and Samantha Gibbins

2004 "The End of the Chalcolithic Period in the South Jordan Valley: New ^{14}C Determinations from Teleilat Ghassul, Jordan." *Radiocarbon* 46/1: 315–23.

Brandfon, Fredric R.

1977 "The Earliest City Wall at Megiddo." *Tel Aviv: Journal of the Institute of Archaeology of Tel Aviv University* 4/1: 79–84.

Braun, Eliot

1985 *En Shadud: Salvage Excavations at a Farming Community in the Jezreel Valley, Israel*. British Archaeological Reports, International Series 249. Oxford: British Archaeological Reports.

1989a "The Problem of the Apsidal House: New Aspects of Early Bronze I Domestic Architecture in Israel, Jordan, and Lebanon." *Palestine Exploration Quarterly* 121: 1–43.

1989b "The Transition from the Chalcolithic to the Early Bronze Age in Northern Israel and Transjordan: Is There a Missing Link?"In *L'urbanisation de la Palestine à l'âge du Bronze ancien: bilan et perspectives des recherches actuelles*, edited by P. de Miroschedji, pp. 7–28 (Actes du Colloque d'Emmaüs, 20–24 octobre 1986). British Archaeological Reports, International Series 527/i. Oxford: British Archaeological Reports.

1990 "Basalt Bowls of the EB I Horizon in the Southern Levant." *Paléorient* 16/1: 87–96.

1993 "Some Observations on the Origins and Iconography of a Cylinder Seal from Bâb edh-Dhrâc." *Bulletin of the American Schools of Oriental Research* 290–291: 121–25.

1996a Cultural Diversity and Change in the Early Bronze I of Israel and Jordan: Towards an Understanding of the Chronological Progression and Patterns of Regionalism in Early Bronze Society. Ph.D. dissertation, Tel Aviv University.

1997 *Yiftaḥ'el: Salvage and Rescue Excavations at a Prehistoric Village in Lower Galilee, Israel*. Israel Antiquities Authority Reports 2. Jerusalem: Israel Antiquities Authority.

2001 "Proto, Early Dynastic Egypt, and Early Bronze I–II of the Southern Levant: Some Uneasy ^{14}C Correlations." *Radiocarbon* 43/3: 1279–95.

2004a *Early Beth Shan (Strata XIX–XIII): G. M. FitzGerald's Deep Cut on the Tell.* University Museum Monograph 121. Philadelphia: University of Pennsylvania Museum of Archaeology and Anthropology.

2004b "More Evidence for Early Bronze Age Glyptics from the Southern Levant." *Levant* 36: 13–30.

2004c "Egypt and the Southern Levant in the Late 4th Millennium B.C.E.: Shifting Patterns of Interaction." In *Egypt at Its Origins: Studies in Memory of Barbara Adams* (Proceedings of the International Conference, "Origin of the State: Predynastic and Early Dynastic Egypt," Krakow, 28 August–1 September 2002), edited by Stan Hendrickx, Renée F. Friedman, Krzysztof M. Ciałowicz, and Marek Chłodnicki, pp. 507–17. Orientalia Lovaniensia Analecta 138. Leuven: Peeters.

2008 "Palmaḥim Quarry." In *The New Encyclopedia of Archaeological Excavations in the Holy Land*, edited by Ephraim Stern, Hillel Geva, and Alan Paris, supplementary volume 5, pp. 1991–93. Jerusalem: Israel Exploration Society.

2009 "Social Development in Early Bronze Age I of the Southern Levant: Reflections on Evidence for Different Modes of Ceramic Production." In *Techniques and People: Anthropological Perspectives on Technology in the Archaeology of the Proto-Historic and Early Historic Periods in the Southern Levant*, edited by Steven A. Rosen and Valentine Roux, pp. 233–52. Mémoires et travaux du Centre de Recherche Français à Jérusalem 9. Paris: De Boccard.

2011a "South Levantine Early Bronze Age Chronological Correlations with Egypt in Light of the Narmer Serekhs from Tel Erani and Arad: New Interpretations." In *Egypt at Its Origins 3* (Proceedings of the Third International Conference "Origin of the State: Predynastic and Early Dynastic Egypt," London, 27 July–1 August 2008), edited by Renée F. Friedman and Peter N. Fiske, pp. 975–1001. Orientalia Lovaniensia Analecta 205. Leuven: Peeters.

2011b "Of Pots and Towns: New Perspectives on EB I of the Southern Levant." In *Daily Life, Materiality, and Complexity in Early Urban Communities of the Southern Levant: Papers in Honor of Walter E. Rast and R. Thomas Schaub*, edited by Meredith S. Chesson, pp. 265–80. Winona Lake: Eisenbrauns.

2011c "Early Interaction between Peoples of the Nile Valley and the Southern Levant." In *Before the Pyramids: The Origins of Egyptian Civilization*, edited by Emily Teeter, pp. 105–22. Oriental Institute Museum Publication 33. Chicago: The Oriental Institute.

2012a "On Some South Levantine Early Bronze Age Ceramic 'Wares' and Styles." *Palestine Exploration Quarterly* 144/1: 4–31.

2012b "Qiryat Ata: New Perspectives on a Late Prehistoric Site in the Southern Levant." *Studies in Ancient Art and Civilization* 16: 7–38.

In press "The Pottery of Early Bronze Age I." In *The Pottery of Israel and Its Ancient Neighbors*, edited by Seymour Gittin. Jerusalem: The Israel Exploration Society and the Israel Antiquities Authority.

Braun, Eliot, and Ram Gophna

2004 "Salvage Excavations at Afridar (Ashqelon, Israel) in Area G." *ʿAtiqot* 45: 185–242.

Braun, Eliot, and E. C. M. van den Brink

1998 "Some Comments on the Late EB I Sequence of Canaan and the Relative Dating of Tomb U-j at Umm el Ga'ab and Graves 313 and 787 from Minshat Abu Omar with Imported Ware: Views from Egypt and Canaan." *Egypt and the Levant* 7: 71–94.

Braun, Eliot; E. C. M. van den Brink; J. Regev; E. Boaretto; and S. Bar

2013 "The Late Chalcolithic to Early Bronze Age I Transition in the Southern Levant: Determining Continuity and Discontinuity of 'Mind the Gap.'" *Paléorient* 39/1: 15–22.

Braun, Yael; E. Kagan; A. Agnon; M. Bar-Matthews; and A. Ayalon

In press "Speleoseismites from Different Fault Systems: Clues to System Coupling." *Israel Journal of Geological Science.*

Breasted, James Henry

1929 "Foreword." In *The Excavation of Armageddon*, by Clarence S. Fisher, pp. vii–xiii. Oriental Institute Communications 4. Chicago: University of Chicago Press.

Chesson, Meredith S.

2001 "Embodied Memories of Place and People: Death and Society in an Early Urban Community." In *Social Memory, Identity, and Death: Anthropological Perspectives on Mortuary Rituals*, edited by Meredith S. Chesson, pp. 100–13. Archeological Papers of the American Anthropological Association 10. Arlington: American Anthropological Association.

Covello-Paran, Karen

2003 "The Early Bronze Age Occupation at Tel Gat-Hefer, Lower Galilee, Areas C and D." *ʿAtiqot* 44: 97–170.

de Vaux, Roland M.

1955 "Les fouilles de Tell el-Farʿah, près Naplouse: cinquième campagne." *Revue biblique* 62: 541–89.

de Vaux, Roland M., and Marie-Joseph Steve

1947 "La première campagne de fouilles à Tell el-Farʿah, près Naplouse." *Revue biblique* 54: 394–433.

1948 "La seconde campagne de fouilles à Tell el-Farʿah, près Naplouse." *Revue biblique* 55: 544–80.

1949 "La deuxième campagne de fouilles à Tell el-Farʿah, près Naplouse." *Revue biblique*: 56: 102–53.

Dever, William G.

1995 "Social Structure in the Early Bronze IV Period in Palestine." In *The Archaeology of Society in the Holy Land*, edited by Thomas Evan Levy, pp. 283–96 London: Leicester University Press.

Dodson, Aidan, and Salima Ikram

2008 *The Tomb in Ancient Egypt: Royal and Private Sepulchres from the Early Dynastic Period to the Romans*. London: Thames & Hudson.

Dothan, M.

1970 "A Burial Cave Near Tel Esur." *Ezor Menashe (Menashe Region)* 2: 1–16. [Internal publication of the Menashe Regional Council; in Hebrew]

1971 "The Late Chalcolithic Period in Palestine: Chronology and Foreign Contacts." *Eretz-Israel* 10: 126–31, xii–xiii. [In Hebrew, with English summary]

Doumet-Serhal, Claude

2006 *The Early Bronze Age in Sidon: "College Site" Excavations (1998-2000-2001)*. Bibliothèque archéologique et historique 178. Beirut: Institut français du Proche-Orient.

Dubis, Elzbieta

1999 "Field K: The Dolmen," pp. 109–10 in "Mādabā Plains Project: Excavations at Tall al-'Umayrī, 1998," by Larry G. Herr, Douglas R. Clark, Lawrence T. Geraty, and Øystein S. LaBianca. *Annual of the Department of Antiquities of Jordan* 43: 99–114.

Dunand, Maurice

1945 *Byblia grammata: documents et recherches sur le développement de l'écriture en Phénicie*. Études et documents d'archéologie 2. Beirut: République libanaise. Ministère de l'éducation nationale et des beaux-arts, direction des antiquités.

1950 "Chronologie des plus anciennes installations de Byblos." *Revue biblique* 47: 583–603.

Dunayevsky, Immanuel, and Aharon Kempinski

1973 "The Megiddo Temples." *Zeitschrift des deutschen Palästina-Vereins* 89: 161–87.

Duncan, J. Garrow

1930 *Corpus of Dated Palestinian Pottery*. Publications of the Egyptian Research Account 49. London: British School of Archaeology in Egypt.

Eisenberg, Emanuel

1996 "Tel Shalem: Soundings in a Fortified Site of the Early Bronze Age Ib." *ʿAtiqot* 30: 1–124.

2001 "Pottery of Strata V–IV, The Early Bronze Age I." In *Tel Te'o: A Neolithic, Chalcolithic, and Early Bronze Age Site in the Hula Valley*, edited by Emanuel Eisenberg, Avi Gopher, and Raphael Greenberg, pp. 116–31. Israel Antiquities Authority Reports 13. Jerusalem: Israel Antiquities Authority.

Eisenberg, Emanuel, and Raphael Greenberg

2006 "Area EY: The Eisenberg–Yogev Excavations, 1981–1982, 1985–1986." In *Bet Yeraḥ: The Early Bronze Age Mound*, Volume 1: *Excavation Reports, 1933–1986*, edited by Raphael Greenberg, Emanuel Eisenberg, Sarit Paz, and Yitzhak Paz, pp. 339–468. Israel Antiquities Authority Reports 30. Jerusalem: Israel Antiquities Authority.

Emery, Walter B.

1961 *Archaic Egypt*. Edinburgh: Penguin.

Engberg, Robert M., and Geoffrey M. Shipton

1934a *Notes on the Chalcolithic and Early Bronze Pottery of Megiddo*. Studies in Ancient Oriental Civilization 10. Chicago: University of Chicago Press.

1934b "Another Sumerian Seal Impression from Megiddo." *Palestine Exploration Fund Quarterly Statement* 66: 90–93.

Esse, Douglas L.

1991 *Subsistence, Trade, and Social Change in Early Bronze Age Palestine*. Studies in Ancient Oriental Civilization 50. Chicago: The Oriental Institute.

Fantalkin, Alexander

2000 "A Salvage Excavation at an Early Bronze Age Settlement on Ha-Shophtim Street, Qiryat ʾAta." *Tel Aviv: Journal of the Institute of Archaeology of Tel Aviv University* 27/1: 28–56.

Finkelstein, Israel, and David Ussishkin

2000a "Area J." In *Megiddo III: The 1992–1996 Seasons*, edited by Israel Finkelstein, David Ussishkin, and Baruch Halpern, pp. 25–74. Monograph Series 18. Tel Aviv: Institute of Archaeology, Tel Aviv University.

2000b "Chapter 24: Archaeological and Historical Conclusions." In Israel Finkelstein, David Ussishkin, and Baruch Halpern, eds. *Megiddo III: The 1992–1996 Seasons*, pp. 25–74, 576–605.

Tel Aviv: Institute of Archaeology, Tel Aviv University.

2003 "The Cache of Egyptianized Vessels from Megiddo: A Stratigraphical Update." *Tel Aviv: Journal of the Institute of Archaeology of Tel Aviv University* 30/1: 27–41.

Finkelstein, Israel; David Ussishkin; and Baruch Halpern, editors

2000 *Megiddo III: The 1992-1996 Seasons.* Monograph Series 18. Tel Aviv: Institute of Archaeology.

2006 *Megiddo IV: The 1998–2000 Seasons.* Monograph Series 24. Tel Aviv: Institute of Archaeology, Tel Aviv University.

Fischer, Peter M.

2008 *Tell Abu Al-Kharaz in the Jordan Valley*, Volume 1: *The Early Bronze Age.* Denkschriften der Gesamtakademie 48. Vienna: Österreichisches Akademie der Wissenschaften.

Fisher, Clarence S.

1929 *The Excavation of Armageddon.* Oriental Institute Communications 4. Chicago: University of Chicago Press.

FitzGerald, G. M.

1934 "Excavations at Beth-Shan in 1933." *Palestine Exploration Quarterly for 1934*: 123–34.

1935 "Beth Shan: Earliest Pottery." *The Museum Journal* [The University Museum, University of Pennsylvania, Philadelphia] 24: 5–22.

1936 "Pottery of the Early Bronze Age" pp. 91–100 in "Jericho: City and Necropolis; Report for Sixth and Concluding Season, 1936," by John Garstang, Immanuel Ben-Dor, and G. M. FitzGerald. *Annals of Archaeology and Anthropology* 23: 67–100.

Frangipane, Marcella, editor

2010 *Economic Centralisation in Formative States. The Archaeological Reconstruction of the Economic System in 4th Millennium Arslantepe.* Studi Preistoria Orientale 3. Rome: Sapienza Università.

Frankfort, Henri

1955 *Stratified Cylinder Seals from the Diyala Region.* Oriental Institute Publications 72. Chicago: University of Chicago Press.

Gal, Zvi, and Karen Covello-Paran

1996 "Excavations at 'Afula, 1989." *ʿAtiqot* 30: 25–67.

Garfinkel, Yosef

1992 *The Pottery Assemblages of the Sha'ar Hagolan and Rabah Stages of Munhata (Israel).* Les cahiers du Centre de recherche français de Jerusalem 6. Paris: Association Paléorient.

1993 "Yarmukian Culture in Israel." *Paléorient* 19/1: 115–34.

1999 *Neolithic and Chalcolithic Pottery of the Southern Levant.* Qedem 39. Jerusalem: The Hebrew University of Jerusalem.

Garrod, D. A. E.

1934 "Notes on the Flint Implements (Appendix II)." In *Notes on the Chalcolithic and Early Bronze Pottery of Megiddo*, edited by Robert M. Engberg and Geoffrey M. Shipton, pp. 78–79. Studies in Ancient Oriental Civilization 10. Chicago: University of Chicago Press.

Garstang, John

1935 "General Report for 1935: The Early Bronze Age," pp. 143–68 in "Jericho: City and Necropolis; Fifth Report," by John Garstang, J. P. Droop, and Joan Crowfoot. *Annals of Archaeology and Anthropology* 22: 143–84.

Genz, Hermann

2001 "Early Bronze Age Potmarks from Khirbat az-Zayraqun: Some Aspects Concerning their Meaning." *Studies in the History and Archaeology of Jordan VII*, pp. 217–29. Proceedings of the Seventh International Conference on the History and Archaeology of Jordan held in Copenhagen, Denmark. Amman: Department of Antiquities.

2002 *Die frühbronzezeitliche Keramik von Hirbet ez-Zeraqon: Mit Studien zur Chronologie und funktionalen Deutung frühbronzezeitlicher Keramik in der südlichen Levante.* Abhandlungen des deutschen Palästina-Vereins 27:2. Wiesbaden: Harrasowitz.

Gersht, D.

2006 "The Flint assemblage from Area K." In *Megiddo IV: The 1998-2000 Seasons*, edited by I. Finkelstein, D. Ussishkin, and B. Halpern, pp. 343–52. Monograph Series 24. Tel Aviv: Institute of Archaeology, Tel Aviv University.

Getzov, Nimrod

2006 *The Tel Bet Yeraḥ Excavations, 1994-1995.* Israel Antiquities Authority Reports 28. Jerusalem: Israel Antiquities Authority.

Getzov, Nimrod; O. Barzilai; G. Le Dosseur; A. Eirikh-Rose; Ofer Marder; N. Marom; and Ianir Milevski

2009 "Nahal Betzet II and Ard el Samra: Two Late Prehistoric Sites and Settlement; Patterns in the Akko Plain." *Mitekufat Haeven - Journal of Israel Prehistoric Society* 39: 81–158.

Getzov, Nimrod; Yotam Teper; and Inbar Ktalav

2008 "Midrakh 'Oz." *Hadashot Arkheologiyot* 120. Online at http://www.hadashot-esi.org.il/report_detail_eng.asp?id=905&mag_id=114. Accessed December 16, 2011.

Glock, A.

1993 "Taanach." In *The New Encyclopedia of Archaeological Excavations in the Holy Land*, edited by Ephraim Stern, pp. 1428–33. Jerusalem: Israel Exploration Society.

Golani, Amir

2003 *Salvage Excavations at the Early Bronze Age Site of Qiryat Ata.* Israel Antiquities Authority Reports 18. Jerusalem: Israel Antiquities Authority.

2004 "Salvage Excavations at the Early Bronze Age Site of Ashqelon, Afridar — Area E." *ʿAtiqot* 45: 9-62.

2006 "Qiryat Ata." *Hadashot Arkheologiyot* 118. Online at http://www.hadashot-esi.org.il/report_detail_eng.asp?id=410&mag_id=111. Accessed December 11, 2011.

Gopher, Avi

1996 *The Nahal Qanah Cave: Earliest Gold in the Southern Levant.* Monograph Series 12. Tel Aviv: Institute of Archaeology, Tel Aviv University.

Gophna, Ram

1974 The Settlement of the Coastal Plain of Eretz Israel during the Early Bronze Age. Ph.D. dissertation, Tel Aviv University. [In Hebrew]

1992 "The Intermediate Bronze Age." In *The Archaeology of Ancient Israel,* edited by Amnon Ben-Tor, pp. 129–58. New Haven: Yale University Press.

Goren, Y., and Sharon Zuckerman

2000 "An Overview of the Typology, Provenance and Technology of the Early Bronze Age I 'Gray Burnished Ware.'" In *Ceramics and Change in the Early Bronze Age of the Southern Levant*, edited by Graham Philip and Douglas Baird, pp. 165–82. Levantine Archaeology 2. Sheffield: Sheffield Academic Press.

Green, John D. M.

2009 "Archaeology and Politics in the Holy Land: The Life and Career of P. L. O. Guy." *Palestine Exploration Quarterly* 141/3: 167–87.

Greenberg, Raphael

1996 "Part III: F. Small Finds." In *Dan I: A Chronicle of the Excavations; The Pottery Neolithic, the Early Bronze Age and the Middle Bronze Age Tombs*, edited by Avraham Biran, David Ilan, and Raphael Greenberg, pp. 139–50. Annual of the Nelson Glueck School of Biblical Archaeology. Jerusalem: Nelson Glueck School of Biblical Archaeology, Hebrew Union College-Jewish Institute of Religion.

2000 "Changes in Ceramic Production between Early Bronze Age II and III in Northern Israel, Based on the Pottery of Tell Hazor and Tell Dan." In *Ceramics and Change in the Early Bronze Age of the Southern Levant*, edited by Graham Philip and Douglas Baird, pp. 18–200. Levantine Archaeology 2. Sheffield: Sheffield Academic Press.

2006 "Notes on the Early Bronze Age Pottery (The 1998–2000 Seasons)." In *Megiddo IV: The 1998-2000 Seasons*, edited by I. Finkelstein, D. Ussishkin, and B. Halpern, pp. 149–65. Monograph Series 24. Tel Aviv: Institute of Archaeology, Tel Aviv University.

Greenberg, Raphael, and Emanuel Eisenberg

2006 "Area BS: The Bar-Adon Excavations, Southeast, 1951–1953." In *Bet Yeraḥ: The Early Bronze Age Mound*, Volume 1: *Excavation Reports, 1933-1986*, edited by Raphael Greenberg, Emanuel Eisenberg, Sarit Paz, and Yitzhak Paz, pp. 117–234. Israel Antiquities Authority Reports 30. Jerusalem: Israel Antiquities Authority.

Greenberg, Raphael; Emanuel Eisenberg; Sarit Paz; and Yitzhak Paz

2006 *Bet Yeraḥ: The Early Bronze Age Mound*, Volume 1: *Excavation Reports, 1933-1986.* Israel Antiquities Authority Reports 30. Jerusalem: Israel Antiquities Authority.

Greenberg, Raphael, and Naomi Porat

1996 "A Third Millennium Levantine Pottery Production Center: Typology, Petrography, and Provenance of the Metallic Ware of Northern Israel and Adjacent Regions." *Bulletin of the American Schools of Oriental Research* 301: 5–24.

Greenhut, Zvi

1995 "EB IV Tombs and Burials in Palestine." *Tel Aviv: Journal of the Institute of Archaeology of Tel Aviv University* 22/1: 3–46.

Guy, P. L. O.

1931 *New Light from Armageddon: Second Provisional Report (1927-29) on the Excavations at Megiddo in Palestine.* Oriental Institute Communications 9. Chicago: University of Chicago Press.

1932 "Balloon Photography and Archaeological Excavation." *Antiquity* 6: 148–55.

Guy, P. L. O., and Robert M. Engberg

1938 *Megiddo Tombs.* Oriental Institute Publications 33. Chicago: University of Chicago Press.

Hanbury-Tenison, J. W.

1986 *The Late Chalcolithic to Early Bronze I Transition in Palestine and Transjordan.* British Archaeological Reports, International Series 311. Oxford: British Archaeological Reports.

Herr, Larry G.; Douglas R. Clark; Lawrence T. Geraty; Randall W. Younker; and Øystein S. LaBianca, editors

2000 *Madaba Plains Project IV: The 1992 Season at Tall al-'Umayri and Subsequent Studies.* Berrien Springs: Andrews University.

Herr, Larry G.; Lawrence T. Geraty; Øystein S. LaBianca; Randall W. Younker; and Douglas R. Clark

1996 "Mādabā Plains Project 1994: Excavations at Tall al-'Umayrī, Tall Jalūl and Vicinity." *Annual of the Department of Antiquities of Jordan* 40: 63–81.

Hofstetter, A.; T. van Eck; and A. Shapira

1996 "Seismic Activity along Fault Branches of the Dead Sea–Jordan Transform System: The Carmel-Tirtza Fault System." *Tectonophysics* 267: 317–30.

Horwitz, L. K.

1985 "Appendix C: The En Shadud Faunal Remains." In *En Shadud: Salvage Excavations at a Farming Community in the Jezreel Valley, Israel*, edited by Eliot Braun, pp. 168–77. British Archaeological Reports, International Series 249. Oxford: British Archaeological Reports.

2003a "Fauna from Tel Qashish." In *Tel Qashish: A Village in the Jezreel Valley; Final Report of the Archaeological Excavations (1978–1987)*, edited by Amnon Ben-Tor, Ruhama Bonfil, and Sharon Zuckerman, pp. 427–43. Qedem Reports 5. Jerusalem: Institute of Archaeology, Hebrew University of Jerusalem and the Israel Exploration Society.

2003b "Early Bronze Age Animal Exploitation at Qiryat Ata." In *Salvage Excavations at Early Bronze Age Site of Qiryat Ata*, edited by Amir Golani, pp. 225–37. Israel Antiquities Authority Reports 18. Jerusalem: Israel Antiquities Authority.

Hrdlicka, A.

1938 "Skeletal Remains." In *Megiddo Tombs*, edited by P. L. O. Guy and Robert M. Engberg, pp. 192–214. Oriental Institute Publications 33. Chicago: University of Chicago Press.

Ilan, David

2002 "Mortuary Practices in Early Bronze Age Canaan." *Near Eastern Archaeology* 65/2: 92–104.

Ilan, Ornit, and Yuval Goren

2003 "The Egyptianized Pottery Vessels of Early Bronze Age Megiddo." *Tel Aviv: Journal of the Institute of Archaeology of Tel Aviv University* 30/1: 42–53.

Joffe, Alexander H.

1993 *Settlement and Society in the Early Bronze Age I and II, Southern Levant: Complementarity and Contradiction in a Small-scale Complex Society.* Monographs in Mediterranean Archaeology 4. Sheffield: Sheffield Academic Press.

2000 "The Early Bronze Age Pottery from Area J." In *Megiddo III: The 1992–1996 Seasons*, edited by Israel Finkelstein, David Ussishkin, and Baruch Halpern, pp. 161–85. Monograph Series 18. Tel Aviv: Institute of Archaeology, Tel Aviv University.

2001 "Early Bronze Age Seal Impressions from the Jezreel Valley and the Problem of Sealing in the Southern Levant." In *Studies in the Archaeology of Israel and Neighboring Lands in Memory of Douglas L. Esse*, edited by Samuel R. Wolff, pp. 355–75. Studies in Ancient Oriental Civilization 59/American Schools of Oriental Research, ASOR Books 5. Chicago and Atlanta: The Oriental Institute.

Kantor, Helene J.

1965 "Egypt and Its Foreign Correlations." In *Chronologies in Old World Archaeology*, edited by R. W. Ehrich, pp. 1–46. 2nd edition. Chicago: University of Chicago Press.

1992 "The Relative Chronology of Egypt and Its Foreign Correlations before the First Intermediate Period." In *Chronologies in Old World Archaeology*, edited by R. W. Ehrich, vol. 1, pp. 3–21, vol. 2, pp. 2–45. 3rd edition. Chicago: University of Chicago Press.

Kafafi, Z. A.

2011 "Jordanian-Egyptian Interaction during the Third Millennium B.C.E. as Evidenced by the Abydos Ware." In *Daily Life, Materiality, and Complexity in Early Urban Communities of the Southern Levant: Papers in Honor of Walter E. Rast and R. Thomas Schaub*, edited by Meredith S. Chesson, pp. 139–52. Winona Lake: Eisenbrauns.

Kenyon, Kathleen M.

1960 *Excavations at Jericho*, Volume 1: *The Tombs Excavated in 1952–4.* London: British School of Archaeology in Jerusalem.

1970 *Archaeology in the Holy Land.* 3rd edition. New York: Praeger.

1979 *Archaeology in the Holy Land.* 4th edition. London: Benn.

Kenyon, Kathleen M., and Thomas A. Holland

1983 *Excavations at Jericho*, Volume 5: *The Pottery Phases of the Tell and Other Finds.* Jerusalem and London: British School of Archaeology in Jerusalem and The British Academy.

Khalaily, Hamoudi

1999 The Flint Assemblage of Layer V at Hagoshrim: A Neolithic Assemblage of the Sixth Millenium B.C. in the Hula Basin. M.A. thesis, The Hebrew University. [In Hebrew]

2004 "An Early Bronze Age Site at Ashqelon, Afridar — Area F." *ʿAtiqot* 45: 121–59.

Lamon, Robert S., and Geoffrey M. Shipton

1939 *Megiddo I. Seasons of 1925–34: Strata I–V*. Oriental Institute Publications 42. Chicago: University of Chicago Press.

Levy, Thomas Evan

1995 "Cult, Metallurgy, and Rank Societies – Chalcolithic Period (ca. 4500–3500 B.C.E.)." In *The Archaeology of Society in the Holy Land*, edited by Thomas Evan Levy, pp. 226–43. London: Leicester University Press.

Levy, Thomas Evan, and Edwin C. M. van den Brink

2002 "Interaction Models, Egypt and the Levantine Periphery." In *Egypt and the Levant: Interrelations from the 4th through the Early 3rd Millennium B.C.E.*, edited by Edwin C. M. van den Brink and Thomas Evan Levy, pp. 3–38. London: Leicester University Press.

Loud, Gordon

1948 *Megiddo II: Seasons of 1935–39*. Oriental Institute Publications 62. Chicago: University of Chicago Press.

Macalister, Robert Alexander Stewart

1912 *The Excavation of Gezer: 1902–1905 and 1907–1909*. 3 volumes. London: John Murray.

Marco, S.; A. Agnon; Israel Finkelstein; and David Ussishkin

2006 "Megiddo Earthquakes." In *Megiddo IV: The 1998–2000 Seasons*, edited by Israel Finkelstein, David Ussishkin, and Baruch Halpern, pp. 568–76. Monograph Series 24. Tel Aviv: Institute of Archaeology, Tel Aviv University.

Marcus, E.

2002 "Early Seafaring and Maritime Activity in the Southern Levant from Prehistory through the Third Millennium B.C.E." In *Egypt and the Levant: Interrelations from the 4th through the Early 3rd Millennium B.C.E.*, edited by Edwin C. M. van den Brink and Thomas Evan Levy, pp. 403–17. London: Leicester University Press.

Marder, Ofer; Eliot Braun; and Ianir Milevski

1995 "The Flint Assemblage of Lower Ḥorvat ʿIllin: Some Technical and Economic Considerations." *ʿAtiqot* 27: 63–93.

Matthews, Donald M.

1997 *The Early Glyptic of Tell Brak: Cylinder Seals of Third Millennium Syria*. Orbis Biblicus et Orientalis 15. Fribourg: University Press; Göttingen: Vandenhoeck & Ruprecht.

May, H. G.

1935 *Material Remains of the Megiddo Cult*. Oriental Institute Publications 26. Chicago: University of Chicago Press.

Mazar, Amihai, editor

2012 *Excavations at Tel Beth-Shean 1989–1996*, Volume IV: *The 4th and 3rd Millennia BCE*. Jerusalem: The Israel Exploration Society and the Hebrew University of Jerusalem.

Mazar, Amihai, and Yael Rotem

2009 "Tel Beth Shean during the EB IB Period: Evidence for Social Complexity in the Late 4th Millennium B.C." *Levant* 41/2: 131–53.

Mazzoni, S.

1986 "The Diffusion of the Palestinian Combed Jars." In *Studies in the History and Archaeology of Palestine*, edited by Shawqi Shaath, vol. 2, pp. 145–58. Proceedings of the First International Symposium on Palestine. Aleppo: Aleppo University Press.

Meyerhof, Ezra L.

1989 *The Bronze Age Necropolis at Kibbutz Hazorea, Israel*. British Archaeological Reports, International Series 534. Oxford: British Archaeological Reports.

Milevski, Ianir

2005 Local Exchange in Early Bronze Age Canaan. Ph.D. dissertation, Institute of Archaeology, Tel Aviv University.

2009 *Early Bronze Age Goods Exchange in the Southern Levant: A Marxist Perspective*. London: Equinox.

Milevski, Ianir; Eliot Braun; Daniel Varga; and Yigal Israel

2012 "A Newly-discovered Early Bronze Age Settlement and Silo Complex at Amaziya, Israel." *Antiquity* 85/331. Available online at http://antiquity.ac.uk/projgall/milevski331/. Accessed December 24, 2011.

Milevski, Ianir; Ofer Marder; Hamoudi Khalaily; and F. Sonntag

2006 "The Flint Assemblage." In *ʿEn Esur (ʿEin Asawir) I: Excavations at a Protohistoric Site in the Coastal Plain of Israel*, edited by Eli Yannai, pp. 179–210. Israel Antiquities Authority Reports 31. Jerusalem: Israel Antiquities Authority.

de Miroschedji, Pierre

2000 "An Early Bronze Age III Pottery Sequence for Southern Israel." In *Ceramics and Change in the Early Bronze Age of the Southern Levant*, edited by Graham Philip and Douglas Baird, pp. 315–46. Levantine Archaeology 2. Sheffield: Sheffield Academic Press.

Niemann, Herman M., and Gunnar Lehmann

2006 "One Hundred Years After: Gottlieb Schumacher, Carl Watzinger and Excavations at Megiddo." *Megiddo IV: The 1998–2000 Seasons*, edited by Israel Finkelstein, David Ussishkin, and Baruch Halpern, pp. 688–93. Monograph Series 24. Tel Aviv: Institute of Archaeology, Tel Aviv University.

Nigro, Lorenzo; Andrea Polcaro; and Maura Sala

2005 *Tell es-Sultan/Gerico, alle soglie della prima urbanizzazione: il villaggio e la necropoli del Bronzo Antico I (3300–3000 a.C.)*. Rome "La Sapienza" Studies on the Archaeology of Palestine and Transjordan 1. Rome: Università di Roma "La Sapienza."

Nigro, Lorenzo, and Maura Sala

2010 *Tell es-Sultan/Jericho in the Early Bronze II (3000–2700 B.C.): The Rise of an Early Palestinian City; A Synthesis of the Results of Four Archaeological Expeditions*. Rome "La Sapienza" Studies on the Archaeology of Palestine and Transjordan 5. Rome: "La Sapienza" Expedition to Palestine and Jordan.

Niton-1

http://www.niton.com/Niton-Analyzers-Products/xl3/goldd-technology.aspx?sflang=en`. Accessed June 21, 2010.

Niton-2

http://www.niton.com/portable-XRF-technology/literature.aspx?CntCatID=5766b693-a8a7-41ef-8b51-41d944618736&sflang=en. Accessed June 21, 2010.

Nof, R. N.; G. Baer; Y. Eyal; and F. Novali

2007 "Recent Crustal Movements along the Carmel Fault System, Israel." Paper presented at ENVISAT (European Environmental Satellite) Symposium, Montreux, Switzerland, 23–27 April 2007. Available online at http://envisat.esa.int/envisatsymposium/proceedings/posters/4P11/463014no.pdf. Accessed December 24, 2011.

Orni, Efraim, and Elisha Efrat

1980 *Geography of Israel*. 4th revised edition. Jerusalem: Israel Universities Press.

Paz, Sarit

2006a "Area MS: The Mazar–Stekelis Excavations, 1944–1945." In *Bet Yeraḥ: The Early Bronze Age Mound*, Volume 1: *Excavation Reports, 1933–1986*, edited by Raphael Greenberg, Emanuel Eisenberg, Sarit Paz, and Yitzhak Paz, pp. 17–52. Israel Antiquities Authority Reports 30. Jerusalem: Israel Antiquities Authority.

2006b "Area SA: The Stekelis–Avi-Yonah Excavations (Circles Building), 1945–1946." In *Bet Yeraḥ: The Early Bronze Age Mound*, Volume 1: *Excavation Reports, 1933–1986*, edited by Raphael Greenberg, Emanuel Eisenberg, Sarit Paz, and Yitzhak Paz, pp. 53–103. Israel Antiquities Authority Reports 30. Jerusalem: Israel Antiquities Authority.

Paz, Yitzhak

2006a "Area GB: The Guy–Bar-Adon Soundings in the Northern Part of the Mound, 1949–1955." In *Bet Yeraḥ: The Early Bronze Age Mound*, Volume 1: *Excavation Reports, 1933–1986*, edited by Raphael Greenberg, Emanuel Eisenberg, Sarit Paz, and Yitzhak Paz, pp. 105–15. Israel Antiquities Authority Reports 30. Jerusalem: Israel Antiquities Authority.

2006b "Area UN: The Ussishkin–Netzer Excavations, 1967." In *Bet Yeraḥ: The Early Bronze Age Mound*, Volume 1: *Excavation Reports, 1933–1986*, edited by Raphael Greenberg, Emanuel Eisenberg, Sarit Paz, and Yitzhak Paz, pp. 277–338. Israel Antiquities Authority Reports 30. Jerusalem: Israel Antiquities Authority.

Perrot, J.

1964/65 *The Prehistoric Period: From the Era of Early Man to the Age of the Patriarchs*. Israel: Israel Defense Forces [General Staff, Chief Education Officer]. [In Hebrew]

Petrie, W. M. Flinders

1891 "Chronology of Pottery." *Palestine Exploration Fund Quarterly Statement for 1891*: 68.

1921 *Corpus of Prehistoric Pottery and Palettes*. British School of Archaeology in Egypt, Publications 32. London: British School of Archaeology in Egypt.

Porat, N.

1989 Composition of Pottery: Application to the Study of the Interrelations between Canaan and Egypt during the 3rd Millennium B.C. Ph.D. dissertation, The Hebrew University of Jerusalem.

Prag, K.

2000 "Tell Iktanu, South Jordan Valley: Early Bronze Age I Ceramics." In *Ceramics and Change in the Early Bronze Age of the Southern Levant*, edited by Graham Philip and Douglas Baird, pp. 91–99. Levantine Archaeology 2. Sheffield Academic Press: Sheffield.

Pritchard, James B.

1958 *The Excavation of Herodian Jericho, 1951*. Annual of the American Schools of Oriental Research 32–33. New Haven: American Schools of Oriental Research.

Raban, Avner

1982 *Map of Nahalal (28) 16-23*. Archaeological Survey of Israel. Jerusalem: Archaeological Survey of Israel.

1999 *Map of Mishmar Ha-ʾEmeq (32)*. Archaeological Survey of Israel. Jerusalem: Archaeological Survey of Israel. [In Hebrew]

Rice, Prudence M.

1987 *Pottery Analysis: A Sourcebook*. Chicago: University of Chicago Press.

Rosen, Steven A.

1997 *Lithics after the Stone Age: A Handbook of Stone Tools from the Levant*. Walnut Creek: AltaMira.

Rotem, Y.

2012 "The Ezrly Bronze Age IB Pottery from Strata M-3 and M-2." In *Excavations at Tel Beth-Shean*, Volume 4: *The 4th and 3rd Millennia B.C.E.*, edited by A. Mazar, pp. 123–235 Jerusalem: The Hebrew University and the Israel Exploration Society.

Roux, Valentine, and Pierre de Miroschedji

2009 "Revisiting the History of the Potter's Wheel in the Southern Levant." *Levant* 41/2: 155–73.

Russell, John

1981 *The Meaning of Modern Art*. New York: Harper & Row.

Sass, Benjamin

2000 "The Small Finds." *Megiddo III: The 1992-1996 Seasons*, edited by in Israel Finkelstein, David Ussishkin, and Baruch Halpern, pp. 349–423. Monograph Series 18. Tel Aviv: Institute of Archaeology, Tel Aviv University.

Schattner, U.; Z. Ben-Avraham; M. Reshef; G. Bar-Am; and M. Lazar

2006 "Oligocene-Miocene Formation of the Haifa Basin: Qishon-Sirhan Rifting Coeval with the Red Sea-Suez Rift System." *Tectonophysics* 419: 1–12. Available online at http://www.sciencedirect.com/science/article/pii/S0040195106001648. Accessed December 24, 2011.

Schaub, R. Thomas, and Walter E. Rast

1989 *Bâb edh Dhrâᶜ: Excavations in the Cemetery Directed by Paul W. Lapp (1965-67)*. Reports of the Expedition to the Dead Sea Plain, Jordan 1. Winona Lake: Eisenbrauns.

Scheftelowitz, Na'ama

2002 "Stratigraphy and Architecture" and "Pottery II: Early Bronze Age." In *Tel Kabri: The 1986-1993 Excavation Seasons*, edited by N. Scheftelowitz and Ronit Oren, pp. 19–34 and 96–108. Monograph Series 20. Tel Aviv: The Institute of Archaeology, Tel Aviv University.

Schick, Tamar

1998 *The Cave of the Warrior: A Fourth Millennium Burial in the Judean Desert*. Israel Antiquities Authority Reports 5. Jerusalem: Israel Antiquities Authority.

Schumacher, Gottlieb

1908 *Tell el-Mutesellim I: Bericht über die 1903 bis 1905 mit Unterstützung Sr. Majestät des deutschen Kaisers und der deutschen Orient-Gesellschaft vom deutschen Verein zur Erforschung Palästinas veranstalteten Ausgrabungen*. Leipzig: Rudolf Haupt.

Sellin, Ernst, and Carl Watzinger

1913 *Jericho: Die Ergebnisse der Ausgrabungen*. Wissenschaftliche Veröffentlichungen der deutschen Orient-Gesellschaft 22. Leipzig: Hinrichs.

Shamir, G.

2007 "Earthquake Epicenter Distribution and Mechanisms in Northern Israel: Report GSI/16/2007" (Internal Report). Unpublished. Geological Survey of Israel: Jerusalem.

Shipton, Geoffrey M.

1938 "The Early Pottery of Megiddo, Season 1937–8." *Journal of the Palestine Oriental Society* 18: 54–56.

1939 *Notes on the Megiddo Pottery of Strata VI–XX*. Studies in Ancient Oriental Civilization 17. Chicago: University of Chicago Press.

Shimelmitz, R.; R. Barkai; and A. Gopher

2000 "A Canaanean Blade Workshop at Har Ḥaruvim, Israel." *Tel Aviv: Journal of the Institute of Archaeology of Tel Aviv University* 27/1: 3–22.

Shimelmitz, R.

2009 "Variability in Specialized Canaanean Blade Production of the Early Bronze Age, Levant." In *Techniques and People: Anthropological Perspectives on Technology in the Archaeology of the Proto-Historic and Early Historic Periods in the Southern Levant*, edited by Steven A. Rosen and Valentine Roux, pp 135–56. Paris: De Boccard.

Stekelis, M.

1966 *The Yarmukian Culture*. Jerusalem: Magness Press. [In Hebrew]

Sukenik, E. L.

1936 "Late Chalcolithic Pottery from 'Affûleh." *Palestine Exploration Fund Quarterly Statement*: 150–54.

1948 "Archaeological Investigations at 'Affula." *Journal of the Palestine Oriental Society* 21: 1–79.

Tufnell, Olga, et al.

1958 *Lachish IV (Tell ed-Duweir): The Bronze Age*. The Wellcome-Marston Archaeological Research Expedition to the Near East 4. London: Oxford University Press.

van den Brink, Edwin C. M., and Eliot Braun

2006 *South Levantine Influences on Egyptian Stone and Pottery Production: Some Rare Examples; Archaeology of Early Northeastern Africa*. Studies in African Archaeology 9. Poznan: Poznan Archaeological Museum.

van den Brink, Edwin C. M., and Uzi 'Ad

2011 "Tel Qashish: Preliminary Report." *Hadashot Arkheologiyot* 123. Available online at http://www.hadashot-esi.org.il/report_detail_eng.asp?id=1894&mag_id=118. Accessed December 16, 2011.

Waheeb, Mohammad

1996 "The First Season of the An-Naq' Project, Ghawr aṣ-Ṣāfī." *Annual of the Department of Antiquities of Jordan* 39: 553–55.

Wampler, Joseph Carson

1947 *Tell En-Nasbeh II*. Berkeley: The Palestine Institute of Pacific School of Religion.

Wapnish, P., and B. Hesse

2000 "Mammal Remains from the Early Bronze Sacred Compound." In *Megiddo III: The 1992–1996 Seasons*, edited by Israel Finkelstein, David Ussishkin, and Baruch Halpern, pp. 429–62. Monograph Series No. 18. Tel Aviv: Institute of Archaeology.

Watzinger, Carl

1929 *Tell el-Mutesellim II: Bericht über die 1903 bis 1905 mit Unterstützung Sr. Majestät des deutschen Kaisers und der deutschen Orient Gesellschaft vom deutschen Verein zur Erforschung Palästinas veranstalteten Ausgrabungen*, Volume 2: *Die Funde*. Leipzig: Hinrichs.

Wilson, John Albert, and Thomas George Allen

1938 "Editors' Preface." *Megiddo Tombs*, edited by P. L. O. Guy and Robert M. Engberg, p. vii. Oriental Institute Publications 33. Chicago: University of Chicago Press.

Wright, G. Ernest

1936 "The Chronology of Palestine in the Early Bronze Age." *Bulletin of the American Schools of Oriental Research* 63: 12–21.

1937 *The Pottery of Palestine from the Earliest Times to the End of the Early Bronze Age*. Publications of the Jerusalem School, Archaeology 1. New Haven: American Schools of Oriental Research.

1958 "The Problem of the Transition between the Chalcolithic and Bronze Ages." *Eretz-Israel* 5: 37*–45*.

1971 "The Archaeology of Palestine from the Neolithic through the Middle Bronze Age." *Journal of the American Oriental Society* 91/2: 276–93.

Yannai, Eli

2006 *'En Esur ('Ein Asawir) I: Excavations at a Protohistoric Site in the Coastal Plain of Israel*. Israel Antiquities Authority Reports 31. Jerusalem: Israel Antiquities Authority.

Yannai, Eli, and Z. Grosinger

2000 "Preliminary Summary of Early Bronze Age Strata and Burials at 'Ein Assawir, Israel." In *Ceramics and Change in the Early Bronze Age of the Southern Levant*, edited by Graham Philip and Douglas Baird, pp. 153–64 in Sheffield: Sheffield Academic Press.

Yannai, Eli; D. Lazar-Shorer; and Z. Grosinger

2006 "The Pottery Assemblages." In *'En Esur ('Ein Asawir) I: Excavations at a Protohistoric Site in the Coastal Plain of Israel*, edited by Eli Yannai, pp. 62–178. Israel Antiquities Authority Reports 31. Jerusalem: Israel Antiquities Authority.

Zbenovich, Vladimir G.

2004 "The Flint Assemblage from Ashqelon, Afridar — Area E." *ʿAtiqot* 45: 63–84.

Zigelman, A.

1978 "A Tomb from the Early EB I at Kefar Glickson." *Ezor Menashe* [Menashe Region] (internal publication of the Menashe Regional Council) 7: 4. [In Hebrew]

Zuckerman, Sharon

2003a "Tel Qashish and the Jezreel Vaslley in the Early Bronze Age." In *Tel Qashish: A Village in the Jezreel Valley; Final Report of the Archaeological Excavations (1978–1987)*, edited by Amnon Ben-Tor, Ruhama Bonfil, and Sharon Zuckerman, pp. 7–9. Qedem Reports 5. Jerusalem: The Institute of Archaeology of the Hebrew University of Jerusalem.

2003b "The Early Bronze Age I Architecture." In *Tel Qashish: A Village in the Jezreel Valley; Final Report of the Archaeological Excavations (1978–1987)*, edited by Amnon Ben-Tor, Ruhama Bonfil, and Sharon Zuckerman, pp. 31–34. Qedem Reports 5. Jerusalem: The Institute of Archaeology of the Hebrew University of Jerusalem.

2003c "The Early Bronze Age I Pottery." In *Tel Qashish: A Village in the Jezreel Valley; Final Report of the Archaeological Excavations (1978–1987)*, edited by Amnon Ben-Tor, Ruhama Bonfil, and Sharon Zuckerman, pp. 35–56. Qedem Reports 5. Jerusalem: The Institute of Archaeology of the Hebrew University of Jerusalem.

2003d "Tel Qashish in the Early Bronze Age I." In *Tel Qashish: A Village in the Jezreel Valley; Final Report of the Archaeological Excavations (1978–1987)*, edited by Amnon Ben-Tor, Ruhama Bonfil, and Sharon Zuckerman, pp. 57–60. Qedem Reports 5. Jerusalem: The Institute of Archaeology of the Hebrew University of Jerusalem.

2003e "The Early Bronze Age II–III Pottery." In *Tel Qashish: A Village in the Jezreel Valley; Final Report of the Archaeological Excavations (1978–1987)*, edited by Amnon Ben-Tor, Ruhama Bonfil, and Sharon Zuckerman, pp. 61–124. Qedem Reports 5. Jerusalem: The Institute of Archaeology of the Hebrew University of Jerusalem.

1

INTRODUCTION TO THE EAST SLOPE

THE PHYSICAL SETTING OF THE EAST SLOPE

Megiddo (modern Tell el-Mutesellim) is located on a portion of the piedmont, small hills on the eastern flank of the Carmel Range directly adjacent to the Jezreel Valley (i.e., the Plain of Esdraelon[1]) (figs. 1–2). The site, once estimated to be at its most extensive about 50 hectares in size (*Megiddo III*, p. 583; fig. 1.2), seems actually to have been significantly smaller as indicated by recent excavations (Matthew Adams, pers. comm.). Nevertheless, it appears to have included not only settlements on the high mound, but also archaeological deposits in select, adjoining precincts, particularly to the south and southeast (Raban 1999, pp. 82*–90*). In addition to the East Slope, deposits to the east encroach on the edge of the broad, Jezreel Plain (*Megiddo IV*, p. 721). Rock-cut tombs occupy the bedrock scarp that defines the lower mound to the east and south. While the East Slope forms a continuous belt of archaeological deposits between the upper and lower mounds (pl. 1), so far as may be discerned at present, it appears to have been a precinct distinct from them, an interpretation reflected in the type of specialized ancient remains unearthed there.

PARAMETERS OF THE EAST SLOPE

The excavated area on the East Slope is very precisely defined according to a grid laid out by the excavators of the Oriental Institute (fig. 3). On the west it follows the contour of the base of the high tell and extends southeastward in a jagged line that at one point reaches as far east as a road which, as it did during the time of excavation, still crosses the lower mound from north to south.[2] In the Chicago Expedition's superimposed grid that divides the site into squares of 25 m, the East Slope includes complete and partial Squares Q15–17, R15–20, S16–19, T16–19, U16–19, V16–20, W16–19. In all the East Slope covers ca. 15,000 sq. m (*Megiddo Tombs*, p. 2) excavated down to bedrock (fig. 3, pl. 2).

EXCAVATION OF THE EAST SLOPE

Excavation of the East Slope was not a primary aim of the Oriental Institute's 1925–1933 expedition, but rather part of its overall strategy applied to excavating the tell, which aimed at systematically "dissecting" the mound and re-depositing it nearby (Breasted 1929, pp. x–xi; Fisher 1929, pp. 9, 27, 40–41, 58). The East Slope (frontispiece, fig. 3, pl. 1) was chosen as an appropriate location for dumping "waste material" removed from excavations because of certain features which, according to the first director of the project, Clarence Fisher (Fisher 1929, p. 25; Guy 1931, fig. 5), made it "most satisfactory." The East Slope was considered "ideal" because of its proximity to the mound and its large, exposed outcrops of bedrock with numerous open, tomb apertures, indicating it was used as a necropolis and thus outside "the actual walled

---

[1] This is the New Testament name for the Valley (Hebrew יזרעאל), sometimes also written Yizrael.

[2] This is correct as of the time this manuscript was written. Plans to re-route the road have existed for years and will eventually move what is now a heavily traveled highway off the tell.

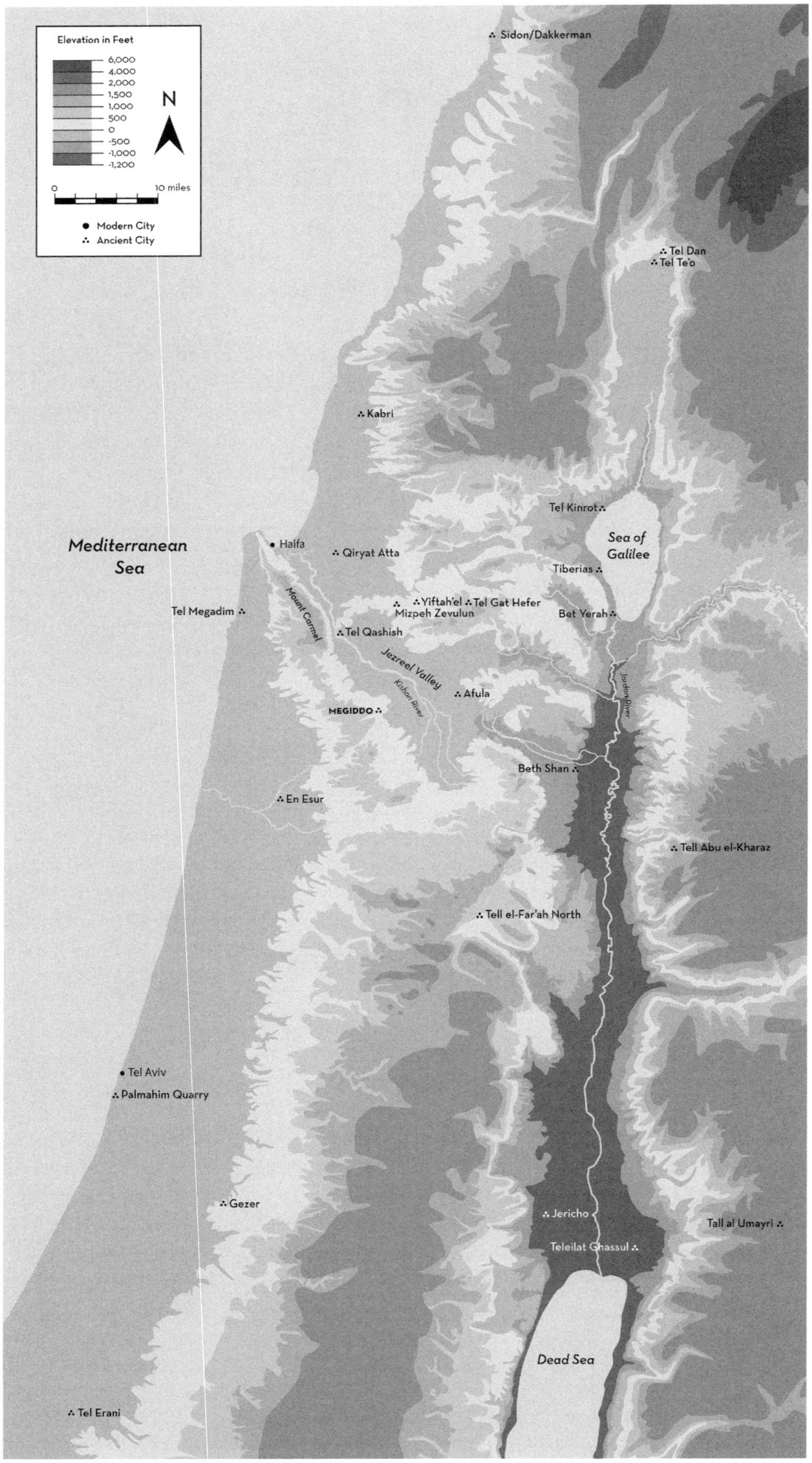

Figure 1. Map of the principal sites discussed and cited in the text

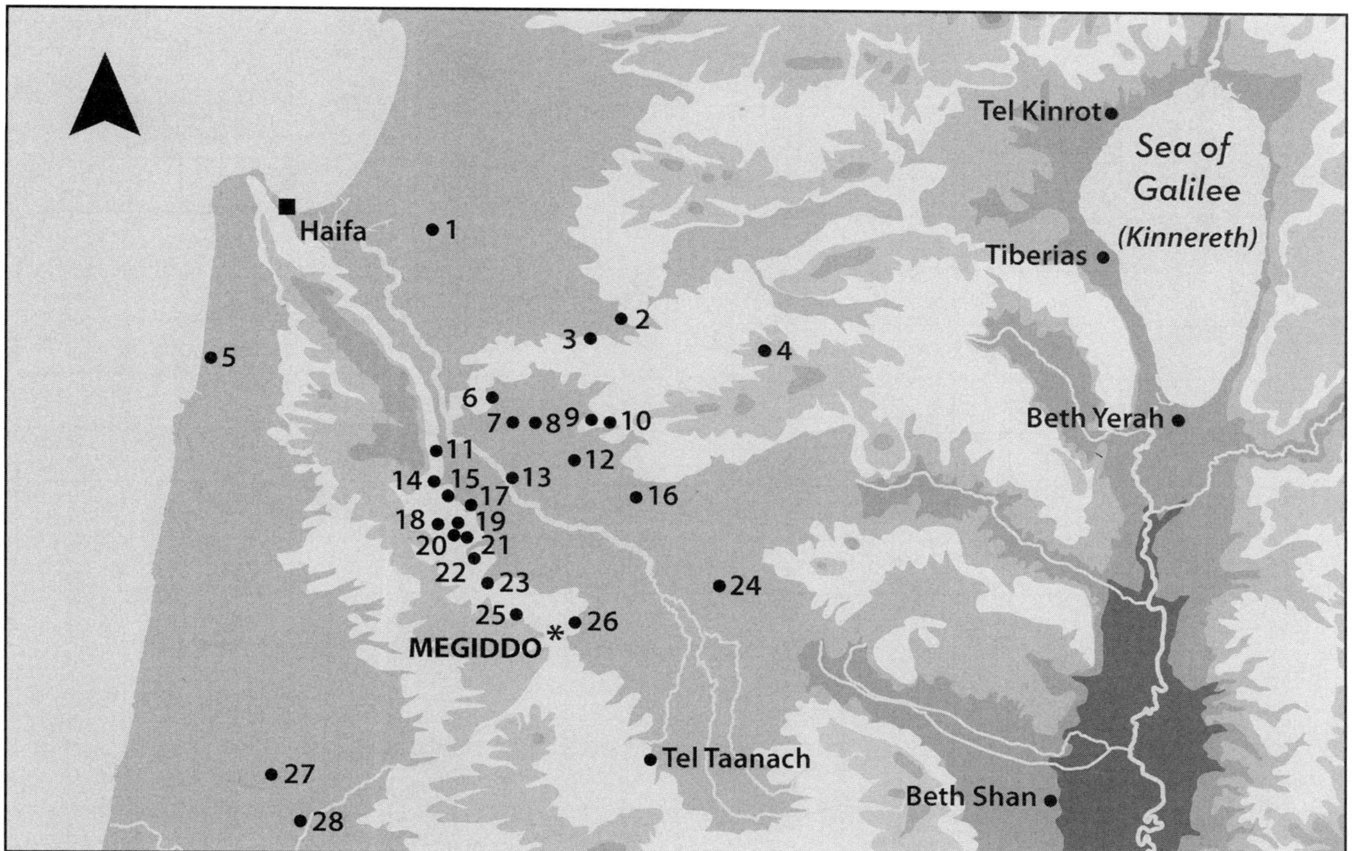

1. Qiryat Ata
2. Yiftahʾel
3. Mizpeh Zevulun
4. Tel Gat Hefer
5. Tel Megadim
6. Beʾer Tivon
7. Tell Risim/Tell er-Rish
8. Kh. Shabana
9. Nahalal Junction East
10. Tel Shimron
11. Tel Qashish
12. Horvat Seifan/Tell el-Beida
13. Tel Shem/Tell es-Shammam
14. Tel Yoqneam
15. ʿEn Levana South
16. ʿEn Shadud
17. ʿEin el Mughaiyir
18. Tel Qiri
19. Hazorea
20. Tel Zariq/Tell Abu Zureiq
21. ʿEn Nahlaot
22. Nahlaʾot
23. Mishmar Ha-emeq
24. ʿAfula
25. Midrakh Oz
26. Edh Dhahar
27. Kefar Glickson
28. ʿEn Esur

Figure 2. Map of Early Bronze Age I sites in the Megiddo region

city in all periods" (pl. 2). Its relatively gentle slope, originally believed to have been merely covered with accumulated debris "eroded" from the higher mound, was also considered as unlikely to yield much in the way of stratified deposits and architecture beyond the obvious terrace walls visible on its surface, which were assumed to be modern in date.

With John D. Rockefeller, Jr.'s, funding, and what he believed to be ample time,[3] Fisher systematically set about excavating a large swath of the East Slope down to bedrock and then dumping soil onto it derived from excavation on the summit, preparatory to reducing the entire high mound. To that purpose he set a large chute on top of the tell that emptied into cars on a small railway below, which then distributed "waste material" along two lines on the East Slope where it had been denuded. As work on the tell apparently proceeded

[3] Notably, Fisher withdrew from the excavation after a short time, probably for health reasons. Especially in the early years of the project the region was particularly insalubrious due to the nearby swamps that acted as breeding grounds for the malaria-carrying anopheles mosquito (Breasted 1929, p. ix).

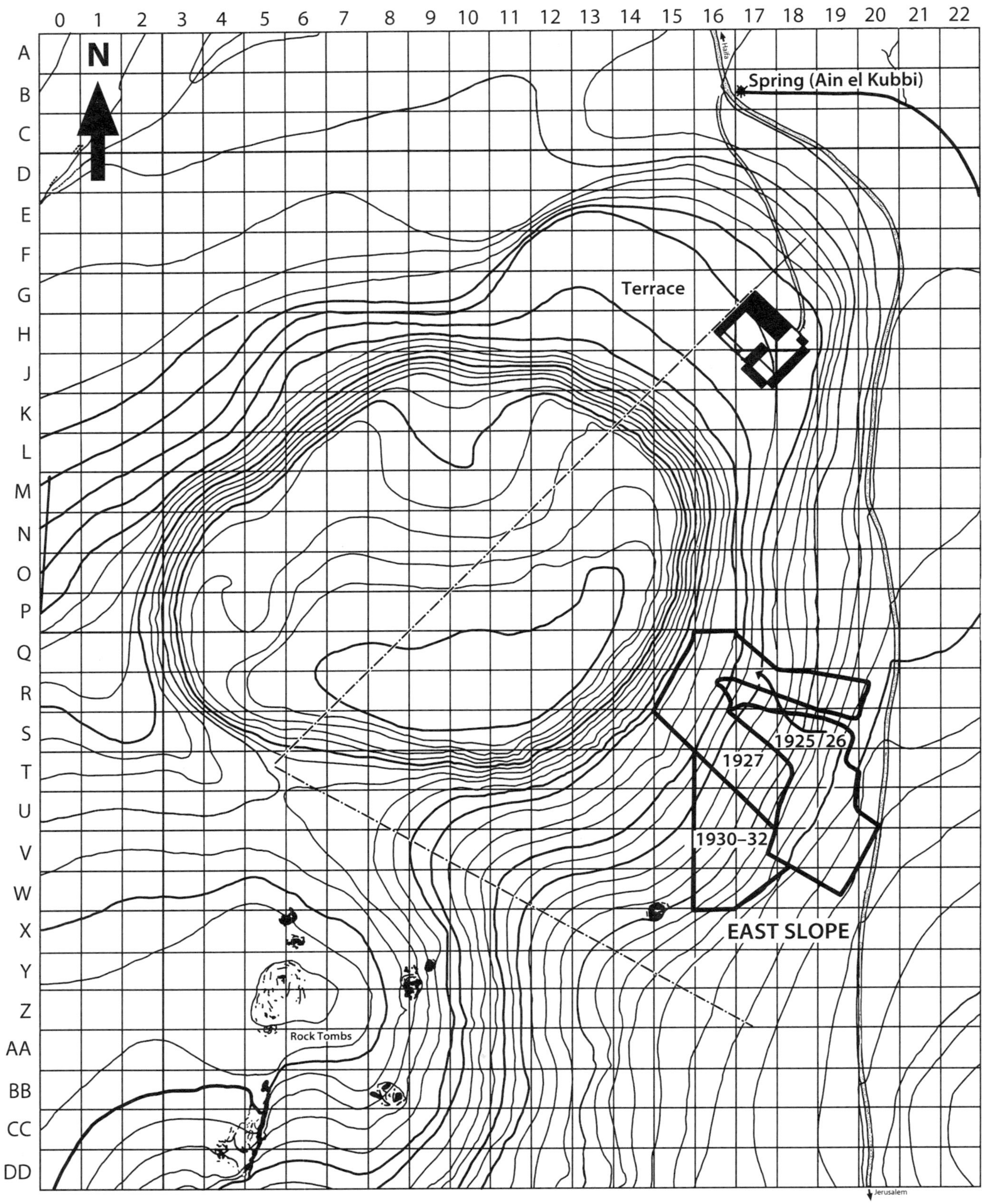

Figure 3. A new rendering of a scanned copy of the published topographical map (*Megiddo Tombs*, fig. 2) of the high mound prepared by Edward L. DeLoach. It illustrates the phases of expansion of the East Slope excavation as work on the high mound demanded. Its original caption reads: "Key Plan of Megiddo, Showing Areas Excavated on the East Slope. Scale 1:5000." Contour lines are at 2-meter intervals

faster than planned, the area originally cleared for dumping proved inadequate and had to be extended to additional precincts of the East Slope, apparently during the campaigns of 1925/26, 1927, and 1930–33. Work on the East Slope, especially in the latest seasons, indicated that, despite its location off the high mound, archaeological deposits there were not as limited as Fisher had assumed.

THE EAST SLOPE TODAY

After exposure most of the precinct was covered by excavation spoil removed from the high mound and its own, displaced archaeological deposits. Today part of the East Slope is the location of two substantial mounds of that spoil, while there remain exposed some bedrock areas honeycombed with tombs marked by fig trees and date palms that germinated from seeds in bird droppings (pls. 2–3). Thus this entire work is based only on information available from documentation and artifacts retained from the excavation.

THE EAST SLOPE IN ARCHAEOLOGICAL RESEARCH

Earliest Research

The early settlement on the East Slope was revealed and first published at a time when the late prehistory of the southern Levant was still pretty much in its infancy (e.g., Albright 1926), and when a series of ceramic-producing cultures, predating those associated with biblical periods (i.e., Neolithic, Chalcolithic/Æneolithic, Early Bronze) were first coming to light and being recognized in excavations, mostly in deep deposits at the major tells of Beth Shan (FitzGerald 1934, 1935) and Jericho (Ben-Dor 1936; FitzGerald 1936; Garstang 1935). Prior to that, the archaeological record of what later came to be known as the Neolithic, Chalcolithic, and Early Bronze Age periods was little known and poorly understood from publications such as those of Schumacher (1908) and Watzinger (1929) at Megiddo, Sellin and Watzinger (1913) at Jericho, and Macalister (1912) at Gezer. Those early works offered only desultory and little-understood evidence of some of the earliest sedentary occupations, mostly derived from artifacts encountered in deep deposits within very limited exposures, or in cave-tombs. Duncan's (1930) "corpus" of pottery types, meant to apply Petrie's (1891) dating principal to pottery of the southern Levant and accomplish what his mentor's (Petrie 1921) corpus of Egyptian pottery more or less did for archaeologists working in the Nile Valley, proved to be less than useful as it was based primarily on pot morphology and on evidence of dubious chronological significance.[4]

Albright's (1935) primary attempt at creating a generalized chrono-cultural periodization for those periods, which suffered from a lack of reliable information, is probably the first example of a serious attempt at a synthesis of evidence for late prehistoric periods. It appears to have whetted scholars' appetites for more reliable data, in particular that of his student G. E. Wright (1936, 1937), then engaged in research for his doctoral thesis. It seems also to have encouraged the excavators of Megiddo and Beth Shan to rapidly publish results of their fieldwork (FitzGerald 1934, 1935).

Primary Impact of the 1934 Report

In contrast to Duncan's synthesis, Engberg and Shipton's 1934 *Notes on the Chalcolthic and Early Bronze Age Pottery of Megiddo* was clearly based on fieldwork done with significant care (p. 2) and which was apparently better documented than much previous excavation, particularly those at Megiddo (*Megiddo IV*, pp. 688–93). It also benefitted from the knowledgeable advice of Pere Vincent of the École Biblique, already a venerable

---

[4] In retrospect, it may be noted that Duncan's work offered an inaccurate and severely conflated chronological sequence of pot types.

figure in the archaeology of the region (Engberg and Shipton 1934a, p. vii), and from the timeliness of its appearance. For its era it was a quite advanced and ground-breaking tract that offered the excavators' interpretation of a chrono-stratigraphic sequence based on pottery types or forms.

For many years most scholars accepted Engberg and Shipton's own assertion that their interpretation "may be relied upon with a considerable degree of faith" (ibid., p. 2), and for decades it had major consequences for archaeological interpretation, especially as it was, in part, also based on observations made from the basal deposits in Schumacher's earlier trench in the high mound (ibid., p. 6). The site's identification with Armageddon (Fisher 1929; Guy 1931) led to its having an inordinately important impact on a discipline fueled by and steeped in biblical associations, while it simultaneously suggested associations of early settlements at Megiddo with other south Levantine sites (Beisan/Beth Shan and Gezer) as well as with broader traditions of the ancient Near East.

While the thrust of the report's intent, clearly stated in its title, was to explicate the pottery sequence from the East Slope, it also offered a fleeting glimpse of late prehistoric architecture as well as something of early artistic, glyptic expression within the greater ancient Near Eastern sphere (Engberg and Shipton 1934a). Although it failed to discuss details of the actual settlement remains and offered no evidence for direct association of artifacts to them beyond claiming ascriptions to seven "stages" (purportedly layered deposits; but see below), the severe limitations of the report did not, unfortunately, prevent other scholars (e.g., Wright 1937) from over-reliance on it. In lieu of a more full account of the excavation results, and what was once a dearth of hard information on contemporary settlement remains, the short monograph came to figure importantly in later narratives on the late prehistory of the southern Levant (e.g., Wright 1958; 1971; Kenyon 1970; 1979; Levy 1995, p. 229).

Terminological Confusion

Engberg and Shipton's use of the terms "Chalcolithic" and "Early Bronze," pertaining to the central finds from the East Slope (i.e., "Stages" VII–I), has sowed not a little confusion in archaeological literature, particularly as the former term appears in the title of the 1934 report but does not represent any chrono-cultural assemblage presently equated with "Chalcolithic" as it is understood in the southern Levant. Their interpretation of that site of Teleilat Ghassul suggested a quite unusual chronological scheme. They wrote:

> The first assertion, that Ghassūl is a Chalcolithic site and therefore largely antedated the localities that constitute the ledge-handle province, can now be modified to some extent. For while perhaps remaining Chalcolithic in nature, the uppermost level, Ghassūl IV, seems beyond all reasonable doubt to have existed until the beginning of the Middle Bronze period (Engberg and Shipton 1934a, p. 48).

Believing that some of the earlier Ghassulian occupations were contemporary to those of the Megiddo Stages, Engberg and Shipton thus titled their report accordingly.[5] Today it is universally accepted that the Chalcolithic period precedes the Early Bronze Age, that one of its type sites, Teleilat el-Ghassul, was abandoned early in the fourth millennium (Bourke et al. 2004, 2007), prior to the beginning of Early Bronze Age I, and that all the cultural material associated with Engberg's and Shipton's Stages I–VII, should be ascribed to the Early Bronze Age.

The confusion caused by this nomenclature reigned until Ernest Wright's seminal 1958 article, based on a greater understanding of the chrono-stratigraphic associations of Teleilat el-Ghassul and Early Bronze Age I tomb groups, laid to rest for most scholars[6] the question of what constitutes Late Chalcolithic and what

[5] It seems likely that Guy, who dated the habitations to "very early periods which go back well into the 4th millennium B.C." (*Megiddo Tombs*, p. 2), did not share these scholars' opinion.

[6] A notable exception was M. Dothan (1971), who clung to the appellation "Late Chalcolithic" for designating what others (e.g., Braun 1985) understood to be an early phase of Early Bronze I. T. E. Levy (1995, p. 229) included Megiddo in his list of major Chalcolithic sites, citing Engberg and Shipton 1934a as his source. Levy's rationale for inclusion of the site that has, to date, yielded only a handful of Ghassulian Chalcolithic objects — all but one from the high mound and only a single example from the East Slope, published in this work for the first time — remains obscure.

identifies Early Bronze I, although Albright (1935, p. 199) in a 1934 speech to the Palestine Oriental Society, rather perspicaciously associated the term "Chalcolithic" primarily with settlement at Tuleilat el-Ghassul.

CURATED ASSEMBLAGES AND DOCUMENTATION

Documentation of the East Slope was in one sense extensive and relatively precise, especially for the era in which the excavations were carried out. However, according to present-day standards the level of information that documentation offers may be deemed rather limited (see below: *Limited Documentation*). Documentation is primarily found in two archives, in the Oriental Institute, in Chicago, and in the Israel Antiquities Authority, in Jerusalem. Happily, those two institutions also curate all the finds retained from the Oriental Institute's Megiddo's excavations. In each instance the archiving of the documents is extraordinarily well organized and curation of the artifacts make them easily accessible, conditions that greatly facilitated preparation of this report.

The Oriental Institute Archive and Artifact Assemblage

Primary documentation of the excavation is, as far as I have been able to ascertain, found in the Oriental Institute, where many original documents are stored. They include a series of small notebooks with brief descriptions of loci, plans, and sections of some features of the excavated East Slope, and a sizable, now digitized, photographic archive.

Artifacts in the Oriental Institute collection are those allotted to it at the time of excavation by the Department of Antiquities of the British Mandatory Government of Palestine from material retained by the excavators. A policy then in effect allowed the Department to generously divide ownership of finds almost equally between itself and excavating institutions. However, the Department did retain the right to keep any object of unique or special interest. In light of this the allotment to the Oriental Institute seems particularly generous, possibly in recognition of its financial mentor, John D. Rockefeller, Jr. (Breasted 1929, p. ix), who funded the Megiddo Expedition as well as construction of the Palestine Archaeological Museum.[7] The Oriental Institute's share of the Megiddo finds includes a large number of ceramics and ground- and chipped-stone objects from the East Slope; that of the Israel Antiquities Authority has some complete vessels, primarily from tombs, numerous sherds, and a few objects in stone.

The Israel Antiquities Authority Archive and Artifact Assemblage

The British Mandatory Department of Antiquities archive, today administered by the Israel Antiquities Authority, contains little documentation of actual fieldwork beyond copies of photographs archived in Chicago. However, it does include museum inventories in two forms, oversized ledgers and large index cards, registers of objects retained by the Department after its division with the Oriental Institute (Fisher 1929, p. 38).

The Israel Antiquities Authority curates a comprehensive collection of artifacts, in particular pottery, that appears to accurately represent the material retrieved and retained from the excavation of the East Slope (Engberg and Shipton 1934a, p. 1 n. 2). Thus in a sense, with some notable exceptions, from the point of view of representativeness both collections seem to be reasonably accurate samples of the types of artifacts recovered, although they are not indicative of quantities recovered. In the Israel Antiquities Authority some small portion of the finds are on display in the Rockefeller Museum, while the remaining artifacts are

[7] The Palestine Archaeological Museum is now known as the Rockefeller Museum and is currently administered by the Israel Antiquities Authority.

stored in "student galleries," where they are organized for the express purpose of allowing qualified persons doing research to view and handle them.

A Limited Database

Documentation for the East Slope is severely limited to some rather cursory written descriptions, plans, sections, and photographs. There is some reason to suggest that because of the way the excavators envisaged the hill, as a repository for eroded soil and only a cemetery, they paid less attention to details than they did for excavation on the high mound.

Fisher (1929, pp. 32–33), in describing documentation for work on the high mound, notes "progress cards" and "survey cards" that made up "the complete record of the work." He further indicated the type of information one would expect to find in such documents:

> Any fragments of jars, handles, rims, and other objects are placed in baskets provided for that purpose at the edge of the work. These are tagged with their provenience number and are carried to the headquarters at the close of the day, or, if of unusual importance or value, at the noonday rest hour. This process continues until the tops of walls appear. Then the method is changed. The pickmen are distributed over the square and begin to follow the walls down to a pavement level. Rooms at once receive regular numbers such as I 15, which would indicate that this room was the fifteenth found in the first or topmost stratum. Objects now found are given the room number and a serial number preceded by an *x*, as are also those found in the indefinite surface layers. This signifies that, while found in the area or room stated, they were not in position and therefore must be used with caution as evidence. Often, before the floor of a room is reached, jars, either singly or in groups, may be found. These are left *in situ* until the position is located on the plan and, if of special interest, a photograph is taken. No object, even in such a position, is ever moved until this record is complete (Fisher 1929, p. 29).

There does not appear to be any parallel documentation for the East Slope as possibly indicated by the rather minimal descriptions of tombs numbered 1–60 excavated by Fisher and published in *Megiddo Tombs*. Descriptions are based on "brief accounts," which, as indicated by John Wilson and Thomas Allen in their preface to *Megiddo Tombs* (p. vii n. 2), were "treated as far as possible in accordance with the principles discussed by Mr. Guy in chap. i." This statement suggests some recorded information was not available to Guy or, more likely, if available, it was not very detailed, especially concerning findspots and locations. Possibly that led Guy (*Megiddo Tombs*, pp. 4–5) to introduce the concept of "locus" (see below), which allowed for localization of objects into excavator-defined units smaller than the large 25 m squares (= 625 sq. m) in the project's grid.

Destined as a dump, the East Slope was originally considered little more than an incline atop which were deposits eroded from the high mound and thus likely to contain a mélange of chrono-cultural deposits (see below) rather than a sequence of superimposed levels, as was encountered on the high tell (*Megiddo Tombs*, p. 2). At least in the early years that attitude appears to have dictated a less-than-exacting mode of excavation, especially as some of the work included moving Schumacher's dump. It is also possible the method described above was not as assiduously applied to excavation on the East Slope as it was on the tell summit, although that seems unlikely as Guy indicated the area with habitations, some superimposed, "demanded very careful excavation" (*Megiddo Tombs*, p. 2).

Most notable in their absence in the documentation are recording techniques of modern excavation methodology such as "basket lists," locus cards, or their equivalents, intended to provide detailed information on findspots of artifacts and their contexts. With almost no exception there are no three-dimensional parameters of excavated deposits, descriptions of soil deposits, notes on architectural elements and their associations to one another. Drawn sections are few and those that exist often lack minute details that would help to provenience artifacts. In short, the early years of work at Megiddo took place in an era before those types of documentation became standard in excavations, and when the ratio of workmen to archaeologists or other field personnel would anyway have precluded such attention to detail in the field (e.g., frontispiece, pl. 13).

Extant only are the most generalized descriptions concerning actual deposits and the architecture encountered in the excavations of the East Slope. They are in a "locus register," which I have transcribed verbatim and included in this publication (*Appendix C*). When possible I have annotated the excavators' descriptions to make them easier to understand. Considering what I know of work at other sites, and in particular the published accounts of Guy and Engberg in *Megiddo Tombs*, which describe some deposits in great detail, it is likely there was additional written documentation for the East Slope not found in the archives of either the Oriental Institute or the Israel Antiquities Authority. One missing document seems to be a "field book," cited in the locus register in an entry for April 8, 1931, which probably contained important information on the location and nature of various loci.

I suspect the present lacuna in the archives is due to some documentation never having been deposited in them as both repositories have continuously operated under strict guidelines that would not have allowed for removal of primary documentation.[8] The apparent loss of documentation may in some part be due to the exigencies of dividing up the retrieved finds between the Oriental Institute and the Department of Antiquities, as well as maintenance of a dig house on site, where such documents might have been stored in hopes of future excavation and research to be carried on there.

Since the end of the excavation in 1938, major historical events have overtaken the region and the site. It has endured periods of political instability just before and after a World War, a local war in 1948 that saw an invasion by an army from Iraq and the de facto division of Mandate Palestine into separate political entities; all factors that could explain such a loss. Alternately, some records may have been retained by one or more of the several excavators[9] and possibly not archived for personal reasons.[10] Whatever the explanation, it appears that some written documentation of work on the East Slope was lost or is, at any rate, not available for study.

Another unfortunate lacuna in documentation is a lack of virtually any significant information on the faunal assemblage excavated at the site. Although now a standard practice in excavation, the collection and study of animal bones does not appear to have been considered an important part of field procedures when the East Slope was excavated. Thus, most unfortunately, there is no faunal assemblage from the excavation that can be studied and little was written about what might have been retrieved (e.g., Engberg and Shipton 1934a, p. 6). A few exceptions are the skeleton, apparently of a bovide, described as a "cow," found near the mouth of Tomb 903 (*Megiddo Tombs*, fig. 8), and some bones of equids, pig, sheep, goats, and a lion (*Megiddo Tombs*, pp. 209–13). There is no indication of specific findspots or precise contexts; some burnt examples are from basal deposits, but apparently most are from tombs and it is impossible to state whether they should be associated with the mortuary-related finds or are intrusive in the contexts reported.

The System of Loci

In the early stages of the excavation at Megiddo, objects and features were given numbers related to their stratigraphic ascriptions according to stratum, with unique, arbitrary numbers assigned to specific features. Objects were then defined as deriving from those features, generally rooms within structures. While that system seemed to be useful for deposits on the high mound, Guy realized it was not applicable to every deposit, especially on the East Slope, where stratigraphic associations were often less than clear. Accordingly, he instituted a new system that designated selected features as "loci" (*Megiddo Tombs*, p. 4).

[8] The archive of the Department of Antiquities of the British Mandate was administered by the government of Jordan between 1948 and 1967, thereafter by the Israel Department of Antiquities and Museums, and lastly by the Israel Antiquities Authority. All parties appear to have assiduously guarded the Mandate-period archive and protected its integrity. Thus it remains an extraordinary source of documentation on archaeological investigations in Palestine from 1919 through 1948.

[9] I have only had access to the personal records of P. L. O. Guy, now in the Central Zionist Archives in Jerusalem, but they contain only a single, tangential reference to the excavation in a letter of a personal nature.

[10] While Guy is listed as the author of *Megiddo Tombs*, Engberg was apparently responsible for the final manuscript (editor's preface to *Megiddo Tombs*, p. vii) and it appears that Guy may not have been consulted on its final form.

A locus in Guy's system may be said to be a three-dimensional unit of excavation or feature so designated by the excavators (see also *Appendix C: The Excavators' Annotations in the Locus Register*). In order to ensure continuity with Fisher's documentation, Guy, who took over the directorship of the excavation from Fisher, took the original list of tombs on the East Slope with its ordinal numbers beginning with 1 and merely continued it from number 201, including all loci, both on the high mound and on the East Slope. Each locus was recorded in a small notebook (pl. 4) with a very brief description. In general, blocks or series of consecutive numbers were assigned to one or the other precinct, either on the high mound or on the East Slope, but occasionally, as demanded, numbers were assigned outside those groups.

In this system rooms were sometimes listed as loci, as occasionally were individual walls or even surfaces. However, not all features, especially walls, were uniquely identified (i.e., assigned numbers) and virtually no documentation was devoted to soil features or fills. What is apparent is that much soil was excavated and not assigned to any particular locus, which may account for the numerous objects that were recovered and maintained but that have no identification numbers that associate them with one or another locus. Because loci descriptions are so cursory, there are virtually no details of findspots within loci and no elevations are indicated except in a few rare instances when particular features can be detected on drawn sections or when photographic documentation is available. Therein lie the major weaknesses of Guy's system of documentation and our ability to accurately reconstruct the archaeological record of the East Slope.

I suspect that objective conditions did not allow the relatively small staff to properly document work on the scale that it progressed. This probably accounts for the cursory notations in the locus list. By contrast, much greater attention was paid to the post-fieldwork treatment of acquisitions, both in Jerusalem and in Chicago. The Department of Antiquities' (of Mandate Palestine) ledgers in and on index cards listed and often illustrated in penciled renderings to scale all objects retained from the excavation (pl. 5) and even some that were discarded. Items retained in Jerusalem were also entered into the Palestine Archaeological Museum inventory and each one was given an index card in its catalog of acquisitions.

Original, hand-entered excavation inventories were created after each season and often include information on provenience (albeit only up to the level of locus) as well as on the ultimate division of the artifacts between the Palestine Archaeological Museum and the Oriental Institute. While most of the objects listed could be located, the existence of some few is preserved only in documentation. The Israel Antiquities Authority, which administers the Rockefeller Museum's objects, has registered them all in a conveniently searchable, computerized database that also indicates their present locations within their stores. A similar system is used by the Oriental Institute, which houses the remainder of the Megiddo collection.

Photographic Documentation

The lack of written documentation places an extraordinary burden on the photographic archive of the excavation. While this archive is not as extensive as might be hoped, it has proved to be the primary source of information on many features found in the field, and sometimes the sole source of information on them. It has allowed me to virtually see the field as it was witnessed by the excavators, albeit only in a limited number of instances. Because it is the most primary, abundant, and specific source of data, much of it is reproduced in this report.

Although general conditions in Palestine were often quite primitive, the expedition made extraordinary efforts to record the excavation in photographs. It imported fine equipment and made the best use of it for shots taken from the ground (pl. 6) and the air. These photos, preserved in scans made from large-scale negatives by the Oriental Institute, are quite professional and indicate a wealth of details, which to some extent ameliorate a lack of direct observations by field personnel.

Although the negatives have lost much of their original intensity through aging, scanning and digitization of them in very high resolution by the Oriental Institute has allowed me to revitalize them through computerized enhancement techniques. Without such technology it is doubtful the process would have been possible, but if so it would have been prohibitively expensive and very time consuming.

Such enhancement, sometimes almost to the point of exaggeration, includes intensive manipulation of digital files, which allows them to be presented in a manner that best illustrates the descriptions in this report. The photographs, which often must serve as evidence in lieu of plans of structures never made (see below), have been extensively annotated for the benefit of the reader. Annotations include the addition of wall numbers and a virtual 5 × 5 m grid superimposed on the excavators' 25 × 25 m squares. These additions have allowed me to locate features in the field with a level of precision necessary for discussion, which was not possible with the excavators' system. As these photographs are the best source of primary evidence for the field, they are also accompanied by detailed captions intended to aid the reader in understanding the evidence they present.

The Balloon Series of Photographs

Because of his experience as chief inspector for the British Mandate Department of Antiquities (Green 2009, pp. 169–70, 173), Guy (1932) placed great faith in aerial photography as a means of documenting excavations. He is responsible for importing equipment that allowed for an extraordinary series of aerial photographs taken with a remotely controlled camera attached to a large balloon (pl. 7). Those photographs remain as a monument to Guy's foresight and the remarkable skills of the expedition photographer, Olaf E. Lind.

Sets of photographs represent four sequential phases of the excavation of the East Slope, which document, among other things, the early architecture located in Squares T16, U16, T17, and U17 (pls. 16–17), the focus of this report. According to a "Level Book" (pl. 8), the first set was taken on June 3, 1931 (e.g., pl. 9), the second (e.g., pl. 10) on April 19, 1932, and a third (e.g., pl. 11) possibly as early as May 2, 1932. The date of the fourth (e.g., pl. 12) aerial photographic session remains obscure, but clearly it occurred sometime prior to final work in Stages IV and V in the 1932 season, which would not have been too much later in time as excavation was generally halted during the hot summer months.

More than two dozen photographs taken in the field are the most direct and often the sole evidence available for details of the finds in Square U16, the precinct in which the most ancient evidence of utilization and occupation of the East Slope was preserved. They make up a unique source of information on such features as fills, plastered floors, earthen surfaces, some stratigraphic relationships, and structures otherwise undocumented. Presumably all field photographs were the work of Olaf Lind. Rather curiously, no ground-level photographs of the East Slope, other than of tombs, were ever published by the excavators. The sole indication of a published field photograph I have come across, a picture of the Stage IV building (virtually the same view as found in pl. 25), is in an obscure Hebrew publication by J. Perrot (1964/65), where it appeared virtually without explanation.

Studio and Recent Photography

Included in the archives of the Oriental Institute are a number of black-and-white photographs of objects from Megiddo. As some of those are of objects presently found in Jerusalem, it appears they were taken at times more or less current with the excavation. Unfortunately, there is no record of the photographer, but I assume they are also the work of Olaf Lind, the expedition's Jerusalem-based photographer. All recent photographs are, unless otherwise stated, the work of E. Braun.

Plans and Sections of the East Slope

Only two basic plans and three sections illustrate some, but not all, structures and features encountered on the East Slope. One plan, depicting most of the East Slope, has only the latest features encountered and is annotated with numerous elevations (fig. 4). The other is a portion of the East Slope centered around Square U16, where the earliest structures were located, and has an accompanying section (figs. 16, 19). These plans, while rather precise in showing select features in two dimensions, are particularly deficient in elevations that indicate a third dimension (see below). A second section, through much of the East Slope (fig. 8), is a compendium of data compiled apparently after work in the area had ceased. A third drawn, completely "schematic" section (fig. 9), was intended to represent Engberg's and Shipton's interpretation of the stratigraphic sequence, but in doing so it misrepresents the evidence and thus does a serious disservice to those wishing to understand the essence of the East Slope in that area.

Absolute elevations, expressed in meters above sea level (asl), are found on only one plan depicting the latest features on the East Slope (fig. 4; see below). Additional, relative elevations derive from two sections, one of the entire East Slope (fig. 8) and another of a house in Square U16 (B/IV/1; see *Chapter 2*, figs. 16, 19). By collating data I have been able to reconstruct a number of absolute elevations on plans I have reworked with a reasonable degree of confidence. Those plans are compilations of original data from several sources. Despite those efforts, I have been unable to obtain information on elevations of many features, especially some depicted in the photographs, and others on plans.

Additional elevations on features not yet unearthed when the first plan (Primary Master Plan) was made were recorded in a level book (pl. 8) and their locations marked on a set of prints made of three aerial photographs. However, they now are useless data as their actual locations, somewhere on the East Slope, cannot be ascertained because those annotated prints are no longer available.[11] However, even when elevations are indicated in absolute numbers, they are often of little help in ascertaining something of the archaeological record as they invariably denote only a single datum. Thus they are relatively uninformative concerning states of preservation of structures in relation to other features.

Excavators' Plans

Two primary plans prepared by the excavators for the East Slope are the sole extant interpretative sources in the archives for the architecture of this area and from which all additional plans illustrating this report are derived. At times they have proved to be slightly inaccurate, but the most disturbing element about them is the absence of constructions that should appear on them. Following is a discussion of each of the extant plans available.

An Unpublished "Primary Master Plan" of the East Slope

The "Primary Master Plan" of the East Slope, partially reproduced in figure 4, is an advanced, composite version that has been heavily interpolated, the excavators choosing to depict only select structures in one or another state of exposure. Although presumably originally drawn in pencil in the field by a draftsman (probably R. S. Lamon) from measurements taken with the aid of a plane table, the earliest version I could find is in portions of a large, black-and-red inked draft, now in several long, narrow strips cut from a large sheet of some shiny, blue-colored fabric in the Oriental Institute Archives.[12]

It is undoubtedly a compilation, mostly of structures visible in the first two series of balloon photographs, as well as some that are no longer visible in them as those features had already been removed. It seems likely some other features were drawn directly from measurements taken on the ground, yet others, I suspect, were taken from tracings of one or another of the aerial photographs. This probably explains the lack of details such as stones in the depictions of man-made constructions; walls were rendered only schematically as in *Megiddo II*. Visible are schematic renderings of bedrock outcrops, tomb locations, shaft openings, caves, other rock-cut features, walls, and additional constructions, some designated by locus numbers. I have redrawn two excavations squares from this plan, which is the area where the earliest buildings were found (fig. 4).

Absolute elevations are marked in some locations while outlines of shadowed areas, understood from thin lines on one plan and corresponding darkened areas on other versions (e.g., figs. 4–6), were drawn adjacent to certain bedrock features to create an impression of a third dimension. However, there are no elevations on these bedrock features and thus the shadow effect offers only an impression of depth but no

[11] Although the level book cited above exists and is replete with numbered elevations, the photographs with numbers corresponding to the numbered data in the book are not extant in either the Jerusalem or the Chicago archive. My assumption is that they are permanently lost.

[12] There are no "original" field plans extant in either archive, which suggests they were deliberately removed or discarded.

accuracy. This is an unusual convention, favored by the excavators of Megiddo,[13] which I believe was influenced or inspired by or, more likely, derived from aerial photographs. It is unfortunate that the original plans drawn in the field are not available as they would allow me to ascertain the accuracy of this plan. Notably, the shadows, albeit carefully drawn, do not correspond to a single angle from which light was directed as they would if they were faithfully representing shadows visible in extant aerial photographs. Sometimes these shadows are on one side of a bedrock outcrop, while in other instances they emphasize a rocky prominence on another side. Thus they appear to be more of an artistic convention and a relative, albeit not very accurate, guide to elevations. Possibly these features are the reason why this plan was never published.

"Generalized Plan of Part of the East Slope": A Published Plan

A "Generalized Plan of Part of the East Slope," published as plate 1 in *Megiddo Tombs*, is based on the Primary Master Plan (fig. 4). It differs from its source in three important features: (1) it lacks elevations as the excavators believed they were not of "high importance" because of the sloping topography (*Megiddo Tombs*, p. 4); (2) individual stones are drawn on it, albeit apparently only schematically; and (3) it lacks indications for shading that produced an isometric effect for specific features found on other plans (e.g., figs. 4–6).

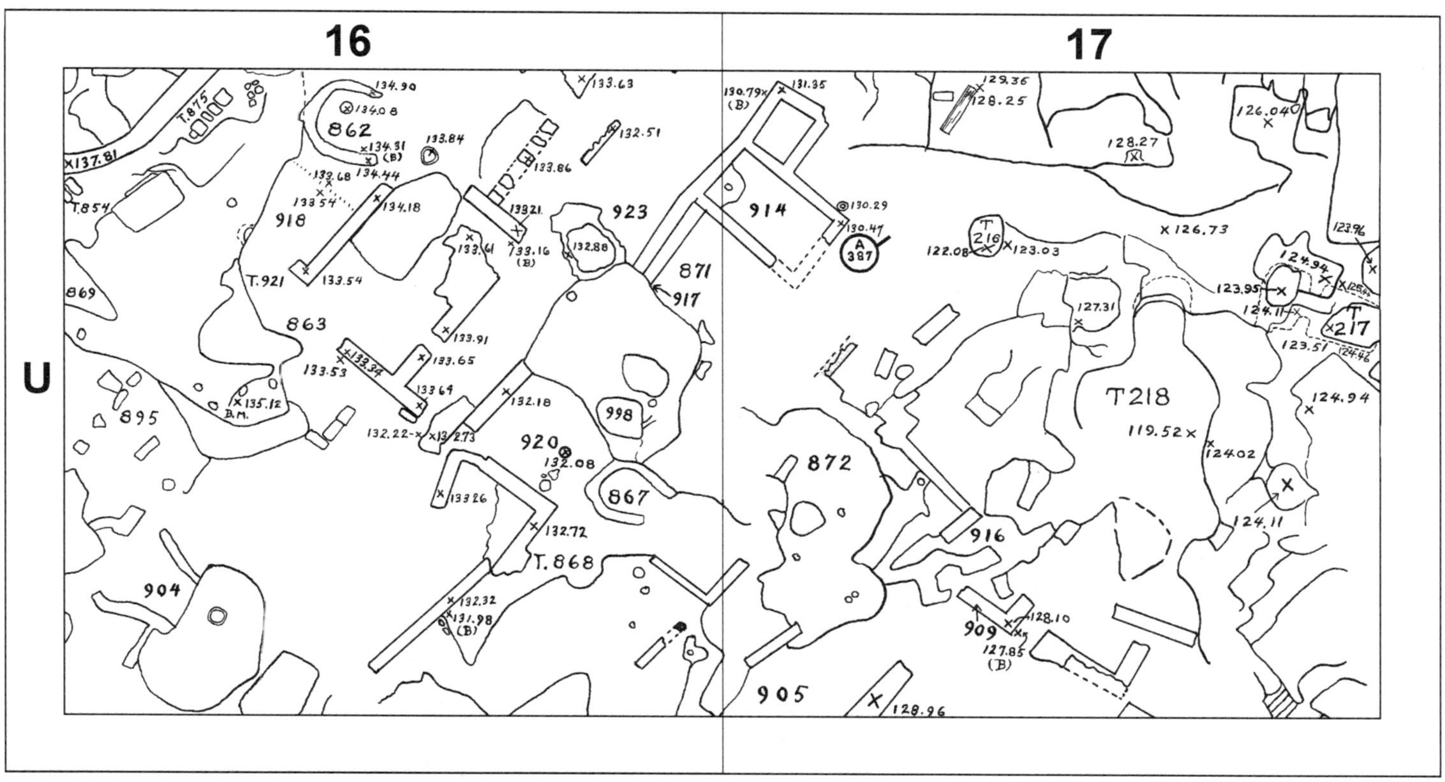

Figure 4. Detail from what I have labeled the excavators' inked "Primary Master Plan" of the East Slope, previously unpublished. This plan represents the latest structures, bedrock outcrops, and other features encountered in the excavation and is the basis for the published plan (*Megiddo Tombs*, pl. 1) and several others in this work (figs. 5–7). It was prepared prior to the first series of balloon photographs. Long, wavy lines represent shadows used to give the beholder a third dimension. This plan is also the primary source for absolute elevations of the later features on the slope

[13] This somewhat unusual convention is analogous to the axonometric, schematic plans published in *Megiddo II*.

An Unpublished Plan of Most of the East Slope

A plan (fig. 5) based on the conventions noted above, with drawn stones, bedrock features, and shading was prepared but has not been previously published. This untitled plan reproduces the structures in the published plan in rows R–U and columns 16–19, in all a block of sixteen large, 25 × 25 m squares. Walls drawn include the outlines of stones and shadows, giving a sense of three dimensions. It has many features found also on Megiddo Special Sheet No. 1 (see below), but includes additional squares and is further annotated with locus numbers. I suspect it is an attempt to show features associated with two levels or strata, labeled

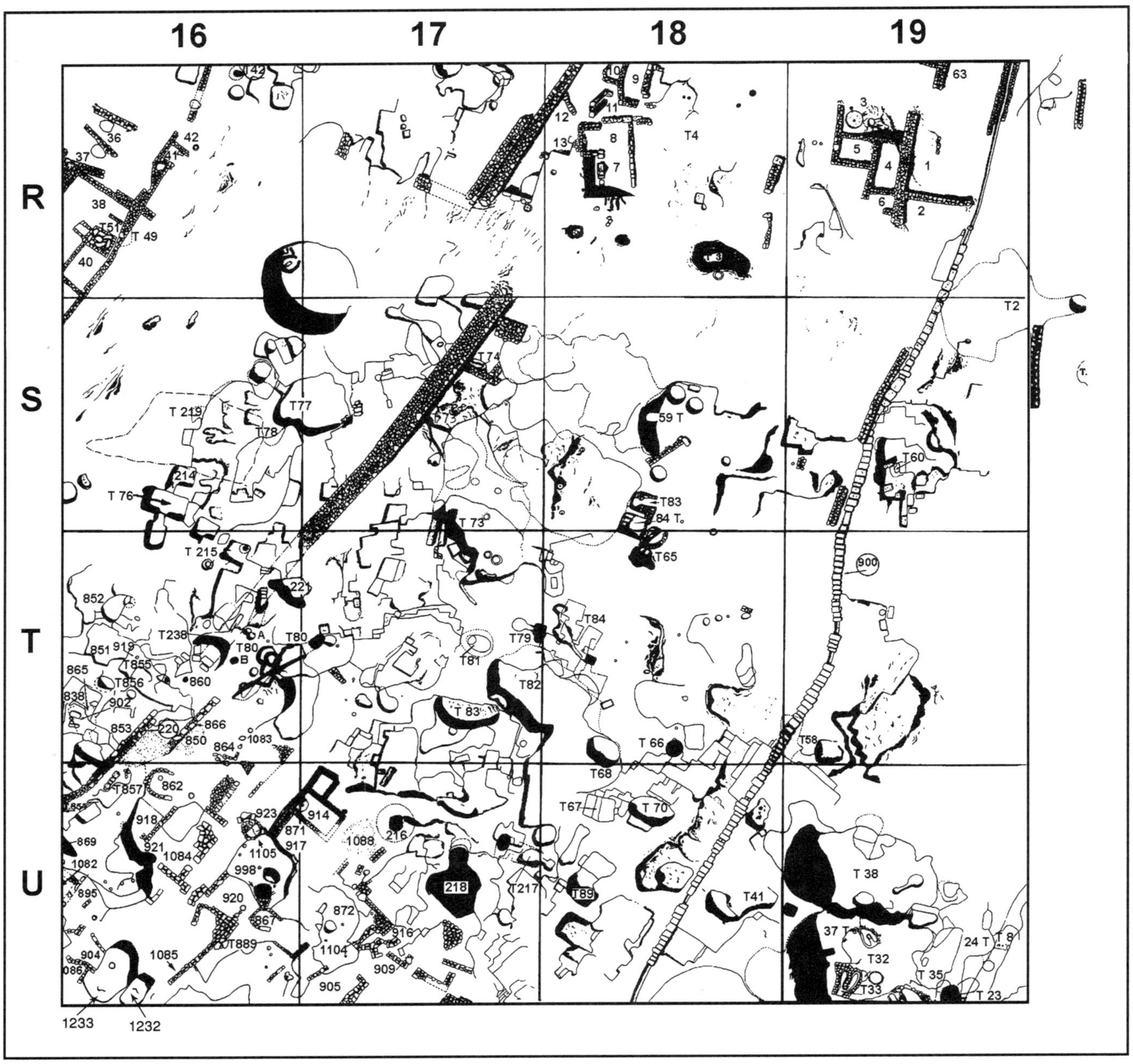

Figure 5. This hitherto unpublished plan of the East Slope was prepared from the more schematic "Primary Master Plan" (fig. 4). It portrays the major areas of work and was apparently prepared prior to the first balloon photographs. It indicates where numerous loci were but has no elevations. A third dimension is indicated, vicariously, by the inclusion of dark shadows. Structures portrayed on this plan should be dated to numerous periods, including Early Bronze Age III

ES[14] II and ES III, referred to in *Megiddo Tombs* (p. 2) but otherwise unacknowledged. (I have enlarged part of that plan [fig. 6] to illustrate details of four squares where most of the evidence for early occupation of the East Slope was unearthed.)

"Megiddo Special Sheet No. 1 Stratum A": A Stratigraphic Anomaly

One archived plan, obviously prepared for publication but never submitted, bears the title "Megiddo Special Sheet No. 1 Stratum A" (fig. 7). It apparently shows the latest stone-built elements in eight squares in rows T–W and columns 16–17. It is reproduced essentially as the excavators might have intended it to be, but I have somewhat embellished it by slightly emphasizing an unidentified line drawn diagonally through it indicating the section shown in figure 8, and by sub-dividing the large excavation grid into units of 5 × 5

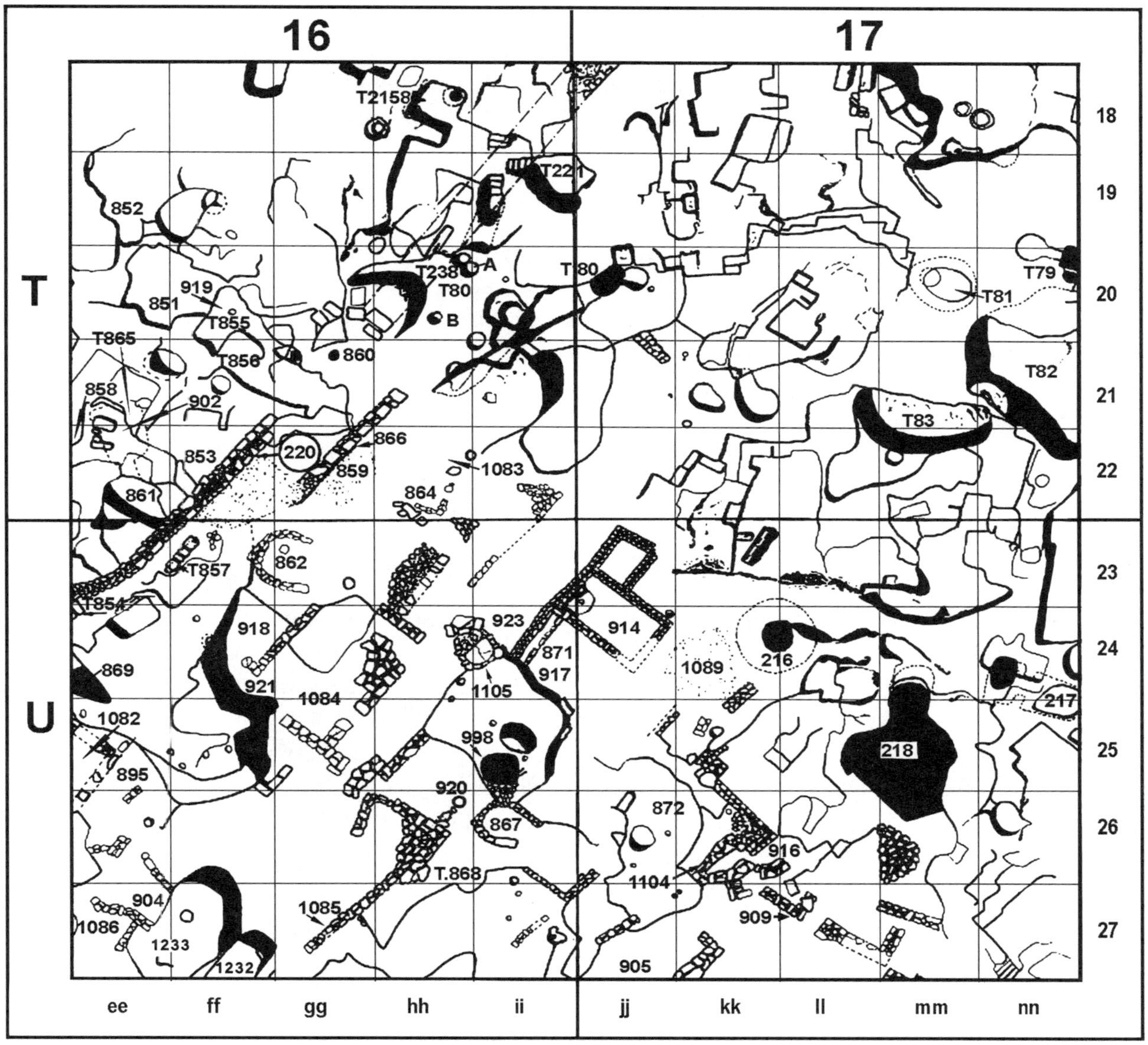

Figure 6. Enlarged detail of figure 5 showing the latest structures and the location of loci overlying the precinct in which the buildings of the early stages were unearthed. A 5 × 5 m grid superimposed on the 25 × 25 m grid of the original excavation has been added to the excavator's plan

[14] "ES" stands for East Slope.

m. I have also labeled this section as C–D, in accordance with the excavator-labeled Section A–B shown in figures 16 and 19.

This plan is particularly noteworthy as the "Stratum A" denotation does not correspond to either of the systems in use for the stratigraphy of the site (Stages I–VII as designated in Engberg and Shipton 1934a, and Strata ES I, II, and III as designated in *Megiddo Tombs*, p. 4). It is, however, found in descriptions of some loci in the unpublished register, but only in the descriptions from the 1931 season (*Appendix C*). Thus it was likely used as a stratigraphic ascription only for a short time and then abandoned. I suspect this might be the latest stratum alluded to by Guy (ibid., p. 4]). The designation "Stratum A" in the plan's title suggests the excavators intended it as a single stratigraphic unit incorporating "late" or the latest structural elements that could be stratigraphically correlated. Notably, all the constructed elements share the same basic orientation and there do not appear to be any superimposed buildings.

Comments by Guy concerning the confusing sequence of deposits on the East Slope in *Megiddo Tombs* suggest why this plan was never published. The locus numbers in the plan suggest many of these structures were unearthed over the years and were not excavated in the same season. Without any information on the absolute or even relative elevations of most of these buildings (excepting those on the line of the section), and with no information regarding associated finds, this plan remains as an interesting attempt by one or another of the excavators to make some stratigraphic sense of the late buildings on the slope.

A Detailed Plan of "Stages V and IV"

The sole detailed plan of the structures attributed by Engberg and Shipton to Stages IV and V, apparently readied for publication by Robert S. Lamon,[15] is only preserved in its final form, beautifully rendered in ink and reproduced photographically (fig. 16). For reasons obscure today, it was omitted from both volumes dealing with the East Slope (Engberg and Shipton 1934a; *Megiddo Tombs*) and never even alluded to in Loud's 1948 *Megiddo II*, which included some artifacts from the East Slope. Curiously, and most unfortunately, there are no drafts of it in the archives, nor are there any explanatory notes. As noted below in *Chapter 2*, there are no indications of why particular walls were included and others, nearby and clearly visible in photographs, were excluded from the plan (see *The Engima of Walls 31, 32, and 26* in *Chapter 2*).

Synthetic Plans

Utilizing the resources described above, in combination with the few applicable data from the "Level Book," I have synthesized a series of plans of the complete sequence of architectural remains in the precinct where the buildings of Stages V and IV are located. These plans represent composites of all available documentation. For purposes of discussion they are also enhanced by a 5 × 5 m grid superimposed on their larger squares to divide them up into significantly smaller units, which allow me to describe locations of features with a reasonable degree of accuracy. In effect, the larger grid was never used by the excavators as an actual guide to excavation; they neither respected confines of squares nor left any balks in their work on the East Slope. They simply cleared extensive areas down to bedrock, in increments of unknown depth. Their grid was a simple, heuristic device roughly based on surveyed points marked by large cubes with cylindrical hollows (cinder blocks or concrete?), clearly visible in aerial photographs (e.g., pls. 9–12), that allowed them to measure with relative ease.

Using those points I have superimposed the smaller grid as an aid when trying to identify specific features in the aerial photographs. The reader will note slight discrepancies in these grids between different plans and sections, especially in the 5 × 5 m grid. This results from several unavoidable errors. A primary error results from the excavators' own difficulties creating a precise grid because of their inability to compensate for the sloping terrain. Thus they ended up with some slightly skewed "squares" in their grid

[15] The plan is initialed RSL.

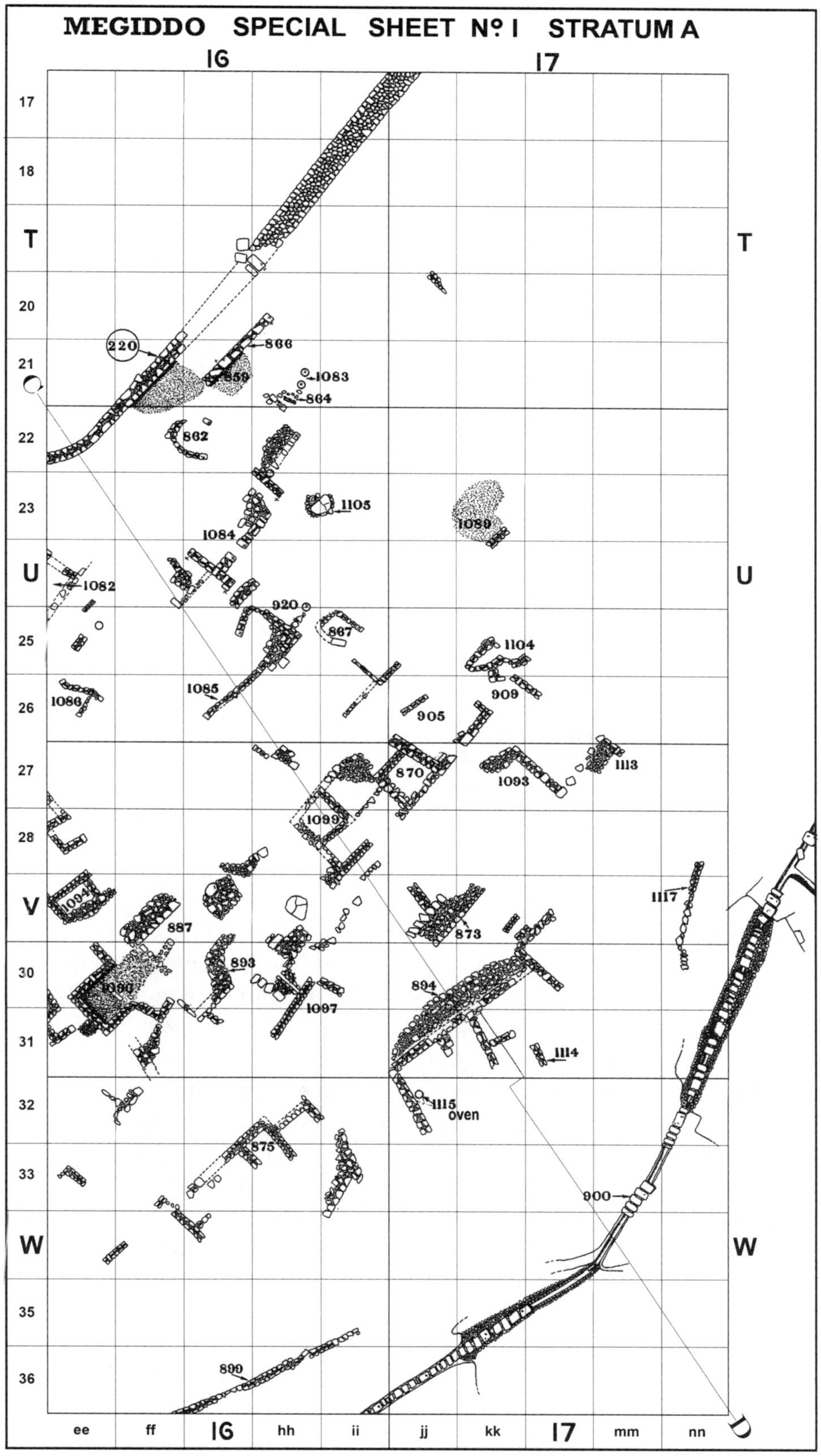

Figure 7. This heretofore unpublished plan, prepared by the excavators, is probably another interpolation of figure 4. Its label, "Megiddo Special Sheet No. 1 Stratum A," reflects some short period when some loci on the East Slope were assigned to "Stratum A." Clearly it represents what the excavators considered to be some coherent, possibly even contemporaneous constructions. Walls excluded are some dating to Early Bronze Age III, and so this represents occupation in "late periods." I have added to the original the letters identifying the position of Section C–D (see fig. 8), and a 5 × 5 m grid superimposed on the 25 × 25 m grid of the original excavation

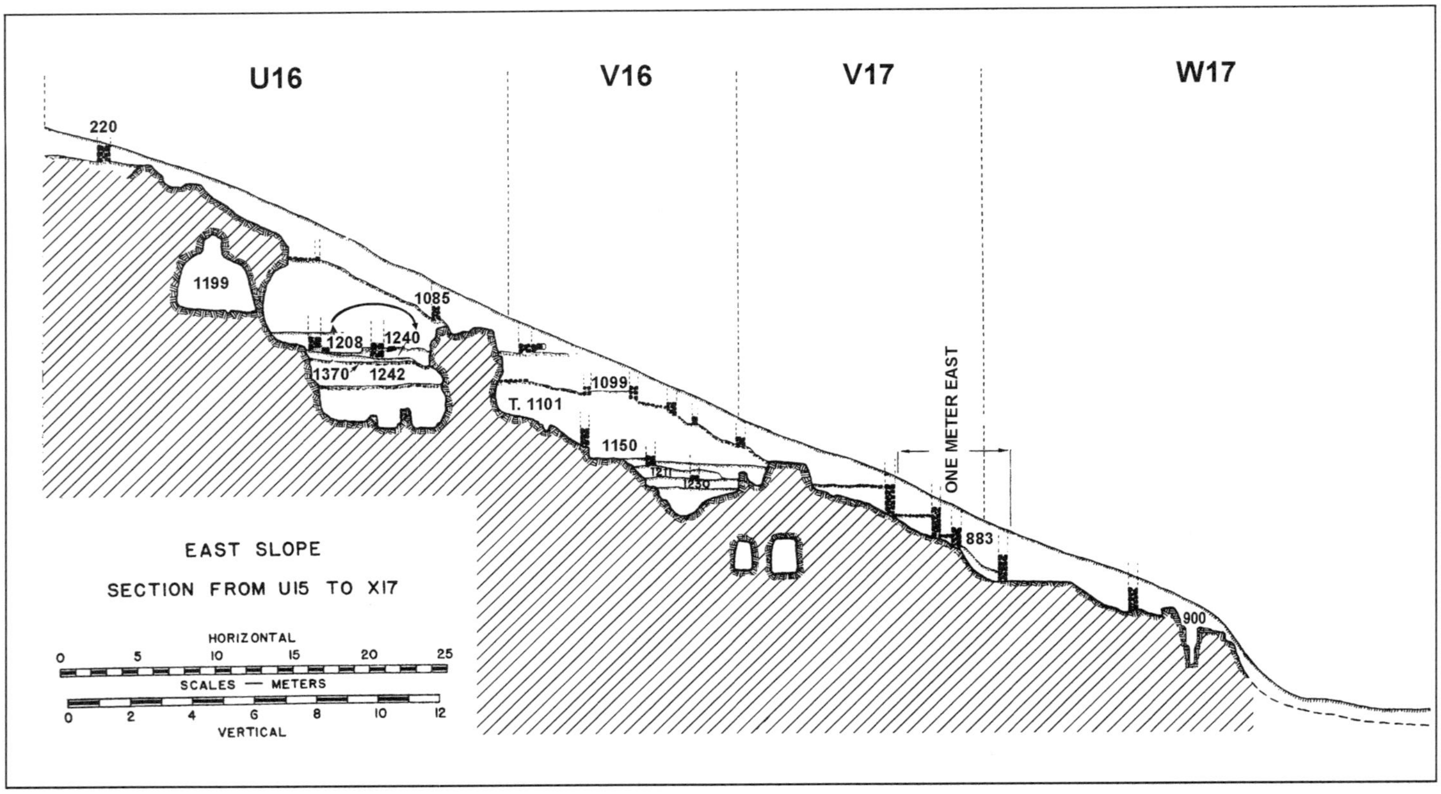

Figure 8. The excavators' drawing of what is latterly labeled Section C–D, purportedly in the area of Square V16. However, it is not actually a section drawn along a single, straight line in the field, as suggested in figure 7. Rather it is a compendium of data from different places, made at different times, facing roughly northeast but approximately in the location of a segment of Section C–D as marked in plate 21. It is one of two illustrations (see fig. 9) for a deep probe below building B/V/1 on the lower terrace

(*Megiddo Tombs*, p. 2), which slightly compounded the error when transferred to the balloon photographs, themselves not taken at precisely right angles to the ground. As I have created the new renderings of the grid on the evidence of grid points from aerial photographs and transposed them to the aerial photographs and new plans using the precision of a computer-generated grid, there was no way to avoid such discrepancies. Outlying portions of some squares conform to squares of correct precision engendered by a computer program, but not always to the original grid, especially if there was no physical marker visible in the photograph. Accordingly, small errors became compounded over large distances. Thus the reader should be aware that particularly on smaller plans the grid lines do not always correspond precisely. They should be understood as merely a simple device for quickly locating features in illustrations.

I have sought to make these synthetic plans as accurate as possible by correcting some few slight errors in the original documentation and by adding structures not drawn but clearly visible in photographs, when I believe them to be pertinent to the discussion of features and structures on them. I have also endeavored to place those additional structures, drawn in outline from the evidence of photographs, in their correct locations, taking into account skewing owing to angles from which photographs were taken. The results, while reasonably accurate, are not as precise as they would have been had those features been measured directly in the field.

In the case of elevations I have attempted to insert them in their correct places but in fact only rarely are their precise locations indicated on plans; in most instances they are not located on single stones as today's conventions dictate, because they appear only on the Primary Master Plan that has only schematic renderings of structures. In other instances I have been forced to extrapolate from the sections to indicate the location of elevations for which I do not know exact positions. The reader should note that in those instances, in order not to leave numbers "floating" on plans, I have taken certain license by linking all elevations to specific points, usually on stones or bedrock as close to the line of the section as possible. However, those linked elevations should be understood as a convention to reflect the ultimate height of a particular feature, which may or may not been at the precise points I have indicated.

Sections

As noted above, only three sections were drawn for the East Slope. They represent several degrees of accuracy.

Section C–D: A Section Drawing through Squares U16, V16, V17, and W17

Following the excavators' assigning letters to one drawn section (see below: *Section A–B*), I have labeled a large drawing of a section as C–D (fig. 8) to conform to the excavator's system of identification. This drawing was apparently prepared for publication and more or less represents a diagonal cut from northwest to southeast across four large squares on the East Slope from the 1925[16] surface, down to bedrock. It corresponds, albeit roughly, to an unlabeled, very faintly marked line I found on "Megiddo Special Sheet No. 1 Stratum A" (fig. 7) and to a black line drawn diagonally across the grid on an annotated aerial photograph indicating the location of tombs on the East Slope (*Megiddo Tombs*, pl. 2). Since most of the features are not germane to the present discussion, I consider in detail only the segment of the section in Square U16 (fig. 23), which is, incidentally, the sole source of relative elevations for a structure attributed to Stage V by the excavators (see *Chapter 2*).

After considerable pondering over some anomalies between the drawing and the evidence of photographs it became obvious the section drawing is probably not precisely a section measured along a nearly straight line[17] of an actual excavation section. Rather it is apparently a belated effort to represent a sequence of major deposits in the East Slope.[18] It is, in fact, a composite illustrating the original surface of the slope, some of its underlying bedrock features including cavities, and a number of late and early architectural remains and associated deposits, more or less in the vicinity of the demarcation found on the large plan of the East Slope (fig. 7). The data it contains were documented at different times during the excavation and combined into a single illustration, probably sometime close to the end of the excavation or perhaps even after the cessation of fieldwork. It also seems likely that some features were drawn in the field, while others may have been drawn from aerial photographs.

The *en-face* view of features at specific points only roughly corresponds to a continuous, straight line marked on the unpublished "Primary Master Plan" (see above). That explains a number of anomalies in the depiction of Loci 1208 and 1242,[19] where they appear as if they were nestled into a narrow bedrock cavity, which, as may be seen in aerial photographs, they were not. The section is drawn with the right side representing downhill, which would not allow a view of the interior of Locus 1199. In plate 21, a photograph annotated with locus numbers, I have attempted to more or less indicate the line of the section, which must have come through the covered portion of Locus 1199, where presumably it had a bell-like aspect, as much of it was open to the sky. It differs slightly in its orientation from that indicated on the published photograph, which indicates the section to have bisected Locus 1226 rather than Locus 1208 as I have done. I am uncertain which is the correct interpretation. This drawn section is also noteworthy as it has the only depictions of Loci 1242 and 1370, two early floors or surfaces beneath structure B/V/1.[20] Locus 1242, marked in plate 21, is an even deeper surface that apparently ran under that building and as far as the bedrock to the east.

Whoever drew the section obviously took some license with reality in order to depict a specific sequence, which is the only graphic record of the final, deep soundings made on the two terraces. It appears that the

[16] This is the year the excavations began.

[17] One short segment is noted to be one meter east of the line in Squares V17 and W17.

[18] It would have been an arbitrary line that did not conform to the grid which, in any event, was merely a heuristic device for measuring, as no balks were left in the excavation to provide sections.

[19] Locus 1240, not visible in the photograph, is a floor or surface under Locus 1226 (*Appendix C*) and under Locus 1208, according to the section.

[20] For an explanation of this nomenclature, see *Chapter 2*.

author of the section was forced to resort to data available from different perspectives rather than from actual measurements of extant features. I suspect that one or more of the excavators were not particularly pleased with the results, which might explain why this section was never published. Notably, this section was drawn using a technique I have not encountered elsewhere in archaeological documents. The scale of the horizontal axis is different from that of the vertical axis.

Section A–B

Section A–B is drawn along the longitudinal axis of a building ascribed by the excavators to Stage IV (figs. 16, 19). As it is one of two structures purportedly associated with that stage, I have identified this, the better preserved building, as B/IV/1,to distinguish it from an adjacent structure, B/IV/2. Section A–B shows the relative elevations of the walls and floor, which I have been able to translate into reasonably accurate asl values by corresponding data derived from a schematic section (see below). With one minor adjustment — the position of a stone cap in a cavity in the bedrock floor, which was not actually directly in line with the position of the section but which nevertheless appears in it — the drawing is a reasonably accurate, albeit simplified plan of this building.

A Schematic Section

The sole published section (Engberg and Shipton 1934a, fig. 1; herein fig. 9) for the East Slope is a schematic representation of the stratigraphic association of structures attributed by the excavators to Stages IV and V, an adjacent bedrock outcrop, and superimposed earthen deposits roughly representing additional earlier and later stages (VII–I). The drawing was obviously intended to give the reader a rough perspective for understanding the stratigraphy, but it does not accurately represent any actual place in the excavation, while some of its features are downright misleading. It purports to demonstrate the excavators' understanding of the stratification they encountered in Square U16, where the bedrock is terraced and where they encountered superimposed deposits.

According to the text (Engberg and Shipton 1934a, p. 6), that part of the section drawing labeled "B," to the left of the high bedrock pylon-like formation, is located on the lower of two terraces wherein the earliest deposits were found. This location is indicated by the excavators' description that noted fills with burnt animal bones and, below an immense boulder (Locus 1234 in small squares gg26 and hh25: fig. 17, pl. 21), an inhumation, apparently (according to this section) on a bedrock shelf, well below a floor of Locus 1242 (associated with Locus 1370?), which they assigned, based on recovered pottery, to Stage VII.

Little is noted in the publication of the deposits labeled as "C," but the second burial shown within a matrix of Stratum VII appears to be the burial noted as Locus 1704 (*Appendix C*), on "rock" (i.e., bedrock) below a floor of Locus 1371 (in small squares hh23, hh24, ii23, ii24 in pl. 21). Thus, despite the upward slope of the bedrock from right to left in "A" of the schematic section, side "B" was actually dug down in what was a lower terrace, downslope from a slightly higher terrace, marked as "C" in this section (see *Chapter 2*).

Broken lines, intended to indicate different deposits assigned to the several stages in this section are, so far as I understand, completely schematic and do not appear to represent actual visibly discernible layers of soil or any distinction between deposits. Rather they are intended to schematically represent somewhat vaguely discerned changes in styles and quantities of ceramic objects purportedly encountered by the excavators in a sequence of digging operations that probed the area, in some restricted places rather deeply, until they reached bedrock (Engberg and Shipton 1934a, p. 6).

The excavators, inferring from their understanding of the sequence of recovered pottery an analogous chrono-stratigraphic sequence, arbitrarily drew broken lines to subdivide what must have been earthen deposits in which they apparently did not distinguish changes worthy of notation. Their description of the ceramic sequence, which suggests the pottery of one period "melted" into that of the subsequent era, is particularly informative on that point. That interpretation is expressed more fully in the publication of a chart of pottery types assigned to the different stages (Engberg and Shipton 1934a, fold-out chart entitled

"Chalcolithic and Early Bronze Age Pottery Types Found at Megiddo"), in which numerous types are assigned ranges within the lifetime of the settlement that cover one or more stages.

Note on the Provenience of Artifacts

Despite Fisher's statement to the contrary (1929, pp. 36–39), apparently less care was applied to the sizable collection of early ceramics and other objects derived from the East Slope than was taken with the pottery from the excavation of the summit, suggesting that documentation of work there was of lesser exactitude. While an unknown quantity of pottery was discarded in the field (Fisher 1929, p. 36[21]), the bulk of saved finds is represented by numerous potsherds and a small collection of flint artifacts, mostly tools. Information on their findspots beyond a general notation of provenience somewhere within deposits on the East Slope is limited to remarkably few items in the curated collections. Even when more specific information exists, at best it indicates a position somewhere within a locus, with no suggestion of a precise spot or relative elevation. The very few notable exceptions are complete or nearly complete ceramic vessels discernible in photographs or, uniquely, marked on one plan (fig. 16, south corner of Locus 1200).

This limited information apparently reflects a prejudice concerning the importance of the excavation on the East Slope particularly expressed by Guy:

> The results, while interesting, need not detain us for long. Fisher has given a summary of his finds in contiguous areas; mine were very similar to his, and both will be fully published in the series known as "Oriental Institute Publications."
>
> The chief feature of the slopes below the tell is, of course, that, owing to the washing-down of débris from higher up, the stratification is rarely reliable. Intrusion and disturbance are the rule, even in tombs and caves, though some good datable groups were discovered. These showed that the occupation of the site went back well into the third millennium B.C. at the least[22] (Guy 1931, pp. 10–11).

The "Megiddo Stages"

Any discussion of the earliest occupations on the East Slope must begin with a definition of its "Stages," a concept introduced by Engberg and Shipton (1934a, pp. 1–6) to explain their interpretation of the evidence of early occupation there. The concept of stage should not be understood as merely the bestowal of parallel nomenclature on deposits on the East Slope to distinguish them from "strata" on the summit of the tell. While these last can be considered to be more or less discrete, chrono-cultural deposits laid down in a sequence one atop the other, the Stages are much more hypothetical constructs encountered on the sloping terrace in different localities.

The supposed divisions or boundaries between those constructs are derived from the excavators' observations of what believed to be the appearance of ceramics and of specific types in sequentially excavated deposits, which they could not be claimed as discrete. They wrote: "In general, as one would expect, it has been observed that the ceramic repertoire of the earliest settled periods consisted mainly in a progression of the stabler types of vessels, with one form melting into the next" (Engberg and Shipton 1934a, p. 2). They noted that in the earliest stages there was no pottery, and after its appearance they claimed to have been able to discern a progression of types. They further wrote: "It will be realized that isolated features should not be used to define any particular stage; an association of features will always be necessary for this definition, depending on predominant forms" (ibid., p. 2). Thus the sequence of Stages I–VII on the East Slope is based solely on Engberg and Shipton's perception of a "pottery sequence" as they discerned it in their excavations and which, they believed, was also reflected in their observations of Shumacher's deep trench in the middle of the high tell (ibid., p. 6). Their report, as we now know, does not present the "practically perfect piece of stratification" they claimed it to be (ibid., p. 2).

---

[21] Occasional references to discarded objects also appear on some entries in artifact inventories.

[22] Later, Guy emended this statement to include the fourth millennium (*Megiddo Tombs*, p. 145).

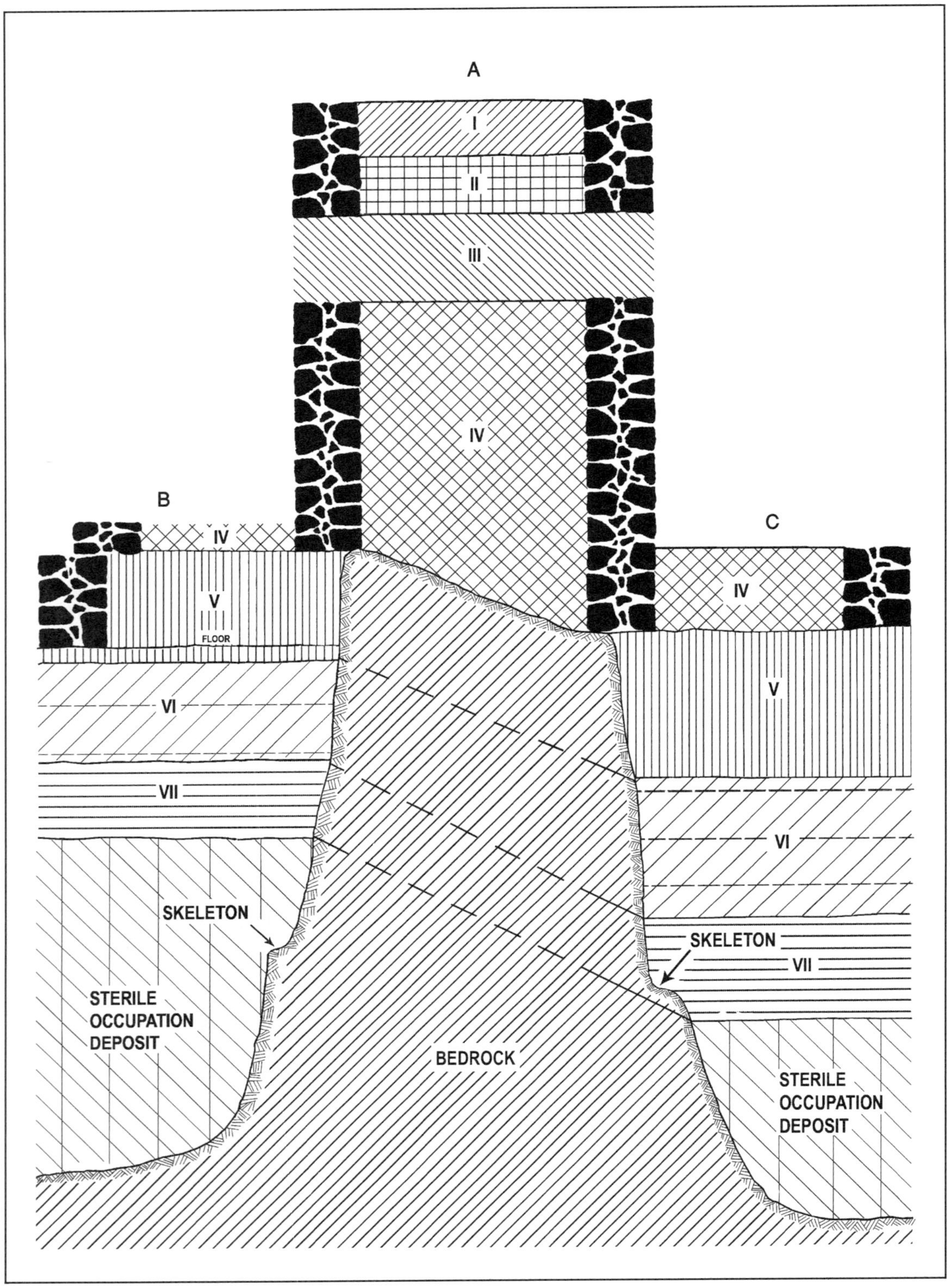

Figure 9. This completely schematic section, published as figure 1 in Engberg and Shipton 1934a to explain their interpretation of the Stages, has been faithfully rendered anew. Notable are the two indications for skeletons, probably evidence of burials of pre-Early Bronze Age periods of occupation or utilization of the East Slope. This is the only visual illustration of these interments. This section reflects results from the two deep soundings below the structures on the upper and lower terraces, which are otherwise documented only in a section drawing (fig. 8) and in the briefest of notations in the locus registry. The superimposed sequences of Stages although clearly marked by different styles of space fillers and labeled with Roman numerals are theoretical constructs that do not appear to reflect actual earthen deposits

Although the published "schematic section" (Engberg and Shipton 1934a, fig. 1; fig. 9) suggests the existence of discrete, superimposed fills equated with the several stages, the evidence was nowhere so definitive. Certainly those responsible for the study of the pottery were able to discern some progression of pot types, which is roughly reflected in Engberg's and Shipton's (1934a) pottery chart, but its equation with specific stages is wholly inaccurate. The broken lines in this section suggesting such deposits are equated with specific stages are merely hypothetical constructs, with two equivocal exceptions.

Stages IV and V are associated with buildings but, contrary to what the section portrays, the stratigraphic relationship of one to the other is anything but clear. Stage IV was not directly superimposed on Stage V, while the architecture of each of these so-called stages, that is, buildings, indicates a complicated history of internal phasing. Thus, deposits associated with the stages are neither archaeological layers of successive settlements within a definite stratigraphic sequence to which specific assemblages of material culture objects could be related (*Megiddo Tombs*, pl. 5 n. *), nor can they be shown to be discrete chrono-cultural deposits.

IN APPRECIATION OF THE EXCAVATORS AND STAFF

With the perspective of nearly nine decades since the end of the East Slope excavation, it is rather too easy to criticize the field methodology of the Megiddo Expedition. It should be noted that, especially in the early years, the staff worked under difficult and often trying physical conditions. In 1925, when work began, Megiddo was adjacent to a malarial swamp, at a time when medical services were primitive (Breasted 1929, pp. ix–x). At least in the earliest years, all members of the expedition seem to have suffered from the insalubrious conditions and the difficulties of being somewhat distant from an urban center with its "modern" amenities. Only after the dig house was built, the nearby swamps drained, and the road improved were some of those pressures removed from the excavation team.

Actually, for the time period during which the excavation was carried out, the methodology of the expedition, as it developed from Fisher to Guy, may be understood as considerably advanced and far more precise than was usual for excavations in the southern Levant. The expedition's field documentation, and especially its treatment of artifacts, were vastly superior to anything done before in the region, and to some done considerably later.

I am convinced that were some of the documents created by the excavators still available (and not apparently irretrievably lost), I would have been able to present in this volume a considerably more precise database and possibly be more definitive concerning the archaeological record of the East Slope. That loss (however incalculable and detrimental to our understanding of its record) cannot be placed directly at the door of the excavators. It does for them and their reputations as great a disservice as it does to those who wish to understand the essence of their work.

It should be noted that Robert Engberg and Geoffrey Shipton were virtually the first to publish something substantial on early sedentary societies[23] of the southern Levant and that they had neither a significant nor a reliable body of literature to consult and by which to evaluate their finds. They had to rely on their own field experience and that of Pere Vincent, then the doyen of Palestinian archaeology, a true scholar and savant of archaeology, but who could not have had much additional knowledge of these late prehistoric periods. Thus these scholars may be forgiven whatever errors and inadequacies we now perceive in their work, and be praised for rushing a reasonable report into press so soon after the termination of work on the East Slope. That is particularly fortunate as, to date, virtually no additional reports on the non-mortuary related remains encountered on the East Slope have been forthcoming.[24]

The reader will find much in the present report that is critical of and which contradicts that which has been previously published by the excavators of the East Slope. That is neither unexpected nor unnatural,

[23] FitzGerald's (1934) short article on the "Deep Cut" at Beth Shan was published that same year, but it was not well illustrated, and even his later report (FitzGerald 1935) lacked details of provenience of artifacts (Braun 2004a) and failed to include plans of the structures encountered in seven superimposed levels of construction.

[24] Some little information on non-mortuary related occupations is to be found in *Megiddo Tombs*.

as I have the benefit of hindsight based on nearly nine decades of archaeological exploration and research by others and more than three decades of personal experience in excavating and learning about the earliest periods represented on the East Slope. Accordingly, I wish to disabuse the reader of any notion that my opinion of the contributions of the excavators of the East Slope is anything but positive and deferential. They were pioneers who paved the way for the later efforts of colleagues and myself. In short I wish to state that I have great admiration for the work of Clarence S. Fisher, P. L. O. Guy, Robert M. Engberg, Geoffrey M. Shipton, and Robert S. Lamon on the East Slope of Megiddo and all the additional members of their staff who toiled so long and made such extraordinary efforts in explicating the history of occupation of the site (pl. 14).

In addition, a few extra words must be dedicated to the vision of P. L. O. Guy and the work of Olaf Lind, the expedition photographer, who left an extraordinary wealth of primary photographic documentation. In particular, the balloon series represents a priceless record of late phases of the East Slope operation, providing primary data unavailable elsewhere. I have relied particularly heavily on those series of aerial photographs, taken at four different phases of excavation, for a reconstruction of the sequence of deposits on the East Slope. Without them it would have been virtually impossible to complete this report.

2

EARLY DEPOSITS ON THE EAST SLOPE

DOMESTIC AND NON-MORTUARY ACTIVITY

Although most of the East Slope served as a necropolis throughout several millennia from early in the history of its utilization, there is evidence that at least certain precincts of it were devoted to non-mortuary related activities and possibly to those related only tangentially to its function as a cemetery. Between bedrock outcrops and natural and man-made cavities that served as tombs, there is evidence of cave dwellings and above-ground constructions dedicated to domestic, storage, industrial, agricultural, and possibly animal husbandry related activities. Those that took place in the early history of utilization of the site are the primary subject of this report. The presence of later, that is, post-Early Bronze Age elements is discussed only in detail for those remains physically superimposed upon the early deposits, which were found in the excavators' Squares U16 and U17.

In order to present a coherent narrative I have adopted a more up-to-date approach than was in vogue during the period of excavation and utilized by the excavators for their preliminary publications. Thus I have imposed an arbitrary system of identification of architectural remains on the original plans, which together with the subdivision of the excavators' 25 × 25 m grid into a virtual grid of 5 × 5 m squares, are essential aids to the present discussion. Whereas heretofore only a few select walls were given identification numbers, that is, locus numbers, I have labeled each wall or segment of construction with a unique and arbitrary number prefixed by the letter "W."

For those walls understood to belong to the early periods, I began with the number 1, while walls associated with significantly later periods were numbered beginning with 500. Occasionally, walls were assigned locus numbers (all greater than 1000) by the excavators; their numbers have been retained but I have added the prefix "W" to them. The new, more detailed grid is indicated by arbitrarily assigned double letters in lower case and numbers of increasing values beginning with the letters "ee" and the number 18 (e.g., figs. 6–7).

Since the earliest structures have been previously identified by the excavators as associated either with Stage IV or Stage V, I have continued to utilize their nomenclature, albeit with additional identification numbers that reflect new interpretations. As I consider juxtapositions of some walls to form coherent units or buildings, when discussing them I designate them by the letter "B" followed by a forward slash, after which appears the stage number assigned to it by the excavators. Because I also recognize the existence of more than one building in Stage IV, each has been given, following another forward slash, a further arbitrary numerical designation of 1, 2, or 3. Phasing within buildings is indicated by a letter, with "a" representing the latest elements and the following letters signifying progressively earlier structures. Thus, the reader will encounter references to B/IV/1a and B/IV/1b, which are two phases of a building the excavators associated with Stage IV. B/IV/1a designates a later phase of a building superimposed upon remains of B/IV/1b.

STRATIGRAPHY OF THE EAST SLOPE: AN OVERVIEW

As noted in *Chapter 1*, the excavators' understanding of the stratigraphy of the East Slope was somewhat limited, which is perhaps best indicated by Guy and Engberg (*Megiddo Tombs*, p. 4), who claimed, "The east slope counted more or less as a stratum ...." They did, however, actually discern three "late" strata, apparently encountered in patches all over the East Slope, rather than a single "blanket" layer or even in contiguous deposits. In addition, they do not appear to have been able to correlate most of the later deposits with anything on the summit of the mound. Accordingly, they created a new nomenclature to ascribe the deposits on the East Slope, which they appropriately gave its initials to. Thus, ES I, II, and III (*Megiddo Tombs*, p. 4) are labels intended to designate three roughly superimposed deposits encountered in places on the East Slope.

However, the excavators never explicated the differences between them nor is there any evidence of their attempting to assign them to one or another chrono-cultural horizon. Indeed, except for the single cryptic reference to these deposits cited above, there does not appear to be evidence of any further work by them on the subject. There was, however, an attempt by someone or perhaps several members of the expedition to sidestep that issue by virtually ignoring it, as may be seen in the publication of the plan of the East Slope in *Megiddo Tombs* (pl. 1). It seems also to be negated in references to "Stratum A" on an unpublished plan (fig. 7; see also *Chapter 1: "Megiddo Special Sheet No. 1 Stratum A": A Stratigraphic Anomaly*, and in the locus list *Appendix C*), which appears to be a conflation of some aspects of ES I–III in a single layer, presumably of contemporary structures.

As there is considerable evidence for "late" deposits, superimposed in some instances directly above the remains of Stage IV and others directly above Stage V, I have conventionally designated them all as +IV. That should be understood as merely an indication of their associations with relatively late activity on the East Slope, mostly dated after the Early Bronze Age. I have, for lack of information on the excavators' identifications of ES I, II, and III, not attempted any correlations for the sequence of "late" deposits I describe. Instead I have stuck to documenting only highly localized sequences, usually in terms of buildings, which reflect the stratigraphy observable in the archived documentation. When possible I have tried to correlate between these sequences, but such observations are based mostly on circumstantial evidence from plans and photographs and do not take into account associations of artifacts from poorly or un-documented contexts.

By contrast with their "late" ES deposits, the excavators, based on their understanding of associated pottery, suggested seven stages to represent considerably earlier chrono-cultural horizons, which they eventually identified with the Chalcolithic and Early Bronze periods. Accordingly, they understood them to deserve an independent nomenclature and in order to distinguish them from the stratigraphy of the summit of the tell, they adopted the term "stages" (as opposed to "strata"), although they essentially were meant to designate similar phenomena. However, as noted in *Chapter 1*, these stages were not, *stricto sensu*, more or less discrete, superimposed deposits. This issue, critical to an understanding of the early deposits on the East Slope, is discussed in detail below.

ARCHITECTURE

As some of the post-Early Bronze Age levels were directly superimposed upon the earliest deposits found on the East Slope, I have endeavored to describe them in the sequence in which they were encountered. They are part of the record of the site and should not, I believe, be completely ignored when considering the earliest levels, as some of the deepest buried of them may have been associated with Early Bronze Age activity. The present discussion centers on those architectural features, some rather imposing, found in Square U16 and its immediate environs, the same precinct in which the early stages were unearthed. Architectural remains in those squares represent a considerable body of evidence, discussed below in order of the latest to the earliest.

PART 1: "LATE" ARCHITECTURAL FEATURES ON THE EAST SLOPE ABOVE THE EXCAVATORS' "STAGES"

The "late" architectural elements described below should be understood as a local sequence only, although some or many elements may have been coeval with numerous others found on the slope in other squares. Together they indicate periods of rather intense utilization of the East Slope in different time spans and for different functions. For a guide to locating the walls of this period in the illustrations, see table A.1.

"Post-Stage IV"

The term "Post-Stage IV" (i.e., +IV) is used here to designate a rather large number of stone-built structures identifiable in plans and balloon photographs within the immediate area of Stages IV and V, and superimposed upon them. These structures were termed "late" by the excavators, but the term is relative and precisely what it was meant to designate remains obscure, as nowhere did they elaborate on or attempt to define the absolute chronology or the chrono-cultural associations of those remains. My assumption is that they should, with a single definitive exception, mostly be associated with the settlement of the East Slope in historical periods, all post-dating the Early Bronze Age.

The Very Latest Features on the East Slope

Descriptions of several loci by the excavators suggest that most of the built structures encountered there were uncovered after soil removal. The very latest of them, those cut into the fill from the surface, are described below. Possibly they could be equated with ES I and Stratum A (see above).

Kilns

Three or possibly four kilns are visible in the photographs taken of the area around Stages IV and V. They appear as small, U-shaped or keyhole-shaped structures. They were not drawn on any plan but they may be easily discerned in the second and third series of aerial photographs and in several others taken at ground level. Two are situated in an exposed area between bedrock outcrops on the southwest border of Square U16 partially in large Square U15 (pl. 11) and in small Squares ee26 and ee27 (pl. 17). Another is visible in the southeast quadrant of large Square T16 and in small Squares hh22 and ii22 (pl. 17) and atop the curved wall of the apsidal-plan building shown in plate 19. What appear to be remains of another, similar installation are discernible in a deep, open pit virtually identical in size and shape to part of the inside of the kiln adjacent to it on the left in plate 17, possibly suggesting its superstructure had already been mostly removed. In plate 19 it may appear as a pit just north of the curvilinear wall of B/IV/1. Another structure that is likely to have been a kiln was found adjacent to and just east of that building (pl. 15); in aerial photographs where it appears as a small oval of sporadic stones, apparently after most of it was removed (e.g., pl. 19, ii23 in pl. 22).

The kilns are deep, subterranean affairs such as Locus 1087 (pl. 15) and were obviously intrusive into previously laid down deposits. Other analogous installations are found on the East Slope indicating that for some of its history that hillside was an area devoted to the manufacture of pottery. Fisher (1929, pp. 49–50) described a workshop complete with tools and other paraphernalia of the potter's craft found in a cave, but failed to offer a date for it beyond the observation that it was founded atop fill dated to the Iron Age and was constructed at a "much later period." The dates for these kilns remain equally obscure.

Grain Pit

A small, stone-lined and partially paved pit, set against the bedrock in Squares hh24 and ii24 (fig. 10), appears to have cut into the soil matrix surrounding B/+IV/1 and B/+IV/2 (see below). No evidence to verify this specific function is available, but stone-lined bins of this type are not atypical at sites in the southern

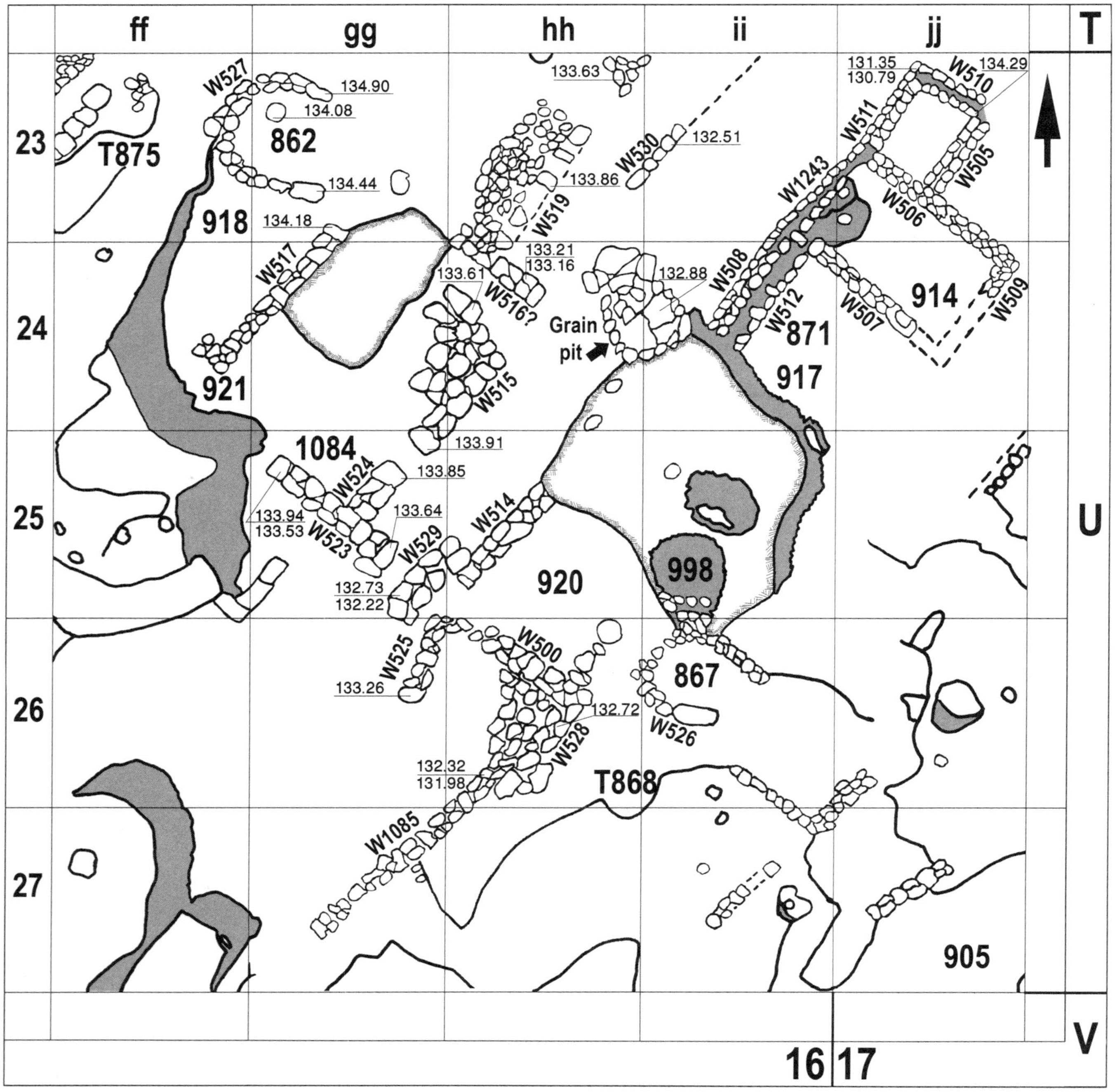

Figure 10. Re-drawn detail of the excavators' Primary Master Plan of the East Slope, indicated as "Stratum A," apparently a conflation of ES I, II, and III in another stratigraphic scheme cited in the *Megiddo Tombs* and in the locus list. Gray shading is the excavators' indication of a third dimension

Levant in many periods from the Neolithic until virtually modern times. Grain storage is one of the presumed functions of such installations.

Additional Late Architectural Features

A number of architectural features appear on the excavators' plan (fig. 10), which could be contemporary with, later, or earlier than the several post-Stage IV buildings discussed below. However, elevations are indicated for only a few of those features, while for others none is known. Thus it is impossible to ascribe them to any relative stratigraphic context because of the sloping terrain and lack of additional information. Most

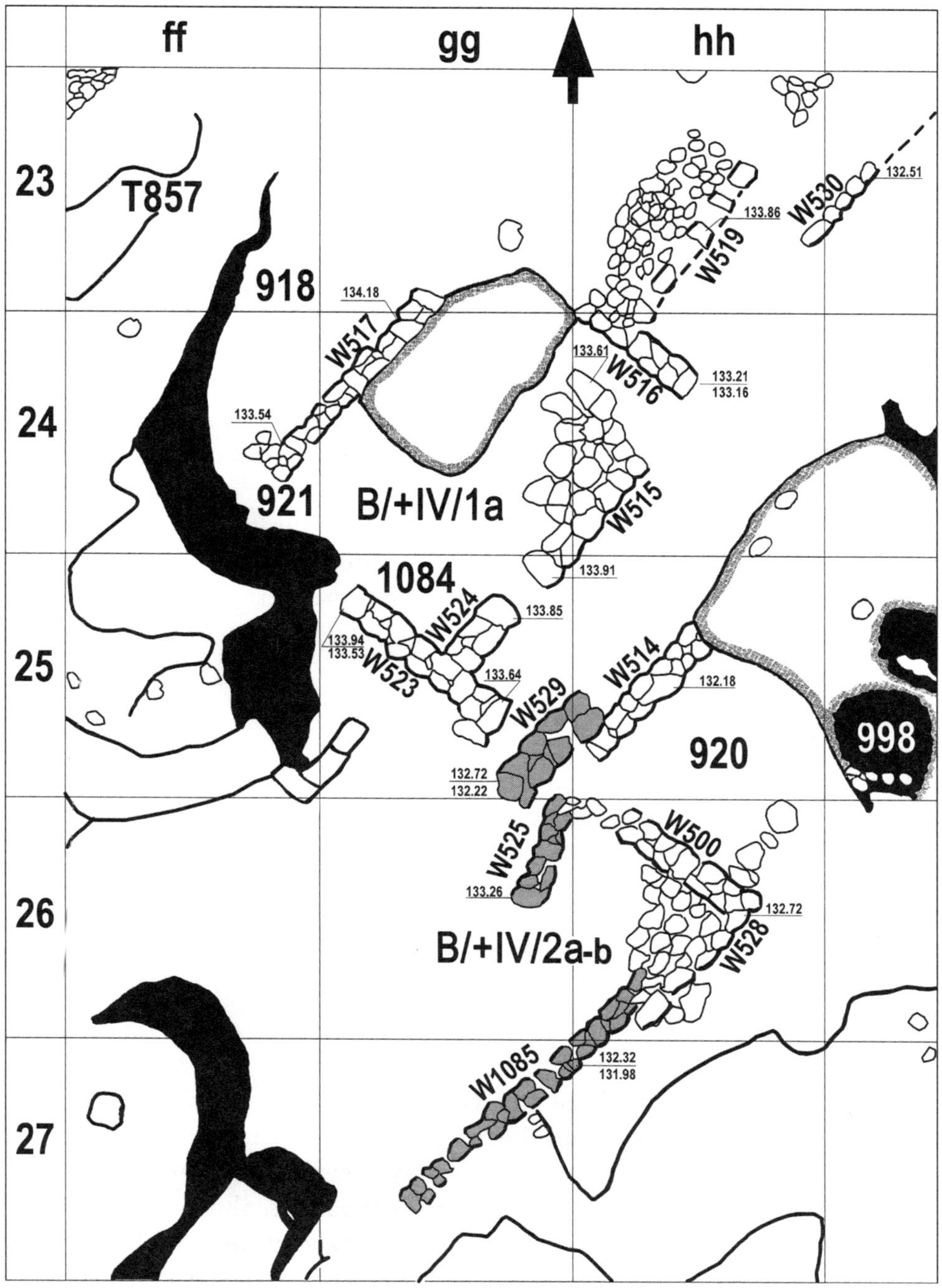

Figure 11. Re-drawn detail indicating two phases of the latest buildings on the upper terrace in Square U16, derived from the excavators' Primary Master Plan. Two structures, B/+IV/1 and B/+IV/2, are interpreted from the remains. Their styles of construction as well as their relative elevations suggest these buildings functioned contemporaneously. The shaded stones of W529 are understood to represent additional construction phases. The remaining walls are assumed to have existed coevally, but may not have all been constructed at the same time

appear to be included in the latest elements in a sequence of construction found on this precinct of the East Slope. Such is W527 of Locus 862 (fig. 10: Squares ff–gg23), a horseshoe-shaped affair of uncertain function, described by the excavators as a "stone enclosure." A similar element is W526 of Locus 867 (fig. 10: Square ii26), described as a "room?" Wall 1085 (Square gg27), noted as "wall etc., late" in the locus list, is interesting for that characterization because it is one of the few walls for which upper and lower elevations are noted and which was given a locus designation. Since its lower elevation at 131.98 is lower than the upper elevation of nearby W528 (132.72), it suggests that the foundation of the latter wall was still farther below. Other walls, mostly single lines of stones or bits of corners of structures, were apparently considered as very late or even modern by the excavators and thus of no import to them for recording the history of utilization of the East Slope. As I have no additional information on these features, and I cannot relate them to specific buildings, I have left them un-numbered on my adaptation of the excavators' plan (fig. 10).

The Latest Buildings and Structures

Insofar as I have been able to ascertain, all the buildings discovered within large Squares U16 and U17 were completely unearthed during excavations and were not visible prior to that.[25] Several, which appear on "Megiddo Special Sheet No. 1 Stratum A,"[26] may be representative of a more or less contemporary occupation as indicated by relative elevations of some of the structures. Available photographic documentation (pl. 16) indicates they are the latest structures encountered in the excavation. However, evidence compiled from the series of aerial photographs and extant plans and elevations suggests that each is likely to have been built in successive phases. Since it is not possible to stratigraphically correlate between them and thus offer a general scheme for this precinct of the excavation, nor is there definitive evidence of chrono-cultural associations for any of them, they are discussed as separate features, that is, buildings or associations of walls roughly identified as coherent architectural structures. Each represents a highly localized sequence based on obvious superimposition and additional evidence or clues suggesting sequential construction.

B/+IV/1

Evidence from this building suggests it had a long history of use with at least three sequential phases during which a single orientation was maintained. It appears to have utilized remains of an earlier building, which, because it cannot be correlated with any additional structures, is conventionally identified as Phase d, although it does not share the same orientation as Phases a–c and may belong to a completely different structure, the remains of which were incorporated into this building. This structure is notable for the large size of the stones — virtual boulders — used in its external walls.

B/+IV/1a

This phase is apparently associated with the excavators' Locus 1084, dated according to them to a "late" chrono-cultural horizon. I understand it to have been the latest in a series of superimposed structures because of its inclusion on Special Sheet No. 1 and because only a few scant remains of it are visible in Squares ff23–25, gg23–25, and hh23–25 (fig. 11) and in the first series of balloon photographs (pl. 16). Its uppermost stratigraphic position is indicated by the relative degree of vertical exposure of a bedrock outcrop (adjacent to W517) within the confines of Locus 1084, which is depicted without a shadow in figure 11. Elsewhere on the same plan shadows on bedrock outcrops are an apparent sign of more considerable above-surface exposure, suggesting this particular outcrop was not very prominent when the plan was drawn. By contrast, that same outcrop is clearly visible as having been significantly exposed in a detail of an aerial photograph (pl. 16), obviously taken at a later date, as indicated by what appears to be an extension of W517 to the southwest.

B/+IV/1a, only poorly preserved, seems minimally to have been a two-roomed, rectilinear structure formed by W515, W516, W517, W519, W523, and W524. The better-preserved southern chamber, perhaps accessed by a doorway on the east between W524 and W515, enclosed a large bedrock outcrop. To the northeast is an additional wall, W519, which appears to be associated with a cobbled surface to its west. That surface is probably directly above another associated with B/+IV/1c (see below), as this latter is notably not visible on the first series of aerial photographs (pl. 16), unless the drawn plan represents not only a status prior to

[25] Various descriptions by the excavators indicate exposed areas of bedrock and apertures of tombs but none suggests standing structures on the East Slope.

[26] Stratum A is possibly a conflation of the excavators' ES I–III strata (see *Chapter 1*).

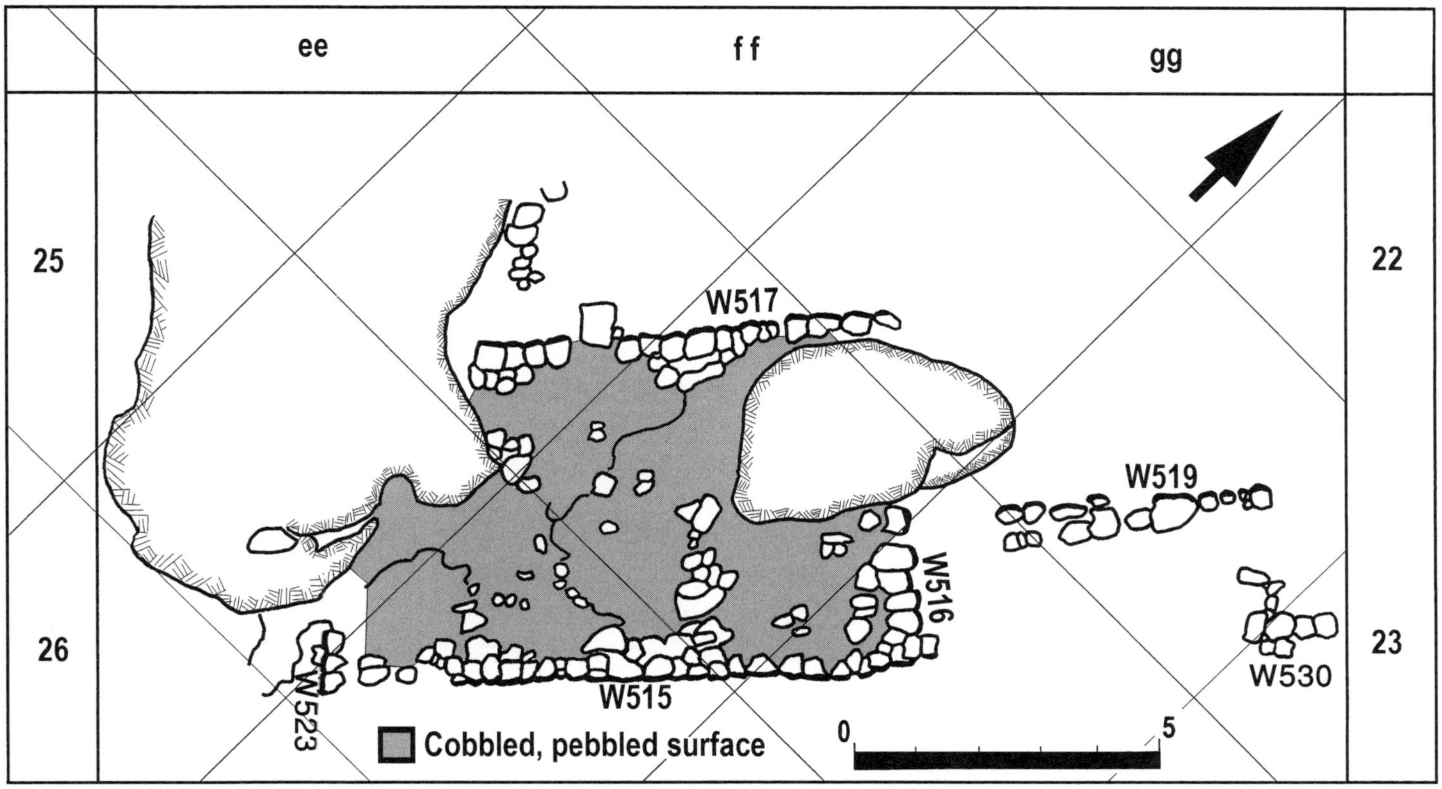

Figure 12. Plan of B/+IV/1a based on an aerial photograph (pl. 16). The gray shading represents stone pavements, one apparently directly atop the other

the balloon photographs but also incorporates some elements revealed at a tardier stage of excavation, as seems to be the case with Section C–D (see *Chapter 1*). Only a few stones of W519, part of a single row of large boulders, are preserved in situ. They are apparently part of the uppermost course of a well-preserved structure below, B/+IV/1b. Several of the stones in W515 and W516 appear to be exceptionally large, enhancing the suggestion that they are the uppermost remains of earlier structural phases (see below). The positions of some of the walls of B/+IV/1a indicate they were re-used segments of walls of the earlier B/IV/1b. Although I have assigned them the same numbers, I do not have absolute proof of this identity. A short wall segment, W530, may also have been associated with this building as its proximity and orientation suggest. So too may W514 have served as the east side of another room, although this wall is probably part of another building, nominally identified as B/+IV/2.

B/+IV/1b

My drawing of the plan of this building (fig. 12) is entirely derived from one of the aerial photographs from the second series (pl. 17). While this phase of the building includes W515, W516, W517, and W519, re-used in Phase a, the structure extends farther to the southwest, where it abuts a large bedrock outcrop. The photograph suggests that the uppermost course or courses of all those walls were removed to expose larger stones in this earlier and significantly more robust building phase. The outer walls of this building, as in an earlier phase (c), were fashioned of large boulders, either chosen for their natural shapes or roughly hewn into approximations of ashlar masonry.

Evidence of remains of internal walls abutting the west side of W515, the plan of the large, rectangular precinct formed by the massive outer walls, seems to indicate an internal, tripartite division into small, rectangular chambers, with the bedrock feature taking up nearly all the northwest half of the northernmost room. One wall, W519, sharing the orientation of W515, appears to be part of a more northerly extension of this structure, although little of it is preserved. I have added W530 to the plan as it appears in the photograph, but I am not certain that it was actually contemporary with this building. Two cobbled surfaces, apparently successive floors, appear also to be associated with this building. They are indicated in my plan by gray shading and are distinguished one from the other by a black line. The aerial photograph shows them only at one stage of excavation and it is uncertain how much more of either surface was preserved. The surface to the south is apparently the later, as it appears to be superimposed upon that to the north, which presumably existed also beneath it.

B/+IV/1c

An even earlier phase of this building is visible in an aerial photograph (pls. 17–18), taken after B/+IV/1b had been partially deconstructed, revealing another edifice of sizable proportions. The same massive masonry forms the external walls of this room, but there are no apparent internal divisions. The photograph suggests the plan of one large, rectangular room paved with cobbles over most of its surface, as well as associated structures to the west and north.

I have drawn a plan of this building and adjacent structures that seem to be associated with it (fig. 13). A low wall or bench-like structure (W520), parallel and adjacent to the north face of W516, seems to be associated with a northerly extension of this building. Parallel walls W519 and W521, partially enclosing another cobbled surface, appear to be remains of what must have been a long, narrow chamber, possibly an indication that this was once a substantially larger complex.

Abutting the west wall (W517) of the large room was what appears to have been a long, narrow wall (W532), which appears in the aerial photograph as a very straight, solid, thick, sharply delineated, high-standing mass of even width. I have virtually ruled out the possibility of this line being a balk as there is no evidence of any such technique having been employed in excavations at the site.[27] Unfortunately, this feature was never drawn on a plan and its identification as a wall is subject to some doubt as only at its most western extent are stones discernible in it. The remainder of this feature was, I presume, constructed of pisé or mudbrick, or at least covered in dark-colored plaster, which would have hidden its internal features. I have identified as a wall (W531) another similar feature to the north. I further suggest that another parallel construction to the south, in which a few stones are visible, albeit much narrower and less straight than these two other features, is a third wall (W533) of similar construction, probably less well preserved. All three of these features (i.e., walls) seem to emerge from the bedrock scarp at virtually right angles with W517, which strengthens this supposition, although only W532 forms a corner with W517. If indeed these features are walls, then there was a sizable, two-room extension to the west of the large building.

Unfortunately, there is no good evidence of any special features that could suggest surfaces or floors in these rooms on the west, but that may be a function of the state of exposure when the photograph, the sole evidence for these features, was taken. Visible in the enlarged detail of the aerial photo (pl. 17) is a circular object (a *tabun*?) in the room formed by W532 and W533, and in the room to the north there is a line of smallish stones abutting the south side of W531 that could possibly have closed the room off from the bedrock outcrop to the west. I have drawn it on the plan but have not given it a number as it is unclear whether it was associated with the building; there are no indications of its elevations or the number of its courses. It might even be an artifact of excavation, a temporary support wall to prevent fill from collapsing into the excavation. Although there is no evidence for the function of this building, its rather robust construction and multi-roomed plan suggest it was likely to have been of some import for those that occupied or utilized it.

[27] In the same photograph (pl. 18) one can see a sloping, rounded scarp, the line of excavation, in the upper right-hand corner where B/+IV/3 was revealed. Another excavation line, apparently straight and vertical, is noticeable just above the label "B/+IV/1," which suggests the excavation removed the fill of this area from the side and not in successive, horizontal increments.

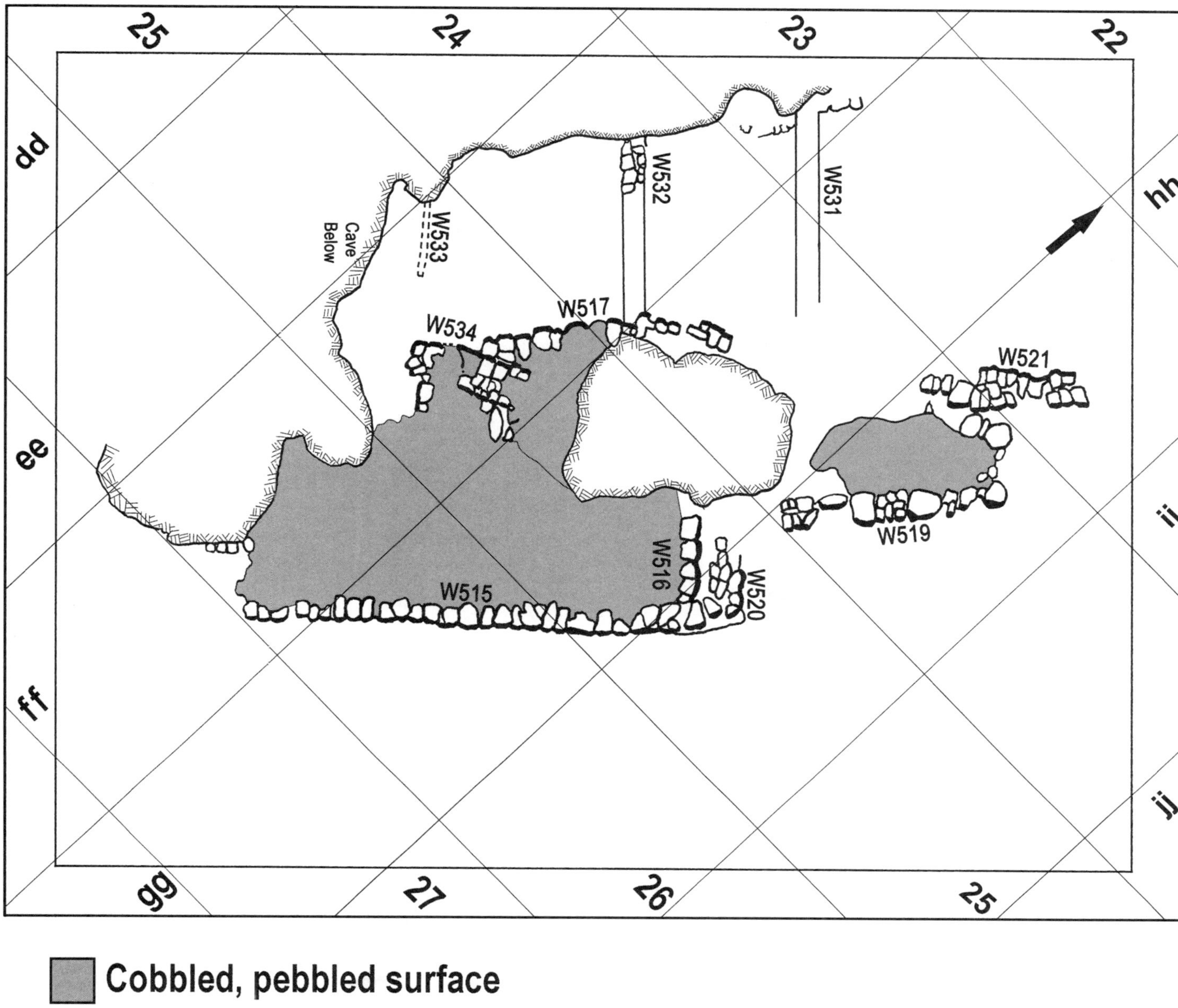

Figure 13. Plan of the earliest phases of B/+IV/1 from an aerial photograph (pl. 17)

B/+IV/1d

Just to the south of the mass of bedrock in the floor of B/+IV/1c, and to the east of the southern end of W517, a wide swath of large stones incorporated into the pavement of B/+IV/1c may be discerned in the aerial photograph (pl. 18). I do not believe this arrangement to be coincidental as the alignment, in two parallel rows of stones oblique to W517 (fig. 13), suggests it is likely to be the top of a wall of an earlier structure with a slightly different orientation. Somewhat hesitatingly, as there is very little evidence for this phase, I have labeled this group of stones W534 and assigned it to B/+IV/1d to indicate its stratigraphic situation within a local sequence. If W534 is indeed remains of an earlier structure, it is not truly part of the sequence of rebuilding, which the later, superimposed phases represent. Neither is it associated with the earliest structures that lie below it, which, rather interestingly, more nearly share the orientation of the buildings above. Unfortunately, nothing more is known of this Phase d structure, although nearby buildings (see below) could have been contemporary.

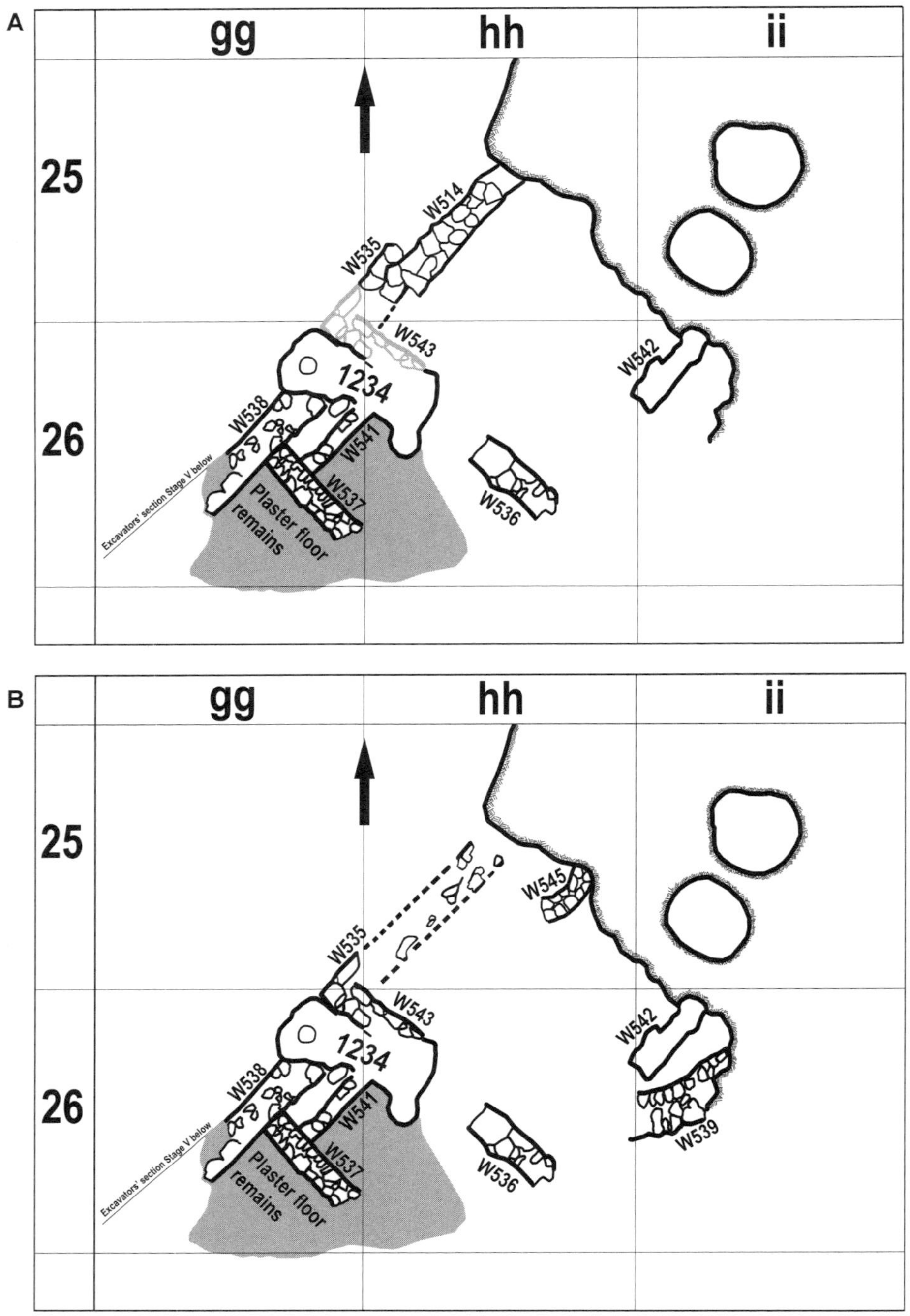

Figure 14. Plans of B/+IV/2, a building constructed up against a bedrock outcrop, from an aerial photograph (pl. 17). The upper register, A, illustrates the latest phases. The walls in gray represent an earlier structure that may, or may not have remained in used in one or another of these phases

Structures Likely to Be Contemporary with One or More of the Several Phases of B/+IV/1

Different phases of several buildings and wall segments (pl. 18), sharing the same alignment as B/+IV/1a, may be contemporary with one or more of its phases. However, each represents a separate, completely local sequence and so the alphabetic values of these buildings do not necessarily indicate contemporaneousness with the equivalent alphabetic phases of B/+IV/1.

B/+IV/2

Located southeast of B/+IV/1, this poorly preserved building, if indeed it deserves such an appellation, exhibited a number of structural phases (fig. 14). A lack of written descriptions and relative elevations, especially of wall foundations, made it extremely difficult to unravel its complex stratigraphy. I have endeavored to understand the essence of the sequence from the photographs of the structure in different stages of exposure. The combined evidence suggests a complicated sequence of construction and reconstruction, with some walls utilized in more than one phase. With a single exception preserved in photographs (see below) there are no records of surfaces associated with its walls. I have associated elements that appear to be in synchronization — whether because of construction style, proximity, or relative position in a sequence — to one or another phase.

In its latest phase, remains of this building were quite proximal to B/+IV/1a, while the style of construction and orientations of its walls suggest they may even have formed a single, complex structure with it. Earlier phases below, however, appear to have been independent of B/+IV/1a. The excavation of B/+IV/2 appears to have yielded a sequence of no less than four successive phases of construction, but because preservation was so poor and the evidence is so equivocal for each phase, the several phases are discussed as groups as they appear on the different plans. All phases of this building were associated with a boulder of massive proportions (Locus 1234) removed later in the excavation. Locus 1234 sealed a number of additional stratified architectural deposits below. Thus the earliest phase of this building is a *terminus ante quem* for the placement of that boulder and the deposits below.

B/+IV/2a–b

Little more than scant remains of W514 of this building was left by the time the first series of aerial photographs (pl. 14) was taken, but the latest phases (a and b) are documented in the excavators' plan (fig. 11). In order to distinguish between features that appear not to belong to the principal building phase, I have shaded them in that plan. However, there is no assurance that the shaded features did not function simultaneously, nor that they were also, at some point in time, not in use during the principal occupation phase of the building.

In my synthetic plans of B/+IV/2a–b I have drawn the stones of walls that originated in an earlier phase and which may have remained in use in the later building in light-gray outlines (fig. 14a). Those same walls are drawn in black when they were apparently integral to the building (fig. 14b) in an earlier phase. Other walls are drawn in black and seem likely to represent two construction phases. As it is unclear which of the phases was the later in the final sequence of construction (fig. 14a), I have not assigned any particular element to one or another phase, but merely designated those features "a–b" (fig. 11). The evidence could even support the reconstruction of a third phase (fig. 14a), but as it is not definitive, that phase remains unattributed.

The short wall segment W529 (fig. 11) appears to be the very latest element constructed atop the southern end of W514, and may have been also associated with the nearby B/+IV/1a, as it appears to form a narrow passageway with the end of W523 to the west, possibly demarcating access to a room or courtyard. It is, however, a somewhat incongruous arrangement when considered with the buildings nearby and thus may not have been directly associated with them, but rather part of a later structure of which nothing additional is preserved.

Several walls, more or less sharing the same alignment, form a nearly rectangular structure that apparently had two rooms in an earlier phase. The more northerly room, the excavators' Locus 920, is bounded by W514 to the northwest and may have been the principal chamber of this building. It was enclosed to the southwest by W500 and to the northeast by a bedrock outcrop. Perhaps the eastern boundary of this room is reflected in the short line of stones abutting W500 to the north. As noted above, the regular mien of these walls is similar to the construction of B/+IV/1a, which suggests they are likely to have existed contemporaneously. Possibly these two building were actually elements composing a single, large, complex structure built around the two opposing bedrock outcrops.

A room to the south is indicated by the well-preserved corner of W500 and W528, which appears to have had an associated cobbled surface. The somewhat misaligned W525 may have enclosed that room to the west, although W529 is better aligned and better built and may have also functioned for that purpose. The relationship of W525 to W514 is obscure. Although they are somewhat misaligned and the relative elevation of the foundation of W525 suggests it is a later element, it seems likely that at least at some period in time they functioned together. The style of construction of W525 and W1085, slightly less robust than that of the additional walls of these phases, may be an indication of the formers' contemporaneousness. Wall 535 may, in part, have functioned in the later phases of this building, but that is uncertain and, as noted above, it has been "ghosted" in light-gray outline (fig. 14a).

B/+IV/2c–d

The early phases of B/+IV/2 are documented solely in aerial photographs (pl. 17). The plans are composite drawings of elements visible in the first through the third series of balloon photographs (fig 14b and pls. 9–11). This building appears to have been a multi-chambered, rectilinear structure in which minimally two phases are discernible, although extant constructions suggest the likelihood of more structural phases. One wall on the northwest, W535, although very poorly preserved at the time of the photograph, appears to have enclosed a large, nearly rectangular room, up to the large mass of bedrock. The stubby, poorly preserved W542 is likely to have been the room's eastern closure wall. Wall 543 and its likely continuation, W536, would have marked the southern extent of the room. A gap between W536 and the massive boulder to the west (Locus 1234) may have been the entryway into the chamber. Within the room is a short segment of a curvilinear wall (W545) only faintly visible in an aerial photograph (pl. 17). Its association with this structure is as unclear as its function. In aspect it appears to be analogous to W539 (see also below), the function and stratigraphic associations of which are equally obscure.

Wall 543 is built up against a massive boulder, which appears to show additional evidence of some construction atop it. It created part of a small room or niche, bordered by W541 and W537. This latter wall also forms a corner with W538, indicating an additional room or courtyard to the south. Wall 541 is a narrow, poorly built element that is likely to have been a late addition; it created a narrow gap between it and parallel W538 to the west, which seems less than what might be normally considered a functional space. However, a spread of potsherds or small stones forming a floor, visible, apparently on the floor of this narrow compartment (pl. 30), could suggest it was used for storage. A photograph (pl. 32) taken at ground level of Stage V, incidentally indicates that W538 was built directly atop a thick, white plaster floor, probably cut by diggers when B/V/1 was excavated. This plaster floor extended over a larger area as may be discerned in the aerial photographs (pl. 19), but I was unable to ascertain the association of it and the additional walls of these phases, as no further details of this part of the excavation are available. Clearly, W538 was built later than the floor, which suggests one or more of the other walls is likely to have been constructed coevally with it.

B/+IV/3

Despite the relative elevations of this building (fig. 15), which place it close to the levels of some of the earliest structures, it appears to have been positioned farther down the incline, as suggested by the lack of any evidence for bedrock in the photographs. Possibly the excavators believed it was mostly in sync with later occupation levels (ES III?) as it appears on their drawn plan, although as the easily discerned low, semicircular excavation scarp in Squares ii23, ii24, and ii25 (pl. 17) indicates, it was exposed on a level lower than that on which the other nearby "late buildings" were founded.

There is a suggestion that some of the structures, wall segments incorporated into later buildings in this precinct of the excavation, may have originated in the Early Bronze Age III. One wall of this building, W1243, appears on the excavators' plan of the early stages (see below). Probably they intended that it should be understood as more or less contemporary with the architecture of Stage IV, as a complete holemouth vessel of the Early Bronze III Age was found nearby, "outside wall of 914" (i.e., a wall of Locus 914; *Appendix C*,

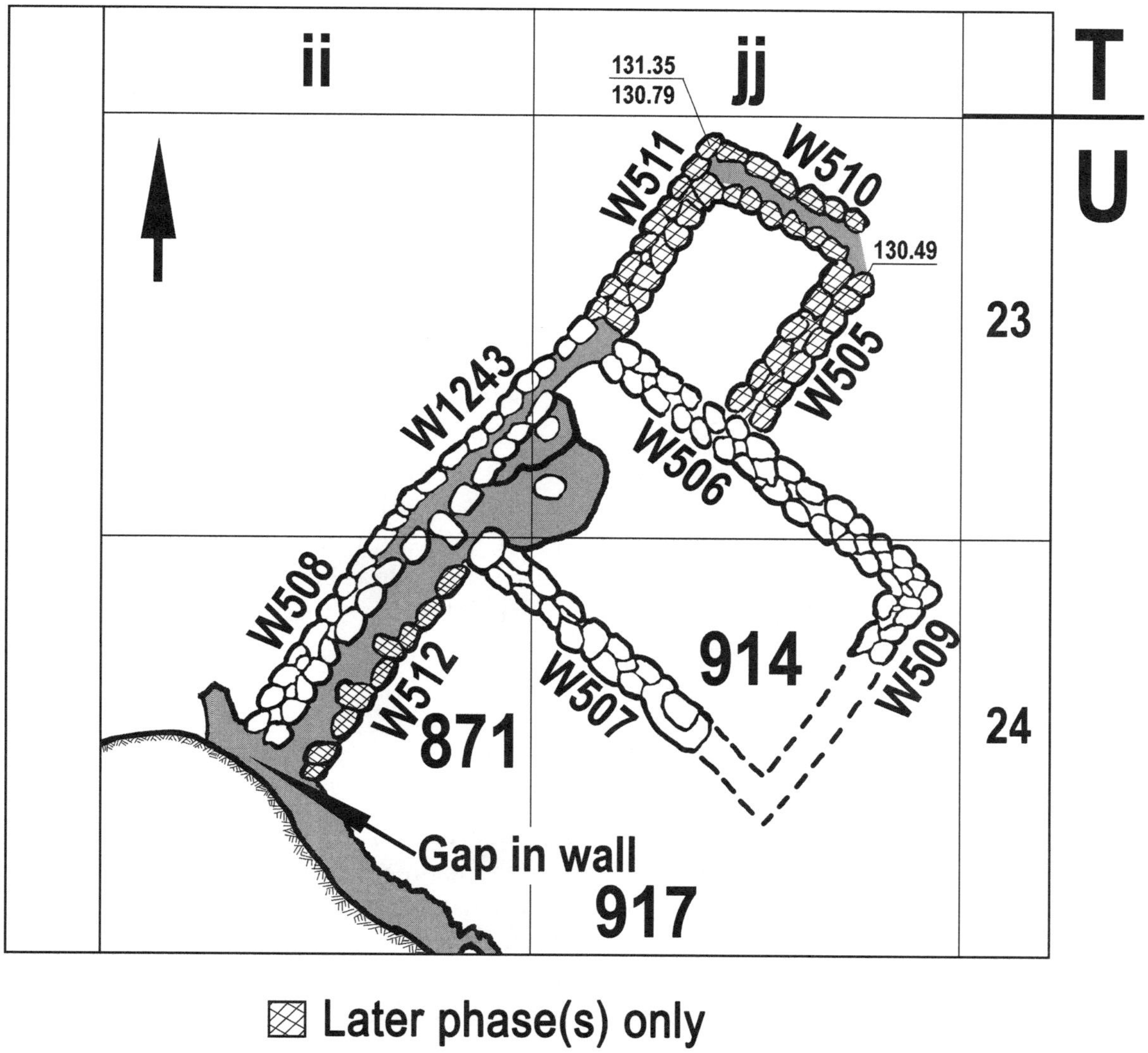

Figure 15. Plan of B/+IV/3, derived from figure 11, with suggested phasing based on sequence of construction

Locus 914). The likely feature in this description is W1243, although there are three additional walls to that room, any one of which might be indicated in the excavator's cursory notation. Curiously, another similar and nearly complete vessel of this type was recovered from below a floor, probably somewhere in this same area (pl. 41), but it has no apparent association with any of these structures.

B/+IV/3a

The central, rectangular room of this building, Locus 914 (figs. 5, 10, 15; pl. 19), is suggested by the excavators' plan (fig. 4) to have remained in use throughout the entire lifetime of the building. Thus it was constructed in an earlier phase and built onto sometime later. The addition is a small, rectangular room to the north of Locus 914, comprised of W505, W510, and W511. Although the excavator's plan (fig. 15) suggests W511 is a direct continuation of W1243, it is clear from the aerial photographs that this northern room is somewhat mis-aligned with room 914, that is, offset to the west (pl. 19). While there are no elevations to confirm my stratigraphic or structural phasing of this building, it seems quite clear the small room was added later. What appears to be a stone with a cavity, perhaps a mortar, is indicated on the excavator's plan just north of the east end of the short, northernmost wall of the small room, W510, at an elevation of 130.20 (fig. 4) (a circle with inner circle, elevation 130.29, is similar to this description, appears just north of the east end of wall W506 of 914; in fig. 5 it appears as a dark, nearly circular patch; in fig. 6 it appears as a circle within a circle, but whether that signifies a floor or merely the top of that feature, is uncertain). Wall 512, a single line of stones that was allowed to remain in place during the entire period covered by the aerial photographs, appears to be some very late construction of uncertain function. On the excavator's plan (fig. 15) I have indicated the very latest walls by filling them with cross hatching. Areas filled in gray represent a shading technique used by the excavators to indicate a third dimension (fig. 10).

B/+IV/3b

In this earlier phase it appears that B/+IV/3 had either two rooms or one room, Locus 914, and a courtyard to its south (Locus 871) effectively formed by W508 and the large bedrock outcrop. This courtyard could have been entered from the west through the narrow gap between bedrock and W508; to the east there is no sign of any form of closure. The core of this building appears to have been the rectangular Locus 914. Its extant walls, W1243, W506, W507, and W509, seem to have been built coevally. W508, possibly constructed somewhat later than W1243, may have been originally associated with this phase and could have even functioned in the later life of this building. Notably, several sherds dated to Early Bronze Age III from this room are found in the assemblage. Together with the holemouth vessel cited above, they are a good indication of the Early Bronze Age III date of the earliest phase of the central room of this building (see below).

An Area of Activity

Additional information on activity in this area in the Early Bronze Age comes from a photograph (pl. 41) of a nearly complete, Early Bronze Age II–III holemouth vessel (P4509; pl. 73a) from Locus 1183. According to the locus list (*Appendix C*), that is fill in Square U17 below Locus 1171, noted as a "room" in Square V17. By contrast, Locus 1183 is noted as in Square U17. While there are no precise visual records of the location of this room, part of a rectilinear structure of at least two rooms is visible in aerial photographs (pls. 9–12), at the juncture of these squares. One of these rooms is likely to have been Locus 1171. Possibly there is additional evidence of occupation nearby in the same period from another such vessel (pl. 72e; 34.2546), found nearly intact in Locus 1152, a small cavity in the bedrock (pl. 41), but that information is equivocal.[28]

PART 2: THE EARLIEST CONSTRUCTIONS ON THE EAST SLOPE: STAGES IV AND V AND BELOW

Evidence of the earliest building on the East Slope indicates the existence, mostly in Square U16, of two adjacent, step-like areas of bedrock rather than a gradual slope. Portions of those contours represent deliberate leveling of the soft limestone by ancient inhabitants. Thus, they utilized or expanded existing cavities and other natural bedrock features and created somewhat crude broad and uneven steps or terraces, which were exposed below earthen fills and the remains of structures of Stage +IV. For a guide to finding the walls of these periods in the illustrations, see table A.1.

Although the excavation of both areas yielded two local sequences of building and utilization, one on each terrace, the excavators assigned them to sequential strata within a single sequence based on a sole point of supposed contact, one short, superimposed wall segment they ascribed to Stage IV above a wall of Stage V. While that specific sequence is undeniable, the validity of the general paradigm of Stage IV above Stage V is questionable because the wall above cannot be assigned to Stage IV with any degree of certainty. Indeed, there is actually good reason to suspect it belongs to some later phase of utilization of the terrace.

[28] It is even possible that the last two of these vessels are one and the same pot as they were recovered from the same area. Notably, I have found no trace of a nearly complete vessel from Locus 1152. The discrepancies in locus numbers may be explained by the fact that Locus 1152 is just a small depression, while the pot was first recovered, still standing in situ, in fill above. Unfortunately, there are no additional records on the excavation of these loci.

If that surmise is correct then the stratigraphic paradigm offered by the excavators is no longer tenable and the whole sequence becomes questionable, especially as the very earliest stages (VII and VI) were represented in the excavation in a few small probes to bedrock below what the excavators called Stages IV and V. As noted in *Chapter 1*, those "stages" are represented only by artifacts and have no associated structures. Following is a detailed discussion of the evidence of architecture and associated deposits, which appear to belie the excavators' seven neatly dovetailing stages coinciding with ceramic horizons morphing one into another over time.

In attempting to reconstruct the stratigraphy of buildings on these bedrock steps I have had to rely almost completely on visual aids, mostly photographs, but a modicum of corollary information available from the plans and sections of these structures also proved to be useful, if not always completely reliable. The absence of any field notes, indications of soil qualities, the studious avoidance of any description of the architectural remains and stratigraphic associations in the publications, beyond the single notation that Stage IV overlapped Stage V (Engberg and Shipton 1934a, p. 3), was a particular hindrance to this task as there is no information on associated floors and/or surfaces hinted at by the excavators.

There is a possibility that some additional information, extant in the 1960s may now be lost, or at least not now available in official archives. A. Ben-Tor (1978, p. 44), in his monograph on glyptics, noted information supplied to him by A. Eitan:

> ... 1) there are sound reasons to suggest a refining and sub-phasing of the stages, as presented by Engberg and Shipton; 2) the impressions published in Engberg and Shipton (1934a: 31–39) originate from a pit onto which they were thrown together with additional ceramic material; 3) the pottery found in this pit should be dated to EB I, and gray-burnished ware is present.

I was unable to verify that information in available documentation but I suspect it refers to deep probes (e.g., below Locus 1371) after most excavation had ceased on the ES. In a personal conversation with A. Eitan (2013), I asked about the provenience of the "pit," but Eitan did not remember offhand and noted there was too much documentation for him to go through and pursue the matter.

Indeed, even when the excavators found some pottery vessels in situ collapsed onto floors where they were abandoned, they eschewed noting or illustrating them in their publication, while there are no known notes concerning these particular discoveries. I am only aware of a very few examples of such finds, and they are documented only in photographs. Thus, it is particularly difficult to evaluate the significance of occasional passing references to floors in available documentation. They could mean that such elements were encountered only in those places documented in the photographs or noted in the locus list, or merely that they were inferred because of relationships of fills to walls, but not actually detected.

The discussion below follows the excavators' basic stratigraphic scheme that maintains a primary distinction between Stages IV and V; in summary, it offers an expanded and much more complicated sequence of building events that belies the existence of only two strata or "stages" of buildings in the early deposits. It also calls into question the very essence of some features of the excavators' sequence in what are basically two slightly sloping bedrock terraces, one upslope from the other. For purposes of discussion I have maintained the excavators' stratigraphic ascriptions as a means of primary identification. The upper terrace and all the architecture on it are ascribed to Stage IV; the lower terrace and its buildings to Stage V.

The Architecture of Stage IV

Stage IV is represented by a sequence of building phases occupying a large, (artificially?) flattened patch of bedrock that forms a kind of step or terrace east of a nearly vertical bedrock scarp in the south of Square T16 and in Square U16. As is now well understood, the deposits assigned by the excavators to Stage IV are the very lowest-lying there, which had been covered by massive deposits discussed above as +IV. Several structures, representing a number of phases, including features quarried into the bedrock, were encountered in these deposits. For reasons that are unclear but which might be related to the relationship of Guy to Engberg and Shipton, plans of this and the lower terrace, "Stage V," were prepared and ready for publication but

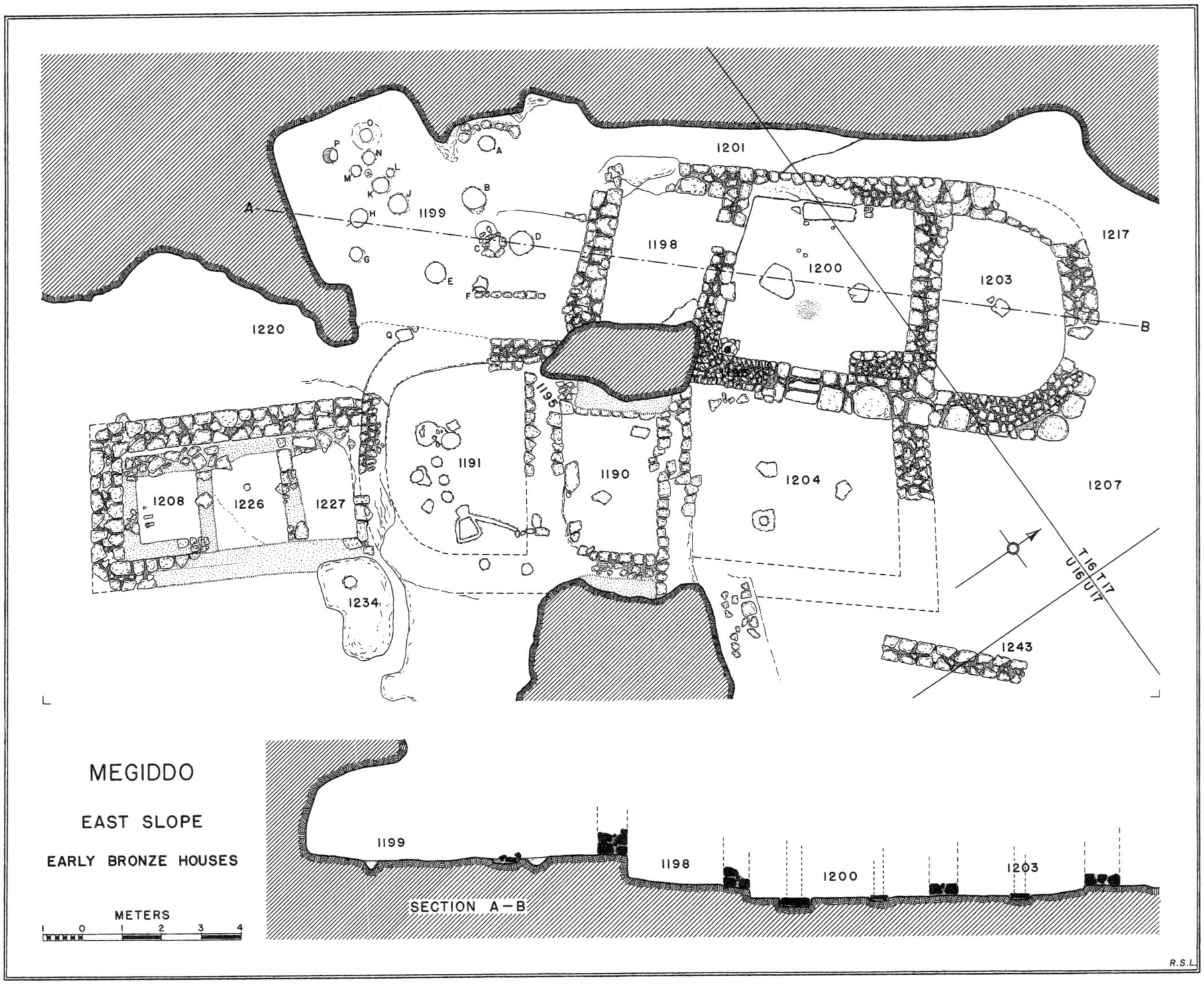

Figure 16. An exact copy of Lamon's original, unpublished plan and section of "Stages IV and V," scanned from a photograph and "cleaned" of imperfections for publication

were never published (fig. 16). Instead, Engberg and Shipton preferred to illustrate the early structures in a photograph (pl. 20; Engberg and Shipton 1934a, fig. 1) from the last balloon series taken of the East Slope.

B/IV/1

This structure, the largest building (fig. 16; pl. 20), has several phases of construction (fig. 20). In an earlier publication (Braun 1989a, fig. 2) I was able, using only evidence from the published detail of the same annotated balloon photograph (pl. 20[29]), to discern that this building was constructed in at least two phases. Now, additional information for this building, one of the best-known and widely discussed examples of Early Bronze Age I architecture in the southern Levant, is available from the archives. It comes from the last two series of balloon photographs (pls. 11–12, 19–20, 21–22) and other photographs taken at ground level from several directions (pls. 23–32, 36–38) and at different times, and from Robert S. Lamon's[30] detailed plan and section of Stages IV and V (fig. 16). They reveal additional important details about this structure, especially in its latest phase. Some details, neither documented in the plan nor discernible in the balloon series, confirm

[29] This figure is a newly produced copy of that published by Engberg and Shipton. Both are details taken from plate 12.

[30] This is indicated by the initials RSL on the plans and sections.

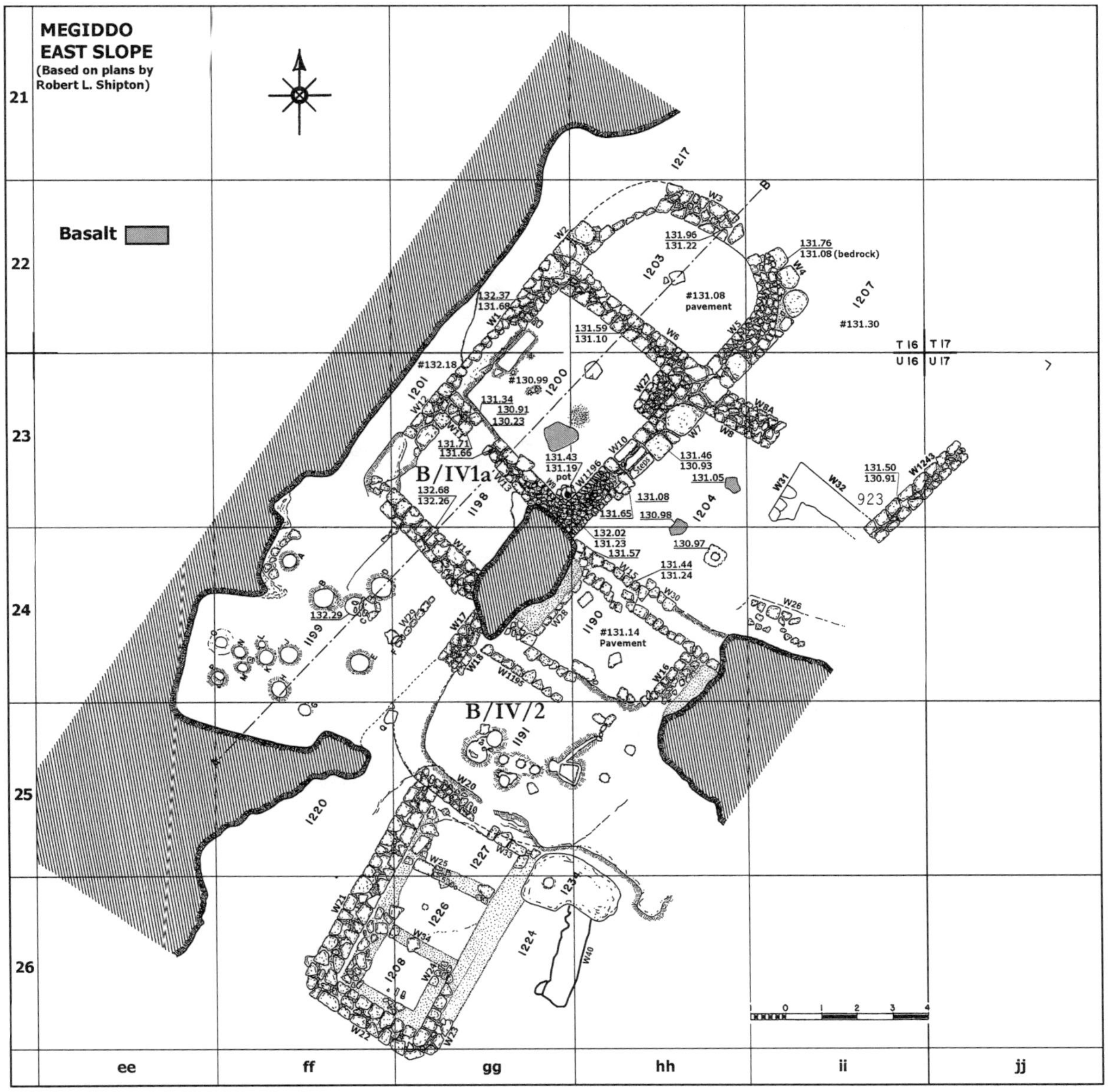

Figure 17. Lamon's plan (see fig. 16), enhanced with elevations, annotated, newly assigned wall numbers, additional walls drawn from the evidence of aerial photographs (pls. 9–12), elevations, and a 5 × 5 m grid superimposed upon it

my initial impression obtained from the published photograph, which is also obvious from Lamon's plan (which I had seen but was not then at liberty to publish), that the building was constructed in two phases. In endeavoring to embellish and correct Lamon's plan with more details available from the photographs, I present the results in several versions of the different construction phases.

B/IV/1a

This latest phase appears to incorporate three construction phases evidenced in the types of stones used. The major phase seems to have been built atop remains of a very robust building, constructed of large boulders, using smaller fieldstones. As the very latest phase seems to be nothing more than a repair of an existing structure using very small fieldstones. I have conflated these two latest phases into one, labeling them Phase a.

In this phase the building was subdivided into three rooms in a linear arrangement (figs. 16–18). The room to the north, Locus 1203, is a single unit unconnected by a doorway to the remaining two communicat-

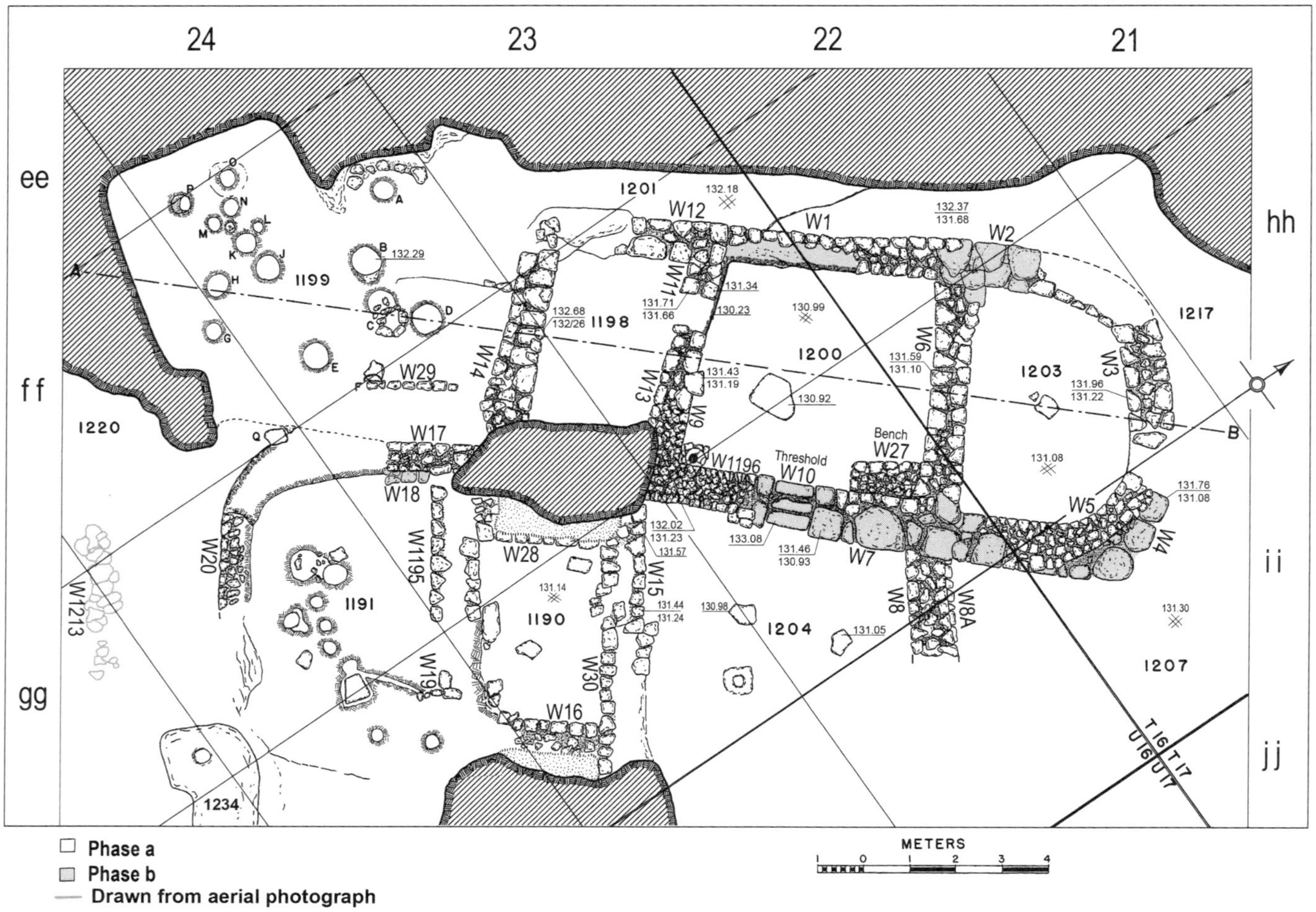

Figure 18. Detail of figure 17 indicating stratigraphic phasing, wall numbers, and adjustments in the alignment of stones in the floor of B/IV/1, according to evidence from aerial photographs. Shaded stones belong to earlier phases

ing rooms (Loci 1200 and 1198). The plan of this structure was determined by significant remains of an earlier phase or phases that were incorporated into it. The latest additions to this structure are wall segments of smallish fieldstones laid atop foundations of large boulders or directly atop bedrock where it was quarried in straight lines. Walls or segments of walls constructed of smaller stones appear to have been repairs to large gaps in walls between remains of an earlier structure. Wall segments W1, W3, W5, W9, and W1196, and possibly portions of W6 (i.e., individual stones; pl. 24) are obvious late "filler" elements that completed the latest plan of this building. Wall 8, which appears to be a number of superimposed upper courses, slightly mis-aligned with a wall below (8A), which served as a foundation, should also probably be assigned to this same construction phase.

Locus 1200, the Central Room

The basic plan of B/IV/1a is tripartite with a central, almost square chamber (Locus 1200) flanked by two smaller rooms (Loci 1198 and 1203). The entrance to the central room from the outside is on the southeast between W7 and W1196, through an impressive doorway with jambs constructed of large stones and boulders (see esp. pls. 24–27). The upper part of the southern doorjamb seems to be a late rebuild, while the opposite side, comprised of boulders, appears to have originally been constructed in an earlier phase (see below). This northern jamb, part of W7, is composed of a large stone that appears as if it might have been roughly dressed or, if naturally shaped, may have been specifically chosen for that function. Additional examples of dressing of stones from the upper mound and a nearby tomb (*Chapter 6*), as well as the evidence of bedrock in this building, indicate stone dressing was not only well within the capabilities of the early inhabitants at the site but was widely practiced at Megiddo when this building was inhabited.

The most striking feature of this building is the imposing entryway. It is composed of three flat stone slabs that form a stairway leading up into the structure together with the doorjambs. Such an imposing central stairway is, so far as I am aware, a unique example in the archaeological record of the southern Levant for its time, although there is evidence for steps in the period. Usually there is just a single step that allows access to houses with floors slightly sunken below ground level, as at nearby ʿEn Shadud (Braun 1985, p. 77).

The walls of this room were fashioned of three types of stones: large boulders, medium-size fieldstones, and small fieldstones, the latter which obviously belong to the latest construction phase. An interesting and highly unusual feature is found in segments of W1, W9, and W11 (fig. 18), which were constructed atop the deeply cut straight lines in underlying bedrock, using the latter features as plinths. These bedrock cuttings are possibly associated with the earlier phase of this building, but could be even older still (see below). Significantly, the tops of these bedrock plinths are not level, indicating they were likely to have been cut out of an uneven, natural surface or higher portions were broken off from them leaving them uneven. If these quarried features predate the construction of an earlier level of the building, it would appear they were used opportunistically in the building's final phase of occupation.

Within Locus 1200, in a corner to the right of the doorway, is a small, bench-like affair (W27) attached to W7 and abutting W6. Benches are familiar appurtenances in houses of the Early Bronze Age, but they are usually longer and may even wrap around several walls (e.g., see below, *Stage V*). From the relative height of the highest step at the entrance, which is somewhat higher than the level of the bedrock within, it is obvious that the floor of the room in this phase is not pictured in any of the photographs; it must have been removed previously because it is pointless to build steps to ascend in order to descend into a room. As the relative height of the top of the bench and the uppermost step seem to be more or less equal, it is not unlikely the bench was hidden beneath the floor during the last phase of occupation of the building. Alternately, the bench-like structure served as the base for some feature above that was no longer preserved.

There is a modicum of evidence for the level of the floor in this phase. It was presumably earthen and was preserved more or less near the base of an intact, holemouth vessel found in the southeast corner of the room (pls. 20–26, 61:7). Although the flat base of this jar is obscured by stones and soil, probably left to hold it together for the photograph, the 43 cm height of the jar indicates it was not placed directly on the flat bedrock surface visible around it but rather on fill above that flattened bedrock. Of note also is W9, the wall behind the jar to the south. Instead of allowing the bedrock outcrop in the southeast corner of the room to serve as the corner, its facade was deliberately shielded in this phase and possibly in earlier phases, by this stone curtain.

As there is no indication of any threshold or gap in W6, the wall that separates this room from the room to the north (Locus 1203), it appears there may not have been communication between them. By contrast, there is a well-defined doorway leading into Locus 1198, a small chamber also partly defined by the bedrock outcrop. Access to it was up a bedrock step (a continuation of the plinth atop which W11 was built) to a significantly higher, flattened but slightly sloping bedrock surface.

Locus 1198, the Southwest Room

This narrow, rectangular room was built integrally and obviously meant to function together with the central room. However, considerably less attention was paid to its construction as may be discerned by its perimeter, which is defined by only three walls and a length of the bedrock outcrop; a natural cavity forms its east side. Significantly, there was no evidence here of a construction analogous to W9, which was meant to shield the bedrock from view in Locus 1200. The excavators' drawn Section A–B (fig. 19) indicates the bedrock floor of this room sloped slightly down from southwest to northeast. Whether it was like that in the last phase of this building is uncertain as there is no sign of a later floor as in Locus 1200, perhaps because nothing was found resting on it, which would mean that even had there been one it was unlikely to have been discerned by the excavators. There is reason to believe that the leveled bedrock surface, which seems a deliberate alteration, is likely to have pre-dated the existence of the building, even in its earlier phase, as

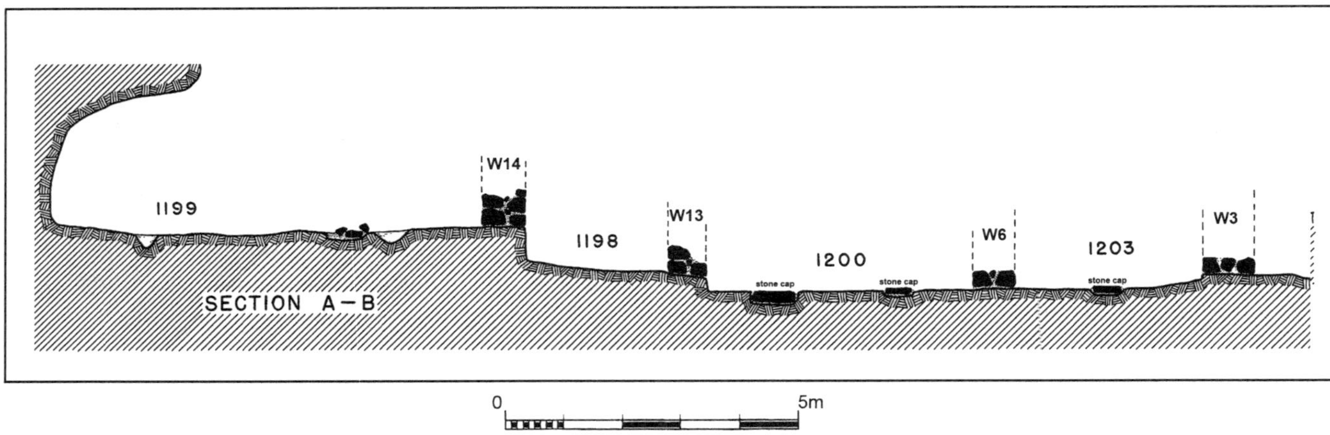

Figure 19. Lamon's Section A–B (see fig. 16) through B/IV/1, with loci and wall numbers. Note the slightly sloping bedrock surfaces in Loci 1198 and 1203. This view represents the earlier phase of the structure. In a later phase there was an earthen surface, not depicted, at least in Locus 1200

there is evidence of a similar surface in the adjacent Locus 1199, outside to the west (see below). Segments of the constructed courses of the walls of this chamber also utilized the quarried bedrock lines as plinths.

Locus 1203, the Northeast Room

The northern chamber of B/IV/1a has a plan in the shape of an uppercase D. While the internal plan of this room is indubitably "apsidal" (i.e., it has two right-angled corners opposing a regularly curving end), the outer lines of W4, built in an earlier phase, give the original building an irregular aspect. Both the plan and photographs indicate that W5 was built atop the much larger stones of W4 of Phase b; so too is the north end of W1 built directly on a segment of W2, which is also ascribable to the earlier Phase b. Thus, the apsidal portion of this room was a late invention, more of an "afterthought" superimposed on remains of an earlier building rather than a deliberate attempt at creating this specific cross between rectilinear and curvilinear styles. As such, this building has less significance for the history of architectural traditions of the Early Bronze Age I than has been suggested by some scholars (*Chapter 7*).

The gap in its curvilinear east end, between W3 and W5, may mark what was once an entrance, but it could also be an artifact of incomplete preservation, due to destruction caused when the kiln built above cut into the wall of the building (see above). Notably, in plate 19 (Square T16) the gap appears as a narrow passageway, but that function is unclear as there is no definitive evidence for it having been an entrance. Neither Lamon's plan (fig. 19) nor the later photographs (pls. 21–24) offer any hint of such a function. Unfortunately, there seems to be no good candidate for an entrance to the room, unless the thin line of stones connecting W2 and W3 preserves the sill of such an aperture. The gap in the full width of the wall can almost certainly be ascribed to the kiln constructed above, which cut into its outer layer (pls. 19, 27). A more likely candidate is a blocked entranceway at the west end of W6, faintly visible in several photographs (pls. 23–24) and plan (fig. 20).

There is no particular indication of where the floor of this latest phase might have been. Possibly it was an earthen surface analogous to that postulated for Locus 1200 or it may have re-used the bedrock surface (fig. 19) that must have been in use in the earlier phase of this building. This floor had a rock-cut depression, filled in by a stone plug to make it level.

B/IV/1b

This earliest phase is represented by walls constructed of large to massive stones (fig. 20a). While two such stones that jut out from the lines of W2 and W7 seem to indicate the existence of W6 in this phase (suggested in the reconstruction by a broken line), it is not otherwise documented and thus it could be merely an artifact of my restoration. Quite possibly the wall segments attributed to this phase, W2, W4, W7, and a few stones below W1196, ghosted on the plan in figure 20b where they approximately lay because they were not visible from above, are however, clearly seen from the northeast as part of W1096 on plate 28. The scant evidence of this phase appear to be remains of a roughly rectangular structure. Its association with the bedrock surface (see below) suggests that it utilized the same rock-cut plinths as those seen in B/IV/1a. Certainly they were associated with the earliest phase of this building but they may even predate its construction.

I associate use of the flattened bedrock surface with B/IV/1b as it was a convenient, possibly even preexisting feature that did not need to be modified by the occupiers of this phase. The large, flat stones visible on this surface are not, as suggested by Lamon's plan (fig. 16), arranged in a straight line through the central, longitudinal axis of the building. Based on the evidence of multiple photographs taken from the ground and from the air, I have redrawn these stones more or less where they should have been located in the plan (figs. 17–18). Their locations as well as their obvious functions belie Lamon's restoration of them in Section A–B (fig. 19), which suggests they are analogous to stone pillar bases commonly encountered in earthen floors in houses of the Early Bronze Age (e.g., Braun 1985, p. 77, figs. 5–6). Clearly, the bedrock surface would have been even more stable than any such stone, while the shallow pits in which the stones lay could have served as means to stabilize pillars and prevent them from slipping on a flat surface. Thus the bedrock surface obviates a need for stone bases.

I believe these stones had a quite different function. They are not bases but rather plugs intended to fill cavities in the floor. Clearly, the cavities have nothing to do with the building, but represent an earlier phase of utilization of the bedrock surface. The largest of these stone caps, somewhat unusually, was of basalt rather than limestone, may have originally had some special significance, as this type of stone had to be brought especially to the site, and may even have been dressed. The pits these stones filled are similar to numerous other shallow indentations and cavities in the bedrock surfaces of the East Slope, labeled by the excavators "pot-holes" and "cupmarks." Most notable are those found in the adjacent Locus 1199 (pl. 37) and those found on this terrace to the east and south in Loci 1191 and 1192 (pl. 38).

Lamon's plan (fig. 16) depicts a narrow, roughly trapezoidal feature adjacent to the rear wall of Locus 1200, but which may be visible as a lighter shaded area in an aerial photograph (pl. 3). At first I suspected it might have been a very large stone, but after analyzing the drawing I believe it is actually intended to portray a trough-like, bedrock-cut feature of unknown depth. This conclusion is based on the convention used to draw stones in Lamon's plan. Stones were outlined and then given a rough, shadow-like effect within. That style contrasts with how this feature was drawn. It is empty within, but the shadow-like effect surrounds it, indicating the artist meant to emphasize the stone surrounding the feature. While such a cavity could have been in use during this phase of the building, my guess is that it could well belong to an earlier period, possibly pre-dating the construction. As such it was probably filled in, as were the other cavities in the bedrock floor. Alternately, the trough might have served a different purpose, perhaps associated with mortuary practices (see below).

Lamon's deliberate depiction of a line of stones below W8 that I have labeled W8A, which juts out to the north of the line of the wall above, suggests the existence of an earlier wall. Whether that mostly hidden segment should also be ascribed to this phase is unclear as the sizes of the stones of which it is constructed are considerably smaller than those in the walls of B/IV/1b. While the association of W8A with W7 (which existed in both phases of B/IV/1) at some point in time is clear, there are additional architectural elements, including B/IV/2 as well as others not found on Lamon's plan, W31 and W32 (figs. 17; pl. 24; see also below), with which one or another of these two phases of W8 may have been associated. A hypothetical reconstruction of most of the features of this phase (see below) suggests the possibility of them having been associated with a cave that occupied most of the area of this building, and Locus 1199, prior to the latest construction.

B/IV/2

Just to the southeast of B/IV/1 are remains of what Engberg and Shipton (1934a, fig. 2 = pl. 20), in the aerial photograph they published, intimated was a second house. Without ever expressly stating so, their addition of a few broken lines virtually reconstructs half of an apse that appears to be the opposite half of

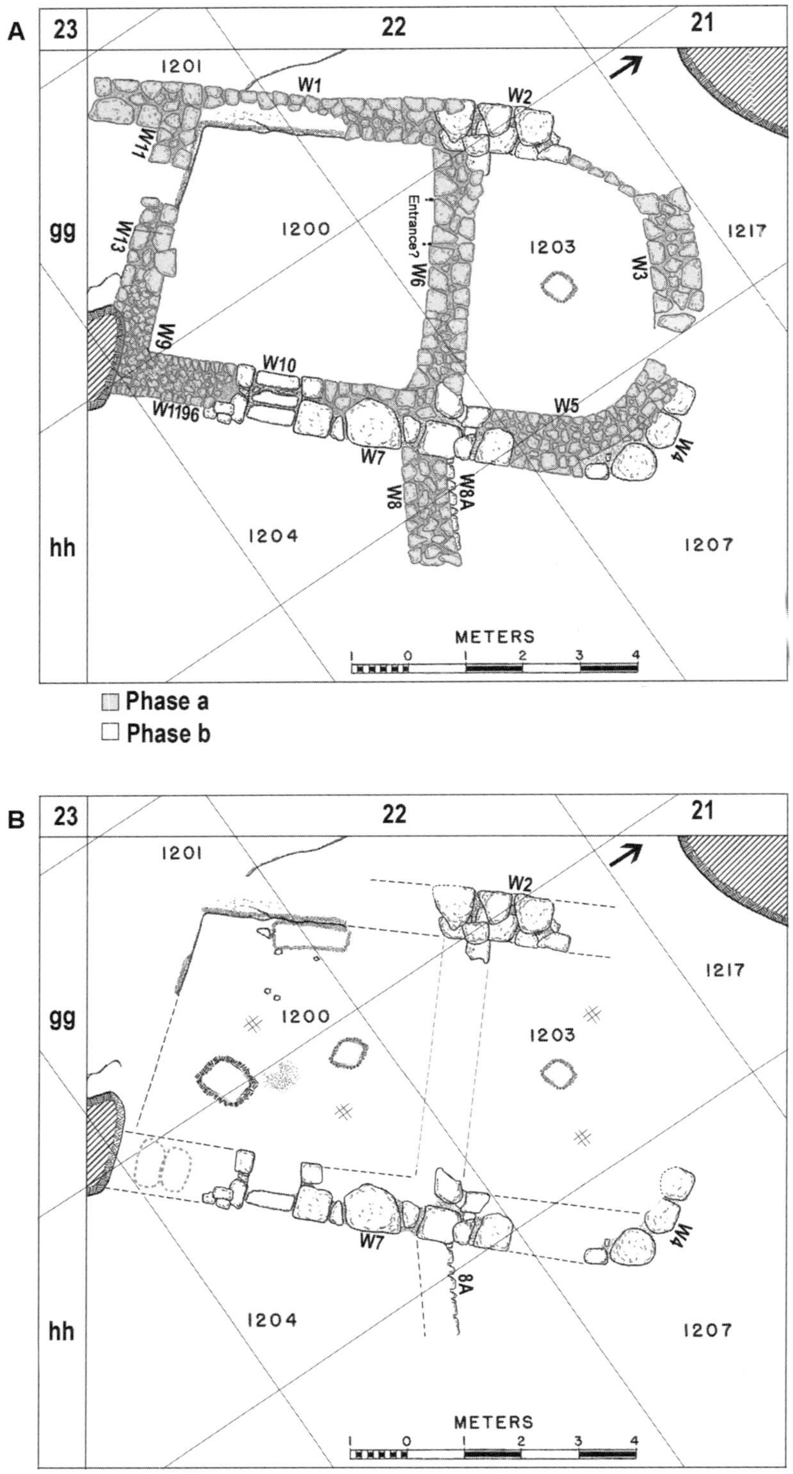

Figure 20. Plans reconstructing early phases of B/IV/1, derived from Lamon's original plan (fig. 16). (*A*) Represents the later phase and (*B*) represents remains of the earliest phase of the structure. Indicated is the possible location of a blocked passage between Loci 1200 and 1203, visible in several photographs (pls. 23–24)

one marked by a line in the quarried bedrock. That, in turn, appears to be continued by a wall segment, W20 (figs. 16–17). All of these features together do, indeed, form a significant segment of an apsidal plan. However, the evidence of untouched photographs, including some taken from ground level, indicates another, more complicated reality that does not uphold the excavators' inferences. My interpretation (fig. 18) suggests that this house had a single rectangular room built between two bedrock outcrops. The structural features to its southwest in Squares gg25 and gg24 probably belong to another, indeterminate phase (see below).

EXCURSUS 1

THE DATING OF LOCUS 1234, A MASSIVE BOULDER

by Eliot Braun

Locus 1234 is an immense boulder, which, when removed by the excavators, was found to have covered early structures. Its importance lies in the date when it was detached from the bedrock, which could possibly be related to tectonic activity that affected the site in Early Bronze Age I (see below, *Excursus 2*). Visible in several photos (pls. 34–35) and on the plan of B/V/2 (fig. 21), the date of that house could shed light on when the massive boulder, Locus 1234, arrived at the spot where the excavators found it. While W1221 is clearly earlier and below remains of B/+IV/2, its stratigraphic relationship to the boulder is not clear. It is impossible to determine definitively from photographs whether the boulder had fallen on top of this wall, or whether W1221 was built abutting it. However, the former scenario seems to be the more appropriate from the detailed evidence (pl. 34), in which I believe I am able to discern the bottom of the boulder.

B/IV/2a–b

There are two phases observable in the remains of this building. The later is better preserved, while the earlier is identifiable only in a single wall segment. One additional wall cannot be assigned to either phase with any level of confidence, while a rock-cut outline of the bedrock surface appears to belong to a phase of quarrying likely to pre-date any construction (see below).

Locus 1204

This large space, defined by the eastern facade of B/IV/1, W8, and W15, may have been an open courtyard during the lifetime of houses B/IV/1 and B/IV/2; possibly it was shared by the two buildings. Although W8 is parallel to W15, I tend to think they might not have been part of a roofed chamber for two reasons. (1) They would have greatly reduced the impact of the grand entrance into B/IV/1, the construction of which shows so much care; and (2) W15 is a rather robust structure that seems likely to have been an exterior wall and not an internal divider. It and W1195 to the south are notably constructed of two parallel lines of stones with gaps between them that are of considerable width.

Lamon's plan (fig. 16) shows two large, presumably flat basalt stones and another with a cavity, possibly a mortar embedded in the floor, but they are associated with the bedrock surface and probably belong to the living surface of an earlier phase. Those features would have been covered by a later earthen floor in this phase of this building. The raised level of the floor is clearly indicated in a photograph (pl. 38, upper left) taken after the removal of these walls to expose the bedrock below. They are two large, flat stones, presumably pillar bases rising up above the bedrock surface.

Locus 1190

The entrance to the small, rectangular Locus 1190 from Locus 1204 may have been preserved in a poorly defined doorway, possibly reflected in a number of disarranged stones of W15 in the plan (see also pl. 28), although there is no definitive doorsill. Alternately, access to this room could have been from the south through the gap between W19 and W1195 (fig. 18), which would have had a step in the bedrock analogous to that between Rooms 1198 and 1200 in B/IV/1.

The remaining walls of this room, W30, the continuation of W15, W16, W1195, and W28, appear to have been built integrally of stones of similar sizes. These walls create a small, nicely rectangular, well-built chamber with unusually broad walls ensconced between two bedrock outcrops. The location to the side of the entrance of B/IV/1a, and the lesser size of this chamber, suggest for it a subordinate and adjunct function to the more imposing building to its west. That these walls are to be associated with B/IV/1a is indicated by details (pls. 28–29, 31), in which extreme close-ups indicate the foundations of W15, W30, and W1195 rested on earthen fill at least 10 cm above the bedrock surface noted by the excavators as a "pavement" at the elevation of 131.14. Clearly the bedrock surface predates the construction of this building phase.

Locus 1191

This space, to the southwest of W16, was interpreted by Lamon as having a plan in the shape of the letter D and was associated by him with the rectangular chamber formed by the walls surrounding Locus 1190. There are several reasons for rejecting this interpretation. Foremost are stratigraphic considerations that indicate the walls enclosing Locus 1190 rested on a layer of soil that covered the bedrock surface (see above, *Locus 1190*). That effectively dissociates the chamber with that surface and calls into question the very *bona fides* of a building of apsidal plan in which the apse is represented by a bedrock cutting in that same surface and a wall segment (W20) that is purported to be a partial continuation of the apse. Wall 20 was actually set down on a narrow bedrock step slightly below the upper surface[31] where it formed its southern border. As the superimposition of W20 above the northern wall of the Stage V building is the lynchpin of the Stage IV–Stage V stratigraphic sequence, its dissociation with Locus 1190 brings into question the excavators' straightforward paradigm of superimposition of Stage IV upon Stage V.

Another reason to question the ascription of W20 to B/IV/2 in any phase is the width of W20 and the stones used to construct it. They are patently different from analogous features in W15, W16, W19, W28, W30, and W1195. These last all appear to form a nicely rectangular structure that has no clear association either with W18 or W20, which were purportedly part of the same building. Notably, the two closure walls of Locus 1190, W15 and W1195, are comprised of two parallel lines of stones separated by large spaces (presumably for rubble-like fill) that are unusually wide and clearly the external confines of this building. W20, if ever it were part of the same structure, would at best be an appended room of very different style of construction.

Earlier Phases in Locus 1191

Additional structural elements suggest an earlier building phase or phases in Locus 1191. The large wall segment W17 abutting the bedrock outcrop to the west of W1195 was purportedly the western side of an apse, and is indeed arranged along a length of the curving quarried line in the bedrock surface. Lamon's plan (fig. 16), however, suggests it continued in a straight line to a large and small stone (at the juncture of squares ff24, ff25, gg24, and gg25) and beyond, to the bedrock outcrop (fig. 17). Notably, W17 is not bonded to form a corner with W1195, while its position suggests it could have enclosed Locus 1199, effectively making it a part of B/IV/1 by utilizing the bedrock scarps as if it were a closure wall. The short segment of W18, parallel but set below and on the east side of W17, sits directly on the bedrock surface. It could have been a bench in an apse, but alternately it could have been remains of an earlier structure that disregarded any advantage of building along the upper edge of the curved line.

The bedrock immediately to the east of the line of W20 did not, as Lamon's plan (fig. 16) suggests, preserve any evidence of a quarried line. The dashed line drawn roughly parallel to the quarried line on the west, purportedly completing the apse's eastern edge, is not in evidence in a photograph of the bedrock

---

[31] It is visible as an uneven step in plate 38 just to the right of the meter stick.

after it was laid bare (pl. 38). Thus it appears to have been merely an element of Lamon's interpretation. In addition, the quarried line of the bedrock, unlike the vertical plinths in B/IV/1, sloped gently inward, giving a bowl-like effect to the bedrock. Thus, all together, there appears to be little evidence to suggest the existence of a true apse in the remains of the bedrock in association with the segment of W20. Quite possibly the quarried bedrock contours are related to other rock-cut features that include channels and sump-like installations, all of which apparently predate the building.

Intermediate Levels Between Stages +IV and V

The question of what, if any, building remains W20 should be associated with, is one that cannot be discerned from Lamon's plans. This wall is a double row of stones set into a natural bedrock step, where the upper terrace ended and the lower terrace began, visible in a photograph after bedrock was cleared of all later deposits (pl. 38). It may have been little more than an attempt to create a more or less level surface or possibly foundations of a wall of which no upper courses survived.

The question of the stratigraphic context of W20 is crucial for the sequence of the excavators' stages. On the one hand it probably should be dated earlier than the walls of Locus 1190, which were built when all or some of the bedrock surface was covered with earthen fill, while on the other hand it is superimposed upon part of the northern wall of B/V/1 (see below). Nearby walls of B/+IV/2 just to the east are all apparently founded at higher elevations and thus must also be later. To what, then, does this small segment of building relate? It is very difficult to give a definitive answer to that question. It may relate to the period of utilization of the bedrock, but that hardly seems likely as there appears to be no special reason to fill out a line of natural bedrock, unless for purposes of construction atop it. That suggests W20 was the sole remainder of a foundation of a wall of which the upper courses were no longer extant when it was exposed. It does not appear to relate to B/IV/2.

That does not mean that W20 was a lone construction with no associations. Two nearby walls may have been associated with it; if this hypothesis is correct, W20 is within a stratigraphic context between the upper phase of Stage IV and Stage V. A wall (W1213), largely undocumented by the excavators except in photographs (pls. 30–31) and in a cryptic description in the locus list (*Appendix C*) stating it is a wall with threshold and door socket, appears likely to have been associated with W20. An aerial photograph (pl. 19) indicates these two walls were nearly parallel and founded roughly at the same elevation. If indeed they were part of the same structure, then it was mostly constructed on earthen fill at least partly covering the lower terrace in which were found the Stage V remains.

Walls W20 and W1213 in turn might also have been associated with another wall segment to the south, W546 (pl. 30), which I initially designated as belonging to the array of Stage +IV buildings (see above) but which in retrospect I suspect could belong to the same phase as W20 and W1213. Two stones in an upper course of W1213, one of which partially obscures the door socket, indicate the possibility of two construction phases, while the placement of the socket, if found in situ, would have marked the approximate level of the earthen surface associated with the earlier building.

There is evidence for an additional phase below W1213 that must also date later than the Stage V building, which appears at least in part to have been sealed below the level of its foundation. Clearly visible in a small, vertical, excavated section above a juglet sitting on the floor of the Stage V building (pl. 31) is a thick, apparently light-colored plaster surface, ca. 40 cm below the foundations of W1213.[32] A close examination of this section indicates this surface is likely to have been a layer of some type of plaster ca. 20 cm thick.[33] It represents a phase definitively later than the Stage V building, seen partly exposed below, but its association with other structures remains obscure.

---

[32] Here I wish to pay homage to the skills of the photographer and the quality of his equipment, and the foresight of Oriental Institute Archivist John A. Larson for scanning the photographs at very high resolution, which allowed for such minute details to be discerned.

[33] Other, similar plaster surfaces are visible in the higher section to the left in this same photograph.

THE ARCHITECTURE OF STAGE V

Stage V was identified on a slightly lower terrace to the south. This terrace began just below a low, sloping scarp in the bedrock, revealed after the removal of W20 (pl. 38). The very northernmost extent of the terrace, in effect the continuation of the scarp, lay below a small segment of W20. Continuing my nomenclature in including these structures apparently ignored by the excavators, but absolutely visible on their plans, I have designated two buildings associated with the excavators' Stage V as B/V/1 and B/V/2.

Enigmatic Structures of Stage V

There are several curious and inexplicable discrepancies between Lamon's plan (fig. 16) of Stage V and the photographic evidence. They are found in the omission of a considerable number of constructions from Lamon's plan that are eminently visible in both aerial and ground-based photographs. I have added these constructions to my synthetic plans and labeled them with wall numbers and, when suggested, given them building designations (fig. 21; pls. 33–35).

B/V/1

Lamon drew the complete plan of this structure (fig. 16, leftmost structure) but possibly he ghosted in portions of it that were not of stone construction. Once again there are no notes concerning the conventions used in the plan, and so I can only guess that the lines of segments of walls and benches, drawn as tiny dots placed close together, were not meant to be analogous to the broken lines used to complete the plans of the Stage IV structures. That could mean he was more certain of the veracity of his reconstructions than in those he suggested for the upper terrace.

Views in the photographs (pls. 31–32) are equally uninformative. The lines of the walls not of stone appear in them, including a line bifurcating the southern segment of W23, which continues at the width of the line of stones in the wall to the south. In Lamon's drawing the non-stone features were filled in with dots, creating a sort of stippled effect. Unfortunately, there are no annotations and no records indicating the precise meaning of this artistic convention, but I believe, from my understanding of the photographs taken at ground level, that it might have been meant to indicate either pisé or possibly mud plaster, but probably not mudbrick. Careful examination of the photographs of this building (pls. 31–35), enlarged to reveal maximum details, reveals no evidence that could suggest mudbrick construction. Alternately, the drawn effect could have been a simple convention to shade those constructions to distinguish them from the surrounding areas.

The building appears on Lamon's plan as if it were a lone feature on the terrace, which it might have been at some point in its existence, but he ignored another building adjacent to it, B/IV/2 (fig. 21), perhaps because he ascribed it to a significantly later period, an interpretation that seems, however, unlikely (see below). B/V/1 is a small, rectangular structure with rounded corners, features commonly found on Early Bronze Age I houses. While its basic external plan is certain, an important detail, as well as the extent of the building's internal features, are somewhat equivocal (fig. 22). Most of the evidence for it derives from details in the ground photographs taken during several phases in its excavation.

As drawn by Lamon the building appears to have had a tripartite division, with benches on three internal walls. That the internal structures along those walls are benches seems likely, as such appurtenances are often found in houses of the Early Bronze Age I. However, Lamon's internal division of the building is less convincing.

Curiously, no evidence for an entrance seems to have been preserved in this structure, although it is likely it would have been in one of the long walls as is usual for the Early Bronze Age, during which there was a marked preference for "broadrooms." It also appears likely the house was semi-subterranean, which might account for preservation of the nearly complete plan of the external walls. In that case it is likely an entrance would have been over a raised sill, in this instance probably the top of a wall foundation, with

EXCURSUS 2

EARLY BRONZE AGE I MEGIDDO AND EARTHQUAKES

by Yael Braun

Megiddo lies within a wide seismogenic zone that runs along the Jezreel Valley, which lies between the Gilboa Fault (GF) and the Carmel Fault (CF) systems (Hofstetter von Eck and Shapira 1996; Schattner et al. 2006; Nof et al. 2007), both branches of the nearby Dead Sea Transform (DST) fault system. This fault zone has been defined by Shamir (2007) as the most seismically active area in the north of Israel and it is believed to have generated many earthquakes in the past that may have affected the archeological site of Megiddo (Marco et al. 2006). An event that caused structural damage to an Early Bronze Age I temple at about 3000 B.C. may be corroborated by geological evidence of a seismic event or series of events that affected the whole region at approximately the same time frame (Y. Braun et al. in press).

perhaps an internal bench functioning as a step.[34] The floor of this building appears to have been an earthen surface at approximately the basal level of the wall foundations, as indicated by the presence of two ceramic vessels found in situ on or just above it.

Lamon's reconstruction of the line of W34 is not very convincing, especially as it would make the southern room (Locus 1208) exceedingly small (ca. 1.80 × 1.65 m) and disallow access to the northern part of the structure unless it were pierced by an entrance, for which there is no indication in the plan. Although clearly drawn as a wall, W34 (fig. 21), this purported divider incorporates only a few largish stones and, at least when photographs were taken (pls. 31–32, 34), it was not well defined. Unfortunately, there is no picture of Locus 1208 after it was excavated and so only its upper elevations, well above the floor of Locus 1226, are discernible in the photographic documentation. If this construction was indeed a wall, it seems likely it functioned as such in a late utilization of this building (see below).

B/V/1 had a rather extraordinary feature, albeit one documented solely in photographs (pls. 30–32, 34). Two large, flattish stones, standing parallel and upright, both apparently of coarse basalt,[35] were found protruding considerably above the level of what may have been a mud-plaster surface[36] that covers the floor and eastern bench in Locus 1208. While their juxtaposition makes them appear as if they were stelae, another, more mundane explanation is possible. The stones are irregularly shaped but one, on the left in plate 34, looks as if it is a large saddle quern; the other, considerably thicker and more massive, may also have a worked surface, suggesting it too was part of a grinding installation. If these stones were actually functioning querns at the time they were abandoned, they might have been so placed simply to prevent them from collecting dust on their working surfaces. Presumably the owners expected to return to the building but never did. Notably, in this same photograph there are two small, nicely worked basalt upper grinding stones (i.e., rubbers). One was either built into the west end of W34, or in a gap between it and W21. The other is resting on the western bench of this room. As it does not appear to have been built into the wall, presumably

[34] I have excavated a house of similar plan with an internal bench at one end at Palmahim Quarry (Braun 1996a, fig. V.E.6/2-A; Braun 2008, p. 1991, Schematic Plan, Stratum 2; 2008). There the entrance, marked by a door socket, utilized the top of the wall foundations as a sill, while the bench functioned as a step down to the floor level ca. 25 cm below.

[35] The specific form of this stone created by numerous air bubbles when it cooled can be discerned when the photographs are examined very closely after being greatly enlarged.

[36] See below for a discussion of this and other features that suggest different phases of utilization in B/V/1.

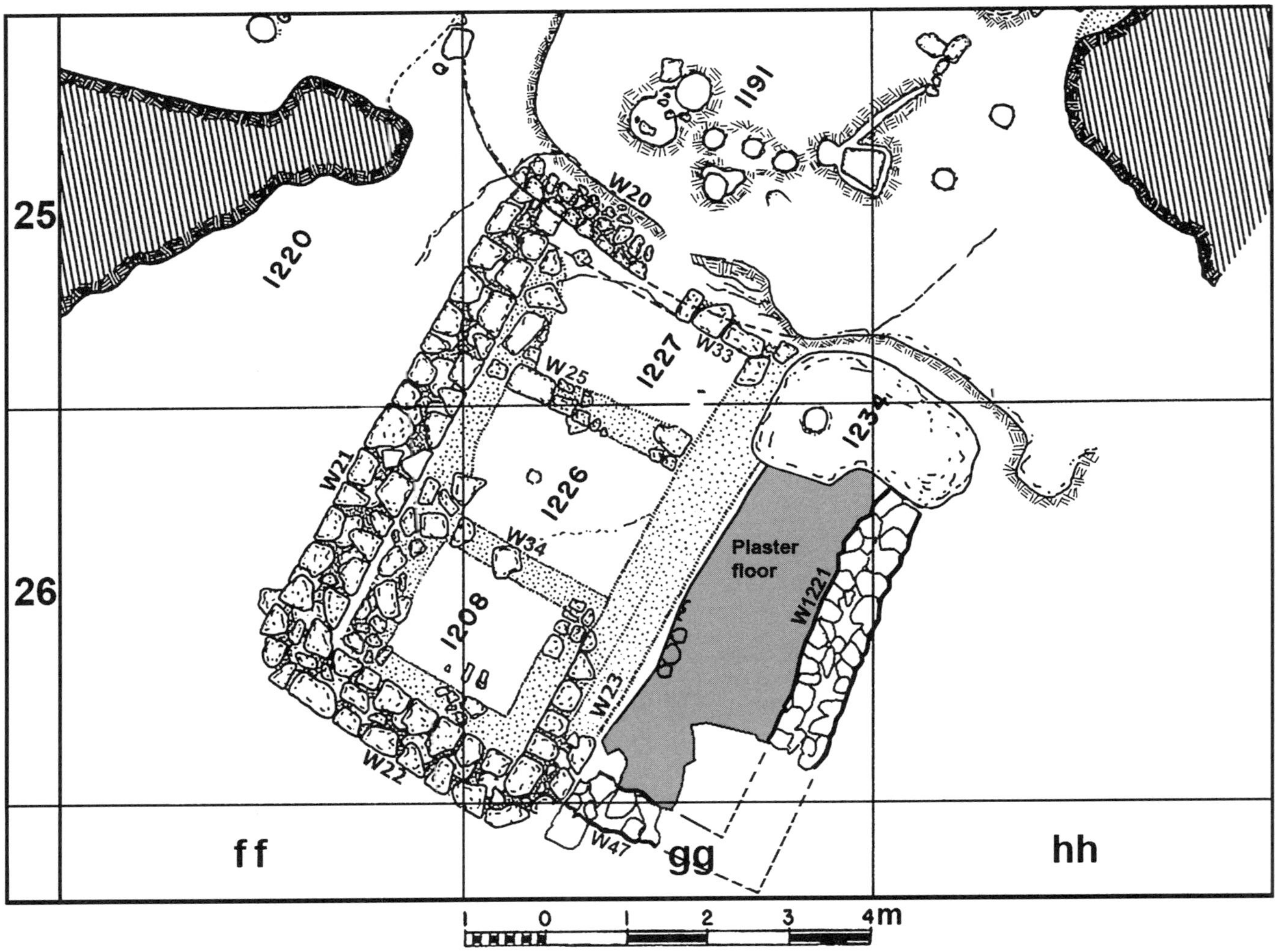

Figure 21. Plan of B/V/1 and W20, based on Lamon's plan and aerial and ground photographs (pls. 22, 34). Wall 20 was assigned by excavators to the southern end of B/IV/2, where it partially overlies W33 (of B/V/1), but it may have other stratigraphic associations (pls. 30–31)

it was deliberately left in the photograph because it was found in the building. That would suggest that at one time the room housed grinding facilities.

Evidence of an Additional, Late Phase of Utilization of Walls of B/V/1

There are some few hints in the photographic documentation that suggest evidence for more than one period of occupation of B/V/1. Unfortunately, they cannot be corroborated for lack of additional data. These features are what appears to be a mud-plaster surface from which the querns protrude (pl. 34), that could be evidence of a late utilization of the walls of this building. An extreme close-up of the earthen section behind W34 in plate 32 shows light-colored patches at a corresponding elevation, which might be a continuation of this floor. It also indicates the method of excavation, which may have cut through the mud plaster in that room, possibly revealing the existence of the surface, which was then cleared to the south without being destroyed. This surface may well be related to another plaster surface in B/V/2, either in continuation of it or associated with it. In the former instance that would necessitate interpreting the non-stone segment of W23 as an artifact of excavation (see above). Additional evidence for this may be seen in an adjacent structure (B/V/2) with a plastered floor (see below).

I would suggest also that W34, if indeed a wall, could also be assigned to this phase. However, a more likely interpretation suggests that the large flat stone in it might have been a pillar base, with no connection to a wall. Such features are commonly encountered in Early Bronze Age I buildings (e.g., Braun 1985, figs.

5–8). By contrast, W25, which divides between Loci 1226 and 1227, seems to be rather better documented (pls. 33–34).

The Function of B/V/1

In addition to the large querns in B/V/1 there are other objects which, most fortunately, are documented in detail in photographs, including the major portion of a pithos bearing the impression of a cylinder seal. The vessel can be definitively identified by its large size, represented in a heap of sherds and by the fragment of its bow rim clearly visible in the straw basket propping up a sign indicating the locus number (pl. 34). On the same floor is a squat, piriform juglet with strap handle (mostly missing) that probably joined the rim (missing but which once crowned a flared neck) with the widest portion of the vessel's body.

At least two small stone rings, probably of basalt (pls. 33–34), of a type commonly associated with Early Bronze I occupations, were found nearby. Several additional "suspiciously" flat cylindrical stones visible and adjacent to these rings in one photograph (pl. 34) are probably additional examples. Together, they suggest a small deposit of such objects, recently identified as loom weights from a similar cache found in an Early Bronze Age I context at Tell Abu el-Kharaz in the Jordan Valley (cf. Fischer 2008, fig. 39). Unfortunately, I have not been able to locate these artifacts; or if I have found them in the extant assemblages (several examples of such objects are extant and illustrated: pl. 75a–b), I have not been able to identify them as deriving from this locus.

The presence of the juglet, the loom weights, and the querns argues for simple, quotidian functions for this building. There is, however, some related information that suggests this straightforward interpretation may be equivocal. There is some possibility that this building, at some point in its history of utilization, may have functioned as a location for mortuary-related activities in Early Bronze Age I. The following reasons suggest such an interpretation:

1. The building, definitively dated to Early Bronze Age I by the finds from it, is located within a large cemetery of that period and is actually only short distances from several rock-cut tombs of that era.
2. The two upright querns seem overly large and out of place in this diminutive building, which, if it were merely a simple household, would more likely have had much smaller facilities for grinding (e.g., Braun 1985, pl. V:B). These stones likely served a larger population, perhaps related to mortuary behavior, which likely included the use or consumption of foodstuffs.
3. The pithos from this room is one of a type commonly found at Megiddo and other sites, where it may be seen to have a very distinct pattern of distribution. It is of special interest because it bears two impressions of a cylinder seal with an animal motif, which might ascribe to it a non-quotidian, mortuary-related function (*Chapter 4*).
4. Weaving of fabrics could possibly be related to fabrication of shrouds, for which there is a modicum of documentation in Early Bronze Age I and earlier times in the southern Levant (e.g., Bar-Adon 1980, pp. 153, 199; Schick 1998, pp. 6–22).
5. With the exception of the Stage IV buildings, some of which may have post-dated B/V/1, no evidence was found of actual houses in this "neighborhood" of the site. That is a somewhat unusual pattern for Early Bronze I settlements, where most houses appear to have been built in clusters.
6. Early Bronze Age I settlements were usually separated physically from places of burial, as was the East Slope from the occupation on the high mound.

B/V/2

Adjacent to the east wall of B/V/1 is a plaster floor associated with a stone wall, W1221, which probably originally formed a right-angled corner with W27 (pl. 34), part of a rectangular chamber. Its place within a stratigraphic sequence remains obscure as there appears to be no written notation for it. I suggest three options for ascribing this substantial structure to a position in the sequence of construction in the lower terrace. As for its chrono-cultural ascription, that remains obscure, although there Early Bronze Age seems likely.

Option 1: A Construction Post-dating B/V/1

In plate 34 the line of the plaster surface may be seen to end at W23. There, it is marked by two stones on the plaster surface, possibly remains of a closure wall that parallels W23. Thus, B/V/2 should be reconstructed as a long, narrow chamber. It is somewhat mis-aligned with W23 and appears to have been built later, as its elevation is significantly above either floor attributed to B/V/1 (see below). As the extant portion of the floor in the photograph is opposite the non-stone built segment of W23, it is possible that when the floor was laid that wall, which must have existed at some point in time, was no longer extant. That would make this building definitively later than B/V/1. The stone arrangement I have labeled W546, which is found at approximately the same elevation on the west side of B/V/1, could have been contemporary to this building. In such a scenario B/V/2 represents a poorly preserved stratum of occupation that post-dates B/V/1.

Option 2: A Construction Post-dating B/V/1 and Contemporaneous Occupation

This option suggests B/V/2 was constructed later than B/V/1 and reutilized the upper courses of some of the former's walls. The photograph in which B/V/2 is clearly visible (pl. 34) was taken as work progressed, showing B/V/1 in a partial state of excavation.[37] It also indicates the B/V/2 surface was cut on its south along a straight line, which suggests that this building was already being dismantled and that the visible remains were only a portion of what was originally exposed.

Thus we do not know the full extent of the plaster surface. I suspect it could even have continued not only to the south as far as W47, but possibly farther to the west, where it may have covered the line of W23 where the non-stone constructed segment is drawn. That could suggest the building in some late phase included most of the walls of B/V/1 and possibly had two chambers, separated, at least partially, by W23, where it is represented by stones (fig. 21). This interpretation suggests that the late mud-plastered surface, which I believe I have discerned in B/V/1 (see above), may have been a continuation of the plastered surface in B/V/2, and that the narrow gap visible between the plaster floor and W23 was probably an artifact of modern excavation intended merely to delineate the east edge of W23. This scenario seems the most likely as W47, abutting but not bonding with W23 (thus making them absolutely contemporary at some point in their mutual histories of utilization), is the likely closure on the south for the eastern extension of this large room.

Option 3: A Construction Pre-dating B/V/1

A third scenario is possible if B/V/2 existed prior to the construction of B/V/1. The gap between the plaster floor of B/V/2 and W23 would then have been made when B/V/1 was constructed. As this latter building appears to have been slightly subterranean, its construction would have required a foundation pit, which, when excavated, would have cut through an existing plaster floor of B/V/2. That would account for the gap between the floor and W23.

Additional Structures that Cannot Be Ascribed to Any Particular Stage

At least three and possibly five walls can be assigned to earlier than the post-Stage IV (i.e., +IV) horizon, but cannot be placed within Engberg and Shipton's stratigraphic scheme of Stages IV and V. They are well documented in the photographs but inexplicably do not appear on Lamon's plan. They suggest the possibil-

[37] Locus 1208 had not yet been excavated down to the floor levels in the additional two rooms.

ity of being associated with one or the other of the intermediate levels between Stages IV and V, although their precise stratigraphic relationship with Stage IV, with which they share the upper terrace, is uncertain.

The Enigma of Walls 31, 32, and 26

Walls 31 and 32 are an anomaly for which I have been unable to find any documentation other than their very clear visibility in the third series of aerial photographs (pls. 11, 19) and photographs taken at ground level (pls. 24, 29). While Lamon placed W1243, a relatively late wall associated with B/+IV/3, on his plan of the stages (fig. 16), apparently because of its Early Bronze Age III date, inexplicably, both W31 and W32 were ignored and most enigmatically, they actually disappear from the last photographs in the balloon series in which later buildings, one actually superimposed on W32, are clearly visible (pl. 12). These two early walls are similarly absent in one view from ground level of the precinct where they were unearthed. That might indicate the plan was made in the field when these features were no longer extant, or that it is derived from the latest aerial photograph. Either scenario would account for these features being missing on the plan.

From what little I have been able to discern, W31 and W32 were removed by trenching. One trench, along the line of W32, seems to have been dug incrementally. It is first visible in plate 119 as a short depression continuing the line of W32 to the west. It is also noticeable in the extreme right foreground of a view of B/IV/1 (pl. 27), where the continuation of W8 is marked by a line of small stones. Unfortunately, the location of W31 and W32 is outside the limits of this view and it is unclear whether either wall was extant when the photograph was taken. In another photograph of the location of these walls (pl. 28), neither wall is visible, although the "robber's trench," which appears to have removed W32, seems to be marked by a narrow, regular patch of soil, presumably some sort of backfill. In that photograph what could possibly be a continuation of W32 protrudes from the left side of W1243, which seems to have been built atop it. This view was apparently photographed shortly after the third series of aerial photographs, as may be discerned by the still-extant kiln above Walls 2 and 3, but prior to the fourth series as the kilns were no longer extant in that series. I have been unable to find any definitive sign of the "robber trench" that removed W31.

Viewing extreme close-ups of W32 in two additional photographs (pls. 24, 29), it appears that only a single course of stones of it was preserved; those to the north appear to have been resting on soil, while the stones in its south may have rested on or very near bedrock. Possibly some few stones to the left of W1243 in plate 38 may be remains of W31. Beyond them is another enigmatic stone construction, seemingly a wall foundation, just below the arrow and more or less parallel to it. As I have no additional information on this feature, and as I am unable to plot it on plan, I have declined to number it. Suffice it to note the existence of this structure and to suggest it may be somehow related to W31 and W32, as it lay at more or less the same elevations.

Another wall segment, W26, more or less at the same elevation and parallel to W32, seems to belong to the same period (figs. 16–17). As I understand them, Walls 26, 31, and 32 are likely to belong to the very earliest structures on the east side of the upper terrace. Conceivably they are additional, albeit scant evidence of an occupation phase between Stage IV and Stage V, but alternate possibilities suggest they were contemporary with Stage V or possibly were constructed even earlier. Clearly they antedate W1243 and are possibly the reason for the excavators' recognition of Stages VI and/or VII, which are earlier than the houses they ascribed to Stage IV, although they claimed no architecture for those stages.

Wall 32, relatively broad and constructed of two rows of largish stones, forms a corner at an acute angle with W31, possibly part of a single rectilinear structure in conjunction with W26, a short wall segment nearly parallel and ca. 2.5 m south of W32. Together these walls could define three sides of a roughly rectangular chamber that extended farther to the east under W1243 and W508. The foundations of the former three walls appear to have been at more or less the same elevations, which in turn are more or less at the foundation level of W8A. Undoubtedly the position of these walls places them prior to B/+IV/3 in the stratigraphic sequence, but their relationship to each other and to the adjacent buildings of Stage IV is far from clear as they are located at the eastern edge of the upper terrace, where the topography slopes down. Thus their precise stratigraphic associations remain obscure.

Curvilinear Wall 539

This well-built wall at the southwestern edge of the terrace on which the Stage IV buildings are located partially encloses an aperture in the bedrock. The wall was exposed over a lengthy period during the excavation and appears in a number of photographs (pls. 19–22, 35[38], 38). Its proximity to the buildings of Stages IV and V and its location directly on bedrock suggest it might have had an association with them. Unfortunately, there is no documentation other than the photographs to categorically indicate that its position lower down the slope does not preclude an association with a "late" chrono-cultural horizon. Accordingly, it was numbered with the post-Early Bronze Age structures.

Locus 1240

The location of this locus may be discerned from only two sources, a terse entry in the locus book (*Appendix A*) indicating it was a floor and a label assigned to a floor in Section C–D (figs. 8, 23). It was exposed in a deep sounding below B/V/2 but, most unfortunately, there is no photographic documentation of that sounding. I suspect it might have been done sometime after the 1932 season, possibly in 1933 when major work on the East Slope had ceased. That would explain the locus numbers used for the deepest deposits, 1370 and 1371, which were assigned in a post-1932 season. There is no description of the nature of the "floor," but from published accounts we know that it was assigned to pre-Stage V and was not associated with any architectural features. Its chrono-cultural attribution remains obscure, but two options seem likely. It is either dated to some phase of Early Bronze Age I, not much earlier than that of B/V/2 (*Chapter 3*), or to one or another phase of the Chalcolithic or Neolithic periods (*Chapter 6*).

Additional Enigmatic Deposits below B/V/2: Earlier Architecture

A single photograph (pl. 38) indicates two walls, W41 and W42, forming what appears to be a corner of a structure (probably in Locus 1241) that had lain buried beneath the massive boulder labeled Locus 1234. The relative positions of these walls, based on my estimation of their locations from that photograph, are suggested[39] in figure 22, where they are drawn schematically. Nothing else is known of these walls other than that they were exposed at the end of the excavation of the East Slope and were probably described as "room under 1234." They lay within a shallow depression in the bedrock to the east of Locus 1240 (probably within Locus 1241), below B/V/2 and, dependent upon the stratigraphic relationship of B/V/2 to B/V/1, they could have be contemporary with or earlier than B/V/1. Were the date of the arrival of Locus 1234, the massive boulder to that location known, it would provide a *teminus post quem* for the building below. That may have been as early as Early Bronze Age I, possibly as the result of an earthquake (see *Excursus 2*).

The Earliest Occupation and Utilization of the East Slope: Quarrying and Activity in Caves

Activity in and on the Bedrock

Excavation of the East Slope exposed bedrock over most of the site (pls. 9–12, 94; *Megiddo Tombs*, pl. 2), which proved to be a very uneven mass with large and small outcrops, quarries,[40] natural and man-made cavities. In addition, it was strewn with massive boulders, that is, detached portions of the bedrock such as Locus 1234. Caves and cavities were utilized for a variety of purposes in different periods, some after en-

[38] It appears as a small segment to the right of and above W1221.

[39] Plotting would imply more precision than deserved in this exercise.

[40] Several quarries visible in the plans and aerial photographs of the East Slope, related to the production of ashlars, are probably to be dated later than the Early Bronze Age, during which time the use of such stones was extremely rare.

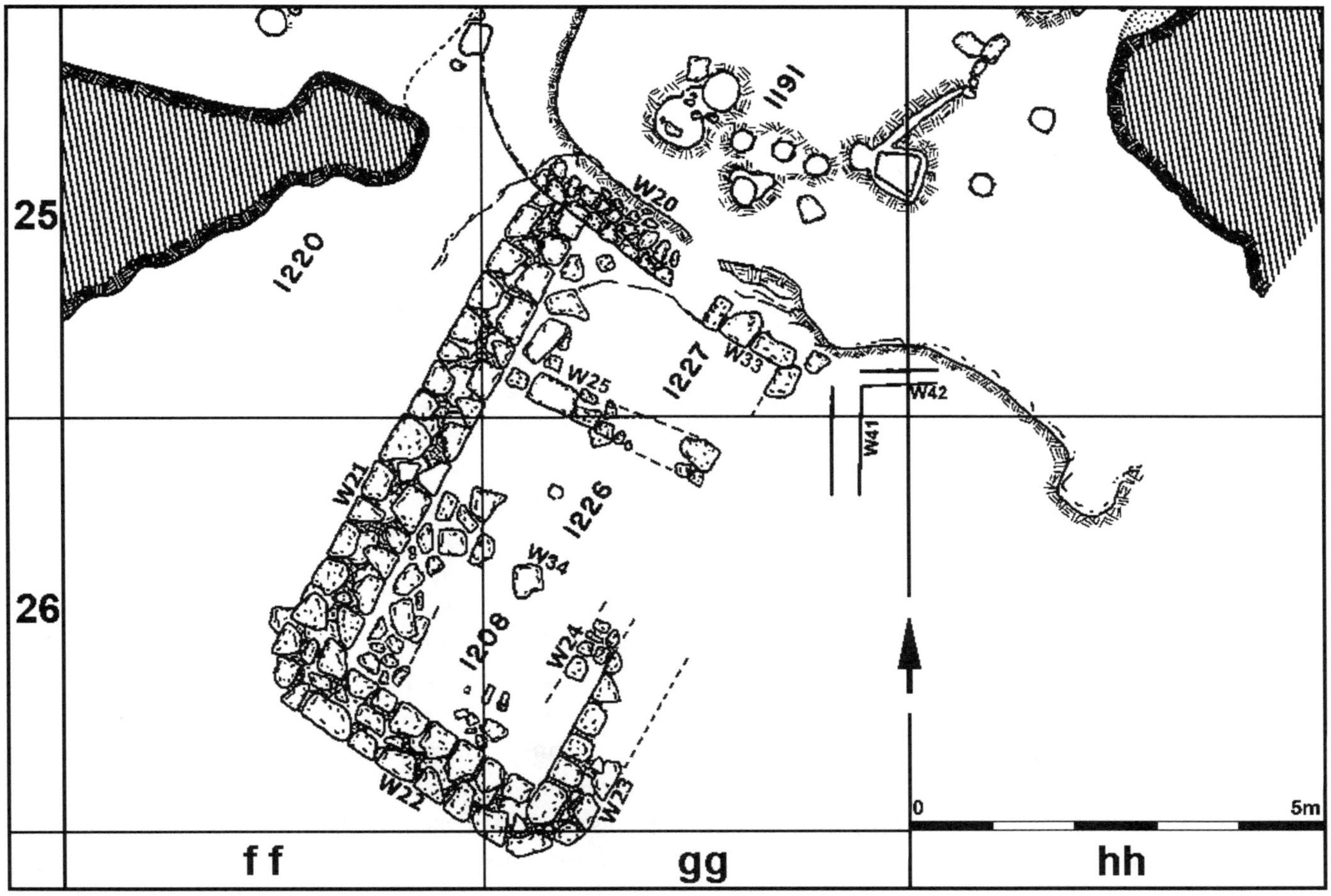

Figure 22. Plan of B/V/1 and two walls, W41 and W42 (drawn in their approximate locations from evidence of photograph pl. 38)

largement and alteration. They include scores of tombs of different periods (see *Megiddo Tombs*), but some were habitations and workshops. The earliest evidence for domestic (i.e., non-mortuary related) activity in this precinct of the site apparently took place in low-lying areas, caves, and possibly, coevally in buildings constructed atop bedrock. As these features may only be placed in localized sequences, the discussion follows the order above solely for the sake of consistency.

Deposits below and Earlier than the Stage IV Buildings

Evidence derived from exposure of the bedrock below the Stage IV buildings indicates human activity there prior to their construction. Following are descriptions of the remains of this activity with my suggestions for interpreting them.

Postulation of a Collapsed Cave on the Upper Terrace in Squares T16 and U16

The state of the bedrock on the upper terrace (fig. 19; pl. 21) at the junction of Squares T16 and U16, as well as evidence of quarrying, have led me to hypothesize the existence of a large natural cave in the area occupied by B/IV/1 and Locus 1199, the open space south of the building. I suggest that the area was originally roofed and that large portions of the roof collapsed. Later, most of the area was cleared and built upon. This interpretation is best understood from photographs in which a more or less vertical bedrock scarp is discernible adjacent to and just west of the western side of B/IV/1 (pls. 23–24, 27–28, 33, 35–36). Nothing of the northern closure of the cave appears to have been preserved, but to the south and west remains of the cave are visible in Locus 1199, which at the time of its excavation still preserved portions of its roof in small cavities in the bedrock to the west and south (fig. 23). The larger of these cavities is a sizable niche with an obviously quarried, rectangular ground plan (fig. 16). On the east, remains of this cave are visible only in the large bedrock outcrop incorporated into Locus 1200 and especially in Locus 1198, in which a small cavity, presumably part of the larger cave, was extant and obviously utilized by the occupiers of B/IV/1.

Rock-cut Features on the Upper Terrace within the Cave

To this same cave I ascribe most, if not all of the quarried bedrock features in B/IV/1, which, so varied and apparently uncoordinated as they are, obviously indicate an incremental history of activity in different periods. This interpretation explains the leveled surfaces and different indentations, "cupmarks," and "pot-holes" cut into the bedrock surfaces, as well as the rock-cut features that divided the space into chambers.

As noted above, the rock-cut features that served as plinths of the walls of B/IV/1 were obviously not quarried for that purpose, but were associated with some earlier activity at that location. I interpret them as analogous to, and probably contemporary with, the rectangular plan of the large niche in Locus 1199. I believe them to have been part of a large burial cave that collapsed and was re-used in the construction of B/IV/1. In that scenario I suggest an explanation for the massive stones found in the earliest phase of B/IV/1. As the original plan of the cave remains unknown, it is not inconceivable that those stones were actually placed there when the cave was still extant to provide a curtain or closure wall to seal off what was likely a large, natural opening.

Clearly, from the extant evidence of the scarp behind the upper terrace and the shape of the bedrock, the cave was a natural feature, quarried and altered as necessary for human needs, probably in a sequence of events. Basic alterations made to the plan of the cave suggest some special function other than as a dwelling, which it appears to have been only in its latest phase of use, especially if the massive walls and the early elements of the imposing entrance were associated with it.

The location of this terrace, within an area already reserved for mortuary purposes in Early Bronze Age I, suggests the cave was associated with mortuary-related activity. I interpret the quarried features of the two southern rooms, which served as high plinths for later walls (features unparalleled in any Early Bronze Age building yet unearthed in the southern Levant) as divisions pre-dating the constructed building, designed to provide burial chambers. Such an explanation would also account for the considerable differences in elevations between the floors of Loci 1198 and 1200, a rather inconvenient feature in a dwelling, but one far less so in a sepulcher.

Similar quarrying is found in adjacent, multi-chambered Tomb 910, albeit on a grander scale (fig. 34; pls. 95–96a) that evidences considerably more skill and care. While the precise date of Tomb 910 remains obscure, as it was cleaned out and re-utilized in a later period (*Chapter 6*), there is a great likelihood of it having been first quarried and used during Early Bronze Age I. Although it is not a typical tomb of the period, Megiddo is an atypical site that features evidence of the type of social organization concomitant in scale and in skill with such quarrying activities (*Chapters 6* and *7*). The quality of the dressed, soft, chalky limestone of the hillside evidenced in this cave on the Stage IV terrace on the East Slope, and in nearby Tomb 910, was well within the obvious masonic capabilities of the Early Bronze I people at Megiddo. Their considerable skills in working stone on a massive scale are best known from objects of finely finished, extremely hard basalt found in the temples of Strata J3 (Stratum XIX) and J4 in Area BB on the tell (*Megiddo IV*, ch. 3, pp. 29–53). Cutting into the soft limestone of the East Slope and dressing its surfaces would have been a much easier task than shaping hard basalt.

The leveled surface of Locus 1199 is dotted with small cavities of various shapes. The largest were given alphabetic labels by the excavators and documented in a photograph (pl. 37). Those that showed evidence of burning were identified as "pot-holes" used for cooking. Two, visible in Section A–B (fig. 19), diminish in circumference below the surface, which gives them a conical aspect that is unlikely to have been intended for pots of the Early Bronze Age or earlier, which invariably had flat or large, rounded bases. These features may have been grinding or pounding installations, although the soft bedrock might not have been particularly good for such functions, while the numerous very small cavities would be unsuitable for such activity.

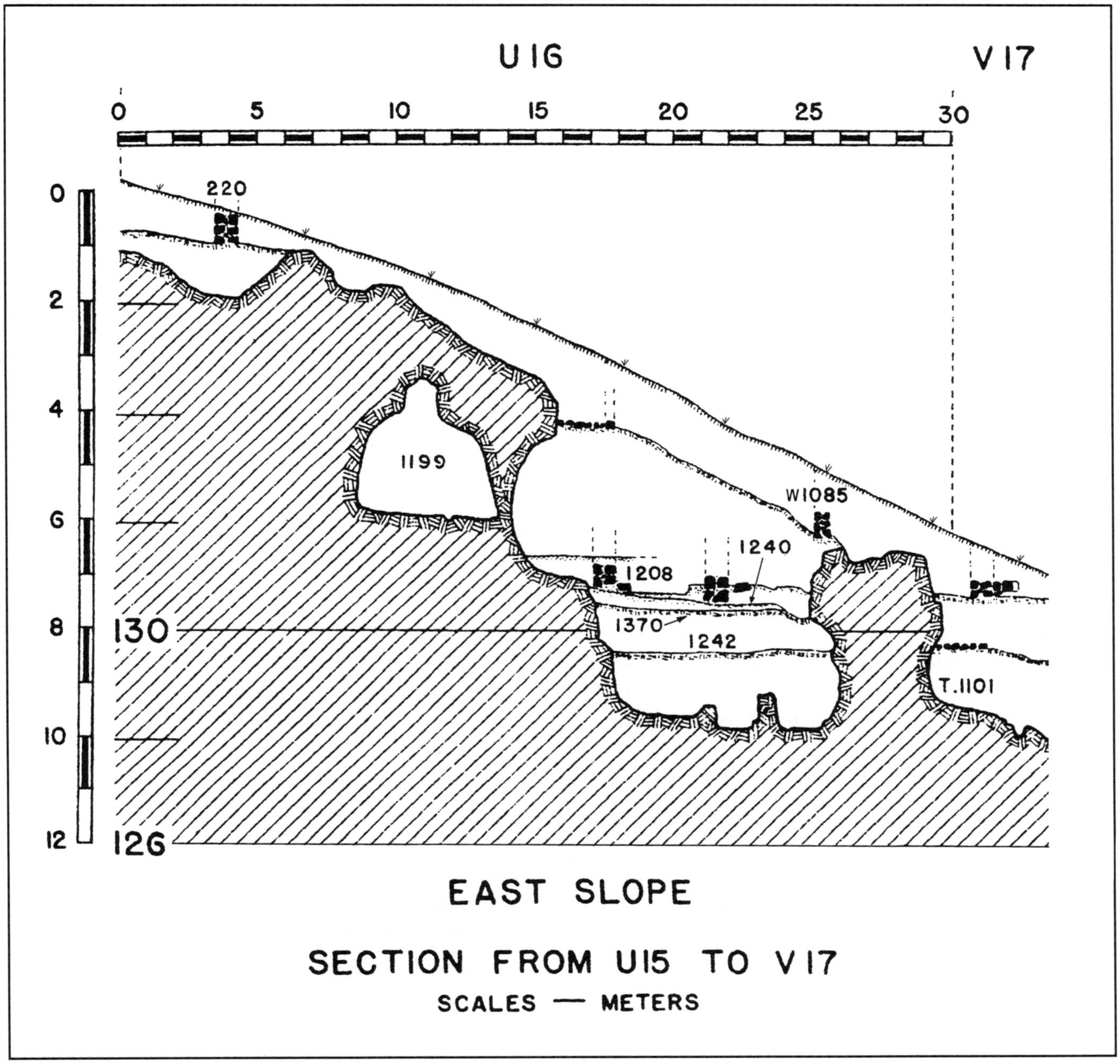

Figure 23. Enlarged detail of a segment of Section C–D with indications of a deep probe below B/V/1. The approximate location of this section, drawn apparently after the end of the excavation, is noted in plate 21

I cannot explain the evidence of burning, but as these features were literally carved into the rock and likely to have been exposed for long periods, it could be the result of activity not associated with their primary functions. I do not know how to interpret the numerous tiny depressions in the bedrock surface visible in the same photograph, but they appear to be small holes, which could be either ancient or possibly even modernly made at the time of excavation.

If, as suggested above, the upper terrace was once the site of an Early Bronze Age I burial cave, then it seems likely it was destroyed in the same earthquake (Act 1) that wreaked violent and instant destruction on the mound in Area BB. The evidence from the cave would place the date of the earthquake sometime late in Early Bronze Age I, presumably when the cave was still in use. Shortly thereafter the cave was cleared of debris (Act 2) and its ruins built over with B/IV/1. That dating is consistent with the time span noted by Shmuel Marco and colleagues (*Megiddo IV*, ch. 31, pp. 568–75, esp. table 31.1:1), which places the event between a very late phase of Early Bronze Age I and Early Bronze Age III. If the latest phase of occupation of

B/IV/1 is dated to late Early Bronze Age I, then the earthquake may also be dated to then. The same tremor or tremors may also explain the partial destruction of the entrance to nearby Tomb 910, which was apparently cleared at the end of Early Bronze Age I (*Chapter 6*).

Such an event could have caused the top of the cave, already weakened by quarrying, to collapse. It could also account for the massive boulders found just a bit farther down the slope, which may be chunks of the cave's roof. One of those boulders, designated by the excavators as Locus 1234, was later removed (see above, *B/V/2*) and proved to have been located above a structure, of which a corner was found (W41, W42; pl. 38, right middle ground). Two even more massive boulders,[41] located just a bit farther down the slope, in the southwest quadrant of Square U16 (pl. 17, largely in Squares ee28 and ff28; pl. 19, bottom center), could be additional debris from the collapsed cave.

That same event may also explain the jagged aspects of the uppermost portions of lengths of the bedrock plinths in B/IV/1. They would have been remains of extant features broken off with the destruction of the cave. Certainly, had they been features deliberately quarried to support superstructures of free-standing walls, they would have been leveled on top. Later builders of B/IV/1 did not bother to quarry, but used existing features on which to found their structures in what was then a broad, more or less flat space, mostly open to the air. Over time the structure morphed into the house with an apsidal end, which the excavators documented in their photographs.

Bedrock Features on the Upper Terrace East of the Collapsed Cave

Clearance of the bedrock around B/IV/2 and the flattened area to the north of it, Locus 1204, revealed numerous rock-cut features from earlier periods, most of which were hidden by the floor of B/IV/2. After the floor's removal, that part of the area cleared to bedrock was shown to have had an artificially leveled, albeit rough-hewn surface with a number of depressions and fissures, most of which appear to be natural (pls. 29, 38).

Below Locus 1190, mostly directly below W28 and W1195, two apparently natural, deep cavities were found (pl. 38), one of which was excavated as Locus 1236. It appears to have been utilized for water storage as it seems to drain a small, rock-cut channel adjacent to it on the south. Directly to its north and also adjacent to it is a small, shallow, rock-cut basin that could have been a settling pool. Additional small cavities and another channel cut into the bedrock surface to the east of Locus 1236 (Loci 1191 and 1192) indicate the bedrock surface was likely to have been an activity area over time, prior to construction of any buildings there.

Deposits Below B/V/1: Interpreting Results of Deep Probes

That the Stage V building was not the earliest deposit is evident from a short segment of Section C–D (fig. 23) drawn by the excavators and from the schematic section published in Engberg and Shipton 1934a (reproduced here as fig. 9). Section C–D is a compound and schematic view and compilation of the Stage V house and deposits encountered below. Unfortunately, there are no photographic records of what appears to have been a deep sounding below a massive boulder, which produced evidence for a floor, Locus 1370 (pl. 21). I have been able to more or less locate the section on a photograph, but I have not been able to place it precisely. That is because it should have been positioned so as to cross Locus 1240, noted as a "rooms under 1226," which is noted as a "room next 1208."

Also somewhat misleading is the bell-shaped form of Locus 1199, which was mostly a large, open-air space to the west of B/IV/1. Section C–D apparently shows a cut through the large, partially rectangular niche with its numerous small depressions, one of which it illustrates. One feature that does seem to be accurate in this section is the identification of Locus 1240 as a surface associated with the foundations of W32, which

[41] That they are not bedrock outcrops is revealed in the locus list, which indicates that Locus 1242 is a "floor going under 1232," described as a "smaller stone over 903." This "smaller stone" is in actual fact a gargantuan boulder, one of two visible in the latest aerial photographs. The other, considerably more massive, was labeled Locus 1233 (pl. 21).

are on the same level. The technique of placing foundations and floors on the same surface is well known in Early Bronze Age construction.

There is little additional indication of excavation activity in these basal deposits. None is indicated in the last series of aerial photographs or in the ground views of Stage V, which depict B/V/1 and B/V/2 in situ. Those on the upper terrace seem to have been exposed in a small probe or sondage (Loci 1370 and 1371), somewhere within the confines of Locus 1204 (pl. 21). As the last locus number given in the 1932 season series is 1243 and there are only a few entries for the East Slope after that, it is clear these loci were exposed sometime quite late in the excavation of the East Slope, possibly at the very end of the 1932 season or, what is more likely, in a later season. Just possibly the numbers of these loci were assigned *ex post facto*. Any of these factors could account for the unfortunate lack of photographic documentation. Virtually nothing is known of these probes, but I suspect they yielded the two inhumations pictured on bedrock in the schematic section in fills well below the stages (fig. 9).

Additional Caves

Numerous caves, some apparently natural and others altered or created by humans, dot the East Slope. Those utilized as tombs and published (*Megiddo Tombs*), albeit beyond the primary scope of this report, are of tangential interest to this study as they are indicative of coeval human activity in this precinct of the site. Several caves are of particular interest for the evidence they indicate of non-mortuary related activity on the East Slope in early periods, likely to be contemporary with the buildings encountered on the upper and lower terraces.

"Tomb" 903 Lower

This large cavity of irregular plan is apparently the remains of a cave, most of the roof of which collapsed (pl. 39). It is located just to the south of the Stage V house, partially in Square U16 (pl. 21), but mostly in Square V16. Below several layers of human bones (Tomb 903 Upper), in a layer of fill nominally called "Tomb 903 Lower," were found animal bones, pottery, and what is described as a "lime floor" (*Megiddo Tombs*, pp. 9–12; pl. 40). The lack of any human remains as well as the pottery objects recovered from this deposit suggest the earliest function of the cave was domestic, or at least not directly associated with burials. The material associated with the "Tomb 903 Upper" gives the earlier phase a *terminus post quem* in Late Early Bronze Age I.

Tomb 910

This multi-chambered complex in Square V17 (*Chapter 6*) was originally a tomb, although the excavators suggested it may have been re-used afterward for domestic purposes (fig. 34; pls. 95–96). Its primary, mortuary function seems certain as access from the vestibule is through a short corridor only ca. 0.8 m high, which would be mightily inconvenient for live residents as they entered and left. The size, multi-roomed plan, and execution of this rock-cut tomb mark it as an extremely impressive monument indicative not only of the level of skills exhibited by the Early Bronze Age stone masons of Megiddo, but also of their social organization.

The excavators suggested the tomb was cleared of most of its non-living occupants prior to re-use. That may be indicated by the empty state in which much of this complex was found. Latterly, or perhaps in areas not cleared of human remains, several skeletons were found scattered within (*Megiddo Tombs*, p. 18). What is apparently an almost complete Early Bronze Age cooking pot (ibid., pl. 4:13) on its floor is of a generic type known to have a range from Early Bronze Age II through III. It provides a *terminus ante quem* for the quarrying and construction of this complex. Another possible *terminus ante quem* for the quarrying of this cave is based on the evidence of a small, nearly complete jar found in the fill of chamber D (ibid., pl. 4:22), if it is accepted as not having been introduced as an heirloom. That vessel should be dated to sometime within the Early Bronze Age I (pl. 57b; *Megiddo Tombs*, pl. 4.22).

Tomb 1122

This relatively commodious cave of very irregular plan, located in Square V17, was probably a natural cavity altered by humans for their utilization. It appears to have had two entrances and an aperture for ventilation (*Megiddo Tombs*, pp. 19–20). It was likely used for domestic purposes, after which it was apparently abandoned. At some date later than the original use of the cave, a shelf-like niche in it received an Early Bronze Age I burial, suggesting a *terminus ante quem* for its occupation.

Tomb 1128

Guy and Engberg (*Megiddo Tombs*, p. 20) suggested this irregular chamber in Square V16, originally a tomb, was re-used for domiciliary purposes in the time span of Stage 0–I, perhaps in Early Bronze Age III. Noting that the entrance to this chamber was horizontal rather than through a vertical or sloping shaft, they likened it to Tomb 910. However, there does not appear to be any corroboratory evidence for this claim of contemporaneousness, while there is a vast difference between the care taken in the quarrying of these two caves.

Tomb 9

Described as a "rough circular pit" (*Megiddo Tombs*, p. 20), this small cavity yielded a single vessel, misidentified by the excavators as "the only piece of Khirbet Kerak ware yet found at Megiddo." The drawing and the color of the sherd indicate it to be part of a specific type of bowl of the class of Gray Burnished Ware, for which there are numerous additional examples in the assemblage of the East Slope (*Chapter 3*, Gray Burnished Ware, Type 1c).

Tomb 52

Based on pottery from this cave, it appears to have been occupied or utilized in the Early Bronze Age III and subsequently in the Late Bronze and Iron Ages. This tomb was located near the East Slope, apparently somewhere on the southeast flank of the high mound. The Early Bronze Age III objects associated with this cave suggest it served for quotidian rather than mortuary functions in that period.

Tombs 1101 and 1102

These "tombs" are part of a larger complex of cavities used in different periods, the latest of which appears to be the Early Iron Age. The basal level of fill within them (fig. 24; pl. 40) yielded evidence of occupation, including small circular cavities in the bedrock described as "pot-holes" similar to those described in Tomb 1106 (see below). A hearth in Locus 1101 and a "basalt slab," apparently worked, were found on the bedrock surface. Additional evidence of domestic activity was encountered in the earliest deposits in Locus 1102, represented by ca. 50 cm of soil containing charcoal, animal bones, and potsherds. The earliest of these last were equated by the excavators with the pottery they associated with Stage IV.

Kiln

A wall and a small, circular construction of stone with a central division, described as a "kiln" (Locus 1143), within Locus 1142, are illustrated in plan and section within the complex of Tombs 1101 and 1102 (fig. 24; pls. 40, 42). There is, however, no additional information on adjacent fills or finds such as wasters or other telltale evidence of the function of this installation that might help date it. Guy and Engberg suggested dating this kiln to at least as early as "somewhat later than Stage IV" (*Megiddo Tombs*, p. 27) or possibly even earlier, which would indicate a date within the Early Bronze Age. Corroboration for an Early Bronze Age date

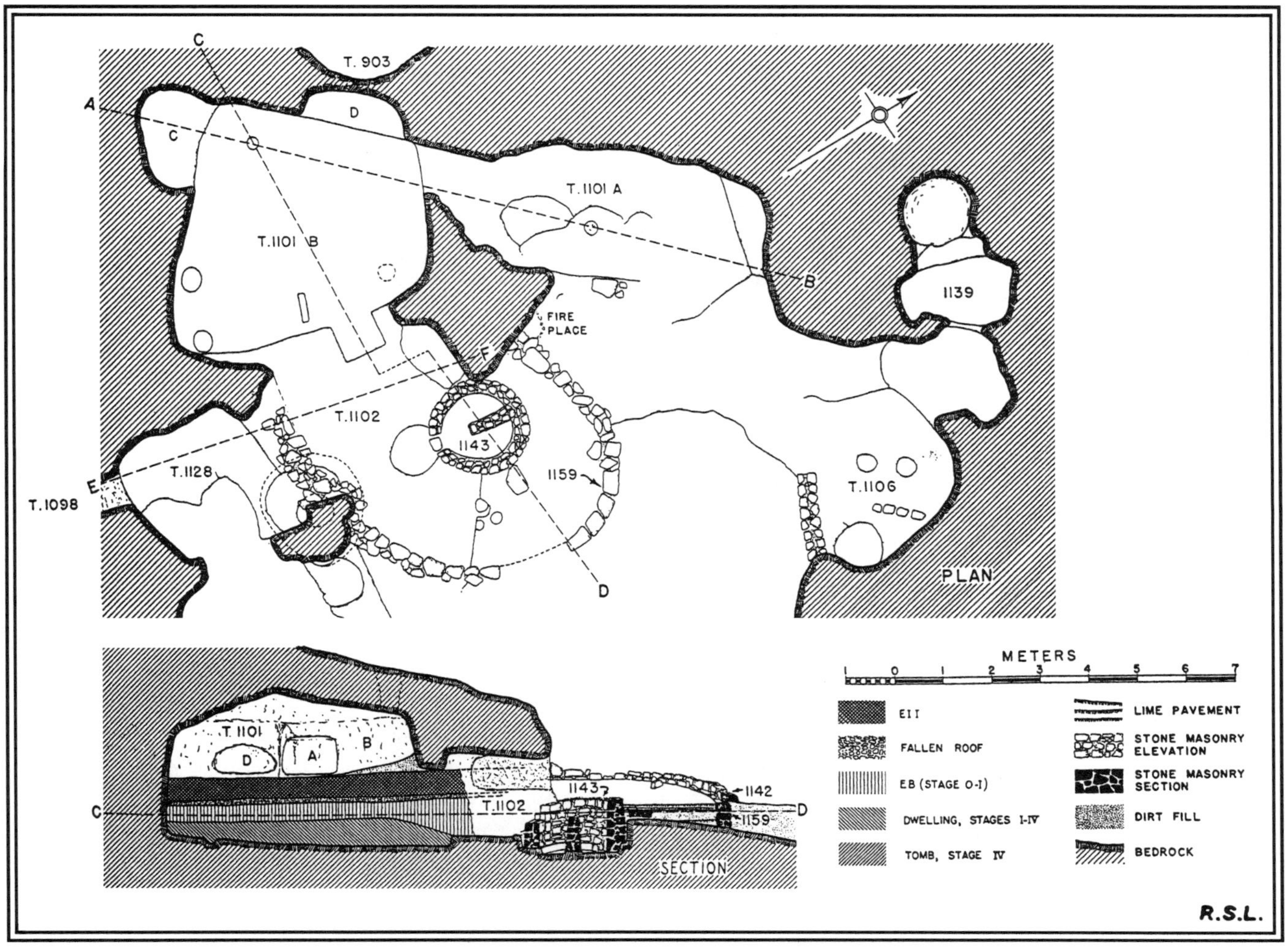

Figure 24. Plan of Locus 1101 (Robert S. Lamon), which in its earliest utilization was apparently a dwelling (after *Megiddo Tombs*, fig. 22)

comes perhaps from a complete holemouth vessel with a rounded bottom encountered nearby in a shallow cavity (pl. 41). It is of a type common in the Early Bronze Age II–III.

In addition, there is a modicum of evidence for pottery production at Megiddo in the Early Bronze Age. It derives from three basalt tournettes found at the site. One is from the high tell in Stratum XVIII (*Megiddo II*, pl. 268:1), another from Stratum XVI (ibid., pl. 268:2), while the third is from Stage IV on the East Slope (Engberg and Shipton 1934a, p. 40). Those from the East Slope and Stratum XVIII appear to belong to a type associated with the Early Bronze Age (Roux and de Miroschedji 2009; *Chapter 3: A Potter's Tournette*) and thus argue for pottery production in that time span; that from Stratum XVI seems to be of a later type and may have been intrusive.

However, the plan of this installation is suspiciously similar to other kilns dotting the hillside, which are dated to "late" periods (i.e., +IV levels; see above), while the drawn section indicates it was located in a partially open area of the cave (fig. 24). That admits of the possibility that it could have been intrusive down to the bedrock floor of Locus 1102 from some much later period. Notably, there is evidence of one or possibly two kilns intruding into the fills of Stage IV. One definitive example sat atop the apsidal wall of B/IV/1 (pl. 19), between Walls 2 and 3, while the other installation lay adjacent to the east face of W5 (pl. 27).

It is, in any event, most unfortunate there is no additional information on the dating of this kiln as there is very limited information on this aspect of the potter's art for the Early Bronze Age southern Levant. The sole examples of installations of this type for the entire Early Bronze Age of the southern Levant are a kiln at Tell el-Farʿah North (de Vaux 1955, pp. 558–63) dated to Early Bronze Age II (the excavator's periode 4) and another at Bet Yerah (S. Paz 2006b, pp. 64–67), dated to Early Bronze Age III. Similar to Locus 1143, that latter installation was partially subterranean and had a central post supporting a portion of its floor pierced with small, circular openings. These last two features were not preserved in the kiln in Tomb 1102.

Tomb 1106

The evidence for the function of this cave in the earliest deposits found there is equivocal. The excavators suggested that below a series of disturbed burials there may have been a primal domestic utilization of the cave, although they conceded it could also have been associated with burials. They further noted two white, rock-cut cavities in the floor of this cave filled with plaster in which were embedded lumps of basalt and traces of ash, which led them to call these installations "pot-holes" associated with cooking. Two intact carinated bowls of gray fabric were discovered in the deeper of these cavities, which probably belie their suggested function. These bowls, associated with a somewhat advanced, albeit not the latest phase of Early Bronze Age I, suggest a relative date for the cave's use.

An Early Bronze Age III Activity Area?

A photograph of a nearly complete holemouth vessel (pls. 41, 72e) introduces an anomaly in the documentation that I cannot explain. The vessel, of an Early Bronze Age II–III type, is attributed to Locus 1183, which is indicated as a "floor under NE part of 1171," and it is placed in Square U17. A quick check of Locus 1171 indicates it was in Square V17, which is probably not a mistake as this is one of the double entries identical in the information they impart. A check of all extant plans, including that of the latest buildings (fig. 5), and the annotated aerial photograph from *Megiddo Tombs*, pl. 2, fails to inform of the location of either locus, while the series of aerial photographs from the second and third series show very little evidence of construction in Square V17 (pl. 42, successively). By the fourth series the square was barren of structures and stripped to bedrock.

Several rectangular rooms visible in Squares U17 and V17, which form part of what appears to be a single structure, apparently built in different phases, are likely candidates for the location of this floor. Unfortunately, no plans were made of this building and there are no means to identify them with Locus 1171. Thus there is evidence of additional activity in the Early Bronze Age III, possibly utilizing some elements of the structures unearthed there in conjunction with the nearby cave. That extends the area of activity in the Early Bronze Age farther down the East slope, although the essence of it and the precise location of the excavators' Locus 1171 remain obscure.

THE STRATIGRAPHY OF THE EARLIEST UTILIZATION AND OCCUPATION OF THE EAST SLOPE: A SUMMARY STATEMENT

As has been demonstrated above, Engberg's and Shipton's (1934a) somewhat simplistic stratigraphic paradigm for the early occupation of the East Slope (Stages VII to I), developed at a time when virtually nothing was known of architectural traditions of the Early Bronze Age and when the study of early pottery-producing cultures of the southern Levant was still in its infancy, is no longer tenable as a reflection of what may be discerned from the evidence of their excavation there. While we remain with a picture of activity prior to the construction of the Stage V and Stage IV buildings, and evidence of early architecture there, those vestiges can no longer be definitively associated with the excavators' numbered stages.

Indeed, those stages must now be understood as heuristic and loosely defined occupation episodes represented by material culture that consists primarily of groups of ceramic types that sequentially came in and out of fashion during a range of time now known to include the developed Early Bronze Age I (see *Chapter 3*) into the Early Bronze Age II and, after a hiatus in occupation, Early Bronze Age III. As most of that pottery was not recovered in situ, and our knowledge of what was recovered in the excavations is based on only retained materials, it is rather difficult to assign chrono-cultural associations to the majority of architectural elements recorded, which represent sedentary occupation. Indeed, the bulk of material retained lacks even a context or findspot within a locus, while most of the ceramic objects are sherds that are merely provenienced to the East Slope.

Below Stages V and IV to Bedrock

Two "Early" Burials

Two burials are possibly the earliest evidence of human activity on the East Slope encountered in the excavation. They appear to be simple inhumations but unfortunately there is little description of them. One (Locus 1703), possibly the earlier, was encountered in a deep probe on the lower terrace. It is indicated as found "under floor 1242" (fig. 23), which could suggest a relationship to that floor, but that seems very unlikely as the floor was strewn with Early Bronze Age I pottery, which appears to be at odds with the description of the matrix in which the burial was found:

> From here down to the bed rock were deep hearth deposits containing burnt animal bones, but no artifacts. In B, at the point indicated in Figure 1,[42] lay a skeleton of this very early period. There was no possibility of its being intrusive, as a large rock weighing about two tons rested on it,[43] while above the rock was the accumulation of Stage VII. (Engberg and Shipton 1934a, p. 6)

The skeleton was in too poor a state to be measured, but from information available it seems likely to have derived from one of the pre-Early Bronze Age I occupations indicated by the assemblage of chipped stones (*Chapter* 5).

The other burial was found on bedrock below the floor designated Locus 1371, which locates it somewhere on the upper terrace beneath B/IV/2 or its courtyard. Engberg and Shipton's schematic section (see fig. 9) places it within the matrix of Stage VII, significantly above the "sterile occupation deposit," but nothing more of this burial is documented. Stage VII, according to the excavators, was distinguished by the relative infrequency of pottery which, if judged from the extant collections, was almost completely derived from the Early Bronze Age I or later. As intramural burials, especially under floors, are very rare in the Early Bronze Age I, and the position of the skeleton on bedrock indicates it is the earliest possible deposit in a localized sequence, it seems likely that it too belongs to some pre-Early Bronze Age episode on the East Slope. That would suggest the little pottery in the matrix was intrusive.

Vestiges of Sedentary Occupation

The few patches of surfaces either fashioned or utilized by humans below the Stage V and IV buildings are the sole indisputable evidence of the earliest attempts at above-ground construction encountered in the excavation of the East Slope. I have no photographic documentation of the deep probes in which they were found, although they are noted briefly in the published text, drawn in Section C–D, and references to them are found in the locus list. They appear to represent more than one episode of activity, but little else may be said of them beyond noting that they are likely to have been associated with actual buildings apparently described as a "room" and given the label Locus 1241, which I believe are to be identified with W41 and W42 (pl. 23). Thus the excavators' Stages VII and VII, which appear drawn on their schematic section (fig. 9), have some justification, although they are not what the excavators suggested in their attempt at documentation.

Perhaps one, another, or all of the earliest walls (W26, W31, and W32) not appearing in Lamon's plan (fig. 16) and documented solely in photographs should be associated with these surfaces; possibly some of them functioned coevally. Unfortunately, they may not be dated because there are no artifacts that can be associated with them. To these same pre-Stages V and IV episodes of human activity may also be assigned

[42] This is the schematic section (fig. 9).

[43] Quite possibly this "large rock" is an enormous boulder identified as Locus 1234.

all the artificial, quarried alterations visible in the bedrock below the buildings of those stages. Judging by the number and types of features, cupmarks, pot-holes, channels, quarried lines, and flattened and leveled surfaces, many of which do not seem to have been coordinated with others nearby, that activity appears to represent sequential episodes, which could have occurred over a considerable span of time.

It is also possible to assign to one or another of these periods the earliest uses of the caves for burials and dwellings. While it is impossible, given available information, to equate any particular feature with a specific chrono-cultural episode, the likely parameters for the entire scope of this activity are probably to be found in the dating of the flint artifacts (*Chapter 5*) and possibly some of the earliest pottery, which offer evidence for early human activity on the East Slope. *Grosso modo*, that suggests a span of time from Early Neolithic to some time in the advanced phases of the Early Bronze Age I (*Chapter 3*).

Stage V

As noted above, the stratigraphic association between the excavators' Stages V and IV is at best highly tenuous and thus each of these stages should be considered as representing a localized stratigraphic sequence. The evidence suggests a single phase of use (but two phases of construction) for B/V/1, which ended sometime in an advanced but not very late phase of Early Bronze Age I. Afterward, portions of it may have been incorporated into B/V/2, which probably should be dated to a slightly later period, indicated by the absolute elevations of B/V/2, as it seems highly unlikely that the construction of B/V/1 cut into B/V/2. The dating of B/V/2 remains obscure, but probably can be limited to within the Early Bronze horizon.

Stage IV: The Earliest Phase(s)

The earliest phase of B/IV/1 on this terrace appears to have utilized the flattened bedrock surfaces and quarried lines of earlier times. One or possibly two phases may be associated with it. The sparse remains of B/IV/1, large boulders, and the elaborate entrance could possibly have preserved remains of a facade of a cave (later collapsed), or of a free-standing building, or both. By contrast, only a few scant wall segments suggest the bedrock below B/IV/2 to the east on the same terrace was utilized during the same time span, possibly as a courtyard or activity area for the cave or the early phase of the building. The flattened, level bedrock surface to the south of this building in Locus 1199 saw its latest use in the Early Bronze Age I, as may be discerned from a nearly complete, Egyptian-style vessel, dated to the late proto-dynastic period found there (see *Chapter 3*). Possibly to this stage we may assign the anomalous walls (W26, W31, W32) under W1243, on the east side of the terrace, which apparently formed a rectangular structure.

Stage IV: The Latest Phase(s)

The later phase of B/IV/1 is represented by a rebuilding of walls that gave the structure its distinctive, "apsidal" plan. Its earthen floor, discernible from evidence of a complete holemouth vessel standing in situ on it on Locus 1200, is indicative of the building's latest use. The date of that is determined by the dating of the vessel, which clearly belongs to the Early Bronze Age horizon and is likely to be dated to Early Bronze Age I or II. Remains of the well-built rectangular structure B/IV/2, adjacent to the east face of the bedrock outcrop incorporated in B/IV/1, belong to this later phase, as may be discerned from the layer of earthen fill covering bedrock below the former's foundations.

Above Stage IV: Activity in Early Bronze Age II and an Early Bronze Age III Occupation

Based on the pottery in Engberg and Shipton's chart (1934a), Stages III–I should be roughly dated to the Early Bronze Age II and Early Bronze Age III. However, evidence for Early Bronze Age II, at the site in general and on the East Slope specifically, is very scant. Evidence for it is found in a minute collection of sherds of "metallic ware," which indicates the likelihood of some activity in that period on the East Slope. Judging by the size of this collection, supposedly a representative sample of what was found by the excavators (pls. 65–66), it seems safe to suggest that activity in that period was as limited on the East Slope as it apparently was on the mound (Esse 1991, pp. 68–76: *Megiddo III*, pp. 585–86). However, the site was very significantly larger than the excavated area for these periods and it is not unlikely that elsewhere within the confines of this large site more significant activity in that period is to be found.

At least W1243 and probably the room identified as Locus 914 were at some point in their history occupied in Early Bronze Age III. They appear to have been part of a settlement that left a not inconsiderable quantity of ceramic refuse on the East Slope. Possibly other areas of the slope, where some structures and large caves were found, were also utilized in that period.

Above Stage IV: Later Horizons

The stratified remains above the pre-Early Bronze Age and earlier deposits represent a complicated and patchy series of sequences of utilization and occupation of the East Slope during different periods. Although a discussion of their chrono-cultural relations lies beyond the scope of this work, it is noteworthy that almost throughout the period of utilization of the precinct discussed above, the same general orientation of buildings was maintained. Some of the structures are quite sizable and indicate intensive activity in one or more periods. In addition, there is evidence of a flourishing pottery industry spread over the East Slope at some time in these "late" periods.

3

ARTIFACTS FROM THE EAST SLOPE

PART 1: POTTERY

Given the limitations of documentation outlined in the preceding chapters, and advancements made in understanding late prehistoric pottery of the southern Levant, one is tempted to question the utility of studying a ceramic assemblage of limited scope and imprecise provenience that has been languishing in storerooms for nearly eight decades. But one should consider the importance that Megiddo continues to play in scholars' perceptions of late fourth- and third-millennium cultures of its northern region (*Chapter 1: Introduction*).

What, then, can be gleaned from the collection of odd bits of ceramics, mostly fragments of pots, broken and discarded on the East Slope in ancient times? The answer is, I believe, analogous to what may be discerned by standing on the eastern edge of the high mound at Megiddo and gazing out over the vast expanse of the Jezreel. As a vantage point it is only a few score meters off the valley floor and offers far from an all-encompassing view. Standing atop the Carmel Range directly to the west would offer a significantly broader perspective. Nevertheless, the top of the mound is a good place to halt and scrutinize the immediate surroundings and ken something of the nature of the valley and its contours in detail. So too does the ceramic assemblage culled from the yield of the East Slope offer a good (if not the best) vantage point from which to examine and analyze the pottery from neighboring sites of the same time span.

But is it really necessary to do this for such a limited collection after such a long delay? In effect, this postponement has actually been propitious for this assemblage as the detailed study offered here would not have been possible even a decade ago, since much of it is based on the fruits of colleagues' labors so splendidly available in recently published excavation results. Thus, in presenting this material I have attempted to integrate the East Slope assemblage into a regional study of the pottery of the Early Bronze Age and then used it to interpret the evidence encountered in the East Slope.

THE ASSEMBLAGE

Pottery available for study from the East Slope is a highly selective collection of a few complete or nearly complete vessels and numerous potsherds derived during the years of excavation. It is likely to be representative of the entire collection that came into the hands of the excavators, as they obviously chose to retain objects that would fulfill such a function. However, no parameters are available for the degree of its representativeness, especially as it is obvious that unknown quantities of ceramics were discarded, probably in the field, and no records kept of them. Thus we remain with a collection of objects culled from what is likely to have been a much larger assemblage for which there is no quantification.

The policies of the Oriental Institute and the Palestine Mandate's Department of Antiquities aided my studies as the finds were divided between only two institutions, allowing me to access them all in Jerusalem and Chicago.[45] Of the ceramic objects retained from the excavation of the East Slope, all are today either on display in the Rockefeller Museum (formerly the Palestine Archaeological Museum), the Israel Museum,

[45] Such would not be the case for Kathleen Kenyon's excavations at Jericho, which distributed finds to numerous institutions (Kenyon and Holland 1983, p. 824).

and the Oriental Institute Museum, or are stored either in the facilities of the Israel Antiquities Authority in Jerusalem or at the Oriental Institute in Chicago.

While the preserved assemblage of ceramics from the East Slope is indicative of major trends and developments that occurred there during more than a millennium, it should not, with a handful of exceptions, be viewed as a source of information on specific chrono-cultural associations of features and deposits. Most of the objects in the preserved assemblage were retrieved from findspots for which there is no information beyond that they come from somewhere on the East Slope. Even when there is information on provenience, it is of dubious import as stratigraphic associations are dependent on findspots expressed in terms of large 25 × 25 m squares or within loci, mostly large, three-dimensional, volumetric designations of fills, indicated by only two-dimensional boundaries roughly defined by wall foundations (i.e., the excavators' "rooms"). Thus for most provenienced objects there are no absolute elevations or associations with features such as surfaces or floors, vital information for determining chrono-cultural associations of architectural remains. Accordingly, with a few notable exceptions captured on film, precise locations of where artifacts were recovered are unknown.

Of themselves the objects bear mute witness to a variety of aspects of ancient human activity related to life at Megiddo in a number of late prehistoric periods. First and foremost they indicate the chrono-cultural range of human activity there, but in addition they contain considerable information, especially when collated with data from other sites, on a whole variety of ancient activities in the Jezreel Valley and its environs during select periods in the late fourth and third millennia B.C. As much of this study is based on typological considerations indicating chrono-cultural associations, the discussion follows a chronological order from earliest to latest period.

Earlier Publication of the Artifacts

Selected examples of the pottery and other artifacts from the East Slope are found in several early publications. They are in Engberg and Shipton's (1934a) monograph, in a small publication by Shipton (1938), and in the *Megiddo Tombs* volume.

Note on Drawing Conventions, Photographs, and Pottery Descriptions

Scholars dealing with ancient pottery know that the black-and-white line drawings used to represent objects in publications tend to standardize shapes by minimizing and sometimes even removing irregularities, minor asymmetries, flaws, and other idiosyncrasies characterizing profiles of objects. Those tendencies are exacerbated by the reduction of drawings to sizes fitting the printed page, with the end result often presenting only an approximation of the original form of such artifacts. That is particularly true of the late prehistoric hand-made pottery of the southern Levant, which was often roughly finished and fired under relatively primitive conditions; neat, black-line outlines of such vessels fail to convey anything of the "feel" of their surfaces.[46] With the advent of computerized, digital technology, which has greatly reduced the cost of publication (making this work possible), those "smoothing out" tendencies have been even further exacerbated.

Gray shading indicates additional coloring atop an underlying fabric. Conventionally the shading is often used to indicate earthen hues of "reds," but in specific instances it may include yellowish and orange hues and more rarely dark gray or brown (e.g., as in select examples of grain-wash or band-slip). Slips of these darker hues seem to have been applied in the same manner as red slips, suggesting the color variations may well have been the result of differences derived from firing.

[46] There are exceptions to this type of drawing (e.g., Bertemes 1986, pls. 10–14), but they are the result of very labor-intensive work that is prohibitively expensive.

Accordingly, the reader is advised that the line drawings presented in this work are highly standardized approximations of objects, accurately scaled to size, and should be understood merely as guidelines for generally recognizing morphology of these ancient objects. While they allow them, *grosso modo*, to be identified as to their chrono-cultural associations, these simplified drawings do not adequately represent their true appearances. Thus in order to allow for a better understanding of the true nature of this pottery I have attempted to include photographs of select objects, which illustrate and give the reader the "feel" of many of the distinctive features of pots and sherds of the different periods. The reader should be aware that many of these photographs show excavators' and museum curators' inked annotations on the objects; often accomplished in a manner that would be deemed unacceptable today. Following is a guide to the markings found on sherds, some of which are noticeable in the photographs:

1. Large Roman numerals indicate the excavators' suggested associations of the objects with the different stages. Thus, for example, "V–III" indicates a particular object, representing a morphological type, is associated, according to the excavators' understanding, with the occupations of Stages V through III. That is, of course, in line with their observations of the pottery forms "melting" from one period into the next (*Chapter 1*), but is not, however, in agreement with our present understanding of the chrono-cultural periodization of the East Slope, which argues for a major occupational gap between the chrono-cultural period represented by the occupation identified by the excavators as Stage IV and that represented by their Stage III. In other words, there is a significant gap between what appears to be evidence of a very late Early Bronze Age I occupation that might have carried over into the very earliest phase of Early Bronze Age II, and what is clearly an Early Bronze Age III occupation.
   Three objects with numbers prefixed by "I" (I.3154, I.3354a–b, I.3383a–b) were registered by the Rockefeller Museum.
2. All numbers beginning with "34." followed by a string of additional digits, are acquisition numbers of the Palestine Archaeological Museum, which officially acquired them in 1934. Digits preceded by "37.," "38.," and "39." are acquisition numbers for the years 1937, 1938, and 1939, respectively.
3. All digits following an "A" are acquisition numbers of the Oriental Institute.
4. Large-scale one- and two-digit numbers, occasionally followed by an uppercase letter (e.g., 23A, 14D), are arbitrary numbers assigned to different morphological types identified in Engberg's and Shipton's (1934a) pottery chart. Such numbers are associated with a chrono-cultural period represented by one or more stages.
5. Additional strings of numbers in small formats, preceded by b (indicating excavation during the 1936/37 season), c (indicating excavation during the 1937/38 season), and d (indicating excavation during the 1938/39 season), P (= Pottery), M (= Miscellaneous), are prefixes for Oriental Institute field numbers given at the time of excavation. Another set of numbers — without prefixes (4736, 4839, 4842, and 4884) — are also Oriental Institute field numbers.

Pottery from before the Early Bronze Age

I have been able to identify only a few sherds datable to a period prior to the Early Bronze Age in the retained assemblage (pl. 43), which I find rather extraordinary and virtually inexplicable, as the assemblage of flint tools (*Chapter 5*) suggests some not inconsiderable activity on the East Slope in those early ceramic-producing periods (i.e., the Late Neolithic through Chalcolithic periods). As those periods are much better represented in the ceramics from Strata XX and XIX (*Megiddo II*) on the mound, their dearth in the East Slope assemblage suggests lesser and only minimal activity there in those periods, although its diminished presence may be due in part to the selective nature of the retained artifact assemblage.

A large ledge handle, long, narrow and crudely fashioned (A16791; pl. 43a), has certain aspects that may distinguish it from similar appurtenances of most Early Bronze Age I pottery, suggesting it dates to sometime within the Late Neolithic (i.e., Pottery Neolithic) through Chalcolithic horizons, as indicated by generic parallels (e.g., Garfinkel 1999, figs. 50:1, 3 [albeit pierced], 4–5, 53:2). An alternate date for this handle comes from a colleague's suggestion[47] that it is a type of very early Early Bronze Age I ledge handle similar to others found in Transjordan (e.g., Hanbury-Tenison 1986, fig. 28:6; Prag 2000, fig. 5:10).

Another likely example of a pre-Early Bronze Age I sherd is a tube handle on a fragment of a vessel wall (A16851; pl. 43b). Tube handles are also known from Early Bronze Age contexts, but are quite rare and tend to be shorter in length. Because of the particularly coarse fabric of this sherd I suggest it should be dated to a pre-Early Bronze Age I period. It is uncertain how to position this sherd, but a likely parallel is found in a horizontally placed tube handle on a bowl from Jericho (Garfinkel 1999, fig. 62:3).

A simple stovepipe neck with tapered rim (34.2593; pl. 43c), of coarse fabric and uneven surface, should also be attributed to an early period. A coil, betraying the method of its construction, is visible internally at the juncture of the neck and rim — something I have failed ever to perceive in a jar of comparable style of the Early Bronze Age I. Another pre-Early Bronze Age I sherd, a portion of a shallow basin with an extraordinarily thick wall, flat, slightly splayed rim, and very thick, rounded, ledge handle (34.2627; pl. 43d) (Engberg and Shipton 1934a, chart: 22E) was found in a late context and ascribed to Stages IV and III. However, its coarse fabric, characterized by evidence of vegetal temper and large grits, are clear indications of its early date. A similar vessel from ʿEn Assawir (Yannai, Lazar-Shorer, and Grosinger 2006, fig. 4.29:13) is dated to the Late Chalcolithic period.

Early Bronze Age I Pottery

A large portion of the retained ceramic assemblage from the East Slope is assigned, on the basis of comparanda, to the Early Bronze Age I. This collection includes a number of styles and wares indicating the East Slope was utilized and occupied during different phases of this period (Braun 1996a, pp. 171–239; 2001; 2012a). The bulk of the assemblage points to occupation in developed and very late phases.

Pottery of the Early Phases of Early Bronze Age I

One very early phase of Early Bronze Age I, identified with Stratum II at Yiftahʾel (Braun 1997), about 20 km north of Megiddo, is represented by only a few sherds of pithoi of a type definitively associated with this chrono-cultural period (e.g., 34.2591/1; pl. 44a). These sherds are notable for their light, buff-colored, gritty, soft fabrics that differ from the better-fired, more dense fabrics of later Early Bronze Age I vessels. Those features as well as the morphology of these sherds are very similar to variations of Type 52 pithoi found at Yiftahʾel and other sites (e.g., Braun 1997, fig. 9.17:1, 4).

No provenience is indicated for these sherds, but the excavators included the pithos rim fragment as Type 16K in their chart (Engberg and Shipton 1934a) and they assigned it to Stages VII and VI. That suggests it was recovered in a deposit they considered relatively early in their sequence. A large, wavy-edged ledge handle of a very similar fabric (A65974; pl. 44b) may also belong to this same horizon. Fragments of similar vessels were ascribed to Stratum XX on the high mound, where Neolithic and Chalcolithic types were also found (*Megiddo II*, pl. 2:12–13[48]). It is difficult to interpret the existence of two sherds as definitive evidence for an occupation in a particular period, but there is additional, albeit somewhat equivocal information that points to activity early in Early Bronze Age I at the site, which may be discerned from a group of specialized bowls of Gray Burnished Ware. How much activity in that period took place on the East Slope remains obscure.

---

[47] I am grateful to an unknown reader of an earlier draft of this work for this suggestion.

[48] This object (A65974) is suspiciously similar to one illustrated in *Megiddo II*, pl. 103: 20 (cf. *Megiddo Tombs*, pl. 81:15), but because it appears on Engberg and Shipton's (1934a) chart, it probably originated on the East Slope.

Gray Burnished Ware

Gray Burnished Ware, a specialized class of pottery and a hallmark of the Early Bronze Age I in the northern region of the southern Levant (Amiran 1969, pp. 47–48; Braun 2012a, pp. 6–11), is crucial for understanding chronology. As certain types are present in the East Slope assemblage, while others are absent, it is possible that indications of its detailed chronological development may be gleaned from this assemblage, notwithstanding the imprecision of available data on findspots of these bowls.

Definition

The presence in the East Slope assemblage of a number of mostly dark-hued bowls of specialized morphology and recognizable, gray-burnished fabric (Engberg and Shipton 1934a, p. 17), known also from other early deposits in and around the Jezreel Valley (e.g., the tell of Afula; Sukenik 1936, p. 151), led G. E. Wright (1937, p. 44), in his seminal publication on the early pottery cultures of the southern Levant, to define the group as "Esdraelon[49] Ware." Bowls of those types are also known as Gray Burnished Ware (Sukenik 1948, p. 21), a name indicating two of its most prominent features.

Gray Burnished Ware is a rather restrictive, relatively homogeneous group of objects defined by only a few obvious attributes.[50] Available data on the chronological and spatial distribution of Gray Burnished Ware indicate it dates to the Early Bronze Age I, that it is basically a regional phenomenon confined to the northwestern portions of the southern Levant, and one that occurred over a span of time. Thus, despite the restrictive definition of Gray Burnished Ware, the group includes a number of morphological types that can be assigned to earlier or later phases within Early Bronze Age I, respectively. I suggest the group as a whole might better termed in the plural ("Gray Burnished Wares"), with each basic type related to a specific time span and associated with a pattern of spatial distribution, but the original term, a long-accepted convention, is maintained here. Some types and sub-types of this group are contemporary, while others apparently represent sequential periods within Early Bronze Age I.

In recent years the *bona fides* of Gray Burnished Ware has been greatly strengthened by petrographic studies (Goren and Zuckerman 2000; Zuckerman 2003a, p. 8) that indicate the likelihood of the different types deriving from a small number of production centers, probably located somewhere in the northern region. Gray Burnished Ware represents a very conscious and deliberate attempt at creating a highly specialized and specific kind of product as the same clays, treated differently, could produce quite disparate results (ibid., p. 8). Today this distinctive ware is understood as a hallmark ceramic of the northern region (Amiran 1969, p. 47; Braun 1989b, pp. 14–15; Braun 1996a, p. 184; Braun 2012a).

The widely disparate geographic distribution of the types has chronological associations and indicates a rather widespread pattern of distribution. At least one exponent of the earliest type, which had the widest pattern of dispersion, is found in sites in northern Israel, the Palestinian territories on the West Bank, and the northern Jordan Valley and its fringes in Israel and Jordan. This ware has not as yet been reported in Syria, but to the northeast one example is known from Kamid el-Loz in the Bakʾaa Valley of Lebanon (Bertemes 1986, pl. 14:3); others were found farther to the south in the Huleh Valley at Tel Teʾo (Eisenberg 2001, fig. 7.2). Farther north the type is known at Kabri (Scheftelowitz 2002, fig. 5.3:4–6), and as far west as Tel Megadim (Sam Wolff, pers. comm.). On the west it is known as far south as Palmahim (Braun 1996a, p. 184). To the east it is found as far south as the Wady Qelt (i.e., at "Herodian Jericho") where it debouches into the Jordan Valley just south of Jericho (Pritchard 1958, pl. 57:29–35, 40–42). In later periods variations

[49] "Esdraelon" is the New Testament name for the Jezreel Valley, in which lie the sites of Megiddo and Afula, where quantities of these vessels were found in excavations during the 1930s.

[50] This discussion follows Rice's (1987, pp. 286–87) definition of traditional wares, which can be broadly or narrowly defined dependent upon the purpose of classification. Gray Burnished Ware is narrowly defined by contrast with other, contemporary groups of ceramics such as "Red Burnished Ware," which is an extraordinarily broad category of objects of virtually any morphology possessing a single eponymous feature.

on the earliest type, as well as other morphological types of this ware, were significantly more limited in their distribution to the region in and around the Jezreel Valley.

Chrono-cultural Associations

Wright (1936; 1937) originally consigned Gray Burnished Ware to a Late Chalcolithic horizon, very possibly under the influence of Engberg and Shipton's (1934a) Chalcolithic attribution of the East Slope pottery. However, in a major revision of his chronological paradigm for early south Levantine ceramics, Wright (1958), basing his opinion primarily on tomb assemblages, latterly reassigned the group to his Early Bronze Age I. Today that opinion has a broad consensus, especially after the excavation of Yiftah'el II (Braun 1997), which yielded no Chalcolithic pottery and an abundance of an early type of Gray Burnished Ware.

Typology of Gray Burnished Ware

Wright (1958), mostly from his knowledge of tomb and mixed chrono-cultural deposits (e.g., the pottery from Afula; Sukenik 1936, 1948), discerned four morphological types of Gray Burnished Ware. Despite a lack of available stratigraphic information at the time of writing, he suggested, almost intuitively, that the different types have chronological significance. Decades of research have shown Wright's observations to be basically sound, although some corrections and additions[51] to his paradigm are necessary. In particular, it is now possible to postulate the existence of additional types and sub-types that augment his work and make it more sensitive to chronological and other disparities. It should be noted, however, that these types are somewhat broadly defined and that within each are considerable variations in features such as fabric color, slip color, quality of burnishing, and morphology. Such differences are entirely in accord with pottery production in these early periods with output from different workshops (Goren and Zuckerman 2000) with a substantial time trajectory.

Type 1 Bowls

Wright's (1958) Type 1 bowls share certain morphological characteristics that define them aside from the specialized treatment of their fabrics. They are invariably carinated or appear so, and have flat protuberances at their external lines of carination. Most are of dark hues, gray to black, but others range in color from mustard yellow to brown to creamy white. Morphological differences appear to be of import to understanding the archaeological record, while the issue of color seems to be less significant and likely due to lack of standardization in firing practices (Braun 1997, p. 54; 2012a). I believe there are three significant, discernible, morphological sub-types of Type 1 (fig. 25), of which only one, Sub-type 1c, is found in the East Slope assemblage.

Sub-type 1a

Bowls of sub-type 1a are carinated and have flat, widely spaced protuberances along their external lines of carination, or, alternately, have S-shaped profiles that appear, by virtue of these protrusions, to be carinated. Only a single example of this type was found on the high mound at Megiddo, in fill of Level J-4, where it is likely to be out of context (Greenberg 2006, fig. 10.2:5[52]); none has been found on the East Slope. Examples of this sub-type in other colored fabrics, painted red and sometimes also burnished (e.g., Braun 1997, fig. 9.4:1, 3), should be considered contemporary imitations of Gray Burnished Ware. Some few examples of Gray Burnished Ware and its imitations are set on high, fenestrated pedestal bases.

[51] Additional, less normative, rarely encountered types (e.g., Sukenik 1948, pl. 2:22–27) appear also to belong to this ware category but none of those is included in the assemblage of the East Slope.

[52] This vessel is somewhat unusual for the diminutive size of its protuberance. Otherwise, it appears to be a good example of this early type, especially in the dark, mottled hues of its slip and the high quality of its burnish.

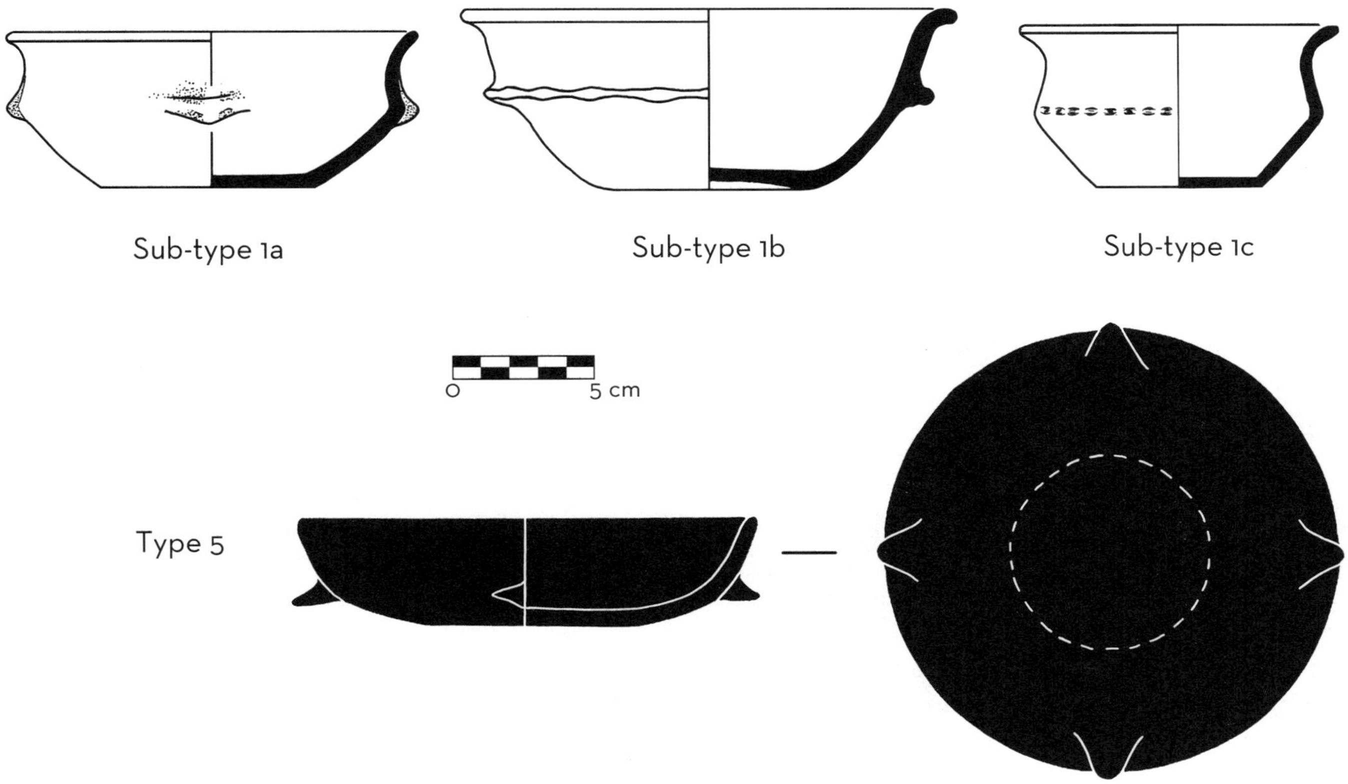

Figure 25. Gray Burnished Ware: Idealized examples of early Types 1 and 5

Sub-type 1b

Sub-type 1b is distinguished by its carinated or carinated-appearing profile resulting from the addition of an external sinuous line of closely spaced, flattened protuberances at the widest part of the body. This sub-type also includes fenestrated, pedestaled examples.

Sub-type 1c

Sub-type 1c (pls. 45a–b, h, and 46a–b), while similar to Sub-type 1b, is distinguished from the latter by its much more subtle adornment at the point of carination; a rope-like decoration is barely emphasized in very low relief. There seems to be considerable variation in this group; one rare example of this decoration is on a simple, curved bowl that lacks even a hint of carination (34.2603; pls. 45b, 46b), while another has a double line of decoration (34.2603/12; pl. 45h). The former type is, so far as I am aware, unparalleled, while the latter is rare but has a parallel at nearby Afula (Gal and Covello-Paran 1996, fig. 4:9).

Type 2 Bowls

Wright's Type 2 bowls seem to be only tangentially related to the other types of Gray Burnished Ware. They are virtually site specific or have a very limited geographic distribution within the mountainous region of biblical Samaria (Amiran 1969, p. 47). Most examples come from tombs in the area of Tell el-Farᶜah North and have notably coarser fabrics and are much less well made than examples of Gray Burnished Ware, suggesting to me they are not, *stricto sensu*, true exponents of it. I suggest that Type 2 bowls at best are coarse approximations of bowls of Type 1. A fenestrated and pedestaled Type 2 bowl from Tell el-Farᶜah North (Amiran 1969, photo 37) illustrates the basic differences between Type 2 and Type 1 bowls. It is crudely shaped, has rope-like decoration instead of protuberances on a straight-sided (not carinated) profile, and exhibits non-contiguous burnish marks. By contrast, Type 1 bowls are notable for the high quality of their continuous burnishing. There are no bowls of Type 2 in the East Slope assemblage.

Type 3 Bowls

Type 3 bowls are distinguished by their carinated profile (pls. 45c–g, 46c–l) and lack of spaced protuberances. Most are simply carinated, but some examples have an additional raised line that enhances the carination (pls 45f,46h, l). Rims, rounded or tapered, vary in this group from slightly to widely splayed. Most examples appear to have been burnished or polished. Bowls of similar forms are also found in lighter-colored fabrics; some, apparently imitations, are only red slipped but others are similarly slipped and also burnished.

Type 4 Bowls

Bowls of Type 4 morphology are generally small with simply curving profiles and horizontal rows of conical protuberances just below their rims (pl. 47). Definitive exponents are gray and burnished and have inverted rims (pls. 47d–f, 48a, g). They appear to be few in number and I suggest they represent a specialized and limited production. True Gray Burnished Ware bowls of this morphology, as Types 1 and 3, appear to have been slipped with slurries of the same pastes as the fabrics from which they were fashioned. A rare variation on Type 4, preserved in a small fragment from the East Slope, has one conical protuberance adjacent to another in the shape of an elongated, horizontal bar (pl. 47d; Engberg and Shipton 1934a, fig. 6:18b).

There are in the East Slope assemblage (pls. 47a–c, 48b–f) and in assemblages from numerous additional sites in the region, many examples of small bowls of similar morphology. While some are of gray fabrics, most others were fashioned of clays that when fired were buff colored. They do not exhibit the same high quality as Type 4 bowls and are not, *stricto sensu*, examples of Gray Burnished Ware (Engberg and Shipton 1934a, p. 19), but should probably be considered imitations of this ware.[53] Some of these last have thin, very dark slips, others are mottled red and/or brown slipped and sometimes polished.

Numerous examples have mottled exterior color schemes of red, brown, and black and occasional examples of them may have been burnished, although that is difficult to determine as preservation of the bowls is generally poor. Some bowls of this basic form were neither slipped nor burnished (e.g., pl. 47b–d). The morphological type, distinctively south Levantine, is basically a hallmark of the northern region, but some few examples of rounded bowls with similar knobs are found in the south (e.g., Wampler 1947, pl. 52:1124) and occasional examples are known in more or less contemporary contexts in Egypt, in pottery and in stone (Engberg and Shipton 1934a, fig. 16:K; van den Brink and Braun 2006).

Type 5 Bowls

A fifth Gray Burnished Ware type bowl (fig. 25), unknown to Wright, seems to be contemporary to Type 1, to which it is morphologically related. Although it has a shallow, curving profile, midway on its wall are four flat, tapering protuberances placed at equidistant intervals. Type 5 bowls have gray fabrics covered by black, burnished slips. What appear to be imitations of this Gray Burnished Ware type are found in different color fabrics, slipped brown or red and not burnished. There are no examples of this ware found at Jezreel Valley sites; the type's distribution appears to be more northerly (Braun 2012a, in press), with one red-slipped example from Aktanit in Lebanon (Amiran 1969, photo 32).

---

[53] While this definition seems likely, it is not provable as most bowls of this general morphology are of non-Gray Burnished Ware fabrics, which could mean that the form was imitated in Gray Burnished Ware.

Additional Types of Gray Burnished Ware

In addition to the five types noted above, there are rare examples of vessels of different morphology produced in the same burnished fabric. They include a rounded bowl with strap handle (Gal and Covello-Paran 1996, figs. 4:16, 7:c), a tiny, cup-like bowl with small lug handle found by me in a construction dump of fill derived from the tell of Afula, and at least two Type 1c bowls with double carination lines; one from the East Slope (34.2603/12; pl. 45h), the other from Afula (Gal and Covello-Paran 1996, fig. 4:9). As these types are represented by fragments and have no good stratigraphic ascriptions, their relative dating remains obscure. A fenestrated, pedestaled, rounded bowl from Nahal Tavor (Amiran 1969, photo 36), dark brown and highly burnished, seems to be another variant.

On the Relative Chronology of Gray Burnished Ware Types

Wright's suggestion that Type 1 bowls appeared earlier than his Types 3 and 4 was a particularly perspicacious observation, made when there was virtually no reliable information available on stratified pottery deposits; most examples came from tomb contexts that have chronological ranges of unknown duration. Type 1 bowls have since been discerned in stratified deposits at ʿEn Esur (Yannai 2006),[54] where they are in contexts definitively earlier than Types 3 and 4. Types 5 and 1 are found in identical stratigraphic contexts at Tel Teʾo, while the presence of Type 1 and no other Gray Burnished Ware types at Yiftahʾel II indicates its association with an early phase of Early Bronze Age I. This observation is further verified by the complete absence of Gray Burnished Ware and other hallmark early Early Bronze Age I types at Tell es-Sultan, ancient Jericho.[55]

Sub-types of Type 1 at Megiddo

Significantly, there are no examples of Sub-types 1a and 1b Gray Burnished Ware in the East Slope assemblage, which supports the interpretation of minimal evidence for activity in an early phase of Early Bronze Age I there (see above). There is, in fact, only minimal evidence for any activity on the site in that period. With the exception of the Yiftahʾel II–type pithos fragments (34.2591/1; see above), the only additional pottery typical to that horizon is a sherd of Sub-type 1b found in Level J-4[56] of the renewed excavations on the high mound (see above). There are, however, several examples of Type 1c in the East Slope assemblage, which suggests the possibility that this sub-type may be assigned to a different chronological niche. Included in this group is one fragment from Tomb 9, erroneously identified by the excavators as Khirbet Kerak Ware (*Megiddo Tombs*, pl. 10:1), and three small fragments picked up on the surface of Area BB (Braun 1985, fig. 36).

If, as I suspect, Sub-type 1c is a somewhat later chronological development, its muted, plastic decoration may be a degeneration of the more pronounced protuberances that adorn Sub-type 1b. Notably, at Yiftahʾel there is only a single example of a vessel with what appears to be similar morphology of Sub-type 1c (Braun 1997, fig. 9.2:7) but its decoration is notably better defined than on the examples of Sub-type 1c from Megiddo. At ʿEn Esur the closest parallels in the early level of Early Bronze Age I, contemporary with Yiftahʾel II, all appear to belong to Sub-type 1b (e.g., Yannai 2006, figs. 4.49, 4.65:2–6, 4.67:1–6), while Sub-type 1c seems to be missing in the Gray Burnished Ware repertoire of that site. As there is so little pottery of that early period in the East Slope assemblage it seems likely that the Sub-type 1c bowls on the East

---

[54] Zuckerman (2003d, p. 58) also cites petrographic differences between the various types.

[55] I refer in particular to holemouth vessels that have rope-like decoration made by diagonal slashes on applied bands of clay (e.g., Pritchard 1958, pl. 27:2–9; Braun in press) on or near their rims. The absence at Tell es-Sultan of these types, as well as a complete lack of Gray Burnished Ware, indicates a chronological gap in occupation in early phases of Early Bronze Age I.

[56] Level J4 refers to Tel Aviv University's renewed excavations stratigraphic designation (*Megiddo III*; *Megiddo IV*) of the original excavators' Stratum XIX temple in Area BB (*Megiddo II*). The preponderance of evidence suggests it should be dated to a late phase within Early Bronze Age I.

Slope probably date to a later period. None was found at ʿEn Shadud, and thus it seems likely the type was already extinct by the time the excavated area of ʿEn Shadud was first occupied in Early Bronze Age I. While it could be argued that ʿEn Shadud was merely not a recipient of the type, that seems little likely as the only additional site where Sub-type 1c bowls are found is at nearby Afula (table 1), which has yielded numerous ceramic parallels with ʿEn Shadud.[57]

Table 1. Gray Burnished Ware types from Megiddo and select parallels

Type	*Megiddo Area J/BB*	*Tel Qashish*	*ʿEn Shadud*	*Afula*	*ʿEn Esur*	*Bet Yerah*
1a	Greenberg 2006, fig. 10.2:5	—	—	Sukenik 1948, pl. 2:1–3, 12	Yannai, Lazar-Shorer, and Grosinger 2006, figs. 4.51:1–2	S. Paz 2006, figs. 3.35:2–4, 3.37:2; Y. Paz 2006, figs. 4.3:3, 4.6:7
1b	Joffe 2000, fig. 8.1:12	Zuckerman 2003c, fig. 17:8	—	Sukenik 1948, pl. 2:4–6, 8–11	Yannai, Lazar-Shorer, and Grosinger 2006, figs. 4.65:3–6, 4.67:1–6	—
1c	Joffe 2000, fig. 8.1:3(?)	Zuckerman 2003c, fig. 23:1–2	—	Sukenik 1948, pl. 2:7 (Stratum VI); Gal and Covello-Paran 1996, fig. 4:7, 9	—	—
2	—	—	—	—	—	—
3	—	—	—	Sukenik 1948, pl. 2:13–21 (Stratum VI); Gal and Covello-Paran 1996, fig. 4:13	—	—
3-P[a]	—	Zuckerman 2003c, fig. 17:9–11	Braun 1985, fig. 19:15	—	Yannai, Lazar-Shorer, and Grosinger 2006, figs. 4.72:10–11, 4.75:9, 12	—
4	—	Zuckerman 2003c, fig. 17:12	—	—	Yannai, Lazar-Shorer, and Grosinger 2006, fig. 4.50.5	—
4-P[a]	—	Zuckerman 2003c, fig. 17:7	Braun 1985: fig. 18:8–9	(Stratum VI) Gal and Covello-Paran 1996, fig. 4:18	Yannai, Lazar-Shorer, and Grosinger 2006, figs. 4.52:13–18, 4.75:8	—

[a] As there are relatively few parallels in gray burnished fabrics, the designation "P" refers to morphological parallels in non-gray fabrics, painted red, brown, or gray, or mottled and not burnished (Braun 1985, p. 61).

Type 3 in the East Slope Assemblage

The lack of precision for the provenience of Type 3 bowls from the East Slope assemblage does not allow for any definitive chronological associations for them but their presence indicates a broad degree of contemporaneousness with specific occupations at Tel Qashish (Zuckerman 2003c, fig. 23), ʿEn Shadud (Braun 1985, fig. 19:10), Qiryat Ata (Golani 2003, fig. 4.25:5), and ʿEn Esur (Yannai, Lazar-Shorer, and Grosinger 2006, fig. 4.61:1–6). Several intact examples of these bowls were found in tombs on the East Slope (e.g., pl. 49).

[57] Incidentally, this information suggests the likelihood of a continuity in occupation of the tell of Afula throughout the period of production of Gray Burnished Ware (Sukenik 1936; 1948; Gal and Covello-Paran 1996).

Type 4 in the East Slope Assemblage

The chronological associations of Type 4 in the East Slope remain somewhat obscure as information on them comes mostly from fragmentary examples lacking good contexts, while only a few examples of this morphological type are genuine exponents of Gray Burnished Ware. Most morphologically similar bowls, including many I have observed at Megiddo and other sites (e.g., Tel Qashish, Qiryat Ata, ʿEn Esur, and ʿEn Shadud), display neither of the group's characteristic traits and are less skillfully made than their Gray Burnished Ware counterparts. What is unclear is whether Zuckerman's (2003d, p. 59) assumption that non-Gray Burnished Ware bowls sharing the morphology of Type 4 are absolutely contemporary with Gray Burnished Ware examples, as there is no stratigraphic proof for that claim.

Perhaps it is significant that the Tomb 903 Lower deposit (i.e., occupation) yielded a number of Type 4 Gray Burnished Ware bowls (*Megiddo Tombs*, pl. 3:31–32; e.g., pl. 48:2–4) as well as non-Gray Burnished Ware bowls of similar morphology. Bowls of the morphology of Type 4 that I have been able to verify as true Gray Burnished Ware are relatively rare and include examples from only two sites, Megiddo (pls. 47:4–6, 48:5) and Afula (Gal and Covello-Paran 1996, figs. 4:18, 7:b). That could suggest some special association between those communities and their fabrication associated with a particular production center. It might also be indicative of limited production within a short time span. As there appear to be so many more examples of non-Gray Burnished Ware bowls of this morphology, it is not inconceivable that some or perhaps many of them post-date the end of production of Gray Burnished Ware.

Chronological Range of Gray Burnished Ware within the Early Bronze Age I and Its Relation to the East Slope

What is the significance of Gray Burnished Ware in the East Slope assemblage? That is difficult to understand as the length of the chronological range of this phenomenon remains unclear. Zuckerman (2003d, p. 59) has suggested that Gray Burnished Ware lasted throughout the Early Bronze I Age (her EB IA and EB IB[58]). However, that seems highly unlikely as the period is thought to have lasted for half a millennium or more (Braun 2001; 2009; Braun and Gophna 2004, pp. 220–25[59]; Braun et al. 2013). That is an inordinately long time span for continued production in a tradition that includes only a few bowl types, and for which there appears to be no parallel in the history of pottery production in the southern Levant. Significant for the occupation and utilization of the East Slope is that, on the one hand, the lack of Sub-types 1a and 1b there de-emphasizes human activity in the Yiftahʾel II period. On the other hand, the presence of Sub-type 1c suggests significantly more activity there during a short but later time span within Early Bronze Age I. The appearance of Types 3 and 4 suggests later and probably continued activity, but they seem unlikely to indicate activity in the very latest phase of Early Bronze Age I, which is found in other ceramic types (see below).

More Advanced Phases: Later Early Bronze I Pottery

The bulk of the Early Bronze I ceramic assemblage dates to later, post-Yiftahʾel II phases. It includes a number of different types of vessels, some of which belong to classes recognized as "wares" (Braun 2012a). Represented are morphological types that appear, on the basis of parallels, to indicate occupation over a considerable span of time. Some of these types are contemporary to Gray Burnished Ware; others date to later periods and suggest the East Slope saw continued activity from late in Early Bronze Age I into Early Bronze Age II. Following are some general remarks on the different features of this collection.

---

[58] This suggested division into two sub-periods, "EB IA" and "EB IB," shared by many scholars, seems much too simplistic a framework for the period; elsewhere I have suggested a more detailed division of pottery types associated with different phases of the sequence of Early Bronze Age I (Braun 1996; 2012b).

[59] Golani (2004, pp. 46–48) has even suggested a significantly longer, 800-year duration for this period, which if correct would make such a scenario even less likely. However, there are serious objections to such an early date for the beginning of Early Bronze Age I; see Braun and Gophna 2004.

Quality of Wares

The pottery from the late phases of Early Bronze Age I can be somewhat arbitrarily divided into three general groupings that recognize differences in potters' skills. They suggest the likelihood of their origins in very different workshops and that they were intended for diverse functions. Simply stated, there are three broad classes of wares: those made by skilled potters, which may be called "fine wares"; those of middling quality made by potters with significant skills but who did not pay very particular attention to a vessel's finish; and vessels carelessly formed and finished, for which minimal skills were required in their fabrication. Vessels of the first class were found in tombs — which indicates an importance attached to funerary offerings — but they are also included in the non-mortuary-related finds from the East Slope assemblage, as are the other two classes of pottery.

Features of the Later Early Bronze Age I Pottery: Fabrics, Technology, and Quality

Most of the non-Gray Burnished Ware ceramic artifacts retained from the East Slope of this period are of light-colored fabrics, often slipped in red and sometimes burnished or polished.[60] While it is impossible to know the precise degree of representativeness of the East Slope sample retained, from my experience in studying the pottery of other sites such as ʿEn Shadud and the publications of Qiryat Ata and Tel Qashish, it would appear to accurately reflect a goodly percentage, if not the bulk of material retrieved during the excavation. The term "red" is somewhat misleading as it is a convention for designating a wide range of the color spectrum from reddish-brown through dark reds to maroon and even orange. All these hues probably resulted from ferruginous clays that when fired under oxidizing conditions tend to produce such colors dependent upon numerous variables (Rice 1987, pp. 109, 335).

Some red-slipped vessels, including burnished examples, seem also to be of consistent shades with little or no variation in their external appearances. That suggests a likelihood, at least in some ceramic production, of improvements in firing technology. The reasons for this remain unknown, but I speculate they are related to the introduction of kiln technology that could account for greater control over the appearance of the final products.[61]

The suggestion in the assemblage, *grosso modo*, is of a basic dichotomy of finer objects and vessels of lesser quality, with the former particularly in evidence in small vessels, especially those slipped and burnished or smoothed and polished. A superior or luxury class of pottery is loosely defined by symmetry of forms and attention to details of external finishes in slips and burnishing. The finest non-Gray Burnished Ware types are small, closed, spouted forms, called "teapots," and medium-sized bowls. Other vessels are nicely finished but cannot be considered as luxury objects, while a third category is of crudely fashioned objects such as small lamp-bowls from the East Slope tombs (e.g., *Megiddo Tombs*, pls. 3:9–11; 4:6, 31, and some larger vessels). Little attention was paid to their external surfaces, some of which preserve impressions of potters' fingerprints.

Red Slip "Wares" — Unburnished

"Unburnished" is a very broad definition that includes a great deal of the pottery in the later Early Bronze Age I assemblage from the East Slope. The term "ware" in this sense should be understood merely as a generalized recognition of the most popular type of external decoration and not in the sense of specialized production such as Gray Burnished Ware. I eschew the term as I have explained elsewhere (Braun 2012a). Red slips on large vessels tended to be applied as relatively thin coats, sometimes in stylized ways (see below, *Grain Wash/Band Slip*) and sometimes seemingly with less care. Certain medium-size and smaller

[60] The distinction between these two types of treatments is subtle and mostly arbitrary. I suggest that burnishing refers to examples with a high to glossy sheen, while polishing leaves a smooth but matte-like finish without the luster of burnishing.

[61] Unfortunately, to date, despite more than a century of excavation in the southern Levant, no evidence whatsoever has been found of an Early Bronze I Age potter's workshop or firing installation.

vessels were more carefully slipped, apparently with coats of what appears to have been thick slurries, the application of which produced surfaces of a single desired color after firing.

Most everted-rim vessels appear to have been treated in this manner, as are medium-size wavy-edged ledge handles (probably from medium-size jars or large bowls). A noticeable trait of some bowls is the lack of slips on their interior surfaces; internally, many have only bands of red just below their rims (e.g., pl. 51d, f, h–i, k–l). Such treatment indicates slips were basically intended for decorative effect rather than to be functional. This group includes vessels with mottled coloration, which appears as patches of lighter and darker hues on the same vessel. It includes bowls of Gray Burnished Ware Type 4 morphology as well as storage jars, simpler bowls, and numerous ledge handles from large specimens of these last. While most of these cannot be considered luxury items, they can be designated as a "second best" class of wares, mostly characterized by some attention to details in form and the addition of slips. However, the quality of finish on these vessels does not attain that in vessels that were slipped and also burnished.

Red Slip "Wares" — Burnished and Polished

Burnish and polish seem to be applied exclusively to small vessels in the later Early Bronze Age I, primarily bowls and jars, some spouted. The evidence of such vessels recovered outside the tombs derives mostly from small fragments, especially spouts and small ledge handles. Some examples are highly burnished such that they have a high sheen (e.g., pls. 55a, 56i), while others appear to be more smoothed and only lightly polished (e.g., pl. 55d) to give them an evenly coated surface only slightly smoother than that of wares that were merely slipped. Burnishing of these red-colored vessels, contrary to that applied to Gray Burnished Ware, was usually done with a small, narrow tool that left smooth and shiny, very often non-contiguous paths interspersed with narrow, un-burnished gaps. Thus, despite morphological similarities between Gray Burnished Ware vessels and some red-burnished examples, there is a marked difference in the burnishing process, suggesting these two categories of pots are products of disparate traditions.

Fabrics of most of these vessels appear to be similar to those of non-burnished items, which may be generally described as relatively coarse-looking because of what appears to be a significant quantity of temper, grits of different sizes and colors. Most appear to be lithic particles or grog, with only two exceptions that indicate the addition of large quantities of vegetal temper (see below, *Egyptian-style Vessels*). In many instances, burnishing was successfully used to cover coarse-looking fabrics. There are, however, a few notable exceptions from the tombs and in the assemblage from the East Slope. One is a bowl of particularly well-levigated fabric, finely fashioned, slipped and burnished externally and on its internal rim (pl. 52d). Although the burnishing produced a high sheen, the gaps between the burnish marks are highly visible.

What is additionally notable is that this particular bowl, as well as another of similar quality, was only slipped externally; inside, the consistency of its smooth, cream-colored surface is actually marred by a few smeared drips of slip that the potter obviously did not feel necessary to remove prior to firing. Another vessel with similar fabric is apparently the body of a gourd jar with a wall of even thickness (A16858; pl. 55d). It is notable for its beautifully symmetrical, squat, globular form and heavy, finely smoothed, lightly polished external slip. In form it is likely to have been similar to examples recovered from the tombs on the East Slope (Engberg and Shipton 1934a, chart, column 26) and numerous others from tombs near ʿEn Esur (i.e., Assawir; Dothan 1970, fig. 3, esp. nos. 12 and 14 with rounded bases), but it is much more finely fashioned and has a completely rounded base, which seems to be rare for this basic form.

Grain Wash/Band Slip

Grain wash, or band slip, decoration, alternately identified by one of these names by most scholars, includes a number of techniques and styles that form a continuum of decorative elements, all of which involve a layer of thinly and unevenly applied paint that allows some portions of the surface, always of a lighter fabric, to remain visible. One technique is that made by clearly defined strokes of a broad brush through which some of the surface of the unadorned fabric remains exposed (pl. 50a–c). Another technique takes the form of groups of parallel stripes juxtaposed at various acute angles, which sometimes gives the impression of bundles of straw (pl. 50d–e). In other instances the bands of paint are diagonally arranged in a lattice pattern (pl. 50f), while the most simple type is a more or less careless attempt at covering most of the surface of a vessel with no definitive pattern to the brush strokes (pl. 50g–h). Grain wash is sometimes confused with broad definitive bands or stripes painted in a lattice pattern (e.g., Nigro, Polcaro, and Sala 2005, p. 177) that leaves rhombs unpainted between straight, diagonal lines. That type of decoration, popular in Early Bronze Age II–III (e.g., Getzov 2006, fig. 3.48:10, 13) and sometimes erroneously identified as band slip (e.g., Y. Paz 2006b, p. 281), may have been a late development that grew out of this type of decoration.

Especially in the archetypical version of this type of painting (i.e., broad, vertical stripes) the effect is suggestive of wood grain, hence one name for this style. The other, equally descriptive name is "band slip," with the word "slip" suggesting less than full coverage of the surface. In general, large vessels were painted with broad vertical bands while smaller vessels were decorated with thinner lines. The paint for these bands ranges in color from brick red to orange, brown, and dark gray, all of which appear to have been dependent upon the firing process. Numerous sherds of such decorated vessels are found in the East Slope assemblage, but all are quite fragmentary (pl. 50a–h).

Light Stripes Left to Drip on Dark-colored Wares

Dripped stripes on dark wares is an unusual style of decorative treatment made by applying relatively thin, vertical stripes with a crude brush (pl. 50i–k). The results left roughly parallel, albeit not very straight lines of light color on dark surfaces. The paint applied was usually runny and often the stripes ended in a drip pattern. Until recently I believed this type of decoration was specific to Megiddo, but one example of it is reported from an Early Bronze Age II assemblage at Bet Yerah (Greenberg and Eisenberg 2006, fig. 5.82:7), where it is probably residual. Some examples have buff-colored stripes on dark gray, while others have light-gray lines on dark-red surfaces. Quite possibly this style was the production of a single workshop during a relatively short span of time. Recently a single sherd of this type has appeared in a late Protodynastic context at the site of Tell el Farkha in the Nile Delta (Marcin Carnowicz, Institute of Archaeology, Jagiellonian University, Krakow, pers. comm.).

Red-striped Decoration

Occasional sherds in the East Slope assemblage have narrow, apparently vertical red stripes placed at large intervals (e.g., pl. 50l). The quality of these sherds and especially the fabrics suggests they belong to vessels dated to Early Bronze Age I.

Incised Decoration

A number of sherds, especially strap handles, were decorated with short, usually oblique or parallel incisions prior to firing (pl. 54a–b, e–f; table 2). This was a popular form of adorning vessels, most of which appear to have been red slipped, though some were also burnished. In addition, a small group of bowls was adorned with graceful, wavy lines incised into exterior walls of these vessels (pl. 51k–m).

Table 2. Handles with incised decoration: Select parallels

Tel Qashish	*ʿEn Shadud*	*Afula*	*ʿEn Esur*	*Bet Yerah*	*Qiryat Ata*
Zuckerman 2003c, fig. 22:7–8	Braun 1985, pl. 10:H, I	Sukenik 1948, pl. 8:12–19	Yannai, Lazar-Shorer, and Grosinger 2006, fig. 4.60:25	Greenberg and Eisenberg 2006, fig. 5.76:18	Golani 2003, figs. 4.10:1–2, 4, 4.11:1

Non-Slipped Plain Wares

The group of non-slipped plain wares is represented by only a small collection of sherds in the East Slope assemblage (e.g., pls. 49; 53b–c; 54j, l, o–p; 60a–b; 61a–c, f). It is difficult, without knowing the representativeness of the sample, to know whether it is an accurate reflection of the entire assemblage encountered. It includes a few handles and a number of small, crudely fashioned, shallow bowls with simple, tapering rims; some, with soot-covered rims, were obviously lamps. Also common are holemouth fragments of coarse, friable brown fabrics that were not slipped. They appear to be a specialized production likely related to their functions. Some of them may have been cooking pots but that is uncertain as the pieces retained do not seem to bear evidence of firing that would indicate their functions.

Pot Types

Small Rounded Bowls

Small rounded bowls (sometimes labeled "hemispherical") with simple, tapered rims are common throughout the Early Bronze Age. They are represented in the East Slope assemblage by numerous fragments (e.g., pl. 51a–b). Some are plain, others were slipped and sometimes burnished, while several examples have soot stains indicating their use as lamps. This type of vessel is ubiquitous throughout the Early Bronze Age and it is thus difficult to ascribe any from the East Slope to a specific chronological context.

Guttered- and Everted-rim Vessels

The group of vessels with guttered and everted rims includes a variation on a type of thickened rim with a narrow pinched or guttered lip. Potters created them for a variety of small, medium, and large, closed and open shapes (e.g., fig. 26; pl. 51c–m; table 3). Most examples of these vessels were slipped red, with some of the finer ones having heavy slips of consistent dark-red hues. Vessels with this type of rim appear to be of different sizes; most if not all may be considered as of good, but not the finest quality. Several examples have a graceful horizontal wavy line decoration on their exteriors (pl. 51k–m), incised prior to slipping, which is, so far as I am aware, paralleled only at Afula. There were numerous examples at ʿEn Shadud of vessels of these types (e.g., Braun 1985, fig. 16). Internally most of these vessels were left without any slip except for a wide band carelessly applied just below their rims. The distribution of this vessel type seems to be within the Jezreel and Zebulon Valleys and as far as the western end of the Megiddo Pass at ʿEn Esur. Several small, delicate examples have ledge handles (e.g., pl. 51d–e).

Table 3. Guttered and everted rim vessels: Select Early Bronze Age parallels

Tel Qashish	*ʿEn Shadud, Strata II-I*	*Afula, Late Chalcolithic*[a]	*Afula, Stratum VI*	*Qiryat Ata, Strata III-II*	*ʿEn Esur, Late EB I*
—	Braun 1985, fig. 22	Sukenik 1948, pl. 6:20–35, including incised decoration	Gal and Covello-Paran 1996, fig. 4:6	Golani 2003, fig. 4.1:16–19	Yannai, Lazar-Shorer, and Grosinger 2006, fig. 4.53

[a] This is now recognized as Early Bronze Age I.

Figure 26. Profiles of vessels with guttered and everted rims (after *Megiddo Tombs*, pl. 3:12–20). No scale

Inverted-rim Bowls

Inverted-rim bowls appear toward the end of Early Bronze Age I and continue on into Early Bronze Age II (pl. 52c). Their rims tend to be wide and sometimes almost carinated where they slope inward. The morphology of these bowls, similar to some of the early types of Early Bronze Age II platters (see below), presages the appearance of this latter type and may well be its ultimate inspiration.

Large Shallow, Carinated Bowls

Large carinated bowls are shallow with short, almost vertical upper walls ending in tapered rims (pl. 52a, c). The type appears toward the end of Early Bronze Age I and seems to presage the appearance of platters, similar in form but larger and shallower, in Early Bronze Age II.

Wide Flat-rim Bowls

Wide bowls with larger, thickened and flattened rims atop relatively shallow, rounded forms were often slipped and sometimes burnished externally, but usually unadorned internally (pl. 52b, d–e). They are found in advanced phases of the Early Bronze I Age and continue on into Early Bronze Age II. An unusual feature in this group, which includes some extremely well-levigated and highly burnished examples (e.g., pl. 52c), is that the slipping and burnishing were applied only externally, while interiors of these vessels were left unslipped and unburnished. One particularly fine example even has drops of red color, apparently unintentionally splashed onto the internal, smooth buff surface of its highly levigated fabric (pl. 52d).

Basins and Vats

Basin or vats (sometimes designated as kraters) have rims similar to rims of holemouth jars (pls. 51n; 61d, e), although they are open rather than closed types. The excavators (Engberg and Shipton 1934a) termed them "holemouth bowls," which is in my opinion an apt name. Rims of large basins are also found in the collection, but with a single exception (pl. 51n) all are very fragmentary. Illustrated in plate 53 are four examples of a small collection of fragments with large, short spouts (table 4). Most appear to have been red slipped or covered with grain wash-style decoration; some larger examples had ledge handles. Occasional examples have dark gray slips.

Table 4. Spouted basins: Select Early Bronze Age parallels

Tel Qashish	*ʿEn Shadud, Strata II–I*	*Beth Shan Stratum M3 (late EB I)*	*Qiryat Ata, Strata III–II*	*ʿEn Esur, Late Early Bronze Age I*
Ben-Tor, Bonfil, and Zuckerman 2003, fig. 15:4	Braun 1985, fig. 18	Sukenik 1948, pl. 6:20–35, including incised decoration	Golani 2003, figs. 4.3:8–13, 4.4	Yannai, Lazar-Shorer, and Grosinger 2006, figs. 4.34:11, 4.75:16, 17

Jugs and Juglets

Numerous fragments of jugs and juglets (pl. 54m, o–p), usually represented by handles (pl. 54g–l), are found in the East Slope assemblage, although few examples, including the juglet from B/V/1 found in situ (see in pls. 31, 34), were well preserved. Unfortunately, I have been unable to locate that particular object for additional illustration, but it appears to have had a somewhat squat, rounded body, a high loop handle, and probably a large, tapered, flaring rim typical of Early Bronze Age I (for examples of the type, see *Megiddo Tombs*, pls. 3:6, 5:2; Amiran 1969, pl. 9:22; similar to pl. 54o–p). Jugs and juglets are highly under-represented in archaeological publications of occupations, presumably because of their fragility; only fragments are generally recovered from occupation contexts and they are rarely illustrated. However, the popularity of these types in the Early Bronze Age I in all contexts is attested to by their presence in tombs of the period, often in great quantities.

Gourd Vessels (amphoriskoi)

Gourd vessels, also called *amphoriskoi*, are found often and sometimes in quantity in tombs. Only fragments of these squat vessels were recovered from the East Slope (pl. 55b–c), but a nearly complete example from Tomb 903 Upper (*Megiddo Tombs*, pl. 3:7; pl. 55:1) illustrates the type. It has a broadly flaring rim attached to its shoulders by a generally straight handle that is round or oval in section. Most examples are red slipped; some are polished and others are burnished. Many have flat bases (e.g., Dothan 1970, figs. 3–4). An extremely well-made round-based body of unusual, finely levigated fabric is ascribed to this morphological group (pl. 55d). This example is notable for its beautifully rounded body and heavy, red-slipped, lightly polished, matt surface.

"Teapots"

"Teapot" is a generic descriptor used to describe virtually all medium-size to small vessels with small spouts. Most of these appear to have been luxury items.

Fine Ware Teapots

The group of fine ware teapots includes a number of small to medium-size vessels, remarkable for their finely proportioned, oval bodies and consistently red hues (pl. 56). Some have dull, smooth finishes, but the finest are highly burnished and have lustrous surfaces. Most complete examples derive from tombs, but one comes from Locus 1088 (pl. 56i), described as a "kiln," although I do not believe that association to indicate the vessel was manufactured at that location.[62] There are numerous fragments in the East Slope assemblage of such vessels, represented by detached spouts. Some examples have no necks and thick rims (pl. 56l), while others have narrow, ridged necks and wide, flaring rims (pl. 56g–h[63]). This last type is one of a highly distinctive morphological group that likely derives from a single production center. Numerous examples are found at Megiddo, Assawir/ʿEn Esur (Dothan 1970, fig. 2; Yannai and Grosinger 2000, fig. 9.7:1–2), Qiryat Ata (Golani 2003, fig. 4.21:1–2), and Tell el-Farʿah North (de Vaux and Steve 1949, fig. 13:8),[64] which suggests there was a lively trade in such vessels.

Examples of neckless teapot types may have horizontal tube handles or raised decorations (pl. 56:9a), while necked types may have two loop handles (pl. 56h). Some spouts are straight but others are definitively bent, which indicates they were not objects for mere display to be used as grave goods but were equally functional (pl. 56a–e). Bent spouts allow liquid contents to be poured without completely upending vessels, preventing spillage through their large apertures. Vessels of this type derive from the northern region, where they are found in quantities, especially in tomb assemblages, but they are also common in mortuary contexts at south-central sites, where they were presumably prized as luxury items. It seems likely the different types were associated with specialized workshops where skilled craftspeople were able to turn them out in some quantity. Red burnished teapots were apparently desirable trade items as they are found in

[62] There is no indication of the date of the kiln, nor the relationship of the material from the same locus to it.

[63] For purposes of illustration the photograph juxtaposes fragments of two different vessels.

[64] This is a significant observation as it is evidence of patterns of distribution of different pottery types. Notably, there is production of a certain type of bowl and closed vessels made from the same form associated with Early Bronze Age I tombs at Tell el Farʿah North in the same contexts that this type of teapot has been found (Braun 2012a, with references). Those bowls have been found at sites on the Coastal Plain as far south as Palmahim Quarry, but to date there is no evidence whatsoever of them at Megiddo.

tombs of the southern region in late contexts of Early Bronze Age I, where they contrast with local pottery of lesser quality.

Plainer Ware "Teapots"

From the large number of spouts found in the assemblage it seems likely the teapot was a popular vessel, both for its practicality and for its other, luxury qualities. Numerous examples were red slipped but not burnished and may have been less elegant in form than the finer examples (e.g., pl. 56f).

Medium-size and Small Jars

Little may be said of the classes of smaller vessels because they are poorly represented in the East Slope assemblage, mostly by only a few minuscule sherds. One sizable jar fragment (pl. 57a) has a thickened, squared-off rim and no neck. It was decorated in the grain-wash style with dark paint over a buff fabric. Others have short necks ending in slightly splayed, tapering rims. Most have relatively thin walls and were decorated, either by slipping or in the grain-wash style. On the basis of parallels from other sites it seems likely that most would have had flat bases. Some had ledge handles. Comparisons of sherds suggest parallels at ʿEn Shadud (Braun 1985, pottery types 16 and 17, table 3).

Another, nearly complete jar pl. 57b), from Tomb 910 — a sepulcher obviously emptied of human remains (*Chapter 6*) — has typical features of Early Bronze Age I vessels, including the morphology of its body, indented ledge handles, and a red burnished exterior. It is notable, however, for its unusual, broken-off base. It may have had a ring base, a fenestrated, or perhaps a high trumpet base. I have been unable to find any parallels to suggest the likely reconstruction of the base.

A Stand

About three quarters of a large, cylindrical stand are extant in the assemblage (pl. 57c). It is an unusual piece that suggests possible cultic associations as it seems too large for a pot stand and in most instances pots of this period have flat bases, thus obviating such a function.

Large Jars

Large jars are poorly represented in the assemblage retained. One example, of which only the base and part of a wall with a handle is preserved, may have been retrieved in situ, but unfortunately a marking on it that may indicate its origin in the field is too indistinct to be read (pl. 57d). This jar is notable for its strap handle (likely one of two) and its external, grain-wash decoration. A handle of another such jar, also with a grain-wash decorated exterior, is notable for its incised decoration (pl. 54f).

Bow-rim Pithoi

Bow-rim pithoi, named for their characteristic rims, are broadly inclusive of some vessels with rims that are not, *stricto sensu*, "bowed" but that are probably associated with similar body forms (e.g., fig. 27, leftmost rim profile; pl. 59d–f). Their distribution seems to be within the Jezreel and Zevulon Valleys and to the west through the Nahal ʿIron (Megiddo) Pass[65] through the Carmel Range as far as the coast, but no farther east. Notably, bow-rim pithoi are totally absent in the ceramic repertoire from contemporary occupations at Beth Shan and the published assemblages from Bet Yerah, while these pithoi, in variations and in quantity,

[65] This is the well-traveled pass through the Carmel range that connects the Jezreel Plain with the Coastal Plain.

have been found at ʿEn Esur, Tel Qashish,[66] Qiryat Ata (table 5), and Tel Megadim on the Mediterranean coast (Gophna 1974, fig. 1:5–6; Sam Wolff, pers. comm.).

Such pithoi can be further defined by overall morphology and decorative elements. There appear to be two basic variants in body shape and style of decoration, and within each type there are great variations in rim morphology (pls. 58–59). For purposes of this discussion I propose calling the major variants Types BR 1 and BR 2. Examples may be slipped or un-slipped. These types may represent chronological or distinctions derived from different workshops but for the present the correct interpretation of these differences remains elusive (Braun 2012b, pp. 21–24).

Type BR 1

Type BR 1 pithoi seem to have nicely proportioned bodies with not overly wide, curving shoulders, to which the eponymous bow rim is attached. The type is also defined by its distinctive rope decoration (pl. 58) applied in arched and/or horizontal segments. The rope effect was made by pinching a thin, raised line of clay so it is triangular in section and then depressing it at short, regular intervals. Only Type BR 1 is definitively present in the assemblage from the East Slope (pl. 58), but that could simply be the result of preservation, as there are numerous rim fragments indicating the generic group, which could include vessels of Type BR 2.

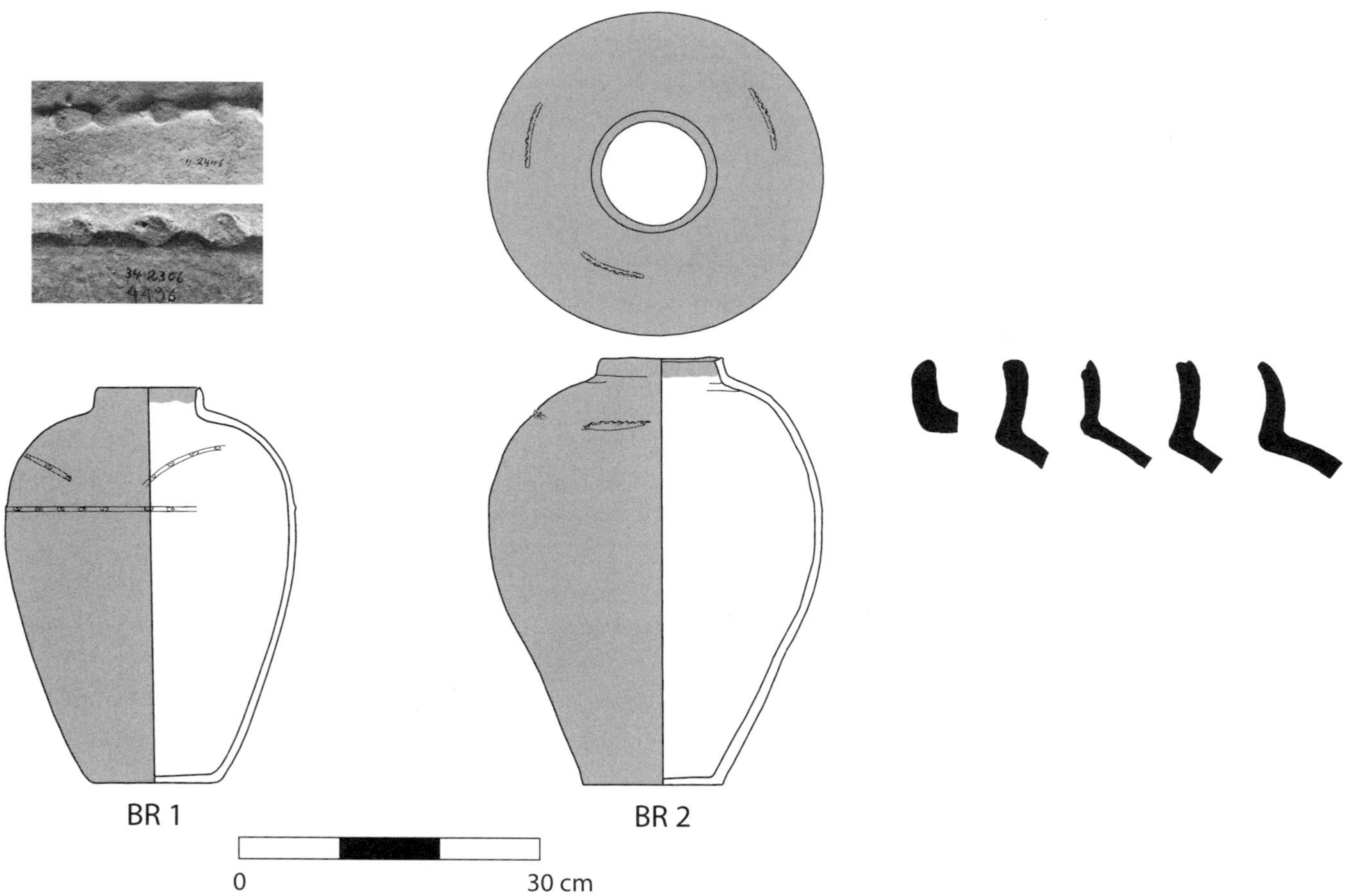

Figure 27. Early Bronze Age bow-rim pithos typology. Left: Ideal Type BR1 pithos (based on Yannai, Lazar-Shorer, and Grosinger 2006, fig. 4.62:5) and examples of rope-like decoration. Center: Ideal Type BR 2 (based on Yannai, Lazar-Shorer, and Grosinger 2006, fig. 4.73:1). Right: Bow-rim variations (after Engberg and Shipton 1934a, chart)

---

[66] In the off-the-tell occupation the type was found in great quantities and appears to have been the sole type of pithos in use there. By contrast, another contemporary occupation at the base of the Mizpeh Zevulun site in Nahal Zippori, other types of pithoi were common, while only a few examples of bow rims were encountered (E. C. M. van den Brink, pers. comm.).

There is an intriguing correlation between this pithos type and architecture at two sites that may prove to be significant, although its precise significance eludes us for the present. The sole well-preserved example of this kind of pithos (34.2587; pls. 58a, 76a, 81c) from the East Slope was found in situ on the earthen floor of B/V/1, a rectangular building with externally rounded corners. This same type of pithos was found in Area D at ʿEn Esur on the floor of a somewhat larger room, similarly rectangular with rounded corners (Yannai 2006, pp. 52–54). Another example of this pithos type, from Qiryat Ata, Area E, was found smashed on the floor of a house (Locus 1028) of rectangular plan with rounded corners (Golani 2003, p. 52, fig. 2.37, plan 2.15; Braun 2012b, pp. 19–24). At ʿEn Shadud a close parallel to the Megiddo seal-impressed vessel of this type (*Chapter 4*) was recovered from Stratum I in Area A. The actual plan of the building at ʿEn Shadud is unclear due to warping;[67] it can be reconstructed as sausage shaped or sub-rectangular with rounded corners (Braun 1985, p. 68, figs. 5–6). At Tel Qashish a large, upper portion of this type of jar was found in Locus 532, a surface purportedly associated with a short, curvilinear wall segment (W315) attributed to the earlier of two phases of Stratum XV (Ben-Tor and Bonfil 2003a, p. 21, section A–A′). This information suggests the possibility of a close chronological association between this type of pithos and a particular phase of Early Bronze Age I (see below).

Type BR 2

Most pithoi of Type BR 2 seem to have narrower bases and broader shoulders than the slimmer Type BR 1 pithoi (pl. 58). The rope-like decoration on this type consists of short, raised segments on the upper shoulders, juxtaposed either horizontally or obliquely.

At Qiryat Ata Type BR 2 pithoi were found on the floor of Locus 4, an Area A house with a sausage-shaped plan, somewhat distant from the Area E house (see above). Located farther downhill, the Area A house not only differs from the latter in plan, but it also is oriented differently, possibly suggesting some less-than-direct association between these buildings. At ʿEn Esur BR 2 pithoi were found in association with a burial beneath the floor of a building that has very rounded corners, such that it approaches a true curvilinear plan (Yannai 2006, p. 59, plan 3.2). At Tel Qashish this type of pithos was found in Locus 532, purportedly a surface in association with the short, curvilinear wall segment W315 (Ben-Tor and Bonfil 2003a, p. 21, section A–A′). However, this large fragment was found in fill that appears in the section drawing to have been below the foundations of that wall. That could suggest the surface should be associated with an even earlier feature, as floors in Early Bronze Age I houses tend to be level with the bottoms of foundations and not below them.

A possible correlation between pithos type and architectural plan, albeit uncertain, is intriguing as there is no indication in available publications of these two pithos types found within the same buildings. If such a correlation should prove to be correct, the evidence could suggest some ethnic or social differentiation between different groups occupying two types of houses, both at ʿEn Esur and at Qiryat Ata. Another possibility is that these dissimilarities reflect slight chronological differences, manifested in architectural traditions and in types of pithoi available.[68] Unfortunately, as there is no indication of the presence of Type BR 2 pithoi either in the East Slope or in the ʿEn Shadud assemblages due to the poor preservation of artifacts, it is impossible to suggest any further evaluation of the East Slope evidence in light of information from other sites.

Dating of Type BR 1

A comparison between vessel 34.2587 from B/V/1 and that from ʿEn Shadud (pl. 81c), each bearing two cylinder-seal impressions, offers compelling reasons to date them as absolutely contemporary (*Chapter 4*). That places B/V/1 within an advanced phase of Early Bronze Age I, but it does not offer any greater chronological precision. If the Stratum I provenience of the ʿEn Shadud bow-rim pithos is an indication, then it

---

[67] That left the layered deposits undulating and far from strictly horizontal.

[68] For instance, a scenario that could account for such differences would be that the two types represent the output of a single workshop over two or more generations.

is somewhat advanced for that site, but that says very little as preservation there was so poor and the site so badly warped it was virtually impossible to ascribe more than a few artifacts to one or the other of two superimposed strata.

Thus, this distinctive pithos, one of the few artifacts found in situ, is likely to date to a horizon in which Gray Burnished Ware Type 3 bowls were still in use, but prior to the latest phases of Early Bronze Age I. That could suggest that B/V/1 dates to relatively early within the sequence on the East Slope, possibly earlier than the latest occupation of the Stage IV house.

Table 5. Bow-rim pithoi: Select parallels

Tel Qashish	*ʿEn Shadud*	*Afula*	*ʿEn Esur*	*Megadim*	*Qiryat Ata*
GENERIC PARALLELS					
Ben-Tor and Bonfil 2003a, figs. 3:11–12, 4:5–6, 6:13, 9:13–14, 10:12–13, 12:12–14, 22:3	Braun 1985, fig. 23:8–12	Sukenik 1948, pl. 4:1–3, 5–7, 9–11	Yannai, Lazar-Shorer, and Grosinger 2006, figs. 4.40:12–18, 4.59, 4.62:8, 4.74:8	Gophna 1974, fig. 1:5–6	Golani 2003, fig. 4.11:2–6
BR 1 PARALLELS					
—	Braun 1985, fig. 34, pl. 8:A	—	Yannai, Lazar-Shorer, and Grosinger 2006, fig. 4.62:5, 7	Gophna 1974, fig. 1:5(?)[a]	Golani 2003, fig. 4.10:3
BR 2 PARALLELS					
Ben-Tor and Bonfil 2003a, fig. 10:11, photo 11	—	—	Yannai, Lazar-Shorer, and Grosinger 2006, fig. 4.73:1, 2	—	Golani 2003, figs. 4.10:1–2, 4 and 4.11:1

[a] This fragment of a bow rim is remarkable for the cylinder-seal impression it bears.

Pithoi with Thickened Rims

Because of poor preservation, large vessels are, unfortunately, under-represented in the East Slope assemblage. There is considerable variation in the forms of rims in this generic group. Most of these vessels were either slipped in red or decorated in one or another of the grain-wash techniques. Variations in these types range from examples that are virtually neckless to others with short, stovepipe-like necks, all with thick walls (e.g., pl. 60:a–f, h).

Rolled-rim Pithoi

Rolled rim pithoi have thick, round-sectioned rims, sometimes atop short necks. Most appear to have been red slipped or decorated in the grain-wash technique (pl. 60h, j). There are many similar examples from ʿEn Shadud (Braun 1985, fig. 25:3–7) and Qiryat Ata (Golani 2003, fig. 4.13:16–18), but which have striations or shallow incisions at regular intervals on their rims. Notably, examples with striations are not found at Megiddo, suggesting possible chronological differences and/or patterns of distribution. Comparanda from sites to the east show patterns of dispersion of these types that differ considerably from the distribution of bow-rim types.

The non-striated type, paralleled at a number of sites, seems to have been first made in the latest phases of Early Bronze Age I (table 6) and then continued to be popular at least in the early phases of Early Bronze Age II (table 7). Thus the chronological range for these non-striated examples seems to transcend the end of Early Bronze Age I and continue into the early phases of Early Bronze Age II. Apparently this utilitarian type vessel was eventually replaced by more elegant, lighter, and probably more functional pithoi of Metallic Ware. Notably, at Bet Yerah, where Metallic Ware was found in quantity, the published evidence suggests the type was not in use or perhaps not very popular in the Early Bronze Age II, but at Tell Abu el-Kharaz, a much smaller site that might not have been able to obtain Metallic Ware as easily as its larger and probably more affluent neighbor to the north, rolled-rim pithoi appear to have a longer history of utilization. One may only speculate whether a similar circumstance led to the type's seeming popularity at Megiddo and whether the fragments we know of could suggest human activity on the East Slope in the early phases of Early Bronze Age II. The absence in the published pottery assemblage of Tel Qashish of the Early Bronze Age I and II levels of pithoi of this type is difficult to explain (table 7). Its absence at that site could suggest a gap between the end of the last Early Bronze Age I level and the succeeding Early Bronze Age II occupation there.

Table 6. Storage jars with necks and thickened rims: Select Early Bronze Age I parallels

Megiddo, Levels J4, J5	*ʿEn Shadud, Advanced Early Bronze Age I*	*Bet Yerah, Period B and Local Stratum 5*	*Qiryat Ata, Strata III–II*[a]	*Beth Shan, Stratum XIII*	*ʿEn Esur, Late Early Bronze Age I*	*Tell Abu el-Kharaz, Phase IB*
Joffe 2000, figs. 8.4:20–23, 8.5:6	Braun 1985, fig. 23:5, 7 (variant with short neck)	Greenberg and Eisenberg 2006, figs. 8.48:5–7; Paz 2006, figs. 7.22:12, 7.24:10	Golani 2003, fig. 4.19:4–5	Braun 2004, figs. 3.22:3, 5, 6; Mazar 2012, pls. (9:1, 2, 10, 16:10, 28:11–19	Yannai, Lazar-Shorer, and Grosinger 2006, figs. 4.62:10–12, 4.76:10	Fischer 2008, figs. 32:4–6, 111:1–2, 112:1, 113, 114:1, 2, 4, 115:1, 2, 4, 5

[a] This is an artificial stratigraphic division as nowhere is Stratum II superimposed upon Stratum III at the site (Braun 2012b). Remains purportedly associated with these two "strata" are found in two different precincts of the site. The stratigraphic division, if valid, remains to be substantiated as it is based on a differentiation of two styles of architecture, one sausage shaped, the other rectangular with curved corners, with the former type plan understood to be associated with the earlier phase (Golani 2003). However, there is a distinct possibility that these two styles were in use coevally, as they may have been at ʿEn Esur (Yannai 2006, plans 2.7–8, 2.10–12, 3.1–2) and possibly ʿEn Shadud (Braun 1985, pp. 67–77). Notably, the pottery associated with these two "strata" at Qiryat Ata is understood as "homogenous," that is, the excavator cannot distinguish between the pottery of Strata III and II, which admits of the contemporaneousness of these strata at the site.

Table 7. Storage jar with neck and thickened rim: Select Early Bronze Age II parallels

Qiryat Ata, Stratum I	*Tell Abu el-Kharaz, Phases II–III*
Golani 2003, fig. 4.34:1–2	Fischer 2008, figs. 44:2–3, 49:1–2

Holemouth Jars

Holemouth jars are ubiquitous at sites of the Early Bronze Age and, despite their many variations in style (e.g., Zuckerman 2003c, fig. 22; Zuckerman 2003d, fig. 66), are often exceedingly difficult to date, especially when not found in good stratigraphic contexts as on the East Slope. Several generic types first appear in the Early Bronze Age I and continue to be made in the following periods. Some examples were used for storage and others, usually marked by fire clouding, and sometimes with shiny temper in their fabrics, can be discerned as cooking vessels. Unfortunately, with the exception of several complete jars, the remaining examples were of small sherds that did not reveal the likely functions of the vessels they represent.

Holemouth Jars with Ridged Rims

Numerous fragments of holemouth jars with ridged rims are found in the East Slope assemblage (pl. 61a–b). Many of them are of coarse, brown fabrics, probably not highly fired, which suggests the likelihood of their having been associated with a single tradition, perhaps even one workshop. The poor quality of fabrics of most examples of this group suggests these vessels were used for storage of non-liquids. Several examples were made of better-quality red-slipped fabrics; their ridges decorated by small, evenly spaced indentations (pl. 61d).

This type is well paralleled at a number of nearby sites but it is not well known or entirely missing in assemblages at others (table 8). The pattern of distribution suggests this particular type has chronological significance. There is only one published example from Qiryat Ata in an Early Bronze Age II level,[69] where it was probably found out of its original context. Significantly, there are no published examples from Tel Qashish but a few are included in the "Late EB I" published types from ʿEn Esur. The type is also found at Afula, where it has no known stratigraphic associations, and at ʿEn Shadud (Braun 1985, pp. 100–01).

Joffe (2000, p. 163) notes the absence of this type, which he describes as "very heavy or elaborately profiled rims," in Level J-2 on the high mound of Megiddo, a very late phase of Early Bronze Age I. The type is also found at Tell el-Farʿah North, where it was assigned to the earlier phase or phases of Early Bronze Age I, identified by the excavators as Énéolithique[70] Supérieur. Thus it appears the type represents an advanced but not very late phase of Early Bronze Age I. Its absence at nearby Tel Qashish and the apparent dearth of examples from Qiryat Ata and ʿEn Esur may suggest chronological differences or, what seems more likely, at least for the latter site, patterns of distribution of select types from different workshops.

Table 8. Holemouth jars with ridged rims: Select Early Bronze Age parallels

Tel Qashish	*ʿEn Shadud, Strata II–I*	*Afula, Late Chalcolithic*[a]	*Qiryat Ata, Stratum I*[b]	*ʿEn Esur, Late Early Bronze Age I*	*Tell el Farʿah North Énéolithique Supérieur*[c]
—	Braun 1985, figs. 21:19–22, 22:1–7	Sukenik 1948, pl. 3:32–35, 38	Golani 2003, fig. 4.28:21	Yannai, Lazar-Shorer, and Grosinger 2006, figs. 4.56:19, 4.76:6	de Vaux and Steve 1947, fig. 2:9; 1948, fig. 5:3

[a] This is now recognized as Early Bronze Age I.

[b] Notably, only a single example is published from this site, compared to numerous examples and variations from ʿEn Shadud, where there are no Early Bronze Age II types. Thus it is likely to be residual in this context, and possibly even a holdover in the Stratum III–II, Early Bronze Age I occupation.

[c] This is roughly equivalent to the Early Bronze Age I, up to but not including its latest phases.

Holemouth Jars with Thickened Rims

Thickened rims appear to have a very long history, beginning in the Early Bronze Age I and continuing on perhaps as late as Early Bronze Age III (fig. 28). Some examples, when well enough preserved, have flat bases (pl. 61f–g). Unfortunately, the sole object found in situ on the late, earthen floor of Locus 1200 (34.2548; pl. 61g), the central room of B/IV/1a, and crucial for dating its use, is of this type. On the basis of morphological parallels it is probably to be dated to the Early Bronze I–II horizon, which also seems to be the case for the potters' mark it bears (see *Chapter 4*). A similar mark is on a small holemouth jug with strap handle found nearby (pl. 61e) in Locus 1199 (*Chapter 2*). Such handles are rarely found on holemouths and this vessel is an unusually small example. Perhaps its diminutive size indicates it had some special function, an association

Figure 28. Generic holemouth rim profiles. The rightmost three are ridged rims (after Engberg and Shipton 1934a, chart). No scale

[69] All parallels derive from Early Bronze Age I contexts.

[70] This term, adopted by de Vaux and Steve (1947, 1948, 1949) in the early reports on excavations at Tell el Farʿah North, is equivalent to Chalcolithique (i.e., Chalcolithic) in later reports.

which in some way may have been shared by the similarly marked larger holemouth. Tables 8 and 9 indicate something of the lengthy chronological range for parallels of this holemouth vessel.

Table 9. Holemouth jar 34.2548 from Locus 1200: Select Early Bronze Age I parallels

Megiddo, Layer J2	*Tel Qashish*	*ʿEn Shadud, Strata II-I*	*Bet Yerah, Period B*	*Qiryat Ata, Strata III-II*	*ʿEn Esur, Late Early Bronze Age I*	*Tell Abu el-Kharaz, Phase IB*
Joffe 2000, fig. 8.1:13	Zuckerman 2003c, fig. 22:9–11	Braun 1985, fig. 21:10–13	Greenberg and Eisenberg 2006, figs. 847.10–11, 8.54:1–3, 8.57:13–16, 8.62:8, 9, 11	Golani 2003, fig. 4.20:8–9, 11–12	Yannai, Lazar-Shorer, and Grosinger 2006, figs. 4.55:11, 4.56, 4.62:13–15, 4.73:3	Fischer 2008, fig. 117:7, 9–10, 12, 15–17, 19

Table 10. Holemouth jar 34.2548 from Locus 1200: Select Early Bronze Age II parallels

Tel Qashish	*Bet Yerah, Period C*	*Qiryat Ata, Stratum I*	*Tell Abu el-Kharaz, Phase IB*	*Tell Shalem*
Ben-Tor and Bonfil 2003b, fig. 57:5, 6	Greenberg and Eisenberg 2006, figs. 8.54:1–3, 8.57:13–16, 8.62:8, 9, 11	Golani 2003, fig. 4.28:1–15	Fischer 2008, figs. 140:1–7, 148:1, 3, 5	Eisenberg 1996, fig.15:1

Ledge Handles

There is a great deal of variation in the types of ledge handles associated with this period (pls. 62–63). While most have wavy exteriors (sometimes described as "wavy lined" or "thumb indented"), some few have smooth profiles. The type with wavy exterior has a long history, now known to begin sometime in the Late (i.e., Ghassulian) Chalcolithic period (Braun, in press) and ending only at the termination of the Early Bronze Age. Such handles are found on most types of vessels from very small bowls to teapots to large kraters and storage jars, but apparently not on pithoi, which seem at Megiddo to have been devoid of handles.

Strap Handles

Strap handles tend to be circular or roughly oval in section rather than flat. They are found on a variety of small vessels including gourd jars, jugs, and juglets (pl. 54). Most were red slipped, some were burnished, and others were decorated with patterns of incisions. Few from the East Slope were well preserved, but a collection of some of the smaller ones, probably from juglets or small jars, but a collection of some of the smaller ones includes "high loop handles," wherein the handles attached to the bodies of the vessels rise up over the tops of the rims where they are attached to them. This is distinctive of Early Bronze Age I vessels and seems to have gone out of favor at the end of the period or shortly thereafter, in an early phase of Early Bronze Age II. Thus "high loop handles" (pl. 54g–p) are one of the hallmarks of Early Bronze Age I pottery.

Egyptian-style Vessels

A single, reasonably well-preserved jar (34.2652; pl. 64a) found in Locus 1199 (the large cavity and adjacent open area to the southwest of B/IV/1) belongs to a class of very coarse vessels of typical Egyptian morphology, known as "granary jars." Although this example was clearly made from local clay (Ilan and Goren 2003, pp. 45–48), its fabric is replete with vegetal temper that very possibly bespeaks the hand of an Egyptian potter (Amiran 1974, fig. 2:1). It is one of two such vessels represented in the East Slope assemblage. The other is known only from a very coarse base fragment, presumably of a similar vessel (34.2653; pl. 64b). Possibly these vessels date to sometime late in the Early Bronze Age I period, for which there is a modicum of evidence of Egyptian associations at Megiddo (Braun and van den Brink 1998; Braun 1993). There may be an association between these objects and a cache of Egyptianized vessels found in association with Level J5 on the high mound (Joffe 2000, pp. 171–75) but its Early Bronze Age I *bona fides* has been questioned by at least one scholar (M. Adams, pers. comm.), who will publish the results of his research in due course. Other Egyptian associations have been noted by Amiran (1992) and Ilan (*Chapter 6*). Most recently a few sherds of Egyptian origin have been discovered by M. Adams (pers. comm.) in excavations on a low hill several hundred meters east of the high mound.

Early Bronze Age I Pottery from the East Slope: A Summary Statement

The sum of the East Slope ceramic assemblage indicates it was the scene of intense activity in the more developed phases of Early Bronze Age I, possibly with some periods of lesser activity. Types of pottery found indicate the site was utilized for different purposes during the latter part of the period, possibly into Early Bronze Age II. Virtually all the pottery is of local types associated with the northern region. Of note are the connections that Megiddo had with sites to the west, through the Nahal ʿIron (i.e., Megiddo) Pass and to sites in the surrounding and inter-connecting Zebulon and Zippori Valleys. There are notably fewer connections with contemporary occupations in the hill country such as Tell el-Farʿah North, associated with a specific kind of pottery I have named TFN Ware (Braun 2012a) that had a widespread distribution in Late Early Bronze Age I. Although TFN Ware is found in considerable quantity at sites on the Coastal Plain as far south as Tel Aviv, there is, somewhat surprisingly, no evidence of it at Megiddo. However, as noted above, a specific type of teapot, prominently featured in the tomb assemblages of Tell el-Farʿah North, is well represented at Megiddo and in tombs in the ʿEn Esur region in the Nahal ʿIron Pass (Dothan 1970).

Some Observations on the Significance of the Early Bronze Age I Pottery from the East Slope

As noted above, pottery offers not only the possibility of determining chronology, but other features of the political and social landscape of pre-literate societies. The significance of studying the limited assemblage from the East Slope lies not in it itself, but rather in its ability to allow for comparisons with other, more complete assemblages from additional sites. One of the most significant aspects of this study is the extreme regionalism in ceramic repertoires suggested by comparanda. Specific types appear to derive from one or only a few centers of production, and their patterns of distribution suggest important links between sites, some of which surely reflect sociopolitical and economic realities of late phases of Early Bronze Age I. In that era Megiddo must surely have been a central site of importance (*Chapter 7*), and relationships suggested by its ceramic repertoire, particularly when contrasted with those of another site of prime importance, Bet Yerah, can be used to help develop an elementary understanding of the social and economic climate of the times.

Another feature of this study suggests that pottery in this period came mostly from specialized workshops devoted to outputs of select types. There seems to have been a long tradition for that mode of production, dating back to the earliest Gray Burnished Wares. That is evidence of an increasing level of social organization, one that matches developments at Megiddo, especially on the high mound (*Chapter 7*).

That ceramic production took place external to settlements seems obvious, as about a century of excavation at Early Bronze Age I sites has failed to produce any evidence of such a workshop or any firing installation. The research on this assemblage offers, albeit only in a very general way, suggestions as to which polities or communities may have had control of these production centers. It remains for archaeologists to find them and solve the riddle of where and how early potters of the southern Levant produced their wares.

Early Bronze Age I–II Pottery

Recent publication of the Early Bronze Age levels at Tell Abu el-Kharaz (Fischer 2008) has demonstrated unequivocally, in a series of extraordinarily well-preserved, superimposed strata, that there is no sharp break in ceramic traditions in the northern region between Early Bronze Age I and Early Bronze Age II. It appears rather that certain ceramic types continue on and eventually are phased out while other types are added, some of which continue on into Early Bronze Age III.

Although most of the high mound at Megiddo appears to have been abandoned during Early Bronze Age II (Esse 1991, p. 75; Joffe 2000, p. 179), there is a small quantity of pottery from the East Slope that bears mute evidence of limited activity there in that period, possibly a continuation of the earlier occupation. Some types that begin in the late phases of Early Bronze Age I and continue into the following period are found in the East Slope assemblage. Although they cannot be associated with any particular architectural feature, they do indicate activity on the East Slope in the time span in which these types remained in use.

Light-faced Painted Ware

A single fragment of "light-faced painted ware" (Kantor 1965; Esse 1991, pp. 107–09), also included in a category sometimes erroneously identified as "Abydos Ware" (Amiran 1969, pp. 59, 62; Braun 2009, p. 28; 2012a), is represented only by a drawing from the object register. Although I have been unable to locate this sherd, the drawing is so explicit and the parallels so compelling, there is no question of the identification of this object. The drawing (pl. 65a) is of a body sherd, presumably part of a jug or juglet, very precisely painted within finely drawn lines. It is decorated with three thin, horizontal bands of dark paint above a register divided into triangles. Those with point facing down are filled with small dots, while alternate triangles with point facing up were left unfilled. Amiran (1969, pl. 17:7–10), Esse (1991, fig. 20), Nigro and Sala (2010, pl. 91:1), and Kafafi (2011, fig. 3) illustrate a number of parallels to this particular style of painting. Another tiny fragment of a similar vessel is attributed to either Stratum XIX or XVIII on the high tell (Kempinski 1989, fig. 10:6). According to the register the sherd was found somewhere in Square Y17, "under 1093." However, its importance lies not in its findspot but in its very existence at the site. This type of pottery is definitively associated with Early Bronze Age II as indicated by its presence in Egypt in the tomb of Djet, the third king of the First Dynasty (Braun 2011a, fig. 1:5; Braun 2012a, pp. 20–24) and later tombs of that dynasty.

"South Levantine Metallic Ware"

"Metallic Ware" (Engberg and Shipton 1934a, p. 20, passim; Porat 1989, pp. 71–75; Esse 1991; Braun 2012a), recently labeled North Canaanite Metallic Ware,[71] or NCMW for short (Greenberg et al. 2006), is a name given to a large assortment of morphological types made of similar, hard-fired fabrics that are a *fossile directeur* of the Early Bronze Age II–III of the southern Levant. Distribution of this ware is mostly confined to sites in the northern reaches of the region (table 11). This type of fabric ranges in color from dark gray to brick red and varying shades of brown. It was apparently made in pottery workshops in the region of Mount Hermon (Greenberg and Porat 1996), where the likely sources for the clay used to make it are found. The name is, I believe, apparently derived from the ringing, "metallic" sound this type of fabric gives off when struck, although some examples the color of tarnished copper perhaps enhance the attractiveness of the name. Vessels made of this hard-fired fabric, which tend to have relatively thin walls, were made by coiling and their exteriors were then smoothed and sometimes combed or polished to a dull sheen.

South Levantine Metallic Ware makes its first appearance either at the very end of the Early Bronze Age I or early in Early Bronze Age II, but it is understood to continue on into Early Bronze Age III, during which its production ceases. Some of the earliest types are small, delicate, platter-like, shallow bowls of dark gray and brown fabrics, precisely those types found in the East Slope assemblage.

[71] The addition of "North" and "Canaanite" to the name of this pottery is as confusing as it is anachronistic in the third millennium B.C. Canaanite is a biblical term appropriate to some ethnic group living in the southern Levant during the second and first millennia B.C. Thus, any ethnic association (probably unintended by the name) is unwarranted as it is unknown whether third-millennium people were ethnically Canaanites. A more appropriate name for this class of pottery would be South Levantine Metallic Ware, which would distinguish it from other similar classes of metallic wares associated with North Levantine sites (Mazzoni 1986; Akkermans and Schwartz 2003, p. 254).

Table 11. Inventory of South Levantine Metallic Ware from the East Slope

Registration No.	*Description*	*Illustration*	*Provenience*
34.2624/1	Platter-bowl, brown to gray, copper-like, gray and white grits, polished, triangular mark scraped on bottom of base	Pl. 66a	East Slope
34.2624/2	Platter-bowl, dark red, gray core, white grits, polished	Pl. 66c	Under Locus 1191
34.2520	Small jar shoulder, strap handle, red-orange, gray core, gray grits, combing, polished	—	Under Locus 1170
34.2624/4	Platter, orange, white and gray grits, polished	Pl. 66b	East Slope
34.2623	Platter, red, gray grits, polished	Pl. 65b	Locus 1168
34.2623/1	Shallow bowl, wide inverted rim, red slipped internally and on external rim, pattern burnished internally, red-brown, white grits, polished	Pl. 65e	Locus 1170
34.2650	Base of closed vessel, gray to brown, white grits, polished externally	—	Locus 1169
34.2513/1	Jug or small jar base, red to gray well levigated, gray core, polished externally	—	Under Locus 1170
34.2624/3 joined to 34.2624/5	Platter-bowl, gray-brown, orange-brown core, white grits, polished, incised potter's mark on bottom of base	Pl. 66f	Tomb 16 or Locus 1092
34.2516	Body sherd of closed vessel, pink-orange and gray, gray and red grits, gray slip externally, polished, crazed	—	East Slope
34.2518/2	Fragment of base of small closed vessel, brown, gray core, gray and white grits, red interior, polished externally	—	Under Locus 1170
34.2517	Base of jug, brown to gray, gray core, vertically combed, polished externally	—	Under Locus 1162
34.2519/4	Base of small jar, orange and brown, gray core, white and gray grits, polished externally	—	East Slope
34.2521	Neck of jug, orange, gray core, orange-brown to gray mottled externally, traces of fine combing, coils highly visible internally, polished externally	Pl. 65c	Locus 1169
34.2614/5	Platter, orange, polished	Pl. 66d	East Slope
A16844	Platter, orange, white and orange grits, polished	—	East Slope
34.2665/2	Body sherd of closed vessel, coiling visible	Pl. 65d	Under Locus 1170

Bowls

One small, finely fashioned, thin-walled platter-bowl (34.2624/3+34.2624/5; pl. 66f) has a dark gray-brown polished exterior, except for the roughly cylindrical, flat base incised with a potter's mark, approximately half of which is preserved. The excavators' notes indicate it was derived from either Tomb 16 or from Locus 1092, which is a kiln found in that cave, but the likelihood of this object being directly associated with a kiln seems virtually nil as vessels of this type of fabric were almost certainly made at centers of production located elsewhere (Greenberg and Porat 1996). A small fragment of another of this vessel type was found on the high mound in fill associated with Level J6, dated to the Early Bronze Age III (Greenberg 2006, fig. 10.11:4), but its diminutive size could allow it to be a residual find.

A sizable portion of a shallower bowl with larger diameter (34.2624/1; pl. 66a) is notable for also having a potter's mark on its flat base. The mark, apparently a triangle (only a portion of it is preserved), rather than incised with a sharp stylus into its surface as was usual, was scraped when the vessel was leather-hard, leaving broad, smooth lines in the coarse surface of the clay. This bowl and a few fragments from the East Slope belong to de Miroschedji's (2000, p. 321) very specific "EB II chocolate-brown, fine Metallic Ware." Additional fragments of other vessels of this ware include the neck of a jug (34.2521; pl. 65c), three bases with fragments of walls, probably of jugs or small jars, a handle and a small portion of the rim of a jug, the rim of a jar and a body sherd of an externally combed vessel of indeterminate mien. Some bowls, which appear to develop from shallow bowl types of the preceding period, are of different fabrics. They are similar to platters but somewhat deeper and smaller (34.2614/3; pl. 66e).

Platters

The appearance of certain types of platters or large, shallow bowls, unknown at sites of the Early Bronze Age I, is an indication of the onset of Early Bronze Age II. Such vessels of this period (e.g., pl. 66a–d) are not over-large and have distinctive features not associated with the Early Bronze Age III types (pl. 70). They have low side-walls joined nearly perpendicularly to their almost flat bases. These vessels were trimmed and given sharply angular carinations at the junctures of rims and walls, possibly suggesting attempts at creating the impression of metal, not only in color. A few diminutive fragments of platters and platter-bowls are found in the East Slope assemblage, several of which appear to be of Metallic Ware. One, from Locus 1199, has a thick, orange slip that was methodically and completely polished to a dull sheen by a thin, flat tool, probably on a tournette. Vessels of similar morphology at Bet Yerah were found in an early Early Bronze Age II context in local Stratum 13 (Greenberg and Eisenberg 2006, fig. 5.78:8, 10, 12) and in other contemporary contexts (e.g., Eisenberg and Greenberg 2006, fig. 8.52:5–6) at the same site.

Closed Vessels

Fragments of medium-size closed vessels of Metallic Ware found in the assemblage include the neck of a jug and a body sherd, on which the coiling technique by which they were fabricated can be clearly seen (34.2521, 34.2665/2; pl. 65c–d). As the internal surface was not meant to be seen, potters made no attempt at smoothing the coils after melding them. By contrast, the external surfaces of this ware were then smoothed to give them a dull sheen; afterward a very fine-toothed comb was sometimes applied to the external surfaces of vessels. Some of these vessels were slipped red.

Early Bronze Age II Jug

Included in this discussion is most of a jug (34.2478; pl. 66g) from Tomb 17 because it is one of the few additional vessels that indicate activity on the East Slope in Early Bronze Age II. Its squat body, broad flat base, and narrow neck are similar to Early Bronze Age I types (Fischer 2008, figs. 267:2–3, 268:5), but its raised vertical decorations place it within the stylistic canons of Early Bronze Age II. Early Bronze Age II jugs with similar decorations tend to be less stout and more svelte in appearance with elongated bodies ending in narrower bases (e.g., Amiran 1969, pl. 17:1–4; Fischer 2008, fig. 289:phase II). The vertical strip, a decorative feature unknown in Early Bronze Age I assemblages, makes its appearance in Early Bronze Age II, when it is particularly popular. This type of decoration is probably inspired by vestigial handles on finely made vessels of Metallic Ware (e.g., Golani 2003, fig. 4.29:1–2). The overall morphology of this crudely fashioned type of jug, especially its handle that rises up slightly over the top of the rim, suggests a somewhat early dating in the period, and that it is likely to be a crude imitation of finer, metallic ware examples.

Early Bronze Age III Pottery

The pottery of the Early Bronze Age III is also represented mostly by small fragments but there are also a number of better-preserved vessels including two complete holemouths. As a rule, slips are less common in this assemblage and there is little evidence of the red slipping and burnishing that distinguishes much of the Early Bronze Age I pottery. Pattern burnishing appears on some of the vessels of this period. The use of the wheel is in evidence on many types, although it is uncertain whether some pots were actually thrown or whether they were merely finished on a wheel. Painting is much in evidence in small and medium-size vessels of different types; red stripes and broad bands were favored.

Small, Wheel-turned Bowls with String-cut Bases

Small, wheel-turned bowls with string-cut bases appear to have been produced in some quantity, with potters making no effort at effacing some of the more obvious evidence of techniques of their craft. The walls of these vessels are of uneven thickness with visible ridges where they were turned on a wheel, while their surfaces are often only barely smoothed (e.g., 34.2488, 34.2477, A65912, A65911; pl. 67d–g). Their bases are very coarse, probably as a result of their being prized off work surfaces when they were dried to states of leather-hardness. This carelessness in finish, as well as the mode of production, suggests the type was mass produced. Most examples appear to be of light-colored fabrics. Additional examples were found in clear Early Bronze Age III contexts on the high mound (*Megiddo II*, pl. 101:1–4; Greenberg 2006, p. 162, figs. 10.4:3–6, 10.52, 10.6:4, 10.7:1–2, 9).

Jugs and Juglets

Fragments of jugs and juglets, including several small stump bases, are typical of the Early Bronze Age III (34.2494, A16752, 34.2496, A65935, A30387 (from Khirbet Kerak, for comparison; pls. 67a, c; 68f–h). Additional stump bases found in the assemblage, almost certainly of jugs, were published by Loud (*Megiddo II*, pl. 100:8–15). They are of varying qualities. Some are extremely coarse but one is noticeably red slipped and burnished to a glass-like sheen (34.2496; pl. 68f). Parallels were found on the high tell and at Bet Yerah (e.g., Greenberg and Eisenberg 2006, fig. 5.84:7–8; Eisenberg and Greenberg 2006, figs. 8.89:1, 8.103:4–5). Some of the larger jugs are wheel-made (34.2503/1; pl. 69d) and morphologically related to small and medium-size jars (A16748, 34.2496/2, 34.2483; pls. 67i; 69b, e). Several small fragments of juglets with a heavy, smooth, satiny slips of dull reds (pl. 66b) could be examples of Khirbet Kerak Ware, but those identifications are uncertain, as they do not bear evidence of distinctive, corroborative features.

Small and Medium-size Jars

Small and medium-size jars are of well-levigated, usually light-colored fabrics and finished on wheels. By comparison with the small bowls, most have relatively thin walls and nicely smoothed exteriors (A16748, A16754, 34.2664, 34.2496/2, A16314, 34.2483; pls. 67i; 68a; 69a–c, e). Some were painted with red stripes. One small, red slipped jar with wide mouth and splayed rim (34.2512; pl. 68b) is decorated with two lines of oblique incisions around its neck. A close parallel from Tel Gat Hefer (Covello-Paran 2003, p. 14) suggests it is dated to Early Bronze Age III. Others, with gracefully curving "S" profiles, are also wheel-made and have string-cut bases (34.2483; pl. 69e).

Goblet

A single example of a small, straight-walled goblet (34.2491; pl. 68c) with simple, tapered rim is notable. Externally it was somewhat carelessly decorated with red bands, while its internal surface was mostly covered with a thin coat of red paint.

Platter-plates

The term "platter-plate" refers to a considerable number of fragments of large, somewhat thick and very shallow vessels notable for their simple rounded rims, large flat bases, and gently rounded, smooth interiors (pl. 70). Many examples have particularly coarse bases suggesting they too (as were small bowls) were made on flat surfaces and then prized off them when the vessels were leather-hard, leaving bits of clay clinging to the surface and corresponding small cavities on the bottoms of their bases (e.g., 34.2463/3, 34.2463/5, A65904; pl. 70b–d). No effort was made to efface these rough surfaces, although the interiors are invariably smooth.

There is considerable variation in size and in morphology of these vessels, as well as in the manner in which they were finished. One group consists of very flat types, red slipped and sometimes pattern burnished (A16741, 34.2463/1; pl. 70i–j), some of which are particularly large. All platters appear to be of light-colored fabrics, buff to brown. Additional examples have been found on the tell (e.g., *Megiddo II*, pl. 6:13–14, 17–18), some in good Early Bronze Age III contexts (Joffe 2000, figs. 8.9:18, 8:10; Greenberg 2006, figs. 10.3:4, 10.7:3). A lack of close parallels at other sites suggests this type may have been locally produced and consumed.

Large Bowls and Basins

Several examples of large, shallow vessels with straight sides are found in this assemblage (pl. 71). Most appear to have had two very wavy ledge handles, typical of Early Bronze Age III (e.g., A16785; pl. 68d). Similar but less well-preserved examples are found on the high mound (*Megiddo II*, pls. 5:19, 6:16; Joffe 2000, fig. 8.9:16).

Holemouth Vessels

Although numerous holemouth vessels with thickened and rounded rims found in the assemblage may date to Early Bronze Age III (pl. 72), they cannot be so ascribed with any great degree of confidence as they could also date to Late Early Bronze Age I or Early Bronze Age II. Numerous examples from Megiddo and other south Levantine sites of this time span bear potters' marks (34.2534, 34.2534/1, 34.2534/2; pl. 72a–b, d; *Chapter 4*), suggesting possible inter-site associations.

One holemouth vessel, found in an open area near a kiln (Locus 1152) (*Chapter 2*), was completely preserved (34.2546; pl. 72e), while another comes from just outside Locus 914 (A16770; pl. 73b). A third example of this type could not be located for the present study but an archival photograph of the restored vessel proved useful. Writing on the vessel, visible in the scanned print (pl. 73a), identifies its excavation number as P4509 and indicates it came from "Locus 1183." According to the locus list this findspot is "floor under NE part of 1171" and is associated with additional loci that appear to be part of a sequence of structures and fills located at the border of Squares U17 and V17. Several walls and bedrock outcrops are visible in the aerial photographs in that location, but there are no more specific records concerning those loci, and so nothing more can be said of this find except that it indicates an area of activity in the Early Bronze Age.

The rounded bases of these holemouth jars are paralleled in Early Bronze Age III contexts on the high mound (*Megiddo II*, pl. 6:8) and at Bet Yerah in Early Bronze Age III (Greenberg and Eisenberg 2006, figs. 5.87:11, 8.89:2), but the type is also associated at the latter site with late phases of Early Bronze Age II (Eisenberg and Greenberg 2006, figs. 8.62:7, 8.68:8, 8.79:7). Those from the East Slope, where there is abundant evidence of Early Bronze Age III pottery and little to suggest human activity in Late Early Bronze Age II, should probably be dated to the later chronological horizon. As none of these examples showed evidence of fire clouding, they appear to have been used for storage and ostensibly were not cooking pots.

Storage Jars and Pithoi

With the exception of holemouths, storage jars and pithoi are sorely under-represented in the East Slope assemblage, perhaps because of poor preservation but possibly because they were not used there. Two fragments of the necks of pithoi are illustrated (A38567, A16806; pl. 69f–g). They bear a typical form of Early Bronze Age III rope-like decoration formed by oblique slashes made at regular intervals into a line of raised decoration where the neck of the vessel was joined to the body.[72] One (A38567) also has traces of thick white encrustation on it, possibly deliberate application of a lime-based slip. The fabrics and morphology of these sherds suggest they are of the same type as others found on the tell in contexts dated to Early Bronze III (*Megiddo II*, pl. 101:30–31; Greenberg 2006, fig. 10.12:9).

Early Bronze Age III Pottery from the East Slope: A Summary Statement

The late assemblage from the East Slope is datable to Early Bronze III but no further precision within that period is possible. What may be absent in the assemblage, or possibly very under-represented, is Khirbet Kerak Ware, one of the hallmarks of the period. Notably, that type of pottery has been found on the high mound (Esse 1991, p. 80; Joffe 2000, p. 174), which might be an indication that Early Bronze Age III activity on the East Slope was more limited in scope or in time. Either explanation or both could account for this particular deficiency. Suffice it to note that the quantity of pottery from this period suggests there was significant human activity within one or more structures located on the East Slope during this period. What appear to be purely functional, quotidian aspects of the different ceramic types from the East Slope in Early Bronze Age III is in agreement with the lack of any tombs from this period. Thus the East Slope, at least for a time, appears to have ceased to be a cemetery, although in the following and later periods it reverted to that function.

PART 2: BONE, GROUNDSTONE, METALLURGICAL ARTIFACTS, AND A POTTERY FIGURINE

TEXTILE-RELATED ARTIFACTS: BONE TOOLS, STONE LOOM WEIGHTS, AND CLOTH IMPRESSION IN POTTERY

Bone Tools

Several bone tools were collected by the excavators, who ascribed them to different stages (Engberg and Shipton 1934a, p. 40, fig. 13). They were recovered in Square U16. One each is ascribed to Stages VII through V, presumably based on their findspots, but unfortunately there are no indications of their precise proveniences. Thus, unfortunately, there is no way of dating these objects (34.2693, 34.2695, 34.2696; pl. 74a–c), either by association to archaeological deposits or by comparanda, as the diminutive sizes and rather simple shapes of these objects do not allow for any specific dating. They appear to be associated with weaving or other tasks related to textile production and suggest that this activity took place somewhere, sometime on the East Slope during early occupations there. Additional evidence of such activity was found in B/V/1, the excavators' Stage V, in a group of small, basalt rings, probably used as loom weights (see below).

Evidence of actual cloth, used probably to cover a work surface on which a small bowl was made, is found in an impression on the interior of that bowl's base (A16852; pl. 74d). This is a somewhat unusual technique, but not entirely unknown in that era. I have found evidence of a similar use of textile impressed into a small bowl from an Early Bronze Age context at Horvat ʿIllin Tahtit in Beth Shemesh, while there are several sherds showing similar impressions from the Northwest Settlement at Lachish (Tufnell et al. 1958, pl. 13:96–97), probably dating to the same general Early Bronze Age I chrono-cultural horizon.

---

[72] In a sense this is a throwback to the style of imitating rope in ceramics that was in vogue during the early phases of Early Bronze Age I.

Metal and Metal-related Objects

A small terra-cotta mold (34.2690; pl. 74e), probably for producing blanks of copper axes, was recovered in fill somewhere within the lower levels in what Engberg and Shipton (1934a, fig. 13) describe as "the stratified area," which is presumably on one of the terraces. In addition, several small copper rods and a thin copper object described as a "spatula" were apparently recovered in fills somewhere on the East Slope (Engberg and Shipton 1934a, fig. 13). They are too poorly preserved to justify illustration here, while their findspots remain obscure. Suffice it to note that any or all of these objects could be related to the Early Bronze Age levels.

Pottery Figurine

A portion of a small figurine, the hindquarters of a quadruped (M2520; pl. 74f), was recovered in Tomb 903 Upper (*Megiddo Tombs*, p. 9, pl. 76:7). Similar figurines are found in many Early Bronze Age I contexts (e.g., Sass 2000, figs. 12.37–38), the period that this object apparently dates to.

Groundstone Artifacts

Engberg and Shipton (1934a, p. 40) reported that "from Stages I to VII the following were common: basalt and limestone rubbers and hammerstones; grinders and fragments of basalt vessels; and whorls of basalt and pottery, especially the former." Unfortunately, there is no information on the precise findspots of these objects. Two basalt "rubbers" or upper grinding stones, two large querns, and several small basalt rings, visible in B/V/1 (pl. 34), are exceptions but their registry numbers are unknown and so they cannot be correlated with the objects discussed below, among which one or more might be included.

EXCURSUS 3

EDS-XRF ANALYSIS OF A TERRA-COTTA MOLD

by Sariel Shalev,
Leon H. Charney School of Marine Sciences
and the Department of Archaeology, University of Haifa

The excavators' identification of this terra-cotta object (34.2690) as a mold for copper axe heads was virtually confirmed by modern technology when it was subjected to EDS-XRF analyses using an XL3T900HE portable Niton instrument (Niton-1; Niton-2). Analyses were made on the internal and external surfaces of this terra-cotta mold using 120-second exposure and an 8 mm beam size (fig. to pl. 74). In two random areas of the inner surface they showed evidence of remains of copper in quantities at least three times higher (0.075 and 0.097 wt% Cu) than the analyses of random places on the object's external surface (between 0.024 and up to 0.026 wt% Cu). The limits of detection for copper is 0.0025 and therefore the counts from the analyses are at least ten times above the LDT (limit of detection) and, accordingly, represent a real effect. Thus it is highly probable that the inner surface of this object was exposed to copper and therefore it may be assumed that this terra-cotta served as an open mold for casting an Early Bronze Age blunt copper axe or adze.

Early Bronze Age Potter's Tournette

A thick stone disk, fashioned of basalt, probably an upper part of a potter's tournette of a type recently documented in the southern Levant (Roux and de Miroschedji 2009, esp. fig. 5A), was associated with Stage IV. Unfortunately, I have been unable to locate the object, which, I suspect, may never have made it to either of the two collections as it was conspicuously reported on and noted as "not illustrated." From its description it appears similar to two additional tournettes from the high tell (*Megiddo II*, pl. 268:1–2), now in the Oriental Institute's collection. The find from the East Slope is described by Engberg and Shipton (1934a, p. 40) as "a pierced basalt disk, 19 × 5 cm, which, because of the glassy wear on one face as well as at the junction of the biconical central piercing, was considered as a possible *tournette*." This description indicates the object had the typical features of an underside of an upper disk, a central piercing surrounded by a large, circular band of a polished surface caused by abrasion where it came into contact with a lower disk (Roux and de Miroschedji 2009). The tournette from Stratum XVIII, apparently almost identical in size and features to that from Stage IV, is illustrated in lieu of the example from the East Slope (pl. 75f).

According to their findspots, the tournettes from Stage IV and Stratum XVIII should be dated to late in the Early Bronze Age I or to an early phase of Early Bronze Age II. However, there seems to be some difficulty in such an interpretation as the pottery of that horizon seems not to show any external evidence of use of the wheel, with the possible exception of external finishing on Metallic Ware objects. By contrast, wheel marks are highly visible on many vessels of the Early Bronze Age III, especially small bowls, small and medium-size jars, and the deeper platters with curving profiles. Notably, these tournettes from Megiddo are closely paralleled in well-provenienced Early Bronze Age III objects from Tel Yarmuth (Roux and de Miroschedji 2009, figs. 3–6, esp. fig. 5).

The tournette's provenience on the East Slope suggests the likelihood of some ceramic production there. It is even possible that the object's presence may somehow be related to the kiln in Locus 1143, although such an ascription must remain in the realm of speculation. Perhaps too, the small, wheel-turned bowls of Early Bronze Age III are additional evidence of local potter's activity (see above).

Potter's Stone Pivot Wheel

A field photograph (fig. to pl. 75) is the sole evidence for an upper portion of a potter's wheel, apparently of basalt, found in Square U17 in a rock-lined cavity in Locus 1185. It is of a type with pivot that probably belongs to a post-Early Bronze Age period (Roux and de Miroschedji 2009, p. 166), perhaps dating to the second millennium B.C. I have been unable to locate this object but an enlarged view of it, derived from the field photograph, is shown in plate 75g.

Basalt Bowl

A basalt bowl (pl. 75e), of a morphological type clearly dated to the Early Bronze Age I, was found on the surface of Square V17. I was unable to locate this object, but a published drawing (*Megiddo I*, pl. 112:7) records its very thick base and high, splayed wall, indicating it is an example of the most common type (Type 1) encountered throughout the southern Levant in this period (Braun 1990). Such bowls are found at sites of all phases of this period and so it may not be dated with any exactitude.

Basalt Loom Weights

Several small loom weights (or spindle whorls), small rings of basalt, are of a type well known from Early Bronze Age I contexts (pl. 75a–d). These are commonly found in Early Bronze Age I contexts throughout the period and are thus of no help in more exact dating. A small cache of these objects was found in B/V/1, which may preserve evidence of a loom having been located there (pls. 33–34).

Grinding Stones

No examples of grinding stones from the East Slope remain in the preserved collections, but several such objects were noted in B/V/1 (pls. 32, 34). Two were large objects, possibly found resting on their sides (*Chapter 2*), while two smaller, apparently loaf-shaped rubbers or upper grinding stones can be seen on plate 34.

4

SEALINGS, POTTERS' MARKS, AND POTMARKS FROM THE EAST SLOPE

INTRODUCTION

The Early Bronze Age artifact inventory from the East Slope of Megiddo includes a number of objects that document examples of forms of non-verbal communication common at other contemporary sites in the southern Levant. Surviving examples include pottery objects that bear seal impressions or motifs either incised into their not-yet-fired fabrics or scratched onto their permanent surfaces. For purposes of the discussion below, incised marks deliberately made in the clay of unfired vessels are considered "potters' marks," a designation indicating their relationship to the manufacturing process and thus their proximity to the potter's craft. They are distinguished from marks incised, drilled, or otherwise engraved into fired ceramics, that is, "potmarks," which could be made by virtually any individual after a vessel was fired.

SEAL IMPRESSIONS

Seal impressions on ceramic vessels from from the East Slope of Early Bronze Age Megiddo have been the subject of numerous publications, beginning with Engberg's and Shipton's treatments of examples recovered in their excavations (1934a, pp. 31–39, figs. 10, 11; 1934b). Although they published only six, seven sealings were found but as one was quite fragmentary it was apparently not deemed worthy of publication.[73] Subsequently, Ben-Tor included it in his in-depth treatment of the subject (1978, fig. 6:39). These impressions, together with two additional sealings discovered on the high tell (*Megiddo II*, pl. 160:4 = *Impression No. 6*; Sass 2000, fig. 12.45), make up the full complement of known cylinder-seal impressions from Megiddo dated to the Early Bronze Age. These sealings and a single cylinder seal-bead of bone (*Megiddo II*, pl. 160:1) are the extent of Early Bronze Age glyptic production known from the site to date. All the impressions were apparently made by rolling cylinders to produce a continuous scene, with the exception of one, which was possibly made from a stamp seal. Those in the former group, when preserved completely enough, have definitive borders. Unfortunately, only one of these examples derives from an in situ context, which indicates its ascription to Early Bronze Age I. However, most of the others can be relatively securely dated to the same period on the basis of their motifs, styles, and fabrics. Although this is a rather modest assemblage[74] for the scale of the exposure of Early Bronze Age I Megiddo, it is a significant collection as the discussion below indicates.

---

[73] This is evident from its eventual disposition after a "division of the spoils" after the excavation. It is the sole impression of the group allotted by the Mandate Department of Antiquities to the Oriental Institute.

[74] Ben-Tor (2003) notes this in comparison with a significantly larger corpus from nearby Tel Qashish, a much smaller site, but that observation seems to be a function of chronology. All but one of the impressions from Tel Qashish belong to the Early Bronze Age II–III group and probably date to a time span when Megiddo was virtually abandoned (Esse 1991, p. 74).

Catalog of Sealings from the East Slope and Two from the High Mound

Impression No. 1

Description:

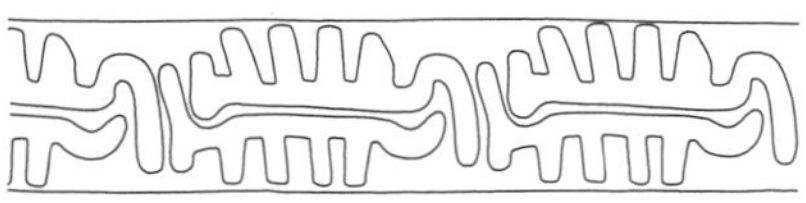

This impression (pl. 76b) was made by a cylinder twice rolled onto the shoulder of a pithos (34.2587), once horizontally and once nearly vertically (pl. 76a).[75] The jar, of a fairly well-levigated, pinkish fabric, has a nicely shaped bow rim and is of a type that has regional and chronological significance (Braun 1985, pp. 50, 51, 62–65, table 3: type 26; *Chapter 3*). The vessel is also notable for its strips of rope-like decoration; raised triangular bands depressed at regular intervals both horizontally and in crescentic segments. The impressions made by the seal are relatively large, with flat planes, probably indicating the cylinder was of wood.

Provenience:

Although the base of this vessel was not preserved, or at least was not mended with the upper parts of the vessel and is no longer to be found, there is no question the pot was found in situ. The broken jar is visible in a photograph as a heap of sherds, apparently on an earthen floor of B/V/1 and in a hemp basket nearby (pls. 33–34). The identification of the vessel is confirmed by a notation on a photograph of the reconstructed vessel and verified by a clearly visible sherd of the bow rim in the basket used for collection of the pottery in the field. The discovery of the impressions took place only after the vessel was cleaned and in the process of restoration (Engberg and Shipton 1934b) as the upper part of the vessel appears to have been covered by some encrustation.

Motif:

Two schematic, five-legged animals in *tête bêche* arrangement make up the motif, which is complete. One animal has a long tail and short head, the other a long head and short tail. These creatures, which defy precise identification, virtually fill the register and are obvious artistic devices to forestall the artist's sense of *horror vacui* in his composition. Presumably they are symbolic representations, but whether of actual quadrupeds or merely schematic renderings of imaginary beasts is obscure as five-legged creatures are not found in nature. A possible explanation for the additional limb may be an artistic attempt at transmitting the idea of kinetic motion of quadrupeds, thus preceding Giacomo Balla's 1912 *Dynamism of a Dog on a Leash* by more than five millennia (Russel 1981, p. 155).

Parallels:

There are no close parallels to this impression on cylinder seals from the southern Levant, although other sealings, some from farther afield, have similar motifs, including five-legged animals. The highly schematic depiction of multi-legged animals combined with a similar sense of *horror vacui* is reminiscent of motifs on several stamp seal impressions found in the énéolithique cemetery at Byblos (Dunand 1945, figs. 5:a–c, 8:c, e–f, h). Multi-legged animals (some with only three limbs) in the same type of artistic, *tête bêche* arrangement, albeit of somewhat less schematic mien, have been found on the East Slope (see Impression No. 2, below) and at nearby ʿEn Shadud. Five-legged animals, similarly schematic, are also found on a stamp seal from Tell el-Farʿah North, dated to Early Bronze Age II by de Vaux and Steve (1948, fig. 3: right).

Functional Parallels:

Another published example of cylinder seal impressions (pl. 81) on a bow-rim pithos suggests a function shared with this pithos as well as close contemporaneousness. Another example of an impression on such

[75] A similar practice is known from ʿEn Shadud (see *Parallels*) and two examples from Sidon (Doumet-Serhal 2006, p. 259).

a pithos is a surface find from Tel Megadim (pl. 81). Notably, both of these impressions have geometric motifs. The sealing from ʿEn Shadud reproduced a chevron pattern, while that from Tel Megadim an "eye" or rhomb motif.

Impression No. 2

DESCRIPTION:

This impression is on a large fragment of the upper wall of a holemouth vessel (34.2752; pl. 77a–b). The vessel has a relatively coarse fabric of dark brown to gray color with light-colored grits and a coarsely finished, slightly pitted surface. The scene, made by a cylinder seal with typical upper and lower borders, appears to be a nearly complete depiction of two animals in a *tête bêche* arrangement, which when rolled would produce a continuous frieze. The impression is distinct but appears to have been made somewhat carelessly, which has led to different interpretations of its details (see *Motif*, below).

PROVENIENCE:

The large fragment is marked as deriving from Square U17 under Locus 1371. Unfortunately, we know neither the exact boundaries of this "nether locus" nor the absolute elevation of its findspot. Ben-Tor's (1978, pp. 43–44) ascription of this locus to Stage V is apparently based on a purported findspot, obviously below the floor level of Stage IV, in a "pit." That claim, based on information supplied by A. Eitan, suggests it and several other sherds with sealings and pot marks derive from the same pit. However, that information cannot be confirmed as we have no greater precision for locating the findspot in documentation presently available. Indeed: that stratigraphic ascription is far from certain for several reasons: 1) The dimensions of Locus 1371 are unknown, beyond the notation that it lay within the bounds of Squares U16 and U17; 2) the sealing, preserved on only a largish sherd, was recovered in non-primary deposition, which means it (as well as the others from the same nether locus) was discarded and need not necessarily have originated in the matrix where it was found; 3) "under 1371" could refer to low-lying deposits above bedrock which was uneven; 4) this sherd (as well as others from this context) could have been intrusive from Stage IV or residual and associated with deposits associated with earlier Walls 26, 31, and 32. If Eitan's information, which cannot be corroborated in presently available documentation, is correct, then a likely location for the pit would be a deep depression in the bedrock some meters to the north of the juncture of Squares U16, U17, V16, and V17. Observable in the last aerial photograph is such a depression bisected by the boundary between Squares U16 and U17 (pl. 12). That provenience, close to bedrock, could explain the excavators' ascription of these impressed sherds to Stage V.

MOTIF:

In the center of the impression is a nearly completely preserved image, a side view of a three-legged animal with head in three-quarters view tapering to a broad, snout-like end. In previous interpretations of the impression a long, horn-like protuberance is shown on left side of the head and coming up over the triangular right ear (pl. 77b). My interpretation (pl. 77c), based on careful examination of the sherd and what I believe to be clearly seen in Z. Radovan's excellent photograph (pl. 77a), suggests the protuberance is actually a second triangular ear (virtually identical in size to that on the right) inadvertently attached to a portion of the foot of the foremost leg of the upside-down animal above and to the left. Careful examination of the end of the leg shows it slopes slightly to the right and does not end where Engberg's and Shipton's drawing (pl. 77b) suggests it does. The general outline of the end of the leg is preserved in very low relief and I suggest that most of what the excavators interpreted as a horn is in actual fact the end of the leg that got pushed off to the left either in the process of rolling or afterward, at some point before the vessel dried. I believe my interpretation is consistent with the clearly defined triangular shape of the left ear and what is only the slightest point of attachment to the unusually shaped "horn."

The animal (with or without horn) has a very long tail, which follows the line of the end of the body and arches up over the back, almost touching the "ear/horn," and then doubles back down where it nearly touches the tail of another, similar animal arranged upside down. In front of the complete animal is another in a *tête bêche* arrangement. Neither of the two flanking animals is complete enough to know how many legs they may have had, but three seems likely. The incomplete animal on the right also has a long, curved tail looping over the animal's back.

These last two animals were probably produced from the same part of the seal and the differences in them may be understood as derived from numerous variables such as viscosity of the clay, quantity and size of temper, pressure applied to the seal when rolled, handling after sealing, shrinkage and cracking during drying and firing processes. These variables could also explain differences between this sealing and its parallel from ʿEn Shadud, which I believe could have been produced from one and the same cylinder.

PARALLELS:

A comparison with the motif of a sealing from nearby ʿEn Shadud (pl. 77) strengthens the interpretation suggested above. In addition to the cylinder seal impression from ʿEn Shadud (Braun 1985, p. 80, fig. 33) there is a partially preserved impression of two animals, one of which is horned, found at nearby Tel Qashish (Ben-Tor 2003, fig. 73:5).

Impression No. 3

DESCRIPTION:

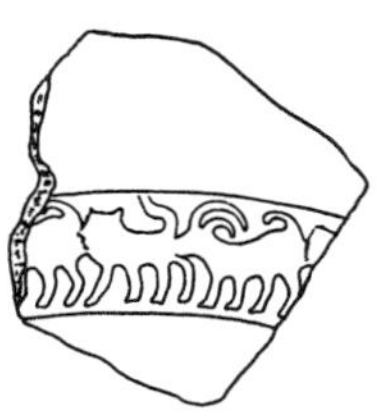

This seal impression is on a small sherd of a vessel (34.2754 / P5554) of indeterminate type (pl. 78a). The seal has flat planes and was evenly impressed leaving the outlines of the motif and the border clearly visible. The fabric of the sherd is buff gray in color with somewhat coarse temper.

PROVENIENCE:

Found in Square U17 under Locus 1371.

MOTIF:

Visible are two quadrupeds in profile with their heads in three-quarters view overlapping the animal in front (to the left). When rolled the seal creates the impression of a file of animals, of which only two are actually depicted on the seal. One animal with two large, curving horns and a small tail that loops up over its back appears to be an ibex or a goat; the other with a long tail and small, pointy ears may depict a feline.

PARALLELS:

Two parallels have been found at Megiddo. Both depict animals in a single file, although the styles of the actual renderings appear to be different. Impression Nos. 4 and 5 below are thematically similar and may even have been intended to represent the same animal types. Another, preserved in a tiny fragment on a minuscule sherd, was found in a late Early Bronze Age I context Early Bronze Age I context near Tel Qashish (E. C. M. van den Brink, pers. comm.).

Impression No. 4

DESCRIPTION:

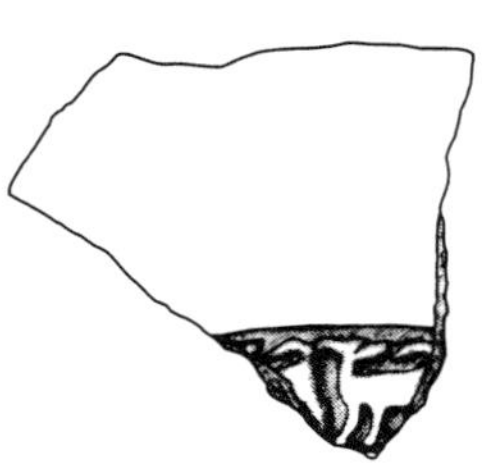

This impression (pl. 78b) is on the edge of a minuscule sherd (A16872), dark buff to brown in color. The fabric is relatively coarse, with numerous small gray and white grits, while the exterior has a surface pitted by a burst air bubble. The impressed side of the sherd is covered with a thin, reddish brown slip or wash that does not cover the reverse side, thus indicating the fragment is part of a closed form. The thickness of the sherd associates it with a medium-size to small vessel but nothing else of its morphology is known, although the fabric would not be inconsistent with having been part of a holemouth vessel. The sealing is in low relief with rounded contours. The red slip must have covered it in its entirety but it has been worn or rubbed off on most of the impression. A low ridge, the margin preserved at the top of its scene, indicates it was made by a cylinder.

Provenience:

This fragment was found on the East Slope but no further information on its findspot was noted by the excavators. Given the diminutive size of the object, the exact provenience would not necessarily have been indicative of its ultimate chrono-cultural origins. It appears, on stylistic grounds, to be dated to Early Bronze Age I.

Motif:

Although only a minuscule portion of the scene is preserved, there is enough for it to be identified as file of animals probably forming a continuous frieze. The more complete image has a thick body atop three visible legs facing to the left. The head, less distinct, is represented by an elongated mass tapering at both ends. Since the legs are more realistic looking, the shape of the head may be the result of either a damaged seal or the careless manner in which it was impressed onto the vessel. The longer end of the head, facing to the right, is almost certainly the snout, suggesting the animal is looking backward. The tail of this animal arches up over its back. The rear end of the animal to the left is completely visible and has a similar tail, which merges with the left side of the head (its horns?) of the animal to the rear. A nondescript raised lump at the left edge of the sherd is probably part of the second animal's head. While the single preserved head and tails of these animals seem to be rather schematic, the legs were rendered a shade more realistically as may discerned in the depiction of a joint in the hind leg of the animal to the left.

It is uncertain what animals were meant to be depicted. While the distinctive posture of the tails is one often identified with felines, the shape of the single preserved head seems to belie such identification. That particular pose and the less-than-distinct features of this animal could be explained by "artistic license" or merely a lack of skill on the part of the carver of the seal. It is one of a number of generic, iconographic representations of quadrupeds found on cylinder seals of the latter phases of Early Bronze Age I that defy more precise identification.

Parallels:

Two sealings from Megiddo are similar in that they have two animals forming a line (see Nos. 3 and 5), but in neither case does any animal look backward. Both, however, have animals with long tails that curve up over their backs. Another, from Tel Dan, shows animals of similar style also walking in single file (Greenberg 1996, figs. 341:22, 343:15).

Impression No. 5

Description:

This impression is on a diminutive sherd (96/H/4/AR1) found on the high mound by the Tel Aviv University Expedition[76] to Megiddo in a more recent excavation (pl. 79a; after Joffe 2001, pp. 355–56).

[76] This expedition renewed work on the high mound and is an ongoing project.

PROVENIENCE:

The sherd was found in a locus containing pottery of Early Bronze Age I and later periods. The context is mixed and thus offers no information on its chrono-cultural origin. Stylistically it appears to be dated to Early Bronze Age I, a dating reinforced by a newly discovered parallel.

MOTIF:

This impression depicts two animals facing left, one slightly in front of the other. The one in front has a nondescript, almost circular face and two large, curving horns similar to the horned animal in Impression No. 3, but there is no tail in evidence for this creature. The other animal has a broad face, a small, tapering snout, two tiny, nearly rectangular ears, and a long tail curving up over its back nearly the entire length of its body. Joffe suggests it might depict a lion or a leopard.

PARALLELS:

A fragment of a sealing preserved on a sherd from an Early Bronze Age I context at a site near Tel Qashish may have been made from the same cylinder that produced this impression (E. C. M. van den Brink, pers. comm.). See also Impression No. 4 above.

Impression No. 6

DESCRIPTION:

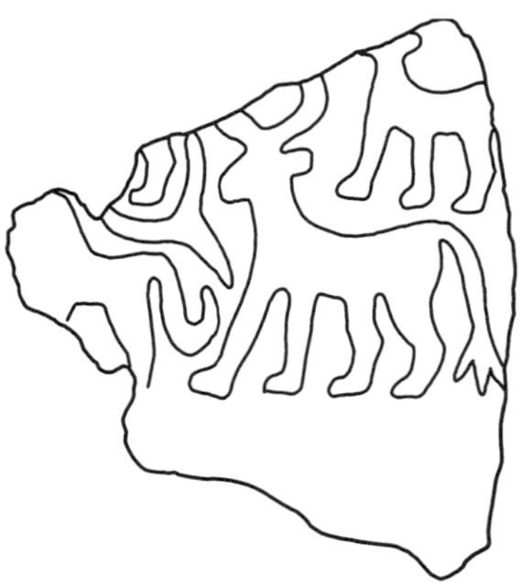

This impression (pl. 79b) was made by a seal impressed on a vessel of indeterminate mien (38.982). The fabric is buff colored with somewhat coarse grits and the exterior is covered by a red slip, similar to many sherds of the Early Bronze Age I. If made by a cylinder seal it is one of the largest known from this period. Its flat planes suggest it was made in the same medium of wood as the seal that produced Impression No. 1.

PROVENIENCE:

The sherd was found in fill associated with Stratum XI on the high mound (*Megiddo II*, pl. 160:4) and, on the basis of parallels to other sealings, assumed by them to have originally derived from Stratum XIX. An Early Bronze Age I ascription on the basis of style seems likely for this object.

MOTIF:

This impression is only partly preserved. Most prominent is a large quadruped with horns, somewhat suggestive of a bovid, albeit with a trident tail. To its left are the hindquarters of another animal with a long, curving tail. Above and to the right of the supposed bovid is another animal, unfortunately less well preserved. Its head seems indistinct, but the extant portion of it could suggest it is facing backward. If the rise of this animal's back is suggestive of its rump (as in the bovid noted below), then it is another depiction of a tri-legged animal. The lower portion of a rear leg of a fourth animal is visible at the upper left of the sherd. Its rendering, so similar to the rear leg of the bovid, suggests considerable skill on the part of the carver. The artist's *horror vacui* is evident in the tripartite space filler between the three animals at the left of the scene. This last element is repeated in Impression No. 7 and is understood to represent a body part of an animal.

This is the sole impression that appears to have what may be construed as a scene intended to portray an event. Its size and the juxtaposition of the animals clearly indicate it was not intended as mere decoration in the way some cylinder seal impressions may have been. Ben-Tor's relegation of the motif into merely two lines of animals in perspective (Ben-Tor 1978, p. 57) seems too simplistic an explanation for the scene. The perspective given to the figures is unparalleled in simple motifs and is not precise as the larger animals intrude into the "line" of those farther to the rear. The composition of the whole appears to depict a scene, perhaps one intended to tell a story related to these animals. While the meaning remains obscure to the modern beholder, it was likely to have been obvious to contemporaries of the vessel when it was made. A depiction of cultic or cult-related activity seems a not unlikely explanation for this scene.

PARALLEL:

There are no good parallels for this impression, but a number of recently published sealings from Sidon have some elements roughly similar to those in this scene. They appear to be space fillers between what were probably more complete renderings of animals (Doumet-Serhal 2006, pls. 167:6, 170:14, 171:20).

Impression No. 7

DESCRIPTION:

This impression (pl. 80a) is on a sherd (34.2753 / P555) of gray fabric with light brown slip, of what is likely to have been a medium-size jar, what the excavators claimed to be of either Type 12N or 16G (Engberg and Shipton 1934a, chart). However, the extant object is just a small sherd with no particular diagnostic features that would allow for identifying the vessel type from which it was broken. Unless the sherd was subsequently further broken and identifiable portions of the vessel lost, I suspect the excavators' type ascription is likely to have been more of an educated guess than a proper identification. Notably, this impression captured the entire sealing, with the extant portion duplicating part of it.

PROVENIENCE:

It was recovered in Square U16 under Locus 1371. Ben-Tor (1978, p. 44) suggested the find spot was a pit, but no extant documentation could be found for that claim.

MOTIF:

The motif is one of detached animal heads with and without horns (Engberg and Shipton 1934a, p. 31). The heads are juxtaposed at different angles and interspersed with filler elements, representing the artist's *horror vacui*. The horned animal heads suggest ibex or goat.

Impression No. 8

DESCRIPTION:

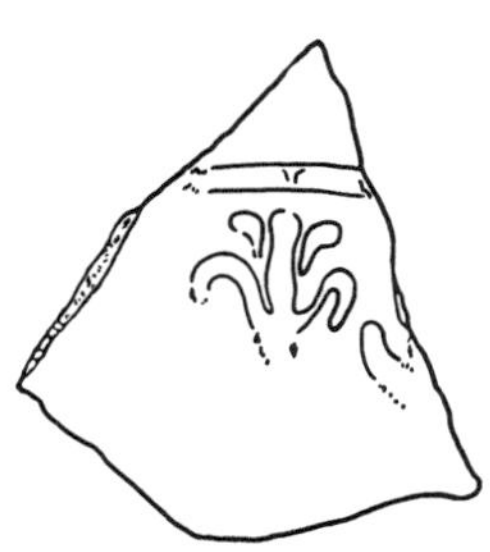

This is a diminutive sherd (A16869; pl. 80b), probably of a jar of small to medium size. Its fabric is gray and somewhat coarse with evidence of temper consistent with pottery associated with Stages VII through IV. The impression has a typical border made by cylinder seals.

PROVENIENCE:

Somewhere on the East Slope; the excavators (Engberg and Shipton 1934a, p. 31) ascribe it to Stage V, but no precise information on its findspot is available. I suspect it may have been found below Locus 1371 (see above, Impression No. 2).

MOTIF:

Visible is part of what appears to be a floral motif, possibly a stalk and leaves.

PARALLELS:

The only good parallel to this is Impression No. 9 (see below). Beck (1967, pp. 55–56) has noted generic parallels with floral motifs from Syria and Mesopotamia.

Impression No. 9

DESCRIPTION:

This is a diminutive sherd (pl. 80c), probably of a jar, small to medium in size. The impression has the typical border made by cylinder seals. The sherd cannot be located and no other information on it is available. [77]

PROVENIENCE:

Probably it is from the same context as the "pit." described by A. Eitan (see above).

MOTIF:

Visible is part of what appears to be a floral motif, possibly a stalk of a plant.

PARALLELS:

The only good parallel to this is also from Megiddo (Impression No. 8). Beck (1967, pp. 55–56) notes generic parallels with floral motifs from Syria and Mesopotamia.

Summary

As all these seals have been described and discussed at length (Engberg and Shipton 1934a, pp. 31–39; 1934b; Beck 1967, pp. 1–5, passim; 1975; 2002; Ben-Tor 1978, passim; Joffe 2001), it is not my intention to review all the revelations of these scholars. Below I briefly address two major aspects of the significance of these sealings, their chrono-cultural ascriptions and the manner in which they reflect on the socioeconomic milieus from which they derive.

Chrono-cultural Ascriptions

Suffice it to note that on the question of dating, all these sealings can, based on evidence of parallels, be reasonably associated with developed phases of the chrono-cultural horizon known as Early Bronze Age I, although I am unconvinced the excavators' claim for a single Stage V ascription for them is correct on several grounds. Such a phase seems ephemeral, considering the evidence reviewed in *Chapters 2* and *3*, and the stylistic differences of the impressions could well represent chronological disparities.

Provenience

With one exception, Impression No. 1, none of these objects derives from an in situ context. All are on fragments, some exceptionally small, of pots that were obviously broken and discarded prior to their deposition in the places where these sherds were found. Unfortunately, we lack detailed information on those findspots, but they may be assumed to be fills of no particular import, as the excavators did not see fit to mark them on these sherds, although they did occasionally do so for other objects. Thus, as Ben-Tor (1978, p. 90) has noted, there is a distinct possibility that these sealings are not all contemporary.

Stylistic and Typological Considerations

With the exception of Impressions Nos. 8 and 9, which may have been made from the same seal, and possibly Nos. 3 and 5, which may have been done by the hand of one and the same artisan, it appears that the remaining five examples are all ultimate products of different practitioners of the glyptic craft. Most

[77] It should be in the Rockefeller collection of the Israel Antiquities Authority, but was apparently lost sometime during the period when the Museum was under control of the British Mandate or until 1967. Beck (2002, p. 235 n. 15) was unable to locate it when she wrote her original version of that article (Beck 1975).

noticeable, of course, are the differences between the iconography of No. 1 and that of Nos. 2–6. Although both Nos. 1 and 2 depict animals in a *tête bêche* arrangement, there is a vast difference in the styles in which these animals were executed. The artists made no attempt at realism in the depiction of highly schematic animals in No. 1 with their rounded contours, while by contrast, individual features in the animals in No. 2 are rendered considerably more realistically in details, although the animals they were meant to portray may never have existed.

The flat-planed, rounded outline style of Impression No. 1 is virtually unique in the southern Levant; the sole exception is found on a jar decorated with a stamp seal from Tell el-Far^cah North (de Vaux and Steve 1948, fig. 3, right), which the excavators ascribed to Bronze Ancien IIa (i.e., an early phase of Early Bronze Age II[78]). As the parallel is not very close and the motifs differ, there is no obvious close association between these objects. Even more distant chronologically (Ben-Tor 1978, p. 71) are the generic parallels in motifs found in the éneolithique cemetery of Byblos, which is probably coeval with the Chalcolithic of the southern Levant (Dunand 1950; Braun 1989b). When considered together, these motifs and their renderings are indicative of a long-lived tradition.

There is, however, evidence that gives us some additional context for this object. It derives from the type of jar and the very fact that it was twice impressed with a single cylinder. The parallel with another, similarly impressed jar from ᶜEn Shadud (pl. 81d) cannot be coincidental and should be understood as evidence of a significant pattern. Additional jars of this type, bearing cylinder seal impressions (e.g., pl. 81a) from Tel Megadim, shed additional light on this practice. Quite clearly these impressions were not meant to be decorative, but imparted some other meaning we are incapable of comprehending.

The correlation suggested by these twice-impressed bow-rim type jars from Megiddo, ᶜEn Shadud, and Tel Megadim suggests contemporaneousness, although it is impossible to identify the precise stage or occupation at Megiddo that parallels Stratum I at ᶜEn Shadud, while the fragment from Tel Megadim was a surface find. The ᶜEn Shadud jar, also found in situ,[79] was in the later of two Early Bronze Age I occupations, which suggests that level was closely contemporary with B/V/1, a correlation that seems not unlikely on the basis of architectural comparanda. The latter site is dated, based on the evidence of what is believed to be a late form of Gray Burnished Ware, to be an advanced, but not the latest phase of Early Bronze Age I (Braun 1985, pp. 99–100). Unfortunately, due to the very fragmentary states of most of the Early Bronze Age I cylinder seal impressions it is impossible to know whether the different styles of expression were in vogue contemporaneously and thus are the products of different "schools" or workshops, or whether they reflect slightly different chronological phases. In any event they appear to be associated with an advanced, but not the latest phase of Early Bronze Age I.

The Social Implications of the Practice of Impressing Seals on Pottery in Early Bronze Age I

The appearance of seal impressions coincides, not unexpectedly, with a period of increased growth and social development at Megiddo, as may be discerned in the sacred precinct. The temples there offer sufficient physical evidence to postulate the existence of a socially stratified site by the end of Early Bronze Age I, especially in Level J4. The presently known distribution of these sealed vessels suggests, I believe, some type of intercourse between sites likely to have developed into something much more sophisticated than mere trade between communities of equal status, especially as Megiddo is so significantly more developed than most nearby communities as the monumental dimensions of the latest (J4) temple and the likely size of the site indicate (*Chapter 7*).

---

[78] The stamp seal impression is on a jar of a type (de Vaux and Steve 1948, fig. 7) paralleled in a late phase of Early Bronze Age I at Tel Beth Shan (cf. Braun 2004a, fig. 3.22:3–6), perhaps suggesting it was no so chronologically distant.

[79] The fill and floor of this room were so extraordinarily warped that there were differences of more than 1 m in elevations between the wall tops and floor levels of this building (Braun 1985, figs. 5, 13, pls. 2, 6) and the restoration of large portions of this vessel, from deposits of vastly different levels within the room, offered proof of this.

What type of a polity Megiddo was in the period in which the seals appeared remains somewhat obscure as the site is only known from the temple precinct and the sparsely utilized East Slope, while the lower mound seems to have been only sparsely settled in developed phases of Early Bronze Age I (Matthew Adams, pers. comm.). Present knowledge of nearby, contemporary, smaller communities at Tel Qashish, ʿEn Shadud, and Qiryat Ata, where additional sealings have been found, suggests some form of relationship between polities of non-equal status. Whether it may be properly described as the relationship of a "city-state" with its dependencies remains to be determined when more of the archaeological record is revealed. How Tel Megadim relates to this phenomenon remains obscure, as it lies in the coastal plain near the shore, at some considerable distance from Megiddo (*Chapter 2: Bow-rim Pithoi*). What seems certain is that the impressions, all associated with ceramic containers of one or another sort, bespeak some type of activity related to commodities and thus must be understood as basically economic in nature.

As some considerable expertise and effort was invested in making a seal and considering that it could be used virtually countless times, it is quite clear the Early Bronze Age I folk who owned them husbanded their use rather carefully. That is suggestive of an elite class of individuals who, by corollary, would have had control over the commodities the sealed vessels contained. That is discernible in the very scarcity of sealings found within the enormous number of potsherds recovered from contemporary or nearly contemporary Early Bronze Age I contexts at Megiddo, ʿEn Shadud (Braun 1985), Qiryat Ata (Golani 2003; Braun 2004b), Tel Qashish (Ben-Tor and Bonfil 2003a; Zuckerman 2003d; E. C. M. van den Brink pers. comm.), and other sites.

That Megiddo had a special relationship with sites in its immediate hinterland seems virtually certain from the finds at ʿEn Shadud and the lower terrace at Tel Qashish and probably also at Qiryat Ata. The relative sizes of these sites suggest Megiddo would have had a primal position in whatever relationship was in effect between them. The sealings suggest some form of local network of economic activity within the Jezreel and its environs,[80] and perhaps beyond to Tel Megadim. If an association with bow-rim pithoi, seen in several sealings, is also attributed to this phenomenon, then such a network seems to have been somewhat far-flung, as it also included ʿEn Esur in the Nahal ʿIron Pass.

Much has been written of the motifs, in particular the animals depicted on south Levantine Early Bronze Age I sealings (e.g., Engberg and Shipton 1934a, pp. 31–39; Beck 1967, p. 41; Beck 1975) and their relation to the iconography of seals of the ancient Near East, especially from the Syro-Mesopotamian sphere of influence. Clearly the Early Bronze Age I folk adopted the idea of sealing and the subject matter which they sought to depict from that milieu, but I believe they did not randomly adopt motifs or make them up, as they appear mostly as variations on the theme of animals, sometimes in a procession and sometimes probably in a symbolic arrangement. While we may only speculate as to the precise meaning these seals imparted and the functions with which they were likely endowed, it seems probable they were associated with some type of formal relationships between Megiddo on the one hand and those additional sites on the other.

The combination of specific motifs and the connection with vessels meant to contain commodities could suggest association with activities related to temples, of which we know a succession at Megiddo in late phases of Early Bronze Age I. The obviously symbolic nature of the faunal motifs, which repeat themselves, suggests a perception (of a belief system?) shared by Early Bronze Age I folk not only at Megiddo but at more far-flung sites. That in turn might suggest a class of temple administrators in charge of activity with economic, social, political, and religious overtones between Megiddo and its lesser neighbors. However, that scenario is highly speculative and other possibilities seem equally plausible. These sealings could be evidence of some form of civil administration[81] with a lesser religious association or they may even have been related to mortuary behavior. This last idea would not be as incongruous as it might seem, if the location of the building in which one sealing on a complete jar were found, had not been B/V/1, been in a precinct of the site surrounded by tombs.

---

[80] Another site that has yielded significant quantities of Late Early Bronze Age I pottery, but where no cylinder seal impressions have been found, is Afula (Sukenik 1936; 1948).

[81] Only a portion of what appears to be the central area of public activity on the high tell in the Early Bronze Age I has been excavated. Other types of public structures such as elite residences, storage areas for exercising economic control, additional temples and even a palace could well be located in adjacent precincts, still covered by later deposits, or even in the lower areas of the mound, yet to be explored.

These sealings are yet another aspect of shared traditions and associations between Early Bronze Age I peoples in the Jezreel Valley, its environs, and beyond (e.g., Me᾿ona; Braun 2004b). They further indicate that both the production of pottery, with which the creation of impressions is intrinsically linked, and the symbolism that accompanied the sealings, were not site-specific phenomena but were shared by and cognizant to peoples over greater regions. This is indication of increased social integration that distinguishes the later phases of Early Bronze Age I from its earlier exponents. The role of Megiddo is likely to have been central to some such regionally integrated social system, which minimally had some economic basis and which likely had political and religious overtones.

To what degree the regions to the north, from whence the symbols and uses to which sealings were put were derived, influenced such a system, remains unclear. What is certain is that the idea caught on and became considerably more popular in Early Bronze Age II–III, as witnessed by the ever-increasing assemblage of south Levantine sealings, examples of which number in the hundreds. That coincides precisely with a floruit of urban and urban-like activity at sites that boast large populations and/or fortifications such as Bet Yerah, Tel Qashish, Qiryat Ata, Tel Kinrot, and Tell Abu el-Kharaz.

POTTERS' MARKS

Deliberate markings incised, scratched, or impressed into the fabrics of not-yet-fired pots can be made with virtually no effort, yet not every pot was so marked. Potters' marks were reserved for specific vessels, very often, but not exclusively, holemouths. While much more common than seal impressions, they too appear to have been reserved for special functions. Those from the East Slope are part of a large corpus dating to the Early Bronze Age of the southern Levant that significantly grows with each new excavation of sites of the period (e.g., Genz 2001, with references[82]). Those from the East Slope, including some previously published (*Megiddo Tombs*, fig. 7), are discussed below. Sufficiently preserved examples, which indicate significant portions of their overall motifs, are illustrated below. Some examples have been published previously and to those I have added a few additions from different places on the East Slope that are sufficiently preserved to reproduce. Yet others are too fragmentary to justify their illustration.

One group of potters' marks seems to be from an ancient cache, a group of sherds deliberately collected and stored within a cave. Fifteen rim fragments, all incised prior to firing, were found in Tomb 903 Lower, which appears to have been used as a habitation or for storage, but was not a tomb. A predominance of holemouth vessels with such marks has also been noted at other sites by Genz (2001), who has suggested such marks were likely associated with one or another commodity. Some of these marks are paralleled at Tell Abu el-Kharaz, where they may be viewed in a form conveniently organized by its excavator, P. Fischer (2008, pp. 391–98). This cache of rim sherds with potters' marks from the East Slope offers an interesting sidelight on their secondary use. For whatever reason, someone took the trouble to collect these broken pieces and store them in the cave, possibly to be used as tokens or chits (pls. 82–83).

Two sherds of holemouths have similar t-shaped arrangements of incisions near their rims (pl. 61e, g), for which there is a good parallel from a late phase of Early Bronze Age I at Tel Beth Shan (Mazar and Rotem 2009, fig. 12:3; Mazar 2012, pls. 5:6, 7:5,). One potter's mark, a four-pointed rosette, is found on two different vessels from what may be associated proveniences. Another is on a wall of a large fragment of a very small holemouth with an unusual high loop handle (roughly oval in section) attached to its rim. A notation by the excavators on this latter vessel reads "863 = 1199," which indicates it was found in the cave to the southwest of B/IV/1 on the upper terrace. However, it would appear, considering the number it was originally given (Locus 863), that it is likely to have been recovered in fills somewhat high up in the deposits. Locus 1199 is the designation given to the same cave when the bedrock floor was visible. The other example of this pot-

[82] Additional information on the pottery of that site is found in Genz 2002.

Figure 29. Sherds bearing potters' marks

	Reg. No.	*Description*	*Provenience*	*Published*	*Photo*
a	P4515	Holemouth fragment	Tomb 903 Lower	*Megiddo Tombs*, fig. 7	—
b	P4514	Holemouth fragment	Tomb 903 Lower	*Megiddo Tombs*, fig. 7	—
c	34.2422 / P4512	Holemouth fragment	Tomb 903 Lower	*Megiddo Tombs*, fig. 7	See pl. 82a
d	34.2426 / P4525	Holemouth fragment	Tomb 903 Lower	*Megiddo Tombs*, fig. 7	See pl. 82b
e	A16762	Holemouth fragment	East Slope	—	See pl. 82c
f	P4510	Holemouth fragment	Tomb 903 Lower	*Megiddo Tombs*, fig. 7	—
g	P4527	Holemouth fragment	Tomb 903 Lower	*Megiddo Tombs*, fig. 7	—
h	P4505	Holemouth fragment	Tomb 903 Lower	*Megiddo Tombs*, fig. 7	—
i	34.2421 / P4511	Holemouth fragment	Tomb 903 Lower	*Megiddo Tombs*, fig. 7	See pl. 82d
j	A65941 / P5055	Holemouth fragment	U16, recess in rock southeast of Locus 1190	—	—
k	P4474	Holemouth fragment	Tomb 903 Lower	*Megiddo Tombs*, fig. 7	—
l	P4526	Holemouth fragment	Tomb 903 Lower	*Megiddo Tombs*, fig. 7	—
m	34.2425 / P4524	Holemouth fragment	Tomb 903 Lower	*Megiddo Tombs*, fig. 7	See pl. 82e
n	P4519	Holemouth fragment	Tomb 903 Lower	*Megiddo Tombs*, fig. 7	—
o	P4522	Holemouth fragment	Tomb 903 Lower	*Megiddo Tombs*, fig. 7	—
p	34.2424 / P4521	Holemouth fragment	Tomb 903 Lower	*Megiddo Tombs*, fig. 7	See pl. 82f
q	P4523	Holemouth fragment	Tomb 903 Lower	*Megiddo Tombs*, fig. 7	—
r	34.2305 / P4495	Holemouth fragment	Tomb 1106	*Megiddo Tombs*, pl. 6:13	See pl. 82g
s	34.2273 / P4133	Holemouth fragment	Tomb 1101-B Lower	*Megiddo Tombs*, pl. 7:5	See pl. 83a
t	34.2292 / P4631	Holemouth fragment	Tomb 1102 Lower	*Megiddo Tombs*, pl. 7:12	See pl. 83b
u	A16757 / P4835	Holemouth fragment	Locus 1168	—	
v	34.2528 / P4711	Holemouth fragment	"under Locus 1170"	—	See pl. 83c
w	A16910 / P4670	Holemouth fragment	U16, Tomb 1162	—	
x	34.2525/2 / P4877	Holemouth fragment	"Under Locus 1168"	—	See pl. 83d
y	34.2619/3	Small bowl. Pinkish fabric, rim painted red externally and internally, two parallel incisions internally; see bowl from Gezer (pl. 84b)	East Slope	—	See pl. 84a
z	A65967 / 4842	Ledge handle, red slipped	East Slope	—	See pl. 62c
aa	34.2639/28	Small handle with incised decoration. Red slipped and polished	East Slope	—	See pls. 54b, 83e
bb	P4259	Object not located. No precise scale	Square U17, Tomb 1141, above step 4	—	—

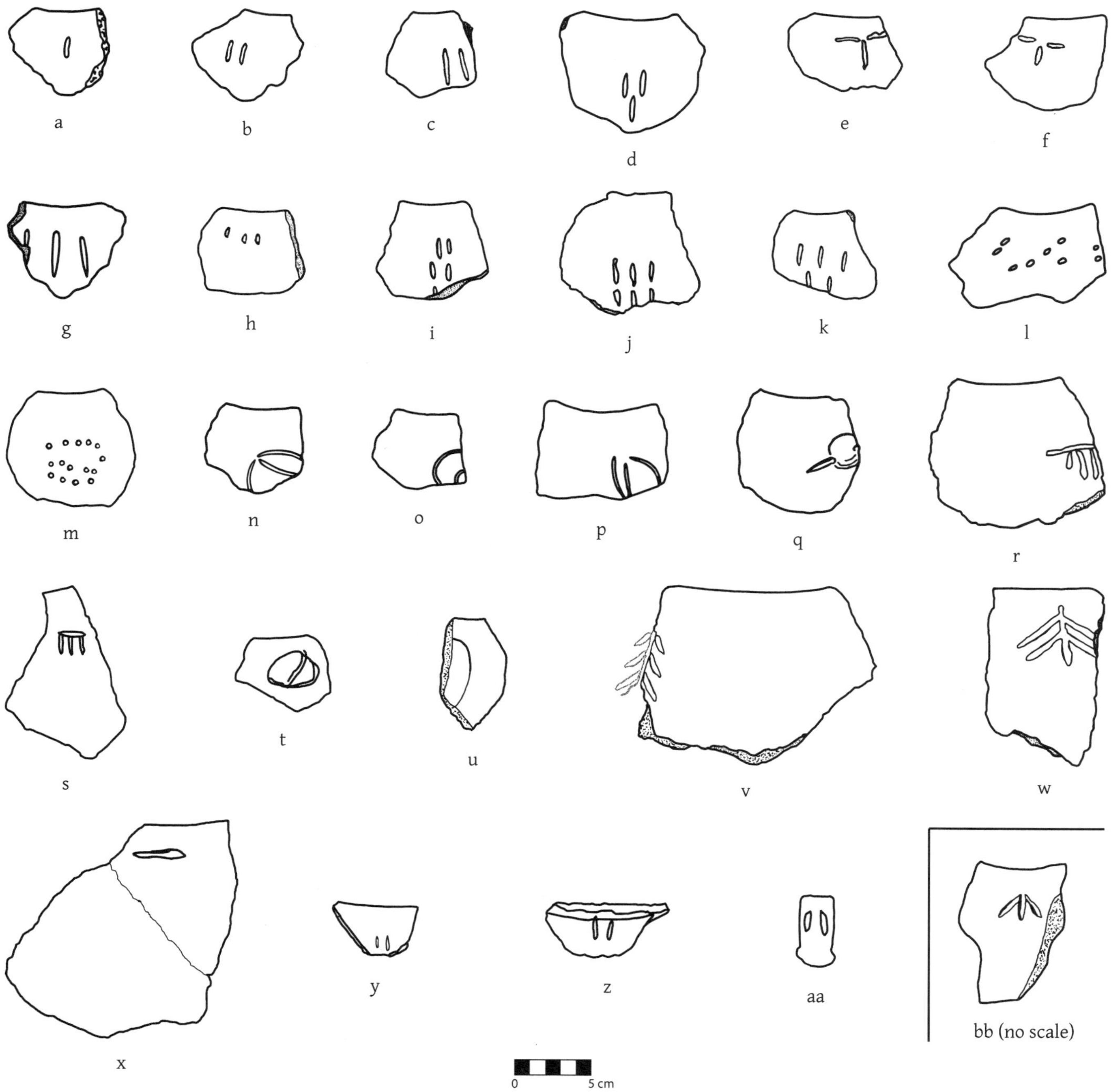

Figure 29. Sherds bearing potters' marks

mark is incised into the wall of a considerably larger, red-slipped holemouth, found in situ on a late floor of B/IV/1, in Locus 1200, apparently on an earthen floor above the bedrock surface. Similar marks are found on generic type holemouths at Beth Shan. One was associated with fill of Stratum XIV (Braun 2004a, fig. 3.17:9); another is from Stratum M-2b, Building MA (Mazar 2012, pl. 20:7) and yet another from Phase IB at Tell Abu el-Kharaz (Fischer 2008, p. 368, fig. 112:1). All are dated to very late phases of Early Bronze Age I. Additional potmarks, some directly paralleled with markings on this group from Megiddo, are from two late Early Bronze I phases at Beth Shan (Mazar 2012, pls. 5:6, 6:4, 7:5, 8, 17:1, 2).

Three chevron-like patterns with central posts, one with at least three pairs of arms, another with two pairs, and the third with one pair (fig. 29v–w, bb respectively) could possibly be related to a single system in which the number of arms has significance. One with two sets of arms is just below the rim on a holemouth with curved base from Locus 4038, ascribed to Stratum XVI on the tell (*Megiddo II*, pl. 6:8). Similar marks with two pairs of arms are found on a holemouth from a late phase of Early Bronze Age I at Bet Yerah (Y. Paz 2006, fig. 7.26:9) and a storage jar from the Stratum I, Early Bronze Age II occupation at Qiryat Ata (Golani 2003, fig. 4.34:7), while another, with one pair of arms on a handle from Bet Yerah, is dated to either Early Bronze Age I or II (S. Paz 2006, fig. 2.336). Similar marks but oriented toward the base of the vessel are found on holemouths from Bet Yerah, where they are dated to the Early Bronze Age II (Eisenberg and Greenberg 2006, fig. 8.72:10) and Early Bronze Age III (Greenberg and Eisenberg 2006, fig. 5.84:1). Another quite similar mark, albeit with the left arms detached, is found on a fragment of another vessel from Bet Yerah also dated to this period (S. Paz 2006, fig. 3.29:9). Additional examples of similar patterns incised into vessels are found at Kabri (Scheftelowitz 2002, fig. 5.9:10–11), where they are dated to the Early Bronze Age.

The repetition of some marks at Megiddo suggests a unified system, at least for the site, while the numerous examples from Bet Yerah (e.g., fig. 30), some with very similar marks, may well indicate some of these signs were generally recognized by Early Bronze Age folk of different communities. Additional examples of such markings from Beth Shan have recently been published (Mazar 2012). This may be particularly true as most of these marked holemouths derive from Early Bronze Age II–III contexts, a time span apparently when Metallic Ware pottery from specialized, probably centralized, workshops was widely distributed over the region.

The sherd of a small open bowl with a red-burnished exterior and a wide band of red paint on the inside of the rim (fig. 29x) was, I thought, a unique example of a potter's mark of two short, parallel incisions on the interior of such a vessel. However, coincidence came to my aid when I happened to notice a complete example of a similar bowl with three similar groups of such markings placed equidistantly on its interior. This complete example, from Gezer, now in the Israel Antiquities Authority's collection (pl. 84b), in a serendipitous coincidence, is stored in the same gallery as the Megiddo collection of Early Bronze Age pottery. Unfortunately, it has no known specific provenience at Gezer, but its complete form is noteworthy for its red painted exterior and wide band of red paint on its interior rim; that of the Megiddo sherd is similarly painted and also burnished externally. That the marks were made very precisely and, in the case of the Gezer example, at regular intervals on the undecorated interior of the bowls suggests some of these vessels may have served some specific, albeit now obscure function. The similarity between these vessels is rather startling, considering the distance between the sites from which they derive. They suggest that both come from the same workshop.

Two handles, one a ledge type (fig. 29y) and the other a small, solid, tubular, high loop handle of a juglet (fig. 29z), are marked by two parallel incisions that appear to be something other than mere decoration, although that observation is uncertain as there are strap handles lined with similar oblique incisions likely intended to be ornamental (pl. 54a, e–f). These two marks may also have conveyed some message to the beholder; however, without benefit of contemporary knowledge of its meaning, it remains obscure.

POTMARKS

Considering the availability of raw materials, pots or potsherds and gravers of stone, or virtually any hard, sharp object, there are surprisingly few potmarks in the preserved assemblage from the East Slope and in general from Early Bronze Age ceramic assemblages. Most in the two collections of objects from the East Slope are illustrated (figs. 30–31). Additional examples include lines incised into sherds after firing that may have been parts of larger compositions but they are too incomplete for illustrations of them to be meaningful. The assemblage of those well enough preserved may be divided into two groups on the basis of motifs. One group includes human and animal representations, while the other portrays inanimate objects. A third group is of representations of objects too poorly preserved to be categorized. The motifs are notable for the tantalizing hints they offer of possible social, economic, and religious activities of the pre-literate society that produced them, which has left such a meager legacy of graphic representations.

Potmarks with Zoomorphic Representations

Insofar as it is possible to discern styles in graffiti, there appears to be no coherency within this group, which suggests the likelihood that these all were ad hoc productions by people of no special artistic inclination or ability. One representation (fig. 31a) is an intriguing fragment of a larger composition that does not allow me to identify the motif. I have placed it in this group because of the wavy lines that suggest appendages associated with animals rather than humans (cf. fig. 31j). The heads of the two animals depicted in another (fig. 31b) are clearly identifiable as of quadrupeds; the one on the left is antlered while the other appears to depict an animal of slightly lesser size either with ears or short horns. Notably, these lines were not made integrally with the head but appended afterward. Although very schematic, there is a possibility that the intention of the depicter was to indicate a male and female of the same species.

The fore portion of another quadruped is an example of a very schematic rendering of some animal of unknown identity. The published rendering (fig. 31c left) differs in details from another (fig. 31c right) recently drawn from a photograph (pl. 85a) of the sherd, which clearly shows its rough exterior and the crudeness of the etching. Not only is the animal portrayed non-realistically, but the image was incised in places by multiple lines, several of which appear to have been false starts or mistakes. The quadruped represented in another potmark (fig. 31d) was, by contrast, rendered on a smooth, painted fabric, the surface of which was somewhat skillfully, carefully, and repeatedly scraped and/or pecked (rather than deeply incised) to produce gently curving contours and broad planes of an animal that could be a donkey, although that identification is far from certain. Animals with two large, curving horns seem to be a common motif as may be clearly discerned in several potmarks (fig. 31e–g). They suggest Engberg's and Shipton's restoration of a complete horned animal preserved on a largish sherd (fig. 31h) is basically correct. The curving horns in the motif of this last suggests that the simple, parallel, curving marks on the sherds depicted in another (fig. 31i–j) may also be fragments of similar representations. One example (fig. 31i), however, differs in the orientation of the curving lines; it could represent an animal viewed *en face*, in which case the double lines would represent single horns.

Two incised sherds, portions of a bowl, probably of the late Early Bronze Age I, from Qiryat Ata (Fantalkin 2000, fig. 17:3–5), also have quadrupeds incised on their external surfaces. This group of decorated objects, with more than a modicum of skill in the renderings of the animals on them, suggests a likely cultic significance for such portrayals.

Potmarks with Anthropomorphic Representations

Only the merest fragment of a motif is preserved on another sherd (fig. 32a). Visible is a stick-like arm, the only certain evidence of a human representation in this group. It is bent at the elbow and ends in fingers touching the side of a large, bulbous object. Beck (2002, p. 27, fig. 6:b), who published a drawing of it juxtaposed it with a rendering of another fragment (fig. 32b), so as to suggest it was meant to portray an upended arm, a pose taken by one figure on the picture pavement ascribed to Stratum XIX in Area BB on the mound (*Megiddo II*, pls. 271–82). That does not, however, seem likely, because the fingers in that figure and two other parallels cited by her (one from Naqada, Upper Egypt; the other from Tel Erani) are extended and splayed and do not touch anything. Accordingly, I suggest the line the fingers touch may well be part of a large, schematic, bulbous body of the individual portrayed.

Beck's suggestion for the meaning of the partial motif visible on the small sherd depicted in figure 32l, that it is a girdle around the waist of a figure, seems most likely, as indicated by three comparanda she suggests, including the same figure from the picture pavement of Stratum XIX. Although the iconography is very simple, if the comparanda for this sherd are truly pertinent, then there is the likelihood of an Egyptian association for the iconography, first noted by Amiran (1992) and later by Braun (1993).

Potmarks with Representations of Boats

Beck (2002, pp. 26–28, fig. 7b) and Marcus (2002, fig. 24:1) identified the partially preserved graffito (fig. 33b) as the end of a boat, with Marcus interpreting additional very schematic lines of another representation (fig. 33a) he identified as the prow of a boat. The suggestion of an Egyptian connection in the simple iconography discussed in detail by Marcus enhances Amiran's and, later, O. Ilan's and Goren's (2003), claims for Egyptian contacts, for which there is only scant evidence. They are particularly notable for a site located so far to the north of the area that witnessed major Egyptian contacts at the end of the Early Bronze Age I period (Braun 2004c; 2011c).

Figure 30. Selection of holemouth vessels bearing potmarks from Early Bronze Age contexts at sites in the northern region of the southern Levant

	Reg. No.	*Site*	*Published*
a	240/7; IAA 51-5253	Bet Yerah	Greenberg and Eisenberg 2006, fig. 5.79:5
b	—	Bet Yerah	Y. Paz 2006, fig. 7.45:5
c	—	Bet Yerah	Getzov 2006, fig. 3.56:6
d	4117-2	Bet Yerah	Eisenberg and Greenberg 2006, fig. 8.61:8
e	370/1	Bet Yerah	Y. Paz 2006, fig. 7.35:10
f	228/3; 51-5100	Bet Yerah	Greenberg and Eisenberg 2006, fig. 5.79:3
g	321/1	Bet Yerah	Y. Paz 2006, fig. 7.32:5
h	—	Bet Yerah	Getzov 2006, fig. 3.56:5
i	2162-1	Qiryat Ata	Golani 2003, fig. 4.28:8
j	909b	Bet Yerah	S. Paz 2006, fig. 3.47:8
k	—	Bet Yerah	Getzov 2006, fig. 3.56:4
l	71/33; 51-1417	Bet Yerah	Greenberg and Eisenberg 2006, fig. 5.87:15
m	832-10	Bet Yerah	Eisenberg and Greenberg 2006, fig. 8.73:12
n	1221-11	Bet Yerah	Eisenberg and Greenberg 2006, fig. 8.84:4
o	KII 1917	Bet Yerah	S. Paz 2006, fig. 3.24:7
p	6066-3	Qiryat Ata	Golani 2003, fig. 4.28:5

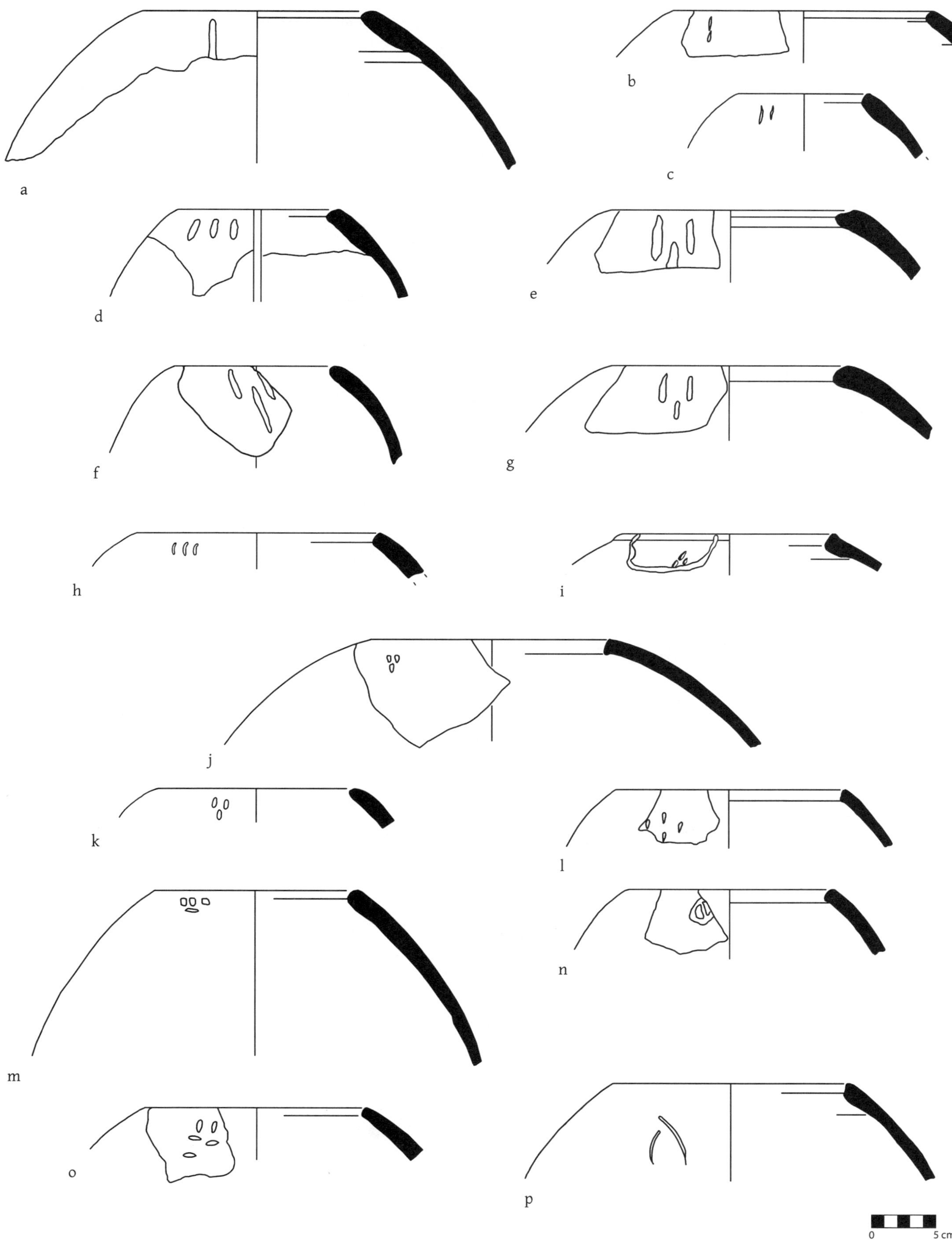

Figure 30. Selection of holemouth vessels bearing potmarks from Early Bronze Age contexts at sites in the northern region of the southern Levant

Figure 31. Potmarks from the East Slope with zoomorphic motifs

	Reg. No.	*Description*	*Provenience*	*Published*
a	—	—	—	Engberg and Shipton 1934a, fig. 10p
b	—	—	—	Engberg and Shipton 1934a, fig. 10n
c1	34.2760 / P5566	Buff, orange brown thin slip or wash	Square U16, Locus 1371	Engberg and Shipton 1934a, fig. 10m
c2	—	—	—	See pl. 85a
d	—	Buff-brown, orange slip	—	Engberg and Shipton 1934a, fig. 10l
e	—	—	—	Engberg and Shipton 1934a, fig. 10o
f	—	—	—	Engberg and Shipton 1934a, fig. 10s
g	34.2762 / P5579	Buff, thick red slip	Square U16, under 1371	Engberg and Shipton 1934a, fig. 10r
h	34.2758	Buff-brown, red slip	Under 1371	Engberg and Shipton 1934a, fig. 10k
i	P5568	Buff-brown, red-brown slip	Under 1371	—
j	A16877	Buff-brown, red slip	East Slope	—

Potmarks with Fragmentary, Obscure Representations

This group includes several examples with graffito, portions of motifs the subjects of which may only be guessed at. One, on the exterior or an Early Bronze Age I bowl (fig. 33c), while quite faint, is a truly complicated series of slight incisions made by a narrow, sharp stylus that removed a thin layer of red paint. At first glance it also appears to be similar to representations of boats with oars, but the resemblance is only superficial and whatever the engraver intended to portray remains unclear. Another carefully incised motif is composed of a highly detailed series of lines on a red painted and polished sherd (fig. 33d); its curved contour could suggest any number of representations of which it was a part. Another small sherd, also with a rather bright red polished surface, bears numerous lines etched into its external surface. Part of a highly detailed motif, which includes a fishbone-like design and some other features (fig. 33e). The less complete rendering prepared specifically for this publication from what remains of the object[83] (fig. 33f), appears to be the more accurate representation.

A jar fragment has several markings on it, which appear to be signs, as they are too few to portray any specific object (fig. 33g). Another sherd, of rather coarse fabric, was apparently incised with a pentagram (fig. 33h). The simplicity of the subject and the quality of the sherd suggest it belongs to a class apart from those discussed above. Examples of this simple geometric motif are found at other sites of the Early Bronze Age (e.g., Braun 1985, fig. 26:12). However, whether they all had the same meaning or were symbols of merely local significance is uncertain. Finally, the most unusual potmark is one very lightly incised into the surface of a red-brown painted ledge handle (fig. 33i). It appears to be a realistic attempt at drawing a tree branch and perhaps shows some artistic discernment by its creator. The style of the handle suggests it should be dated to the Early Bronze Age I. A body sherd from ʿEn Shadud was incised with a similar, albeit less fluid rendition of this design (Braun 1985, fig. 26:14).

[83] Part of the sherd has broken off and been lost since it was first drawn.

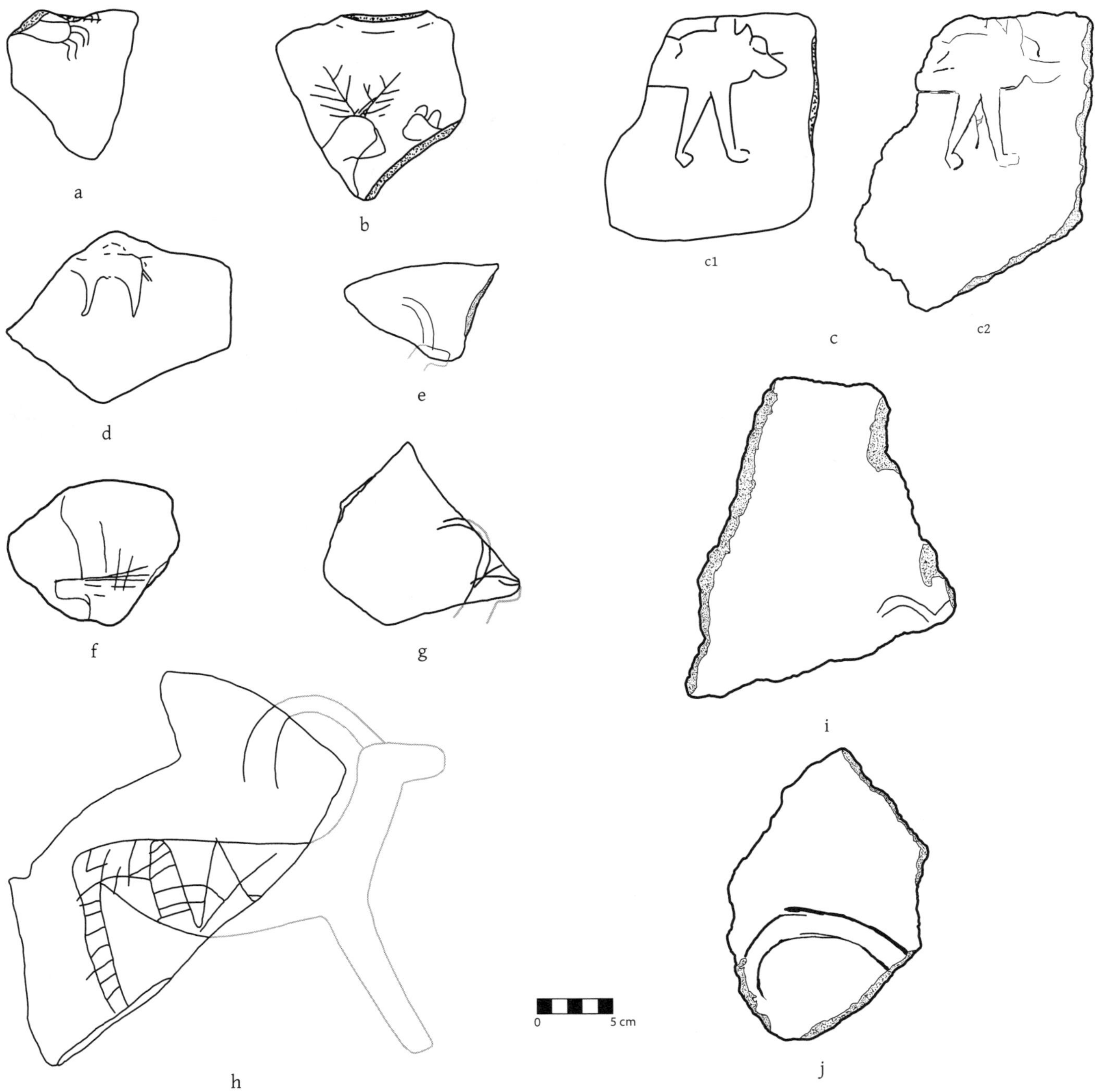

Figure 31. Potmarks from the East Slope with zoomorphic motifs (a–h after Engberg and Shipton 1934a, fig. 10)

Discussion

As these potmarks have been found only on sherds, some of which are particularly small, there is no way of knowing whether they were originally incised or scratched onto the surfaces of complete vessels or of mere sherds. I venture to suggest most of these were originally marked on complete vessels for one or perhaps several purposes. The less-than-prosaic and somewhat complicated motifs of most examples, as opposed to the rather simplified potters' marks and the pentagram and branch symbols, suggest these drawings had specific and special significance.

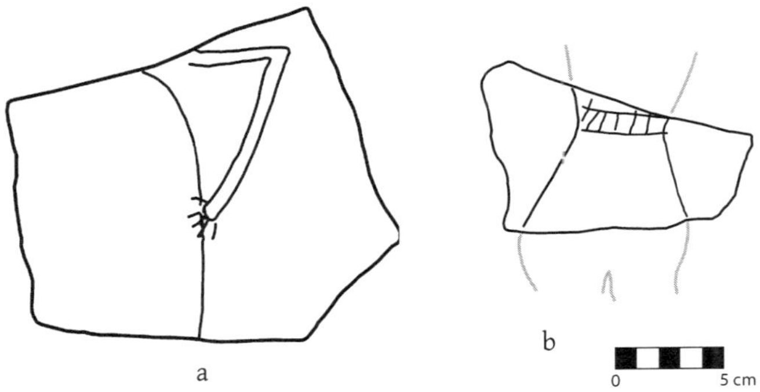

Figure 32. Potmarks from the East Slope with anthropomorphic motifs (after Engberg and Shipton 1934a, fig. 10t, j)

The roughly identifiable animals in this group, that is, those with antlers or horns, are, so far as may be discerned, non-domesticated species with the possible exception of a representation of a donkey. Domesticated species associated with the Early Bronze Age in the region (e.g., Horwitz 1985; 2003a, p. 443; 2003b), and in particular with Megiddo (Wapnish and Hesse 2000, p. 430) are caprids, cattle, and pigs, which is true for what little is known of Megiddo in this period. Thus there is a suggestion of wild animals being particularly chosen as motifs for this form of expression. Two possible scenarios suggest themselves. One is that the subjects of these depictions were somehow associated with hunting, perhaps as some sort of votive token, although as there is very little evidence of such activity in the Early Bronze Age I (Horwitz 1985; 2003a; 2003b; Wapnish and Hesse 2000, table 14.1), that seems the lesser possibility. A more likely scenario suggests the motifs are borrowed from the Syro-Mesopotamian world, perhaps in a way analogous to the influence that seems to have affected glyptic production (see above). That would explain the appearance of the antlered animal, which is found with some frequency on seals from that region (e.g., Matthews 1997, pl. 21:232, 233, pl. 18:502, 514, pl. 41: 558, 559). The animal with the curved horn motif is not only well known there (e.g., Frankfort 1955, pl. 5:25–27,29, pl. 18:190–91, 193, passim), but is also found on cylinder seals (see above, esp. pl. 79) and has a long history of utilization in the southern Levant, dating back at least to the Chalcolithic period (Bar-Adon 1980, cat. nos. 8, 17, 18). Such a relationship, with the world of Syro-Mesopotamian motifs however tentative, suggests associations that may reflect on the belief system of the southern Levant in the late fourth and early third millennia. The possibility of a donkey rendered on one sherd could indicate an association with trade, for

Figure 33. Potmarks from the East Slope with boats and uncertain motifs

	Reg. No.	*Description*	*Published*
a	A16873 / P5560	Body sherd, buff, red slip. Prow of a boat?	Engberg and Shipton 1934a, fig. 10:G
b	P5561	End of a boat(?), buff, red-brown slip (under 1371)	Engberg and Shipton 1934a, fig. 10:H; Marcus 2002, fig. 24:1a
c	A65949	Bowl rim fragment, buff, red-brown slip, with potmark of uncertain motif (boat?) Early Bronze I	—
d	A16870	Red painted and polished sherd	—
e	A16874	Sherd with bright red polished surface, numerous lines etched into its external surface. Part of a highly detailed fishbone-like design and some other features. Redrawn by A. Altenhofen. From below Locus 1371 (This designation indicates the excavators' ascription of this sherd to Stage VI as it came out of a deep probe below B/IV/2)	Engberg and Shipton 1934a, fig. 10:F
f	—	Rim fragment of a jar. Early Bronze Age, partial motif	—
g	A16871	Body sherd, buff-gray, dark red slip (Square U16, under Locus 1371)	—
h	34.2765 / P5573	Sherd. Pentagram potmark. Probably of the Early Bronze Age	Engberg and Shipton 1934a, fig. 10:U
i	A65974	Buff, red-brown-gray slip, friable fabric, ledge handle of a large vessel, Tree branch(?) potmark on underside of lug	See pl. 44b

which there is growing evidence, both in the faunal record and in the identification of goods moving over the Early Bronze Age I landscape (Amiran 1985; Milevski 2005, pp. 241–59; 2009).

Little may be said of the group of sherds incised with incomplete and therefore obscure motifs. Suffice it to note that considerable effort was made to incise specific motifs or representations in two sherds notable for their particularly well-finished exteriors. While the findspots of these fragments on the East Slope offer no help in dating, as none of them was large enough to have been recovered in an in situ context, the very fact that they were recovered on the East Slope could suggest some special association, perhaps with mortuary behavior, as much of this hillside was devoted to "habitations" for the deceased in that era. Alternately, this hillside could have been a repository or dumping area for discarded objects derived from other areas of the site.

Whatever the explanation, it seems safe to note that a small group of mundane objects (pots or portions thereof) became special when they were incised with the different motifs. Those motifs, in turn, together with the limited glyptic production and the pictures on the pavement of Stratum XVIII (*Megiddo II*), are a kind of pinhole that admits a tiny ray of light into the *camera obscura* of the spiritual world and the belief system of the Early Bronze Age peoples of the southern Levant.

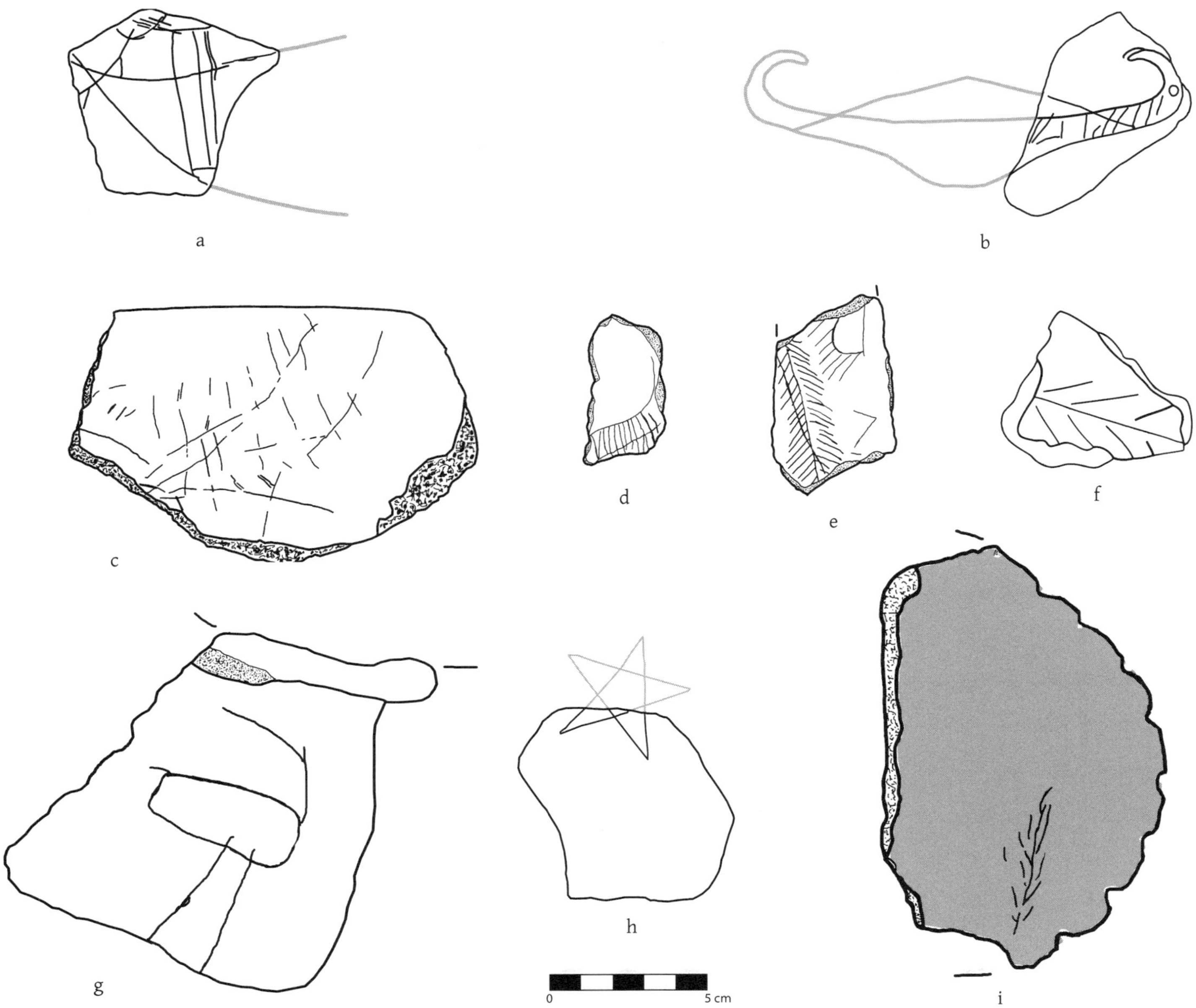

Figure 33. Potmarks from the East Slope with boats and uncertain motifs

5

THE CHIPPED STONE COLLECTION FROM THE ORIENTAL INSTITUTE'S EXCAVATION OF THE EAST SLOPE AND THE HIGH MOUND

Ofer Marder

INTRODUCTION

This report considers the entire collection of chipped stone artifacts found in the Oriental Institute's excavations of the East Slope, as well as items uncovered in Stratum XX on the high mound. The bulk of this collection was originally published by Dorothy Garrod (1934), who carefully described it in her pioneering study of the flint artifacts from the East Slope, while the remainder was included in the publications of *Megiddo Tombs* and *Megiddo II*. Its purpose is to review this material in light of recent scholarship with the hope that it will shed some additional light on the earliest occupation of the site.

Analysis of lithic artifacts from multi-level tell sites is always a challenging task and it is considerably more so when objects derive from old excavations such as that of Megiddo, excavated between 1925 and 1938 (Rosen 1997, p. 35; Milevski et al. 2006, p. 184). Difficulties are further exacerbated for analysis of the chipped stone collection from the East Slope as there is no reliable stratigraphic scheme for deposits on this gradient that lies just beyond the southeast flank of the high mound (*Chapters 1, 7*, frontispiece, fig. 3, pl. 1). The very location of the East Slope in relation to the tell, in addition to its naturally sloping, jagged aspect, numerous re-buildings, and intrusions that wreaked havoc on the deposits there and stymied the excavators' attempts at discerning a sequence of deposits, also allowed slope wash from the summit to further contaminate its deposits. Therefore it seems most of the archaeological remains of the early periods on the East Slope, including what was considered by Guy (1931, p. 10) as representative (i.e., from reliable contexts) for dating, were exposed to severe disturbances, although a few living surfaces and datable groups of artifacts can be discerned in the extant record (*Chapter 2*: the upper and lower terraces).

EVALUATION OF COLLECTION AND CONTEXTS

Excavation methods, as practiced in the early years of the twentieth century at Megiddo (e.g., frontispiece) with many non-skilled workers, are less than optimally conducive to collection of flint artifacts. This was especially true for an area intended for dumping (i.e., the East Slope) deemed less than worthy of minute attention to detail (*Chapter 1*) than excavation precincts on the high mound. Thus collection techniques for flint artifacts were haphazard at best, although it is to their credit that the excavators were interested in collecting chipped stone and including it in their publications.

In addition to the desultory collection of flint artifacts at Megiddo, their contexts, when noted, are of little help in dating them as these diminutive objects were subjected to a variety of post-depositional processes including construction activities, transformation of soil, trampling, and bioturbation of artifacts as result of rodent activity. All such impingements tended to displace these small items to a much greater degree than such artifacts as potsherds (*Chapter 3*; see also Rosen 1986; Rosen 1997, p. 35, for a detailed discussion of this subject), such that even were precise findspots recorded, they might not always have been indicative of the chrono-cultural origins of the objects. Additional problems in evaluating the collection derive from excavation methodology that did not demand total artifact collection, but rather opted for retention only of "nice pieces" (i.e., tools, particularly blades, which are most often sickles). For instance, waste materials (i.e., debitage and debris) were only occasionally collected, counted, and then subsequently discarded. Garrod (1934, p. 83) described just such a procedure in her report, noting specifically about the artifacts from Stage IV that: "A large number of unutilized chips and fragments was thrown away." Apparently, such procedures were applied throughout the entire excavated area including the deposits the excavators assigned to Stages III–VII. Garrod (1934, pp. 85, 88, 90) indicated that something between a small to large amount of waste material was discarded from the original collection.

Because of all the above-mentioned factors, only a very limited number of items from the excavations is available for study. Included is a relatively small quantity of debitage (51.6%; inclusive of cores) and debris (3.4%). The unusually large percentage of tools (45%; table 12) is indicative of the very selective type of collection of flint artifacts. Accordingly, a pure typological approach to the study of the collection was the only meaningful way to approach and report on this material, especially as there are no data on precise findspots. Therefore the analysis presented here treats the flint artifacts as a simple collection of material from the site that indicates human utilization during different periods. This study focuses on presenting an inventory made up primarily of diagnostic tools.

DESCRIPTION OF THE COLLECTION

The chipped stone from the Oriental Institute's excavation is an especially small (n = 438) assemblage that consists mainly of tools. When considered by the different excavation areas the frequencies of tools varies between 30.9 and 73.0 percent (table 12). Two major components representing two chronological horizons are discerned in the chipped-stone collection. They include Early Pottery Neolithic (i.e., Yarmukian) elements and other artifacts typical of the Early Bronze Age. Artifacts of the Early Bronze component clearly dominate the collections from the East Slope and the surface (44.7% and 31.9% respectively; table 13), while the Early Pottery Neolithic, Yarmukian collection is prominent in Stratum XX (32.7%; table 13). In addition, elements of earlier Neolithic and Chalcolithic horizons are also encountered in the assemblage.

Stratum XX

The Stratum XX assemblage consists mainly of Early Pottery Neolithic elements but also includes artifacts typical of the Early Bronze Age. In addition, it appears that some few artifacts can be attributed to the Pre-Pottery Neolithic B, Late Neolithic (i.e., Pottery Neolithic), and Chalcolithic periods. Following is a review of the most salient features of the assemblage of this stratum. In this section Early Pottery Neolithic material is described, including diagnostic artifacts found both on the East Slope and in material collected from the surface. All sickle blades except three fragments (32 of 35) were analyzed. As the Early Bronze Age component from Stratum XX is so minor, it is discussed with the contemporary finds from the East Slope and surface contexts.

The Early Pottery Neolithic Component

The Early Pottery Neolithic component consists of diagnostic tool types such as sickles and projectile points, bifacial knives and unmodified denticulated blades. The most frequent diagnostic tool type is the denticulated sickle blade. Examples were fashioned from a variety of types of flint, although it seems that buff as well as dark brown to black colored types were preferred (9 and 7 respectively of 32). Other examples are of banded gray, gray semi-translucent, and chocolate green-black flint. Four sickles were burnt. Nearly half the sickles are complete specimens (14 of 32). The Yarmukian sickle blades are narrow (pl. 86b–c, e–f; Garrod 1934, figs. 22:L; 23:E–F; 24:B; 25:A–B) with average lengths of 48.5 ± 6.9 SD, while their widths are 13.5

± 2.8 SD on average and their thicknesses on average 3.8 ± 1.1 SD. They were made from both bi-directional (n = 15) and uni-polar blade blanks (n = 9); these last commonly display three scars on their dorsal surfaces. The remainder display indeterminate (n = 5) or multi-directional scar patterning (n = 3). The numbers of their scars range between two and five. Sickles in this collection (n = 35) are deeply denticulated and typical of the Yarmukian culture (Stekelis 1966).

Denticulation is restricted to one edge of the blade (pl. 86b–c, e–f) except for two "saw-like" artifacts displaying denticulation on both sides. Most sickle blades show regular, deep, bifacial denticulation (n = 25; pl. 86b–c, f), while the remainder exhibit shallow denticulation produced by regular, bifacial, pressure retouch (pl. 86e; Garrod 1934, fig. 23:E; Guy and Engberg 1938, pl. 79:2). Their working edges are highly standardized, displaying dense denticulation, usually between five and ten teeth on complete objects. These sickles were rarely re-sharpened. A single, notable exception is one on which an attempt was made to fix its working edge by truncating it through irregular, semi-abrupt retouch of its working edges. The backs of these sickles (n = 12) are usually plain (pl. 86f; e.g., Garrod 1934, figs. 23:F, 24:B) or occasionally (n = 7) altered by semi-abrupt (pl. 86e), abrupt retouch (n = 6) (pl. 86c), or a combination of semi-abrupt with abrupt retouch on the same edge (n = 3). The remaining sickles (n = 4) were modified by regular (e.g., pl. 86b) or irregular retouch. Most sickles (n = 12) were proximally truncated. The remaining tools of this group (n = 7) were truncated at their distal ends (pl. 86c; e.g., Garrod 1934, fig. 23:E), bi-truncated (n = 6) (pl. 86f), or truncated at an indeterminate end (n = 2). Commonly (n = 10), the distal end is plain (pl. 86b, e). Truncated extremities of these sickles are mostly straight (n = 28 of 33) (e.g., pl. 86c, f) and were modified almost exclusively (n = 19) by abrupt (pl. 86c–d, f, see distal extremity) or semi-abrupt retouch (n = 11; pl. 86f, see proximal extremity).

The Early Pottery Neolithic component also includes five projectile points. One is a small, complete Byblos point (pl. 86a); another a large, distally broken Byblos point made on high-quality reddish vein banded flint and partially modified by pressure retouch (pl. 87a; Garrod 1934, fig. 23:J). The remaining examples are three fragments, also partially modified by pressure retouch. In addition to these tools, worth noting is an elongated blade (102 mm in length) made on chocolate-colored flint, which was modified by pressure retouch on its left edge. This tool is possibly a result of an unsuccessful attempt to recycle an elongated projectile point.

Bifacial knives are another important group of tools in this collection, which is composed of three examples, all broken at both ends. One retains a small remnant of cortex, while the remaining two, notable for being of pinkish flint, probably unfinished, were partially modified by pressure retouch. Such tools are known in Pre-Pottery Neolithic C contexts and particularly characteristic of the Early Pottery Neolithic (Khalaily 1999). Five denticulated blades with fine, dense denticulation can also be attributed to the Early Pottery Neolithic assemblage. The remaining elements in this collection include a blade modified by pressure retouch, several splinters, and a bladelet, all of obsidian.

The East Slope

The Early Pottery Neolithic component, consisting of only a handful of artifacts (n = 12; table 13), indicates some minimal use of the East Slope in that period and is analogous in its scarcity to Early Pottery Neolithic ceramic elements from there. The Early Bronze Age component is far better represented (n=43; tables 12–13), by numerous artifacts derived from fills below the surface and within tombs. This collection consists mainly of canaanean sickle blades (n = 17; pls. 88a–b, 89a–b, 90c), canaanean retouched blades (n = 4; pls. 88c, 90b), fan scrapers (n = 3; pls. 91a, 92a–b), and additional tools such as borers and knives made of canaanean blanks (n = 5; pl. 88d–f). Recovered in addition were unmodified, elongated canaanean blade blanks and cortical backed blades (n = 14; pl. 90a, c).

Of particular note are two fan scrapers. One atypical example was made on coarse-grained flint that displays only limited irregular retouch on its dorsal surface (pl. 92a). Another, of Eocene flint, is faceted and exhibits irregular "retouch" that may actually be edge damage rather than the result of deliberate working (pl. 92b). It was found in Tomb 903 Lower (*Megiddo Tombs*, pl. 80:8), believed to be a habitation, in an Early Bronze Age context. In addition, there are two distinct, distally broken, tanged items made of Eocene canaanean blanks. One (pl. 88d) has gloss on its right edge, while the second (pl. 88e), lacking gloss, is an unfinished item with a shallow notch. Such items, rare in Early Bronze Age I and II assemblages (e.g., Bankirer 2003, fig. 6.4:6), were hafted and probably used as reaping knifes.

In addition, a large, thick, retouched flake made of Eocene flint of the type common on canaanean blades was found. It displays a bi-polar, dorsal scar pattern that appears to have been removed as a result of rejuvenation of a canaanean blade core debitage surface (pl. 91b). Another noteworthy tool is an intensively polished graver made on burnt flint, scarred with potlids (pl. 91c). Its shape is pencil-like; one end tapers to a point, the other is somewhat rounded and thicker but flattened or beveled on one side. Its function is unclear; possibly it was used as retouching tool for modifying flint artifacts, for incising decoration into pottery, or for engraving cortexes of fan scrapers (e.g., Marder et al. 1995, fig. 11:1–3).

The Early Bronze Age Canaanean Component: From the East Slope, Surface Collections and Stratum XX

The canaanean assemblage is composed almost exclusively of fine-grained flint, possibly of Eocene origin. Only in two cases was coarse-grained flint (possibly also of Eocene origin) used for the production of sickle blades. It exhibits a variety of colors including light brown to light gray-brown flint with reddish veins and dark brown. No burnt canaanean artifacts were found, which is an exceptional phenomenon, taking into account that in many assemblages burnt items are common (e.g., Marder et al. 1995, p. 88; Khalaily 2004, p. 145; Bankirer 2003, p. 176). It is more than possible that either fragments of burnt canaanean blades were not saved during the excavation, or they were discarded during the previous lithic analysis (see above). Worth noting is one canaanean sickle blade and one canaanean blade blank with remains of a black substance, possibly asphalt or some similar material on one edge as well as on its ventral surface (see below).

Seventeen canaanean blade blanks out of twenty were carefully analyzed. Most are distally broken (9 of 17) and exhibit faceted striking platforms (12 of 17) and trapezoidal cross sections (13 of 17; pl. 90a; Garrod 1934, fig. 21:C). Their dorsal scar patterns are usually uni-polar (n = 8; pl. 90a) and occasionally bi-polar (n = 1) or multi-directional (n = 1). However, it is noteworthy that in seven cases it was impossible to determine scar patterns and therefore it is possible bi-directional scar patterns are more common than records indicate. The number of scars on dorsal surfaces are usually three or four (n = 15 of 17).

Twelve canaanean retouched blades were recorded. Most are broken (n = 11) and consist mainly of medial fragments; they have trapezoidal (n = 6) or triangular cross sections (n = 6). The majority display uni-polar (n = 5; pl. 88c) or bi-polar (n = 4; pl. 90b) scar patterns, with three scars on their dorsal surfaces (n = 7 of 12). Retouch appears almost evenly (n = 7) on one or two edges (n = 5) and their dorsal or ventral surfaces (9 and 7 respectively). In only two cases was retouch found on both surfaces (pl. 90b). Commonly blade edges were modified by nibbling or by regular and irregular retouch, which was continuously or sporadically applied to tools' edges (pls. 88c, 90b). Rare instances of abrupt or semi-abrupt retouch (n = 2 of 12) as well as scalar retouch (n = 1 of 12) are also found in this assemblage.

Thirty-two canaanean sickle blades were found. However, only twenty-nine were systematically analyzed as the remaining items were too fragmented to yield any definitive data. With the exception of two items, all were broken, usually medially (n = 23; pls. 88a–b, 90c). The remainder were broken distally (n = 4; pl. 91b). Analogously to retouched canaanean blades, canaanean sickle blades display uni-polar (n = 12; pls. 88b, 89a–b, 90c) as well as bi-polar dorsal scar patterns (n = 7). However, there is also a high frequency of items on which dorsal scar patterns could not be determined (n = 10; pl. 88a). Gloss usually appears on two edges (n = 17; e.g., pl. 88a–b) or, less commonly, on one edge (n = 12; e.g., pl. 90c), and almost entirely on both dorsal and ventral surfaces (excluding three examples). The sickles' working edges are usually plain and display evidence of damage (n = 22; e.g., pl. 89a) or are finely denticulated (n = 16; e.g., pl. 88a). The remaining working edges display either fine (n = 6) or irregular retouch (n = 2; e.g., pl. 89b).

Canaanean blade (n = 12) widths vary at 20.5 ± 1.8 mm SD, while their thicknesses are 6.0 ± 1.8 mm SD on average. The metrical attributes of the canaanean retouched blades (n = 16) have similar averages but tend to be somewhat thinner. Their widths are 20.4 ± 2.5 SD, while their thicknesses are 5 ± 3.1 mm SD on average. By contrast, canaanean sickle blades (n = 29) are narrower and thinner in comparison to other type of blades.

Their widths are 19.2 ± 3.6 mm SD, while their thicknesses are 4.7 ± 1.6 mm SD on average. It seems that thinner and less wide blanks, with either uni-polar or bi-polar dorsal scar patterns were preferred for sickles. Most of them are medially broken. By contrast, un-retouched canaanean blades are thicker, wider, larger, distally broken, and display mainly uni-polar dorsal scar patterns. They were not deliberately segmented.

Since the sample is small it is not clear if un-retouched canaanean blades are blanks and were kept for further use, or alternatively their dimensions made them less suitable as sickle or retouched blades and consequently were discarded. Canaanean retouched blades possibly show intermediate characteristics between the two groups; they are less wide in comparison to sickles, but similarly they display both uni-polar and bi-polar scar patterns and were segmented and modified by retouch.

The phenomenon of medially broken canaanean sickle blades and less intensely canaanean retouched blades, which were probably deliberately segmented in order to insert blanks inside hafts, is well recorded for Early Bronze Age assemblages (e.g., Marder et al. 1995, p. 77; Rosen 1997, p. 45; Khalaily 2004, p. 145). Moreover, it seems that similar to Megiddo in most of the Early Bronze Age I–II sites, narrower blanks were selected for sickle production (for detail analysis, see Bankirer 2003, fig. 5.8–10; Zbenovich 2004, fig. 14).

Additional Chrono-Cultural Components

A Small Pre-Pottery Neolithic Component

Four tools are believed to date to this early period, three of which were fashioned of purple/violet-colored flint. One is a cortical-backed sickle blade (pl. 86g); another a sickle blade fragment. A third, also fashioned of similar colored flint, is best described as an "epsilon blade." The last is a pointed, blank blade. Most of these tools were prepared using bi-directional technology.

A Late Pottery Neolithic Artifact

A single, short, wide, rectangular (39 × 15 × 5 mm) sickle blade with deep, non-standardized denticulation is assigned to the Late Neolithic Period, probably the Wadi Rabah phase (pl. 86d). Other evidence of this period and other post-Yarmukian phases of the Late Neolithic period is found in pottery of Stratum XX (*Megiddo II*, pl. 2:9–17, 30–36).

A Small Chalcolithic Component

Of particular interest is a group of three sickle blades (pl. 87b–c), one micro-endscraper, one bladelet core (pl. 87d), and two retouched bladelets, all of which can be assigned to a Chalcolithic occupation on the tell. Human activity in this period is also discerned from the typical Chalcolithic pottery found there (Shipton 1939, pl. 15:2–9).

A Small Post-Early Bronze Age Component

This component consists of geometric sickles as well as other geometric pieces. Their shapes are triangular, rhomboidal, trapezoidal, or rectangular. These items are usually bi-truncated, backed by abrupt or semi-abrupt retouch and the sickles' opposite edges are modified by dense, regular retouch, which forms fine denticulated working edges (pl. 87e–f). These tools, found in tombs as well as on the high mound, can be attributed to Middle Bronze through Iron Age assemblages (*Megiddo Tombs*, pls. 120:15–19; 150:20–21; Gersht 2006, fig. 17.5–7).

DISCUSSION

This study of the flint collection from Oriental Institute's excavations of Megiddo has serious limitations because of recovery techniques, modes of sampling, and an innate inability to attribute the artifacts to specific archaeological contexts. Nevertheless, this chipped assemblage reflects at least four and possibly as many as seven archaeological occupations of the site and its environs. Most diagnostic artifacts within the collection can be attributed either to the Early Pottery Neolithic or to the Early Bronze Age. In addition, a few Pre-Pottery Neolithic as well as Late Neolithic and Chalcolithic sickle blades and blanks were recovered. Moreover, several badly eroded Levallois flakes and possibly Upper/Epipaleolithic endscrapers (see Garrod 1934, fig. 22:P) in the collection suggest occasional visits of hunter-gatherer groups of that chrono-cultural horizon to the environs, probably because of the permanent water source.

The Early Pottery Neolithic assemblage is a typical domestic Yarmukian tool-kit repertoire, including large numbers of sickle blades, points, several bifacial knives, denticulated blades, and three items made of obsidian. All in all, their relative abundance, despite the collection methods, suggests a substantial Yarmukian occupation on the mound, found in deep deposits there, but probably badly disturbed by Early Bronze Age deposits that often went down to bedrock (see Garfinkel 1993; 1999).

Evidence of considerable Late Neolithic occupation is also indicated by a collection of pottery typical of that chrono-cultural milieu (*Megiddo II*, pl. 2:37–42) and a figurine (pl. 93) of the Yarmukian type (Stekelis 1966, figs. 43–44; Garfinkel 1992, figs. 36–37; Gopher 1996, fig. 3.1:1–7; Getzov 2009, figs. 28, 29:9, 13). A similar picture of that occupation can be derived from the early excavation reports, from those of renewed excavations in Area J (*Megiddo IV*) and also from an unpublished survey by Y. Teper (pers. comm.). In addition, E. Braun notes that in a visit to the tell several decades ago he noticed a number of denticulated flint blades eroding from the walls of the Stratum XIX temple (newly designated Level J3 in *Megiddo III* and *Megiddo IV*), suggesting that its builders quarried soil from earlier deposits from which they made mudbricks.

Notably, the Early Bronze assemblage includes only a small quantity of artifacts and does not reflect the intensity of the Early Bronze occupation and human utilization of Megiddo, known from both the mound and the East Slope (Gersht 2006; Blockman and Groman-Yeroslavski 2006; Braun, this volume).

From the evidence of extant material several important points should be noted. It seems that at least some canaanean blades were produced on-site and were not imported as final products. That is evident from the existence of canaanean core trimming elements (CTE) (see table 12, under type "other") as well as possible ridge blades and canaanean cortical and *outrepasse* blade blanks. They suggest that at least some of the stages of flint knapping, such as blank removal and rejuvenation of core surfaces, which leave telltale debitage on-site. The only known additional knapping site in the vicinity of Megiddo is Har Haruvim (Shimelmitz, Barkai, and Gopher 2000; Shimelmitz 2009), several kilometers to the southwest, but that site seems not be associated with Early Bronze Age I and the artifacts from it are most notable of a medium-grained variety of eggshell-colored flint, not common in the Megiddo collection recovered in the Oriental Institute's excavation.

Of note is a single canaanean sickle blade with remains of a black substance, possibly asphalt or some like substance adhering to it. It may be one of the earliest instances of evidence for the use of adhesive materials and for such a purpose in the northern region during the Early Bronze Age. By contrast, a similar phenomenon is well documented from the central and southern parts of Israel, where asphalt chunks as well as adhesive remains on canaanean blade blanks and pottery vessels are well documented (Marder et al. 1995).

ACKNOWLEDGMENTS

I would like to offer my gratitude to Eliot Braun for his valuable advice on earlier versions of this chapter. I am grateful to Yorke Rowan for his kind hospitality and valuable professional advice during my stay in Chicago. Thanks are also due Yosef Garfinkel for his advice on the finds of the Pottery Neolithic finds and to Omri Barzilai, Hamudi Khalaily, and Ianir Milevski for their help in this study. I am also grateful to Leonid Zeiger for his excellent renderings of the flint objects, to Silvia Krapiwko for her skilled digitization of them, to Alegre Savariego, curator of the IAA Rockefeller Museum collection and to Helen MacDonald and John Larson of the Oriental Institute for their help in accessing the collections.

Table 12. Waste frequencies

Type	*East Slope*		*Stratum XX*		*Surface*		*Total*	
	N	%	N	%	N	%	N	%
Primary Elements	0	0.0	15	8.5	1	0.4	16	7.1
Flakes	4	17.4	74	42.0	7	3.1	85	37.6
Blades/Bladelets	4	17.4	63	35.8	10	4.4	77	34.1
Canaanean Blades	14	60.9	1	0.6	5	2.2	20	8.8
Burin Spalls	0	0.0	1	0.6	0	0.0	1	0.4
Core Tablets	0	0.0	5	2.8	0	0.0	5	2.2
Ridge Blades	0	0.0	7	4.0	4	1.8	11	4.9
CTE - Others	1	4.3	8	4.5	0	0.0	9	4.0
Overpassed	0	0.0	1	0.6	0	0.0	1	0.4
Bifacial Spalls	0	0.0	1	0.6	0	0.0	1	0.4
TOTAL DEBITAGE	23	100.0	176	100.0	27	11.9	226	100.0
Chips	0	0.0	11	100.0	3	75.0	14	93.3
Chunks	0	0.0	0	0.0	1	25.0	1	6.7
TOTAL DEBRIS	0	0.0	11	100.0	4	100.0	15	100.0
DEBITAGE	23	25.8	176	64.0	27	34.6	226	51.1
DEBRIS	0	0.0	11	4.0	4	5.1	15	3.4
TOOLS	65	73.0	85	30.9	47	60.3	197	44.5
CORES	1	1.1	3	1.1	0	0.0	4	1.0
TOTAL	**89**	**100.0**	**275**	**100.0**	**78**	**100.0**	**442**	**100.0**

Table 13. Tool frequencies

Type	*East Slope*		*Stratum XX*		*Surface-General*		*Total*	
	N	%	N	%	N	%	N	%
Projectile Points	1	1.5	3	3.5	1	2.1	5	2.5
Early Pottery Neolithic Sickle Blades	11	16.9	20	23.5	4	8.5	35	17.8
Bifacial Knives	0	0.0	3	3.5	0	0.0	3	1.5
Recycled Tools	0	0.0	3	3.5	0	0.0	3	1.5
Bifacial	0	0.0	1	1.2	0	0.0	1	0.5
Fan Scrapers	3	4.6	0	0.0	1	2.1	4	2.0
Canaanean Sickle Blades	17	26.2	4	4.7	11	23.4	32	16.2
Canaanean Retouched Blades	4	6.2	5	5.9	3	6.4	12	6.1
Tools on canaanean Blanks	5	7.7	0	0.0	0	0.0	5	2.5
End Scrapers	4	6.2	6	7.1	2	4.3	12	6.1
Awls	0	0.0	2	2.4	1	2.1	3	1.5
Borers	3	4.6	3	3.5	1	2.1	7	3.6
Burins	4	6.2	4	4.7	1	2.1	9	4.6
Truncations	2	3.1	1	1.2	1	2.1	4	2.0
Retouched Flakes	0	0.0	2	2.4	1	2.1	3	1.5
Retouched Blades	4	6.2	17	20.0	4	8.5	25	12.7
Denticulates/Notches	2	3.1	5	5.9	3	6.4	10	5.1
Chalcolithic Sickle Blades	2	3.1	1	1.2	0	0.0	3	1.5
Pre-pottery Neolithic B Sickle Blades	1	1.5	3	3.5	0	0.0	4	2.0
Large Geometric Sickle Blades	0	0.0	0	0.0	9	19.1	9	4.6
Large Geometric Retouched Pieces	0	0.0	0	0.0	1	2.1	1	0.5
Sickle Blades Other	0	0.0	1	1.2	2	4.3	3	1.5
Varia	2	3.1	1	1.2	1	2.1	4	2.0
Total	**65**	**100.0**	**85**	**100.0**	**47**	**100.0**	**197**	**100.0**

6

THE EARLY BRONZE AGE TOMBS OF MEGIDDO: A REAPPRAISAL

David Ilan

INTRODUCTION

Very little has been published about the tombs associated with the Early Bronze Age "Stages" of Megiddo, excavated on the East Slope (Engberg and Shipton 1934a; *Megiddo Tombs*). That is partly because the results of their excavations were never published in full and partly because the sepulchers were disturbed by secondary use, later quarrying, and re-deposition of fills within them. Now, with new revelations about Early Bronze Age Megiddo emanating from the ongoing Tel Aviv University excavations at the site, and more recent synthetic studies of Early Bronze Age burial practices (e.g., Chesson 2001; Ilan 2002), it is worth re-examining the Early Bronze Age tombs of Megiddo; at least one of them is very special indeed.

As shown in previous chapters, the existence of the "Stages" is not borne out by the stratigraphic evidence, meager as it is. Braun prefers to discuss the contexts in terms of periods, referencing material that displays sequencing in confined, local contexts and by means of typological analogy. While Braun's analysis is now the latest word regarding context, I have elected, in places, to make reference to the original "Stages" nomenclature in order to facilitate coordination with the original publications.

SYNTHETIC DESCRIPTION OF THE TOMBS (TABLE 14)

The present author has little to add to the detailed description of the Early Bronze Age I tombs on the southeastern slope. For this information the reader is referred to the *Megiddo Tombs* volume and to *Chapter 2* and plate 94. Following is a synthetic description, arrived at with the benefit of subsequent research, hindsight, and the new insights gleaned by Braun's re-examination of archived records.

Very little remained of the original tomb chambers and burial assemblages by the time of their excavation due to multiple modifications of bedrock and successive use in later periods. This can be seen, even from a distance, in an aerial photograph (pl. 94). Nevertheless, by locating findspots of complete vessels and by determining the locations of human skeletal material associated with Early Bronze Age material culture, we can identify something of how the tombs were laid out and utilized. From the outset it should be noted that the depositional contexts of the ceramic finds suggest that all the tombs under discussion were carved and utilized in the late Early Bronze Age I (EB IB) and used secondarily and sporadically in Early Bronze Age III and later, though apparently not for burial in these later periods. The typology of these early tombs and the stratigraphic evidence from them is discussed in more detail below.

As far as we can discern from what is published (*Megiddo Tombs*, pp. 9–27), and from the unpublished archives, most of the Early Bronze Age I tombs had rather rounded contours, either natural or carved, as was the tradition throughout the southern Levant in that period (Ilan 2002). Subsequent modification, perhaps in the Early Bronze Age I itself, created broad niches and supplemental cavities that emanated from primary burial chambers (e.g., in Tombs 903, 1101–06, and 1141–45). Some chambers were more rectangular (e.g., Tomb 1128) than others. Tomb entrances seem to have been horizontal and in some cases sloping (e.g., Tombs 910, 1128). Shaft entrances were not the norm, as they came to be in the Intermediate Bronze Age tombs (Greenhut 1995).[84] Some loci, rather than having been planned as tombs, may have been utilized for mortuary functions only on an ad hoc basis. Tomb 1103, for example, was simply a cleft in the bedrock that contained a mass of bones spilling over its edges (*Megiddo Tombs*, pp. 18–19).

The finest sepulcher, Tomb 910 (fig. 34, pl. 95a), is comprised of a courtyard entrance and an antechamber (Chamber C) leading into a short passage that opens onto a central chamber (A), from which several other chambers are accessed (labeled B, D, E, F, G, and H in fig. 34). Guy and Engberg (*Megiddo Tombs*, p. 17) noted that "the cutting of this tomb as a whole is better than that of any other on the east slope. The walls of the chambers are very straight and in several cases make good right angles with one another." The passages between the entry court and the antechamber (Chamber C) and from Chamber C to Chamber A, and from Chamber A to Chamber B are marked by low, finely carved sills. Indeed the carving is so fine that tool marks were not even visible (fig. 96a). Here and there, where the chalky bedrock was faulty, gaps were filled with dressed stones and then plastered with great expertise. The walls tapered slightly inward from bottom to top. Unlike the situation in many tombs on the East Slope, some of the ceilings of Tomb 910 were still intact.

This tomb is similar in form to the Intermediate Bronze Age chamber tombs typical of Megiddo that Greenhut (1995) has designated as "Megiddo Type F." However, the roster of contents from this sepulcher (table 16), meager though it is, discounts the possibility that it was fashioned in so late a period. Perhaps Tomb 910 was the prototype for the shaft-and-chamber tombs so common at Megiddo in the Intermediate Bronze Age. A total of ten complete vessels was found in this tomb, of which two clearly date to the late Early Bronze I horizon (*Megiddo Tombs*, pl. 4:22, 35), two, from Chamber E, to the Early Bronze Age III (*Megiddo Tombs*, pl. 4:5, 13), five also probably date to Early Bronze Age I, but could be of later period within the Early Bronze Age (*Megiddo Tombs*, pl. 4:6, 9, 14, 31, 35), while another is probably of the Intermediate Bronze Age (ibid., pl. 4:30).

Of the tombs assigned to their excavators' Stages I–III, one, Tomb 52, is notable for its lack of any mention of bones (*Megiddo Tombs*, pp. 20–22). Unfortunately, there is no additional documentation available for it beyond the brief published account. Two additional sepulchers (Tombs 1106 and 1141–45) contained Early Bronze Age I, Early Bronze Age III, and, in the case of Tombs 1141–45, also Late Bronze Age material. Human remains in them were disturbed or could not be directly associated with objects, such that it is not possible to determine which vessels were contemporary with what skeletal material. Bones in them could date to Early Bronze Age I, III, or even later periods. However, the small corpus of Early Bronze Age III artifacts from them seems domestic- or industry-related (*Megiddo Tombs*, pp. 22–23, 94–99, pls. 6:8; 49:12–13; and *Chapter 3*) and so we may conclude the Early Bronze Age mortuary-associated material from the East Slope is likely confined to Early Bronze Age I.

[84] I prefer the term "Intermediate Bronze Age" rather than the excavator's "Middle Bronze I" or "Early Bronze IV" (cf. Gophna 1992 contra Dever 1995).

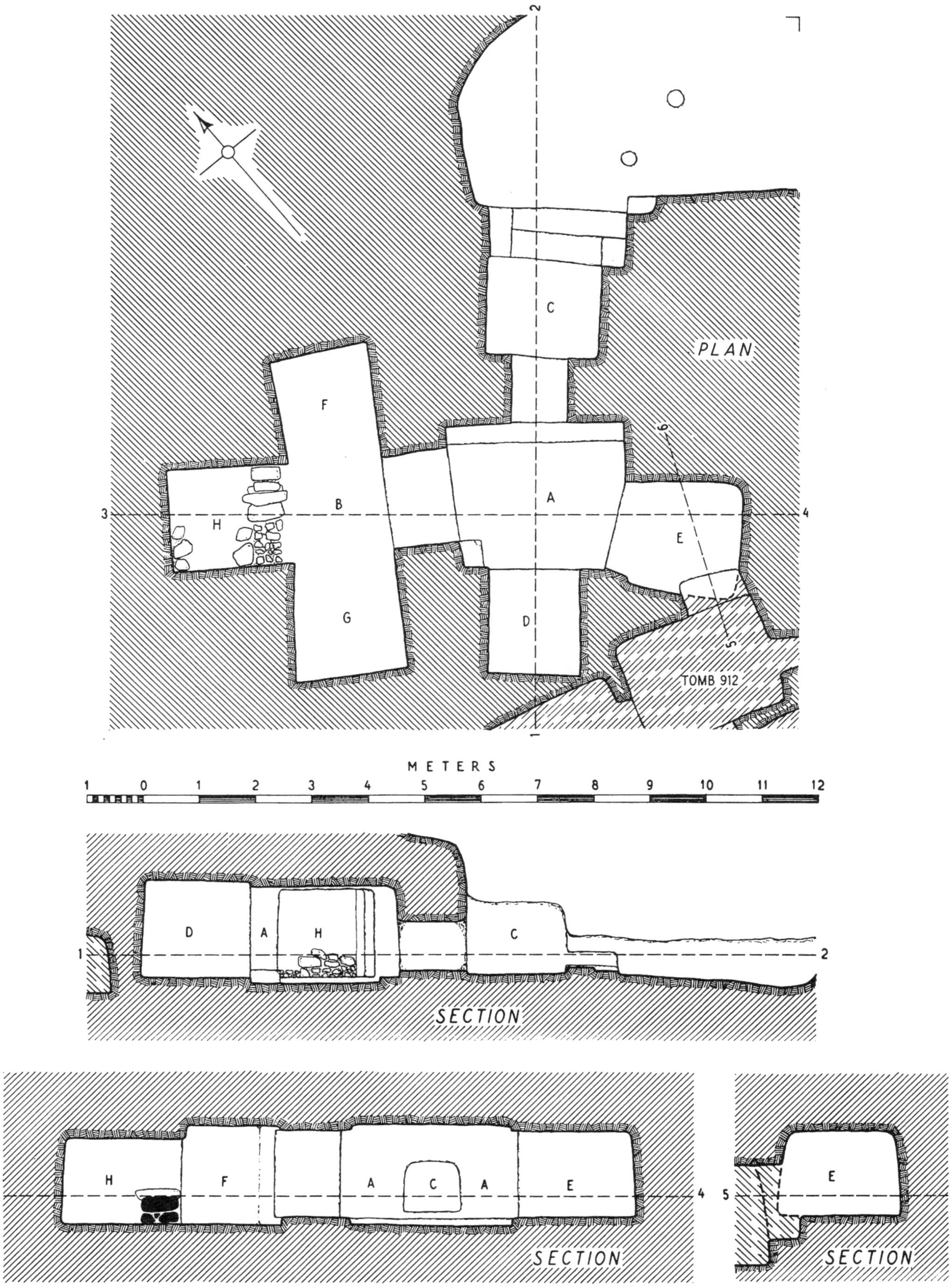

Figure 34. Plan and sections of Tomb 910. Note the elaborate layout with sharply angular features of the cave (after *Megiddo Tombs*, fig. 14)

Table 14. Early Bronze Age tombs on the East Slope of Megiddo (based on Guy 1938, p. 139, table 1)

Tomb	*Square*	*Stage*	*Size/ Dimensions (in meters)*	*Entry*	*Minimum Number of Individuals*	*No. of Complete Early Bronze Age Vessels*	*Comments*
9	V19	Probably IV–V	< 1 m diameter	Pit	0	1	Attributed to Stages I–III and identified as having Khirbet Kerak[a] Ware, but probably Gray Burnished Ware Type 1c (*Chapter 3*; Wright 1958; Goren and Zuckerman 2000). May not be a tomb
52[b]	R13	I–III	?	?	?	5	Early Bronze Age III — "ceramic types not found in tell strata"; includes Late Bronze Age and Iron Age phases
903 Upper	V16	IV–V	8 × 4	Shape not clear, NE corner	60	6	Mass of human skeletal material, non-articulated and in non-primary deposit
903 Lower	V16	V–VII	8 × 4	As above	0	10	No burials
910	V17	IV–V	41 sq. m	Horizontal, via ante-chamber	?	8: A = 4, B = 1, C = 0, D = 1, E = 0,[c] F = 0, G = 2, H = 0	Eight chambers (A–H); skeletal remains on the floors of every chamber — probably what was left behind after transfer of the majority of the bones, perhaps to Tomb 903
1101 Lower –1102	V16	IV	Very large complex	Probably horizontal	14[d]	0	Initially (Early Bronze Age I, no burials) followed by a putative "Stage IV" burial (probably Intermediate Bronze Age), superseded by Iron Age I burials and burial goods in Tomb 1101 Upper
1103	V16	IV–V	4.6 × 0.5–1.6 × 2 deep	Open cleft	20	0	Cleft in rock, partly natural, partly carved, contains a few Early Bronze Age I sherds
1106	V16	IV–VII, I–IV?	ca. 3 × 5	Via Tomb 1101–1102	8	3	Part of a large space modified extensively in subsequent Intermediate Bronze Age and early Iron Age I periods (Tombs 1101, 1102); difficult to know which skeletal material goes with which phase
1122	V17	IV–VII	7 × 6; 3 high	Irregular depressions in bedrock	1	3 (on shelf)	Partly natural, partly carved. Stone bowl and flint blade suggest initial domestic use. Reused as tomb in Late Bronze Age II
1126	V16	VII?	See 903	Via Tomb 903	1	0	Associated with Tomb 903 Lower(?); but possibly earlier; flexed burial, adult male
1127	V16	VII?	See 903	Via Tomb 903	1	0	Associated with Tomb 903 Lower(?); but possibly earlier; flexed burial, adolescent
1128	V16	IV	3.5 × 3.5	Horizontal; no shaft	5	9	Perhaps the most homogeneous group of Early Bronze Age I ceramics
1141–45	U17	I–IV	ca. 12 sq. m	Either shaft or stepped dromos	1	1	Amorphous chamber with lobes. Reuse in Early Bronze Age III and Late Bronze Age I and construction of partition wall

[a] This table includes contexts that were clearly of a mortuary nature in the Early Bronze Age, particularly in Early Bronze Age I. Other caves and hollows must have functioned as tombs and mortuary facilities at this time as well.

[b] Tomb 52 is not plotted in the plan in *Megiddo Tombs* (pl. 1), nor does the volume contain any plan or photo of the tomb, only a brief description of its contents. It is located on the steep southeast flank of the mound, actually outside the precinct designated as the East Slope.

[c] The single complete vessel present in Chamber E (*Megiddo Tombs*, pl. 4:30) dates to the Intermediate Bronze Age.

[d] According to the report on the skeletal remains, nine individuals were attributed to the Early Bronze Age phase of this tomb (Hrdlicka 1938, p. 192 and n. 2). In any case, some skeletal material may belong to the early Iron Age assemblage discovered in the upper horizons of Tomb 1101 (*Megiddo Tombs*, pp. 24–27).

Table 15. Early Bronze Age pottery from the Early Bronze Age tombs of Megiddo, published in *Megiddo Tombs*

Tomb	*No. Complete Vessels*	*No. Fragments Published*	*Types Present*[a]	*Remarks*
9	1	0	Bowl, Gray Burnished Ware, Braun Type 1c (*Chapter 3*)	Parallels: Goren and Zuckerman 2000; or Type A (Yannai 2007, pp. 84–86); Early Bronze Age I
52	5	0	2 small deep bowls, 1 small carinated bowl, 1 jug, 1 bottle	Three vessels appear to be examples of "dribble-painted ware" (Greenberg 2000, p. 191; Stage 0–1, Early Bronze Age IIIb–Early Bronze Age IV)
903 Upper	6	2	2 shallow bowls, 1 deep bowl, 1 high-looped handled cup, 1 amphoriskos, 1 storage jar (fragment)	Early Bronze Age I; two items (*Megiddo Tombs*, pl. 3:3–4) are probably Early Bronze Age III
903 Lower[b]	12	29	3 shallow bowls, 14 deep bowls, 1 krater-bowl, 5 carinated bowls, (red wash and Gray Burnished Ware Type 3), 2 bowls with conoid projections (Gray Burnished Ware Type 4), 1 krater-bowl, 2 amphoriskoi, 1 holemouth jar, 9 storage jars, 3 high-loop handled cups, one teapot	Early Bronze Age I; one Late Bronze Age I intrusion
910	8	32	6 small shallow bowls, 1 large shallow bowl, 2 small deep bowls, 9 large deep bowls, 1 krater-bowl, 4 carinated bowls (red wash and Gray Burnished Ware Type 3), 5 amphoriskoi, 3 holemouth jars, 6 storage jars, 2 stands	Early Bronze Age I; at least one complete vessel dates to the Early Bronze Age III: *Megiddo Tombs*, pl. 4:13; almost all material is from "fill," not from floor
1101 lower	15	8	2 platters, 1 platter bowl, 1 "plate," 1 small deep bowl ("dribble-painted ware"), 2 rounded bowls, 2 straight-sided bowls, 5 holemouth jars, 3 amphoriskoi, 2 storage jars, 2 pithoi, 1 jug	Stage 0–1 (Early Bronze Age III–Intermediate Bronze Age)
1102 lower	5	2	1 platter, 1 straight-sided bowl, 1 pithos, 1 storage jar, 2 small jars, 1 incised sherd	Stage 0–1 (Early Bronze Age III–Early Bronze Age IV)
1103	0	0	0	"a few sherds of Stages IV–V" (Early Bronze Age I)
1106	3	6	2 carinated bowls (Gray Burnished Ware Type 3), 1 shallow bowl, 4 sherds with potters' marks, 2 sherds with rope decoration	One basalt pedestaled bowl with conoid projections (Braun 1990, p. 91, fig. 3a) two items attributed to Stages I–IV (Early Bronze Age I–III)
1122 (shelf)	2	1	1 amphoriskos, 1 high-looped handled cup, 1 deep bowl	Early Bronze Age I; Tomb 1122 Upper contains Late Bronze Age II vessels
1128	9	1	3 small shallow bowls, 1 deep bowl, 1 small deep bowl, 1 carinated bowl (red wash), 1 amphoriskos, 1 teapot, 1 loop-handle jug	Early Bronze Age I; higher fill contains two complete bowls and one upper pithos section of Stages I–IV and later intrusions
1141–1145	1	1	1 high-loop handle jug, 1 sherd with potter's mark (not necessarily Early Bronze Age I)	Early Bronze Age I; attributed to Stages I–IV; most material is Late Bronze Age I

[a] Ceramic typology refers to *Chapter 3* of this volume.

[b] Tomb 903 Lower is not a tomb, per se. However, the present writer is suggesting that it may be of a mortuary nature.

Table 16. Complete vessels from Megiddo Tomb 910

Period	Megiddo Tombs, *pl. 4 number*	*Vessels*
Early Bronze Age I	22, 25	1 jar, 1 deep bowl
Early Bronze Age (probably Early Bronze Age I)	6, 9, 14, 31, 35	3 small shallow bowls, 1 medium shallow bowl, 1 small deep bowl
Early Bronze Age III	5, 13	1 large shallow bowl, 1 cooking pot
Intermediate Bronze Age A	30	1 amphoriskos
TOTAL VESSELS:	10	—

FORMATION PROCESSES OF THE TOMBS

Many of the tombs that yielded Early Bronze Age I material also contained much later burial assemblages, from the Intermediate, Middle, and Late Bronze and Iron Ages. Such tombs often showed evidence for subsequent modification of stone-carved spaces (e.g., Tombs 1141, 31, 63, 1122, 52, 1101+1102). Aerial photographs published by Engberg and Shipton (1934a, fig. 2), in *Megiddo Tombs* (pl. 2), and in this volume (pls. 9–12, 16–22) show a great deal of quarrying activity on the East Slope, which must have taken place over several millennia of human utilization after the Early Bronze Age. Thus, only the tombs containing solely Early Bronze Age I material can be assumed to have been anything near their original states at the time of excavation.

Almost all the Early Bronze Age I tombs containing complete vessels were located in Squares V16 and V17. Guy and Engberg (*Megiddo Tombs*, pp. 9, 135) suggested that the tombs in these squares were utilized as repositories for funerary remains collected from other tombs that were modified and reused in subsequent periods. More specifically, the tombs with the most skeletal material have few complete vessels (Tomb 903 Upper, Tomb 1103; see table 15), while the tombs with more vessels yielded fewer skeletal remains (Tomb 903 Lower, Tomb 1128). In general, such small numbers of finds are not commensurate with the large numbers of individuals usual in tombs of this period. That is most starkly evident in Tomb 903 Upper, which contained a minimum of sixty individuals. The skeletal material was piled into a 4.0 × 2.5 m pit in no discernible order, even spilling out of it. By contrast, despite the opulence of its plan and execution, Tomb 910 contained relatively few skeletal fragments, albeit in all chambers (pls. 95b, 96a).

All this information suggests that skeletal remains were transferred, mainly to Tombs 903 Upper and 1103, but with little or no effort to transfer burial goods as well. Tomb 1128 may have contained the only intact burial assemblage. Guy and Engberg suggest that it may have been the Middle Bronze Age I (i.e., Intermediate Bronze Age) people who did the transferring to facilitate reuse of tombs, though there are no sherds of that period in Tomb 903 Upper. Actually, the *terminus ad quem* for the transfer of the bones is the Early Bronze Age III, the levels of which sealed some of the Early Bronze Age I contexts below.

The intact, flexed, single burials of Tombs 1126 and 1127 were described (*Megiddo Tombs*, p. 12) as "intrusive below" the surface of Tomb 903 Lower (Locus 1242). They were not accompanied by objects of any kind, save for a single "rough flint lying between the knees of the skeleton" in Tomb 1127. However, a substantial number of late Early Bronze Age I vessels and sherds were recovered, including nearly a score of sherds with potmarks (*Chapter 4*), which rested upon the floor of Tomb 903 Lower (Locus 1242). This context was interpreted by the excavators as representing domestic remains, which may well be the case since it included animal bones, which do not generally accompany Early Bronze Age burials (Ilan 2002). Moreover, we know of no intact primary burials in this region and no burials lacking grave goods from the late Early Bronze Age I. There is reason to believe that these are pre-Early Bronze Age I burials (*Chapter 2*).[85] The assemblage on the floor (Locus 1242) above the burials does, however, look very much like an Early Bronze I burial assemblage; perhaps we are seeing two distinct phases, the latter of which was sealed by the collapse of the cave's roof.

[85] For evidence of pre-Early Bronze Age I occupation at Megiddo, see *Chapters 1* and *5*.

INTERPRETATIONS

The excavators of the East Slope pointed out that in several cases the bedrock and surfaces just above the bedrock seem to show domestic remains of the Early Bronze Age I (their erstwhile "Chalcolithic"). Superimposed above these were burials, which in some instances were superseded by domestic levels of later periods (*Megiddo Tombs*, pp. 18, 20, 22, 135). On the face of things then, the Early Bronze Age I material from the caves may be divided into two types of contexts, mortuary and habitation/workshop. Mortuary contexts tend to contain higher frequencies of smaller vessels, fewer large storage vessels, more complete vessels, and more jewelry and metal utensils. Habitation or workshop contexts tend to contain more large storage vessels (versus a lower frequency of small vessels), flint tools, and ground stone vessels. The nearby architecture, apsidal and rectilinear, is usually interpreted as being of a domestic character (e.g., Braun 1989; Zuckerman 2003b, pp. 31–34; *Chapter 3*).

We know that in the Early Bronze Age I inhumation took place almost solely in formal cemeteries located beyond settlement limits (note a lack of burials within nearby, roughly contemporaneous settlements at ʿEn Esur (Yannai 2007), Qiryat Ata (Golani 2003), and Tel Qashish (Zuckerman 2003d).[86] Given patterns observed throughout the southern Levant in the Early Bronze Age I, domestic architecture and mortuary assemblages are not likely to coexist within the same precinct. A process of residences replacing tombs in the same location is also doubtful; we have no documented example of such a sequence. How, then, are we to understand the relationship between these two aspects of activity within the same precinct? We are left with two options:

(a) Both the architecture and the "domestic" finds of some caves comprise an earlier residential phase of the Early Bronze Age IB. The tombs date to the latest phase of the Early Bronze Age IB. This interpretation implies that the late Early Bronze Age IB settlement was much reduced in area from the preceding phase, the western edge of the cemetery forming the settlement limit. Though reduced in size the site was graced with major new architecture on the tell (fortification Wall 4045 of Stratum XVIII and the Level J-4 temple).

(b) The architecture is contemporaneous with the tombs, which implies that Structures B/V/1, B/V/2, B/IV/1, and B/IV/2 (*Chapter 2*, fig. 17) are mortuary related (chapels? temples?). The quotidian material in the caves would then have had mortuary functions as well. In this scenario the entire Early Bronze Age I sequence on the East Slope would have a continuing funerary function. It must be admitted, however, that mortuary structures of this kind, erected within a cemetery, remain, for the present, undocumented in the southern Levant.

Both scenarios have intriguing spatial and ritual implications. Either one would reflect a unique nexus of cemetery and architecture. Furthermore, no matter which interpretation is adopted, the tombs of the southeastern slope lay about 100–150 meters east of the temples of Area BB/J. Perhaps the temples on the tell have a mortuary association as well.

The first scenario described above would mean that monumental Tomb 910 is more or less synchronous with the monumental temple of Stratum J-4, the largest Early Bronze Age structure yet discovered of its time in the Levant (Finkelstein and Ussishkin 2003). Tomb 910 is, for the present, the most elaborate rock-cut tomb known in the Bronze Age of the southern Levant. Its plan, fine masonry, broad horizontal entrance, and branching chambers are unique for this period. More than anything else it resembles, in concept, the subterranean parts of Early Dynastic tombs in Egypt, at Umm el Qaab — the tombs of Qaa and Den, for example — and particularly the complex substructures at Saqqara — Tombs S3503, S2302 (Ruaben), and the grand tomb of Hotepsekhemwy, for example (see summary treatments in Dodson and Ikram 2008, pp. 134–41; Emery 1961, pp. 54–95, and references in both). It is likely that Tomb 910 was that of a high-status person,

[86] A few exceptions can be found, mainly in the Early Bronze Age IA of northern southern Levant, in the form of infant burials (Ilan 2002, p. 94).

perhaps a ruler, and his family. The other tombs may belong to less-exalted residents of Megiddo, perhaps even royal retainers and their families.

SUMMARY

Approximately ten discrete, stone-carved or modified tombs dating to the Early Bronze Age I were discerned on the southeastern slope of Megiddo. Originally there may have been more, but they were disturbed, robbed, re-quarried, and reused over a period of just under three thousand years. Already by Early Bronze Age III it would seem that many of the bones had been transferred to two or three repositories, all in Square V16. Thus there is no clear evidence for mortuary activity after Early Bronze Age I until the Intermediate Bronze Age; most Early Bronze Age III remains appear to be related to non-mortuary activities, habitations or work-spaces (*Chapter 3*).

Early Bronze Age I burials appear to have been multiple and successive, as is usual throughout the southern Levant in the Early Bronze Age. The typical "funerary kit" seems to have been comprised mainly of small bowls and amphoriskoi, with a few larger bowls, jars, and jugs. Metals and jewelry were not found in the tombs, suggesting that such objects were looted prior to excavation, probably in antiquity.

The East Slope may have begun as a residential area, later to be converted into a cemetery, toward the end of the Early Bronze Age I. Alternately, the area may have long been a cemetery, perhaps from its earliest use. If so, what have been interpreted as domestic remains in both caves and above-ground constructions may also have been mortuary related. In either case the architecture of B/V and B/IV may well have been the loci of funerary rituals rather than simple domiciles.

Tomb 910 is the finest tomb known ever to have been carved in the Bronze Age southern Levant. It is in the same league as the Stratum J4 temple recently revealed by the Tel Aviv University expedition on the mound (*Megiddo IV*). Tomb 910 must have belonged to an elite person or lineage. I have suggested a possible Egyptian connection, but that hypothesis will require verification through further research and perhaps future discoveries.

ACKNOWLEDGMENTS

I thank Eliot Braun for inviting me to make this contribution. I am also grateful to Gil Stein, Director of the Oriental Institute, for permission and his encouragement to publish this material. Natan Ben Ari provided much input on the subject of Early Bronze Age I burial assemblages. I must mention Israel Finkelstein, David Ussishkin, and Baruch Halpern, co-directors of the new Megiddo expedition, for inviting me to supervise an excavation area of my own in the 1990s — a great opportunity to study Megiddo's treasures over an extended period of time and up close. Finally, I remember my beloved wife, Ornit Ilan, who had her own adventure with Early Bronze Age I Megiddo before being taken from us, just as she entered her scholarly stride.

7

HUMAN ACTIVITY ON THE EAST SLOPE: A SUMMARY

PART 1: THE EAST SLOPE AS A ZONE OF INTERMITTENT ACTIVITY IN ANCIENT TIMES

Although human utilization of the East Slope seems to have begun as early as that on the adjacent high mound, its craggy bedrock formation, apparently replete with natural cavities, as well as its low-lying location, relegated it to a position of less-than-primary importance. It appears to have been always extramural and a kind of adjunct to occupation on the mound. Because of its proximity to the settlement on the mound and the bedrock limestone that could be quarried relatively easily, from very early times, perhaps even from the Neolithic period, the East Slope was considered as a fit place for the repose of the deceased. That may be seen from two burials in deep deposits (see below) and the numerous tombs from Early Bronze Age I and later that dotted the slope. The hillside was used intermittently and for long periods as a burial ground, but in other times it appears to have been devoted to additional, quotidian functions. These involved utilization and re-utilization of its natural cavities as well as construction of buildings and quarrying. Part 1 is a summary of that activity as may be discerned from the Oriental Institute's excavations of the East Slope.

EARLY HUMAN UTILIZATION OF THE EAST SLOPE

Although evidence for human activity is scant, it seems likely that the East Slope was first exploited in the late prehistoric periods, as there is no indication of any artifacts prior to the Neolithic horizon. There is evidence that desultory activity there began during the Pre-Pottery Neolithic and continued, in some minor way, during several subsequent periods until early in Early Bronze Age I. Beginning in developed phases of that era there is evidence for intense utilization of the East Slope.

Pre-Pottery Neolithic Period

Some few artifacts that may be dated to this period (*Chapter 5*) suggest the possibility of human activity on the tell and the East Slope in the Pre-Pottery Neolithic period.

Early Pottery Neolithic Period

The Early Pottery Neolithic period is represented by only a handful of distinctive tools and possibly one or even both burials found in the deep probes above bedrock in the lower terrace (fig. 9). However, there are deposits on the high mound, in what the excavators labeled Stratum XX (Shipton 1939; *Megiddo II*), that are likely to have been laid down coevally. They are substantial enough to suggest at least minimal sedentary occupation of the site during that time span.

Late Pottery Neolithic–Early Chalcolithic Horizon

The Late Pottery Neolithic and Early Chalcolithic horizons are represented by only a few distinctive tools (*Chapter 5*) and possibly the burials found in the deep probes above bedrock in the lower terrace. Some of the surfaces and constructions encountered below the Stage V house might also be attributed to this period.

Early Deposits below Stage V

The few patches of surfaces either fashioned or utilized by humans below the Stage V building are the sole, indisputable evidence of pre-Stage V attempts at above-ground construction encountered in the excavation. They appear to represent more than one episode of activity, but little else may be said of them beyond noting that they are likely to have been associated with actual buildings. Perhaps one, another, or all of the earliest walls not appearing in Lamon's plan and documented solely in photographs should be associated with these surfaces; some of them may even have functioned coevally.

Probably all the artificial, quarried alterations in the bedrock below the buildings of the upper and lower terraces should be assigned to pre- or very early phases of Early Bronze Age I episodes of human activity. Judging by the number and types of features, cupmarks, pot-holes, channels, quarried lines, and flattened and leveled surfaces, many of which do not seem to have been coordinated with others nearby, that activity represents sequential episodes that occurred over a considerable span of time. They are likely to correspond to the periods represented by datable artifacts (see table 17 and below). It is also possible to assign to one or another of these periods the earliest uses of the caves for burials, dwellings, or some non-mortuary-related activity, such as storage or animal shelters. While it is impossible, given available information, to associate any specific feature with a particular prehistoric episode, the likely chrono-cultural parameters for the entire scope of this activity are probably to be found in the dating of flint artifacts (*Chapter 5*) and possibly some of the earliest pottery.

Early Bronze Age I

Yiftahʾel II (Early) Phase of Early Bronze Age I

A mere handful of sherds suggest some very limited activity on the East Slope in the Yiftahʾel II (early) phase. However, considering what is known of the quality of the pottery of this phase (Braun 1997), which is particularly coarse and liable to augmented fragmentation, it is quite possible that considerably more of this material was discarded during the excavation. The extant fragments, portions of large storage jars, suggest the likelihood of a sedentary occupation in that period. The location of its nucleus remains unknown, but it could have been either on the slope or possibly on the higher mound.

Advanced Phases of Early Bronze Age I: Deposits Roughly Corresponding to the Excavator's Stage V

Sometime during the advanced phases of Early Bronze Age I, activity on East Slope intensified greatly, apparently concomitant with developments on the high mound. The East Slope deposits are mostly represented by fills on the lower terrace, probably associated with a small, rectangular building, and a few remains found within its parameters, in situ, which are probably closely or absolutely contemporary with ʿEn Shadud II. Additional structures adjacent to the small building may also belong to this same occupation or be dated somewhat later. Parallels in pottery place these deposits within an advanced, but not the latest phase of Early Bronze Age I, probably at a time associated with the final production of Gray Burnished Ware, represented by Type 3 bowls and morphological parallels of Type 4 bowls (*Chapter 2*; Braun 2012a; in press).

Early Phase or Phases of the Excavators' Stage IV on the Upper Terrace

Below the apsidal building of Stage IV was a quarried cave and possibly associated walls of large boulders. These features represent either one or perhaps two episodes of use of the terrace. A date within an advanced phase of Early Bronze I seems particularly in line with the quarried bedrock wall features, which are likely to have been associated with a burial cave that collapsed (*Chapter 6*), perhaps within the general time span of Stage V. Possibly the stepped entrance with lintels of B/IV/1 was crafted in this era, although it appears to have continued in use in the latest phase of the building. Possibly also the courtyard directly east of the entrance was used coevally. That open space may also have been associated with the anomalous building just a few meters to its east, represented by the corner formed by the juncture of Walls 31, 32 and 26.[87]

Latest Phase of the Excavators' Stage IV on the Upper Terrace

The latest phase of B/IV/1 is represented by a rebuilding of walls that gave the structure its distinctive "apsidal" plan and a raised, earthen floor in one room, discernible from evidence of a complete holemouth vessel standing on it, in situ. The chronological evidence, albeit equivocal, could suggest a date as late as the initial phases of Early Bronze Age II, which is also represented by a small assemblage of Metallic Ware vessels. Pottery from in and around the central room includes a largish fragment of a shallow bowl (pl. 52c), a minute fragment of an Early Bronze Age II platter (pl. 66d), and an Egyptian-style vessel (pl. 64a) from adjacent Locus 1199, all of which seem to point to activity during that time span.

Early Bronze Age II

A handful of Early Bronze Age II pots, of fine metallic ware, suggest either some continuity from the end of Early Bronze Age I or merely some minor activity there. That appears to have been followed by a gap in occupation until sometime in Early Bronze Age III.

Early Bronze Age III

Only at some point during Early Bronze Age III is there evidence for a re-established human presence on the East Slope. While cultic activity was renewed in the three large megaron temples on the high mound (*Megiddo II*), there is no evidence for coeval mortuary activity on the East Slope. There are, however, several buildings and evidence for the utilization of caves in this period; one possibly for ceramic production. The pottery available for study includes quotidian types, large, coarse, shallow bowls and some smaller vessels, with more typical types of platters and storage jars represented by only small fragments. Absent in the East Slope repertoire is the eponymous Khirbet Kerak Ware, but it is uncertain whether this reflects some chronological or functional reality. Thus the East Slope in the Early Bronze Age III period seems to have been an extramural or outlying occupation reserved for dwellings, perhaps storage and possibly ceramic production.

Activity in this period is represented by several complete vessels, one associated with Locus 914, and another found in a bedrock depression, possibly in association with a kiln. A considerable number of typical sherds recovered, many of them sizable fragments, suggests a significant utilization of the East Slope in that time span. In addition to Locus 914, a rectangular room, there are numerous other Stage +IV walls that could have been in use during this period. The functions of these structures, whether for domiciliary or other activities such as pottery production are uncertain owing to a dearth of direct evidence, while available information is of equivocal utility as it cannot be directly associated with one or another structure. Notably, there does not appear to be any evidence for mortuary-related activity on the East Slope in this period.

---

[87] This is one of the early buildings that does not appear on Lamon's plan and which disappeared from the last series of aerial photographs.

East Slope in Post Early Bronze Age III (Later) Periods

By the Intermediate Bronze Age (the excavators' MB I) the East Slope saw a return to one of its earliest functions, providing shelter for the dead. Thereafter, numerous tombs were cut into the bedrock and used and re-used in many periods. The stratified remains above the pre-Early Bronze Age and earlier deposits represent a complicated and patchy series of sequences of utilization and occupation of the East Slope during different periods, apparently from the Intermediate Bronze Age until very late times. Although a discussion of their chrono-cultural associations lies beyond the scope of this work, it should be noted that the post-Early Bronze Age activity on the East Slope lasted several millennia.

It is notable that successive buildings maintained the orientations of the earliest structures, which were dictated by natural and rock-cut features of the terraces. That is probably due as much to the desultory utilization of the slope and the sparse occupation there as to erosion. Archaeological deposits on the East Slope never attained great depth (fig. 8) because there was a lack of construction debris; extant evidence indicates that only select areas were utilized at any given time.

The sequence of post-Early Bronze Age I buildings there is intriguing. The dimensions of the largest, some constructed of very sizable ashlars, suggest they were not simple dwellings but may have been constructed for public purposes. Presumably those structures had specific functions but, most unfortunately, we have no information as to what those functions might have been. Other buildings, represented by numerous wall segments and portions of rectilinear structures, suggest the possibility they were domiciles, perhaps for overflow of populations settled on the high mound.

Evidence for the late utilization of the East Slope is also found in the numerous tombs (*Megiddo Tombs*), used and re-used for burials and other purposes. Excavation of those cavities — natural, man-made and/or modified — yielded information on a ceramic industry in one or more periods, indicated not only by a socket of a potter's wheel, a potter's workshop, and one kiln found within caves, but also by several kilns constructed on the surface. Those same cavities would also have provided shelter for man and beast, commodities that fed them, and the appurtenances associated with their activities. Quarries for ashlars are clearly seen in aerial photographs of the exposed bedrock (pl. 9, Square T16, northwest corner; pl. 10, Square W16, northeast quadrant), while a long, rock-cut, covered channel was unearthed low down on the eastern part of the slope (fig. 5, rows 18, 19). Thus the East Slope was the scene of much industry and other activity, probably during and after its use as a cemetery.

PART 2: EARLY ARCHITECTURE AND ARTIFACTS OF THE EAST SLOPE IN CONTEXT

Evidence for dating the early buildings comes mostly from associated artifacts, but in only a few instances are such associations definitive. They, and additional information derived from architectural traditions, allow us to roughly place these finds within their chrono-cultural contexts.

Very Earliest Buildings

There is no proper documentation on the very earliest buildings, that is, wall foundations, encountered in deposits, apparently below the excavators' Stage V and IV structures, besides non-annotated photographs. As there is only scant information on adjacent deposits (theoretically those which the excavators assigned to Stages VI–VII), which were apparently reached in the very final phases of two deep soundings where bedrock was very low-lying, there remain several options for dating the structures. The dearth of pottery from periods earlier than advanced phases of Early Bronze Age I in the saved assemblage does not argue well for any of the constructions to have dated to those periods, and so they may have belonged to an early phase of late Early Bronze Age I, although in the absence of any definitive information, the earlier options should not be dismissed out of hand.

Stage V Buildings (B/V/1 and B/V/2)

This small, rectangular structure, the plan of which is nearly completely preserved, is dated on the basis of pottery recovered in situ from its floor. The bow-rim jar with the cylinder-seal impressions must be closely or absolutely contemporary with Stratum II at ʿEn Shadud. That correlation may be further suggested by evidence of shared architectural traditions (see below). The function of this building and that of the adjacent structure to its east remain obscure. They could, based on their locations and relative isolation, be related to the significant mortuary activity known in this period from adjacent tombs, although most of the objects found within can be related to more quotidian functions related to human occupation, weaving, and the grinding of foodstuffs.

Stage IV Buildings (B/IV/1 and B/IV/2)

The single holemouth jar found on the floor of the central room of B/IV/1 is dated to sometime within the Early Bronze Age, while additional ceramic fragments could suggest a date between a late phase of Early Bronze Age I and even an initial phase of Early Bronze Age II, for which there is a modicum of evidence in the assemblage. Nothing of the function of this structure can be deduced from the evidence of artifacts, but its location, within a cemetery active in more or less that same time span, as well as its elaborate entrance, may suggest it was related to mortuary activity. It should be noted that in this same period there is evidence of very considerable activity, apparently of a sacred nature, on the high mound in Area BB/J.

Excepting dolmens and tumuli, there is only a modicum of information on mortuary-related structures in the Early Bonze Age I, and they appear to be mostly actual tombs. Examples include a constructed chamber tomb at Bâb edh Dhrâʿ (Schaub and Rast 1989, pp. 209–33, 325–90), another at Tall al ʿUmayri (Herr et al. 1996, p. 75; Dubis 1999), and several additional, semi-subterranean sepulchers at Ghor es Safi (Waheeb 1996). Thus Ilan's suggestion (*Chapter 6*) that these buildings may have functioned as mortuary temples, especially considering the high degree of social organization evident on the high mound, seems quite reasonable. As noted in *Chapter 3*, there is a modicum of evidence that B/V/1 could be interpreted as having a mortuary association. However, Ilan's suggestion of an Egyptian inspiration seems less likely, although there is some evidence of Egyptian associations at the site in the same time span (Braun 1993, with references).

Buildings of the East Slope and the Early Bronze Age I Architectural Traditions of the Southern Levant

Stage V (B/V/1) Structure

The small, rectangular building of Stage V has certain features that are often associated with Early Bronze Age building practices (Braun 1989a) and which place it within the mainstream of prevailing traditions. Its overall plan may have been that of a broadroom, with its entrance in one of the long walls, although that is not certain. The externally rounded corners of this structure are a normative feature, documented at a number of Early Bronze Age I and II sites (e.g., Braun 1985, pp. 76–77; 1996b, plan 1; Golani 2003, plans 2.2, 2.11, 2.12). What appear to be internal benches adjacent to the walls are also common features in Early Bronze Age I and II houses as is the semi-subterranean floor level.

B/IV/1a (the Stage V Structure) and the Myth of Apsidal Architecture in Early Bronze Age I

Since the 1934 publication of the aerial photograph in which the apsidal plan of this structure is easily discernible, that plan type has come to be considered a hallmark of Early Bronze Age I, although later excavations at ʿEn Shadud and then Yiftahʾel prompted me to question the very *bona fides* of this highly specialized plan as such (Braun 1989a). It is now eminently clear that the curvilinear wall was a late addition and that the building was not originally conceived as an exponent of this specific plan. Rather, in its latest phase it appears to be a hybrid, probably resulting from a curvilinear tradition of construction appended onto a pre-existing, rectilinear constraint, the shape of which was dictated by previously quarried bedrock.

Curvilinear architectural precepts appear to have been first adopted from more northerly regions such as Byblos and Sidon/Dakkerman in the early, Yiftahʾel II phase of Early Bronze Age I (Braun 1989a; 1997, pp. 103–04). Such a tradition, which spread to large areas within the southern Levant, prevailed, however, for only a short time. An earlier and underlying, long-standing tradition of rectilinear architecture in the Levant soon re-exerted its influence such that curvilinear tradition became modified and was adapted to a basically rectilinear (i.e., broadroom) template. That is evident in later Early Bronze Age I occupations at Kabri 9 (Scheftelowitz 2000, pp. 21–24), Qiryat Ata III (Golani 2003, plan 2.3), Tiberias (E. Yannai, pers. comm.[88]), a site near Tel Qashish (van den Brink and ʿAd 2011), another near the site of Mizpeh Zevulun in Nahal[89] Zippori (ca. 1 km south of Yiftahʾel and Mishmar Ha-emeq; N. Getzov, pers. comm.), where some houses have curved ends and others only rounded corners.

Their entrances in long walls and their central pillar bases, in essence make these structures broadrooms with similarities to more typically rectilinear examples, such as the Stratum XIX temple on the high tell. Precisely where the latest phase of B/IV/1 fits into those traditions seems unclear but as it is a kind of hybrid, for which there is no really good parallel, it should be understood as a virtually unique example of an apsidal structure, which has little importance in understanding the architectural traditions of the Early Bronze Age of the southern Levant.[90] Thus the idea of the apsidal plan as typical of Early Bronze Age I architecture, which was born in the 1934 preliminary publication, should at last be laid to rest.

Although rare, in addition to the Stage IV building, there are other instances of Early Bronze Age people either adapting their architecture to extant man-made or natural features as in B/IV/1. One example is the curvilinear end of a sausage-shaped house at Qiryat Ata (Golani 2003, fig. 2.12), in which part of one apse was quarried into bedrock. Another is in Field D at Tall al-ʿUmayri, in Jordan's Madaba Plains region, where bedrock was hewn to permit construction of walls of a sepulcher (Herr et al. 2000, pp. 99–100).

Early Bronze Age I Artifacts in Context

The artifact assemblage of this time span derives from fills outside the slopes and is, in large part, closely paralleled in nearby tombs. However, even given the likelihood that some of that material could have originated in those very sepulchers, parallels from other sites indicate most of the types recovered were also commonly found in domestic contexts. Thus it is virtually impossible to ascertain anything of the function of the buildings from their extant artifact assemblages. What may be noted is that virtually all objects from this period are distinctly northern in aspect (Braun 1985, table no. 3) and, so far as I have been able to ascertain, there are only a few elements that are of conceptually foreign inspiration in the assemblage. They include two Egyptian-inspired ceramic vessels and cylinder-seal impressions; all apparently locally produced, but which evidently devolved from Egyptian and Syro-Mesopotamian prototypes.

[88] A number of such structures dated to late phases of Early Bronze Age I have been uncovered in salvage excavations in the south of Tiberias near the lake front (Sea of Galilee) at the foot of the tomb of Rabbi Meir Baal Ha-ness.

[89] Nahal is a Hebrew word for valley or watercourse, both of which describe this location. The site of Mizpeh Zevulun, located on a high hill on the left bank of this perennial stream, is noted for its Early Bronze Age II occupation that has yielded a number of cylinder seal impressions (Joffe 2001).

[90] Another, similar type building at Byblos has an analogous history of construction (Braun 1989, p. 10).

Artifacts definitively associated with this period all appear to have had quotidian functions, probably related to domestic use. They, too, have some good parallels in assemblages of other northern sites, although the distinctions between north and south in this period are considerably lesser than in earlier phases. The group of large, shallow bowls is suggestive of local production.

Architecture and Artifact Assemblages of Early Bronze Age III

Early Bronze Age III Building (B/IV/1 and B/IV/2)

The simple, rectangular structure Locus 914 is clearly dated to Early Bronze Age III by the complete, intact holemouth found just "outside" its wall. Additional pottery of this period, from there and nearby, suggests a relatively intensive and non-mortuary related occupation that may have been associated with the manufacture of ceramic vessels.

Pottery of the Early Bronze Age III found in some caves includes holemouths and vats, types not usually associated with tombs in that period, suggesting these were not grave goods. More typical types of vessels associated with the few tombs known of this period (e.g., Tombs A and F at Jericho; Garstang 1935, pls. 3–7) are diminutive bowls, small jars, and especially jugs and juglets (Kenyon 1960, figs. 51–62). Such types are not very common in this assemblage and do not appear to have been found in concentrations that suggest their associations to burials. Quite possibly, as suggested by Ilan (*Chapter 6*), other burial practices prevailed in this period, either in the type of treatment of the dead or in the location of tombs, which left the East Slope open for other, quotidian functions. Only subsequently did the necropolis come back into use in the Intermediate Bronze Age.

PART 3: MEGIDDO IN LATE PHASES OF EARLY BRONZE AGE I: A HYPOTHESIS

From what is known of the East Slope and the high mound, it is quite clear that in late phases of Early Bronze Age I something quite extraordinary took place at Megiddo and at additional sites.[91] The evidence suggests developments took place over a period of time, perhaps during several generations, which likely witnessed a gradual increase in the social complexity of the community established at the site. Evidence for this is in the sequence of temples on the high mound (*Megiddo III* and *IV*). This was the period when Early Bronze Age society went from the virtually egalitarian village level to one of hierarchical, social complexity.

Monumental Megiddo

In particular, the temple sequence, culminating in the construction of the monumental temple of Level J4[92] (pls. 97–98; Adams 2009; in press) — the largest and most impressive single structure at Megiddo found to date — points to a significant degree of sophistication matched by economic resources related to a cultic center. They, in turn, are corollated by evidence of monumental Tomb 910 and very intensive mortuary utilization of the East Slope, all of which indicate a floruit of human activity, just prior to its virtual abandonment at the end of Early Bronze Age I or very early in Early Bronze Age II.

Quite possibly, Early Bronze Age Megiddo of the J2–J4 temple horizon, and perhaps the site in all its periods, reached its zenith then, some time around the end of the fourth millennium, or very early in the third millennium (Braun 2001; Braun et al. 2013). That same period may well have witnessed the building

[91] Megiddo was not unique in this period but shared a stage with one or more select, "large players," major agglomerations of populations which have yielded evidence of complex social structures such as Bet Yerah and perhaps Tel Erani (Braun 2011b).

[92] It was found in Area J, which is Tel Aviv University's designation for the Oriental Institute's Area BB that has been slightly enlarged.

of the earliest phase of the stone wall of Stratum XVIII (*Megiddo II*, figs. 152–55; Brandfon 1977), another monumental construction obviously associated with the sacred precinct. Together, those elements allow us to consider Megiddo as having had a central, well-developed, economically prosperous social organization, probably derived from cultic and possibly also mortuary functions provided for a large, regional population known from a considerable number of additional, contemporary occupations (see below).

As relatively little is known of domestic occupation at the site in this period, it is somewhat difficult to define the role of Megiddo in late Early Bronze Age I from the point of view of its social organization. For the present we know definitively only of cultic and mortuary activity, which suggest, by the sizable structures and features associated with them, that the site likely serviced a population of very significant size. Although recent investigations of the "lower mound" have suggested that considerably less than the 50 hectares postulated by its latest excavators were actually occupied in Early Bronze Age I (M. Adams, pers. comm.), there is no doubt that Megiddo was a central, cultic facility, with the East Slope serving as a burial ground for elites and others in this period. Possibly it also served additional contemporary populations[93] that did not inhabit the site, which may explain some of the known features associated with this period.

A modicum of evidence of administration, likely associated with a temple priesthood or an elite class (presumably buried in the monumental tomb or tombs), is hinted at by the small assemblage of Early Bronze Age I seal impressions found at Megiddo and other nearby communities. It is no coincidence that similar finds come from ʿEn Shadud (*Chapter 4*) and more recently a village at the foot of Tel Qashish[94] (van den Brink and ʿAd 2011; E. C. M. van den Brink, pers. comm.). They suggest some type of economic relationship, apparently based on control of significant quantities of comestibles stored in ceramic containers, which necessitated this type of administrative tool.

If Megiddo should prove, after extensive investigations on the lower mound being carried out by M. Adams, to have been inhabited by only a relatively small population, then the monumental remains of the late Early Bronze Age I at the site must be considered as having functioned as an administrative, cultic, and mortuary center for a bevy of nearby and perhaps somewhat more distant communities. That is not surprising as Megiddo, with its own abundant water source, dominates the main western gateway to the Jezreel Valley, a plain of considerable size and great fertility with numerous additional water sources and a climate eminently conducive to agriculture.

The Sociopolitical Context of Megiddo

During the late Early Bronze Age I, the Jezreel hosted a large number of communities, many directly neighboring to Megiddo (fig. 2). Others are not very distant and all would be in contact with such an important site, perhaps relying on it for cultic and economic services. These contacts would have brought the wealth that is so highly visible in the monumental temples and tomb or tombs. The lists of sites is likely to be greater than those known, as others have not yet been excavated or perhaps remain to be discovered beneath the blanket of soil that covers much of the valley.[95] Sites known to be contemporary include: Edh Dhahar (Raban 1999, p. 86*), ʿAfula (Sukenik 1948; Gal and Covello-Paran 1996) ʿEn Shadud (Braun 1985), Tel Yoqneam (Raban 1982, p. 12), Tel Tabʾun (ibid., p. 24), Tel Shem/Tell es-Shammam (ibid., p. 34), Tell Risim/Tell er-Rish (ibid., p. 37), Kh. Shabana (ibid., pp. 37–38), Horvat Seifan/Tell el-Beida (ibid., p. 58), Nahalal Junction East (ibid., p. 66), Site 16-23/95/2 (ibid., p. 68), Tel Shimron (ibid., p. 69–71), Mishmar Ha-emeq (Raban 1999, p. 62*; N. Getzov, pers. comm.), Tel Qiri (Baruch 1987), Tel Qashish (Ben-Tor and Bonfil 2003a; Zuckerman 2003d) and its environs (van den Brink and ʿAd 2011), Hazorea (Anati et al. 1973, p. 73), ʿEn Levana South

---

[93] It was certainly not the sole burial place for the region in this time as attested by cave-tombs at Hazorea (Meyerhof 1989), Kefar Glickson (Zigelman 1978), and Midrakh Oz (Raban 1999, p. 76*; Getzov, Teper, and Ktalav 2008).

[94] This refers to a tiny fragment of an impression, very similar to another from Megiddo, found in a late Early Bronze Age I domestic occupation some small distance from the tell.

[95] Other sites likely remain unknown, either because they have not yet been discovered or their existence awaits publication. Notably, the center of the valley has a heavy cover of alluvium (Orni and Efrat 1980, p. 96) and if such sites were not located on natural prominences then they may lie buried and undiscovered.

(Raban 1999, p. 41*), ʿEin el Mughaiyir (ibid., p. 42*), ʿEn Nahlaot southwest (ibid., p. 52*), Tel Zariq/Tell Abu Zureiq (ibid., p. 54*), Nahlaʾot (ibid., p. 55*), and Mizpeh Zevulun (E. C. M. van den Brink, pers. comm.).

The Arslantepe VI-A Paradigm of Social Organization

Such a description would suggest that a paradigm for the social organization of Arslantepe VIA,[96] dated to the late fourth millennium B.C. (Frangipane 2010, pp. 36–38) and noted as having a "particular character," is pertinent to our understanding of Early Bronze Age I Megiddo. Stratum VIA at Arslantepe is represented by monumental architecture, temples, buildings of public nature, and dwellings of elites. Their excavation has yielded abundant evidence of administration (impressed cretulae[97]) and for contacts with a population of substantial numbers, but which is not represented in the archaeological record of the site itself.

Notably, Arslantepe VIA lacks evidence for habitations of lower classes, activity areas, and other features usually associated with what is often described as early "urbanism"[98] (Braun 2011b), that is, some form of complex, hierarchical, social structure associated with a single, sizable, sedentary community. Thus, Frangipane has described the site in this period as lacking an "urban environment." Nevertheless, the sheer monumentality of the structures of Arslantepe VIA, and the abundant evidence for redistribution of provender encountered there, have led her (2010) to reconstruct the site's prosperity on a food-based economy, and to postulate its associations with nearby, rural, dependent communities.

Frangipane's description may well be relevant for understanding the role of Late Early Bronze Age I Megiddo. At present there is no significant evidence for dwellings housing a population of lower classes that would have provided the wealth needed to construct the series of temples in Area BB/J. Megiddo, too, may have lacked an "urban environment." Such a paradigm of organization, first promulgated by Dunayevsky and Kempinski (1973), albeit without significant elaboration on the subject, might also explain the presence of the massive Stratum XVIII wall found on the east edge of Area BB, the sacred precinct. If indeed it dates to the same time span, it would have been sufficient to protect the inhabited part of the site and the elites that administered it and presumably resided there. If this paradigm is indeed correct, then no additional fortifications should be expected at the site from this period.

The monumentality of the excavated Late Early Bronze Age I structures suggests that Megiddo, as Arslantepe VIA, would have housed central institutions that interacted with extra-mural, rural populations, resident in numerous smaller and less socially developed communities within the Jezreel Valley, and perhaps even farther abroad at Qiryat Ata, ʿEn Esur, and Tel Megadim. Although at Arslantepe there was abundant evidence for the redistribution of food, for which an argument is made that it was the basis for the site's economic prosperity (Frangipane 2010), there is far less evidence for similar social organization in the excavated sectors at Megiddo, perhaps because exposure on the high mound is apparently limited to the sacred enclosure, while the East Slope was merely an adjunct to the sacred precinct. We do not know if at Megiddo there are any additional public structures or domiciles of elites as at Arslantepe.

Nevertheless, there may be some corollary hints of a similar type of economic, food-based system in the pottery repertoires of a number of excavated, contemporary settlements. The very particular pattern of distribution of the bow-rim pithoi (*Chapter 3*), which spread north into the Zevulun Valley and westward into and beyond the ʿIron (Megiddo) Pass, may well indicate something of the economic relations of the Late Early Bronze Age I community at Megiddo. Such pithoi, found in considerable quantities at ʿEn Shadud, Tel

---

[96] This is a large tell site in Malatya, central Anatolia, present-day Turkey.

[97] This is the excavators' term for what are often described as sealings or bullae.

[98] The Early Bronze Age I remains at Megiddo are significantly more impressive than those of Arad III and more deserving of the term "urbanism" (Braun 2011a). At Megiddo, transition to a more socially complex society may have taken place as early as the time of Level J3, as suggested by the sizable temple of that period. In any event it is now known to have taken place somewhat earlier than previously thought (e.g., Amiran 1979).

Qasish, Qiryat Ata, ʿEn Esur, and Tel Megadim, further suggest the importance of foodstuffs, for which these jars would clearly have been employed for storage. The occasional appearances of seal impressions, some on these very pithoi, seem to further enhance this hypothesis with the suggestion they were used as tools of administration.

Such a hypothesis would suggest that Megiddo was a center or a nucleus of control and administration based on religious and economic functions and that it thrived on attachments of smaller dependencies. Such functions would have allowed for the type of aggregated wealth that must have been necessary to create the monumental features known at the site. That paradigm might also explain what appears to have been a very rapid decline at the end of Early Bronze Age I, as has been suggested by Frangipane for the end of the Stratum VIA settlement at Arslantepe. Frangipane suggests that a major reason for the rather abrupt collapse of that polity was that after having been destroyed it did not immediately regain its former status owing to its lack of an "urban environment." Quite simply, it had no internal base of support; no inhabitants to rebuild and repopulate it.

Similar conditions may have prevailed at the end of Early Bronze Age I at Megiddo, which may have been destroyed in an earthquake. With no local population to immediately rebuild, it took several generations for the site to come back into its own; this only happened in Early Bronze Age III, when the sacred precinct was renewed and activity resumed on the East Slope. That trajectory may be contrasted sharply with the occupation of Bet Yerah (Greenberg et al. 2006), which apparently had a large population, that is, an "urban environment," in Late Early Bronze Age I and which continued to be occupied as a thriving community well into Early Bronze Age III. The abrupt demise of Megiddo may also explain the rapid rise in the region of what appear to be smaller polities in Early Bronze Age II, several of which were fortified, such as Tel Qashish (Zuckerman 2003d), Qiryat Ata (Golani 2006), and Tel Taanach (Glock 1993, p. 1432).[99]

These developments at Megiddo suggest the likelihood that more than one type of complex, social organization developed in the southern Levant in this period, and that "urbanism" and its social equivalent, occurred somewhat earlier than scholars were previously wont to admit (e.g., Amiran 1970; Joffe 1993, pp. 24–29[100]). More recently I have argued for these changes to have occurred in late phases of Early Bronze Age I (Braun 2004b, p. 27; 2011b), based on observations from a number of sites. A newly excavated site offers additional suggestions of a possible economic arrangement between several small sites and a larger, central polity at the end of Early Bronze Age I (Milevski et al. 2011). It further enhances the interpretation in this hypothesis.

PART 4: ABANDONING EARLIER STRATIGRAPHIC PARADIGMS

From the detailed review of the evidence derived from the East Slope excavation documented in the preceding chapters, it is clear that radical changes are necessary in any perception of the importance and meaning of the evidence of the "Megiddo Stages" as introduced by the excavators in 1934. That point is particularly stressed as so many chrono-cultural constructs for the archaeological record of the south Levantine Early Bronze Age have relied upon them; indeed have cited them as a backbone of the Early Bronze Age chrono-cultural sequence (e.g., Wright 1937; 1958). Such a change in perception is, however, a natural development as it was clear from the earliest reports that the stratigraphic sequence was an artificial and tentative construction made when the discipline was in its very early, serious phases.[101] Nearly eight decades of excavation, research, and publication since Engberg's and Shiptons' 1934(a) monograph, have greatly altered understanding of the early periods represented in the archaeological record of the East Slope.

[99] For their locations, see figs. 1–2.

[100] Joffe, writing in 1993, placed the major change at the beginning of Early Bronze Age II but more recent research tends to lower the date of this change to sometime late in Early Bronze Age I (Braun 2009).

[101] For a brief review of this early research, see Braun 2011b, pp. 264–65.

Engberg's and Shipton's (1934a) stratigraphic paradigm for the early occupation of the East Slope, encompassing seven consecutive stages, was constructed from information available after work was completed in spring 1933 (*Megiddo Tombs*, p. 2) and prior to excavation of the earliest levels in Area BB on the tell. Those scholars appear to have rushed their work to press for reasons that are not obvious, but possibly related to the change of excavation directors and perhaps some prior commitment to publish preliminary reports. Their small monograph, mostly devoted to pottery studies, studiously excluded plans and other basic information for reasons that are similarly obscure, but which possibly avoided confronting a divergence between the stratigraphic paradigms of Guy (as noted in *Megiddo Tombs*,[102] p. 2), in which the entire East Slope was considered as "more or less a single stratum," and the sequence they purported to perceive based on structures and ceramic horizons. Notably, their work suggested a continuous sequence from what they called "Chalcolithic," now recognized as somewhat advanced Early Bronze Age I (Braun 1985, pp. 99–100; 1989b) through Early Bronze Age III.

It is now clear, from copious evidence, that neither Guy's nor Engberg's and Shipton's stratigraphic paradigms do justice to the confusion of archaeological deposits they encountered on the East Slope; the reality was infinitely more complicated. Therefore, those paradigms should be abandoned, although unfortunately there is no really good replacement system by which to characterize the stratigraphy of the slope. That deficiency derives from the nature of the finds, which were located on a slope with very uneven bedrock features and which was reused, reshaped, plundered, and quarried for its bedrock and building materials over several millennia. In addition, for the most part the finds do not represent in situ deposits, as some of them may well have eroded from the adjacent high mound and subsequently been deposited on the slope. Furthermore, the limitations of the excavation records and the saved artifact assemblages allow for only a silhouette of the archaeological profile of the slope.

It is also clear that there was, in a number of places, especially above the Early Bronze Age remains, a considerable sequence of deposits including several buildings of particularly impressive dimensions. I have designated those structures as "Stage +IV" and attempted to indicate their positions within highly localized sequences, while noting they cannot be combined into a unified system pertinent to the entire slope. Thus the archaeological deposits on the East Slope should be understood as a patchwork of superimposed deposits above a naturally terraced, but also jagged and uneven, human altered, bedrock gradient. Erosion, human activity, intrusions, and depositions all wreaked havoc on an archaeological record that appears not to have been the richest even as it accumulated, especially in the early periods. Accordingly, it is deemed best to abandon the paradigm of seven superimposed stages for a wholly different approach to conceptualizing early human activity on the East Slope.

PART 5: A NEW PARADIGM FOR THE ARCHAEOLOGICAL RECORD OF THE EAST SLOPE

While it is no longer useful to refer to the archaeological record of the East Slope in terms of stages, it is possible to do so by referring to chrono-cultural periods represented by sets of artifacts and, occasionally, their associations with specific structures or rock-cut features. Although they obviously represent sequential episodes in the human utilization of the site, they often do not derive from superimposed deposits. Table 17 is an outline of human activity on the East Slope from its earliest manifestation until the end of the Early Bronze Age.

---

[102] Presumably this was Guy's contribution to the manuscript (Wilson and Allen 1938), probably written much prior to the date of publication.

Table 17. Human utilization of the East Slope of Megiddo

Chrono-Cultural Horizon	*Equivalent "Stages"/"Strata"*	*Principal Remains*
Early Pottery Neolithic	VII	Two flexed burials(?), flint tools
Later Pottery Neolithic to Early Chalcolithic	VII	Two flexed burials(?), few ceramics, flint tools
Chalcolithic	–	Virtually no evidence
Yiftah'el Phase, Early Bronze Age I	VI?	Few ceramics
Late phases of Early Bronze Age I	V, IV	Buildings, ceramics, flint tools, rock-cut tombs, cave tombs
Early phase of Early Bronze Age II	IV	Buildings(?), ceramics
Early Bronze Age II	Gap for most of period	Small collection of ceramics
Early Bronze Age III	III	Building, ceramics
Post-Early Bronze Age III	ES I–III/Stratum A	Buildings, tombs, ceramics, quarries, rock-cut water/drainage, channels, installations, and other features

PART 6: THE ARCHAEOLOGICAL RECORD OF THE EAST SLOPE: AN EPITAPH

Between 1925 and 1933 the East Slope was systematically excavated. By spring of 1933, much of it had been stripped of its ground cover, its archaeological deposits with its secrets revealed by the University of Chicago's Oriental Institute. Shortly thereafter its yield of artifacts was sorted, some of that booty was retained, and apparently much more discarded. Objects in the retained assemblage were registered and divided according to custom into two lots of relatively equal importance and then, each in its new home in Jerusalem or Chicago, was further registered, recorded, and curated. By 1938 a large portion of the newly exposed bedrock of the East Slope was hidden anew beneath two immense mounds of spoil from its own soil deposits and those from excavation of the high mound. Only a small precinct of the East Slope lay exposed, where several empty tombs were left open for birds to come and plant seeds that grew into the trees which presently mark their locations (pl. 3).

PART 7: EPILOGUE

As I complete this volume the lower mound of Megiddo is being systematically studied through survey and excavation by a very competent young colleague, Matthew Adams, for the New Megiddo Expedition. His work represents the first significant attempt, after surveying by the late Avner Raban (1999, pp. 82*–90*), at discerning the full extent of Early Bronze Age occupation off the high mound, which will place the evidence from the East Slope into even better context.

ELIOT BRAUN
Har Adar, Israel
Passover, 2013

APPENDICES

A. LOCATIONS OF LOCI ACCORDING TO THE 5 × 5 M GRID

Table A.1. Locations of loci in Squares T16, U16, T17, and U17
(5 × 5 grid figure references figures 6–7, 10–15, 17–18, 20–22 and plates 7 and 22)

Locus No.	*According to the 5 × 5 m grid*			
79	nn20	—	—	—
80	hh20	ii20	jj20	—
81	mm20	—	—	—
82	nn21	—	—	—
83	mm21	mm22	—	—
158	hh18	—	—	—
216	kk24	ll24	—	—
217	nn24	nn25	—	—
218	mm24	mm25	mm26	ll25
220	ff22	ff23	ee22	—
221	ii19	Jj19	—	—
238	hh20	—	—	—
851	ee20	ff20	—	—
852	ee19	—	—	—
853	ff22	—	—	—
854	ee23	—	—	—
855	ff220	—	—	—
856	ff21	—	—	—
856	gg22	—	—	—
857	ff23	—	—	—
858	ee21	ee22	—	—
859	gg22	—	—	—
860	gg21	—	—	—
861	ee22	—	—	—
862	ff23	gg23	—	—
864	hh22	—	—	—
865	ee21	—	—	—
867	ii26	—	—	—
868	hh26	—	—	—
869	ee24	—	—	—
871	ii24	jj24	—	—

Locus No.	*According to the 5 × 5 m grid*			
872	jj25	jj26	kk26	—
875	ff23	—	—	—
895	ee25	—	—	—
902	ff21	—	—	—
904	ee27	ee26	—	—
905	jj27	—	—	—
909	ll27	—	—	—
914	jj23	jj24	—	—
917	ii24	Jj24	—	—
918	ff24	—	—	—
919	ff20	—	—	—
920	hh25	hh26	—	—
921	ff24	—	—	—
923	ii23	ii24	—	—
998	hh25	ii25	—	—
1082	ee25	—	—	—
1083	hh22	—	—	—
1084	gg25	gg24	—	—
1085	gg27	—	—	—
1086	ee27	—	—	—
1089	kk24	—	—	—
1094	gg24	gg25	—	—
1104	jj26	jj27	—	—
1105	hh24	ii24	—	—
1190	hh24	gg24	—	—
1191	gg25	gg24	hh25	—
1198	gg23	gg24	—	—
1199	ff24	ff23	ee24	gg24
1200	gg23	hh23	—	—
1201	gg23	—	—	—
1203	hh22	—	—	—

Table A.1. Locations of loci in Squares T16, U16, T17, and U17 (*cont.*)

Locus No.	*According to the 5 × 5 m grid*			
1204	hh23	hh24	—	—
1207	ii21	—	—	—
1208	ff26	gg26	—	—
1217	hh21	—	—	—
1220	ff25	—	—	—
1224	gg26	—	—	—
1226	gg25	gg26	—	—

Locus No.	*According to the 5 × 5 m grid*			
1227	gg25	—	—	—
1232	gg27	ff27	—	—
1234	gg26	hh26	gg25	hh25
1240	ff26	gg26	—	—
1242	gg27	ff27	—	—
1243	ii23	jj23	—	—

B. LOCATIONS OF WALLS ACCORDING TO THE 5 × 5 M GRID AND IN ILLUSTRATIONS

Table B.1. Walls of post-Stage IV structures on the East Slope: Locations and labeled illustrations

Wall No.	*Square*	*Square*	*Square*	*Illustration*
500	hh26	—	—	Figs. 10–11
501	—	—	—	—
502	—	—	—	—
503	—	—	—	—
504	—	—	—	—
505	jj23	—	—	Figs. 10, 15
506	jj23	jj24	—	Figs. 10, 15; pl. 28
507	ii24	jj24	—	Figs. 10, 15; pl. 28
508	ii24	ii23	—	Figs. 10, 15; pl. 28
509	jj24	—	—	Figs. 10, 15
510	jj23	—	—	Figs. 10, 15
511	jj23	—	—	Figs. 10, 15
512	ii24	—	—	Figs. 10, 15; pl. 28
513	—	—	—	—
514	hh25	—	—	Figs. 10–11, 14; pl. 16
515	ff26	gg26	gg25	Figs. 10–11, 12–13
516	gg25	—	—	Figs. 10–11, 12–13
517	ff24	gg24	—	Figs. 10–11, 12–13
518	—	—	—	—
519	hh24	—	—	Figs. 10–11, 12–13
520	hh25	—	—	Fig. 13
521	hh23	hh24	—	Fig. 13
522	—	—	—	—
523	gg25	—	—	Figs. 10–11
524	gg25	—	—	Figs. 10–11
525	gg26	—	—	Figs. 10–11
526	iIi26	—	—	Fig. 10
527	ff23	gg23	—	Fig. 10
528	hh26	—	—	Figs. 10–11
529	gg25	hh25	—	Figs. 10–11
530	hh23	ii23	—	Figs. 10–11
531	ff23	gg24	gg23	Fig. 13
532	ff24	—	—	Fig. 13
533	ff25	—	—	Fig. 13
534	ff25	—	—	Fig. 13
535	gg25	hh25	gg26	Fig. 14; pl. 16
536	hh26	—	—	Fig. 14
537	gg26	—	—	Fig. 14
538	gg26	—	—	Figs. 14, 31
539	ii26	—	—	Fig. 14; pl. 22
540	gg26	—	—	—
541	g26	—	—	Fig. 14
542	ii26	—	—	Fig. 14
543	gg26	hh26	—	Fig. 14
544	—	—	—	—
545	hh25	—	—	Fig. 14
546	ff25	ff25	—	Pl. 27
1085	gg27	hh27	hh26	Figs. 10–11, 22–23
1195	gg24	—	—	—
1213	gg26	—	—	Pls. 27, 31–32
1243	ii23	jj23	—	Figs. 22, 16–17; pls. 16, 22, 24, 28–29, 38

Table B.2. Walls of the earliest structures on the East Slope: Locations and labeled illustrations

Wall No.	*Location in 5 × 5 m Grid*				Illustration
	Square	*Square*	*Square*	*Square*	
1	gg22	gg23	—	—	Figs. 17–18, 20; pls. 22–25, 27
2	gg22	hh22	—	—	Figs. 17–18, 20, 27; pls. 22–24, 25
3[a]	hh22	—	—	—	Figs. 17–20; pls. 22–25
4[b]	hh22	ii22	ii23	—	Figs. 17–18, 20, 24; pls. 1, 24–25
5[c]	ii22	hh22	—	—	Figs. 17–18, 20; pls. 21–26, 27
6	hh22	hh23	gg22	—	Figs. 17–20; pls. 22–25, 27
7	hh23	—	—	—	Figs. 17–18, 20; pls. 22, 24–25, 27–28
8	hh23	ii23	—	—	Figs. 17–18, 20; pls. 15, 22, 24, 27–29, 38
8A	hh23	ii23	—	—	Figs. 17–18, 20; pls. 22, 28
9	—	—	—	—	Fig. 20; pl. 25
10	hh23[d]	—	—	—	Figs. 17–18, 20; pls. 22, 24, 28
11	gg23	—	—	—	Figs. 17–18, 20; pls. 22–23, 25
12	gg23	—	—	—	Figs. 17–18; pls. 22, 24
13	gg23	—	—	—	Figs. 17–20; pls. 22–23, 24–25
14	gg23	gg24	ff23	—	Figs. 17–19; pls. 22, 24
15	hh24	—	—	—	Figs. 17–18; pls. 22, 28–29
16	hh24	—	—	—	Figs. 17–18; pls. 22, 29
17	gg24	—	—	—	Figs. 17–18; pls. 22, 29, 38
18	gg24	—	—	—	Figs. 17–18; pl. 22
19[e]	hh25	—	—	—	Fig. 17; pl. 22
20	gg25	—	—	—	Figs. 17–18, 21–22; pls. 22, 29–31, 34
21	ff26	ff25	gg25	—	Figs. 17, 21–22; pls. 22, 33
22	ff26	gg26	—	—	Figs. 17, 21–22; pls. 22, 32
23	gg26	—	—	—	Figs. 17, 21–22; pls. 22, 32, 35
24[f]	gg26	—	—	—	Figs. 17, 22; pl. 21
25	gg26	gg25	—	—	Figs. 17, 21; pls. 22, 33
26	ii24	—	—	—	Fig. 17; pls. 22, 24, 28
27	hh23	—	—	—	Fig. 17; pls. 22–24, 34
28	gg24	hh24	—	—	Fig. 17; pls. 22, 28–29
29	gg24	—	—	—	Figs. 17–18; pls. 22, 29
30	hh24	—	—	—	Fig. 17; pls. 22, 24, 28
31	ii23	—	—	—	Fig. 17; pls. 22, 24, 29, 38
32	ii23	—	—	—	Fig. 17; pls. 22, 24, 28[g], 29, 35
33	gg25	—	—	—	Figs. 17, 21; pl. 22
34	gg26	—	—	—	Figs. 21–22; pls. 32, 34
39	ii26	hh26	—	—	Pl. 22
40	hh26	—	—	—	Fig. 17; pl. 22
41	gg25	gg26	—	—	Fig. 22; pl. 38
42	gg25	gg26	hh25	hh26	Fig. 22; pl. 38
47	—	—	—	—	Fig. 21
1125	—	—	—	—	Pl. 38
1195	gg24	—	—	—	Fig. 17; pls. 28–29. 32–33
1196	hh23	—	—	—	Figs. 17, 20; pls. 24–25, 27–28
1213	gg26	—	—	—	Pl. 18
1221	gg26	hh26	—	—	Fig. 21; pl. 34

[a] This is part of the excavators' "Locus" 1196.
[b] This is part of the excavators' "Locus" 1196.
[c] This is part of the excavators' Wall 1196.
[d] This is a flight of three steps leading up into the building.
[e] Possibly a continuation of W1195 to the east.
[f] Possibly a bench.
[g] Location of robber trench.

C. MEGIDDO EAST SLOPE LOCUS REGISTER BASED ON NOTEBOOKS AND LOCUS/OBJECT CARDS AND PHOTOGRAPHS IN THE ORIENTAL INSTITUTE

INTRODUCTION

This master list of the loci on the East Slope is based on a series of notebooks in the archives of the Oriental Institute and is as complete as I have been able to make it, but it does not represent all the loci assigned to work there as the numbers at the end indicate. It begins with Locus 55; the lower numbers were assigned in seasons prior to the inception of the locus system, as noted in the first page of the first notebook. There is some confusion in those numbers as they appear to represent two systems, one for non-mortuary features; the other prefixed with the letter "T" for tombs. They appear on a previously unpublished plan (fig. 6) and obviously represent two parallel notation systems. After 1927, and from the number 55, P. L. O. Guy instituted a unitary system in which all loci, including tombs, were given consecutive numbers. For a time tombs continued to be identified with the letter "T," but that identification was not always strictly correct as some "tombs" were merely caves or cavities with no evidence of mortuary associations.

There are some gaps in information on numbering between 1250 and 1828 for the East Slope. Most of those numbered loci are to be found on the high mound as work effectively was discontinued on the East Slope in 1932, when the numbering reached at least to 1243. However, I speculate that some of the deep soundings might have been made after the major work was done in order to present a section of the East Slope (*Chapter 1*). Possibly that hypothesis is borne out by the date entries for Loci 1704 and 1828. They appear in parallel entries (see below) as 1932 and 1934, respectively. In addition, Locus 1703 seems to have been a later operation, but for that there is no parallel dating entry. Thus there is some reason to believe they were excavated in the latter time span, probably when work was virtually abandoned on the East Slope, which would explain their relatively high numbers.

However, an alternate explanation would be that the numbers above 1243 were latterly assigned, *ex post facto*, to work done much earlier, perhaps to allow for loci assignments in the drawn section so as to label features encountered there, but otherwise undocumented. I know of no other likely explanation for parallel entries or the disparate datings. In any event it is highly unlikely that many locus numbers were generated for the East Slope after 1932, as after that season most of the area then became an active dump.

Some of the loci in the list are very briefly described. When there are no annotations, it appears the excavators deemed them unnecessary. The descriptions were all entered in hand and in most instances there is only one entry for each locus. Most of the locus numbers in the notebooks were also entered by hand (pl. 4 left), but the group of parallel entries was generated by a rotating stamp that each time it was imprinted created a higher, consecutive number (pl. 4 right). These entries are often annotated with "Site Photo" numbers. As there are no explanatory notes, it is impossible to state the reason for these double entries. Occasionally one entry offers information not found in its parallel, while there are even a few instances of discrepancies between entries. They are noted below. References to "ES I–III" are to a stratigraphic system cited by the excavators (Guy and Engberg 1938), but otherwise never utilized (*Chapter 2: The Stratigraphy of the East Slope*). Those levels are the latest on the East Slope and were considered by them as "late," which may best be interpreted as later than the Early Bronze Age, and probably post Iron Age, but with no further precision.

THE EXCAVATORS' ANNOTATIONS IN THE LOCUS REGISTER

Following are a number of points explaining the excavators' annotations:

1. Some of these locus numbers appear in figure 6 with the prefix "T" for tomb; other large numbers, probably assigned prior to 1927 (see above), representing something akin to loci(?), are indicated without the "T" prefix. Some have the same numbers as tombs suggesting they were part of a different recording system. That is especially likely as a note in the locus book (page 1) indicates a "Tomb Register," but that is not presently found in the extant archives.
2. The following tombs were excavated on the East Slope before the new system of locus numbers was adopted in 1927:
    a) 1925: Tombs 1–5 inclusive
    b) 1926: Tombs 6–59 inclusive
    c) 1927: Tombs 60–84 inclusive
3. They noted that squares in which these tombs occurred are noted in the early pages of the tombs register.
4. "Under the system of numbering which begins overleaf a consecutive serial number is given to each "locus" irrespective of what that locus is. Tombs are distinguished by the prefix 'T'."
5. At the end of the Locus Book there is a page with "General Notes": "All loci in this book from 201 to 900 have been compared with the field book, and checked as to the squares in which they occur, but their strata remain for the most part undetermined" (date stamped: 8 Apr. 1931). Additional notes below state: a) "S. A. photos entered up to and including S. A. 945, S. B. 985" and b) in block letters in yellow crayon: "Published by May X."
6. Most of the work on the East Slope appears to have been terminated by the time Locus 1243 was assigned at the end of the season.[1] After that the following only occasional numbers were used for work on the summit of the tell (see above). Work on the East Slope apparently continued only sporadically after that as indicated by the use of numbers 1370, 1371, 1703, 1704, and 1828, for what are probably deep probes (see below) in limited areas down to bedrock on the upper and lower terraces (fig. 23, pl. 21).
7. I have made a few additions to this list, based on information from plans, sections, annotations in level books, and on sherds and locus/object cards. Those additions appear in italics, while additional, explanatory information has been relegated to footnotes so as not to overburden the table. The column marked "figure(s)" indicates where the loci are illustrated.

[1] An annotation in the flyleaf of the notebook indicates that the number 1244 was apparently to be used for the next season.

Table C.1. Excavators' annotated locus list

Locus No.	*Area*	*Square*[a]	*Notes*	*Year*	*Illustration*
55	—	R15	—	1926	—
56	—	R15	—	1926	—
57	—	R15	—	1926	—
58	—	R15	—	1926	Fig. 6
59	—	R15	—	1926	Fig. 6
60	—	R15	—	1926	Fig. 6
61	—	R15	—	1926	—
62	—	R15	—	1926	—
63	—	Q19	—	1926	Fig. 6
64	—	Q19	—	1926	—
65	—	Q19[b]	—	1926	Fig. 6
Pit 65	—	*T18*	*Entry on a series of locus/object cards indicates a pit south of Tomb 64*[c]	—	Fig. 6
66	—	Q19	—	1926	Fig. 6
South of 83		T17			
214	Rock, ES	S16	Tomb	1927	Fig. 6
215	Rock	T16	Tomb	1927	Fig. 6
216	Rock	U17	Cistern	1927	Figs. 5–6
217	Rock	U17	Tomb	1927	Figs. 4–16
218	Rock	U17	Cave	1927	Figs. 4–16
219	Rock	S16	Tomb	1927	Fig. 4
220	IV?	S17	Wall	1927	Figs. 4, 6–7, 23
South of 220	—	*T17*	*No information; flint artifacts registered*	1927	—
Fill east of Wall 220	—	*T17*	*No information; flint artifacts registered*	—	—
221	ES I	S15	Tomb	1927	Fig. 6
222	ES I	S15	Room	1927	—
223	ES I	S15	Room	1927	—
224	ES I	S15	Room	1927	—
225	ES I	S15	Room	1927	—
226	ES I	S15	Room	1927	—
227	ES I	S15	Room	1927	—
228	ES I	S15	Room[d]	1927	—
229	ES I	S15	Room	1927	—
230	ES I	S15	Room	1927	—
231	ES I	R15	Room	1927	—
232	Above ES I	S15	Tomb[e]	1927	—

[a] This refers to the master grid of 25 × 25 m that covers the entire site (fig. 3).
[b] Tomb 64 is published (*Megiddo Tombs*, p. 127) as located in Squares S–T18; on locus/object cards it is noted as in T18.
[c] This system of numbering for this pit, which does not correspond to the information on Locus 65, is unknown from additional sources in the archives and its significance as well as its precise location remain obscure.
[d] Does not appear on plan. Object register suggests it was located in southeast of Square S15.
[e] This appears to have been a cist tomb.

Table C.1. Excavators' annotated locus list (*cont.*)

Locus No.	*Area*	*Square*	*Notes*	*Year*	*Illustration*
Below 232	—		*Fill that yielded objects*	—	—
233	Rock	S15	Tomb	1927	—
234	Rock	S15	Tomb	1927	—
235	Rock	S15	Tomb, offering place associated with tombs	1927	—
236	Rock	T16	Tomb	1927	—
237	?[f]	Q15	Tomb	1927	—
238	ES II	R15	Room	1927	Fig. 6
239	ES II	S15	Room (*associated with Locus 241; believed contemporary with Locus 49*)	1927	—
240	ES II	S15	Room (*below Locus 227*)	1927	—
241	ES II	S15	Room (*associated with Locus 239*)	1927	—
242	ES II	S15	Room	1927	—
243	ES II	S15	Room	1927	—
244	Above ES II	S15	Tomb	1927	—
245	ES II	S15	Area	1927	—
246	ES II	S15	Area	1927	—
247	Below ES II 238	S15	Tomb (jar)	1927	—
248	—	—	*No record; deliberately skipped?*	1927	—
249	ES II	S15	Room (*"walls only a few cms high, floor of flattish stones on layer of nari[g] stone"; north-west of Locus 239; believed to be contemporary with Locus 239; interpreted as "kitchen or bakehouse"*)	1927	—
250	Rock	R15	Drain (jar)	1927	—
251	Rock	S15	Tomb	1927	—
252	Rock	S15	Tomb	1927	—
253	Rock	R15	Tomb	1927	—
254	Rock	S15	Tomb	1927	—
255	Rock	S15	Tomb	1927	—
256	Floor above rock, ES III	S15	—	1927	—
257	Rock	S15	Tomb (pot)	1927	—
258	Rock	R15	Tomb	1927	—
259	ES III	S15	Room	1927	—
Below 259	*ES III*	*S15*	*Fill to bedrock (yielded large collection of flint)*	1927	—
260	ES III	S15	Room	1927	—

[f] Illegible notation.

[g] "Nari" is a local term used for an uppermost layer of soft, chalky limestone made harder by deposits of calcium derived from exposure to rain (Orni and Efrat 1980, p. 57).

Table C.1. Excavators' annotated locus list (*cont.*)

Locus No.	*Area*	*Square*	*Notes*	*Year*	*Illustration*
Below 260			*Fill to bedrock*		
678	ES	V18	Pottery kiln dug in 1926	1930	—
851	ES	T16	Rock cutting	1930	Figs. 5–6
852	ES	T16	Rock cutting	1930	Figs. 5–6
853	ES	T16	Above T. 861, below Wall 220 in limestone filling	1930	Figs. 5–6
854	ES	U16	Tomb with three cover stones	1930	Figs. 5–6
855	ES	T16	Double burial at least	1930	Figs. 5–6
856	ES	T16	Single burial	1930	Figs. 5–6
857	ES	U16	Tomb with 4 cover stones; no pots	1930	Figs. 5–6, 11
858	ES	T16	Rock cutting	1930	Fig. 6
859	ES	T16	Line – floor, stone pit in rock	1930	Figs. 6–7
860	ES	T16	Tomb	1930	Figs. 5–6
861	ES	T16	Rock chamber, no roof	1930	Fig. 6
862	ES	U16	Stone enclosure	1930	Figs. 5–7, 10
863	ES	U16	Cave	1930	Fig. 5
864	ES	T16	Large stone	1930	Figs. 5–7
865	ES	T16	Tomb, Rock cut tomb-chamber	1930	Figs. 5–6
866	ES	T16	Wall parallel with 220	1930	Figs. 5–7
867	ES	U16	Room?	1930	Figs. 5–7, 10
868	ES	U16	Tomb, child burial-MB	1930	Figs. 5–6, 10; pl. 21
869	ES	U16	Hole in rock	1930	Figs. 5–6
870	ES	V17	Room ("*filling*")	1930	Fig. 7
871	ES	U16	Room: Rock on SW, walls on 2 other sides	1930	Figs. 5–6, 10, 15; pl. 21
872	ES	U17	Rock cutting	1930	Figs. 5–6
873	ES	V17	Room? In rock	1930	Fig. 7
874			*No Record, deliberately skipped ?*	1930	—
875	ES	W16	Room	1931	Figs. 5, 7, 10
876	ES	W16	Tomb, burial	1931	—
877	ES	W16	Shaft tomb	1931	—
878	ES	W16	Shaft tomb	1931	—
879	ES	W16	Quarry	1931	—
880	ES	W16	Tomb, shaft tomb	1931	—
881	ES	W16	Cave, Neolithic floor	1931	—
882	ES	W17	Room with stone floor	1931	—
883	ES	W17	Room on rock	1931	Fig. 6
884	ES	V16	Shaft tomb	1931	—
885	ES	W17	Room with floor	1931	—
886	ES	W17	Room	1931	—
887	ES	V16	Room?	1931	Fig. 7
888	ES	V16	Quarry	1931	—

Table C.1. Excavators' annotated locus list (*cont.*)

Locus No.	*Area*	*Square*	*Notes*	*Year*	*Illustration*
889	ES	W17	Rock cutting	1931	Fig. 5
890	ES	W16	Rock cutting	1931	—
891	ES	V16	Shaft tomb	1931	—
892	ES	W17	Stone floor	1931	—
893	ES	V16	Stone floor	1931	Fig. 7
894	ES	V17	Stone floor	1931	Fig. 7
895	ES	U16	Rock cutting	1931	Figs. 5–6
896	ES	V16	Rock trough with hole	1931	—
897	ES	W16	Raised cup mark	1931	—
898	ES	W16	Rock trough with wall	1931	—
899	ES	W16	Wall across 879	1931	Fig. 7
900	ES	W17[h]	Rock-cut water channel	1931	Figs. 5, 7–8
901	ES	W16	Quarry	1931	—
902	ES	T16	Quarry	1931	Figs. 5–6
903	ES	V16	Tomb, rock cutting(?) with burials(?)	1931	Fig. 24; pls. 21, 39
904	ES	U16	Rock cutting with floor	1931	Figs. 5–6
Under 904	ES	U16	—	—	—
905	ES	U17	Room: half rock (and house)	1931	Figs. 5–7
906	ES	V17	Quarry	1931	—
907	ES	V18	Rock grave, no objects	1931	Fig. 34; pl. 95a
908	ES	W17	Inscription: rock	1931	—
909	ES	U17	Wall	1931	Figs. 5–7
910	ES	V17	Rock tomb	1931	—
911	ES	V17	Shaft tomb	1931	—
912	ES	V17	Shaft tomb	1931	—
913	ES	V17	Shaft, no tomb	1931	—
914	ES	U17	Room with four ovens(?[i]) in NE corner	1931	Figs. 5–6, 10; pl. 21
915	ES	V17	Adult burial with frags of pottery	1931	—
916	ES	U17	Hole	1931	Figs. 5–6
917	ES	U18	Gap in wall	1931	Figs. 5–6, 10; pl. 21
918	ES	U16	Room with oven	1931	Figs. 5–6, 10–11
919	ES	T16	Rock cutting under T. 855	1931	Figs. 5–6
920	ES	U16	Room	1931	Figs. 5–7, 10–11
921	ES	U16	Simple burial with pots	1931	Figs. 5–6, 10–11; pl. 21
922	ES	V17	Shaft tomb	1931	—
923	ES	U16	Room	1931	Figs. 5–6, 17
973	ES	V16	Hole into T. 911 D	1931	—
989	ES	W16	Shaft tomb	1931	—

[h] Notation is not very legible, probably reads: "etc."

[i] Possible reading; not very legible.

Table C.1. Excavators' annotated locus list (*cont.*)

Locus No.	*Area*	*Square*	*Notes*	*Year*	*Illustration*
998	ES	U16	Cistern	1931	Figs. 5–6, 10–11
1014	ES	V16	Shaft tomb	1931	—
1082	ES A	U16	Room ½ rock	1931	Figs. 5–7
1083	ES A	U16	2 ovens	1931	Figs. 5–7
1084	ES A	U16	Complex of late walls and floors	1931	Figs. 5–7, 10–11
Under 1084	ES III	U16	—	—	—
1085	ES A	U16	Wall etc., late	1931	Figs. 5–8, 23
1086	ES A	U16	Late walls above 904	1931	Figs. 5–7
1087	ES	U16	"Kiln"	1931	
Under 1087	ES	U16	—	1931	—
1088	ES	U16	"Kiln"	—	Fig. 5
West of 1088, floor	ES	U16	—	—	—
1087–1088	ES	U16	—	—	—
Under 1088	ES	U16	P4566 potmark on handle	—	—
1089	ES A	U17	Lime floor	1931	Figs. 6–7
1090	ES	U16	Tomb	1931	—
1091	ES	U16	Quarry	1931	—
1092	ES	T16	"kiln"	1931	—
1093	ES A	V17	Wall, late	1931	Fig. 7
1094	ES A	V16	Floor, late	1931	Fig. 7
1095	ES	V16	Area under 1094	1931	—
1096	ES A	V16	Late house	1931	Fig. 7
1097	ES A	V16	Wall over T. 14 and house	1931	Fig. 7
1098	ES	V16	Shaft tomb	1931	Fig. 24
1099	ES A	V16	Room	1931	Figs. 5, 7
1100	ES	W16	Shaft	1931	—
1101	ES	V16	Cave with burials	1931	Figs. 5, 23; pls. 21, 40
1102	ES	V16	Cave, upper pottery only (with 1101[j])	1931	Fig. 24; pl. 21
1103	ES	V16	Human bones (on rock[k])	1931	—
1104	ES A	U17	Walls	1931	Figs. 5–7
1105	ES A	U16	Grain pit	1931	Figs. 5–7
1106	ES	V16	Cave	1931	Fig. 24
1107	ES	V17	Room	1931	—
1108	ES	V17	Room	1931	—
1109	ES	U17	Room	1931	—
1110	ES	U17	Room	1931	—
1111	ES	U17	Room	1931	—
1112	ES	W16	Cistern	1931	—

[j] Derived from Tomb list in notebook.
[k] Derived from Tomb list in notebook.

Table C.1. Excavators' annotated locus list (*cont.*)

Locus No.	*Area*	*Square*	*Notes*	*Year*	*Illustration*
1113	ES A	V17	Room	1931	Fig. 7
1114	ES A	V17	Wall	1931	Fig. 7
1115	ES A	W17	Oven	1931	Fig. 7
1116	—	—	*No record; deliberately skipped?*	1931	—
1117	ES A	V17	Wall	1931	Fig. 7
1118	ES A	W16	Large stone	1931	—
1119	ES	V16	Shaft	1932	—
1120	ES	V17	Shaft tomb	1932	—
1121	ES	V16	Cistern	1932	—
1122	ES	V17	Tomb	1932	—
1123	ES	V17	Hole	1932	—
1124	ES	V16	Cistern	1932	—
1125	ES	V16	Animal in T. 903	1932	Pl. 39
1126	ES	V16	Adult burial in T. 903	1932	Pl. 21
1127	ES	V16	Child burial in T. 903	1932	Pl. 21
1128	ES	V16	Chamber breaking into T. 1101	1932	Fig. 24
1129	ES	V17	Cave under 900	1932	—
1130	ES	W17	Channel under 900	1932	—
1131	ES	W17	Wall	1932	—
1132	ES	V17	Room	1932	—
1133	ES	—	*No record; deliberately skipped?*	1932	—
1134	ES	—	*No record; deliberately skipped?*	1932	—
1135	ES	V17	Room and house	1932	—
1136	ES	U17	Room	1932	—
1137	ES	V17	Room - 1108	1932	—
1138	ES	V17	Room or court of house 1135	1932	—
1139	ES	U16	Hole	1932	Fig. 24
1140	ES	U17	Room under 1109	1932	—
1141	ES	U17	Hole in rock with burial	1932	—
1142	ES	V16	Upper wall, round 1143	1932	Fig. 24 section; pl. 41
1143	ES	V16	Kiln	1932	Fig. 24; pl. 41
1144	ES	U17	Remains of walls	1932	—
1145	ES	U17	Rock tomb	1932	—
1146	ES	V17	Cave with smaller cave behind	1932	—
1147	ES	V17	Rock hole with steps	1932	—
1148	ES	V17	Room part rock over 1211	1932	—
1149	ES	V16	Room part rock	1932	—
1150	ES	V16	Room part rock	1932	Fig. 5
1151	ES	V16	Room, mud walls over 1212	1932	—
1152	ES	V16	Cup mark with pot	1932	Pl. 41
1153	ES	V16	Room part rock	1932	—

Table C.1. Excavators' annotated locus list (*cont.*)

Locus No.	*Area*	*Square*	*Notes*	*Year*	*Illustration*
1154	ES	V16	Rock hole	1932	—
1155	ES	U17	Rock hole	1932	—
1156	ES	U16	Oven	1932	—
1157	ES	U16	Room	1932	—
West of 1157	ES	U16	—	—	—
1158	ES	V16	Wall in 1106	1932	—
1159	ES	V16	Wall under 1142	1932	Fig. 24 section
1160	ES	U16	Oven	1932	—
1161	ES	U16	Oven	1932	—
1162	ES	U16	Stone floor} bracketed with 1163	1932	—
1163	ES	U16	Wall }bracketed with 1162	1932	—
1164	ES	U16	Wall	1932	—
1165	ES	U16	Room over 1169	1932	—
Just over 1166	ES	U16	—	1932	—
1166	ES	U16	Room with stone floor	1932	—
Just under 1166	ES III	U16	—	1932	—
ca. 30 cm under 1166	*ES*	*U16*	—	—	—
1167	ES	W17	Room	1932	—
1168	ES	U16	Room under 918 and over 1194	1932	—
Under 1168	ES	U16	—	—	—
1169	ES	U16	Room under 1165 and over 1198	1932	—
1170	ES	U16	Room over 1200	1932	—
1171	ES	V17	Room	1932	—
1172	ES	V17	Room and house	1932	—
1173	ES	U17	Room	1932	—
1174	ES	V17	Room	1932	—
1175	ES	V17	Large stone in 1172	1932	—
1176	ES	U17	Drain from E corner of 1172	1932	—
1177	ES	U17	Large stone under 1140	1932	—
1178	ES	U17	Tomb, partly rock	1932	—
1179	ES	U16	Fr. of wall SW of 1164	1932	—
1180	ES	V17	Room under 1172	1932	—
1181	ES	V17	Room under 1180	1932	—
1182	ES	U17	Small enclosure,[1] part rock over 1185	1932	—

[1] Writes "inclosure"; "rock" follows "part," but it could be some other word; written in scrawl.

Table C.1. Excavators' annotated locus list (*cont.*)

Locus No.	*Area*	*Square*	*Notes*	*Year*	*Illustration*
1183	ES	U17	Floor under NE part of 1171. *A nearly complete holemouth vessel (P4509) with bulging body and slightly tapered, pointed base was retrieved from this floor, but this information does not correspond to that for Locus 1171, which is indicated as located in Square V17*	1932	—
1184	ES	U17	Rounded enclosure under NE part of 1171 and NE of 1183 (Photo indicates it has a flexed burial)	1932	—
1185	ES	U17	Small enclosure under 1182 of 1183	1932	—
1186	ES	U17	Cistern	1932	—
1187	ES	U16	Area over 1208	1932	Pl. 25
1188	ES	V17	Wall in rock	1932	—
1189	ES	U16	Wall under 904	1932	—
1190	ES	U16	Room	1932	Figs. 16–18; pl. 17
1191	ES	U16	Room (*has a bedrock surface pitted with channels, plugged cavity, and cupmarks*)	1932	Figs. 16–18, 22; pls. 21, 29, 33, 38
1192	ES	U16	Room	1932	Pl. 38
1193	ES	T16	Floor NW of kiln 1092	1932	—
1194	ES	T16	Rounded wall probably ?[m] 1092	1932	—
1195	ES	U16	SW wall of 1190	1932	Pls. 28–29, 32, 33
1196	ES	U16	SE wall of 1200	1932	Pls. 25–28
1197	ES	T16	Wall	1932	—
1198	ES	U16	Room under 1169	1932	Figs. 16–19; pls. 22–25
1199	ES	U16	Room under 1168	1932	Figs. 4, 16–19, 23; pls. 21, 33, 37
1200	ES	U16	Room under 1170 (and house[n])	1932	Figs. 16–19, 20; pls. 21, 23, 24, 27
1201	ES	U16	Rock panage NW of house 1200	1932	Figs. 16–18, 20
1202	ES	T16	Wall E of kiln 1092	1932	—
1203	ES	T16	Room NE of 1200	1932	Figs. 16–19, 20; pls. 21, 23–25
1204	ES	U16	Room NE of 1190	1932	Figs. 16–19, 20; pls. 24–25, 27–28
1205	ES	T16	Wall W of 1092 under 1193	1932	—
1206	ES	U16	Structure of kiln 1210	1932	—
1207	ES	T16	Room E of 1203	1932	Figs. 16–18, 20; pls. 21, 27
1208	ES	U16	Room under 1187	1932	Figs. 4, 16–18, 21–23; pls. 21, 31–32, 34
1209	ES	V16	Small kiln	1932	—
1210	ES	U16	Kiln under 1206	1932	—

[m] Appears as a tiny, very carelessly written x.

[n] From additional entry.

Table C.1. Excavators' annotated locus list (*cont.*)

Locus No.	*Area*	*Square*	*Notes*	*Year*	*Illustration*
1211	ES	V17	Room under 1148	1932	—
1212	ES	V16	Room under 1151; *existence of floor noted on marked sherd (A15791; pl. 43a)*	1932	—
1213	ES	U16	Wall with threshold and door socket	1932	Pl. 32
1214	ES	U17	Room N of 914	1932	—
1215	ES	U17	Small circular structure	1932	—
1216	ES	V16	Wall SE of 1212	1932	—
1217	ES	T16	Area NW of 1203	1932	Figs. 16–18; pls. 21, 25
1218	ES	U16	Square hole under 909	1932	—
1219	ES	U16	Curved enclosure	1932	—
1220	ES	U16	Earth floor; *associated with W40*	1932	Figs. 16–18, 21–22; pls. 21, 35
1221	ES	U16	Wall (rubble)	1932	Fig. 21; pls. 34–35
1222	ES	U17	Earth floor	1932	—
1223	ES	V16	Ring hole in rock between T. 1101 & T. 1128	1932	—
1224	ES	U16	Lime floor under 1220	1932	Pl. 35
1225	ES	U16	Wall-angle	1932	—
1226	ES	U16	Room next 1208	1932	Figs. 16–18, 21–23; pls. 21, 33
1227	ES	U16	Room next 1226	1932	Figs. 16–18, 21–22; pls. 21, 33
1228	ES	U16	Floor with cupmarks	1932	—
Under 1228 (70 cm under)	ES	U16	—	—	—
1229	ES	U17	Rock hole under 1184	1932	—
1230	ES	V16	Floor under 1212	1932	—
1231	ES	V17	Cistern	1932	—
1232	ES	U16	Smaller stone over 903	1932	Fig. 16; pl. 21
1232 under-to 30–80 cm	ES	U16	—	—	—
1233	ES	U16	Larger stone over 903	1932	Fig. 16; pl. 21
1234	ES	U16	Stone E of 1227	1932	Figs. 14–18; pls. 21, 29, 34–35
1235	ES	U16	Stone floor under 1207	1932	—
1236	ES	U16	Rock hole under 1195	1932	Pl. 38
1237	ES	U17	Earth floor under 914	1932	—
1238	ES	U16	Floor under 871	1932	—
1239	ES	U16	Floor with stone on edge	1932	—
1240	ES	U16	Floor under 1226	1932	Figs. 4, 23; pl. 38
1241	ES	U16	Room under 1234	1932	Pl. 38
1242	ES	U16	Floor going under 1232	1932	Figs. 5, 23; pl. 21
1243	ES	U17	NW (older) Wall of 914	1932	Figs. 16–18, 29, 38

Table C.1. Excavators' annotated locus list (*cont.*)

Locus No.	*Area*	*Square*	*Notes*	*Year*	*Illustration*
—	—	—	—	1932	—
1250	SE of tell	JJ21	Burial beside new road SE of tell	1932	—
1370	ES	U16	Floor under 1240	1932	Figs. 4, 23; pl. 21
1371	ES	U16/ U17[o]	Floor under 1204, 871, 914	1932	Pl. 21
Under 1371	ES	U17/ U16	Pit (see Ben-Tor 1978, citing pers. comm. A Eitan; see also *Chapter 4, Impression No. 3*)		
1703	ES	U16	Burial under floor 1242	1932	—
1704	ES	U16	Burial on rock under floor of 1371 (B.946)[p]	1932–1934[q]	—
1828	ES	X17	Cave, full length adult burial	1932–1934[r]	—
1884	ES	U11	*Unknown locus, not indicated in register and not within the East Slope Excavation, but definitively off the mound on its southern flank. Indication from a sherd marked as ES*	—	—
U17, south-east corner	ES	—	—	1927	—

[o] Sherd impressed with a cylinder seal (*Chapter 4, Impression No. 3*, pl. 78a) indicates a provenience in Squares U17/U16 under Locus 1371.

[p] This appears in the 1934 dated entry.

[q] Entered twice with two different dates.

[r] Entered twice with two different dates.

Table C.2. Loci in figures not noted in excavators' locus list

Locus No.	*Illustration*	*Locus No.*	*Illustration*	*Locus No.*	*Illustration*
1	Fig. 5	32	Fig. 5	74	Fig. 5
2	Fig. 5	33	Fig. 5	76	Fig. 5
3	Fig. 5	35	Fig. 5	78	Fig. 5
4	Fig. 5; pl. 15	36	Fig. 5	79	Figs. 5–6
5	Fig. 5	37	Fig. 5	80	Figs. 5–6
6	Fig. 5	38	Fig. 5	81	Figs. 5–6
7	Fig. 5	40	Fig. 5	82	Figs. 5–6
8	Fig. 5; pl. 15	41	Fig. 5	83	Figs. 5–6
9	Fig. 5	42	Fig. 5	84	Fig. 5
10	Fig. 5	49	Fig. 5	89	Fig. 5
11	Fig. 5	51	Fig. 5	113	Fig. 7
12	Fig. 5	67	Fig. 5	387	Fig. 5
13	Fig. 5	68	Fig. 5	838	Fig. 5
23	Fig. 5	70	Fig. 5	850[a]	Fig. 5
24	Fig. 5	73	Fig. 5	2158[b]	Fig. 6

[a] This may be an error because the excavators' locus list indicates it is located in Square O9, on the mound, but in this plan it is located in the south central precinct of Square T16.

[b] Apparently excavated at some very late date in the excavation, well after work on the East Slope had ceased.

INDEX OF ACQUISITION AND FIELD NUMBERS*

Acquisition/Field No.	Description	Reference
A16314	Jar	97; pl. 69c
A16730 / P4599	Bowl	Pl. 71a
A16732 / P2856	Bowl	Pl. 71b
A16741 / P3904	Platter-plate	98; fig. to pl. 70; pl. 70i
A16748 / P4664	Jar	97 (2x); pl. 67i
A16752 / P3693	Jug/juglet	97; pl. 67c
A16754 / P4850	Jar	97; pl. 68a
A16757 / P4835	Holemouth sherd	114 fig. 29u
A16762	Holemouth sherd	114 fig. 29e; pl. 82c
A16770 / P3293	Holemouth vessel	98; pl. 73b
A16781 / P2729	Ledge handle	Pl. 62l
A16785	Ledge handle	98; pl. 68d
A16790 / P4946	Ledge handle	Pl. 63a
A16791	Ledge handle	71, 169 table C.1; pl. 43a
A16794	Ledge handle	Pl. 62p
A16795 / P4910	Jar sherd	Pl. 57b
A16796	Ledge handle	Pl. 62e
A16797	Ledge handle	Pl. 62b
A16806 / P3949	Pithos fragment	99; pl. 69g
A16822	Bowl sherd	Pl. 45c
A16829 / P4541	Bowl sherd	Pls. 47c, 48g
A16844	Platter	95 table 11
A16851	Tube handle	72; pl. 43b
A16852 / P4942	Bowl	99; pl. 74d
A16858 / P4081	Gourd jar	81; pl. 55d
A16869 / P5558	Sherd	109; pl. 80b
A16870	Sherd	122 fig. 33d
A16871	Sherd	122 fig. 33g
A16872 / P5557	Sherd	106; pl. 78b
A16873 / P5560	Sherd	122 fig. 33a
A16874 / P5559	Sherd	122 fig. 33e
A16877	Sherd	120 fig. 31j
A16880 / P5347	Sherd	Pl. 50f
A16881	Sherd	Pl. 50b
A16884 / M3661	Spindle whorl or loom weight	Pl. 75b
A16885 / M3662	Loom weight	Pl. 75a
A16910 / P4670	Holemouth sherd	114 fig. 29w
A22492	Tournette	Pl. 75f
A22559 / c94	Figurine	Pl. 93
A30387 / BY 471	Jug/juglet (from Khirbet Kerak, for comparison)	97; pl. 68h
A38567	Pithos fragment	99 (2x); pl. 69f
A65900 / P4738	Bowl sherd	Pl. 52b
A65901 / P4681	Platter-plate	Pl. 70h
A65904	Platter-plate	98; pl. 70d
A65911 / P4659	Bowl	97; pl. 67g
A65912 / P3691	Bowl	97; pl. 67f
A65921 / P4700	Platter-plate	Pl. 70e
A65935 / P3964	Jug/juglet	97; pl. 68g
A65938	Holemouth vessel	Pl. 61b
A65941 / P5055	Holemouth sherd	114 fig. 29j
A65947 / P3037	Bowl sherd	Pl. 51e
A65948 / 4736	Ledge handle	Pl. 62a
A65949	Bowl rim	122 fig. 33c
A65961 / 4839	Ledge handle	Pl. 63c
A65957 / P2793	Ledge handle	Pls. 62q, 63e
A65967 / 4842	Ledge handle	114 fig. 29z; pl. 62c
A65968 / P5337	Ledge handle	Pl. 62f
A65973 / P2792	Ledge handle	Pl. 62d
A65974	Ledge handle	72 n. 48 (2x), 122 fig. 33i; pl. 44b
A65976	Ledge handle	Pl. 62o
A65981	Ledge handle	Pl. 62m
A65984 / 4884	Holemouth vessel	Pl. 61a
A65987 / P5338	Ledge handle	Pl. 63b
A65989	Bowl sherd	Pl. 51g
A65992	Bowl sherd	Pl. 51d

*For prefixes, see page 71.

Acquisition/Field No.	Description	Reference
A65995	Bowl sherd	Pl. 47d
A66017 / P4951	Bowl sherd	Pl. 51a
b? 117 / 37.859	Sickle blade	Pl. 89b
B.264 (Gezer)	Bowl	Pl. 84b
c94 *see* A22559		
d374 *see* 39.575		
d625 *see* 39.617		
I.3154	Sickle blade	Pl. 87f
I.3354a–b	Sickle blade	Pl. 87e
I.3383a–b	Sickle blade	Pl. 86d
M2520	Figurine	100; pl. 74f
M2555	Loom weight	Pl. 75c
M2558	Bowl	Pl. 75e
M2635	Loom weight	Pl. 75d
M3554 *see* 34.2458		
M3556	Sickle blade	Pl. 86g
M3661 *see* A16884		
M3362 *see* A16885		
M3693 *see* 34.2702		
M3717 / 34.2706	Bladelet core	Pl. 87d
M3832 *see* 34.2698		
M3914 *see* 34.2708		
M3938 *see* 34.2722		
M3942 *see* 34.2723		
M3945 *see* 34.2724a–b		
M4846 *see* 34.2728		
M4847 *see* 34.2729		
M4849 *see* 34.2732		
M4858 *see* 34.2740		
M4859 *see* 34.2741a–b		
M4860 *see* 34.2742a–b		
M4870 *see* 34.2693		
M4873 *see* 34.2695		
M4874 *see* 34.2696		
M5856 / 34.2737	Sickle blade	Pl. 88f
P555 *see* 34.2753		
P1263 *see* 34.2465		
P2729 *see* A16781		
P2792 *see* A65973		
P2856 *see* A16732		
P2859 *see* 34.2488		
P3037 *see* A65947		

Acquisition/Field No.	Description	Reference
P3293 *see* A16770		
P3685 *see* 34.2463/3		
P3685 *see* 34.2463/3		
P3690 *see* 34.2477		
P3691 *see* A65912		
P3693 *see* A16752		
P3770 *see* 34.2555		
P3904 *see* A16741		
P3949 *see* A16806		
P3964 *see* A65935		
P4081 *see* A16858		
P4133 *see* 34.2273		
P4171 *see* 34.2469/1		
P4259	Sherd	114 fig. 29bb
P4474	Holemouth sherd	114 fig. 29k
P4481 *see* 34.2546		
P4486 *see* 34.2419		
P4487 *see* 34.2420		
P4488	Bowl	Pl. 49
P4489	Bowl	Pl. 49
P4495 *see* 34.2305		
P4505	Holemouth sherd	114 fig. 29h
P4509	Holemouth vessel	38; pl. 73a
P4510	Holemouth sherd	114 fig. 29
P4511 *see* 34.2421		
P4512 *see* 34.2422		
P4514	Holemouth sherd	114 fig. 29b
P4515	Holemouth sherd	114 fig. 29a
P4519	Holemouth sherd	114 fig. 29n
P4521 *see* 34.2424		
P4522	Holemouth sherd	114 fig. 29o
P4523	Holemouth sherd	114 fig. 29q
P4524 *see* 34.2425		
P4525 *see* 34.2426		
P4526	Holemouth sherd	114 fig. 29l
P4527	Holemouth sherd	114 fig. 29g
P4528 *see* 34.2428		
P4529 *see* 34.2633		
P4530 *see* 34.2429		
P4531 *see* 34.2631		
P4538 *see* 34.2587		
P4541	Bowl sherd	Pl. 47b
P4541 *see* A16829		
P4547 *see* 34.2629		

Acquisition/Field No.	*Description*	*Reference*
P4631 *see* 34.2292		
P4599 *see* A16730		
P4638	Sherd	Pl. 65a
P4659 *see* A65911		
P4664 *see* A16748		
P4670 *see* A16910		
P4681 *see* A65901		
P4690 *see* 34.2648		
P4700 *see* A65921		
P4711 *see* 34.2528		
P4722 *see* 34.2510		
P4731 *see* 34.2665/2		
P4736 *see* 34.2623/1		
P4738 *see* A65900		
P4787 *see* 34.2664		
P4807 *see* 34.2512		
P4817 *see* 34.2660/2		
P4824 *see* 34.2472/1		
P4829 *see* 34.2491		
P4833 *see* 34.2623		
P4835 *see* A16757		
P4850 *see* A16754		
P4877 *see* 34.2525/2		
P4904 *see* 34.2494		
P4908 *see* 34.2652		
P4909 *see* 34.2548		
P4910 *see* A16795		
P4942 *see* A16851		
P4942 *see* A16852		
P4951 *see* A66017		
P4952 *see* 34.2618/1		
P4978 *see* 34.2483		
P5055 *see* A65941		
P5062 *see* 34.2511/7		
P5338 *see* A65987		
P5252 *see* 34.2445		
P5337 *see* A65968		
P5338 *see* A65987		
P5347 *see* A16880		
P5554 *see* 34.2754		
P5557 *see* A16872		
P5558 *see* A16869		
P5559 *see* A16874		
P5560 *see* A16873		

Acquisition/Field No.	*Description*	*Reference*
P5561	Sherd	122 fig. 33b
P5566 *see* 34.2760		
P5568	Sherd	120 fig. 31i
P5573 *see* 34.2765		
P5579 *see* 34.2762		
P5580 *see* 34.2637		
P5583 *see* 34.2668		
34.2273 / P4133	Holemouth sherd	114 fig. 29s; pl. 83a
34.2292 / P4631	Holemouth sherd	114 fig. 29t; pl. 83b
34.2305 / P4495	Holemouth sherd	114 fig. 29n; pl. 82g
34.2419 / P4486	Holemouth vessel	Pl. 61f
34.2420/ P4487	Basin	Pl. 51n
34.2421 / P4511	Holemouth sherd	114 fig. 29i; pl. 82d
34.2422 / P4512	Holemouth sherd	114 fig. 29c; pl. 82a
34.2424 / P4521	Holemouth sherd	114 fig. 29p; pl. 82f
34.2425 / P4524	Holemouth sherd	114 fig. 29m; pl. 82e
34.2426 / P4525	Holemouth sherd	114 fig. 29d; 82b
34.2428 / P4528	Handle	Pl. 54e
34.2429 / P4530	Spouted vessel	Pl. 56g
34.2432	Bowl sherd	Pl. 47a
34.2432/8	Bowl sherd	Pl. 47b
34.2439	Bowl sherd	Pls. 45a, 46j
34.2445	Ledge handle	Pl. 63d
34.2445 / P5252	Ledge handle	Pl. 62j
34.2449 + 34.2455/9	Bowl sherd	Pl. 46k
34.2453	Handle	Pl. 54n
34.2455	Bowl sherd	Pl. 46e
34.2455/12	Bowl sherd	Pl. 45g
34.2458 / M3554	Fan scraper	Pl. 92b
34.2463/1	Platter-plate	98; pl. 70j
34.2463/3 / P3685	Platter-plate	98; pl. 70b
34.2463/5	Platter-plate	98; pl. 70c
34.2465 / P1263	Bowl	Pl. 71c
34.2469/1 / P4171	Bowl sherd	Pl. 52e
34.2472/1 / P4824	Platter-plate	Pl. 70a
34.2472/2	Platter-plate	Pl. 70f
34.2477	Bowl	97; pl. 67e
34.2477 / P3690	Bowl	Pl. 67h
34.2478	Jug	96; pl. 66g

Acquisition/Field No.	Description	Reference
34.2481	Ledge handle	Pl. 68e
34.2483 / P4978	Jar	97; pl. 69e
34.2488 / P2859	Bowl	97; pl. 67d
34.2491 / P4829	Goblet	97; pl. 68c
34.2494 / P4904	Jug	97; pl. 67a
34.2495/2	Pithos	Pl. 59f
34.2496	Jug	97 (2x); pl. 68f
34.2496/2	Jar	97; pl. 69b
34.2502 /5	Spouted vessel	Pl. 56h
34.2503/1	Jug	97; pl. 69d
34.2510 / P4722	Handle	Pl. 54d
34.2511/5	Sherd	Pl. 50c
34.2511/7 / P5062	Handle	Pl. 54f
34.2512 / P4807	Jar	97; pl. 68b
34.2513/1	Jug	95 table 11
34.2516	Body sherd	95 table 11
34.2517	Jug base	95 table 11
34.2518/2	base sherd	95 table 11
34.2519/4	Jar base	95 table 11
34.2520	Small jar sherd	95 table 11
34.2521 / P4797	Sherd	95 table 11, 96 (2x); pl. 65c
34.2525/2 / P4877	Sherd	114 fig. 29x; pl. 83d
34.2528 / P4711	Holemouth sherd	114 fig. 29v; pl. 83c
34.2534	Holemouth vessel	98; pl. 72b
34.2534/1	Holemouth vessel	98; pl. 72a
34.2534/2	Holemouth vessel	98; pl. 72d
34.2536/2	Holemouth vessel	Pl. 61c
34.2543/8	Gourd jar	Pl. 55b
34.2546 / P4481	Holemouth vessel	98; pls. 41, 72e
34.2546/1	Holemouth vessel	Pl. 72c
34.2547	Holemouth vessel	Pl. 61e
34.2548 / P4909	Holemouth vessel	91, 92 tables 9–10; pl. 61g
34.2550/1	Sherd	Pl. 50h
34.2552	Jar sherd	Pl. 57d
34.2555 / P3770	Holemouth vessel	Pl. 72f
34.2559/2	Ledge handle	Pl. 62h
34.2571/3	Ledge handle	Pl. 62n
34.2574/2	Ledge handle	Pl. 62g
34.2575/2	Ledge handle	Pl. 62i
34.2576/8	Ledge handle	Pl. 62k
34.2578	Handle	Pl. 54a
34.2582/1	Jar	Pl. 60g
34.2584/1	Jar	Pl. 60j
34.2584/2	Jar	Pl. 60h
34.2586/2	Pithos	Pl. 59b
34.2587	Pithos	88 (2x), 104; pls. 58a, 76a–b, 81c
34.2587 / P4538	Pithos	Pl. 58
34.2589/2	Jar	Pl. 60a
34.2589/5	Jar	Pl. 60b
34.2591/1	Pithos sherd	77; pl. 44a
34.2591/6	Jar	Pl. 60c
34.2592/1	Jar	Pl. 60e
34.2593	Sherd	72; pl. 43c
34.2593/32	Bowl sherd	Pl. 45d
34.2594/1	Jar	Pl. 60d
34.2594/2	Pithos	Pl. 60k
34.2595	Jar	Pl. 60i
34.2596/1	Pithos	Pl. 59c
34.2596/3	Jar	Pl. 60f
34.2597/4	Pithos	Pl. 59e
34.2597/6	Pithos	Pl. 59d
34.2598	Pithos	Pl. 59a
34.2599/13	Bowl sherd	Pls. 45e, 46h
34.2599/22	Bowl sherd	Pl. 46d
34.2599/27	Bowl sherd	Pl. 46c
34.2599/31	Bowl sherd	Pl. 46i
34.2599/32	Bowl sherd	Pl. 46g
34.26[or 0]37/24	Handle	Pl. 54h
34.2600/2	Bowl sherd	Pl. 46f
34.2601	Bowl sherd	Pl. 46l
34.2601/6	Bowl sherd	Pl. 45f
34.2603	Bowl sherd	75; pls. 45b, 46b
34.2603/12	Bowl sherd	75, 77; pl. 45h
34.2603/2	Bowl sherd	Pl. 46a
34.2605	Bowl sherd	Pl. 47f
34.2605/1	Bowl sherd	Pl. 48d
34.2605/2	Bowl sherd	Pl. 48b
34.2605/4	Bowl sherd	Pl. 48e
34.2605/6	Bowl sherd	Pl. 48a
34.2605/8	Bowl sherd	Pl. 48c
34.2605/9	Bowl sherd	Pl. 48f
34.2609/1	Bowl sherd	Pl. 51f
34.2609/16	Bowl sherd	Pl. 51i
34.2609/18	Bowl sherd	Pl. 51l

Acquisition/Field No.	Description	Reference
34.2609/19	Bowl sherd	Pl. 51m
34.2609/2	Bowl sherd	Pl. 51c
34.2609/22	Bowl sherd	Pl. 51k
34.2609/23	Bowl sherd	Pl. 51j
34.2609/8	Bowl sherd	Pl. 51h
34.2614/1	Bowl sherd	Pl. 52a
34.2614/2	Sherd	Pls. 50g, 52c
34.2614/3	Platter-bowl	96; pl. 66e
34.2614/5	Platter-bowl	95 table 11; pl. 66d
34.2618/1 / P4952	Bowl sherd	Pl. 52d
34.2619/3	Bowl sherd	114 fig. 29y; pl. 84a
34.2623 / P4833	Sherd	95 table 11; pl. 65b
34.2623/1 / P4736	Sherd	95 table 11; pl. 65e
34.2624/1	Platter /shallow bowl	95 table 11, 96; pl. 66a
34.2624/2	Platter-bowl	95 table 11; pl. 66c
34.2624/3 + 34.2624/5	Platter-bowl	95 table 11 (2x); pl. 66f
34.2624/4	Platter sherd	95 table 11; pl. 66b
34.2625/2	Platter-plate	Pl. 70
34.2626/10	Spouted vessel	Pl. 56b
34.2627	Sherd	72; pl. 43d
34.2628/11	Spouted vessel	Pl. 56a
34.2628/13	Spouted vessel	Pl. 56e
34.2628/15	Spouted vessel	Pl. 56d
34.2629 / P4547	Spouted vessel	Pl. 56j
34.2631 / P4531	Spouted vessel	Pl. 56i
34.2633 / P4529	Juglet fragment	Pl. 54o
34.2636/2	Spouted vessel	Pl. 56f
34.2637 / P5580	Juglet fragment	Pl. 54p
34.2639	Handle	Pl. 54c
34.2639/26	Handle	Pl. 54i
34.2639/28	Handle	114 fig. 29aa; pls. 54b, 83e
34.2639/29	Handle	Pl. 54j
34.2639/31	Handle	Pl. 54k
34.2639/32	Handle	Pl. 54g
34.2642	Gourd jar	Pl. 55a
34.2643/9	Gourd jar	Pl. 55c
34.2645/2	Spouted basin	Pl. 53d
34.2645/3	Spouted basin	Pl. 53b

Acquisition/Field No.	Description	Reference
34.2645/5	Spouted basin	Pl. 53a
34.2646	Spouted basin	Pl. 53c
34.2648 / P4690	Jug/juglet	Pl. 67b
34.2650	Vessel sherd	95 table 11
34.2652 / P4908	Jar	92; pl. 64a
34.2653	Jar fragment	92; pl. 64b
34.2655	Stand	Pl. 57c
34.2658	Bowl sherd	Pl. 51b
34.2660/2 / P4817	Sherd	Pl. 50k
34.2660/3	Sherd	Pl. 50j
34.2664 / P4787	Jar	97; pl. 69a
34.2665/2 / P4731	Body sherd	95 table 11, 96; pl. 65d
34.2668 / P5583	Jar sherd	Pl. 57a
34.2677	Sherd	Pl. 50l
34.2681/1	Spouted vessel	Pl. 56c
34.2689/21	Handle	Pl. 54l
34.2690	Terra-cotta mold	100 (2x); pl. 74e
34.2693 / M4870	Bone tool	99; pl. 74a
34.2695 / M4873	Bone tool	99; pl. 74b
34.2696 / M4874	Bone tool	99; pl. 74c
34.2698 / M3832	Sickle blade	Pl. 88a
34.2702 /M3693	Sickle blade	Pl. 88e
34.2708 / M3914	Canaanean blade	Pl. 90a
34.27087a–b	Sickle blade	Pl. 86b
34.2722 / M3938	Fan scraper	Pl. 92a
34.2723 / M3942	Flake	Pl. 91b
34.2724a–b / M3945	Byblos point	Pl. 87a
34.2728 / M4846	Canaanean blade	Pl. 90b
34.2729 / M4847	Sickle blade	Pl. 88d
34.2732 / M4849	Sickle blade	Pl. 89a
34.2740 / M4858	Fan scraper	Pl. 91a
34.2741a–b / M4859	Sickle blade	Pl. 86e
34.2742a–b / M4860	Sickle blade	Pl. 86f
34.2752	Sherd	105; pl. 77a–b
34.2753 / P555	Jar sherd	109; pl. 80a
34.2754 / P5554	Sherd, seal impres-sion	106; pl. 78a
34.2758	Sherd	120 fig. 31h
34.2760 / P5566	Sherd	120 fig. 31c1; pl. 85a
34.2762 / P5579	Sherd	120 fig. 31
34.2765 / P5573	Sherd	122 fig. 33h
37.859 *see* b? 117		
38.982	Sherd	Pl. 79b

Acquisition/Field No.	Description	Reference
39.575 / d374	Canaanean sickle blade	Pl. 90c
39.617 / d625	Graver	Pl. 91c
39.626a–b	Byblos point	Pl. 86a
96/H/4/AR1	Sherd	107; pl. 79a
4736 *see* A65948		
4839 *see* A65961		
4842 *see* A65967		
4884 *see* A65984		

PLATES

Aerial view of the high mound of Megiddo of unknown date. This cropped view was scanned from a damaged print with a stamp of the "Photogrammetric Institute," Jerusalem, indicating it was taken from an airplane and is not one of Olaf Lind's balloon photographs taken by the expedition. The arrow indicating north is overlaid on an arrow stamped on the print from which this copy was scanned. Judging from the state of the East Slope, much of which was already covered with soil from the high mound, and in which no structures are visible, it is likely to have been taken in the late 1930s, well after the former area had been excavated. This estimate is confirmed by the size of the trees and the developed state of the dig house compound. Most of the lower mound, extending to the right of the paved road, is not visible in this photograph

View of the mound taken from the southeast, probably in winter (note the clouds) and sometime late in the excavation. Judging by the size of the spoil heaps, it was probably well after 1932, when work on the East Slope essentially ceased. Visible to the left of the massive spoil heaps are bedrock outcrops where numerous tombs on the East Slope were exposed (cf. pl. 3)

View of the spoil heaps and exposed bedrock on the East Slope in winter 2008, taken from the east. Note the trees and shrubs growing from the empty tombs, from seeds left by bird droppings

Plate 4

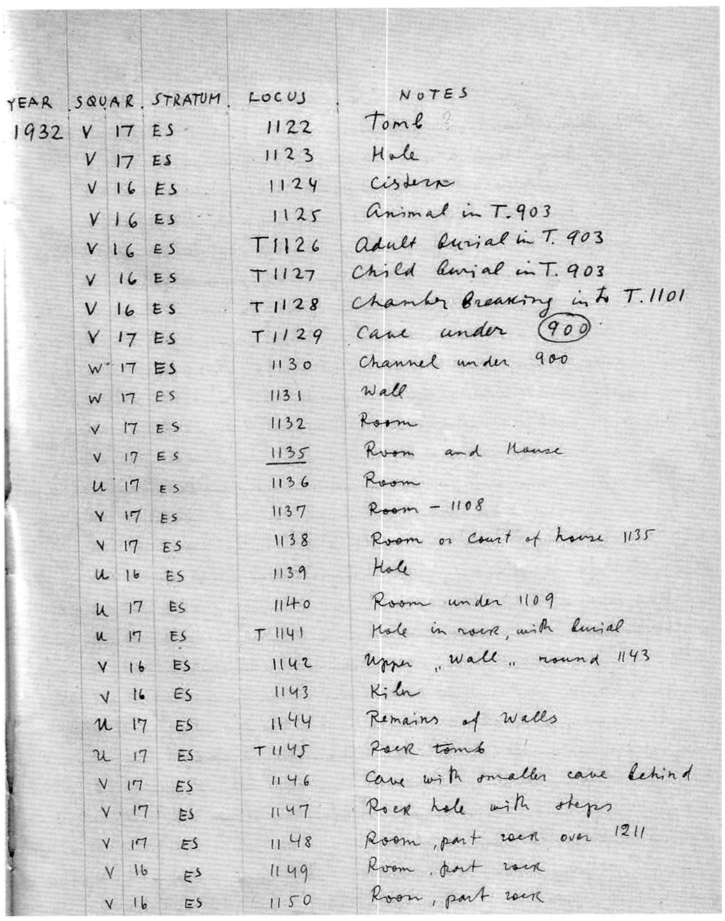

YEAR	SQUARE	STRATUM	LOCUS	NOTES
1932	V	17 ES	1122	Tomb ?
	V	17 ES	1123	Hole
	V	16 ES	1124	Cistern
	V	16 ES	1125	Animal in T. 903
	V	16 ES	T1126	Adult burial in T. 903
	V	16 ES	T1127	Child burial in T. 903
	V	16 ES	T1128	Chamber breaking in to T. 1101
	V	17 ES	T1129	Cave under 900
	W	17 ES	1130	Channel under 900
	W	17 ES	1131	Wall
	V	17 ES	1132	Room
	V	17 ES	1135	Room and House
	U	17 ES	1136	Room
	V	17 ES	1137	Room - 1108
	V	17 ES	1138	Room or Court of house 1135
	U	16 ES	1139	Hole
	U	17 ES	1140	Room under 1109
	U	17 ES	T 1141	Hole in rock, with burial
	V	16 ES	1142	Upper " wall " round 1143
	V	16 ES	1143	Kiln
	U	17 ES	1144	Remains of walls
	U	17 ES	T1145	Rock tomb
	V	17 ES	1146	Cave with smaller cave behind
	V	17 ES	1147	Rock hole with steps
	V	17 ES	1148	Room, part rock over 1211
	V	16 ES	1149	Room, part rock
	V	16 ES	1150	Room, part rock

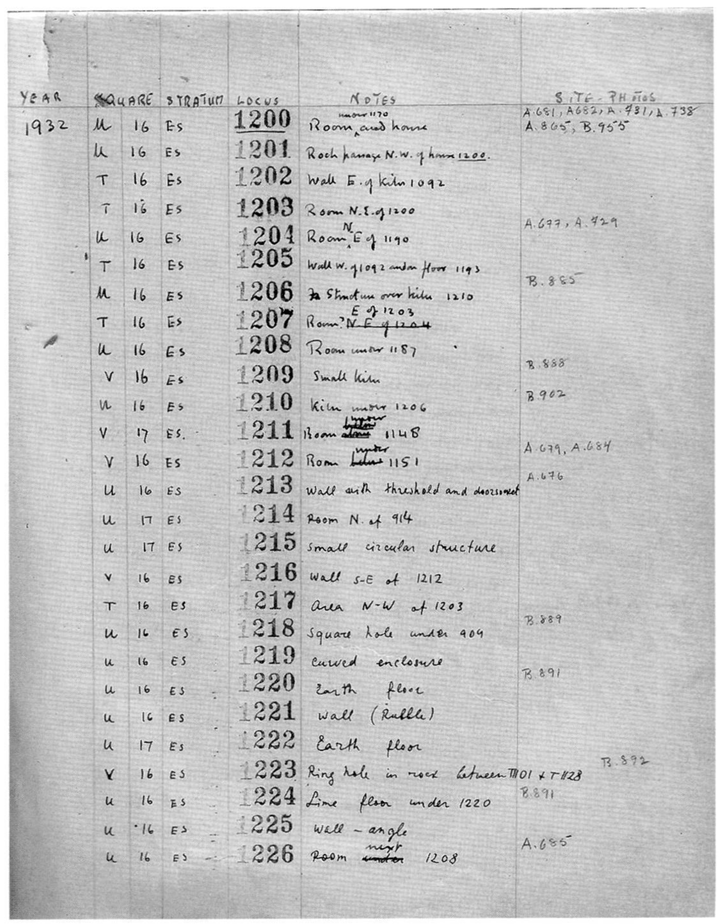

YEAR	SQUARE	STRATUM	LOCUS	NOTES	SITE PHOTOS
1932	U	16 ES	1200	Room and house (under 1170)	A.681, A.682, A.931, A.738 / A.845, B.955
	U	16 ES	1201	Rock passage N.W. of house 1200.	
	T	16 ES	1202	Wall E. of Kiln 1092	
	T	16 ES	1203	Room N.E. of 1200	
	U	16 ES	1204	Room N.E. of 1190	A.677, A.929
	T	16 ES	1205	Wall W. of 1092 under floor 1193	
	U	16 ES	1206	Structure over kiln 1210	B.865
	T	16 ES	1207	Room? E of 1203	
	U	16 ES	1208	Room under 1187	
	V	16 ES	1209	Small kiln	B.888
	U	16 ES	1210	Kiln under 1206	B.902
	V	17 ES.	1211	Room under 1148	
	V	16 ES	1212	Room under 1151	A.679, A.684
	U	16 ES	1213	Wall with threshold and doorsocket	A.676
	U	17 ES	1214	Room N. of 914	
	U	17 ES	1215	Small circular structure	
	V	16 ES	1216	Wall S-E of 1212	
	T	16 ES	1217	Area N-W of 1203	
	U	16 ES	1218	Square hole under 909	B.889
	U	16 ES	1219	Curved enclosure	
	U	16 ES	1220	Earth floor	B.891
	U	16 ES	1221	Wall (Rubble)	
	U	17 ES	1222	Earth floor	
	V	16 ES	1223	Ring hole in rock between T1101 & T828	B.892
	U	16 ES	1224	Lime floor under 1220	B.891
	U	16 ES	1225	Well - angle	
	U	16 ES	1226	Room next 1208	A.685

Two pages from the 1932 Locus Register, each with information on the East Slope denoted by the square identifications. Note the brevity of the entries and the hand-written and stamp-generated loci numbers on different pages. The latter group represents some double entries (see *Appendix C*)

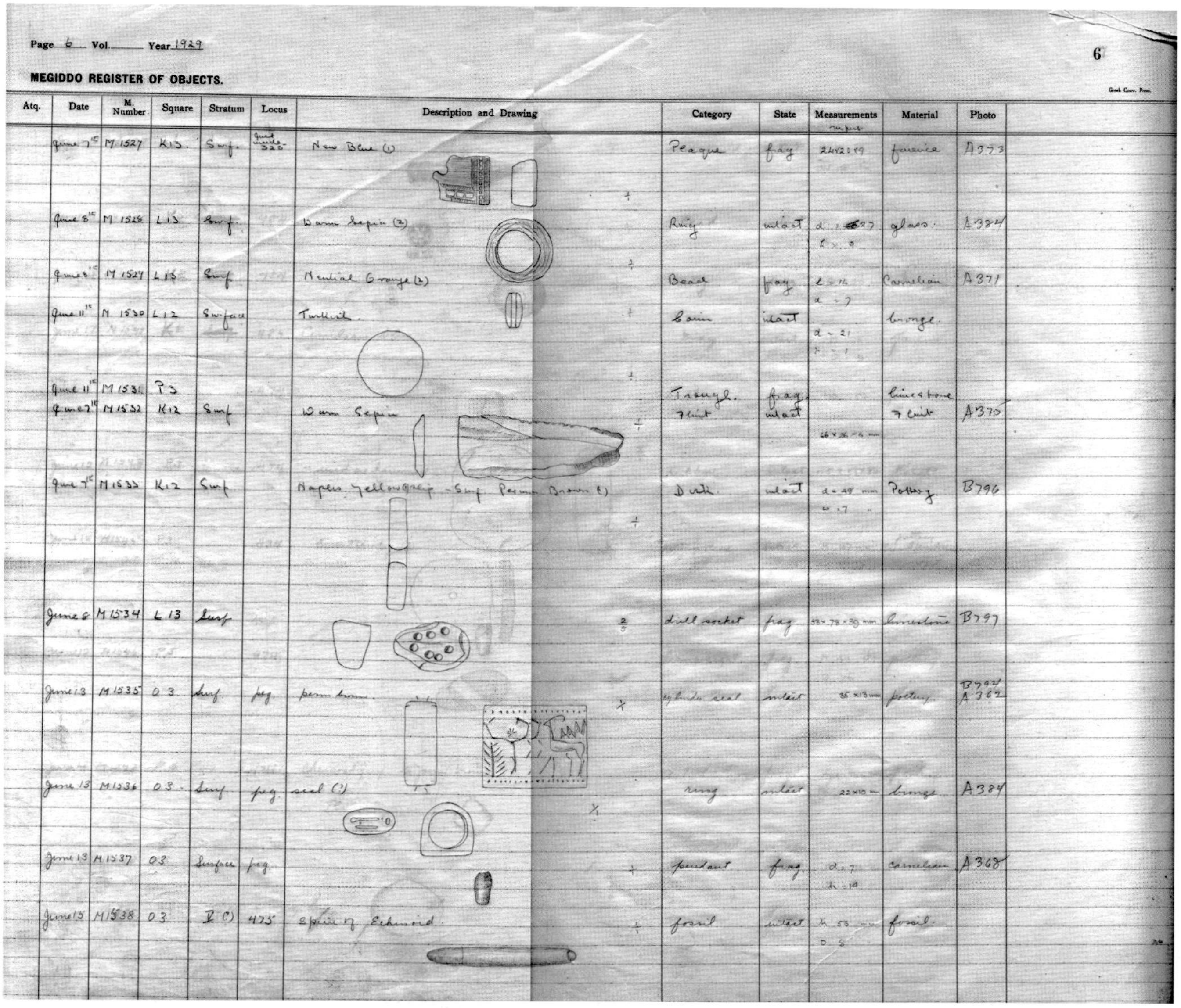

Page 6 Vol. Year 1929

6

MEGIDDO REGISTER OF OBJECTS.

Atq.	Date	M. Number	Square	Stratum	Locus	Description and Drawing	Category	State	Measurements	Material	Photo
	June 7th	M 1527	K13.	Surf.	just inside 320	New Blue (1)	Peaque	frag	24×20×9	faience	A373
	June 8th	M 1528	L13	Surf.		Warm Sepia (2)	Ring	intact	d = 27	glass.	A384
	June 8th	M 1529	L13	Surf.		Neutral Orange (2)	Bead	frag	l = 14, d = 7	Carnelian	A371
	June 11th	M 1530	L12	Surface		Turtlish.	Coin	intact	d = 21	bronze.	
	June 11th	M 1531	P3				Truogh.	frag.		limestone	
	June 7th	M 1532	K12	Surf		Warm Sepia	Flint	intact	66 × 26 × 6 mm	Flint	A375
	June 7th	M 1533	K12	Surf		Napels Yellow Grey - Surf. Permanent Brown (?)	Dish.	intact	d = 49 mm, w = 7 "	Pottery.	B796
	June 8	M 1534	L 13	Surf			drill socket	frag	53 × 78 × 30 mm	limestone	B797
	June 13	M 1535	O 3	Surf	frag	perm brown	cylinder seal	intact	35 × 13 mm	pottery.	B797, A362
	June 13	M 1536	O 3	Surf	frag	seal (?)	ring	intact	22 × 10 mm	bronze	A384
	June 13	M 1537	O 3	Surface	frag		pendant	frag.	d = 7, h = 14	carnelian	A368
	June 15	M 1538	O 3	V (?)	475	Spine of Eckinoid.	fossil	intact	h 55 mm, D 8	fossil.	

Page from the large-format Megiddo Artifact Ledgers of the Palestine Archaeological Museum

Photographer, presumably Olaf E. Lind, at work on the summit of the tell. Lind's work provides the most immediate source of information on fieldwork in the absence of any but the most brief written accounts in the locus list (*Appendix C*)

Balloon with attached camera used for taking aerial photographs of mound and East Slope. Use of this technology was the inspiration of P. L. O. Guy (1932), who went to great trouble to import all the necessary equipment. At left, unidentified, center, Robert S. Lamon, and right, William E. Staples (OIM photograph P.18637 by Olaf E. Lind, November 5, 1929)

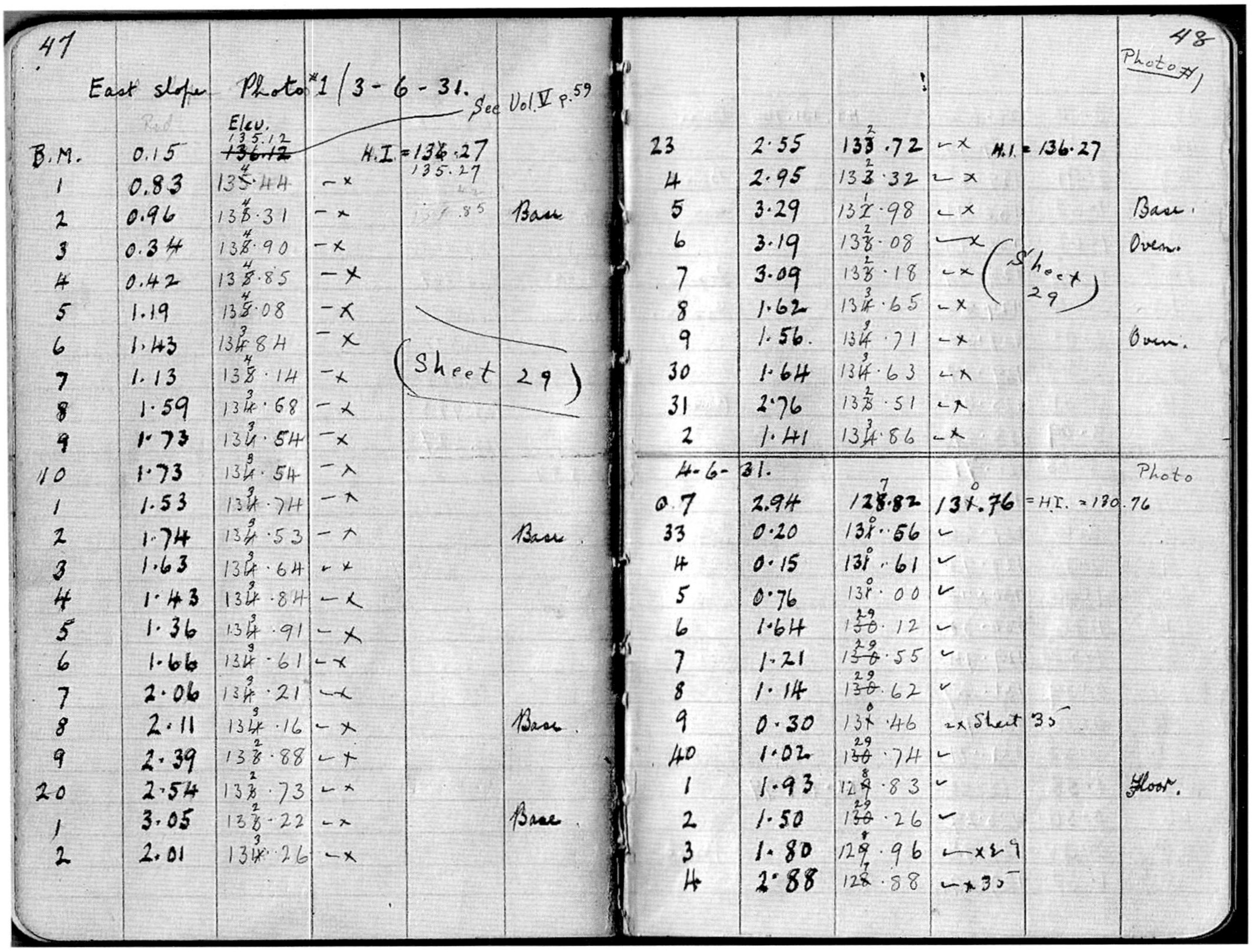

Pages 47 and 48 of the level books indicating elevations taken on the East Slope and marked on a print of one of the first series of balloon photographs taken probably in March of 1931. No corresponding annotated prints of those photographs are to be found in the extant archives of the Oriental Institute and the Israel Antiquities Authority

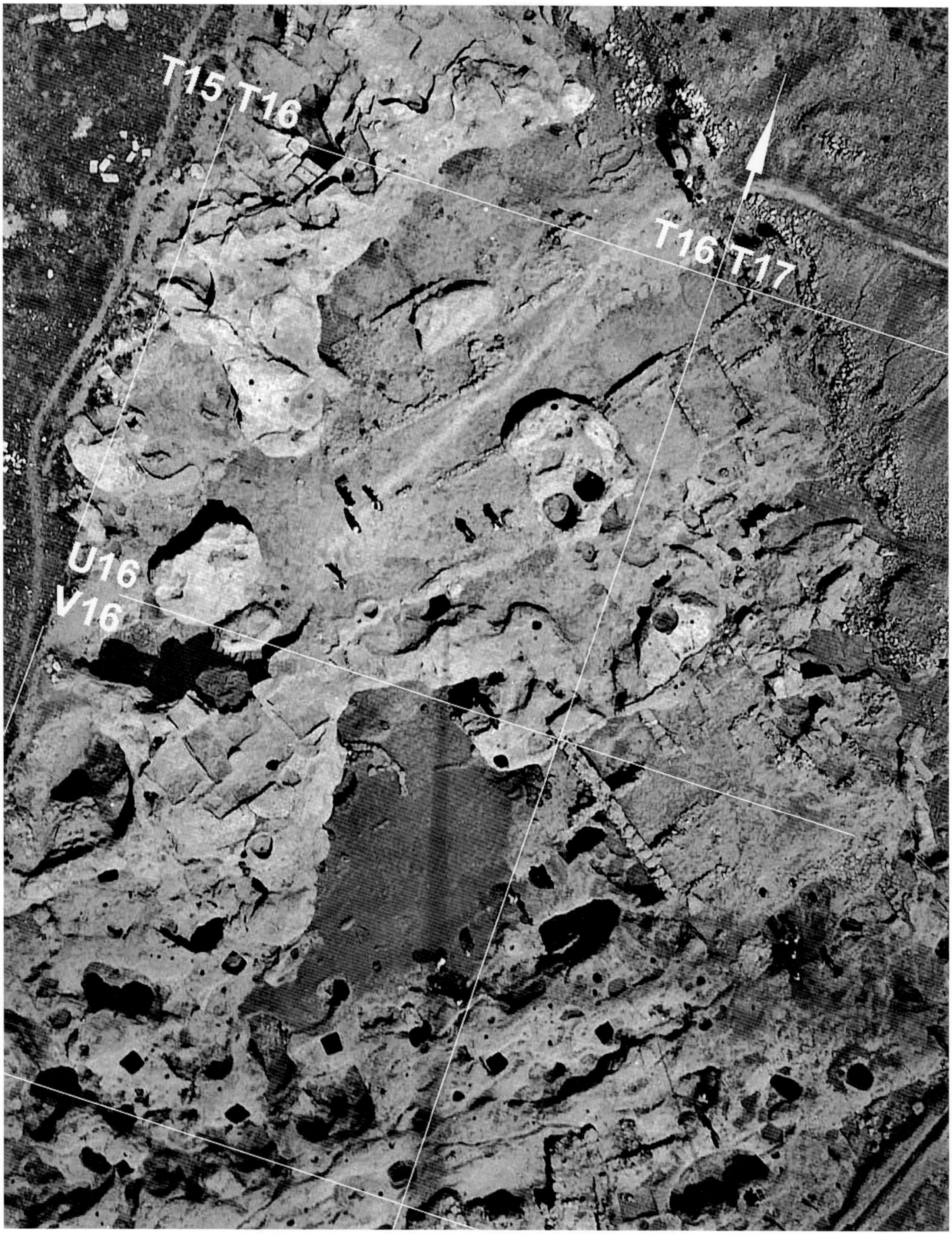

Detail from a photograph showing the squares where most of the evidence for early occupation there was found, from a photograph in the first series of balloon photographs taken of the East Slope. This photograph was taken after a general plan of the East Slope was drawn and embellished in several versions (figs. 4–7). The squares indicated correspond closely, but not precisely, with the excavators' grid, which was somewhat inaccurate due to their inability to correct for the sloping topography. This and subsequent aerial photographs were intended to obviate the need for drawn plans

Detail from a photograph showing the squares where most of the evidence for early occupation was found, from a photograph in the second series of balloon photographs taken of the East Slope. Numerous walls and constructed features visible in this photograph are otherwise undocumented. Note the extensive exposure of bedrock with cavities, many of them tombs. The squares indicated, superimposed on the original balloon photograph, correspond closely, but not precisely, with the excavators' grid

Detail from a photograph in the third series of balloon photographs taken of the East Slope showing the area where most of the earliest finds were made. Numerous buildings and structures from different periods are visible as well as bedrock outcrops with cavities. Buildings of Early Bronze Age appear prominently in the lower left-hand quadrant of the photograph in Squares T16, U16, and U17

Detail from a photograph in the fourth and final series of balloon photographs taken of the East Slope. The earliest buildings, dated to Early Bronze Age I and III, are visible in the upper right-hand quadrant. Much of the remainder of the photograph pictures extensive exposure of the bedrock with its many cavities, some of them tombs. Stone walls visible there, some of them representing free-standing structures, others encircling cavities, are undated and remain otherwise undocumented. Visible is a slight, long, narrow shadow in Square U16 made by one of the guy ropes that tethered the balloon, held by a figure below. The squares indicated correspond closely to the excavators' grid, designated by markers (rectangular blocks pierced by cylindrical holes) in the field

Excavating on the East Slope. Here a crowd of workers in the middle ground is seen laboring away with heavy tools. They are standing atop a wall of a building, while behind them other workers are tipping their spoil over a bedrock scarp. Work is apparently taking place within a large square marked by measuring poles, but no effort appears to have been made to excavate horizontally or trim the sections

Megiddo Expedition staff. (top row, from left to right) Ralph B. Barker, Charles Kent, Reis Hamid, Robert S. Lamon, Olaf E. Lind, Geoffrey M. Shipton; (bottom row, from left to right) Mrs. De Loach, Edward L. De Loach, Yemina Guy, Philip Guy, Mrs. Staples, William E. Staples. May 22, 1929

Robert M. Engberg and Egyptian boatsman on Nile River, February 1932. Photo by Leslie F. Thompson

Photograph, facing west, of remains of a kiln, Locus 1087, in Square U16, one of the latest features encountered on the East Slope. It was partially built over the northwest wall B/IV/1 and is one of a series of similar installations that intruded into the earliest deposits where structures were found on the upper terrace

Detail of a balloon photograph from the first series showing most of the excavators' Square U16 and partial Square U17. Lower case letters and numbers 23–26 indicate the superimposed 5 × 5 m grid, marked in thin black lines. Two buildings, B/+IV/1a and B/+IV/3, are clearly visible. Notable are the dimensions of the stones used in the construction of the external walls and two, superimposed stone-paved surfaces of B/+IV/1

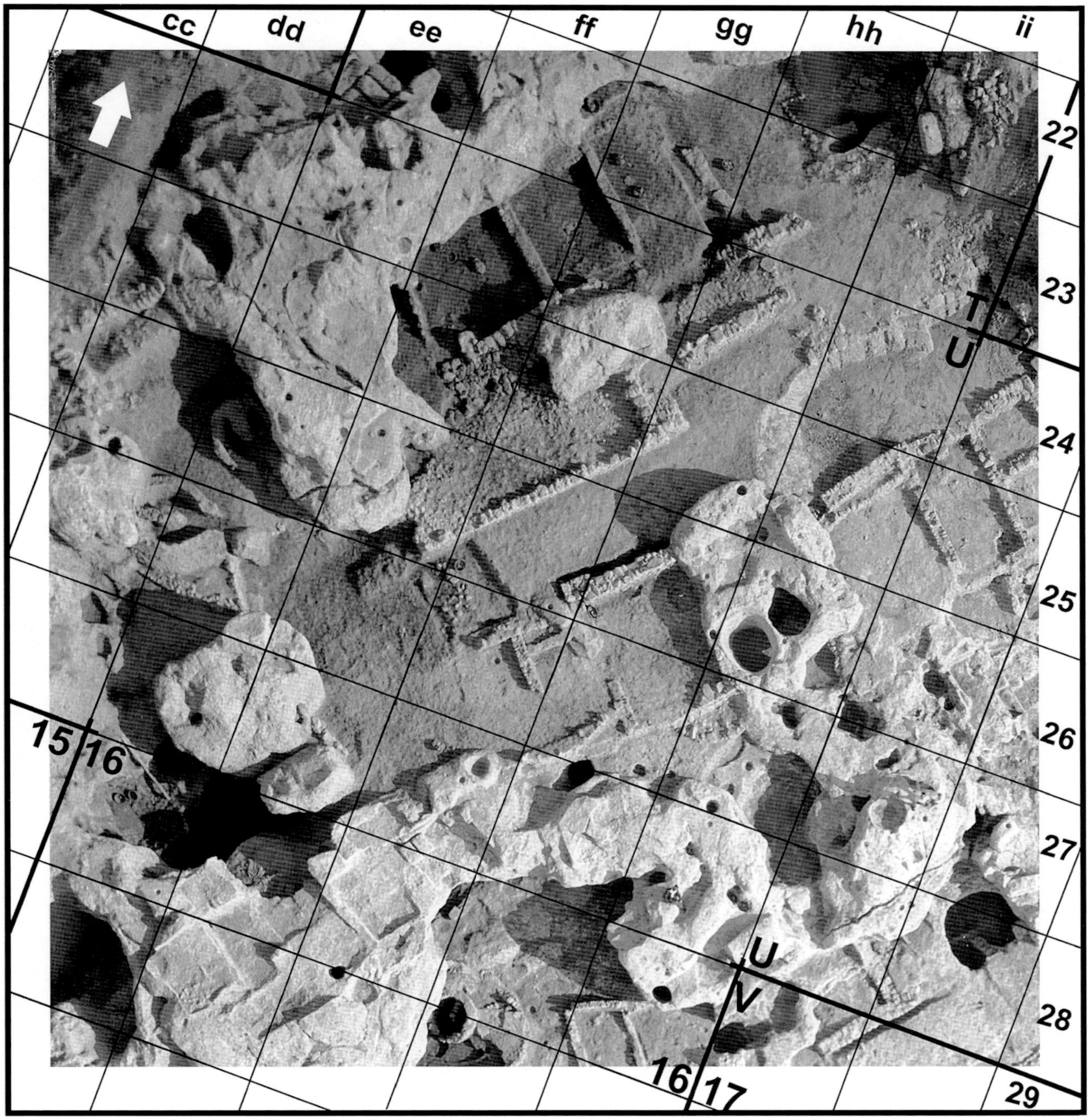

Detail of an aerial photograph from the second series of balloon photographs showing the upper terrace. Note particularly B/+IV/1 (Squares ff24, ff25, gg25, gg26) and the dimensions of the stones in its walls. Visible also are numerous additional structures and rock-cut installations and cavities. Something of the method of excavation on the East Slope can be discerned in the sloping, earthen scarp in Squares ii23, ii24, ii25

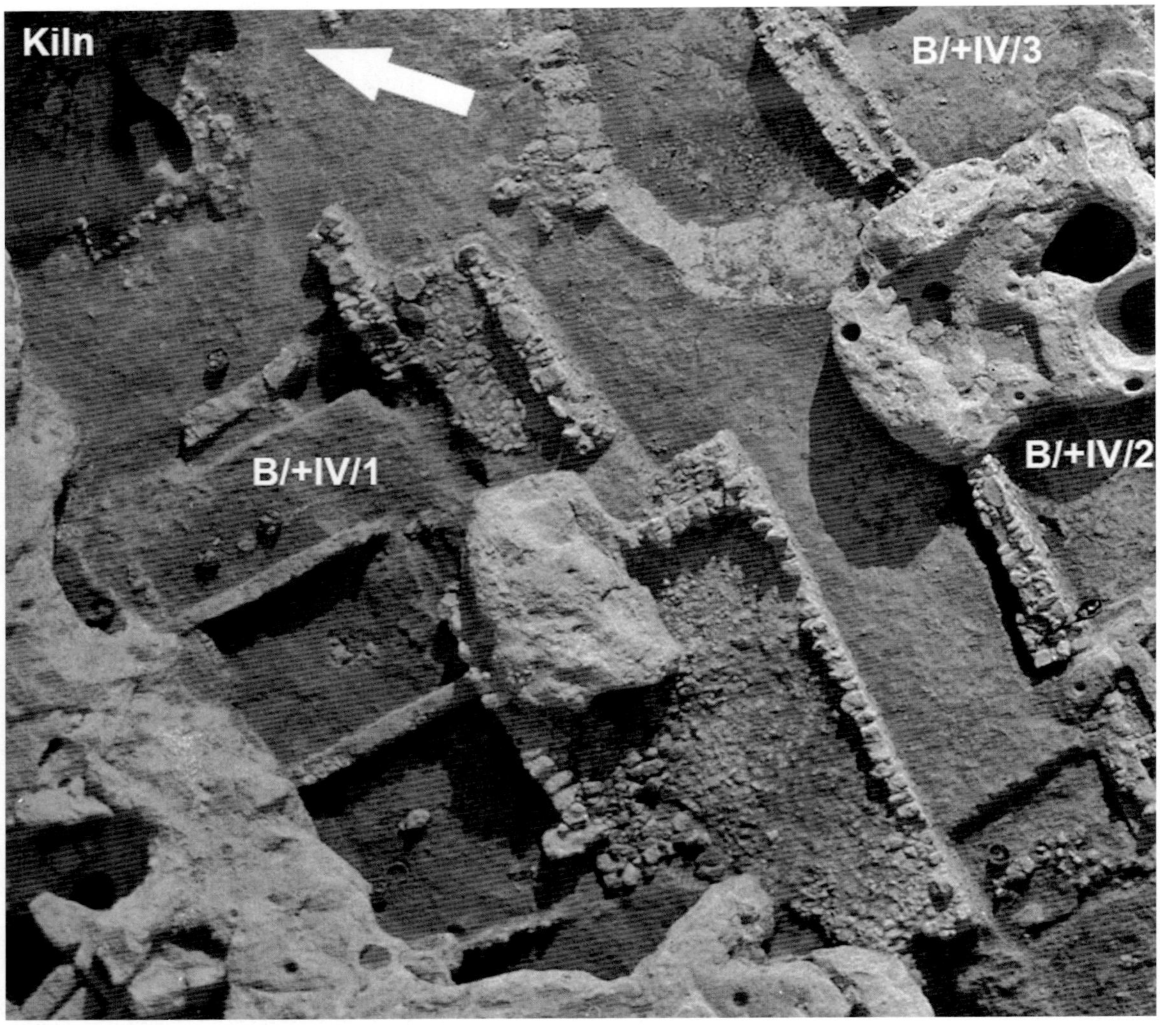

Detail of an aerial photograph of B/+IV/1/c–d (pl. 17) with boulders used in the construction of the outer walls. Note the excavation scarp created by soil removal to the left of B/+IV/3

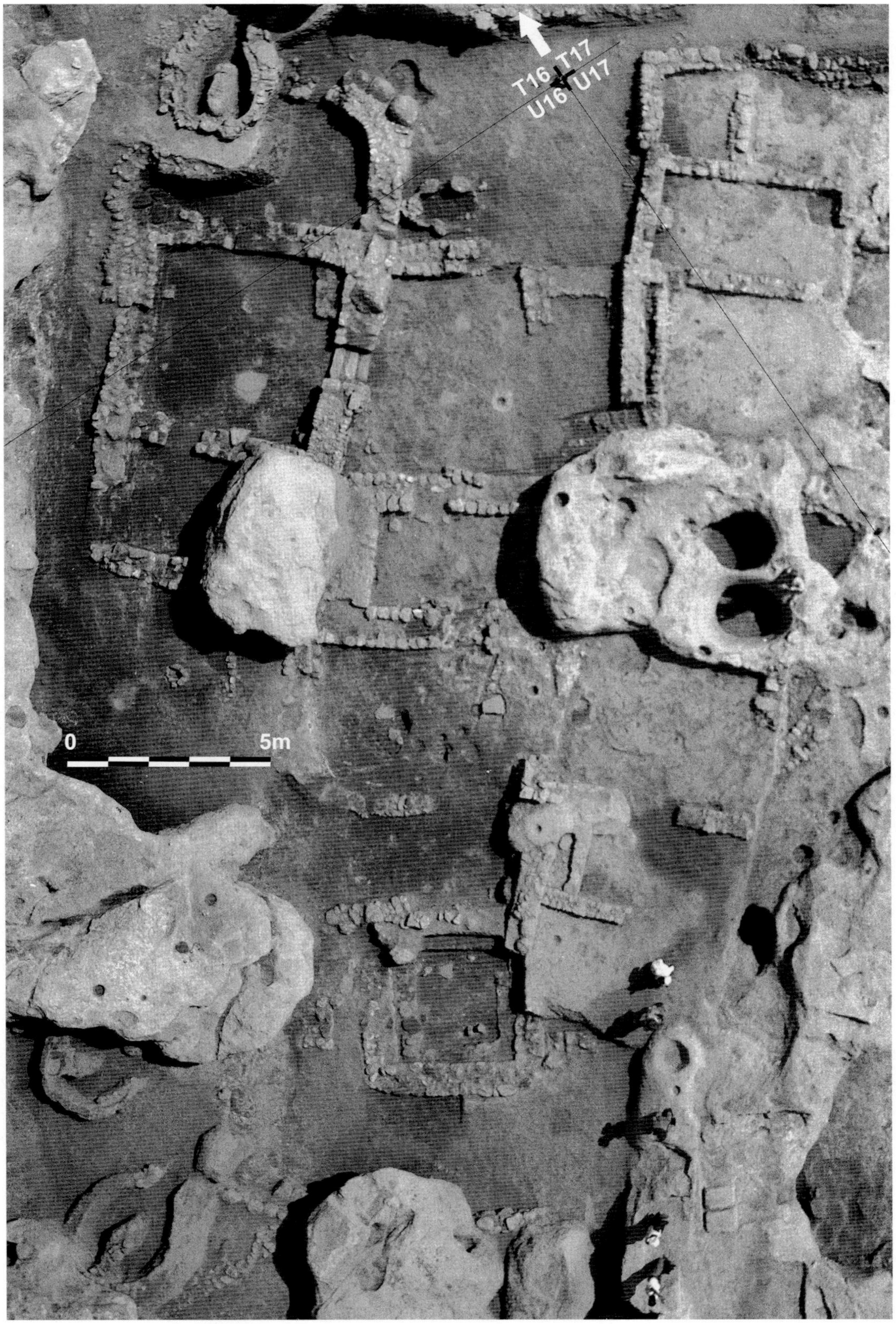

Detail of a photograph from the third balloon series showing all the upper terrace with B/IV/1 and B/IV/2 and part of the lower terrace with the southern half of B/V/1. Note the kiln built over the northwestern wall of B/IV/1 in the upper left background and two kilns in the lower left hand corner, below the large bedrock outcrop. Visible in this photograph are a number of walls that appear to be earlier than B/IV/1, but which are no longer extant in later balloon photography. Note also the lighter shaded area in the square room at the east (center left), which may be evidence of the trough-like feature marked on the building's plan

Newly annotated copy of a detail of an aerial photograph from the final balloon series, as published by Engberg and Shipton (1934a, fig. 2)

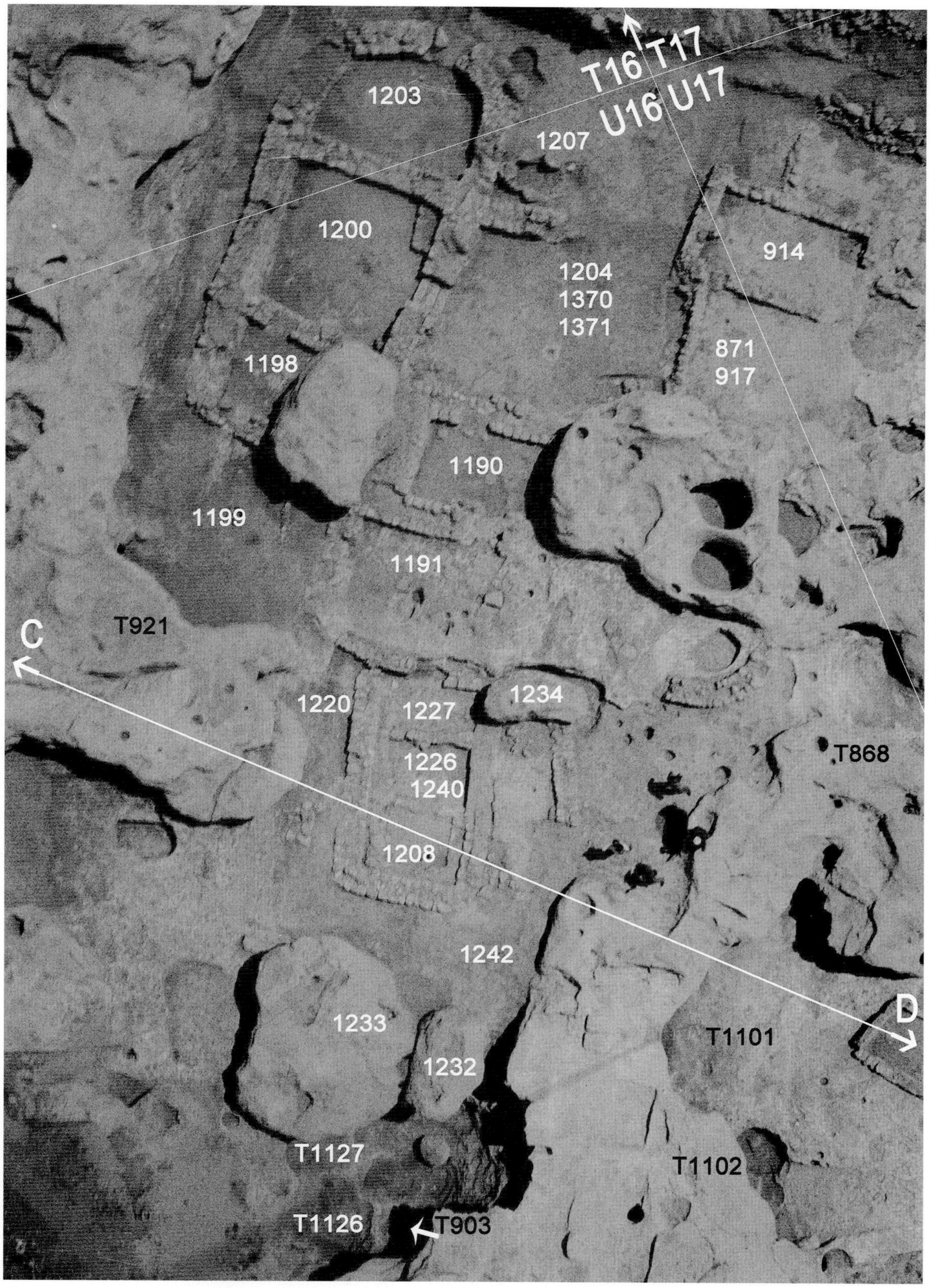

Detail of aerial photograph from the final balloon series, annotated with locus numbers. A white line marks the approximate location of a segment of Section C–D (fig. 23). Note that the area to the left of the labels of Loci 1204, 1370, and 1371 is devoid of structures. There is no trace of Walls 31 and 32 (figs. 12, 17; pl. 17)

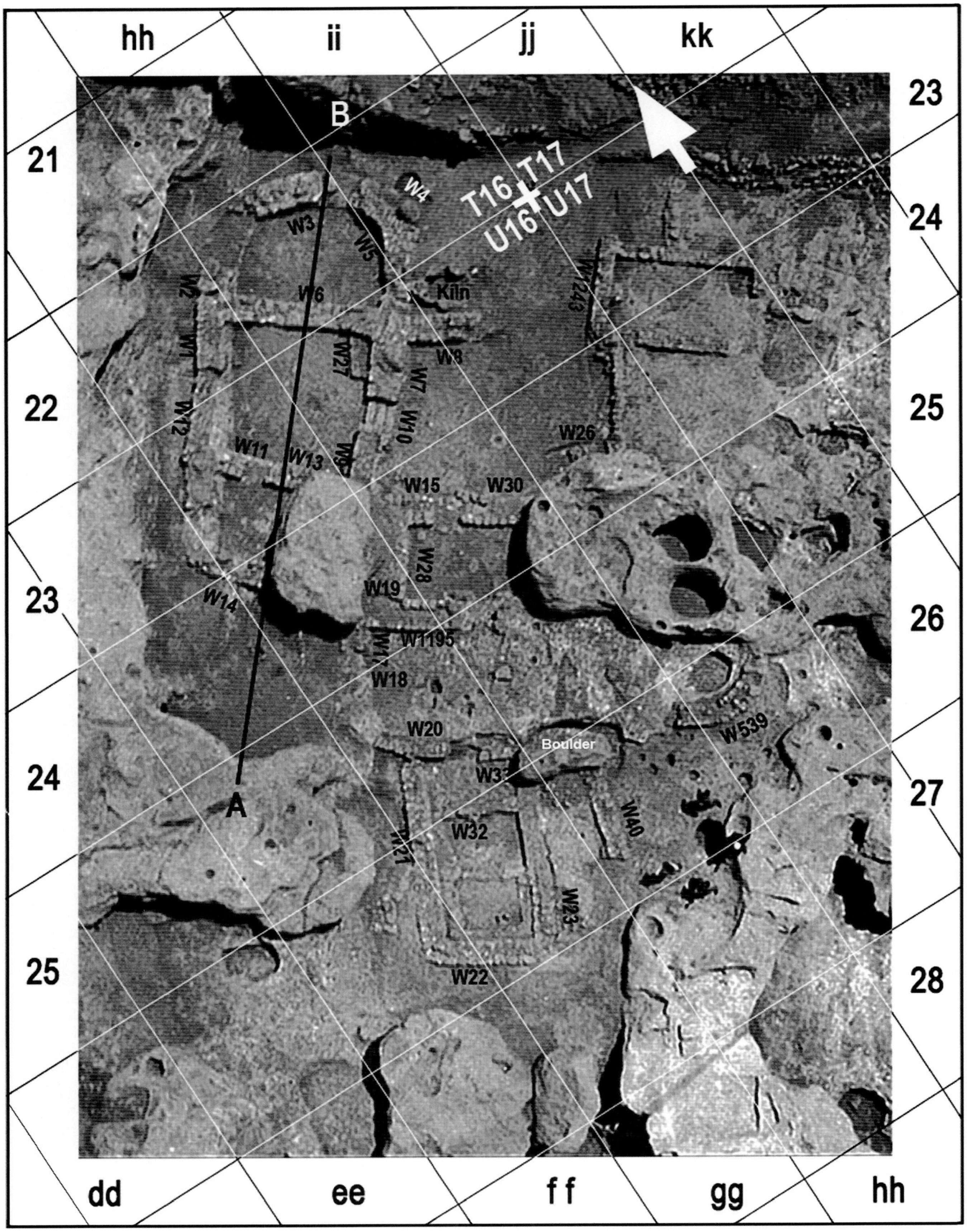

Detail of aerial photograph (see pl. 21) from the final balloon series annotated with wall numbers and overlaid with a grid

Annotated photograph of B/IV/1 from south with wall and locus numbers. Note what may be a doorsill or blocked entranceway in W6

Annotated photograph of B/IV/1 from west. Note the holemouth vessel standing in situ at the juncture of Walls 13 and 1196. The figure in pith helmet is pointing to a flat stone cap, apparently covering up a depression in the bedrock surface. Walls 31 and 32, which form a corner, are in clear evidence below the excavated surface of Locus 1204. An entranceway may be visible in W6

Annotated photograph of B/IV/1 from north. Note the massive stones beneath smaller rebuilds in W3, W4, and W1196, which belong to an earlier, perhaps even pre-B/IV/1 phase (fig. 11), possibly associated with a cave that once existed there

Detail of plate 25 showing a complete holemouth vessel in situ on a patch of the latest earthen floor (mostly removed) of B/IV/1

Photograph of the northwestern quadrant of the upper terrace taken from the southeast. Note steps at entrance to B/IV/1, intrusive kilns still in situ, and massive boulders built into Walls 5 and 7. It is hypothesized that these are remains of what was a curtain wall sealing off a cave that once existed there, prior to an earthquake, which may have caused its collapse. Still visible in this photograph is the kiln built atop the curvilinear wall of B/IV/1

Photograph of southwestern quadrant of the upper terrace taken from northeast. Notably, Walls 31 and 32 are no longer visible in this photograph. The possible robber trench of W32, marked on the plan, seems to coincide with a discoloration of the soil, as if it were back-filled. What appears as a small buttress to the left of W1243, elsewhere undocumented, may be a continuation of W32

Photograph of southwestern quadrant of upper terrace taken from south. Note the wide walls of B/IV/2 (Walls 15, 30, and 1195), which suggest they demarcated the exterior of this structure. Walls 31 and 32 are clearly visible in this photograph, taken sometime prior to the third aerial photograph (cf. pl. 30). Blowups of this photograph indicate that W1195 is at least partially resting on a thin layer of soil above bedrock

Detail of a photograph of B/V/1 greatly enlarged to show walls not drawn on Lamon's plans, which indicate several phases of building. Note the partially hidden door socket in W1213, probably denoting two phases of utilization, and its elevations relative to W546

Photograph of the southern end of B/V/1, overlain with later deposits. Visible are two large grinding stones standing upright in its lower right-hand corner and a small, loaf-shaped grinding stone lying on what appears to be a bench adjacent to the label for Locus 1208. Note also the plaster surface above B/V/1 in the section, which may have been contemporary with one or both phases of W1213

Photograph of the southern half of B/V/1 taken from the southwest. Note the two flattened surfaces in Locus 1208. They could represent late phases of occupation associated with B/V/2 or, alternately, be merely artifacts of excavation. One major dump from the high mound is visible in the left background; to the right are visible an expanse of the Plain of Jezreel and beyond a portion of the Nazareth Ridge. Flooding on plain, indicated by reflections from water, as well as definitions of clouds suggest the photograph was taken in winter. Coarse tool marks in the cut sections indicate no effort was made to smooth them for determining details of soil deposits

Photograph showing details of B/V/1 during excavation. Visible in the fill of Locus 1226 is a stone ring, probably a loom weight, a small juglet, and a pithos collapsed on its earthen floor. In the right foreground is a small patch of the plaster surface of B/V/2

Annotated photograph showing virtually all of B/V/1 and associated floor of B/V/2 to its right, during excavation. Note the floor or surface to the left of this building, associated with W1221. Wall 27 seems to abut, but not be joined to this building. One or another or perhaps both of the flattened surfaces in Locus 1208 (see also pl. 32) may be late phases of this building associated with B/V/2

Annotated photograph showing B/V/2, not drawn on Lamon's plan of Stage V. This photograph was taken prior to plate 33, which may explain why the excavators did not associate it with any phase of B/V/1.
Possibly B/V/2, with its apparently plastered surface, was coeval with one or two, that seem to be visible in Locus 1208 in plates 32 and 34

Photograph showing B/IV/1 from north. Note holemouth vessel in situ, on remains of earthen floor of latest phase of building, and bedrock features, which originated in earlier phase. Clearly this building was associated with a cave, possibly natural, that partially collapsed, leaving two chambers of unequal size in Locus 1199 in the background

Photograph of bedrock surface of Locus 1199 with quarried features, so-called "cupmarks" and "potholes." A nearly complete, Egyptian-style "granary jar" was found in this locus. The bedrock surface extends into the covered portions of the cave and beyond, to the east, where it was utilized in one or more phases of B/IV/1

Plate 38

Photograph of bedrock below B/IV/2 at the southwestern end of the upper terrace. Loci 1240 and 1241 are on lower terrace after removal of the remains of B/V/1 and B/V/2. Note walls in depression in the bedrock on lower terrace in right mid-ground. They lay below a massive boulder, Locus 1234, and were only revealed after its removal. Two walls, W41 and W42, apparently form a corner of a structure, which is clearly dated early, prior to the arrival of the boulder to that spot. Their dates remain obscure

Photograph of Tomb 903 Lower, occupation phase dated prior to the cave's use as tomb

Exact copy of the excavators' annotated photograph of Locus 1101, showing its earliest utilization; identified as dwelling by the excavators. No human remains were found in the lowest deposits

Photograph of Locus 1142, indicated by the excavators to have been a kiln. The intact pot in the left background, in Locus 1152, is a holemouth typical of the Early Bronze Age III. Its association with the kiln is uncertain

a

b

Two details of aerial photos, especially of Square V17, showing buildings that may be associated with Locus 1171: (*a*) from the second series of aerial photographs and (*b*) from the third series. A complete Early Bronze Age II–III holemouth vessel was found in Square U17 under a floor

Plate 43. Pre-Early Bronze Age I pottery

	Reg. No.	*Description*	*Provenience*	*Parallels*
a	A16791	Large ledge handle. Buff-brown, coarse, friable fabric, crudely fashioned	East Slope, V16, under floor of Locus 1212	Garfinkel 1999, figs. 50:1, 3–5, 53:2; Hanbury-Tenison 1986, fig. 28:6; Prag 2000, fig. 5:10
b	A16851	Tube handle. Buff, coarse, friable fabric	V16, Tomb 1212	Garfinkel 1999, fig. 62:3
c	34.2593	Stovepipe neck with tapered rim. Coil visible on interior at juncture of neck and rim. Buff, coarse ware, uneven surface	East Slope	—
d	34.2627	Fragment of thick-walled, shallow basin. Flat, slightly splayed rim; thick, rounded ledge handle. Buff to pink coarse fabric with vegetal temper and large grits	East Slope	—

a

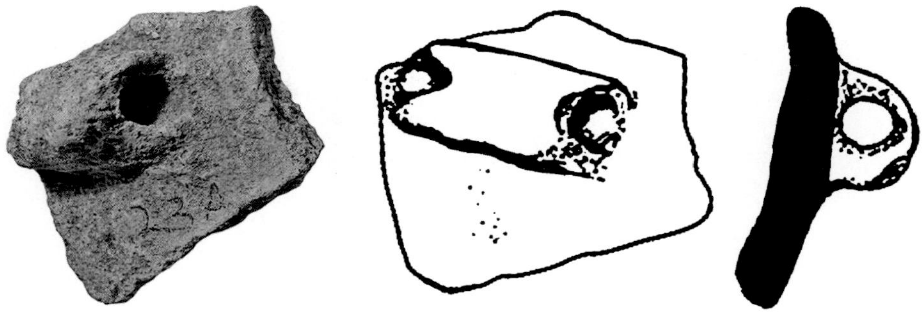

b

c

d

Pre-Early Bronze Age I pottery

Plate 44. Pottery of a very early (Yiftah'el II) phase of the Early Bronze Age I

	Reg. No.	*Description*	*Provenience*
a	34.2591/1	Pithos rim fragment. Buff, friable ware, thin light brown slip	East Slope
b	A65974	Ledge handle of large vessel. Buff, friable ware, thin red-brown-gray slip. NB: This mark is scratched on and is not a "potter's mark," i.e., not necessarily made by potter; rather it is a pot mark	East Slope

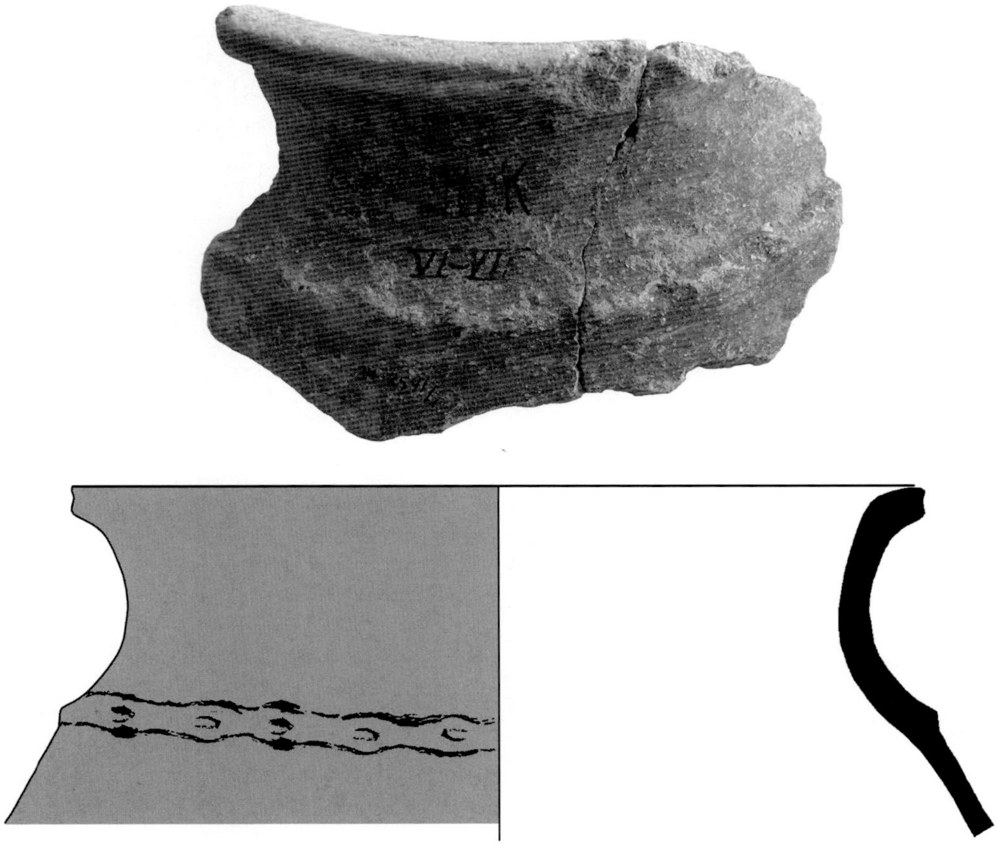

a

b

Pottery of a very early (Yiftahʾel II) phase of the Early Bronze Age I

Plate 45. Early Bronze Age I examples of Gray Burnished Ware bowls

	Reg. No.	*Type*	*Remarks*	*Provenience*	*Parallels*
a	34.2439	3	Carinated. See also plate 46j	Tomb 903 Lower	—
b	34.2603	3	Rare, rounded (non-carinated) morphology. Gray, burnished. See also plate 46b	East Slope	None known
c	A16822	3	Gray, traces of burnishing	Tomb 914	—
d	34.2593/32	3	Highly burnished	East Slope	—
e	34.2599/13	3	Gray, traces of burnishing	East Slope	—
f	34.2601/6	3	Accentuated carination	East Slope	—
g	34.2455/12	3	Gray, traces of burnishing	Tomb 903 Lower	—
h	34.2603/12	3	Double line of rope-like decoration, rare example	East Slope	Gal and Covello-Paran 1996, fig. 4:9

a

b

c

d

e

f

g

h

Early Bronze Age I examples of Gray Burnished Ware

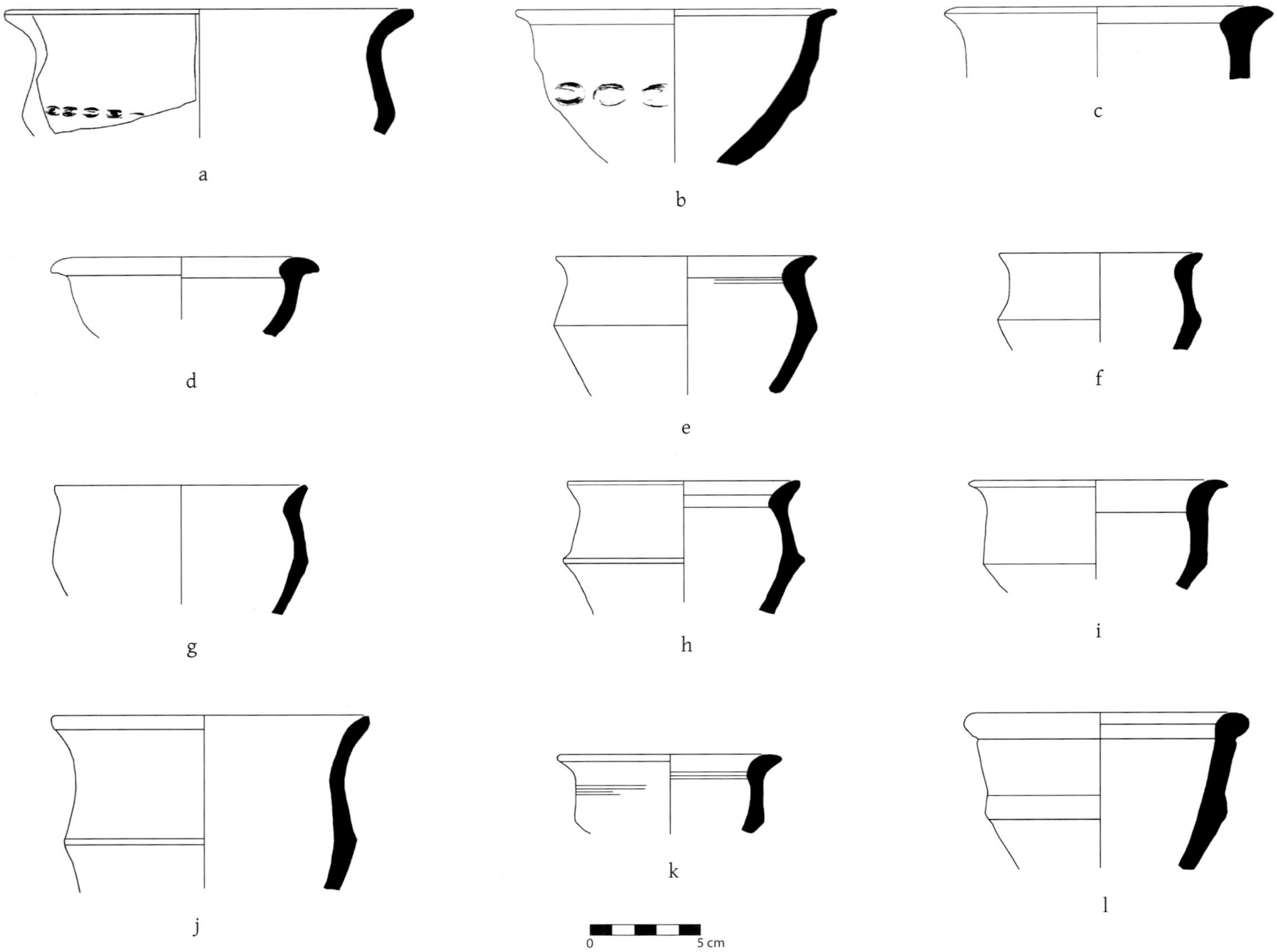

Early Bronze Age I Gray Burnished Ware bowls Types 1c and 3

	Reg. No.	*Type*	*Description*	*Provenience*	*Published*
a	34.2603/2	1c	Mottled medium gray to buff, traces of external burnishing	East Slope	–
b	34.2603	1c	Rare, rounded (non-carinated) morphology. Gray, burnished. See also plate 45b	East Slope	–
c	34.2599/27	3	Light and dark gray, burnished	East Slope	–
d	34.2599/22	3	Light and dark gray traces of burnishing internally	East Slope	–
e	34.2455	3	Gray, very coarse interior wall	East Slope	–
f	34.2600/2	3	Pale gray, pale orange to pale gray core, traces of self slip and burnishing	East Slope	–
g	34.2599/32	3	Gray to brown externally, brown internally, traces of burnishing	East Slope	–
h	34.2599/13	3	Gray, traces of burnishing	East Slope	–
i	34.2599/31	3	Pale gray, dark gray core, mottled brown to orange buff slip and burnished	East Slope	–
j	34.2439	3	Light and dark gray, burnished externally and internally. See also plate 45a	Tomb 903 Lower	–
k	34.2449 + 34.2455/9	3	Gray burnished	Tomb 903 Lower	–
l	34.2601	3	Light gray, burnished	East Slope	–

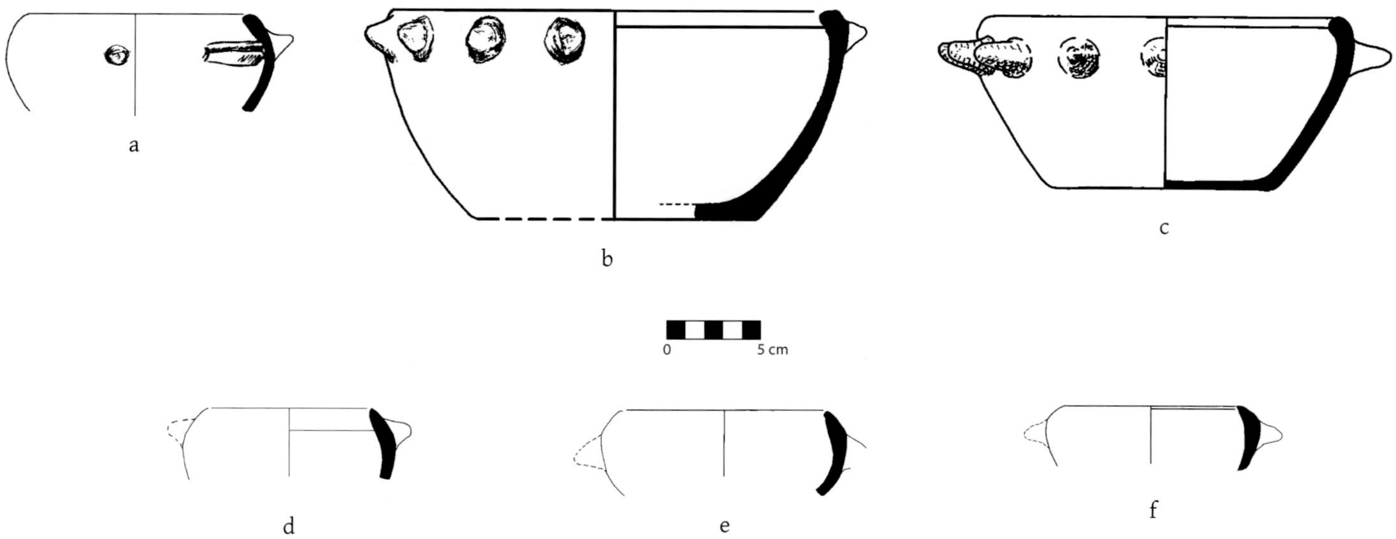

Early Bronze Age I Gray Burnished Ware Type 4 and non-Gray Burnished Ware parallels

	Reg. No.	*Type*	*Description/Comments*	*Provenience*	*Publication*
a	34.2432	4	Gray, gray slip, traces of burnishing; rare variant with bar-like and conical protuberances	East Slope	Engberg and Shipton 1934a, fig. 6:18b
b	34.2432/8	4	Light gray, burnished	Tomb 903 Lower	*Megiddo Tombs*, pl. 3:31
c	A16829 / P4541	4	Dark gray, burnished. See plate 48g	V16, Tomb 903 Lower	*Megiddo Tombs*, pl. 3:32
d	A65995	—	Imitation. Light gray, orange slip, no traces of burnishing	East Slope	—
e	—	—	Buff-brown, no traces of slip or burnishing	East Slope	—
f	34.2605	—	Imitation. Light gray, dark gray and brown slip, polished	East Slope	—

Plate 48. Early Bronze Age I Gray Burnished Ware Type 4 bowl and morphological parallels in non-Gray Burnished Ware fabrics

	Reg. No.	*Type*	*Description/Comments*	*Provenience*	*Publication*
a	34.2605/6	4	Dark gray, traces of burnishing	East Slope	—
b	34.2605/2	—	Imitation. Light gray, brown slip	Tomb 903 Lower	—
c	34.2605/8	—	Imitation. Light gray-buff, brown, black, gray mottled slip	Tomb 903 Lower	—
d	34.2605/1	—	Imitation. Gray, red-brown slip	Tomb 903 Lower	—
e	34.2605/4	—	Light gray, dark gray and dark brown slip	East Slope	—
f	34.2605/9	—	Light gray, brown gray mottled slip	East Slope	—
g	A16829 / P4541	4	Gray Burnished Ware. Light gray, burnished. See plate 47c	Tomb 903 Lower	*Megiddo Tombs*, pls. 3:32, 76:11

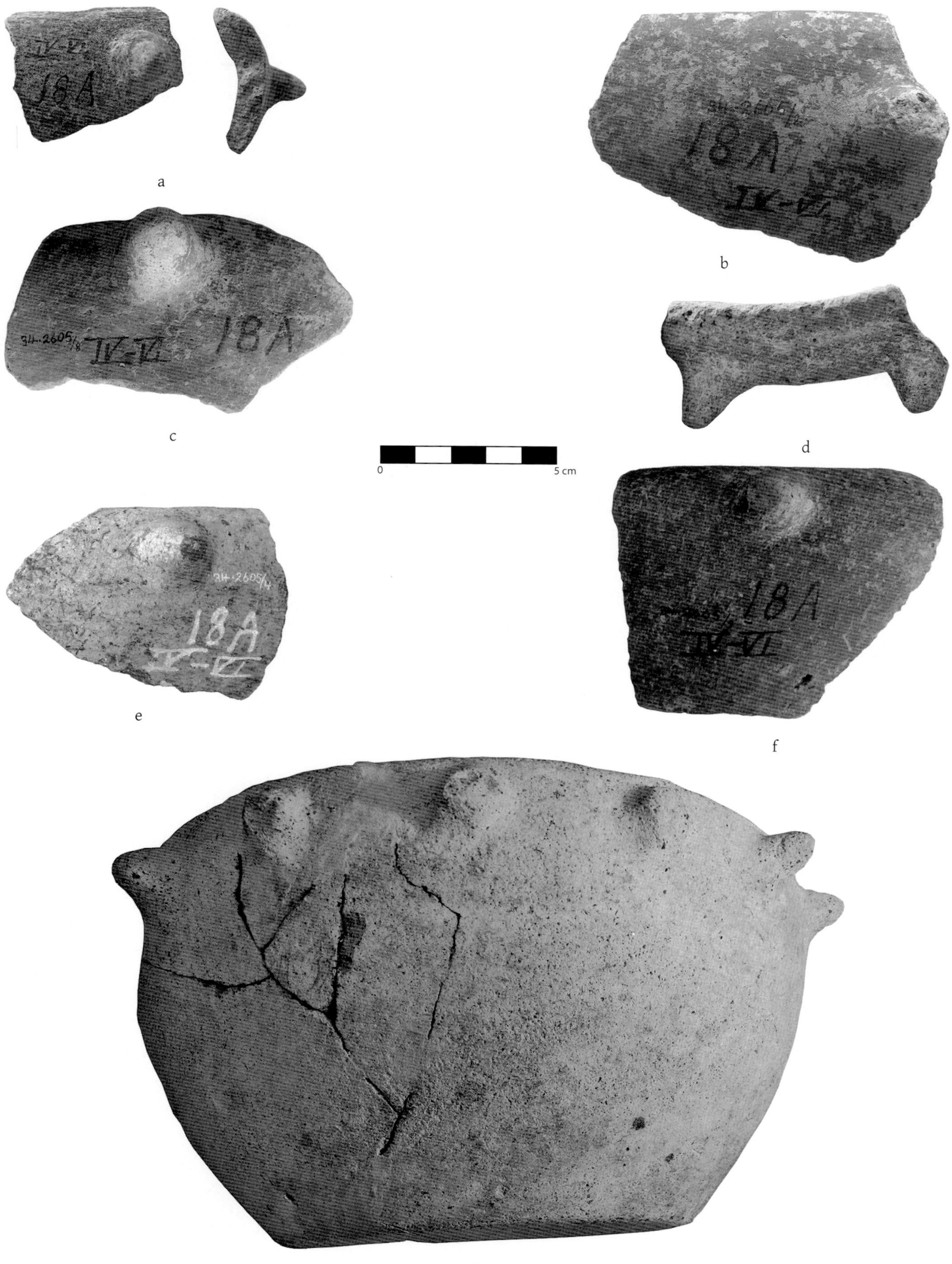

Early Bronze Age I Gray Burnished Ware Type 4 bowl and morphological parallels in non-Gray Burnished Ware fabrics

Two Type 3 carinated bowls found in Tomb 1106. Their colors range from gray-buff to light gray and their surfaces are rather coarse. P4488 above P4489. Published *Megiddo Tombs*, fig. 20

Plate 50. Examples of Early Bronze Age ceramic painted styles from the East Slope

	Reg. No.	*Provenience*	*Published*
GRAIN WASH/BAND SLIP, VERTICAL BANDS			
a	—	East Slope	Engberg and Shipton 1934a, fig. 8:J
b	A16881	East Slope	—
c	34.2511/5	East Slope	—
d	—	East Slope	Engberg and Shipton 1934a, fig. 8:G
e	—	East Slope	Engberg and Shipton 1934a, fig. 8:F
GRAIN WASH/BAND SLIP, LATTICE PATTERN			
f	A16880 / P5347	V17, Tomb 910G fill	—
GRAIN WASH/BAND SLIP			
g	34.2614/2	East Slope	—
h	34.2550/1	East Slope	—
LIGHT STRIPES LEFT TO DRIP ON DARK-COLORED WARES			
i	—	East Slope	Engberg and Shipton 1934a, fig. 8:L
j	34.2660/3	East Slope	—
k	34.2660/2 / P4817	U16, Locus 1168	—
RED PAINTED STRIPES ON LIGHT COLORED FABRIC			
l	34.2677	East Slope	—

Examples of Early Bronze Age ceramic painted styles from the East Slope

Plate 51. Early Bronze Age I open vessels from the East Slope

	Reg. No.	*Description*	*Provenience*	*Published*
a	A66017/ P4951	Small, rounded bowl. Buff-brown, thin red-brown slip	U16, Locus 1220	—
b	34.2658	Small, rounded bowl. Buff-brown, red slip	East Slope	—
c	34.2609/2	Guttered- and everted-rim vessel. Buff brown, red slipped externally	East Slope	—
d	A65992	Guttered- and everted-rim vessel with ledge handles. Buff gray, brown core, red slip, polished. Band of red on interior, just below rim	East Slope	—
e	A65947 / P3037	Guttered- and everted-rim vessel with ledge handles. Buff gray, red slip	V17, Tomb 910	—
f	34.2609/1	Guttered- and everted-rim vessel. Brown, red slip. Band of red on interior, just below rim	East Slope	—
g	A65989	Guttered- and everted-rim vessel. Buff-gray, red slip	East Slope	—
h	34.2609/8	Guttered- and everted-rim vessel. Gray to brown, gray slipped externally, red slipped internally on rim	East Slope	—
i	34.2609/16	Guttered- and everted-rim vessel. Gray to brown, gray slipped externally, red slipped internally on rim	East Slope	—
j	34.2609/23	Guttered- and everted-rim vessel. Orange, red slip	East Slope	—
k	34.2609/22	Guttered- and everted-rim vessel. Buff, red slip. Wavy line incised on exterior	East Slope	—
l	34.2609/18	Guttered- and everted-rim vessel. Brown buff, red slip. Wavy line incised on exterior. Band of red on interior, just below rim	East Slope	—
m	34.2609/19	Guttered- and everted-rim vessel. Brown, red slip. Wavy line incised on exterior. Band of red on interior, just below rim	East Slope	—
n	34.2420 / P4487	Large basin. Buff-orange, red grain wash	Tomb 903 Lower	*Megiddo Tombs*, pls. 3:33, 76:12

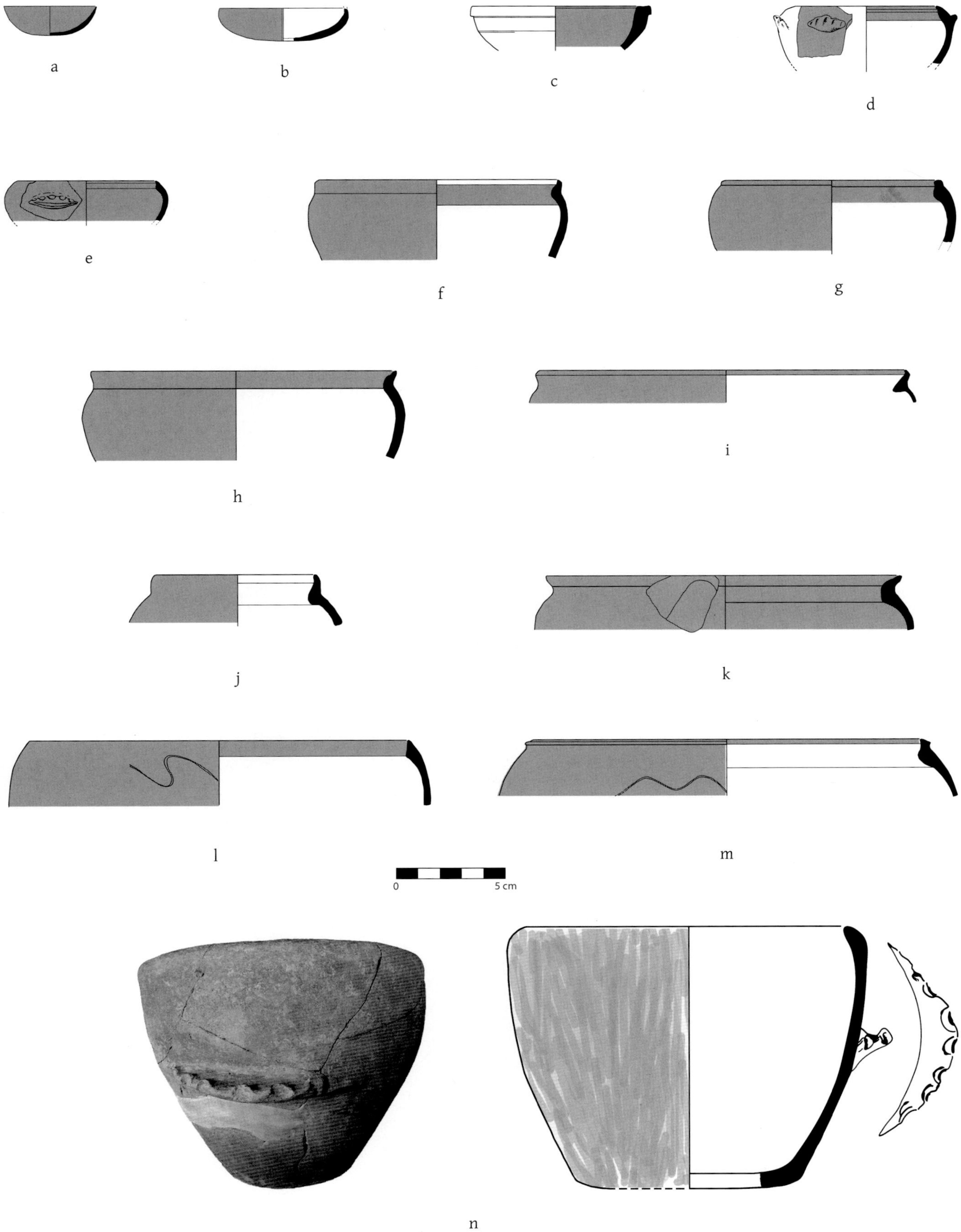

Early Bronze Age I open vessels from the East Slope

Plate 52. Early Bronze Age I bowls

	Reg. No.	*Description*	*Provenience*	*Published*
a	34.2614/1	Inverted-rim bowl. Buff, red slip	East Slope	—
b	A65900 / P4738	Wide flat-rim bowl. Buff, red slip	U16, Locus 1170	—
c	34.2614/2	Inverted-rim bowl. Buff-pink, grain wash exterior Extremely well levigated and highly burnished	Locus 1200	—
d	34.2618/1 / P4952	Wide flat-rim bowl. Buff, red burnished externally	Locus 1220	—
e	34.2469/1 / P4171	Wide flat-rim bowl. Buff, red slip	East Slope	—

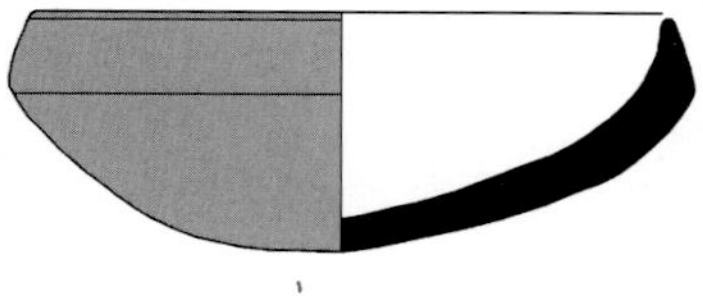

a

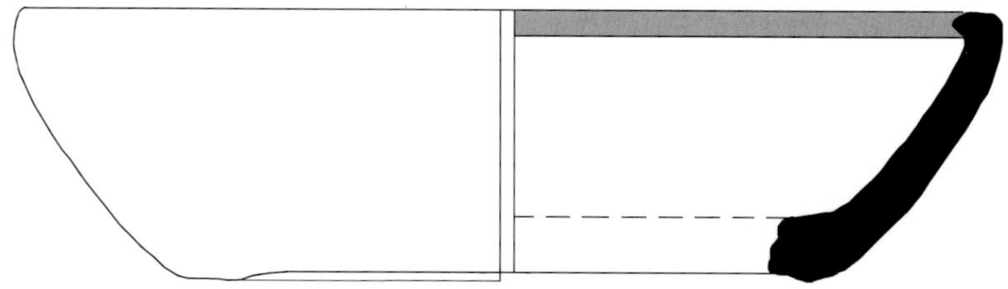

b

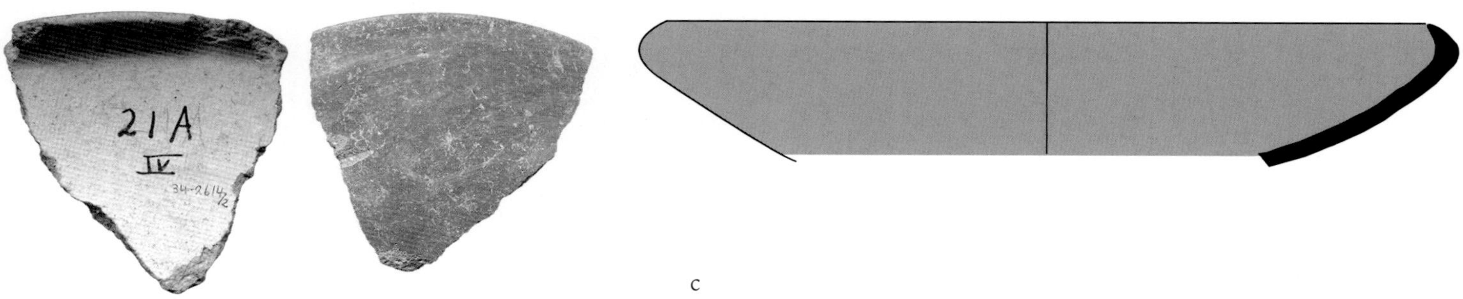

c

d

e

Early Bronze Age I bowls

Plate 53. Early Bronze Age I spouted basins and vats

	Reg. No.	*Description*	*Provenience*
a	34.2645/5	Buff-brown, gray core, red slip	East Slope
b	34.2645/3	Buff, red slip	East Slope
c	34.2646	Brown	East Slope
d	34.2645/2	Buff, red slip	East Slope

a

b

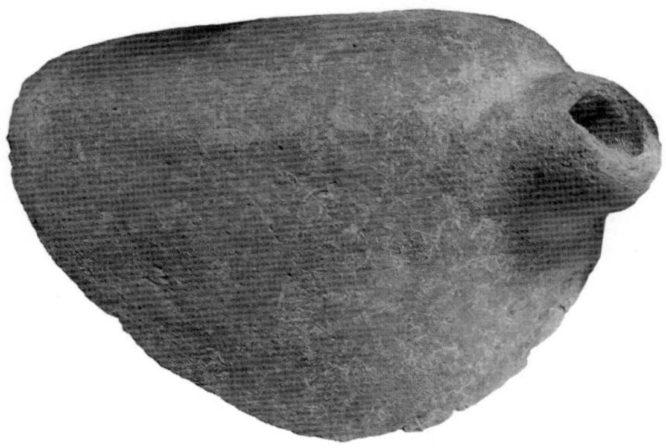

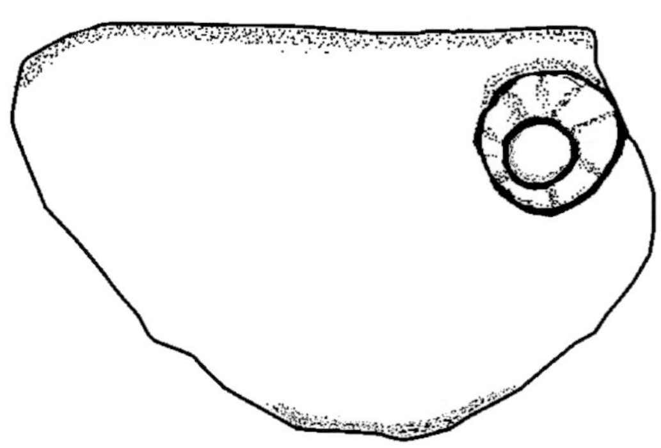

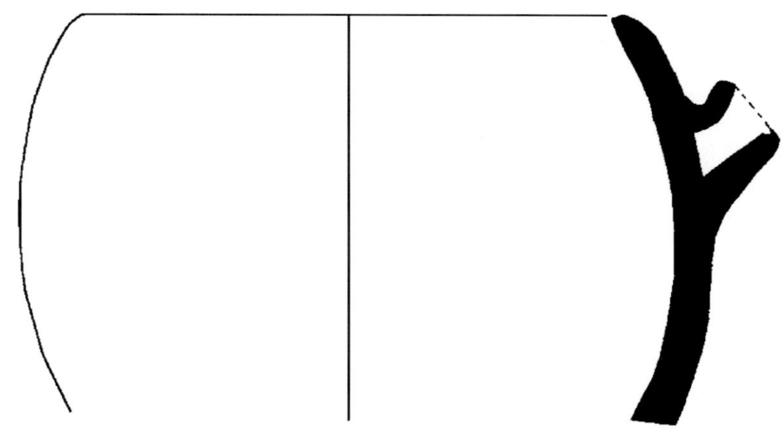

c

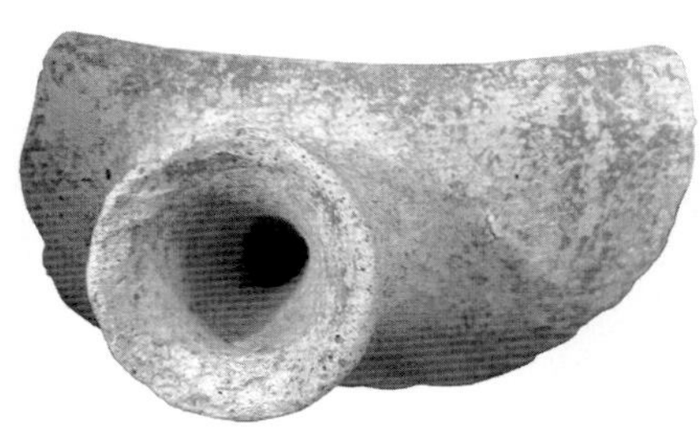

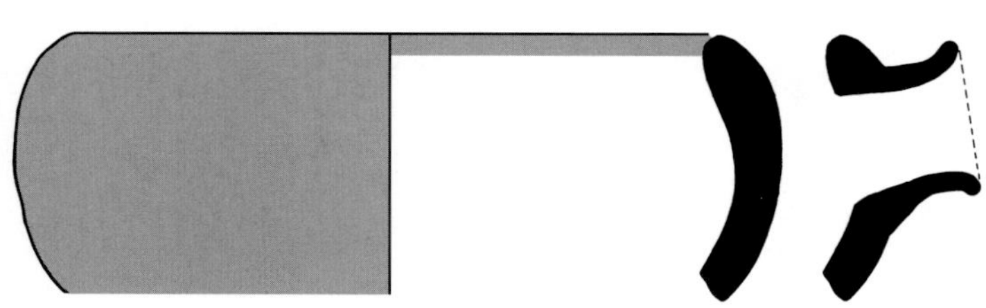

d

Early Bronze Age I spouted basins and vats

Plate 54. Early Bronze Age I strap handles and juglets

	Reg. No.	*Description*	*Provenience*	*Published*
a	34.2578	Small handle with incised decoration. Red slip, polished	East Slope	—
b	34.2639/28	Small handle with potter's mark. Red slip. See also figure 29aa, plate 83e	East Slope	—
c	34.2639	Small handle of a juglet. Red slip	East Slope	—
d	34.2510 / P4722	Rare, double stranded strap handle. Red slip	East Slope	—
e	34.2428 / P4528	Strap handle, incised decoration. Red slip	Locus 903 Lower	—
f	34.2511/7 / P5062	Strap handle of a large vessel. Grain wash and incised decoration	East Slope	Engberg and Shipton 1934a, fig. 9 (shown attached to body sherds)
g	34.2639/32	High loop handle, probably of juglet. Buff, red slip	East Slope	—
h	34.26[or 0]37/24	High loop handle, probably of juglet. Buf, red slip	East Slope	—
i	34.2639/26	High loop handle, probably of juglet. Buff, red slip	East Slope	—
j	34.2639/29	High loop handle, probably of juglet. Buff, red slip	East Slope	—
k	34.2639/31	High loop handle, probably of juglet. Buff, red slip	East Slope	—
l	34.2689/21	High loop handle, probably of juglet. Buff	East Slope	—
m	—'	Fragment of a juglet. Buff-brown, traces of red slip	East Slope	—
n	34.2453	Fragment of juglet. Buff. Red slip, polished	East Slope	—
o	34.2633 / P4529	Juglet. Buff-pink	Tomb 903 Lower	*Megiddo Tombs*, pls. 3:46, 76:16
p	34.2637 / P5580	Fragment of juglet. Buff	East Slope	—

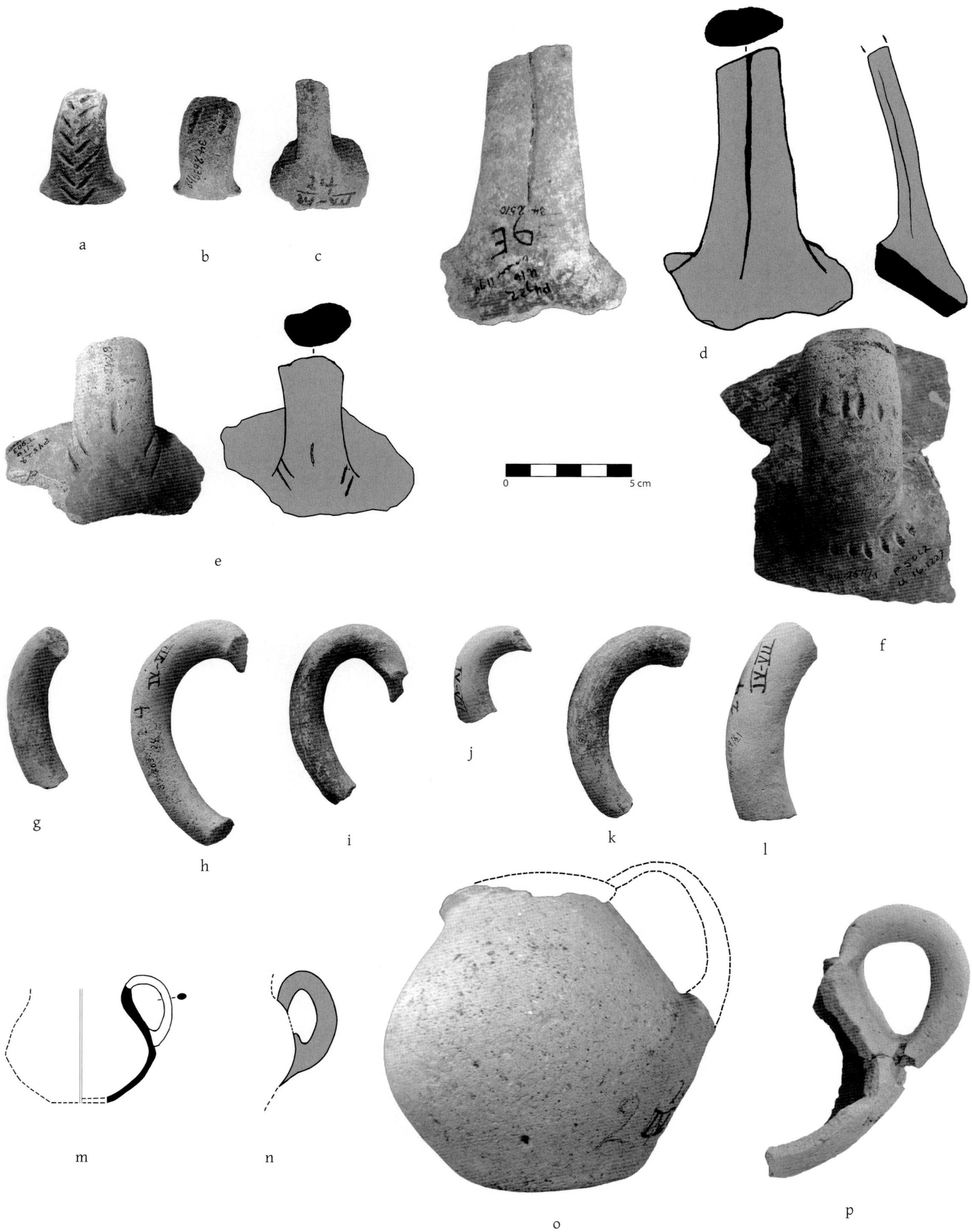

Early Bronze Age I strap handles and juglets

Plate 55. Early Bronze Age I gourd jars (*amphoriskoi*)

	Reg. No.	*Description*	*Provenience*	*Published*
a	34.2642	Buff-, red slip, burnish	Tomb 903 Upper	Engberg and Shipton 1934a, fig. 6; *Megiddo Tombs*, pls. 3:7, 76:2
b	34.2543/8	Buff-brown, red slip	East Slope	—
c	34.2643/9	Buff-brown	East Slope	—
d	A16858 / P4081	Buff, well levigated, thick red slip, lightly polished	V17, Tomb 1122	*Megiddo Tombs*, pl. 5:1

a

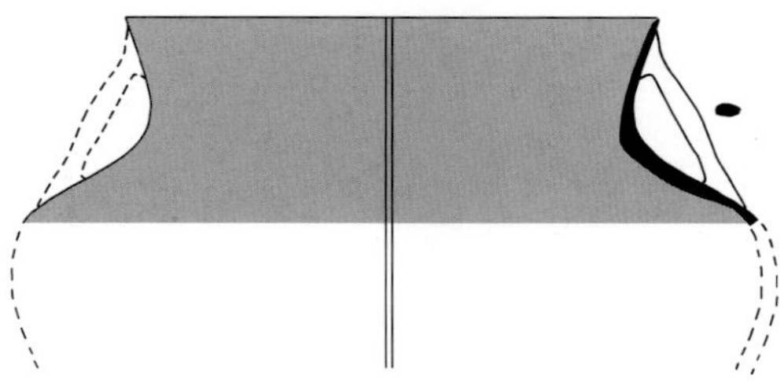

b

c

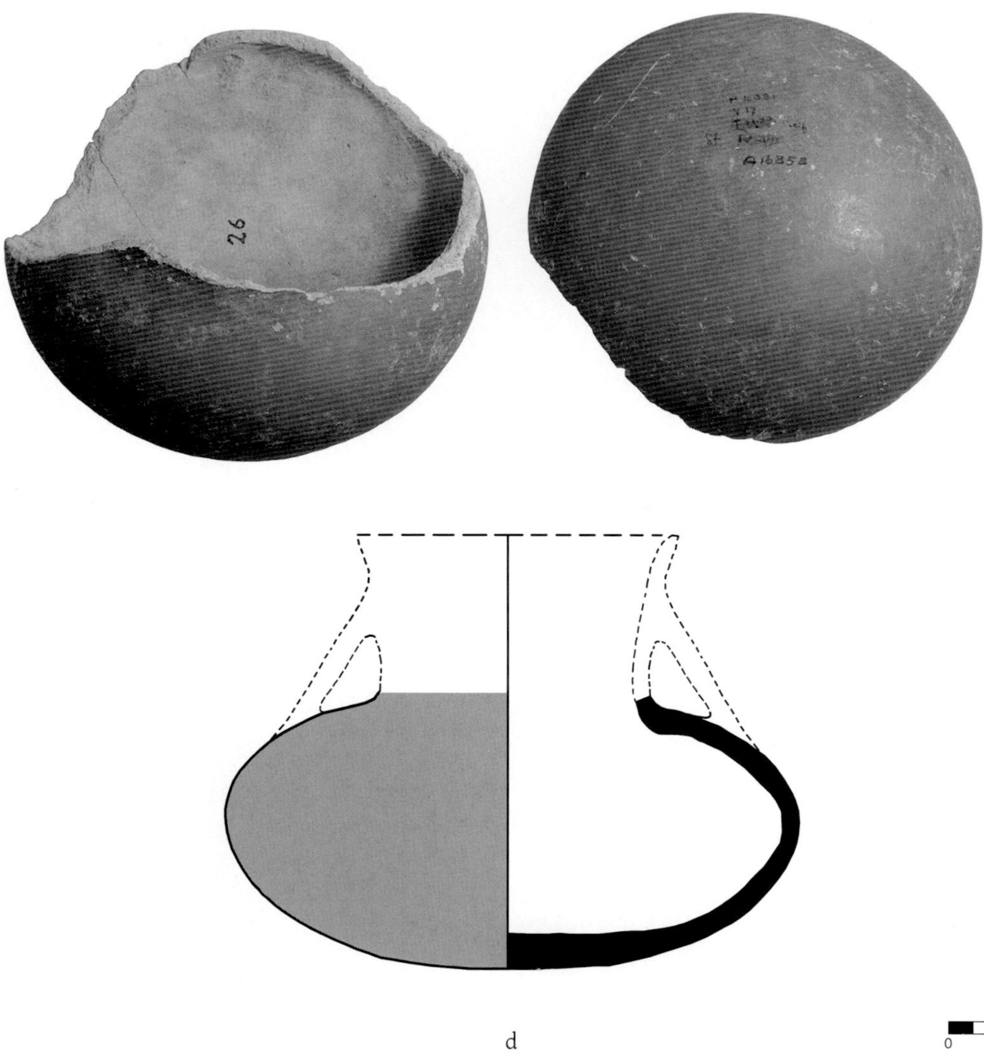

d

0 5 cm

Early Bronze Age I gourd jars (*amphoriskoi*)

Plate 56. Early Bronze Age I small and medium-size spouted vessels ("teapots")

	Reg. No.	*Description*	*Provenience*	*Published*
a	34.2628/11	Small, bent spout. Buff, red slip	East Slope	—
b	34.2626/10	Small, bent spout. Buff-brown, red slip	East Slope	—
c	34.2681/1	Small, bent spout. Buff-brown, red slip, burnished	East Slope	—
d	34.2628/15	Small, bent spout. Buff, red slip, polished	East Slope	—
e	34.2628/13	Small, bent spout. Buff, red slip	East Slope	—
f	34.2636/2	Buff-brown, red slip, burnished. Plain ware	East Slope	—
g	34.2429 / P4530	Buff, red slip, burnished	Tomb 903 Lower	—
h	34.2502 /5	Narrow, ridged neck and wide, flaring rim. Ridged neck, buff-brown, red slip	East Slope	—
i	34.2631 / P4531	Narrow, ridged neck and wide, flaring rim. Two loop handles. Buff-brown, red slip, burnished	Tomb 903 Lower	*Megiddo Tombs*, pls. 3:49, 76:15
j	34.2629 / P4547	No neck, thick rim. Horizontal tube handles. Brown, thick red slip, highly burnished. Missing spout. Fine ware	Locus 1088	—

a

b

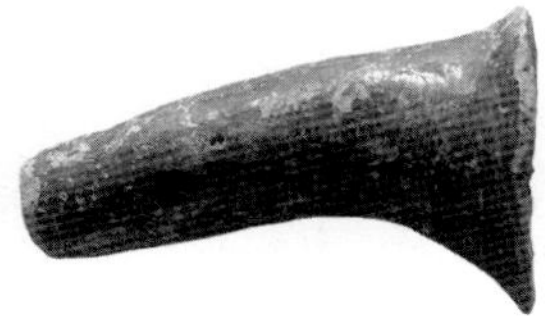
c

d

e

0 5 cm

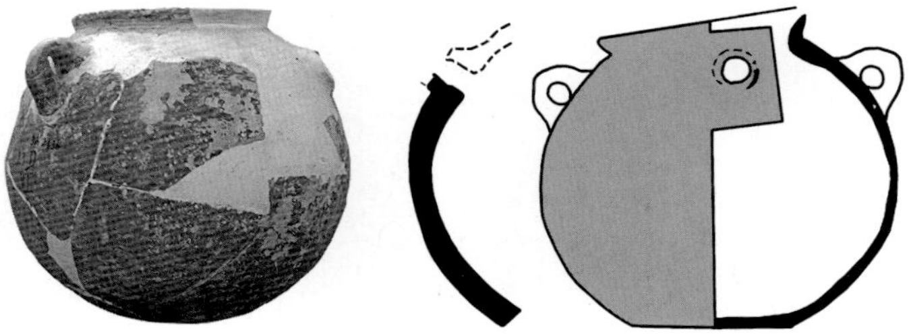
f

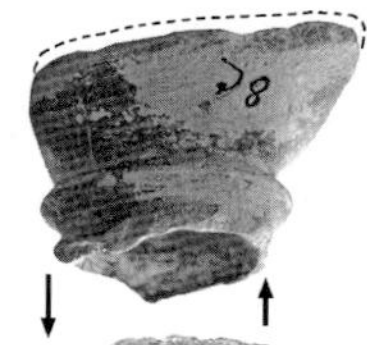
h

i

g

j

0 5 cm

Early Bronze Age I small and medium-size spouted vessels ("teapots")

Plate 57. Early Bronze Age I jars and stand

	Reg. No.	*Description*	*Provenience*	*Published*
a	34.2668 / P5583	Jar fragment. Thickened, squared-off rim and no neck. Buff, dark brown grain wash	East Slope	—
b	A16795 / P4910	Jar with high ("trumpet"?) base (no longer extant). Indented ledge handles. Buff-brown, red slip, burnished	V17, Tomb 910D	*Megiddo Tombs*, pls. 4:22, 83:2
c	34.2655	Stand, base only. Brown, red slip	East Slope	—
d	34.2552	Large jar. Buff, grain wash	East Slope	—

a

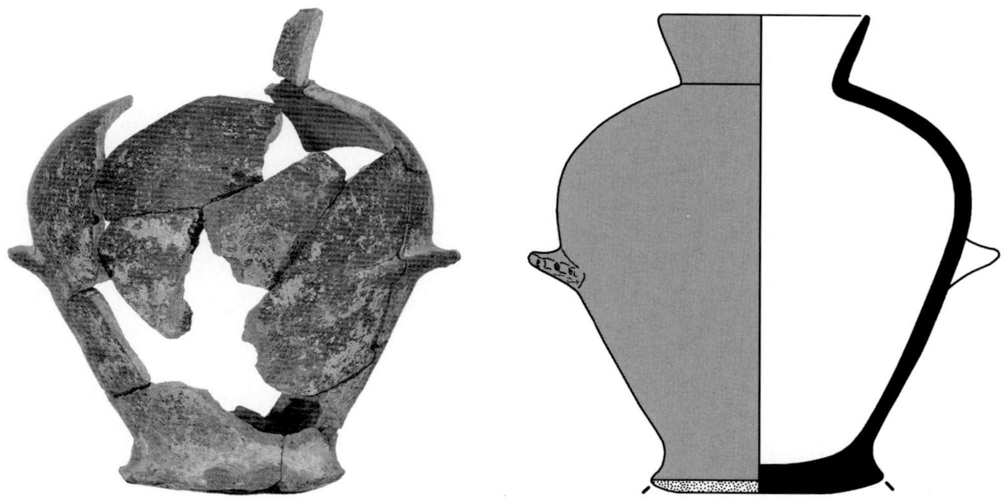

b

0 5 cm

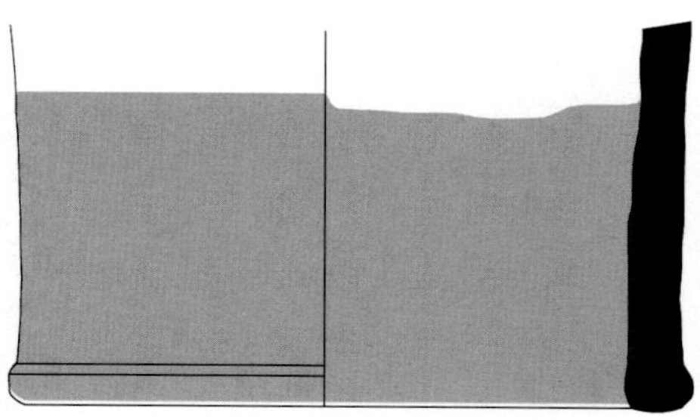

c

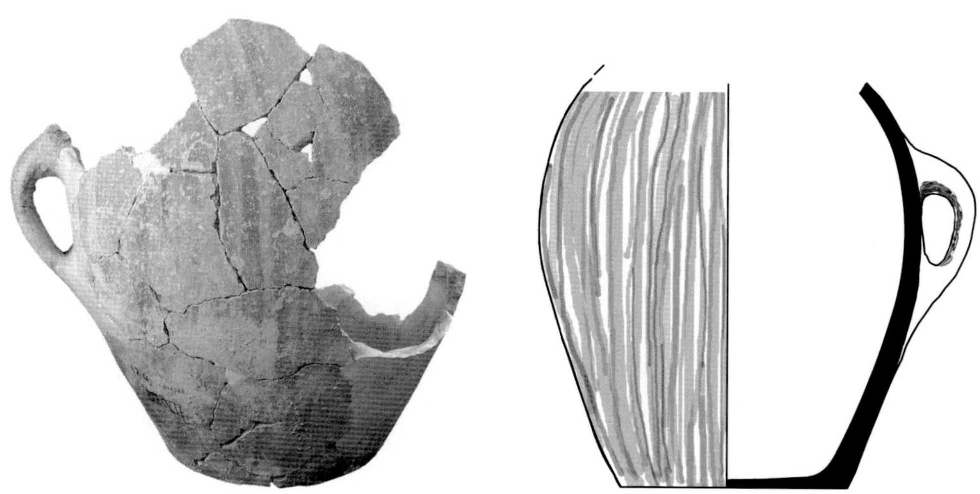

d

0 25 cm

Early Bronze Age I jars and stand

Plate 58. Early Bronze Age I bow-rim pithos

Reg. No.	*Description*	*Provenience*
34.2587 / P4538	Restored pithos with cylinder seal impressions. Fairly well-levigated, pinkish fabric. Rope-like decoraton. See plate 76 for seal impression. Photo by Z. Radovan (courtesy the Israel Antiquities Authority)	B/V/1

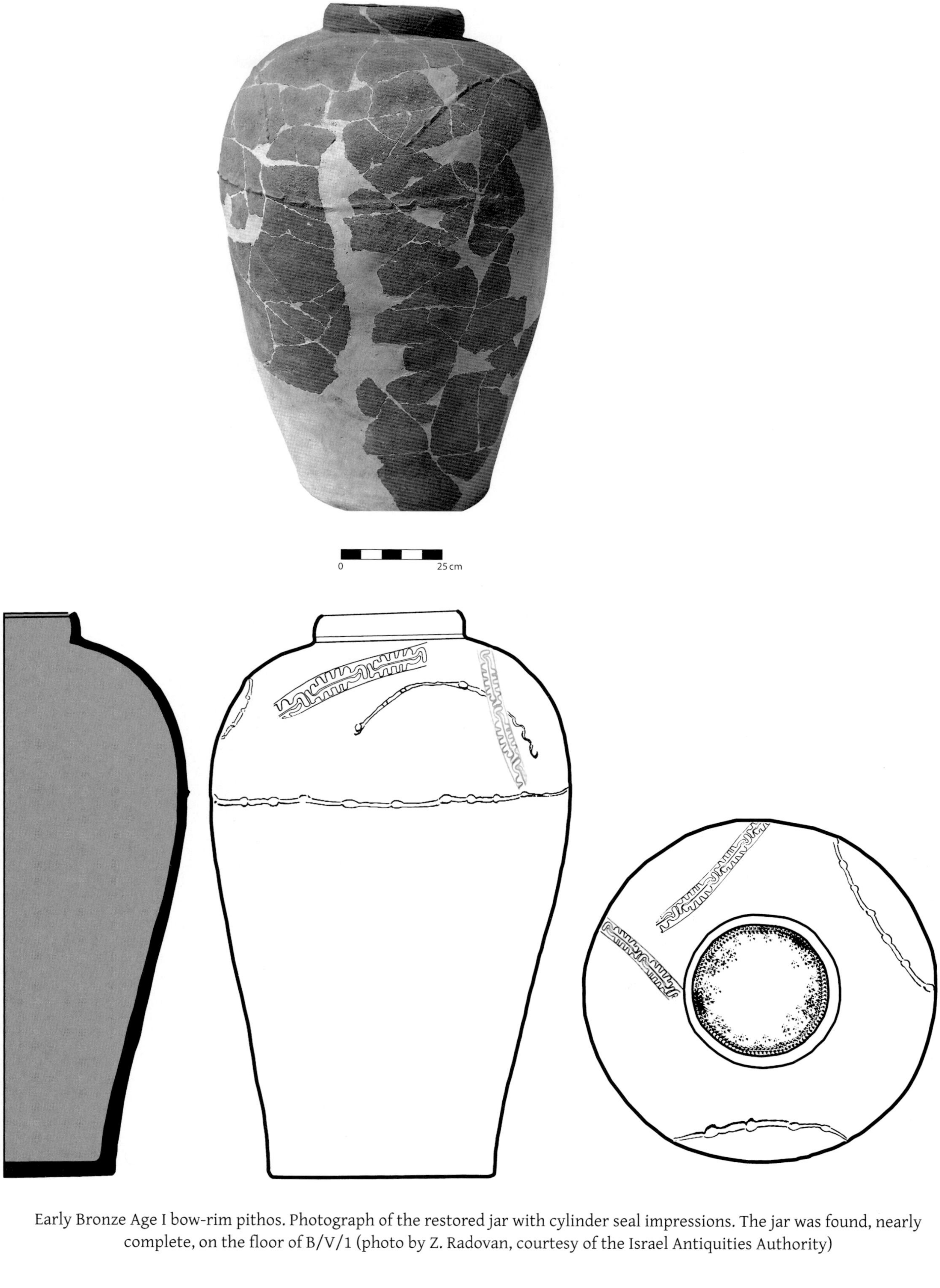

Early Bronze Age I bow-rim pithos. Photograph of the restored jar with cylinder seal impressions. The jar was found, nearly complete, on the floor of B/V/1 (photo by Z. Radovan, courtesy of the Israel Antiquities Authority)

Plate 59. Early Bronze Age I bow-rim pithoi

	Reg. No.	*Description*	*Provenience*
a	34.2598	Buff, red slip	East Slope
b	34.2586/2	Buff, traces of red slip	East Slope
c	34.2596/1	Pink-orange	East Slope
d	34.2597/6	Buff-gray, red slip	East Slope
e	34.2597/4	Orange, gray core, red slip	East Slope
f	34.2495/2	Buff to brown, gray core, red slip	East Slope

a

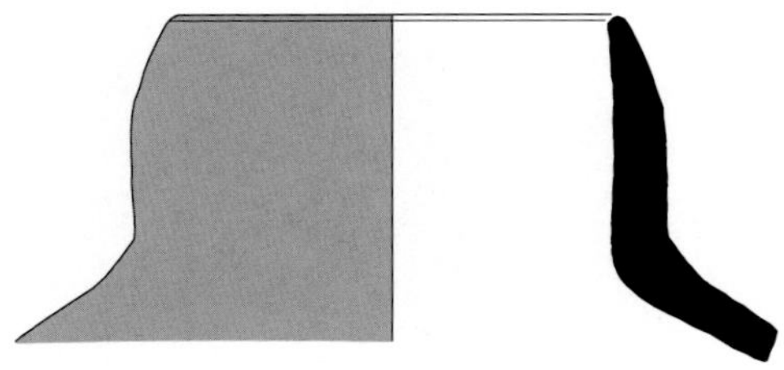

b

c

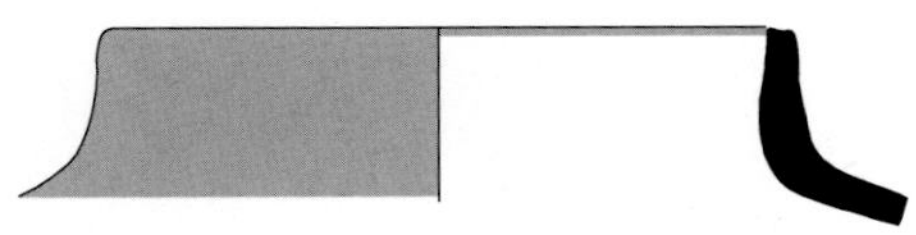

d

e

f

Early Bronze Age I bow-rim pithoi

Plate 60. Early Bronze Age I large jars and pithoi

	Reg. No.	*Description*	*Provenience*
a	34.2589/2	Buff-orange, red slip	Under Locus 1170
b	34.2589/5	Buff	East Slope
c	34.2591/6	Buff, gray core, red slip	East Slope
d	34.2594/1	Buff-pink, red slip	East Slope
e	34.2592/1	Buff to brown, gray core, red slip	East Slope
f	34.2596/3	Buff-gray, red slip	East Slope
g	34.2582/1	Buff, red slip	East Slope
h	34.2584/2	Buff, gray core. Red slip	East Slope
i	34.2595	Orange, gray core	East Slope
j	34.2584/1	Buff-orange, red slip	Under Locus 1170
k	34.2594/2	Buff, traces of red slip	East Slope

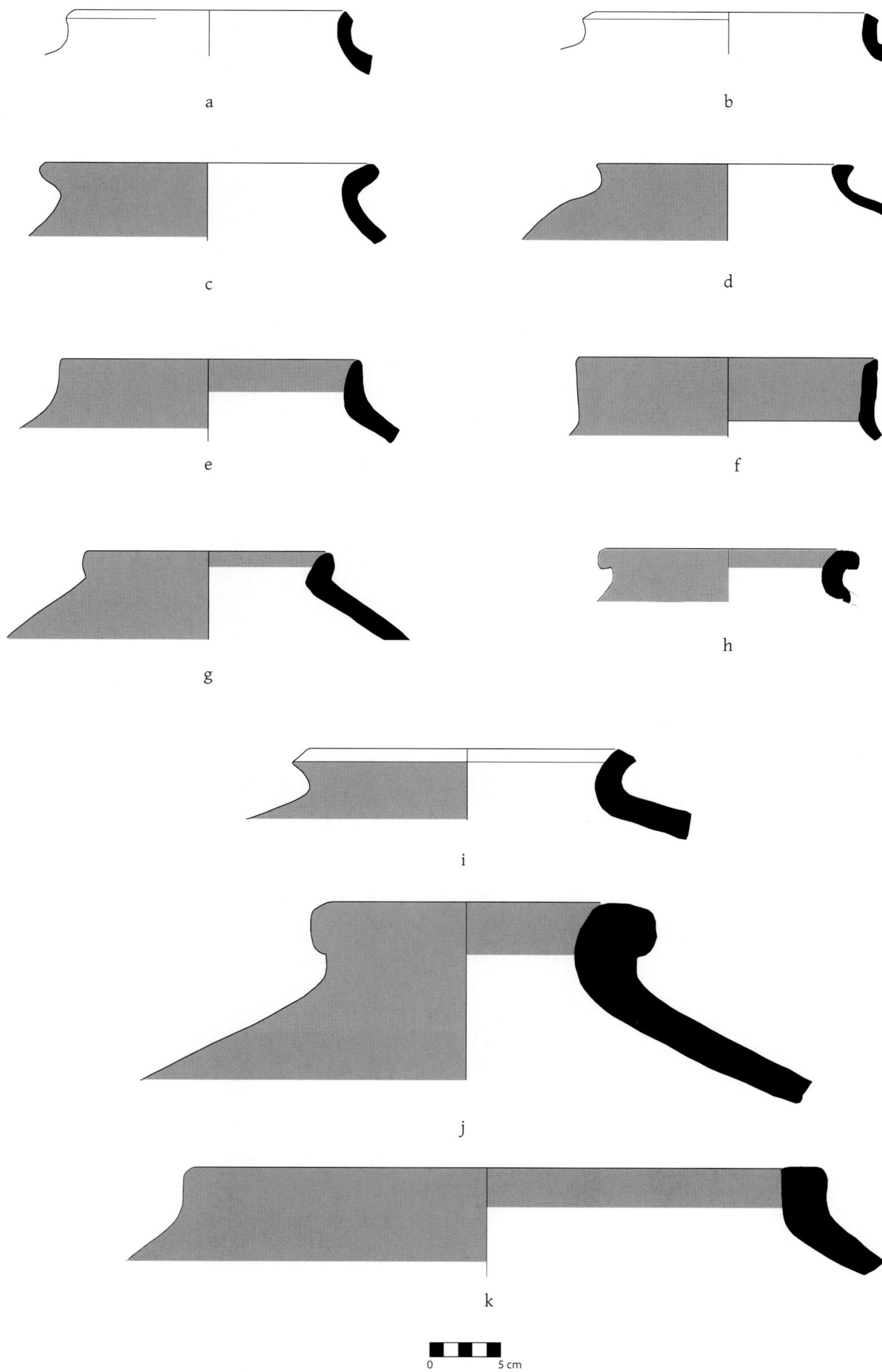

Early Bronze Age I large jars and pithoi

Plate 61. Early Bronze Age I holemouth vessels

	Reg. No.	*Description*	*Provenience*	*Published*
a	A65984 / 4884	Ridged rim. Brown	U11, Locus 218	—
b	A65938	Ridged rim. Brown, red slip	U16, Locus 1190	—
c	34.2536/2	Buff-yellow	East Slope	—
d	—	Buff	East Slope	—
e	34.2547	Small holemouth jug. Brown-gray. Potter's mark	Locus 1199	—
f	34.2419 / P4486	Flat base. Brown	U11, Locus 1884	*Megiddo Tombs*, pls. 3:36, 76:13
g	34.2548 / P4909	Small holemouth jar. Thickened rim. Gray, red slip. Potter's mark	Locus 1200	—

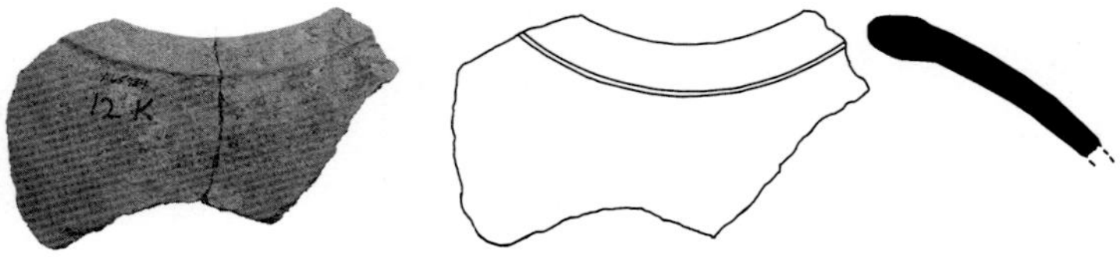

a

b

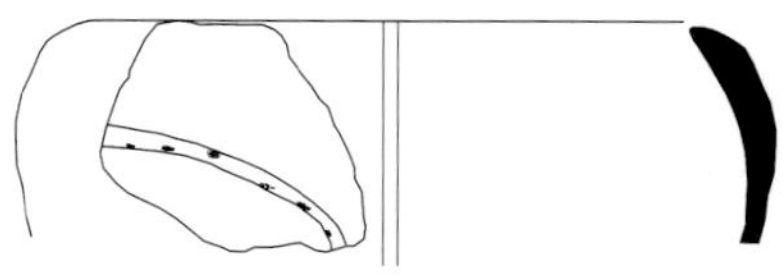

c

d

e

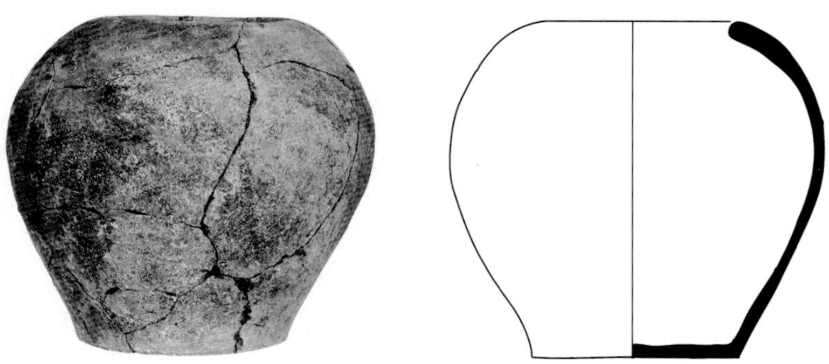

f

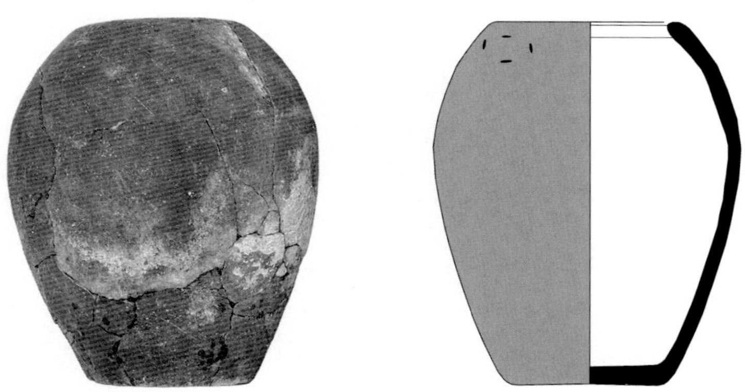

g

Early Bronze Age I holemouth vessels

Plate 62. Assorted Early Bronze Age I ledge handles

	Reg. No.	*Description*	*Provenience*	*Parallel*
a	A65948 / 4736	Buff-gray, red slip	S17	—
b	A16797	Buff, red slip	East Slope	—
c	A65967 / 4842	Buff-gray, red slip	T17	Golani 2003, fig. 4.9.1
d	A65973 / P2792	Buff, red slip	T16	—
e	A16796	Buff, brown slip	East Slope	—
f	A65968 / P5337	Buff-yellow, red slip (grain wash?)	Tomb 910	Braun 1985, fig. 25:4; Golani 2003, fig. 4.21:5
g	34.2574/2	Buff, red slip	East Slope	—
h	34.2559/2	On bowl, buff-gray, red, gray mottled slip	East Slope	—
i	34.2575/2	Buff-gray, red slip	East Slope	—
j	34.2445 / P5252	Buff-gray, red slip	East Slope	—
k	34.2576/8	Buff, red slip	East Slope	—
l	A16781 / P2729	Buff-brown, red-orange slip	T16, Tomb 919	—
m	A65981	Buff, red slip	East Slope	—
n	34.2571/3	Buff-gray, red slip	East Slope	—
o	A65976	Buff-gray, red slip	East Slope	—
p	A16794	Buff	East Slope	
q	A65957 / P2793	Buff. See also plate 63e	T16, Locus 919	Photo by Anna Ressman

Assorted Early Bronze Age I ledge handles

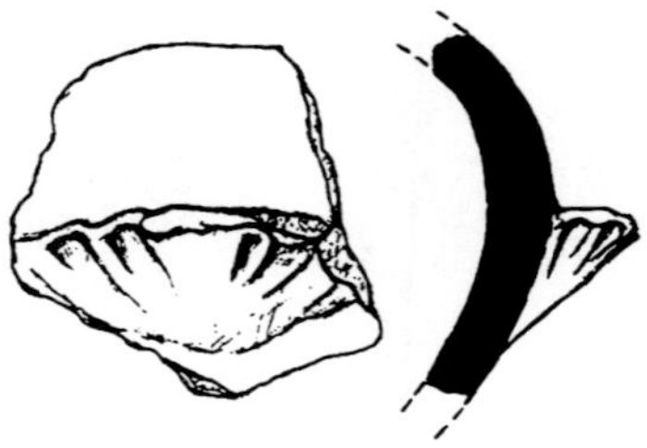

a

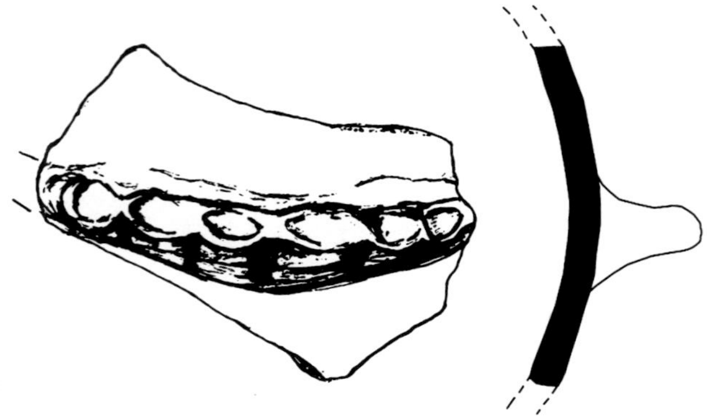

b

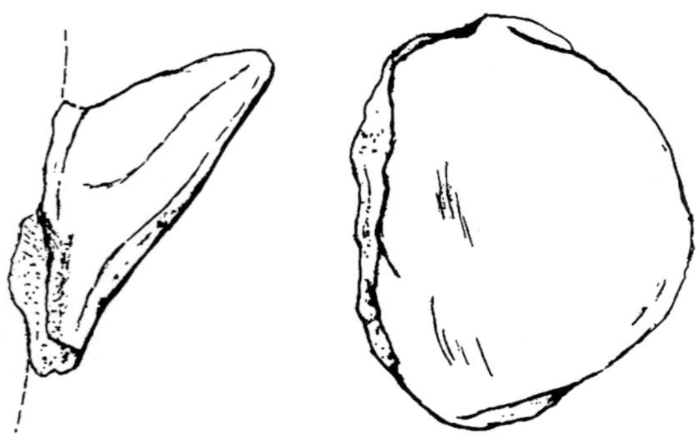

c

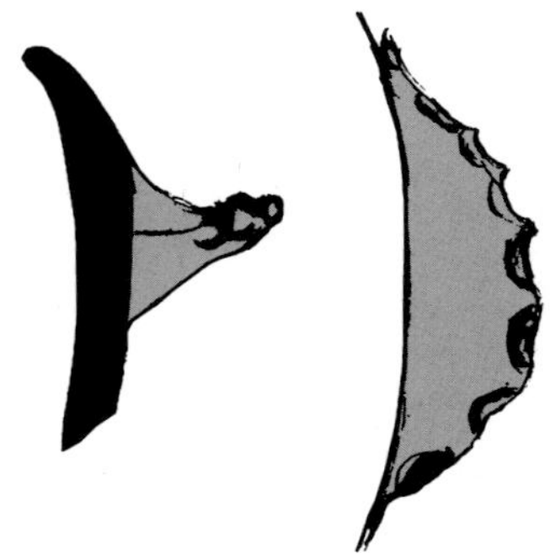

d

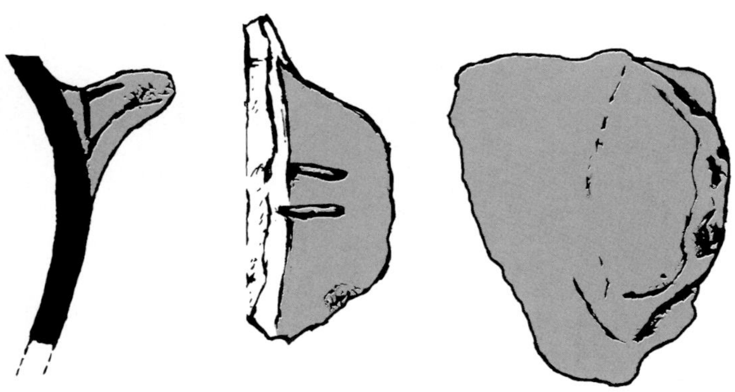

e

0 5 cm

Assorted Early Bronze Age I ledge handles

	Reg. No.	*Description*	*Provenience*	*Parallel*
a	A16790 / P4946	Buff	V16, Tomb 1212	—
b	A65987 / P5338	Buff, red slipped externally	Tomb 910G fill	*Megiddo Tombs*, pl. 82:16
c	A65961 / 4839	Buff	T17	—
d	34.2445	Buff-gray, red slip	East Slope	—
e	A65957 / P2793	Buff, red slip. Two parallel incisions prior to firing. See also pl. 62q	T16, Locus 919	Golani 2003, fig. 4.9.1

a

0 5 cm

b

Egyptian-style, locally produced pottery

	Reg. No.	*Description*	*Provenience*	*Published*
a	34.2652 / P4908	Egyptian-style vessel (granary jar) of local clay, coarse fabric, buff, vegetal temper	Locus 1199	Engberg and Shipton 1934a, fig. 6
b	34.2653	Base of Egyptian-style vessel (probably of granary jar of local clay), coarse fabric, buff, gray core, vegetal temper	East Slope	—

Plate 65. Early Bronze Age II pottery

	Reg. No.	*Description*	*Provenience*	*Paralells*
a	P4638[a]	Sherd of what is probably light-faced painted ware	Y17, under Locus 1093	Amiran 1969, pl. 17:7–10; Esse 1991, fig. 20; Nigro and Sala 2010, pl. 91:1; Kafafi 2011, fig. 3
b	34.2623 / P4833	Platter, red, gray grits, polished. Metallic Ware	U16, Locus 1168	—
c	34.2521 / P4797	Neck of jug, orange, gray core, orange-brown to gray mottled externally, traces of fine combing, coils highly visible internally, polished externally. Metallic Ware	U16, Locus 1169	—
d	34.2665/2 / P4731	Body sherd of closed vessel. Gray surface, orange interior, coiling visible internally. Metallic Ware	U16, under Locus 1170	—
e	34.2623/1 / P4736	Shallow bowl, wide inverted rim, red slip internally and on external rim, pattern burnished internally, red-brown, white grits, polished. Metallic Ware	U16, Locus 1170	—

[a] This is an excavation number taken from the record card. There is no museum number as the sherd could not be found.

a

b

c

d

e

0 5 cm

Early Bronze Age II pottery

Plate 66. Early Bronze Age II pottery

	Reg. No.	*Description*	*Provenience*	*Paralell*
a	34.2624/1	Platter/shallow bowl. Gray-brown, orange-brown core. Metallic Ware. Potter's mark scraped on bottom of base when vessel was leather-hard. Gray and white grits, polished	East Slope	—
b	34.2624/4	Platter-bowl, dark red, gray core, white grits, polished. Metallic Ware	East Slope	—
c	34.2624/2	Platter-bowl, dark red, gray core, white grits, polished. Metallic Ware	East Slope, under Locus 1191	—
d	34.2614/5	Platter-like bowl, buff, gray grits, red slip and horizontally burnished	Locus 1200	—
e	34.2614/3	Platter-like bowl. Buff, red slip	V17, under Locus 1171	—
f	34.2624/3 + 34.2624/5	Platter-bowl, roughly cylindrical, polished, flat base incised with a potter's mark. Gray-brown, orange-brown core, white grits	Tomb 16, East of Locus 1092	Greenberg 2006, fig. 10.11:4
g	34.2478	Jug. Squat body, broad, flat base, narrow neck, raised vertical decorations. Crudely fashioned. Orange-brown. Metallic Ware	Tomb 17	Fischer 2008, figs. 267:2–3, 268:5, 289: phase II; Amiran 1969, pl. 17:1–4; Golani 2003, fig. 4.29:1–2

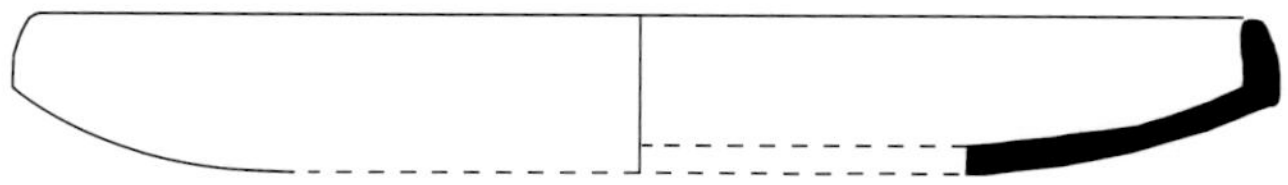

a

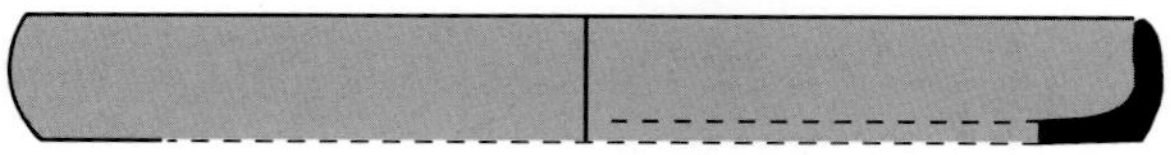

b

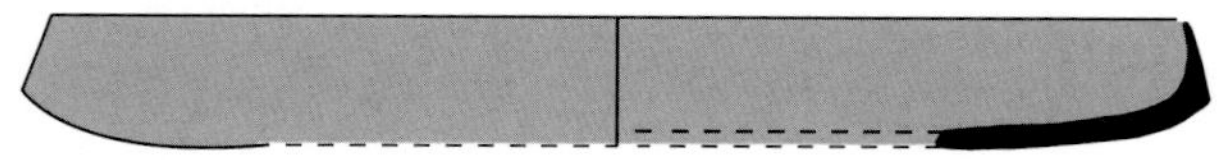

c

d

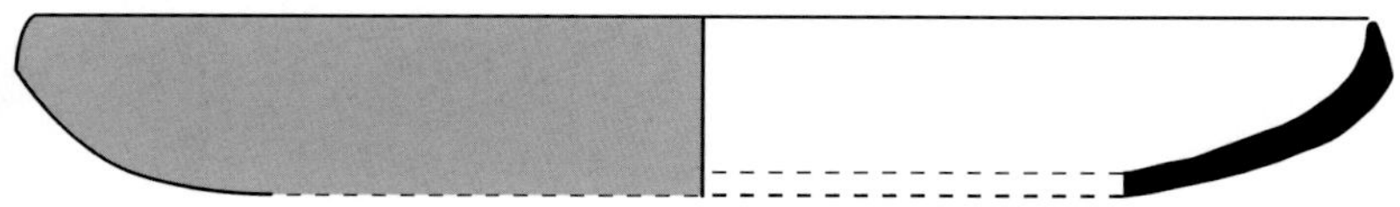

e

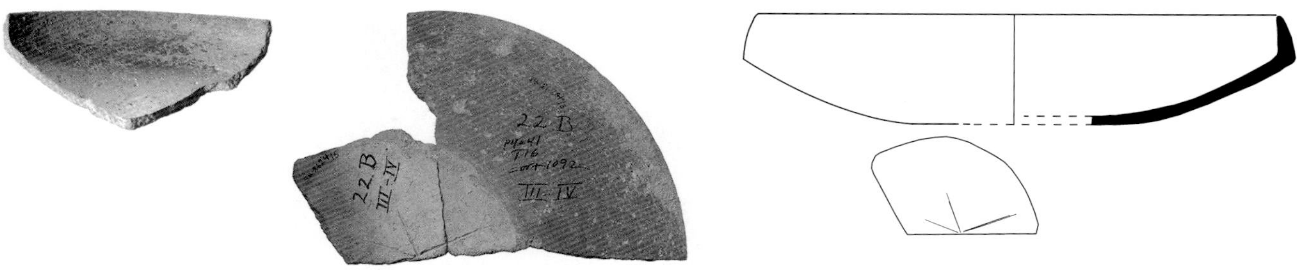

f

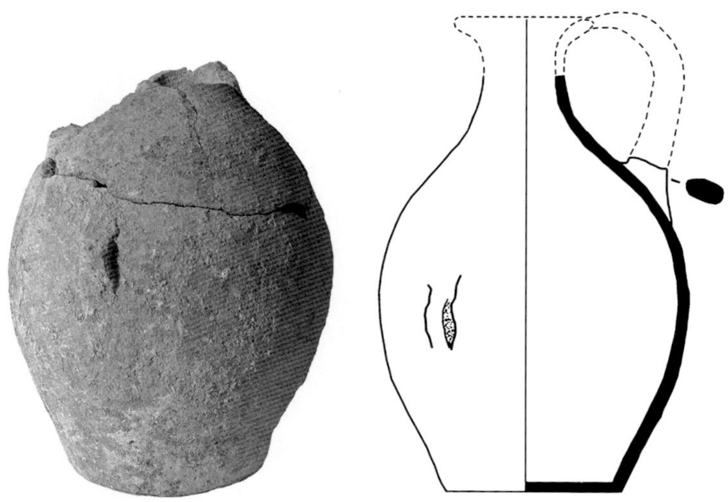

g

Early Bronze Age II pottery

Plate 67. Selected Early Bronze Age III pottery

	Reg. No.	Description	Provenience	Published
a	34.2494 / P4904	Jug/juglet. Brown	Locus 1187	—
b	34.2648 / P4690	Juglet. Heavy, smooth. Buff, heavy red slip, polished	U16, under Locus 1162	—
c	A16752/ P3693	Jug/juglet. Brown	U16, Tomb 923	—
d	34.2488 / P2859	Small, wheel-turned bowl with string-cut base. Buff, coarsely finished, wheel marks	Locus 871	—
e	34.2477	Small, wheel-turned bowl with string-cut base. Buff, coarsely finished, wheel marks	East Slope	—
f	A65912 / P3691	Small, wheel-turned bowl with string-cut base. Buff, coarsely finished, wheel marks	U17, Locus 914	—
g	A65911 / P4659	Small, wheel-turned bowl with string-cut base. Buff, coarsely finished, wheel marks, traces of splattered red paint	V16, Locus 1153	—
h	34.2477 / P3690	Small, wheel-turned bowl with string-cut base. Buff, coarsely finished	U17, Locus 914	—
i	A16748 / P4664	Jar with string-cut base. Smoothed exterior. Buff-pink. Joins A16747 (base)	U16, Locus 1157	—

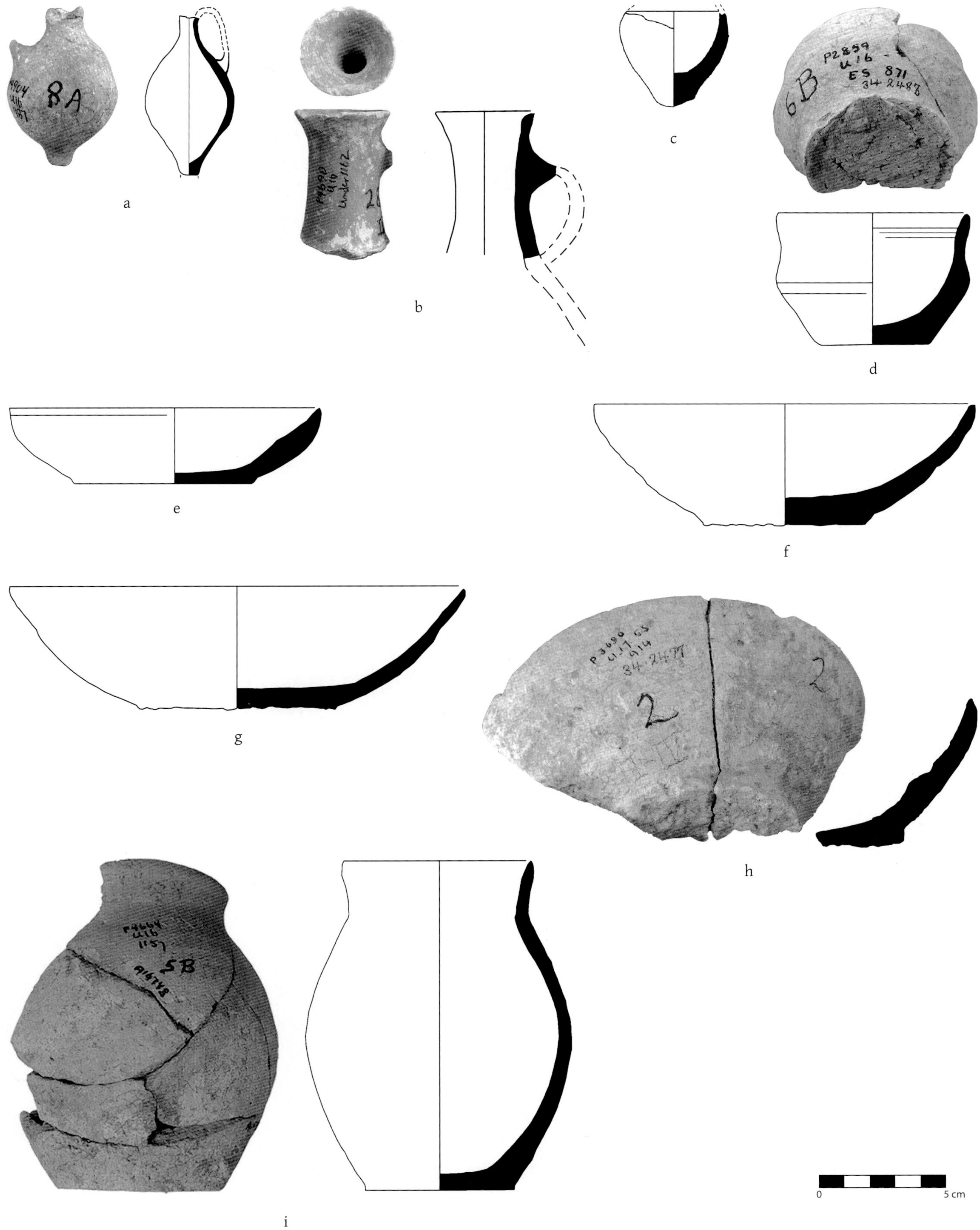

Selected Early Bronze Age III pottery

Plate 68. Selected Early Bronze Age III pottery

	Reg. No.	Description	Provenience	Parallel
a	A16754 / P4850	Jar. Smoothed exterior. Buff	U16, Tomb 1168	—
b	34.2512 / P4807	Small jar with wide mouth and splayed rim. Buff, thin red slip, incised decoration	U16, Locus 1169	Covello-Paran 2003, p. 14
c	34.2491 / P4829	Goblet. Straight walled with simple, tapered rim. Buff, red painted bands on exterior, thin coat of red paint on interior	U16, Tomb 1168	—
d	A16785	Very wavy ledge handle. Brown-buff, traces of thick white slip	East Slope	—
e	34.2481	Sherd with ledge handle. Buff, red paint	East Slope	—
f	34.2496	Jug/juglet. Pink-orange, red, highly burnished	East Slope	—
g	A65935 / P3964	Jug/juglet. Brown	U16, Locus 863	—
h	A30387 / BY 471	Jug/juglet. Brown, red slip, burnished (for comparison)	Khirbet Kerak, L11/21	—

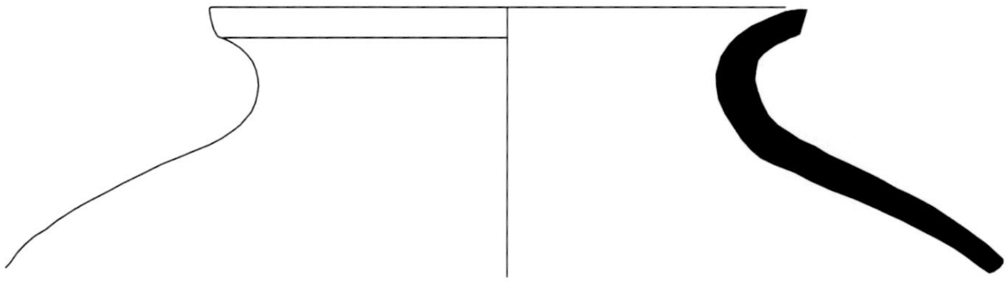

a

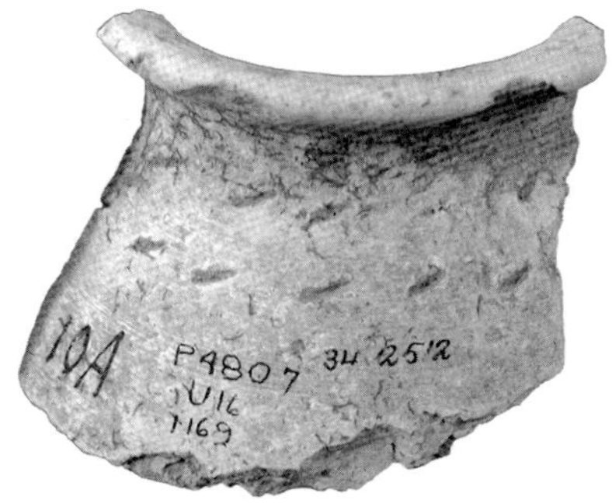

b

c

d

e

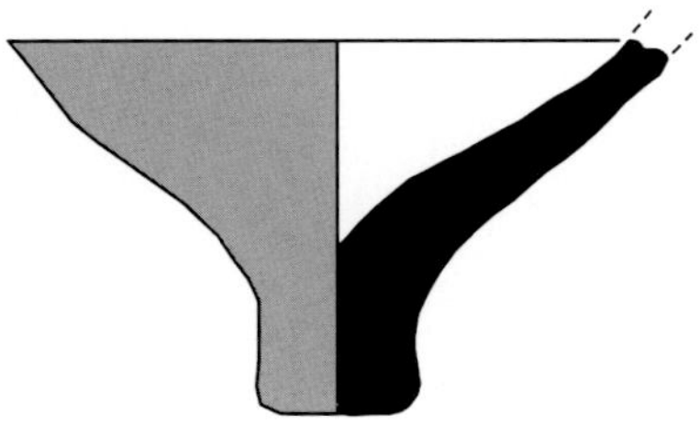

f

g

h

Selected Early Bronze Age III pottery

Plate 69. Early Bronze Age III fragments of small jars, a jug, and pithoi

	Reg. No.	*Description*	*Provenience*	*Published*
a	34.2664 / P4787	Jar. Smoothed exterior. Buff-gray, red painted	East Slope	—
b	34.2496/2	Jar. Smoothed exterior. Buff-gray, red painted	V16, Tomb 1101-A, Lower	—
c	A16314	Jar. Smoothed exterior. Buff, red painted	Tomb 52	—
d	34.2503/1	Jug. Wheel-made. Buff	East Slope	—
e	34.2483 / P4978	Jar. Smoothed exterior. Wheel-made, string-cut base. Buff -pink, red painted	V16, Locus 1212, under floor of Locus 1151	—
f	A38567	Fragment of pithos neck. Rope-like decoration. Orange, traces of thick white slip	Locus 3160	—
g	A16806 / P3949	Fragment of pithos neck. Rope-like decoration. Brown, brown slip	V16, Tomb 1099	—

a

b

c

d

f

e

g

Early Bronze Age III fragments of small jars, jug, and pithoi

Plate 70. Early Bronze Age III platter-plates

	Reg. No.	*Description*	*Provenience*	*Published*
a	34.2472/1 / P4824	Buff, red slip, pattern burnish. Lattice pattern decoration on interior	U16, Locus 1168	—
b	34.2463/3 / P3685	Buff- pink	U17, Locus 914	—
c	34.2463/5	Buff, red slip	East Slope	—
d	A65904	Buff, red slip	East Slope	—
e	A65921 / P4700	Buff, red slip	U16, under Locus 1170	—
f	34.2472/2	Buff, red slip	East Slope	—
g	34.2625/2	Buff	East Slope	—
h	A65901 / P4681	Buff-pink	U16, Locus 1162	—
i	A16741 / P3904	Buff, red slip, pattern burnish. Lattice pattern decoration on interior.	U16, under Locus 1086, Tomb 871	—
j	34.2463/1	Buff	East Slope	—

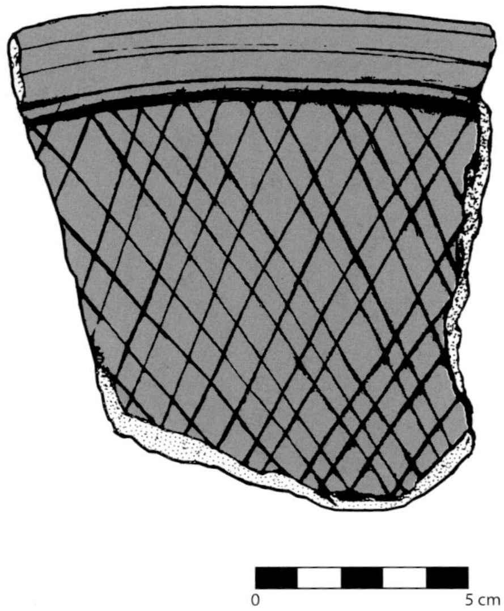

Figure to plate 70. Detail of A16741 interior

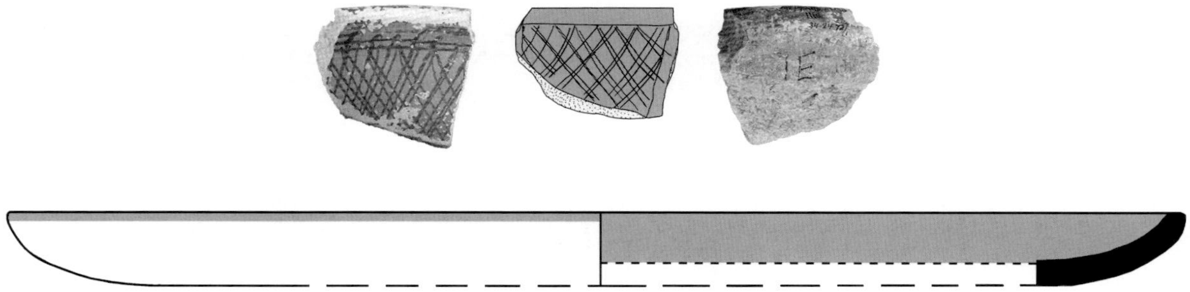

a

b

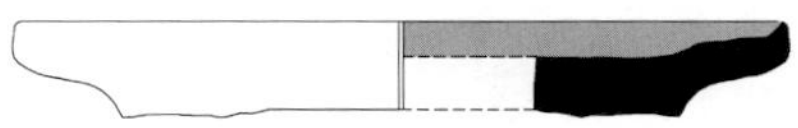

c

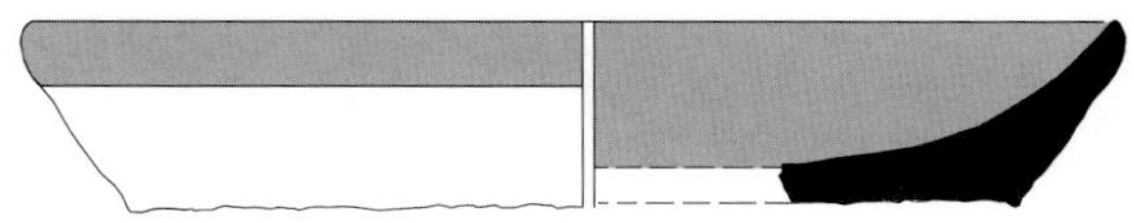

d

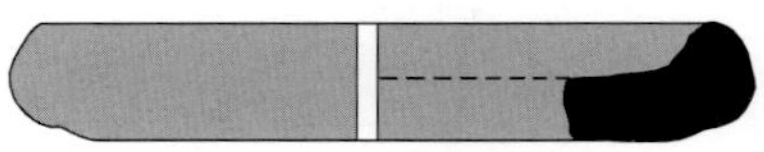

e

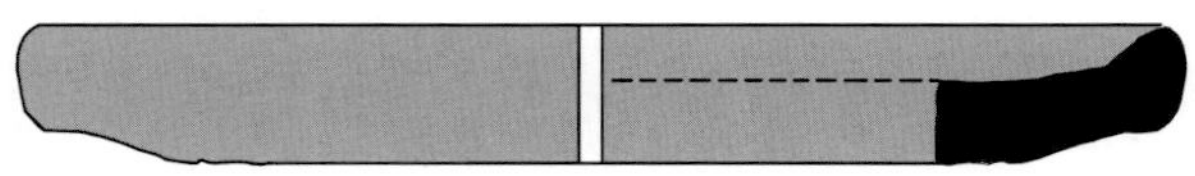

f

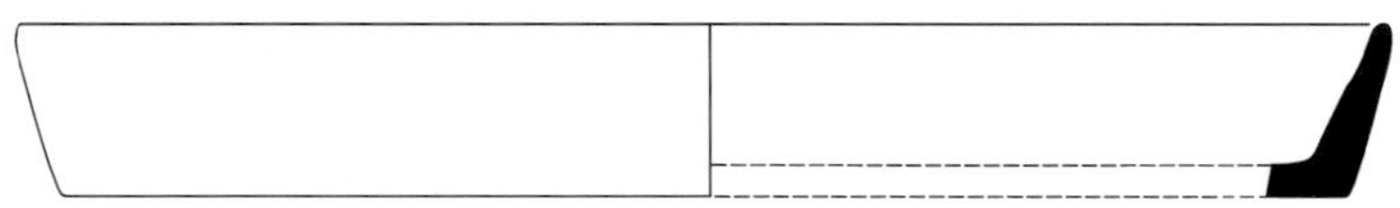

g

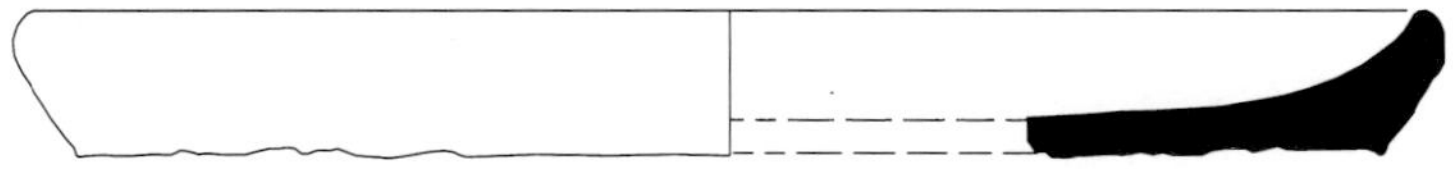

h

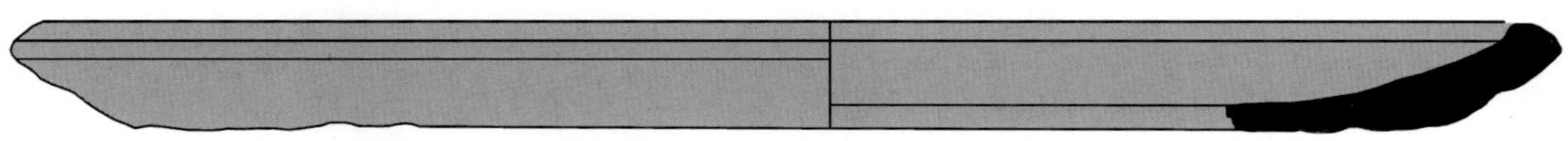

i

j

Early Bronze Age III platter-plates

Plate 71. Early Bronze Age III large bowls and basins

	Reg. No.	*Description*	*Provenience*	*Published*
a	A16730 / P4599	Buff. Wavy ledge handles, red washed interior	U16, Tomb 918	—
b	A16732 / P2856	Buff. Wavy ledge handles	U16, Tomb 918	—
c	34.2465 / P1263	Buff-white. Wavy ledge handles, red washed interior	East Slope	—

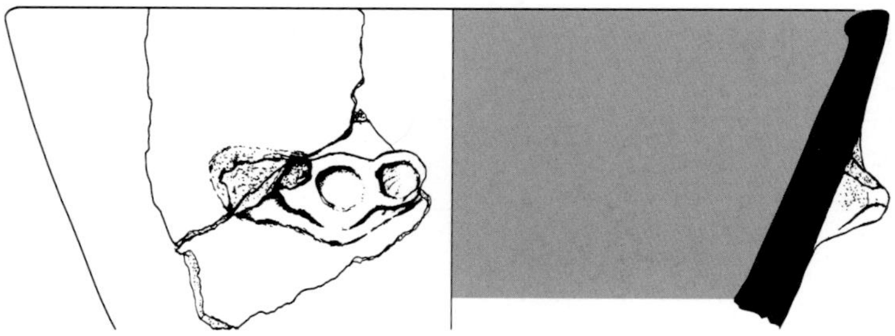

a

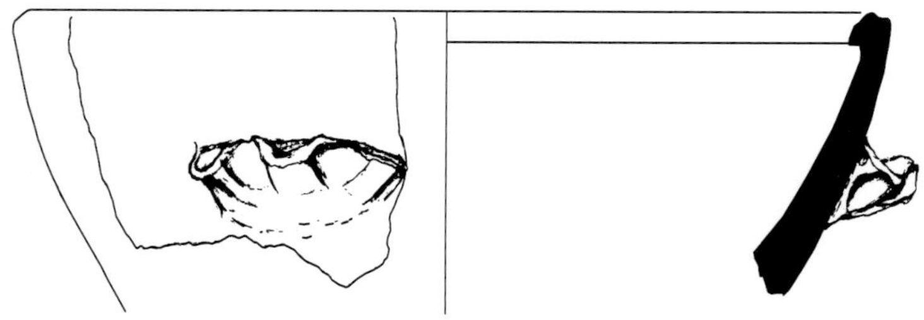

b

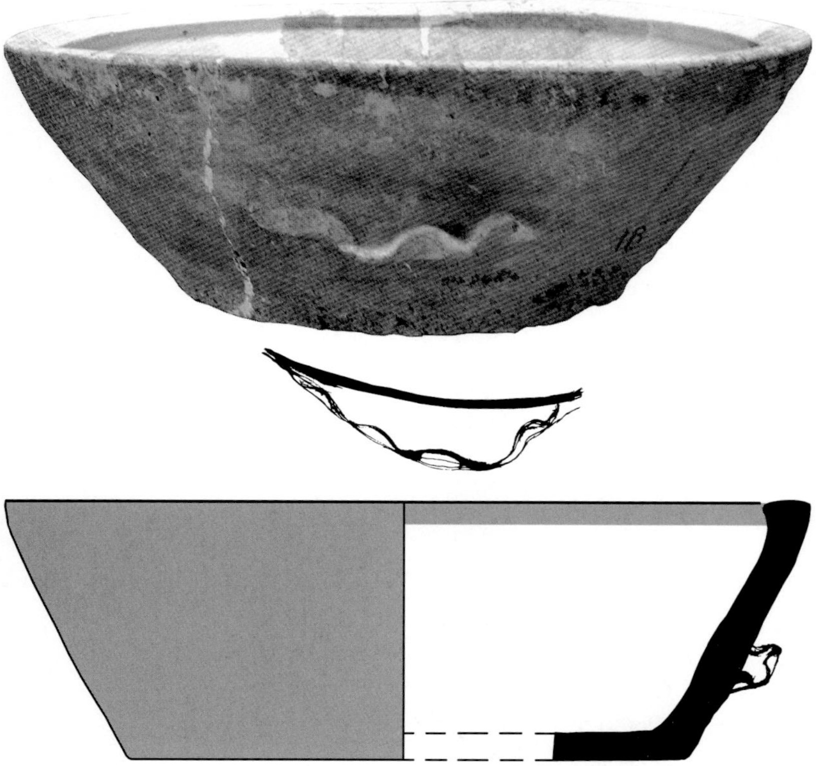

c

Early Bronze Age III large bowls and basins

Plate 72. Early Bronze Age I–III holemouth vessels

	Reg. No.	*Description*	*Provenience*	*Published*
a	34.2534/1	Buff-gray. Traces of red slip. Incised decoration. Early Bronze Age III	Under locus 1162	—
b	34.2534	Buff-gray. Red slip. Potter's mark. Late Early Bronze Age I–III	East Slope	—
c	34.2546/1	Brown-gray. Late Early Bronze Age I–III	East Slope	—
d	34.2534/2	Brown-gray. Potter's mark. Late Early Bronze Age I–III	East Slope	—
e	34.2546 / P4481	Gray. N.B. Locus list has "cup mark," which was the excavators' notation; it does not fit the usual definition of cup mark; they are modernly considered to be small, relatively shallow, circular, man-made depressions in bedrock or large boulders. This is much larger. Note also that two immense boulders in one of the squares are merely labeled as "rock" in the locus list	Locus 1152, a depression in the bedrock (pl. 41)	—
f	34.2555 / P3770	Gray to brown in large patches	Tomb 910A	—

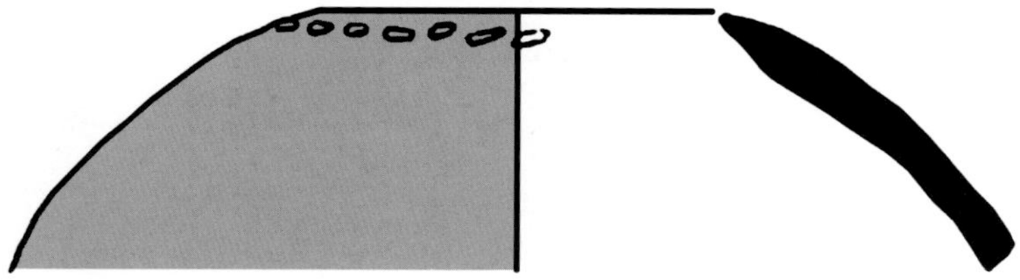

a

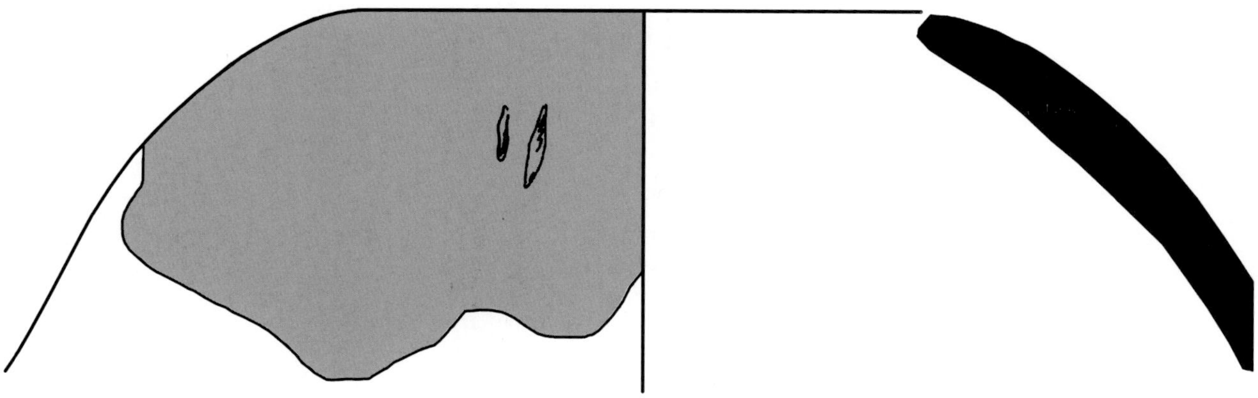

b

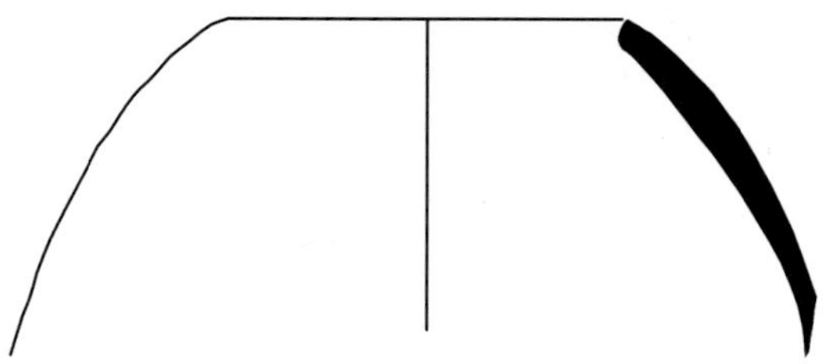

c

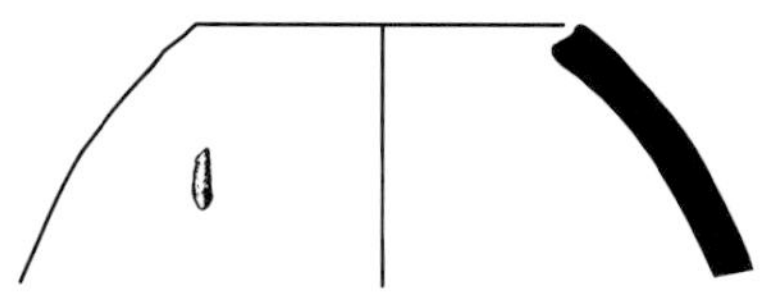

d

e

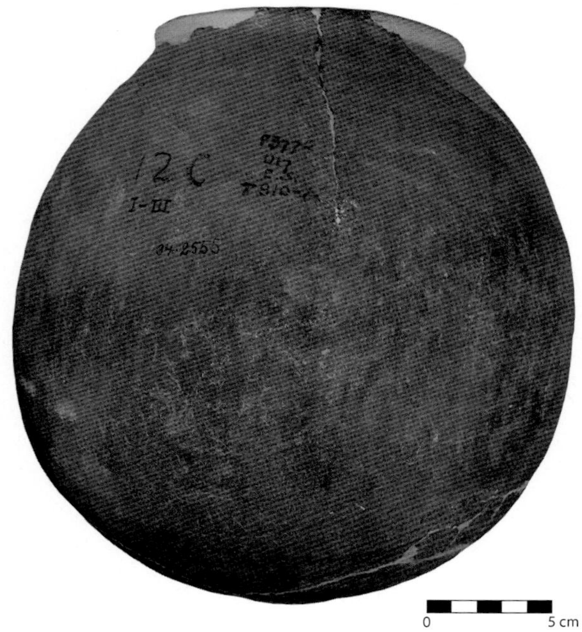

f

Early Bronze Age I–III holemouth vessels

Plate 73. Early Bronze Age III holemouth vessels

	Reg. No.	Description	Provenience	Published
a	P4509	Buff-gray	U17, Locus 1183 (under Locus 1171)[a]	
b	A16770 / P3293	Buff. Striations on upper half of interior, throwmarks visible on base of exterior	U17, outside wall of Tomb 914	

[a] It is uncertain where this locus, noted merely as a "room," was located as it does not appear on any extant plan. Presumably it is a phase of, or associated with, the building marked as Locus 914, located in the same square.

a

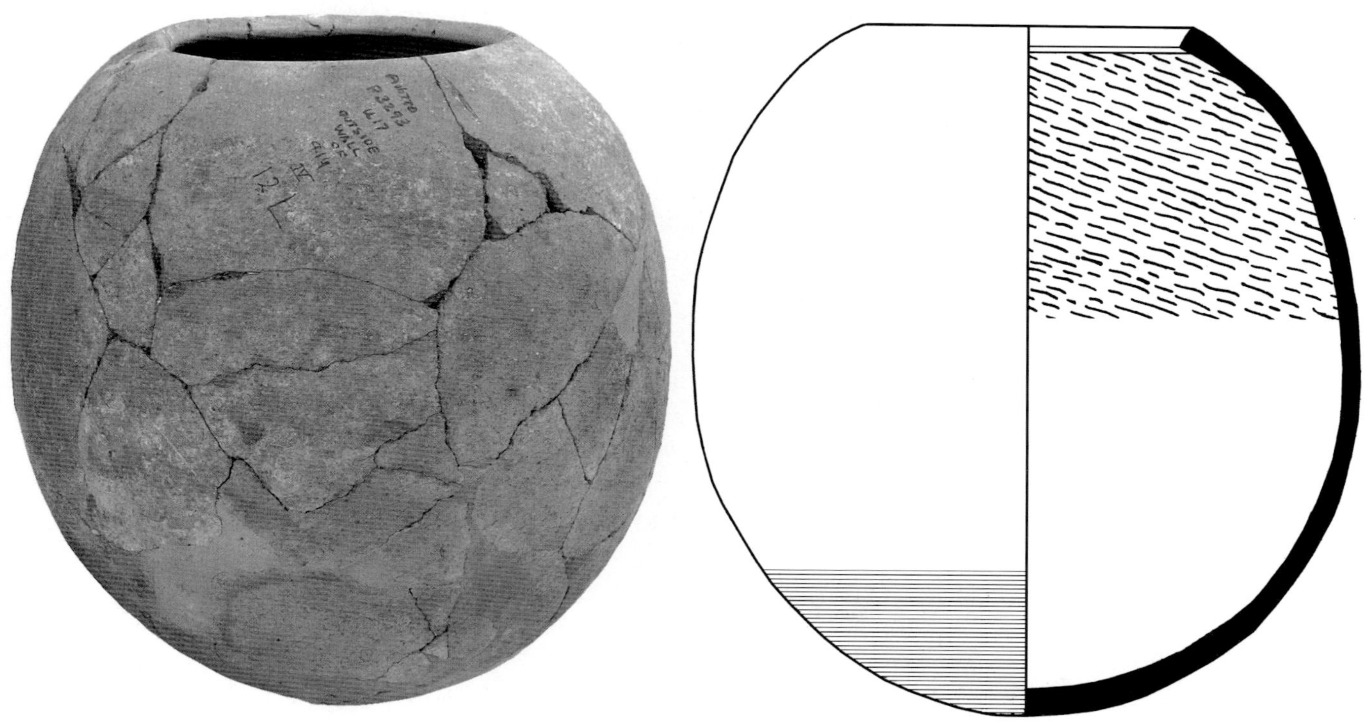

b

Early Bronze Age III holemouth vessels

Plate 74. Varia: bone tools, terra-cotta mold, figurine

	Reg. No.	*Description*	*Provenience*	*Published*	*Paralell*
a	34.2693 / M4870	Bone tool. Neolithic to Early Bronze Age	U16, "Stage V"	—	—
b	34.2695 / M4873	Bone tool. Neolithic to Early Bronze Age	U16, "Stage VI"	Engberg and Shipton 1934a, fig. 13:M	—
c	34.2696 / M4874	Bone tool. Neolithic to Early Bronze Age	U16, "Stage VII"	Engberg and Shipton 1934a, fig. 13:N	—
d	A16852 / P4942	Ceramic bowl with cloth impression on interior. Buff-brown, red slip. Early Bronze Age I(?)	Tomb 914	—	Tufnell et al. 1958, pl. 13:96–97
e	34.2690	Terra-cotta mold for copper axhead blanks. Early Bronze Age I	East Slope	Engberg and Shipton 1934a, fig. 13:A	—
f	M2520	Ceramic figurine, hindquarters of a quadruped. Early Bronze Age I	Tomb 903 Upper	*Megiddo Tombs*, pl. 76:7; May 1935, pl. 37	—

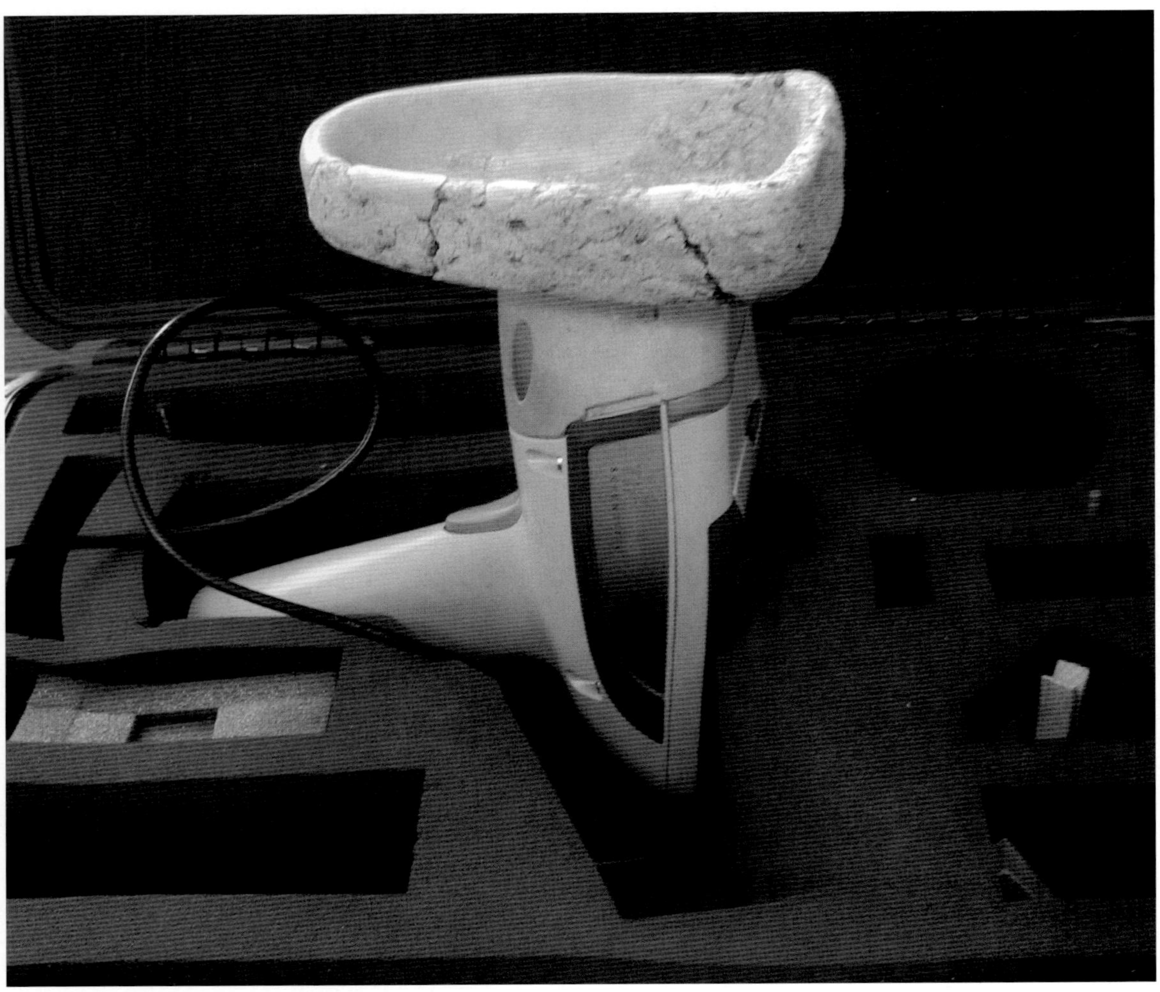

Figure to plate 74. Terra-cotta mold 34.2690 being analyzed for evidence of copper residue

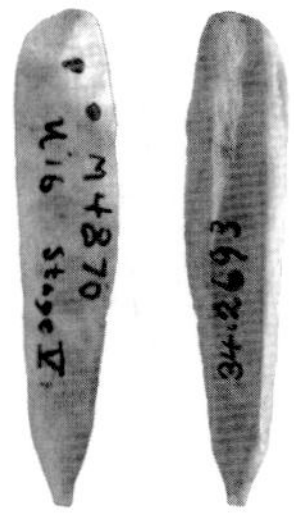
a

b

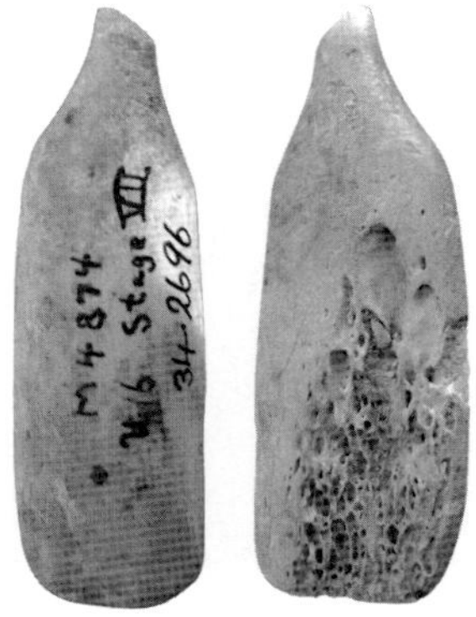
c

d

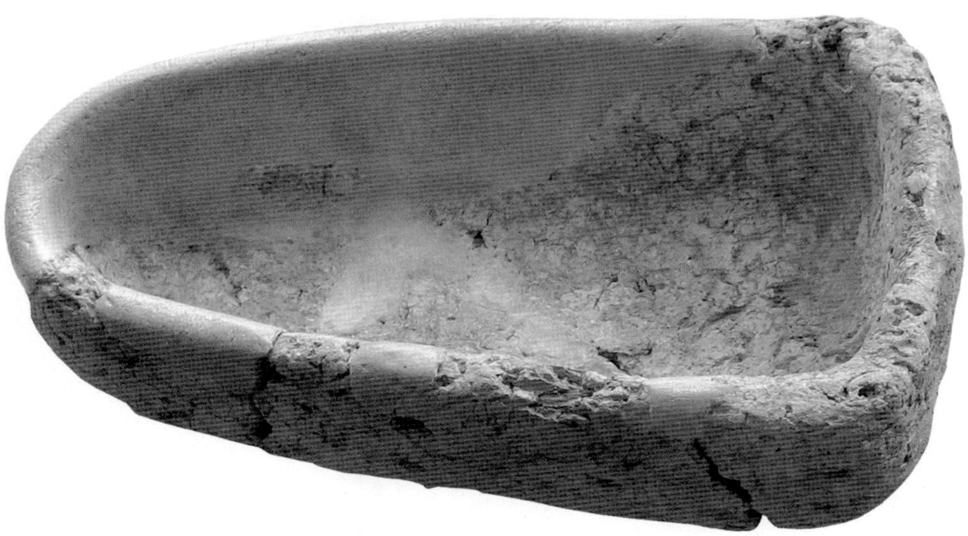
e

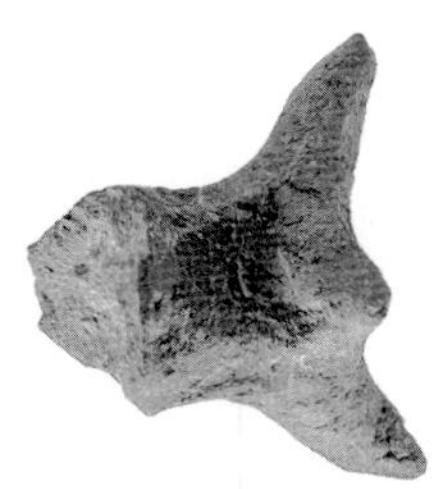
f

Varia: bone tools, terra-cotta mold, figurine

Plate 75. Objects in basalt

	Reg. No.	Description	Provenience	Published
a	A16885 / M3662	Loom weight. Early Bronze Age I	U16, Tomb 1226	—
b	A16884 / M3661	Loom weight or spindle whorl. Early Bronze Age I	U16, Tomb 1226	—
c	M2555	Loom weight. Early Bronze Age I	Tomb 903 Upper	*Megiddo Tombs*, p. 170, pl. 76:5
d	M2635	Loom weight. Early Bronze Age I	Tomb 903	—
e	M2558	Bowl. Early Bronze Age I	V17, surface	*Megiddo I*, pl. 112:7
f	A22492	Tournette or potters' wheel. Basalt, cf. *g*. For comparison only	N16, Locus 4014, Stratum XVIII	—
g	—	Basalt(?) stone pivot for potter's wheel (Image enlarged from field shot in figure below)	U17, Locus 1185	—

Figure to plate 75. A view of Locus 1185 with a stone for potter's wheel (*g*) in situ

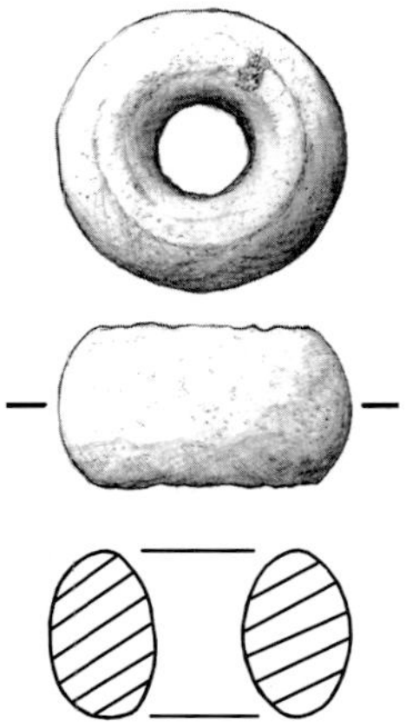
a

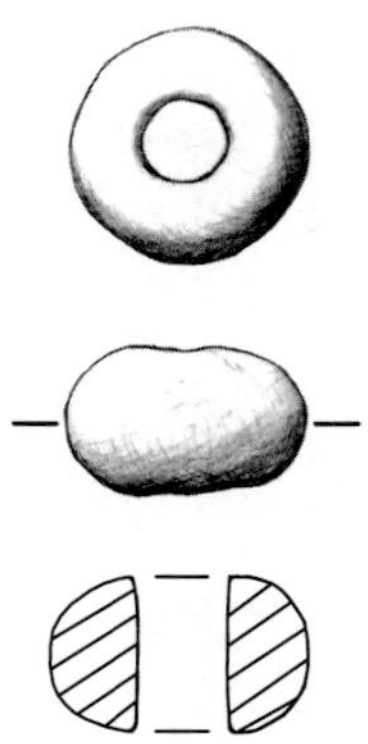
b

c

d

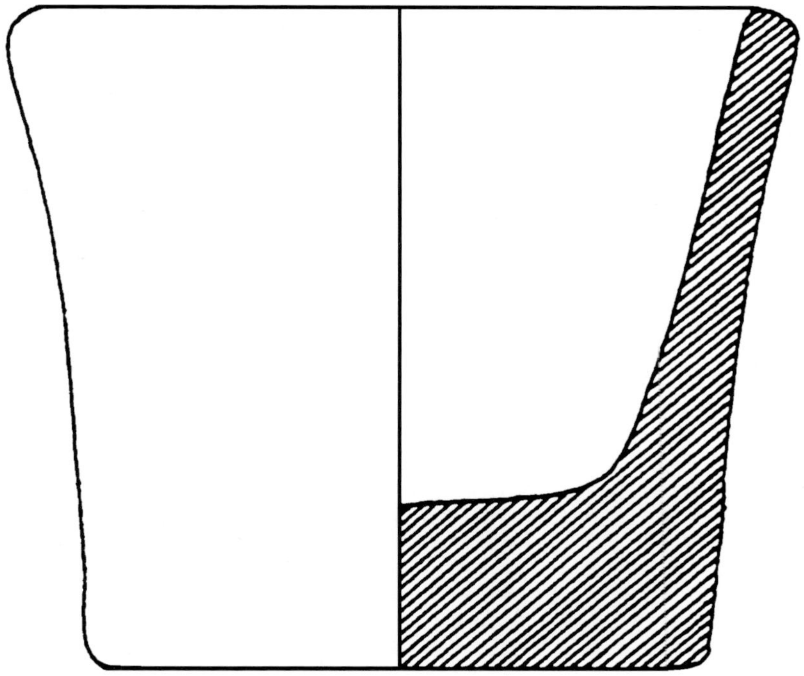
e

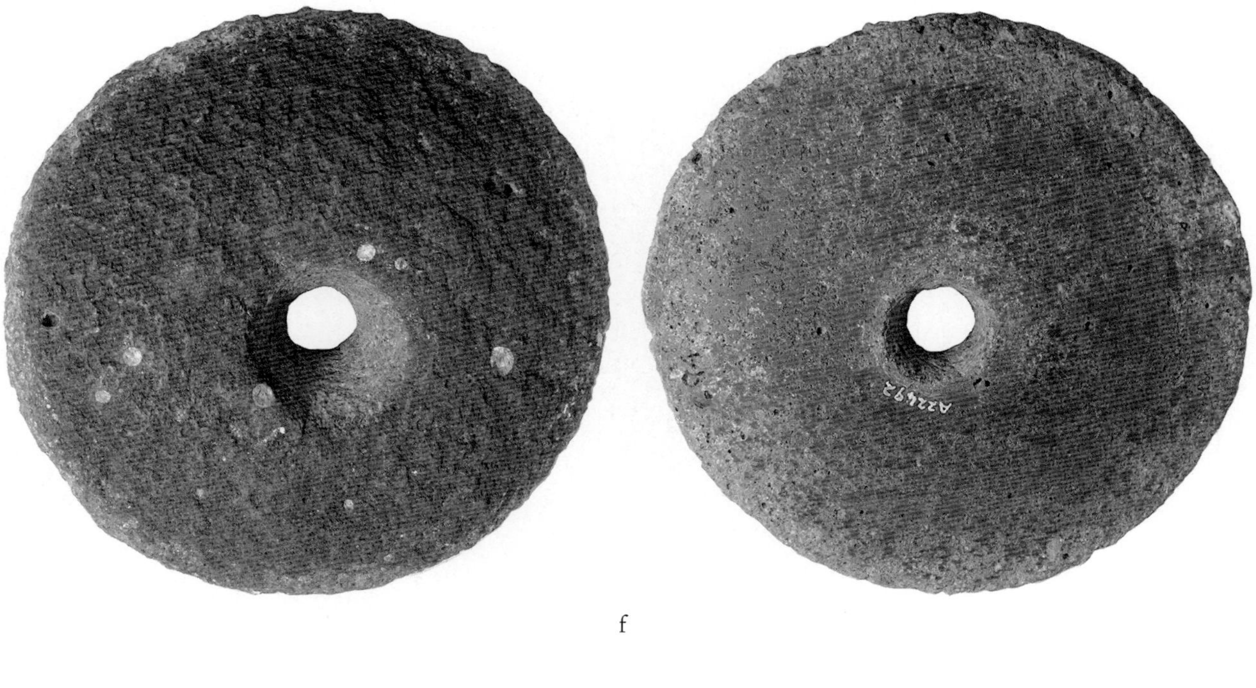
f

g (scale unknown)

Objects in basalt

a

b

(*a*) Detail of bow-rim pithos 34.2587 from B/V/1, with two impressions made with the same seal (Impression No. 1) and (*b*) detail of a photograph of a cylinder seal impression (Impression No. 1) on storage jar 34.2587 found on floor of B/V/1 (photo by Z. Radovan, courtesy of the Israel Antiquities Authority), and a rendering of the sealing after Engberg and Shipton 1934b, fig. 2

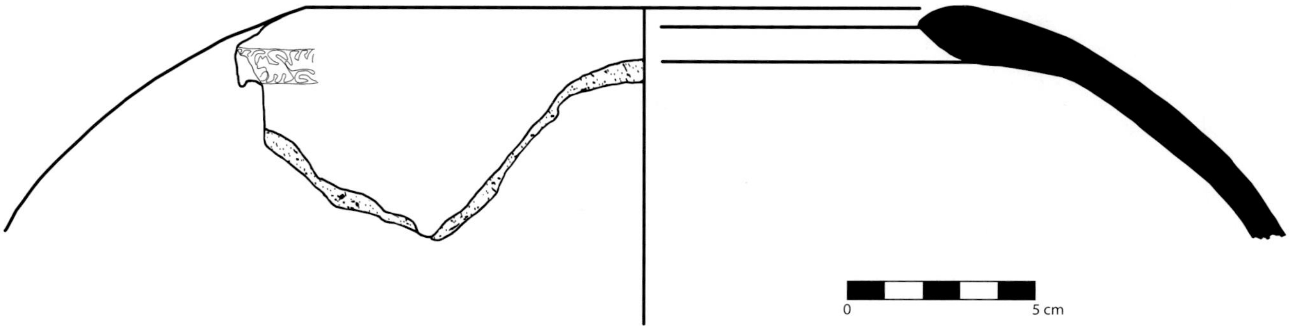

a

1

2

3

b

c

(*a*) Rendering of holemouth fragment 34.2752 with cylinder seal impression (Impression No. 2) (after a rendering by M. Ben Gal in Braun 1985, fig. 33:1D); (*b 1*) Detail of a photograph by Z. Radovan (courtesy of the Israel Antiquities Authority); (*b 2*) rendering after Engberg and Shipton 1934a, fig. 10:B; (*b 3*) suggested corrections (in gray) for the rendering of the impression; and (*c*) Cylinder seal impressions from ʿEn Shadud, possibly made from seal Impression No. 2 (photo by Ts. Segiv, courtesy of the Israel Antiquities Authority; rendering by M. Ben Gal after Braun 1985, fig. 33)

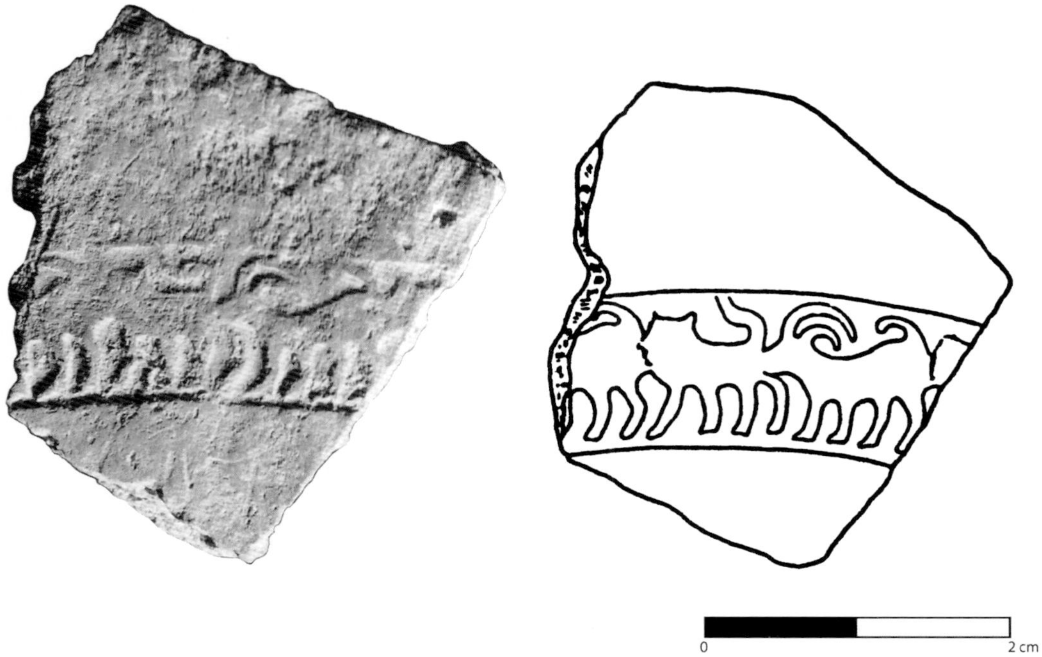

a

b

(*a*) Cylinder seal impression Impression No. 3 on sherd 34.2754 (photo by Z. Radovan, courtesy of the Israel Antiquities Authority; rendering after Engberg and Shipton 1934a, fig. 10:C); and (*b*) cylinder seal impression Impression No. 4 on sherd A16872 / P5557 (rendering of impression by A. Altenhofen)

a

b

0 2 cm

(*a*) Cylinder seal impression Impression No. 5 on jar sherd 96/H/4/AR1* (rendering after *Megiddo III*, p. 409, fig. 12.45) and (*b*) Seal impression Impression No. 6 on sherd 38.982, from the excavation of the upper mound (photo courtesy of Bella Gershovich, Israel Museum, collection the Israel Antiquities Authority; rendering after *Megiddo II*, pl. 160:4)

*Field number assigned by the Tel Aviv University Megiddo Expedition: Excavated 1994, Area H, Locus 4, Artifact 1.

a

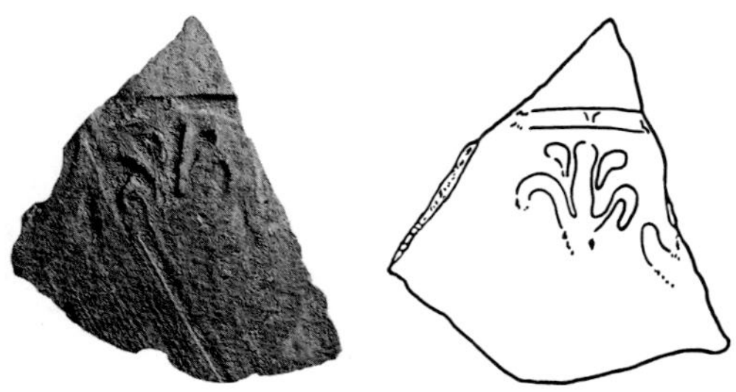

b

c

0 2 cm

(*a*) Cylinder seal impression Impression No. 7 on jar sherd 34.2753 / P555 (photo by Z. Radovan, courtesy of the Israel Antiquities Authority; rendering after Engberg and Shipton 1934a, fig. 10:A); (*b*) Cylinder seal impression Impression No. 8 on jar sherd A16869 / P5558 (rendering after Engberg and Shipton 1934a, fig. 10:E; and (*c*) Cylinder seal impression Impression No. 9 on sherd (rendering after Engberg and Shipton 1934a, fig. 10:D)

a

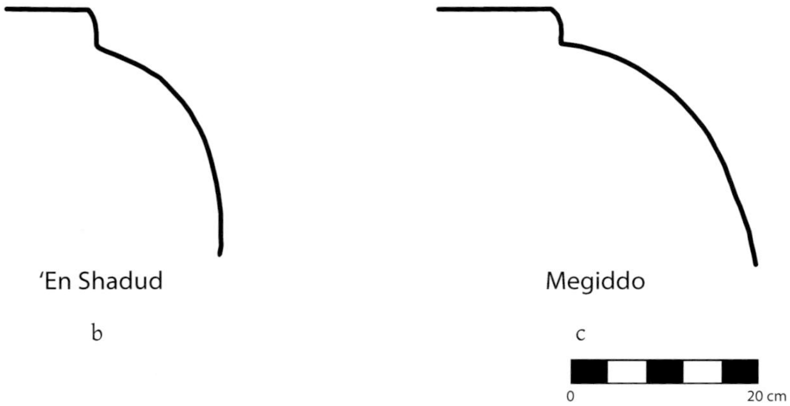

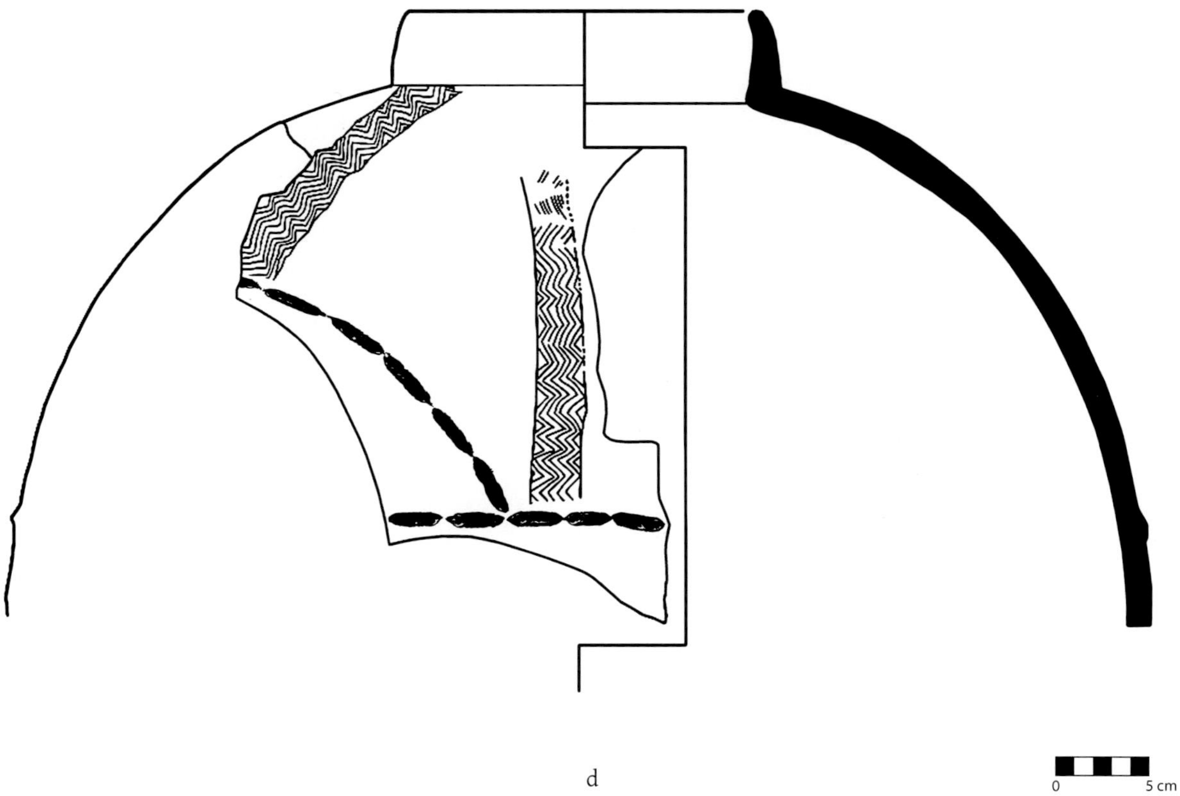

d

Details of bow-rim pithoi with cylinder seal impressions:
(*a*) Photograph and detail of a bow-rim pithos fragment with a geometric impression of a cylinder seal, a surface find from Tel Megadim (reproduced courtesy of R. Gophna [1974, fig. 1:5–6] and S. Wolff). No scale;
(*b*) Profile of a bow-rim pithos (Type BR-1) from ʿEn Shadud; (*c*) Profile of bow-rim pithos 34.2587 (Type BR-1) from Megiddo, B/V/1 (pl. 76); (*d*) Rendering of a bow-rim pithos (Type BR-1) with two cylinder seal impressions from Early Bronze Age I 'En Shadud, Stratum II

Plate 82. Sherds bearing potters' marks

	Reg. No.	*Description*	*Provenience*	*Published*
a	34.2422 / P4512	Holemouth fragment	Tomb 903 Lower	*Megiddo Tombs*, fig. 7
b	34.2426 / P4525	Holemouth fragment	Tomb 903 Lower	*Megiddo Tombs*, fig. 7
c	A16762	Holemouth fragment	East Slope	—
d	34.2421 / P4511	Holemouth fragment	Tomb 903 Lower	*Megiddo Tombs*, fig. 7
e	34.2425 / P4524	Holemouth fragment	Tomb 903 Lower	*Megiddo Tombs*, fig. 7
f	34.2424 / P4521	Holemouth fragment	Tomb 903 Lower	*Megiddo Tombs*, fig. 7
g	34.2305 / P4495	Holemouth fragment	Tomb 1106	*Megiddo Tombs*, pl. 6:13

a

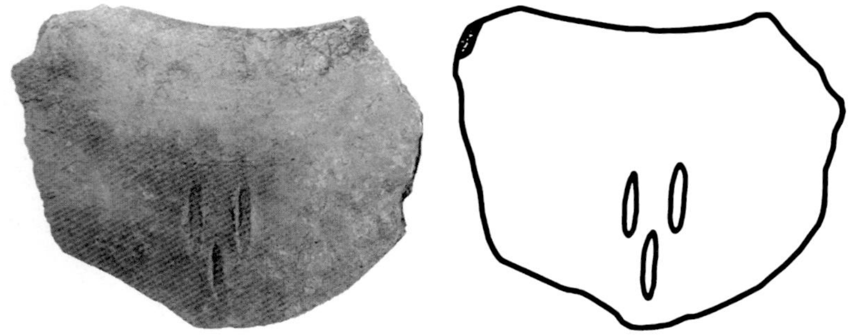

b

c

d

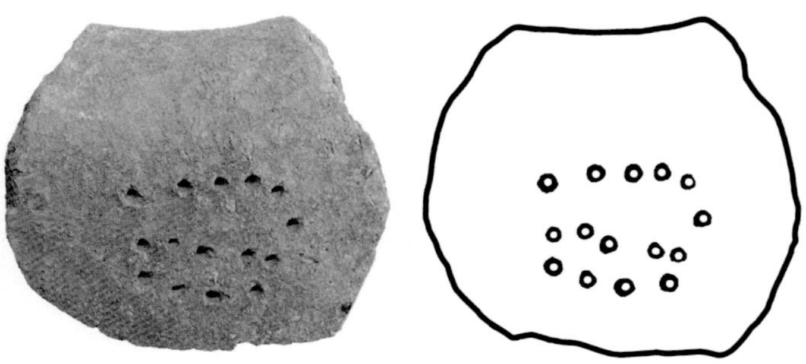

e

f

g

Sherds bearing potters' marks

Plate 83. Sherds and handle bearing potters' marks

	Reg. No.	*Description*	*Provenience*	*Published*
a	34.2273 / P4133	Holemouth fragment	Tomb 1101-B Lower	*Megiddo Tombs*, pl. 7:5
b	34.2292 / P4631	Holemouth fragment	Tomb 1102 Lower	*Megiddo Tombs*, pl. 7:12
c	34.2528 / P4711	Holemouth fragment	"under Locus 1170"	—
d	34.2525/2 / P4877	Holemouth fragment	East Slope / "under Locus 1168"	—
e	34.2639/28	Small handle with incised decoration. Red slip and polished. See also figure 29aa, plate 54b	East Slope	—

a

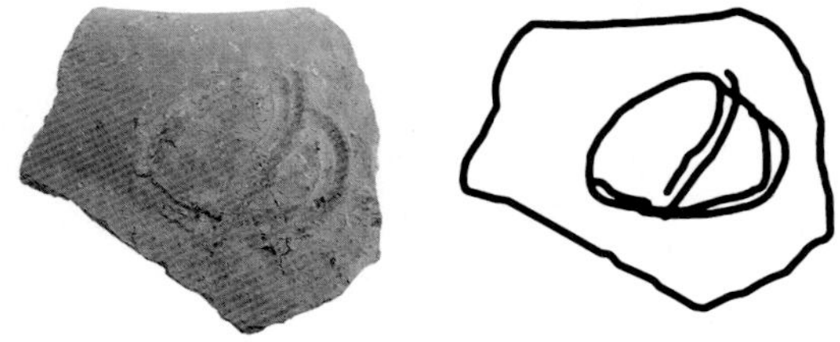

b

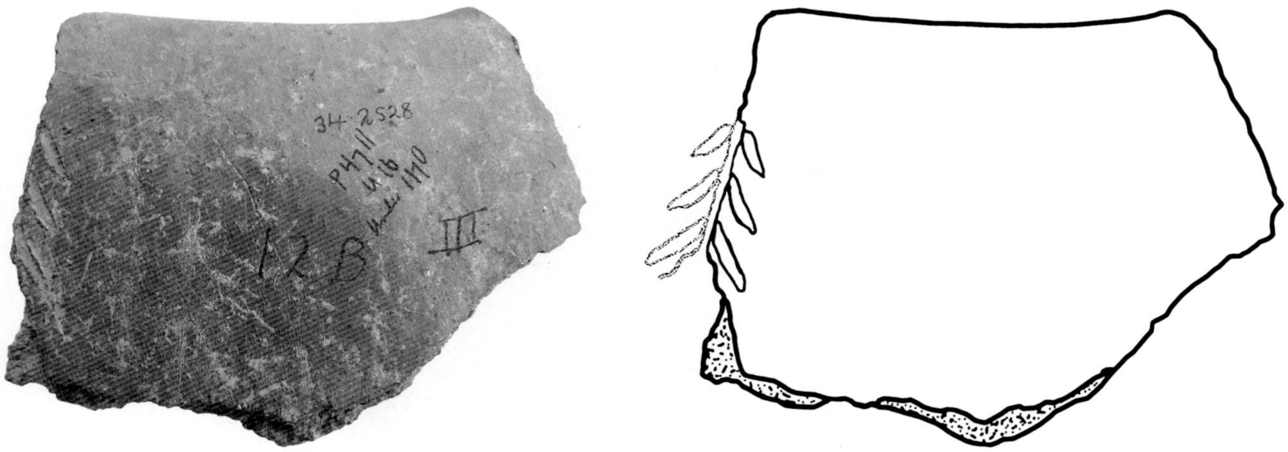

c

d

e

Sherds and handle bearing potters' marks

a

b

0 2 cm

Bowls with internally incised markings: (*a*) fragment a small bowl from Megiddo (34.2619/3), of pinkish fabric with red painted exterior rim and two parallel incisions (see fig. 29y); (*b*) small bowl from Gezer (B.264), probably dated to Early Bronze Age I, with three series of four parallel incisions, at equal distances. The external surface is red painted and burnished

a

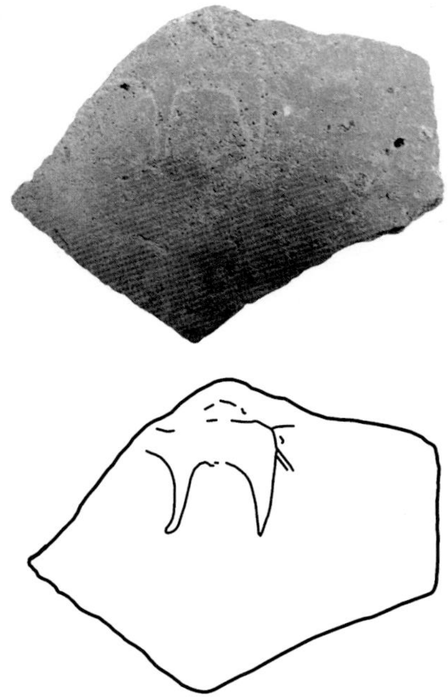

c

b

d

Potmarks from the East Slope with zoomorphic and anthropomorphic motifs

	Reg. No.	*Description*	*Provenience*	*Published*
a	34.2760 / P5566	Sherd with potmark depicting portion of a quadruped (photo by Z. Radovan, courtesy of the Israel Antiquities Authority); see figure 31c	—	Cf. Engberg and Shipton 1934a, fig. 10:M
b	—	Quadruped	—	Engberg and Shipton 1934a, fig. 10:L
c	—	Sherd with incisions possibly representing long, curved horns	—	Engberg and Shipton 1934a, fig. 10:R
d	—	Stick-like human arm	—	Engberg and Shipton 1934a, fig. 10:T

Plate 86. Megiddo Stratum XX lithics: Byblos point and Early Pottery Neolithic (Yarmukian) sickle blades

	Reg. No.	*Description*	*Provenience*	*Published*
a	39.626a–b	Byblos point	—	—
b	34.27087a–b	Sickle blade	—	Engberg and Shipton 1934a, fig. 22:L
c	—	Sickle blade	—	—
d	I.3383a–b*	Sickle blade	—	—
e	34.2741a–b / M4859	Sickle blade	—	—
f	34.2742a–b / M4860	Sickle blade	—	—
g	M3556	PPNB cortical-backed sickle blade	—	*Megiddo Tombs*, pl. 79:20

*This sickle blade and two others (pl. 87e–f) were registered by the Rockefeller Museum.

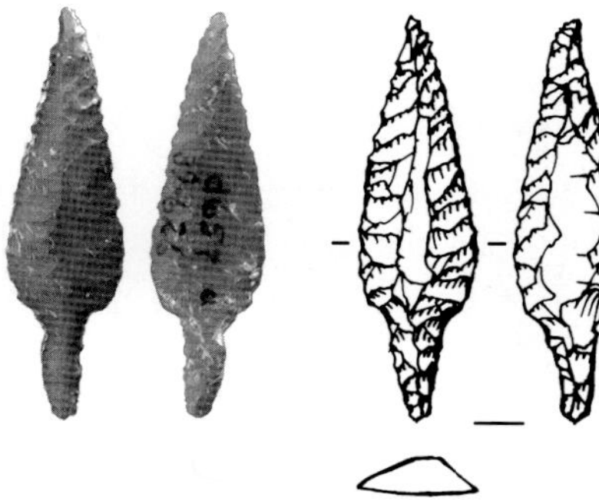

a

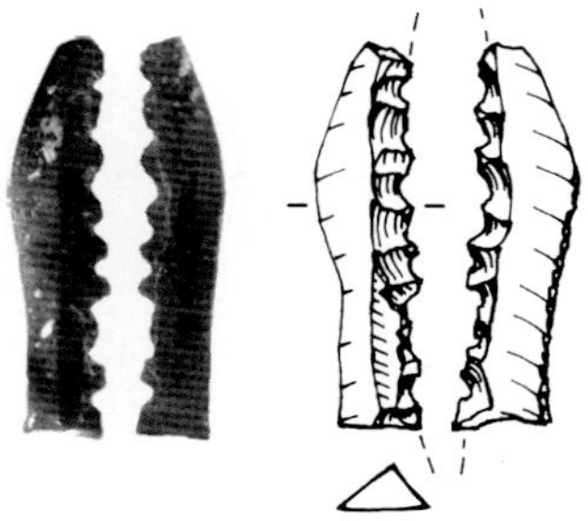

b

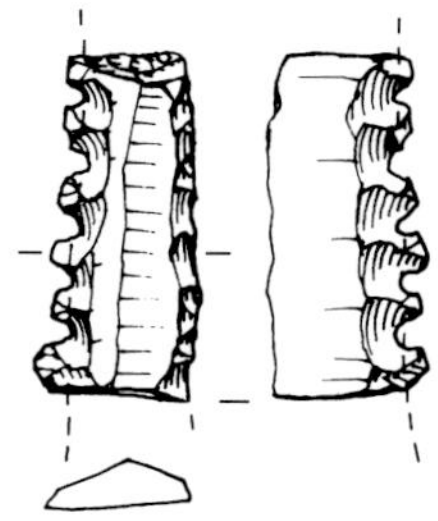

c

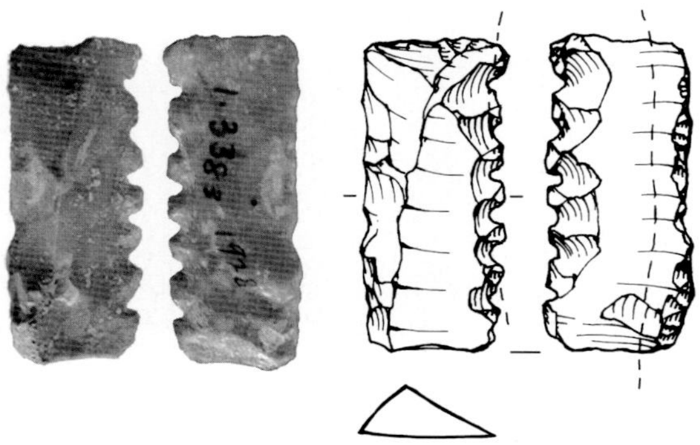

d

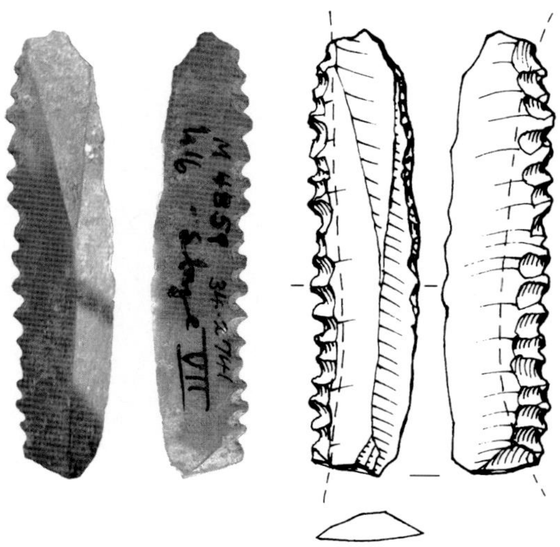

e

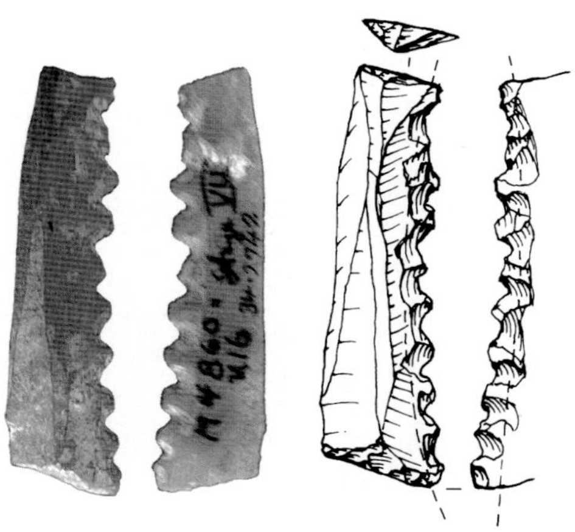

f

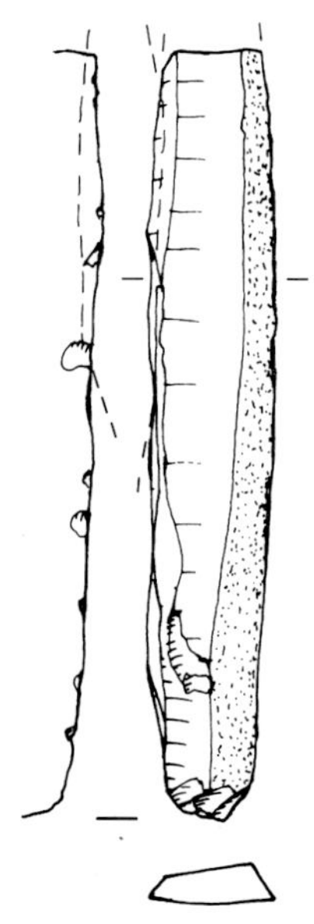

g

Megiddo Stratum XX lithics: Byblos point and Early Pottery Neolithic sickle blades

Plate 87. Megiddo Stratum XX lithics: Byblos point, sickle blades, and bladelet core

	Reg. No.	*Description*	*Provenience*	*Published*
a	34.2724a–b / M3945	Byblos point	U16, Locus 1208	Engberg and Shipton 1934a, fig. 23:J
b	—	Chalcolithic sickle blade	—	—
c	—	Chalcolithic sickle blade	—	—
d	M3717 / 34.2706	Bladelet core	—	Engberg and Shipton 1934a, fig. 22:T
e	I.3354a–b	Geometric sickle blade	U16, Locus 1228	—
f	I.3154	Geometric sickle blade	U16	—

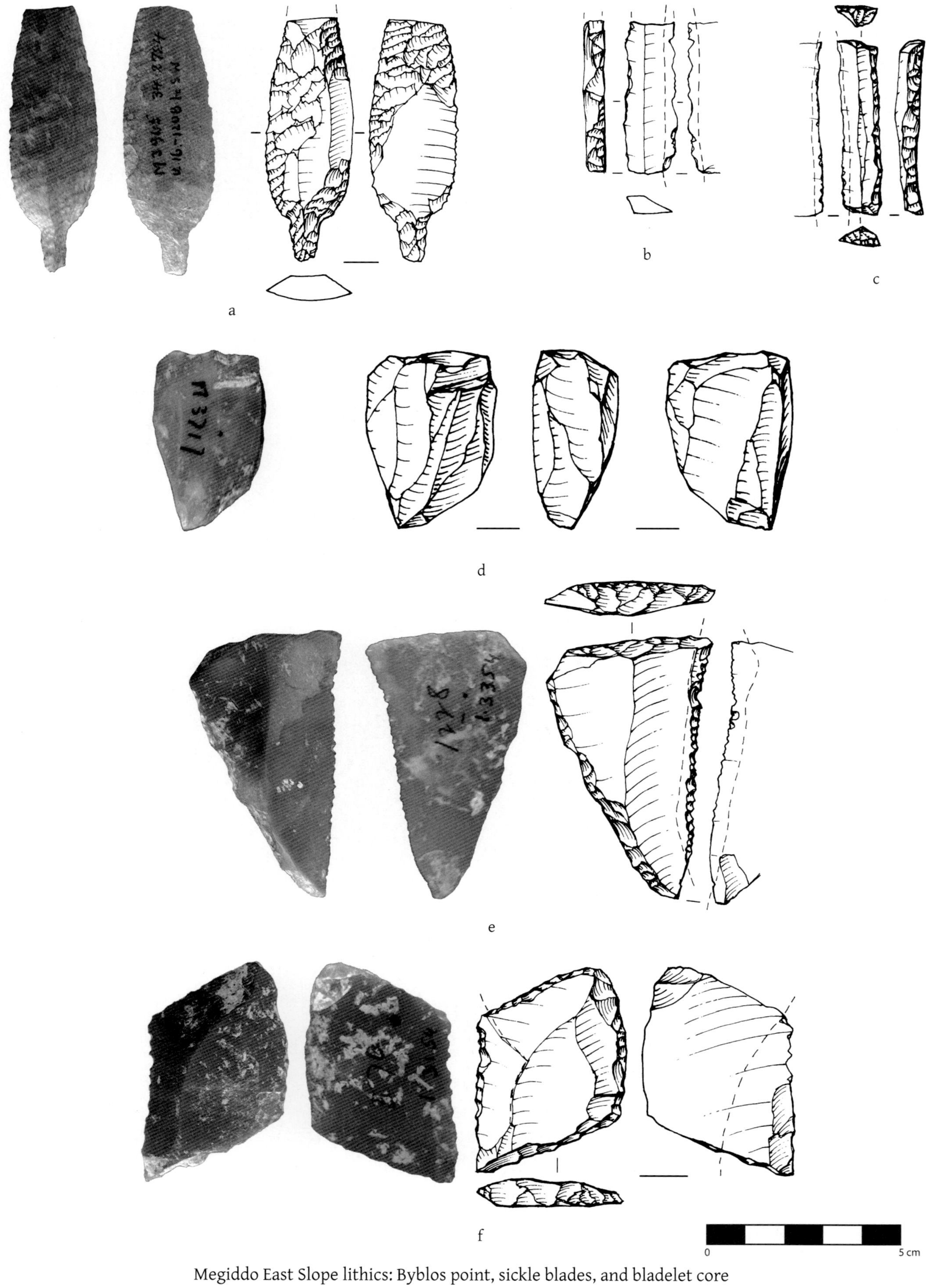

Megiddo East Slope lithics: Byblos point, sickle blades, and bladelet core

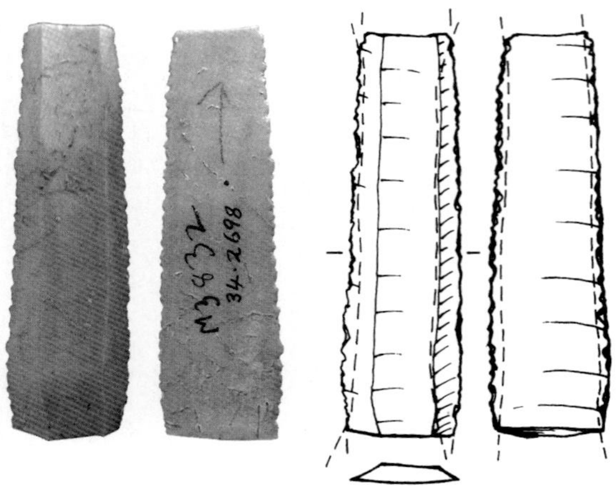

a

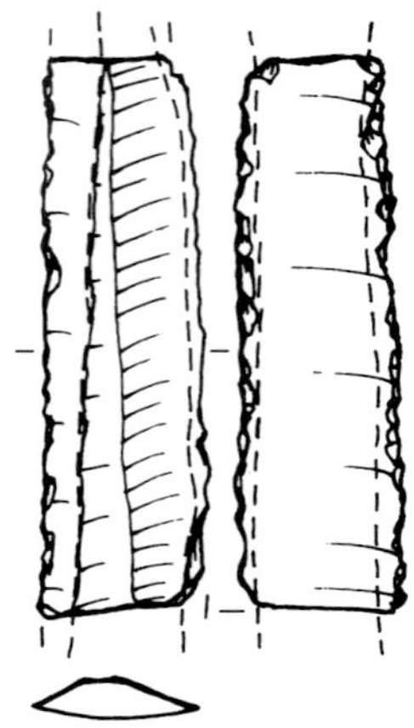

b

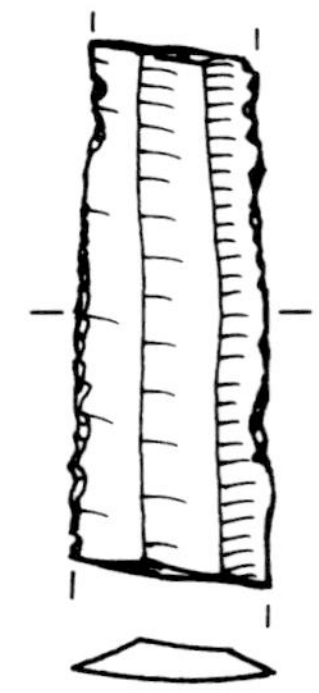

c

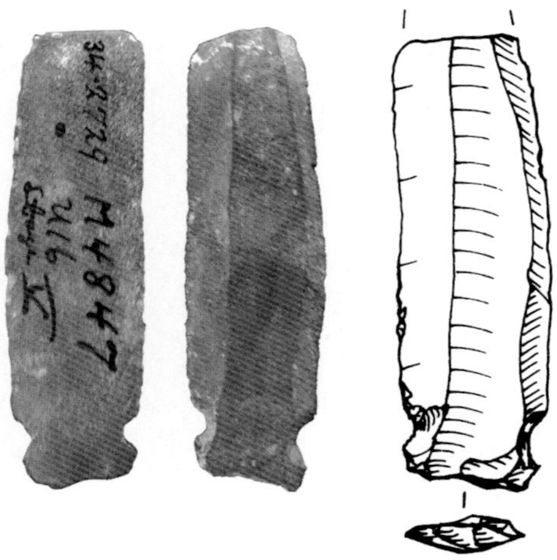

d

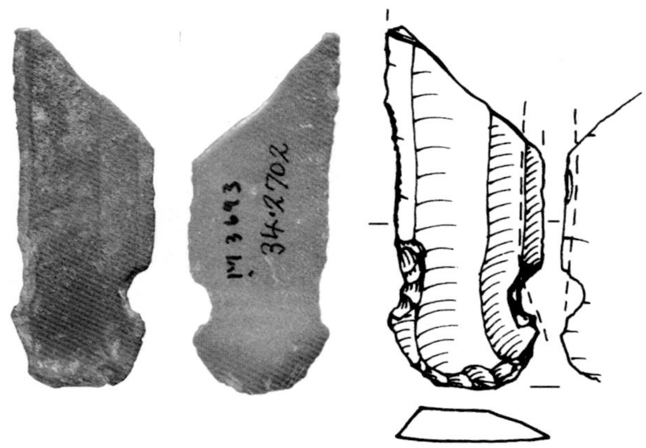

e

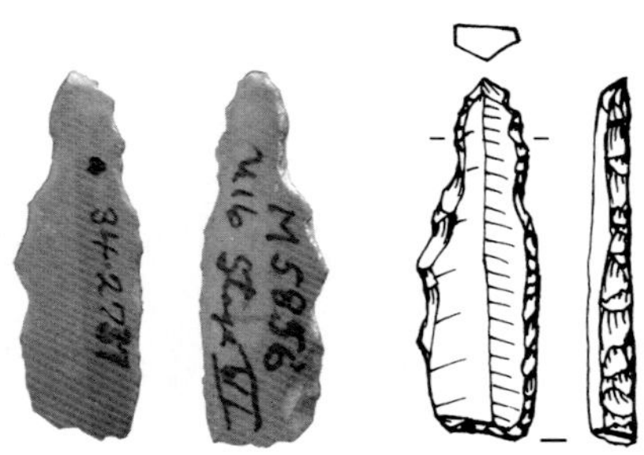

f

Megiddo East Slope lithics: Canaanean blades and borer

	Reg. No.	*Description*	*Provenience*	*Published*
a	34.2698 / M3832	Sickle blade	—	—
b	—	Sickle blade	—	—
c	—	Retouched blade	—	—
d	34.2729 / M4847	Tanged blade	U16	Engberg and Shipton 1934a, fig. 23:G
e	34.2702 /M3693	Tanged reaping knife	—	—
f	M5856 / 34.2737	Borer	U16	—

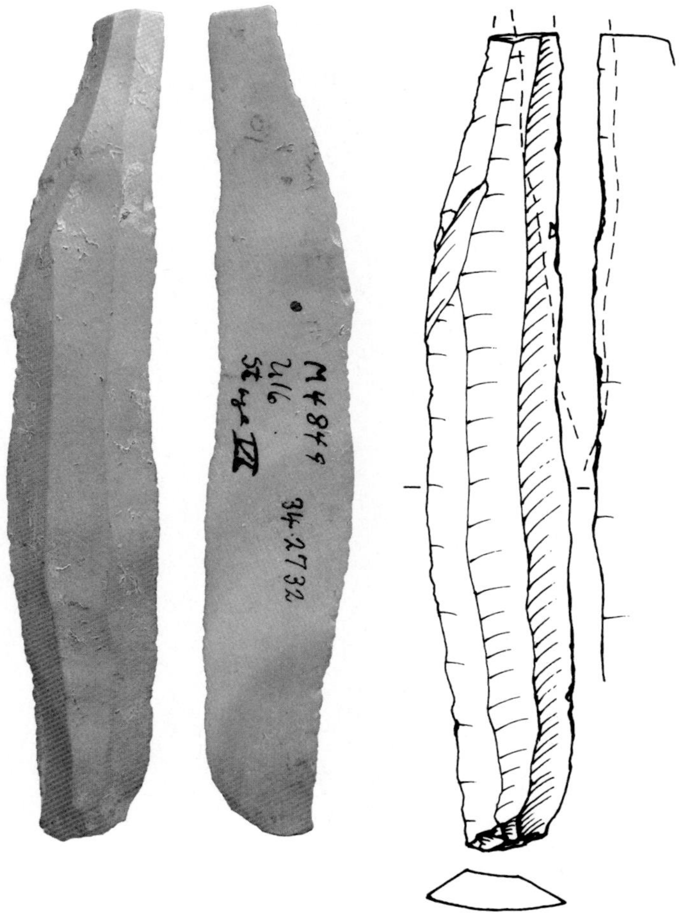

a

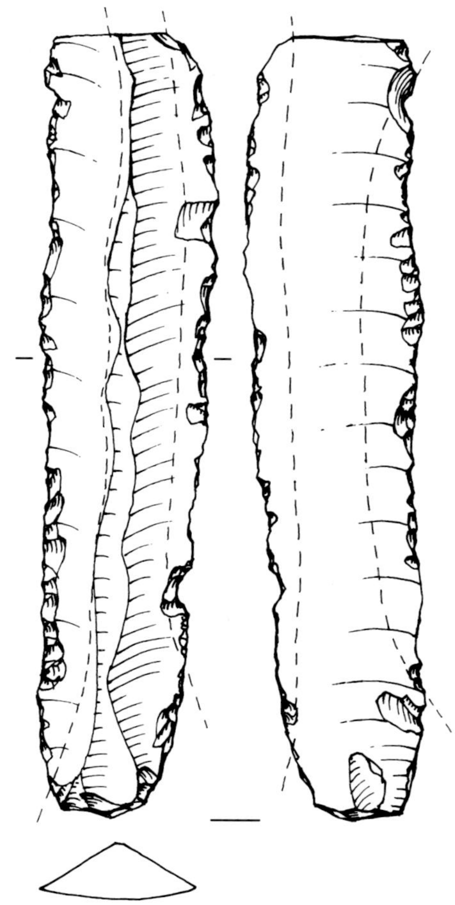

b

Megiddo East Slope lithics: Canaanean sickle blades

	Reg. No.	*Description*	*Provenience*	*Published*
a	34.2732 / M4849	Sickle blade	U16	Engberg and Shipton 1934a, pl. 24:A
b	b? 117 / 37.859	Sickle blade	—	—

Plate 90. Megiddo East Slope lithics: Canaanean blades

	Reg. No.	*Description*	*Provenience*	*Published*
a	34.2708 / M3914	Canaanean blade (blank)	U16, Locus 1200, floor	Engberg and Shipton 1934a, fig. 22:A
b	34.2728 / M4846	Retouched canaanean blade	U16	Engberg and Shipton 1934a, fig. 23:D
c	39.575 / d374	Cortical backed canaanean sickle blade	—	—

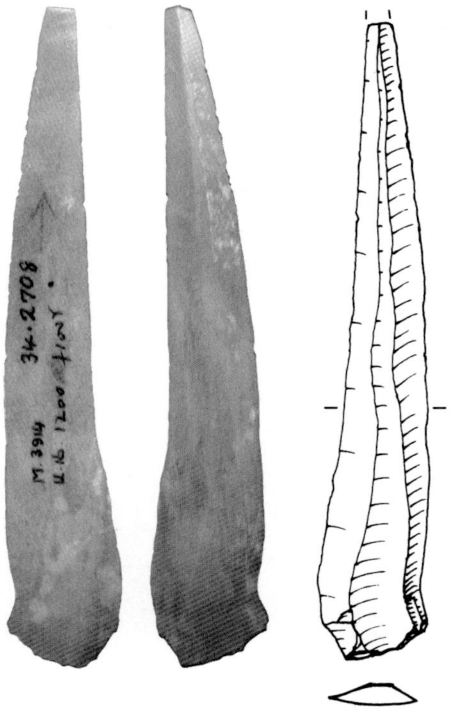

a

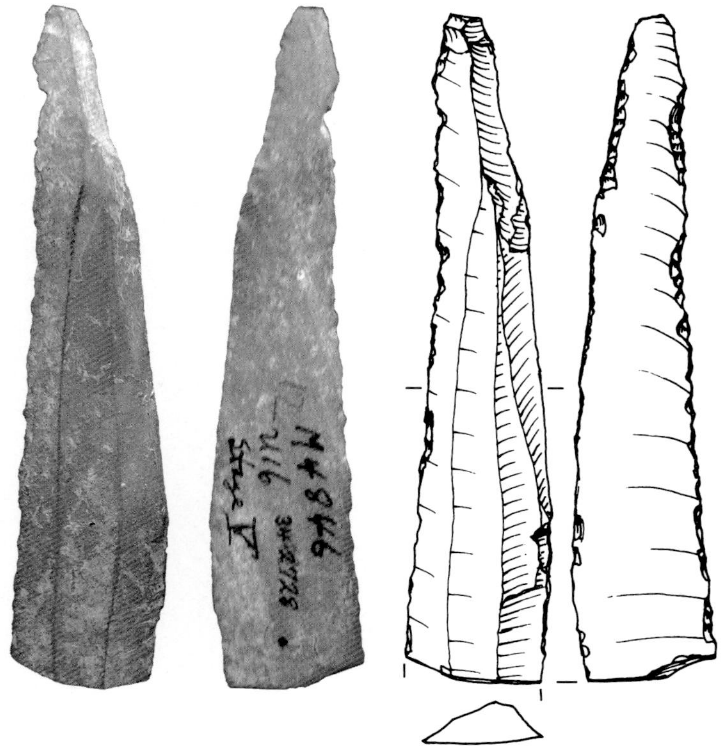

b

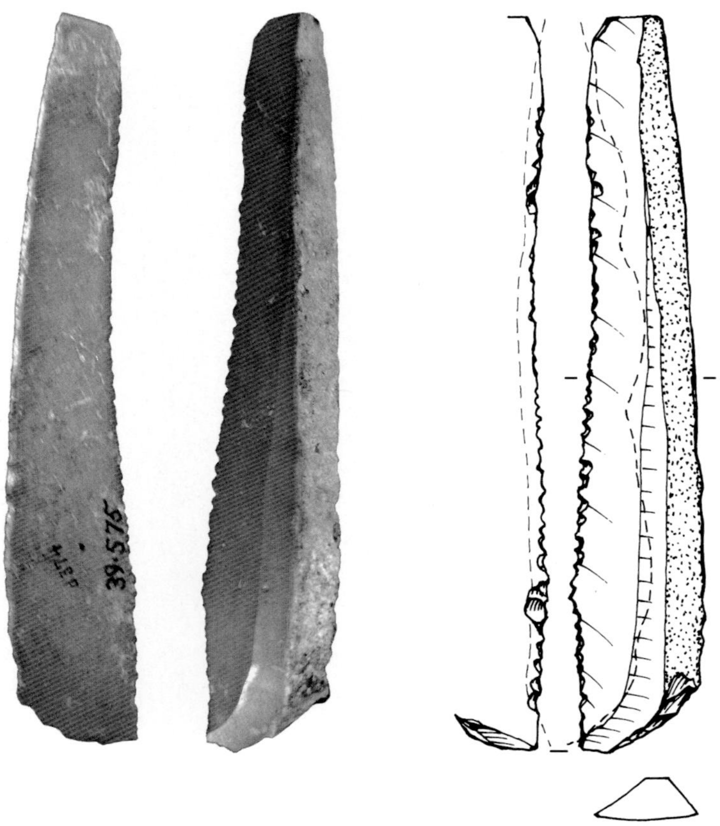

c

Megiddo East Slope lithics: Canaanean blades

Plate 91. Megiddo East Slope lithics: Atypical fan scraper, retouched flake, and polished graver

	Reg. No.	*Description*	*Provenience*	*Published*
a	34.2740 / M4858	Atypical fan scraper	U16	Engberg and Shipton 1934a, fig. 24:K
b	34.2723 / M3942	Retouched flake on canaanean material	U16, Locus 1208 to S.W.	Engberg and Shipton 1934a, fig. 23:A
c	39.617 / d625	Polished graver	—	—

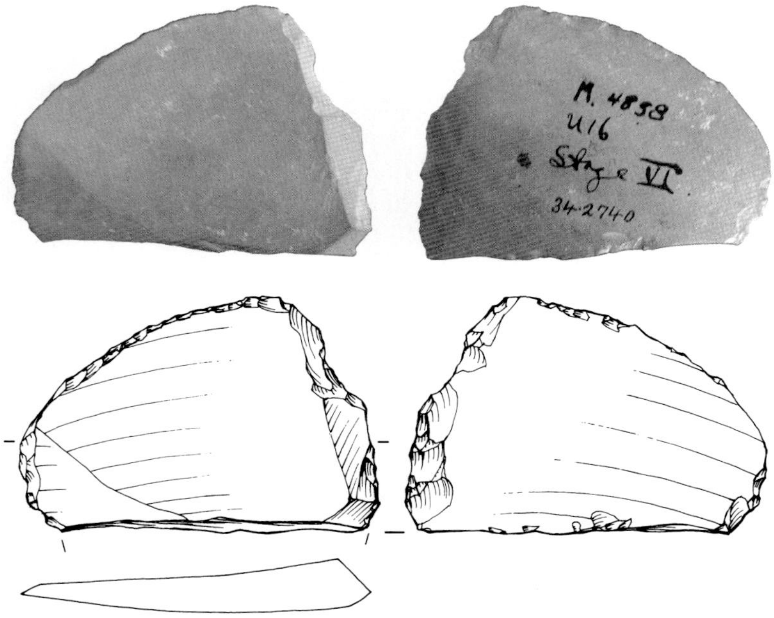

a

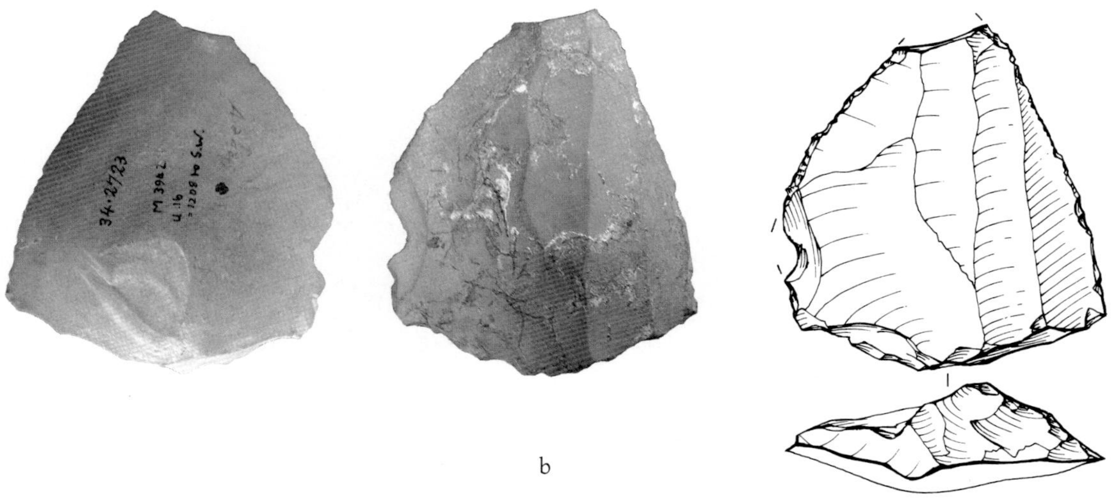

b

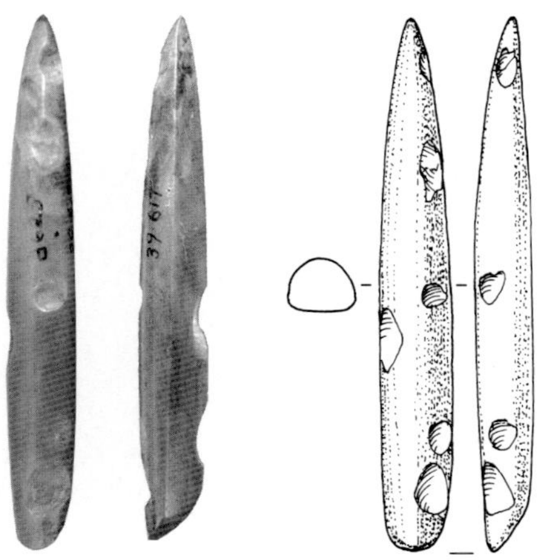

c

Megiddo East Slope lithics: Atypical fan scraper, retouched flake, and polished graver

Plate 92. Megiddo East Slope lithics: Atypical fan scraper and fan scraper

	Reg. No.	*Description*	*Provenience*	*Published*
a	34.2722 / M3938	Atypical fan scraper	U16, Locus 1208, floor	Engberg and Shipton 1934a, fig. 23:B
b	34.2458 / M3554	Fan scraper	Tomb 903 Lower	*Megiddo Tombs*, pl. 80:8

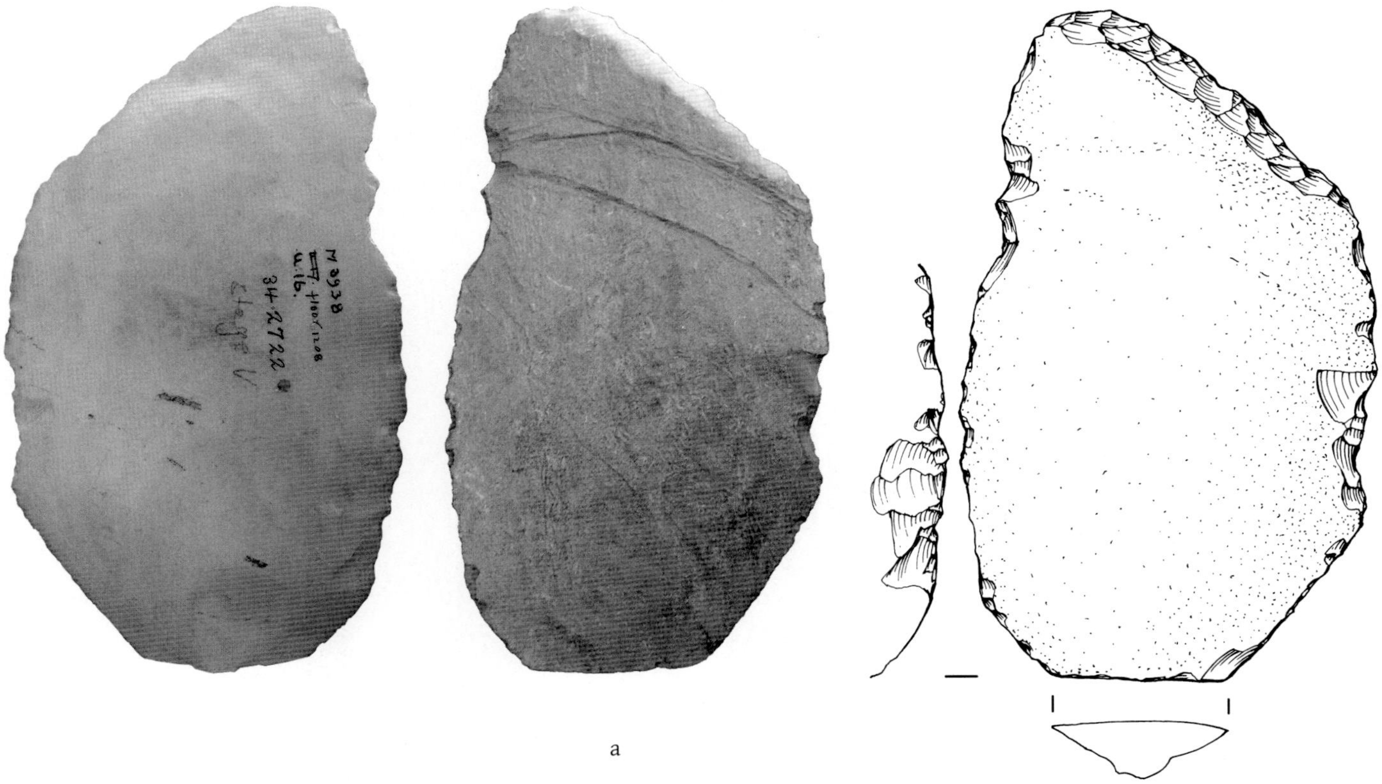

a

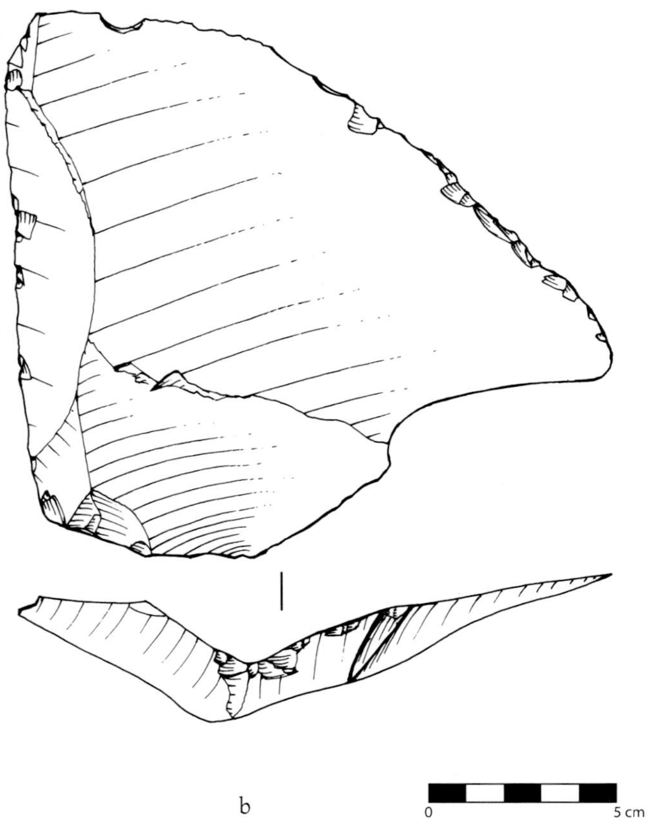

b

Megiddo East Slope lithics: Atypical fan scraper and fan scraper

Head of Yarmukian-type figurine. Baked clay, 6.0 × 2.5 cm. OIM A22559 / c94 (N15, Locus 4008). Photos by Anna Ressman

Reproduction of an aerial photograph of the East Slope showing location of the Early Bronze Age tombs (after *Megiddo Tombs*, pl. 1)

a

b

(*a*) The entry court and antechamber of Tomb 910, looking southwest. Note the flat walls and sharply defined corners of the rock cutting (*Megiddo Tombs*, fig. 11); and (*b*) Sharply carved lintels of Tomb 910 (*Megiddo Tombs*, fig. 12). There is no further indication, beyond the sign in the photograph, of precisely where the photograph was taken

a

b

(*a*) Chamber A in Tomb 910 with skeletal material in situ (*Megiddo Tombs*, fig. 13); it is unknown whether the cave was filled with soil or was found empty, as this photograph may suggest; and (*b*) close up of human remains in Chamber A, Tomb 910

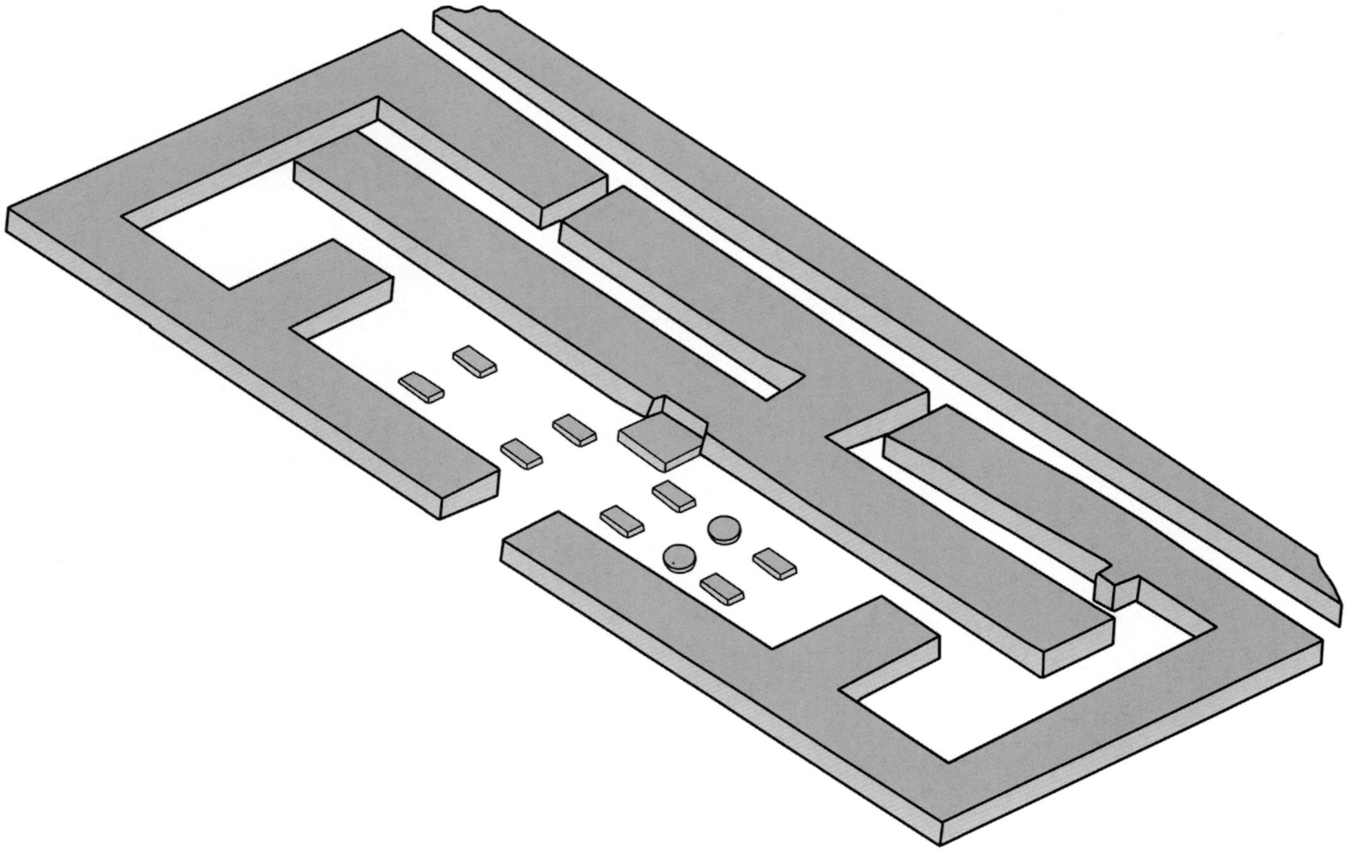

Isometric rendering of the monumental J-4 temple on the high mound (after *Megiddo IV*, fig. 3.29). The building is believed to have been more than 50 m in length; the flat, basalt stones in the floor, ca. 2 m long

Annotated photograph (E. Braun) of a portion of the partly excavated monumental temple at Megiddo, ca. 2008. Note the massive finely worked basalt blocks and the two enormous disks, one nearly completely buried in the baulk. The section where that disk may be seen has been deliberately lightened to allow for details to be discerned. Note also the massive, nearly 3 m wide walls and the large stones used in their construction. A raised platform with white plaster is presumed to have been an altar. Large flat stones along the longitudinal axis of this building may be pillar bases of a late phase